MODERN SOCIOLOGICAL THEORY

FIFTH EDITION

George Ritzer
University of Maryland

Boston   Burr Ridge, IL   Dubuque, IA   Madison, WI   New York   San Francisco   St. Louis
Bangkok   Bogotá   Caracas   Lisbon   London   Madrid
Mexico City   Milan   New Delhi   Seoul   Singapore   Sydney   Taipei   Toronto

McGraw-Hill Higher Education

A Division of The **McGraw-Hill** *Companies*

MODERN SOCIOLOGICAL THEORY

This book is printed on acid-free paper.

1 2 3 4 5 6 7 8 9 0   DOC/DOC   9 0 9 8 7 6 5 4 3 2 1 0

ISBN 0-07-229604-6

Editorial director: *Phillip A. Butcher*
Sponsoring editor: *Sally Constable*
Developmental editor: *Katherine Blake*
Marketing manager: *Leslie A. Kraham*
Project manager: *Carrie Sestak*
Production supervisor: *Rose Hepburn*
Freelance design coordinator: *Gino Cieslik*
Photo research coordinator: *Sharon Miller*
Compositor: *GAC Indianapolis*
Typeface: *10/12 Times Roman*
Printer: *R. R. Donnelley & Sons Company*

Library of Congress Cataloging-in-Publication Data

Ritzer, George.
    Modern sociological theory / George Ritzer.—5th ed.
      p. cm.
    ISBN 0-07-229604-6
    Includes bibliographical references and indexes.
    1. Sociology—History. 2. Schools of sociology—History.
  I. Title.
  HM435.R482   2000
  301′.01 20   99-44807

http://www.mhhe.com

PERMISSIONS ACKNOWLEDGMENTS

Chapter 2 James Coleman, excerpt from a review of Harold Garfinkel's *Studies in Ethnomethodology* from *American Sociological Review* 33 (1968). © 1968 by the American Sociological Association. Reprinted with the permission of the author and the American Sociological Association. • Steven Seidman, excerpt from "Symposium: Queer Theory/Sociology: A Dialogue" from *Sociological Theory* 12 (1994). © 1994 by the American Sociological Association. Reprinted with the permission of the author and the American Sociological Association.

Chapter 3 Robert K. Merton, excerpts from "Remembering the Young Talcott Parsons" from *American Sociologist* 15 (1980). © 1979 by the American Sociological Association. Reprinted with the permission of the author the American Sociological Association. • Figures 3.1 and 3.3: "Structure of the General Action System" and "Society, Its Subsystems and the Functional Imperatives" from Talcott Parsons and Gerald Platt, *The American University.* © 1973 by The President and Fellows of Harvard College. Reprinted with the permission of the Harvard University Press. • Figure 3.2: "Parson's Action Schema" adapted from Talcott Parsons, *Societies: Evolutionary and Comparative Perspectives.* © 1966. Adapted with the permission of Prentice-Hall, Inc., Upper Saddle River, NJ. • Robert K. Merton, "An Autobiographical Sketch." © 1981 by Robert K. Merton. Reprinted with the permission of Robert K. Merton.

Chapter 5 Richard A. Ball, excerpt from "Sociology and General Systems Theory" from *American Sociologist* 13 (1978). © 1978 by the American Sociological Association. Reprinted with the permission of the author and the American Sociological Association.

Chapter 6 George Herbert Mead, excerpts from *Mind, Self and Society: From the Standpoint of a Social Behaviorist.* © 1934 by The University of Chicago, renewed © 1962 by Charles W. Morris. Reprinted with the permission of The University of Chicago Press. • George Gonos, excerpt from "'Situation' versus 'Frame': The 'Interactionist' and the 'Structuralist' Analyses of Everyday Life" from American Sociological Review 42 (1977). © 1977 by the American Sociological Association. Reprinted with the permission of the author and the American Sociological Association. • Figure 10.1: "An Overview of the Components of Mead's Theoretical System" from John Baldwin, *George Herbert Mead: A Unifying Theory of Sociology.* © 1986 by Sage Publications, Inc. Reprinted with the permission of the publishers.

Chapter 7 Figure 7.1: "Breaching in Tic-Tac-Toe" from Michael Lynch, "Pictures of Nothing? Visual Constructs in Social Theory" from *Sociological Theory* 9 (Spring 1991). © 1991 by the American Sociological Association. Reprinted with the permission of the author and the American Sociological Association. • Philip Manning and George Ray, excerpts from "Shyness, Self-Confidence and Social Interaction" from *Social Psychology Quarterly* 56 (1993). © 1993 by the American Sociological Association. Reprinted with the permission of the authors and the American Sociological Association. • R. J. Anderson, J. A. Hughes and W. W. Sharrock, excerpt from "Executive Problem Finding: Some Material and Initial Observations" from *Social Psychology Quarterly* 50 (1987). © 1987 by the American Sociological Association. Reprinted with the permission of the authors and the American Sociological Association. • Marilyn R. Whalen and Don H. Zimmerman, excerpt from "Sequential and Institutional Contexts in Calls for Help" from *Social Psychology Quarterly* 50 (1987). © 1987 by the American Sociological Association. Reprinted with the permission of the authors and the American Sociological Association. • Jack Whalen, Don H. Zimmerman and Marilyn R. Whalen, excerpt from "When Words Fail: A Single Case Analysis" from *Social Problems* 35 (1988). © 1988 by the American Sociological Association. Reprinted with the permission of the authors and the American Sociological Association. • Paul Atkinson, excerpt from "Ethnomethodology: A Critical Review" from *Annual Review of Sociology* 14 (1988). © 1988 by Annual Reviews, Inc. Reprinted with the permission of Annual Reviews, Inc. • Richard A. Hilbert, excerpt from "Ethnomethodology and the Micro-Macro Order" from *American Sociological Review* 55 (1990). © 1990 by the American Sociological Association. Reprinted with the permission of the author and the American Sociological Association.

Chapter 8 Debra Friedman and Michael Hechter, excerpt from "The Contribution of Rational Choice Theory to Macrosociological Research" from *Sociological Theory* 6 (1988). © 1988 by the American Sociological Association. Reprinted with the permission of the authors and the American Sociological Association. • George C. Homans, excerpts from *Social Behavior: Its Elementary Forms.* © 1961 by Harcourt, Inc., renewed 1989 by George Caspar Homans. Reprinted with the permission of Harcourt, Inc. • George C. Homans, excerpts from *Social Behavior: Its Elementary Forms, Revised Edition.* © 1974 by Harcourt, Inc. Reprinted with the permission of the publishers. • Peter Blau, excerpts from *Exchange and Power in Social Life.* © 1964. Reprinted with the permission of Allyn & Bacon, Inc. • Karen S. Cook et al., excerpt from "The Distribution of Power in Exchange Networks: Theory and Experimental Results" from *American Journal of Sociology* 89 (1983). © 1983 by The University of Chicago. Reprinted with the permission of The University of Chicago Press. • Figure 8.1: "Ronald Burt's Integrative Model" from Ronald Burt, *Toward a Structural Theory of Action: Network Models of Social Structure, Perception and Action.* © 1982 by Academic Press, Inc. Reprinted with the permission of the author and Academic Press, Inc. • James Coleman, excerpt from "Rationality and Society" from *Rationality and Society* 1 (1989). © 1989 by Sage Publications, Inc. Reprinted with the permission of the publishers. • James Coleman, excerpts from "A Vision for Society" from *Society* 32 (1994). © 1994 by Transaction, Inc. Reprinted with the permission of the publishers. All rights reserved. • Norman Denzin, excerpt from "Harold and Agnes: A Feminist Narrative Undoing" from *Sociological Theory* 9 (1990). © 1990 by the American Sociological Association. Reprinted with the permission of the author and the American Sociological Association.

Chapter 10 Figure 10.3: "Coleman's Integrative Method" adapted from James Coleman, "Social Theory, Social Research and a Theory of Action" from *American Journal of Sociology* 91 (1986). © 1986 by The University of Chicago. Reprinted with the permission of The University of Chicago Press. • Figure 10.4: "Liska's Macro-to-Micro and Micro-to-Macro Model" from Allen E. Liska, "The Significance of Aggregate Dependent Variables and Contextual Independent Variables for Linking Macro to Micro Theories" from *Social Psychology Quarterly* 53 (December 1990). © 1990 by the American Sociological Association. Reprinted with the permission of Allen E. Liska and the American Sociological Association. • Norbert Elias, excerpts from *The Civilizing Process* (1939/1994). Reprinted with the permission of Blackwell Publishers, Oxford. • Norbert Elias, excerpts from *The Civilizing Process: Part 2, Power and Civility* (1939/1982) Reprinted with the permission of Blackwell Publishers, Oxford.

Chapter 11 Pierre Bourdieu, excerpt from "Social Space and Symbolic Power" from *Sociological Theory* 7 (1989). © 1989 by the American Sociological Association. Reprinted with the permission of the American Sociological Association.

Chapter 12 Ulrich Beck, excerpts from *Risk Society: Towards a New Modernity.* © 1992 by Sage Publications. Ltd. Reprinted with the permission of the publishers. • Sheila Rothenberg and Robert S. Rothenberg, excerpt from "The Pleasures of Paris" from *USA Today Magazine* (March 1993). © 1993 by The Society for the Advancement of Education. Reprinted with the permission of USA Today. • Zygmunt Bauman, excerpts from *Modernity and the Holocaust .* © 1989 by Zygmunt Bauman. Reprinted with the permission of Cornell University Press.

Chapter 13 William Bogard, excerpt from "Closing Down the Social: Baudrillard's Challenge to Contemporary Sociology" from *Sociological Theory* 8 (1990). © 1990 by the American Sociological Association. Reprinted with the permission of the author and the American Sociological Association. • Fredric Jameson, excerpts from "Postmodernism, or the Cultural Logic of Late Capitalism" from *New Left Review* 146 (1984). © 1984. Reprinted with the permission of New Left Review.

Appendix Thomas L. Hankin, excerpt from "In Defense of Biography: The Use of Biography in the History of Science" from *History of Science* 17 (1979). © 1979. Reprinted with the permission of the author. • Reba Rowe Lewis, excerpt from "Forging New Syntheses: Theories and Theorists" from *American Sociologist* (Fall/Winter 1991). © 1991 by the American Sociological Association. Reprinted with the permission of the author and the American Sociological Association.

Photo Credits 8 Culver Pictures 14 Culver Pictures 18 Corbis 22 The Granger Collection 28 The Granger Collection 34 The Granger Collection 37 Corbis 40 Culver Pictures 54 Courtesy of the University of Chicago 60 Courtesy of the American Sociological Association 67 Brown Brothers 98 The Granger Collection 112 Courtesy of the American Sociological Association 120 Courtesy of Jeffrey Alexander 162 Courtesy of Immanuel Wallerstein 206 Courtesy of the University of Chicago 228 Courtesy of the American Sociological Association 246 © Robert Dingwall/Courtesy of Harold Garfinkel 280 Christopher Johnson 286 Courtesy of the American Sociological Association 292 Courtesy of the University of Washington 300 Courtesy of the American Sociological Association 325 Courtesy of Jessie Bernhard 330 Courtesy of Dorothy E. Smith 339 Courtesy of Patricia Hill Collins 372 Courtesy of Randall Collins 376 Courtesy of Eric Dunning 398 Carlos Freire/RAPHO/Liaison Agency 430 Courtesy of Anthony Giddens 446 Courtesy of German Information Center 466 Corbis 496 Courtesy of George Ritzer

ABOUT
THE AUTHOR

GEORGE RITZER is Professor of Sociology at the University of Maryland. His major areas of interest are sociological theory and the sociology of consumption. He has served as Chair of the American Sociological Association's Sections on Theoretical Sociology (1989–1990) and Organizations and Occupations (1980–1981). Professor Ritzer has been Distinguished Scholar-Teacher at the University of Maryland and has been awarded a Teaching Excellence award. He has held the UNESCO Chair in Social Theory at the Russian Academy of Sciences and a Fulbright-Hays Fellowship. He has been Scholar-in-Residence at the Netherlands Institute for Advanced Study and the Swedish Collegium for Advanced Study in the Social Sciences.

Dr. Ritzer's main theoretical interests lie in metatheory as well as applied social theory. In metatheory, his contributions include *Metatheorizing in Sociology* (Lexington Books, 1991), *Sociology: A Multiple Paradigm Science* (Allyn and Bacon, 1975, 1980), and *Toward an Integrated Sociological Paradigm* (Allyn and Bacon, 1981). His major works in the application of social theory, especially to consumption, include *The McDonaldization of Society* (Pine Forge Press, 1993, 1996), *Expressing America: A Critique of the Global Credit Card Society* (Pine Forge Press, 1995), *The McDonaldization Thesis* (Sage, 1998), and *Enchanting a Disenchanted World: Revolutionizing the Means of Consumption* (Pine Forge Press, 1999). Professor Ritzer's work has been translated into many different languages; there are a dozen translations of *The McDonaldization of Society* alone.

In 1997 McGraw-Hill published the first edition of Professor Ritzer's *Postmodern Social Theory.* In 2000 McGraw-Hill will publish the fifth edition of Dr. Ritzer's *Sociological Theory* and the third edition of his *Classical Sociological Theory.*

To Jeremy, with Love

CONTENTS

LIST OF BIOGRAPHICAL AND AUTOBIOGRAPHICAL SKETCHES   xviii

PREFACE   xix

PART 1   **INTRODUCTION**   1

1   **A HISTORICAL SKETCH OF SOCIOLOGICAL THEORY: THE EARLY YEARS**   3

INTRODUCTION   4

SOCIAL FORCES IN THE DEVELOPMENT OF SOCIOLOGICAL THEORY   6

    Political Revolutions   6

    The Industrial Revolution and the Rise of Capitalism   6

    The Rise of Socialism   7

    Feminism   7

    Urbanization   8

    Religious Change   9

    The Growth of Science   9

INTELLECTUAL FORCES AND THE RISE OF SOCIOLOGICAL THEORY   9

    The Enlightenment   10

    The Conservative Reaction to The Enlightenment   11

    The Development of French Sociology   13

    The Development of German Sociology   20

    The Origins of British Sociology   36

    The Key Figure in Early Italian Sociology   42

    Turn-of-the-Century Developments in European Marxism   43

2   **A HISTORICAL SKETCH OF SOCIOLOGICAL THEORY: THE LATER YEARS**   45

EARLY AMERICAN SOCIOLOGICAL THEORY   46

    Politics   46

    Social Change and Intellectual Currents   46

    The Chicago School   52

WOMEN IN EARLY SOCIOLOGY   57

SOCIOLOGICAL THEORY TO MID-CENTURY   58
  The Rise of Harvard, the Ivy League, and Structural
    Functionalism   58
  The Chicago School in Decline   63
  Developments in Marxian Theory   64
  Karl Mannhiem and the Sociology of Knowledge   65
SOCIOLOGICAL THEORY FROM MID-CENTURY   66
  Structural Functionalism: Peak and Decline   66
  Radical Sociology in America: C. Wright Mills   68
  The Development of Conflict Theory   69
  The Birth of Exchange Theory   70
  Dramaturgical Analysis: The Work of Erving Goffman   71
  The Development of Sociologies of Everyday Life   72
  The Rise and Fall (?) of Marxian Sociology   76
  The Challenge of Feminist Theory   77
  Structuralism and Poststructuralism   79
RECENT DEVELOPMENTS IN SOCIOLOGICAL THEORY   80
  Micro-Macro Integration   80
  Agency-Structure Integration   81
  Theoretical Syntheses   82
THEORIES OF MODERNITY AND POSTMODERNITY   83
  The Defenders of Modernity   83
  The Proponents of Postmodernity   84
THEORIES TO WATCH IN THE EARLY TWENTY-FIRST CENTURY   85
  Multicultural Social Theory   85
  Postmodern and Post-Postmodern Social Theories   86
  Theories of Consumption   87
  Others   88

PART 2   MODERN SOCIOLOGICAL THEORY:
         THE MAJOR SCHOOLS   91

    3   STRUCTURAL FUNCTIONALISM, NEOFUNCTIONALISM,
         AND CONFLICT THEORY   93

STUCTURAL FUNCTIONALISM   94
  The Functional Theory of Stratification and Its Critics   95
  Talcott Parson's Structural Functionalism   97
  Robert Merton's Structural Functionalism   108
  The Major Criticisms   114
NEOFUNCTIONALISM   117
CONFLICT THEORY   122
  The Work of Ralf Dahrendorf   123
  The Major Criticisms and Efforts to Deal with Them   126

A More Integrative Conflict Theory   128

4   VARIETIES OF NEO-MARXIAN THEORY   135

ECONOMIC DETERMINISM   135
HEGELIAN MARXISM   136
    Georg Lukács   137
    Antonio Gramsci   139
CRITICAL THEORY   140
    The Major Critiques of Social and Intellectual Life   140
    The Major Contributions   144
    Criticisms of Critical Theory   147
    The Ideas of Jurgen Habermas   148
    Critical Theory Today   151
NEO-MARXIAN ECONOMIC SOCIOLOGY   152
    Capital and Labor   152
    Fordism and Post-Fordism   159
HISTORICALLY ORIENTED MARXISM   161
    The Modern World-System   162
POST-MARXIST THEORY   168
    Analytical Marxism   168
    Postmodern Marxian Theory   173
    After Marxism   176
    Criticisms of Post-Marxism   178

5   SYSTEMS THEORY   181

SOCIOLOGY AND MODERN SYSTEMS THEORY   181
    Gains from Systems Theory   181
    Some General Principles   183
    Applications to the Social World   184
NIKLAS LUHMANN'S GENERAL SYSTEM THEORY   185
    Autopoietic Systems   186
    Society and Psychic Systems   188
    Double Contingency   190
    Evolution of Social Systems   191
    Differentiation   192
    Luhmann's Sociology of Knowledge   197
    Criticisms   198

6   SYMBOLIC INTERACTIONISM   201

THE MAJOR HISTORICAL ROOTS   202
    Pragmatism   202
    Behaviorism   203
    Between Reductionism and Sociologism   204

THE IDEAS OF GEORGE HERBERT MEAD   205
    The Priority of the Social   205
    The Act   208
    Gestures   210
    Significant Symbols   211
    Mental Processes and the Mind   212
    Self   215
    Society   219
SYMBOLIC INTERACTIONISM: THE BASIC PRINCIPLES   221
    Capacity for Thought   221
    Thinking and Interaction   222
    Learning Meanings and Symbols   223
    Action and Interaction   224
    Making Choices   224
    The Self and the Work of Erving Goffman   225
    Groups and Societies   233
CRITICISMS   235
TOWARD A MORE SYNTHETIC AND INTEGRATIVE SYMBOLIC
    INTERACTIONISM   236
    Redefining Mead and Blumer   237
    Micro-Macro Integration   239
    Symbolic Interactionism and Cultural Studies   240
THE FUTURE OF SYMBOLIC INTERACTIONISM   242

7   ETHNOMETHODOLOGY   245

DEFINING ETHNOMETHODOLOGY   245
THE DIVERSIFICATION OF ETHNOMETHODOLOGY   249
SOME EARLY EXAMPLES   251
    Breaching Experiments   251
    Accomplishing Gender   253
CONVERSATION ANALYSIS   253
    Telephone Conversations: Identification and Recognition   254
    Initiating Laughter   255
    Generating Applause   256
    Booing   257
    The Interactive Emergence of Sentences and Stories   258
    Formulations   259
    Integration of Talk and Nonvocal Activities   260
    Doing Shyness (and Self-Confidence)   260
STUDIES OF INSTITUTIONS   261
    Job Interviews   261
    Executive Negotiations   262
    Calls to Emergency Centers   262
    Dispute Resolution in Mediation Hearings   263

CRITICISMS OF TRADITIONAL SOCIOLOGY   264
STRESSES AND STRAINS IN ETHNOMETHODOLOGY   266
SYNTHESIS AND INTEGRATION   267
    Ethnomethodology and Symbolic Interactionism   268
    Ethnomethodology and the Micro-Macro Order   269

8   EXCHANGE, NETWORK, AND RATIONAL CHOICE THEORIES   271

EXCHANGE THEORY   271
    Behaviorism   271
    Rational Choice Theory   272
    The Social Psychology of Groups   273
    The Exchange Theory of George Homans   274
    Peter Blau's Exchange Theory   282
    The Work of Richard Emerson and His Disciples 286
NETWORK THEORY   293
RATIONAL CHOICE THEORY   296
    Foundations of Social Theory   297

9   CONTEMPORARY FEMINIST THEORY
By Patricia Madoo Lengermann and Jill Niebrugge–Brantley   307

THE BASIC THEORETICAL QUESTIONS   308
SOCIOLOGICAL THEORIES OF GENDER: 1960–PRESENT   310
    Macro-Social Theories of Gender   310
    Micro-Social Theories of Gender   314
VARIETIES OF CONTEMPORARY FEMINIST THEORY   315
    Gender Difference   317
    Gender Inequality   320
    Gender Oppression   324
    Structural Oppression   331
    Feminism and Postmodernism   340
A FEMINIST SOCIOLOGICAL THEORY   343
    A Feminist Sociology of Knowledge   344
    The Macro-Social Order   345
    The Micro-Social Order   348
    Subjectivity   350
TOWARD AN INTEGRATIVE THEORY   352

PART 3   RECENT INTEGRATIVE DEVELOPMENTS
    IN SOCIOLOGICAL THEORY   357

10   MICRO-MACRO INTEGRATION   359

MICRO-MACRO EXTREMISM   359

THE MOVEMENT TOWARD MICRO-MACRO INTEGRATION   361
EXAMPLES OF MICRO-MACRO INTEGRATION   362
    Integrated Sociological Paradigm   362
    Multidimensional Sociology   365
    Subjective Levels of Analysis   367
    Micro-to-Macro Model   369
    The Micro Foundations of Macrosociology   371
BACK TO THE FUTURE: NORBERT ELIAS'S FIGURATIONAL
    SOCIOLOGY   374
    The History of Manners   376
    Power and Civility   381

11   AGENCY-STRUCTURE INTEGRATION   387

INTRODUCTION   387
MAJOR EXAMPLES OF AGENCY-STRUCTURE INTEGRATION   388
    Structuration Theory   388
    Culture and Agency   393
    Habitus and Field   396
    Colonization of the Life-World   408
MAJOR DIFFERENCES IN THE AGENCY-STRUCTURE LITERATURE   413
AGENCY-STRUCTURE AND MICRO-MACRO LINKAGES   415
    Basic Similarities   415
    Fundamental Differences   415

**PART 4   FROM MODERN TO POSTMODERN SOCIAL THEORY
AND BEYOND   419**

12   CONTEMPORARY THEORIES OF MODERNITY   421

CLASSICAL THEORISTS ON MODERNITY   421
THE JUGGERNAUT OF MODERNITY   423
    Modernity and Its Consequences   424
    Modernity and Identity   427
    Modernity and Intimacy   428
THE RISK SOCIETY   429
    Creating the Risks   431
    Coping with the Risks   432
McDONALDIZATION, GLOBALIZATION/AMERICANIZATION, AND
    THE NEW MEANS OF CONSUMPTION   432
    McDonaldization   432
    Globalization or Americanization?   434
    The New Means of Consumption   435
    Risky or Not?   439

MODERNITY AND THE HOLOCAUST   440
    A Product of Modernity   440
    The Role of Bureaucracy   441
    The Holocaust and McDonaldization   442
MODERNITY'S UNFINISHED PROJECT   444
    Habermas versus Postmodernists   447
INFORMATIONALISM AND THE NETWORK SOCIETY   449

**13   STRUCTURALISM, POSTSTRUCTURALISM, AND THE
EMERGENCE OF POSTMODERN SOCIAL THEORY**   **453**

STRUCTURALISM   454
    Roots in Linguistics   455
    Anthropological Structuralism: Claude Lévi-Strauss   456
    Structural Marxism   456
POSTSTRUCTURALISM   457
    The Ideas of Michel Foucault   459
POSTMODERN SOCIAL THEORY   468
    Moderate Postmodern Social Theory: Fredric Jameson   472
    Extreme Postmodern Social Theory: Jean Baudrillard   477
    Postmodern Social Theory and Sociological Theory   479
    Applying Postmodern Social Theory   480
CRITICISMS AND POST-POSTMODERN SOCIAL THEORY   483

**APPENDIX   SOCIOLOGICAL METATHEORIZING AND A
METATHEORETICAL SCHEMA FOR ANALYZING
SOCIOLOGICAL THEORY**   **489**

METATHEORIZING IN SOCIOLOGY   489
    Pierre Bourdieu's Reflexive Sociology   493
THE IDEAS OF THOMAS KUHN   494
SOCIOLOGY: A MULTIPLE-PARADIGM SCIENCE   496
TOWARD A MORE INTEGRATED SOCIOLOGICAL PARADIGM   498
    Levels of Social Analysis: An Overview   499
    Levels of Social Analysis: A Model   501
REFERENCES   507
INDEXES   603
    Name Index   603
    Subject Index   609

LIST OF BIOGRAPHICAL AND
AUTOBIOGRAPHICAL SKETCHES

Abdel Rahman Ibn-Khaldun	8
Auguste Comte	14
Emile Durkheim	18
Karl Marx	22
Max Weber	28
Georg Simmel	34
Sigmund Freud	37
Herbert Spencer	40
Robert Park	54
Pitirim A. Sorokin	60
C. Wright Mills	67
Talcott Parsons	98
Robert K. Merton: An Autobiographical Sketch	112
Jeffrey C. Alexander: An Autobiographical Sketch	120
Immanuel Wallerstein	162
George Herbert Mead	206
Erving Goffman	228
Harold Garfinkel	246
George Caspar Homans: An Autobiographical Sketch	280
Peter M. Blau	286
Richard Emerson	292
James S. Coleman	300
Jessie Bernard	325
Dorothy E. Smith	330
Patricia Hill Collins	339
Randall Collins: An Autobiographical Sketch	372
Norbert Elias	376
Pierre Bourdieu	398
Anthony Giddens	430
Jurgen Habermas	446
Michel Foucault	466
George Ritzer: Autobiography as a Metatheoretical Tool	496

PREFACE

With this fifth edition, *Modern Sociological Theory* moves into its third decade and its second century. In preparing this revision I have, once again, been impressed with the vibrancy of the field. The biggest change in this edition is the return of systems theory (a portion of a chapter was devoted to it in the third edition of this book) to which Chapter 5 is devoted. This is made necessary by the increasing international visibility of, and attention to, the work of the leading German systems theorist, Niklas Luhmann. The bulk of the chapter is dedicated to his thinking. Other substantial changes include the addition of sections on applying postmodern ideas, criticisms of postmodernism, the rise of post-postmodernism (Chapter 13), and a discussion of the new means of consumption as well as Manuel Castells's thinking on the informational society (Chapter 12). Then there innumerable minor changes to the text either to bring it up to date or to clarify an argument. And literally hundreds of recent citations have been added to the text (and bibliography) so that the book reflects the latest scholarship.

However, with the book already well over 500 pages, the goal here has been not so much to expand the text (although that has occurred in a number of places) as to prevent it from growing too much longer and perhaps even to shorten it a bit. I'm not sure I've succeeded in the latter, but there have been substantial cuts throughout the text, especially in sections dealing with theories that are not as lively as they once were. An effort has also been made to cut text that does not materially advance the argument. I have also tried to make the book easier to read, primarily by adding many headings and subheadings.

This is the least dramatic of the revisions of this book, in part because of the need not to lengthen the book, but also as a reflection of a hiatus, a period of consolidation, in social theorizing at the approach of the new millennium. That is not to say that there is not much new theorizing going on, but in the main it is within extant categories and there have been no new theoretical creations of overwhelming import since the last edition. To put it another way, there has been nothing in the last few years to rival the emergence of micro-macro and agency-structure theories, as well as postmodern social theory, in the 1980s and early 1990s. Some theories have grown "hotter" (e.g. rational choice theory, as well as systems theory), while others (neofunctionalism, metatheorizing) have "cooled," at least for the time being. But these changes do not constitute a radical alteration of the theoretical landscape. This may be the beginning of a longer period of consolidation, or it may be a lull before the efflorescence of a new set of social theories.

Once again, I want to thank Patricia Lengermann and Jill Niebrugge-Brantley for revising their path-breaking chapter on contemporary feminist theory. Not only has their chapter made this book much stronger, it has had a strong influence on theorizing independent of this book. I also thank Douglas Goodman and Matthias Junge for coauthoring the section on Niklas Luhmann's systems theory. Were it not for the presence of Dr. Junge at the University of Maryland on a post-doc from the University of Cheminitz (with his native-speaking knowledge of German), and the combined expertise of Goodman and Junge, that section would not have been written. Thanks also to a long list of reviewers—Maboud Ansari, David Ashley, J. I. ("Hans") Bakker, Keith Gotham, Peter Kivisto, J. Knotterus, James Marshall, Neil McLaughlin, Martin Orr, Robert Perrin, Jane A. Rinehart, Susan Roxburgh, Teresa L. Schied, and Peter Singelmann. I would also like to thank the people at McGraw-Hill, especially Sally Constable, Kathy Blake, and Carrie Sestak. Thanks, also, to my assistants, Jan Geesin and Zinnia Cho, who did the library work that made this book possible and to my son, Jeremy Ritzer, who did the index.

George Ritzer

PART ONE

INTRODUCTION

1

A HISTORICAL SKETCH OF
SOCIOLOGICAL THEORY:
THE EARLY YEARS

INTRODUCTION
SOCIAL FORCES IN THE DEVELOPMENT
OF SOCIOLOGICAL THEORY
    Political Revolutions
    The Industrial Revolution and the Rise of Capitalism
    The Rise of Socialism
    Feminism
    Urbanization
    Religious Change
    The Growth of Science
INTELLECTUAL FORCES AND THE RISE
OF SOCIOLOGICAL THEORY
    The Enlightenment
    The Conservative Reaction to the Enlightenment
    The Development of French Sociology
    The Development of German Sociology
    The Origins of British Sociology
    The Key Figure in Early Italian Sociology
    Turn-of-the-Century Developments in European Marxism

A useful way to begin a book designed to introduce modern sociological theory is with several one-line summaries of various theories:

- The modern world is an iron cage of rational systems from which there is no escape.
- Capitalism tends to sow the seeds of its own destruction.
- The modern world has less moral cohesion than earlier societies had.
- The city spawns a particular type of personality.
- In their social lives, people tend to put on a variety of theatrical performances.
- The social world is defined by principles of reciprocity in give-and-take relationships.
- People create the social worlds that ultimately come to enslave them.
- People always retain the capacity to change the social worlds that constrain them.
- Society is an integrated system of social structures and functions.
- Society is a "juggernaut" with the ever-present possibility of running amok.

- While it appears that the Western world has undergone a process of liberalization, in fact it has grown increasingly oppressive.
- The world has entered a new postmodern era increasingly defined by the inauthentic, the fake, by simulations of reality.

This book is devoted to helping the reader to better understand these theoretical ideas, as well as the larger theories from which they are drawn.

INTRODUCTION

Presenting a history of sociological theory is an important task (S. Turner, 1998), but because we devote only two chapters (1 and 2) to it, what we offer is a highly selective historical sketch (Giddens, 1995). The idea is to provide the reader with a scaffolding which should help in putting the later detailed discussions of theorists and theories in a larger context. As the reader proceeds through the later chapters, it will prove useful to return to these two overview chapters and place the discussions in their context. (It will be especially useful to glance back occasionally to Figures 1.1 and 2.1, which are schematic representations of the histories covered in those chapters.)

The theories treated in the body of this book have a *wide range* of application, deal with *centrally important social issues,* and have *stood the test of time.* These criteria constitute our definition of *sociological theory.*[1] The focus is on the important theoretical work of *sociologists* or the work done by those in other fields that has come to be *defined as important in sociology.* To put it succinctly, this is a book about the "big ideas" in sociology that have stood the test of time (or promise to), idea systems that deal with major social issues and that are far-reaching in scope.

One cannot establish the precise date when sociological theory began. People have been thinking about, and developing theories of, social life since early in history. But we will not go back to the early historic times of the Greeks or Romans or even to the Middle Ages. We will not even go back to the seventeenth century, although Olson (1993) has traced the sociological tradition to the mid-1600s and the work of James Harrington on the relationship between the economy and the polity. This is not because people in those epochs did not have sociologically relevant ideas, but because the return on our investment in time would be small; we would spend a lot of time getting very few ideas that are relevant to modern sociology. In any case, none of the thinkers associated with those eras thought of themselves, and few are now thought of, as sociologists. (For discussion of one exception, see the biographical sketch of Ibn-Khaldun.) It is only in the 1800s that we begin to find thinkers who can be clearly identified as sociologists. These are the classical sociological thinkers we shall be interested in (Camic,

---

[1]Such a definition stands in contrast to the formal, "scientific" definitions that are often used in theory texts of this type. A scientific definition might be that a theory is a set of interrelated propositions that allow for the systematization of knowledge, explanation, and prediction of social life and the generation of new research hypotheses (Faia, 1986). Although such a definition has a number of attractions, it simply does not fit many of the idea systems to be discussed in this book. In other words, most classical (and contemporary) theories fall short on one or more of the formal components of theory, but they are nonetheless considered theories by most sociologists.

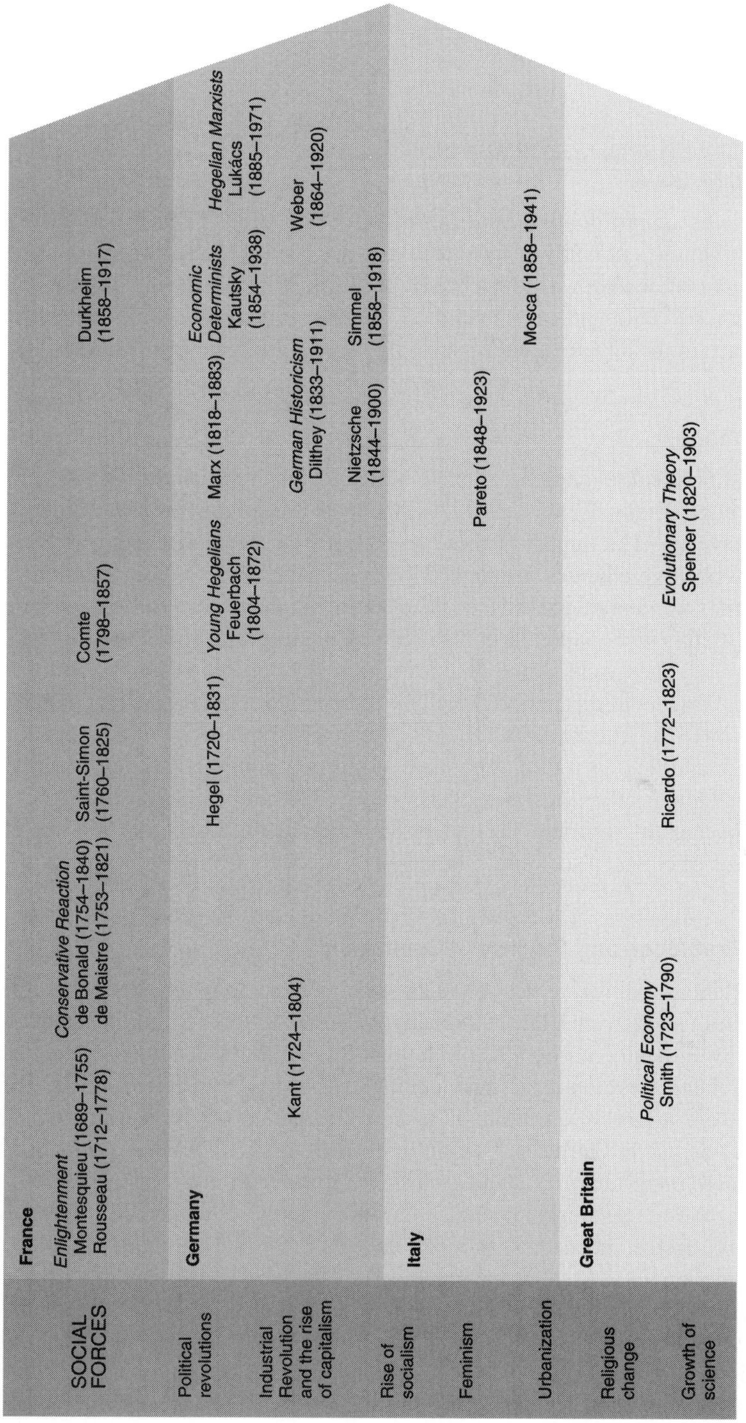

FIGURE 1.1
Sociological Theory: The Early Years

1997; for a debate about what makes theory classical, see Connell, 1997; Collins, 1997b), and we begin by examining the main social and intellectual forces that shaped their ideas.

SOCIAL FORCES IN THE DEVELOPMENT OF SOCIOLOGICAL THEORY

All intellectual fields are profoundly shaped by their social settings. This is particularly true of sociology, which is not only derived from that setting but takes the social setting as its basic subject matter. We will focus briefly on a few of the most important social conditions of the nineteenth and early twentieth centuries, conditions that were of the utmost significance in the development of sociology.

Political Revolutions

The long series of political revolutions ushered in by the French Revolution in 1789 and carrying over through the nineteenth century was the most immediate factor in the rise of sociological theorizing. The impact of these revolutions on many societies was enormous, and many positive changes resulted. However, what attracted the attention of many early theorists was not the positive consequences, but the negative effects of such changes. These writers were particularly disturbed by the resulting chaos and disorder, especially in France. They were united in a desire to restore order to society. Some of the more extreme thinkers of this period literally wanted a return to the peaceful and relatively orderly days of the Middle Ages. The more sophisticated thinkers recognized that social change had made such a return impossible. Thus they sought instead to find new bases of order in societies that had been overturned by the political revolutions of the eighteenth and nineteenth centuries. This interest in the issue of social order was one of the major concerns of classical sociological theorists, especially Comte and Durkheim.

The Industrial Revolution and the Rise of Capitalism

At least as important as political revolution in the shaping of sociological theory was the Industrial Revolution, which swept through many Western societies, mainly in the nineteenth and early twentieth centuries. The Industrial Revolution was not a single event but many interrelated developments that culminated in the transformation of the Western world from a largely agricultural to an overwhelmingly industrial system. Large numbers of people left farms and agricultural work for the industrial occupations offered in the burgeoning factories. The factories themselves were transformed by a long series of technological improvements. Large economic bureaucracies arose to provide the many services needed by industry and the emerging capitalist economic system. In this economy, the ideal was a free marketplace where the many products of an industrial system could be exchanged. Within this system, a few profited greatly while the majority worked long hours for low wages. A reaction against the industrial system and against capitalism in general followed and led to the labor movement as well as to various radical movements aimed at overthrowing the capitalist system.

The Industrial Revolution, capitalism, and the reaction against them all involved an enormous upheaval in Western society, an upheaval that affected sociologists greatly. Four major figures in the early history of sociological theory—Karl Marx, Max Weber, Emile Durkheim, and Georg Simmel—were preoccupied, as were many lesser thinkers, with these changes and the problems they created for society as a whole. They spent their lives studying these problems, and in many cases they endeavored to develop programs that would help solve them.

The Rise of Socialism

One set of changes aimed at coping with the excesses of the industrial system and capitalism can be combined under the heading "socialism." Although some sociologists favored socialism as a solution to industrial problems, most were personally and intellectually opposed to it. On the one side, Karl Marx was an active supporter of the overthrow of the capitalist system and its replacement by a socialist system. Although he did not develop a theory of socialism per se, he spent a great deal of time criticizing various aspects of capitalist society. In addition, he engaged in a variety of political activities that he hoped would help bring about the rise of socialist societies.

However, Marx was atypical in the early years of sociological theory. Most of the early theorists, such as Weber and Durkheim, were opposed to socialism (at least as it was envisioned by Marx). Although they recognized the problems within capitalist society, they sought social reform within capitalism rather than the social revolution argued for by Marx. They feared socialism more than they did capitalism. This fear played a far greater role in shaping sociological theory than did Marx's support of the socialist alternative to capitalism. In fact, as we will see, in many cases sociological theory developed in reaction *against* Marxian and, more generally, socialist theory.

Feminism

In one sense there has always been a feminist perspective. Wherever women are subordinated—and they have been subordinated almost always and everywhere—they seem to have recognized and protested that situation in some form (Lerner, 1993). While precursors can be traced to the 1630s, high points of feminist activity and writing occurred in the liberationist moments of modern Western history; a first flurry of productivity in the 1780s and 1790s with the debates surrounding the American and French revolutions; a far more organized, focused effort in the 1850s as part of the mobilization against slavery and for political rights for the middle class; and the massive mobilization for women's suffrage and for industrial and civic reform legislation in the early twentieth century, especially the Progressive Era in the United States.

All of this had an impact on the development of sociology, in particular on the work of a number of women in or associated with the field—Harriet Martineau, Charlotte Perkins Gilman, Jane Addams, Florence Kelley, Anna Julia Cooper, Ida Wells-Barnett, Marianne Weber, and Beatrice Potter Webb, to name just a few. But their creations were, over time, pushed to the periphery of the profession, annexed or discounted or written out of sociology's public record by the men who were organizing sociology as a professional

---

ABDEL RAHMAN IBN-KHALDUN: A Biographical Sketch

There is a tendency to think of sociology as exclusively a comparatively modern, Western phenomenon. In fact, however, scholars were doing sociology long ago and in other parts of the world. One example is Abdel Rahman Ibn-Khaldun.

Ibn-Khaldun was born in Tunis, North Africa, on May 27, 1332 (Faghirzadeh, 1982). Born to an educated family, Ibn-Khaldun was schooled in the Koran (the Muslim holy book), mathematics, and history. In his lifetime, he served a variety of sultans in Tunis, Morocco, Spain, and Algeria as ambassador, chamberlain, and member of the scholar's council. He also spent two years in prison in Morocco for his belief that state rulers were not divine leaders. After approximately two decades of political activity, Ibn-Khaldun returned to North Africa, where he undertook an intensive five-year period of study and writing. Works produced during this period increased his fame and led to a lectureship at the center of Islamic study, Al-Azhar Mosque University in Cairo. In his well-attended lectures on society and sociology, Ibn-Khaldun stressed the importance of linking sociological thought and historical observation.

By the time he died in 1406, Ibn-Khaldun had produced a corpus of work that had many ideas in common with contemporary sociology. He was committed to the scientific study of society, empirical research, and the search for causes of social phenomena. He devoted considerable attention to various social institutions (for example, politics, economy) and their interrelationships. He was interested in comparing primitive and modern societies. Ibn-Khaldun did not have a dramatic impact on classical sociology, but as scholars in general, and Islamic scholars in particular, rediscover his work, he may come to be seen as being of greater historical significance.

---

power base. Feminist concerns filtered into sociology only on the margins, in the work of marginal male theorists or of the increasingly marginalized female theorists. The men who assumed centrality in the profession—from Spencer, through Weber and Durkheim—made basically conservative responses to the feminist arguments going on around them, making issues of gender an inconsequential topic to which they responded conventionally rather than critically in what they identified and publicly promoted as sociology. They responded in this way even as women were writing a significant body of sociological theory. The history of this gender politics in the profession, which is also part of the history of male response to feminist claims, is only now being written (for example, see Deegan, 1988; Fitzpatrick, 1990; Gordon, 1994; Lengermann and Niebrugge-Brantley, 1998; Rosenberg, 1982).

Urbanization

Partly as a result of the Industrial Revolution, large numbers of people in the nineteenth and twentieth centuries were uprooted from their rural homes and moved to urban settings. This massive migration was caused, in large part, by the jobs created by the industrial system in the urban areas. But it presented many difficulties for those people who had to adjust to urban life. In addition, the expansion of the cities produced a seemingly endless list of urban problems—overcrowding, pollution, noise, traffic, and so forth. The nature of urban life and its problems attracted the attention of many early sociologists, especially Max Weber and Georg Simmel. In fact, the first major school of American sociology, the Chicago school, was in large part defined by its concern for the city and its interest in using Chicago as a laboratory in which to study urbanization and its problems.

Religious Change

Social changes brought on by political revolutions, the Industrial Revolution, and urbanization had a profound effect on religiosity. Many early sociologists came from religious backgrounds and were actively, and in some cases professionally, involved in religion (Hinkle and Hinkle, 1954). They brought to sociology the same objectives as they had in their religious lives. They wished to improve people's lives (Vidich and Lyman, 1985). For some (such as Comte), sociology was transformed into a religion. For others, their sociological theories bore an unmistakable religious imprint. Durkheim wrote one of his major works on religion. A large portion of Weber's work also was devoted to the religions of the world. Marx, too, had an interest in religiosity, but his orientation was far more critical.

The Growth of Science

As sociological theory was being developed, there was an increasing emphasis on science, not only in colleges and universities but in society as a whole. The technological products of science were permeating every sector of life, and science was acquiring enormous prestige. Those associated with the most successful sciences (physics, biology, and chemistry) were accorded honored places in society. Sociologists (especially Comte and Durkheim) from the beginning were preoccupied with science, and many wanted to model sociology after the successful physical and biological sciences. However, a debate soon developed between those who wholeheartedly accepted the scientific model and those (such as Weber) who thought that distinctive characteristics of social life made a wholesale adoption of a scientific model difficult and unwise (Lepenies, 1988). The issue of the relationship between sociology and science is debated to this day, although even a glance at the major journals in the field indicates the predominance of those who favor sociology as a science.

INTELLECTUAL FORCES AND THE RISE OF SOCIOLOGICAL THEORY

Although social factors are important, the primary focus of this chapter is the intellectual forces that played a central role in shaping sociological theory. In the real world, of course, intellectual factors cannot be separated from social forces. For example, in the discussion of the Enlightenment that follows, we will find that that movement was intimately related to, and in many cases provided the intellectual basis for, the social changes discussed above.

The many intellectual forces that shaped the development of social theories are discussed within the national context where their influence was primarily felt (Levine, 1995). We begin with the Enlightenment and its influences on the development of sociological theory in France.

The Enlightenment

It is the view of many observers that the Enlightenment constitutes a critical development in terms of the later evolution of sociology (Hawthorn, 1976; Hughes, Martin, and Sharrock, 1995; Nisbet, 1967; Zeitlin, 1981, 1990, 1994, 1996). The Enlightenment was a period of remarkable intellectual development and change in philosophical thought.[2] A number of long-standing ideas and beliefs—many of which related to social life—were overthrown and replaced during the Enlightenment. The most prominent thinkers associated with the Enlightenment were the French philosophers Charles Montesquieu (1689–1755) and Jean Jacques Rousseau (1712–1778). The influence of the Enlightenment on sociological theory, however, was more indirect and negative than it was direct and positive. As Irving Zeitlin puts it, "Early sociology developed as a reaction to the Enlightenment" (1981:10).

The thinkers associated with the Enlightenment were influenced, above all, by two intellectual currents—seventeenth-century philosophy and science.

Seventeenth-century philosophy was associated with the work of thinkers such as René Descartes, Thomas Hobbes, and John Locke. The emphasis was on producing grand, general, and very abstract systems of ideas that made rational sense. The later thinkers associated with the Enlightenment did not reject the idea that systems of ideas should be general and should make rational sense, but they did make greater efforts to derive their ideas from the real world and to test them there. In other words, they wanted to combine empirical research with reason (Seidman, 1983:36–37). The model for this was science, especially Newtonian physics. At this point, we see the emergence of the application of the scientific method to social issues. Not only did Enlightenment thinkers want their ideas to be, at least in part, derived from the real world, but they also wanted them to be useful to the social world, especially in the critical analysis of that world.

Overall, the Enlightenment was characterized by the belief that people could comprehend and control the universe by means of reason and empirical research. The view was that because the physical world was dominated by natural laws, it was likely that the social world was, too. Thus it was up to the philosopher, using reason and research, to discover these social laws. Once they understood how the social world worked, the Enlightenment thinkers had a practical goal—the creation of a "better," more rational world.

With an emphasis on reason, the Enlightenment philosophers were inclined to reject beliefs in traditional authority. When these thinkers examined traditional values and institutions, they often found them to be irrational—that is, contrary to human nature and

---

[2]This section is based on the work of Irving Zeitlin (1981, 1990, 1994, 1996). Although Zeitlin's analysis is presented here for its coherence, it has a number of limitations: there are better analyses of the Enlightenment, there are many other factors involved in shaping the development of sociology, and Zeitlin tends to overstate his case in places (for example, on the impact of Marx). But on the whole, Zeitlin provides us with a useful starting point, given our objectives in this chapter.

inhibitive of human growth and development. The mission of the practical and change-oriented philosophers of the Enlightenment was to overcome these irrational systems. The theorist who was most directly and positively influenced by Enlightenment thinking was Karl Marx, but he formed his early theoretical ideas in Germany.

The Conservative Reaction to the Enlightenment

On the surface, we might think that French classical sociological theory, like Marx's theory, was directly and positively influenced by the Enlightenment. French sociology became rational, empirical, scientific, and change-oriented, but not before it was also shaped by a set of ideas developed in reaction to the Enlightenment. In Seidman's view, "The ideology of the counter-Enlightenment represented a virtual inversion of Enlightenment liberalism. In place of modernist premises, we can detect in the Enlightenment critics a strong anti-modernist sentiment" (1983:51). As we will see, sociology in general, and French sociology in particular, has from the beginning been an uncomfortable mix of Enlightenment and counter-Enlightenment ideas.

The most extreme form of opposition to Enlightenment ideas was French Catholic counterrevolutionary philosophy, as represented by the ideas of Louis de Bonald (1754–1840) and Joseph de Maistre (1753–1821) (Reedy, 1994). These men were reacting against not only the Enlightenment but also the French Revolution, which they saw partly as a product of the kind of thinking characteristic of the Enlightenment. De Bonald, for example, was disturbed by the revolutionary changes and yearned for a return to the peace and harmony of the Middle Ages. In this view, God was the source of society; therefore, reason, which was so important to the Enlightenment philosophers, was seen as inferior to traditional religious beliefs. Furthermore, it was believed that because God had created society, people should not tamper with it and should not try to change a holy creation. By extension, de Bonald opposed anything that undermined such traditional institutions as patriarchy, the monogamous family, the monarchy, and the Catholic Church.

Although de Bonald represented a rather extreme form of the conservative reaction, his work constitutes a useful introduction to its general premises. The conservatives turned away from what they considered to be the "naive" rationalism of the Enlightenment. They not only recognized the irrational aspects of social life but also assigned them positive value. Thus they regarded such phenomena as tradition, imagination, emotionalism, and religion as useful and necessary components of social life. In that they disliked upheaval and sought to retain the existing order, they deplored developments such as the French Revolution and the Industrial Revolution, which they saw as disruptive forces. The conservatives tended to emphasize social order, an emphasis that became one of the central themes of the work of several sociological theorists.

Zeitlin (1981) outlined ten major propositions that he sees as emerging from the conservative reaction and providing the basis for the development of classical French sociological theory.

1 Whereas Enlightenment thinkers tended to emphasize the individual, the conservative reaction led to a major sociological interest in, and emphasis on, society and other large-scale phenomena. Society was viewed as something more than simply an aggregate of individuals. Society was seen as having an existence of its own with its own laws of development and deep roots in the past.

2 Society was the most important unit of analysis; it was seen as more important than the individual. It was society that produced the individual, primarily through the process of socialization.

3 The individual was not even seen as the most basic element within society. A society consisted of such component parts as roles, positions, relationships, structures, and institutions. The individuals were seen as doing little more than filling these units within society.

4 The parts of society were seen as interrelated and interdependent. Indeed, these interrelationships were a major basis of society. This view led to a conservative political orientation. That is, because the parts were held to be interrelated, it followed that tampering with one part could well lead to the undermining of other parts and, ultimately, of the system as a whole. This meant that changes in the social system should be made with extreme care.

5 Change was seen as a threat not only to society and its components but also to the individuals in society. The various components of society were seen as satisfying people's needs. When institutions were disrupted, people were likely to suffer, and their suffering was likely to lead to social disorder.

6 The general tendency was to see the various large-scale components of society as useful for both society and the individuals in it. As a result, there was little desire to look for the negative effects of existing social structures and social institutions.

7 Small units, such as the family, the neighborhood, and religious and occupational groups, also were seen as essential to individuals and society. They provided the intimate, face-to-face environments that people needed in order to survive in modern societies.

8 There was a tendency to see various modern social changes, such as industrialization, urbanization, and bureaucratization, as having disorganizing effects. These changes were viewed with fear and anxiety, and there was an emphasis on developing ways of dealing with their disruptive effects.

9 While most of these feared changes were leading to a more rational society, the conservative reaction led to an emphasis on the importance of nonrational factors (ritual, ceremony, and worship, for example) in social life.

10 Finally, the conservatives supported the existence of a hierarchical system in society. It was seen as important to society that there be a differential system of status and reward.

These ten propositions, derived from the conservative reaction to the Enlightenment, should be seen as the immediate intellectual basis of the development of sociological theory in France. Many of these ideas made their way into early sociological thought, although some of the Enlightenment ideas (empiricism, for example) were also influential.[3]

---

[3]Although we have emphasized the discontinuities between the Enlightenment and the counter-Enlightenment, Seidman makes the point that there also are continuities and linkages. First, the counter-Enlightenment carried on the scientific tradition developed in the Enlightenment. Second, it picked up the Enlightenment emphasis on collectivities (as opposed to individuals) and greatly extended it. Third, both had an interest in the problems of the modern world, especially its negative effects on individuals.

The Development of French Sociology

We turn now to the actual founding of sociology as a distinctive discipline—specifically, to the work of three French thinkers, Claude Saint-Simon, Auguste Comte, and especially Emile Durkheim.

Claude Henri Saint-Simon (1760–1825)   Saint-Simon was older than Auguste Comte, and in fact Comte, in his early years, served as Saint-Simon's secretary and disciple. There is a very strong similarity between the ideas of these two thinkers, and yet a bitter debate developed between them that led to their eventual split (Pickering, 1993; Thompson, 1975).

The most interesting aspect of Saint-Simon was his significance to the development of *both* conservative (like Comte's) and radical Marxian theory. On the conservative side, Saint-Simon wanted to preserve society as it was, but he did not seek a return to life as it had been in the Middle Ages, as did de Bonald and de Maistre. In addition, he was a *positivist* (Durkheim, 1928/1962:142), which meant that he believed that the study of social phenomena should employ the same scientific techniques as were used in the natural sciences. On the radical side, Saint-Simon saw the need for socialist reforms, especially the centralized planning of the economic system. But Saint-Simon did not go nearly as far as Marx did later. Although he, like Marx, saw the capitalists superseding the feudal nobility, he felt it inconceivable that the working class would come to replace the capitalists. Many of Saint-Simon's ideas are found in Comte's work, but Comte developed them in a more systematic fashion (Pickering, 1997).

Auguste Comte (1798–1857)   Comte was the first to use the term *sociology* (Pickering, forthcoming).[4] He had an enormous influence on later sociological theorists (especially Herbert Spencer and Emile Durkheim). And he believed that the study of sociology should be scientific, just as many classical theorists did and most contemporary sociologists do (Lenzer, 1975).

Comte was greatly disturbed by the anarchy that pervaded French society and was critical of those thinkers who had spawned both the Enlightenment and the revolution. He developed his scientific view, "positivism," or "positive philosophy," to combat what he considered to be the negative and destructive philosophy of the Enlightenment. Comte was in line with, and influenced by, the French counterrevolutionary Catholics (especially de Bonald and de Maistre). However, his work can be set apart from theirs on at least two grounds. First, he did not think it possible to return to the Middle Ages; advances of science and industry made that impossible. Second, he developed a much more sophisticated theoretical system than his predecessors, one that was adequate to shape a good portion of early sociology.

Comte developed *social physics,* or what in 1832 he called *sociology* (Pickering, forthcoming). The use of the term *social physics* made it clear that Comte sought to model sociology after the "hard sciences." This new science, which in his view would ultimately become *the* dominant science, was to be concerned with both social statics

---

[4]While he recognizes that Comte created the label "sociology," Eriksson (1993) has challenged the idea that Comte is the progenitor of modern, scientific sociology. Rather, Eriksson sees people like Adam Smith and more generally the Scottish Moralists, as the true source of modern sociology. See also, L. Hill (1996) on the importance of Adam Ferguson; and Ullmann-Margalit (1997) on Ferguson and Adam Smith.

AUGUSTE COMTE: A Biographical Sketch

Auguste Comte was born in Montpelier, France, on January 19, 1798 (Pickering, 1993:7). His parents were middle class and his father eventually rose to the position of official local agent for the tax collector. Although a precocious student, Comte never received a college-level degree. He and his whole class were dismissed from the Ecole Polytechnique for their rebelliousness and their political ideas. This expulsion had an adverse effect on Comte's academic career. In 1817 he became secretary (and "adopted son" [Manuel, 1962:251]) to Claude Henri Saint-Simon, a philosopher forty years Comte's senior. They worked closely together for several years and Comte acknowledged his great debt to Saint-Simon: "I certainly owe a great deal intellectually to Saint-Simon . . . he contributed powerfully to launching me in the philosophic direction that I clearly created for myself today and which I will follow without hesitation all my life" (Durkheim, 1928/1962:144). But in 1824 they had a falling out because Comte believed that Saint-Simon wanted to omit Comte's name from one of his contributions. Comte later wrote of his relationship with Saint-Simon as "catastrophic" (Pickering, 1993:238) and described him as a "depraved juggler" (Durkheim, 1928/1962:144). In 1852, Comte said of Saint-Simon, "I owed nothing to this personage" (Pickering, 1993:240).

Heilbron (1995) describes Comte as short (perhaps 5 feet, 2 inches), a bit cross-eyed, and very insecure in social situations, especially involving women. He was also alienated from society as a whole. These facts may help account for the fact that Comte married Caroline Massin (the marriage lasted from 1825 to 1842). She was an illegitimate child whom Comte later called a "prostitute," although that label has been questioned recently (Pickering, 1997:37). Comte's personal insecurities stood in contrast to his great security about his own intellectual capacities, and it appears as if this self-esteem was well founded:

> Comte's prodigious memory is famous. Endowed with a photographic memory he could recite backwards the words of any page he had read but once. His powers of concentration were such that he could sketch out an entire book without putting pen to paper. His lectures were all delivered without notes. When he sat down to write out his books he wrote everything from memory. (Schweber, 1991:134)

(existing social structures) and social dynamics (social change). Although both involved the search for laws of social life, he felt that social dynamics was more important than social statics. This focus on change reflected his interest in social reform, particularly reform of the ills created by the French Revolution and the Enlightenment. Comte did not urge revolutionary change, because he felt the natural evolution of society would make things better. Reforms were needed only to assist the process a bit.

This leads us to the cornerstone of Comte's approach—his evolutionary theory, or the *law of the three stages.* The theory proposes that there are three intellectual stages through which the world has gone throughout its history. According to Comte, not only does the world go through this process, but groups, societies, sciences, individuals, and even minds go through the same three stages. The *theological* stage is the first, and it characterized the world prior to 1300. During this period, the major idea system

In 1826, Comte concocted a scheme by which he would present a series of seventy-two public lectures (to be held in his apartment) on his philosophy. The course drew a distinguished audience, but it was halted after three lectures when Comte suffered a nervous breakdown. He continued to suffer from mental problems, and once in 1827 he tried (unsuccessfully) to commit suicide by throwing himself into the Seine River.

Although he could not get a regular position at the Ecole Polytechnique, Comte did get a minor position as a teaching assistant there in 1832. In 1837, Comte was given the additional post of admissions examiner, and this, for the first time, gave him an adequate income (he had often been economically dependent on his family until this time). During this period, Comte worked on the six-volume work for which he is best known, *Cours de Philosophie Positive,* which was finally published in its entirety in 1842 (the first volume had been published in 1830). In that work Comte outlined his view that sociology was the ultimate science. He also attacked the Ecole Polytechnique, and the result was that in 1844 his assistantship there was not renewed. By 1851 he had completed the four-volume *Systeme de Politique Positive,* which had a more practical intent, offering a grand plan for the reorganization of society.

Heilbron argues that a major break took place in Comte's life in 1838 and it was then that he lost hope that anyone would take his work on science in general, and sociology in particular, seriously. It was also at that point that he embarked on his life of "cerebral hygiene"; that is, Comte began to avoid reading the work of other people, with the result that he became hopelessly out of touch with recent intellectual developments. It was after 1838 that he began developing his bizarre ideas about reforming society that found expression in *Systeme de Politique Positive.* Comte came to fancy himself as the high priest of a new religion of humanity; he believed in a world that eventually would be led by sociologist-priests. (Comte had been strongly influenced by his Catholic background.) Interestingly, in spite of such outrageous ideas, Comte eventually developed a considerable following in France, as well as in a number of other countries.

Auguste Comte died on September 5, 1857.

emphasized the belief that supernatural powers, religious figures, modeled after humankind, are at the root of everything. In particular, the social and physical world is seen as produced by God. The second stage is the *metaphysical* stage, which occurred roughly between 1300 and 1800. This era was characterized by the belief that abstract forces like "nature," rather than personalized gods, explain virtually everything. Finally, in 1800 the world entered the *positivistic* stage, characterized by belief in science. People now tended to give up the search for absolute causes (God or nature) and concentrated instead on observation of the social and physical world in the search for the laws governing them.

It is clear that in his theory of the world Comte focused on intellectual factors. Indeed, he argued that intellectual disorder was the cause of social disorder. The disorder stemmed from earlier idea systems (theological and metaphysical) that continued to exist in the positivistic (scientific) age. Only when positivism gained total control would social upheavals cease. Because this was an evolutionary process, there was no need to foment social upheaval and revolution. Positivism would come, although perhaps not as quickly as some would like. Here Comte's social reformism and his sociology coincide. Sociology could expedite the arrival of positivism and hence bring order to the social world. Above all, Comte did not want to seem to be espousing revolution. There was, in his view, enough disorder in the world. In any case, from Comte's point of view, it was intellectual change that was needed, so there was little reason for social and political revolution.

We have already encountered several of Comte's positions that were to be of great significance to the development of classical sociology—his basic conservatism, reformism, and scientism, and his evolutionary view of the world. Several other aspects of his work deserve mention because they also were to play a major role in the development of sociological theory. For example, his sociology does *not* focus on the individual but rather takes as its basic unit of analysis larger entities such as the family. He also urged that we look at *both* social structure and social change. Of great importance to later sociological theory, especially the work of Spencer and Parsons, is Comte's stress on the systematic character of society—the links among and between the various components of society. He also accorded great importance to the role of consensus in society. He saw little merit in the idea that society is characterized by inevitable conflict between workers and capitalists. In addition, Comte emphasized the need to engage in abstract theorizing and to go out and do sociological research. He urged that sociologists use observation, experimentation, and comparative historical analysis. Finally, Comte believed that sociology ultimately would become the dominant scientific force in the world because of its distinctive ability to interpret social laws and to develop reforms aimed at patching up problems within the system.

Comte was in the forefront of the development of positivistic sociology (Bryant, 1985; Halfpenny, 1982). To Jonathan Turner, Comte's positivism emphasized that "the social universe is amenable to the development of abstract laws that can be tested through the careful collection of data," and "these abstract laws will denote the basic and generic properties of the social universe and they will specify their 'natural relations'" (1985:24). As we will see, a number of classical theorists (especially Spencer and Durkheim) shared Comte's interest in the discovery of the laws of social life. While positivism remains important in contemporary sociology, it has come under attack from a number of quarters (Morrow, 1994).

Even though Comte lacked a solid academic base on which to build a school of Comtian sociological theory, he nevertheless laid a basis for the development of a significant stream of sociological theory. But his long-term significance is dwarfed by that of his successor in French sociology and the inheritor of a number of its ideas, Emile Durkheim. (For a debate over the canonization of Durkheim, as well as other classical theorists discussed in this chapter, see Parker, 1997; Mouzelis, 1997.)

Emile Durkheim (1858–1917)   While the Enlightenment was a negative influence, it also had a number of positive effects on Durkheim's work (for example, the emphasis on science and social reformism). However, Durkheim is best seen as the inheritor of the conservative tradition, especially as it was manifested in Comte's work. But whereas

Comte had remained outside of academia, Durkheim developed an increasingly strong academic base as his career progressed. Durkheim legitimized sociology in France, and his work ultimately became a dominant force in the development of sociology in general and of sociological theory in particular (R. Jones, forthcoming).

Durkheim was politically liberal, but he took a more conservative position intellectually. Like Comte and the Catholic counterrevolutionaries, Durkheim feared and hated social disorder. His work was informed by the disorders produced by the general social changes discussed earlier in this chapter, as well as by others (such as industrial strikes, disruption of the ruling class, church–state discord, the rise of political anti-Semitism) more specific to the France of Durkheim's time (Karady, 1983). In fact, most of his work was devoted to the study of social order. His view was that social disorders were *not* a necessary part of the modern world and could be reduced by social reforms. Whereas Marx saw the problems of the modern world as inherent in society, Durkheim (along with most other classical theorists) did not. As a result, Marx's ideas on the need for social revolution stood in sharp contrast to the reformism of Durkheim and the others. As classical sociological theory developed, it was the Durkheimian interest in order and reform that came to dominate, while the Marxian position was eclipsed.

Social Facts   Durkheim developed a distinctive conception of the subject matter of sociology and then tested it in an empirical study. In *The Rules of Sociological Method* (1895/1964), Durkheim argued that it is the special task of sociology to study what he called *social facts*. He conceived of social facts as forces (Takla and Pope, 1985) and structures that are external to, and coercive of, the individual. The study of these large-scale structures and forces—for example, institutionalized law and shared moral beliefs—and their impact on people became the concern of many later sociological theorists (Parsons, for example). In *Suicide* (1897/1951), Durkheim reasoned that if he could link such an individual behavior as suicide to social causes (social facts), he would have made a persuasive case for the importance of the discipline of sociology. But Durkheim did not examine why individual *A* or *B* committed suicide; rather, he was interested in the causes of differences in suicide rates among groups, regions, countries, and different categories of people (for example, married and single). His basic argument was that it was the nature of, and changes in, social facts that led to differences in suicide rates. For example, a war or an economic depression would create a collective mood of depression that would in turn lead to increases in suicide rates. There is much more to be said on this subject, but the key point is that Durkheim developed a distinctive view of sociology and sought to demonstrate its usefulness in a scientific study of suicide.

In *The Rules of Sociological Method*, Durkheim differentiated between two types of social facts—material and nonmaterial. Although he dealt with both in the course of his work, his main focus was on *nonmaterial social facts* (for example, culture, social institutions) rather than *material social facts* (for example, bureaucracy, law). This concern for nonmaterial social facts was already clear in his earliest major work, *The Division of Labor in Society* (1893/1964). His focus there was a comparative analysis of what held society together in the primitive and modern cases. He concluded that earlier societies were held together primarily by nonmaterial social facts, specifically, a strongly held common morality, or what he called a strong *collective conscience*. How-

EMILE DURKHEIM: A Biographical Sketch

 Emile Durkheim was born on April 15, 1858, in Epinal, France. He was descended from a long line of rabbis and himself studied to be a rabbi, but by the time he was in his teens, he had largely disavowed his heritage (Strenski, 1997:4). From that time on, his lifelong interest in religion was more academic than theological (Mestrovic, 1988). He was dissatisfied not only with his religious training but also with his general education and its emphasis on literary and esthetic matters. He longed for schooling in scientific methods and in the moral principles needed to guide social life. He rejected a traditional academic career in philosophy and sought instead to acquire the scientific training needed to contribute to the moral guidance of society. Although he was interested in scientific sociology, there was no field of sociology at that time, so between 1882 and 1887 he taught philosophy in a number of provincial schools in the Paris area.

His appetite for science was whetted further by a trip to Germany, where he was exposed to the scientific psychology being pioneered by Wilhelm Wundt (Durkheim, 1887/1993). In the years immediately after his visit to Germany, Durkheim published a good deal, basing his work, in part, on his experiences there (R. Jones, 1994). These publications helped him gain a position in the department of philosophy at the University of Bordeaux in 1887. There Durkheim offered the first course in social science in a French university. This was a particularly impressive accomplishment, because only a decade earlier, a furor had erupted in a French university by the mention of Auguste Comte in a student dissertation. Durkheim's main responsibility, however, was teaching courses in education to schoolteachers, and his most important course was in the area of moral education. His goal was to communicate a moral system to the educators, who he hoped would then pass the system on to young people in an effort to help reverse the moral degeneration he saw around him in French society.

The years that followed were characterized by a series of personal successes for Durkheim. In 1893 he published his French doctoral thesis, *The Division of Labor in Society,* as well as his Latin thesis on Montesquieu (Durkheim, 1892/1997; W. Miller, 1993). His major methodological statement, *The Rules of Sociological Method,* appeared in 1895, followed (in 1897) by his empirical application of those methods in the study *Suicide.* By 1896 he had become a full professor at Bordeaux. In 1902 he was summoned to the famous French university the Sorbonne, and in 1906 he was named professor of the science of education, a title that was changed in 1913 to professor of the science of education *and sociology.* The other of his most famous works, *The Elementary Forms of Religious Life,* was published in 1912.

Durkheim is most often thought of today as a political conservative, and his influence within sociology certainly has been a conservative one. But in his time, he was considered a liberal, and this was exemplified by the active public role he played in the defense of Alfred Dreyfus, the Jewish army captain whose court-martial for treason was felt by many to be anti-Semitic (Farrell, 1997).

ever, because of the complexities of modern society, there had been a decline in the strength of the collective conscience. The primary bond in the modern world was an intricate division of labor, which tied people to others in dependency relationships. However, Durkheim felt that the modern division of labor brought with it several

Durkheim was deeply offended by the Dreyfus affair, particularly its anti-Semitism. But Durkheim did not attribute this anti-Semitism to racism among the French people. Characteristically, he saw it as a symptom of the moral sickness confronting French society as a whole (Birnbaum and Todd, 1995). He said:

> When society undergoes suffering, it feels the need to find someone whom it can hold responsible for its sickness, on whom it can avenge its misfortunes: and those against whom public opinion already discriminates are naturally designated for this role. These are the pariahs who serve as expiatory victims. What confirms me in this interpretation is the way in which the result of Dreyfus's trial was greeted in 1894. There was a surge of joy in the boulevards. People celebrated as a triumph what should have been a cause for public mourning. At last they knew whom to blame for the economic troubles and moral distress in which they lived. The trouble came from the Jews. The charge had been officially proved. By this very fact alone, things already seemed to be getting better and people felt consoled.
>
> (Lukes, 1972:345)

Thus, Durkheim's interest in the Dreyfus affair stemmed from his deep and lifelong interest in morality and the moral crisis confronting modern society.

To Durkheim, the answer to the Dreyfus affair and crises like it lay in ending the moral disorder in society. Because that could not be done quickly or easily, Durkheim suggested more specific actions such as severe repression of those who incite hatred of others and government efforts to show the public how it is being misled. He urged people to "have the courage to proclaim aloud what they think, and to unite together in order to achieve victory in the struggle against public madness" (Lukes, 1972:347).

Durkheim's (1928/1962) interest in socialism is also taken as evidence against the idea that he was a conservative, but his kind of socialism was very different from the kind that interested Marx and his followers. In fact, Durkheim labeled Marxism as a set of "disputable and out-of-date hypotheses" (Lukes, 1972:323). To Durkheim, socialism represented a movement aimed at the moral regeneration of society through scientific morality, and he was not interested in short-term political methods or the economic aspects of socialism. He did not see the proletariat as the salvation of society, and he was greatly opposed to agitation or violence. Socialism for Durkheim was very different from what we usually think of as socialism; it simply represented a system in which the moral principles discovered by scientific sociology were to be applied.

Durkheim, as we will see throughout this book, had a profound influence on the development of sociology, but his influence was not restricted to it (Halls, 1996). Much of his impact on other fields came through the journal *L'année sociologique,* which he founded in 1898. An intellectual circle arose around the journal with Durkheim at its center. Through it, he and his ideas influenced such fields as anthropology, history, linguistics, and—somewhat ironically, considering his early attacks on the field—psychology.

Durkheim died on November 15, 1917, a celebrated figure in French intellectual circles, but it was not until over twenty years later, with the publication of Talcott Parsons's *The Structure of Social Action* (1937), that his work became a significant influence on American sociology.

"pathologies"; it was, in other words, an inadequate method of holding society together. Given his conservative sociology, Durkheim did not feel that revolution was needed to solve these problems. Rather, he suggested a variety of reforms that could "patch up" the modern system and keep it functioning. Although he recognized that there was no going back to the age when a powerful collective conscience predominated, he did feel that the common morality could be strengthened in modern society and that people thereby could cope better with the pathologies that they were experiencing.

Religion   In his later work, nonmaterial social facts occupied an even more central position. In fact, he came to focus on perhaps the ultimate form of a nonmaterial social fact—religion—in his last major work, *The Elementary Forms of Religious Life* (1912/1965). Durkheim examined primitive society in order to find the roots of religion. He believed that he would be better able to find those roots in the comparative simplicity of primitive society than in the complexity of the modern world. What he found, he felt, was that the source of religion was society itself. Society comes to define certain things as religious and others as profane. Specifically, in the case he studied, the clan was the source of a primitive kind of religion, *totemism,* in which things like plants and animals are deified. Totemism, in turn, was seen as a specific type of nonmaterial social fact, a form of the collective conscience. In the end, Durkheim came to argue that society and religion (or, more generally, the collective conscience) were one and the same. Religion was the way society expressed itself in the form of a nonmaterial social fact. In a sense, then, Durkheim came to deify society and its major products. Clearly, in deifying society, Durkheim took a highly conservative stance: one would not want to overturn a deity *or* its societal source. Because he identified society with God, Durkheim was not inclined to urge social revolution. Instead, he was a social reformer seeking ways of improving the functioning of society. In these and other ways, Durkheim was clearly in line with French conservative sociology. The fact that he avoided many of its excesses helped make him the most significant figure in French sociology.

These books and other important works helped carve out a distinctive domain for sociology in the academic world of turn-of-the-century France, and they earned Durkheim the leading position in that growing field. In 1898, Durkheim set up a scholarly journal devoted to sociology, *L'année sociologique* (Besnard, 1983a). It became a powerful force in the development and spread of sociological ideas. Durkheim was intent on fostering the growth of sociology, and he used his journal as a focal point for the development of a group of disciples. They would later extend his ideas and carry them to many other locales and into the study of other aspects of the social world (for example, sociology of law and sociology of the city) (Besnard, 1983a:1). By 1910, Durkheim had established a strong center of sociology in France, and the academic institutionalization of sociology was well under way in that nation (Heilbron, 1995).

The Development of German Sociology

Whereas the early history of French sociology is a fairly coherent story of the progression from the Enlightenment and the French Revolution to the conservative reaction and to the increasingly important sociological ideas of Saint-Simon, Comte, and Durkheim, German sociology was fragmented from the beginning. A split developed between Marx (and his supporters), who remained on the edge of sociology, and the early giants of mainstream German sociology, Max Weber and Georg Simmel.[5] However, although

---

[5]For an argument against this and the view of continuity between Marxian and mainstream sociology, see Seidman (1983).

Marxian theory itself was deemed unacceptable, its ideas found their way in a variety of positive and negative ways into mainstream German sociology.

The Roots and Nature of the Theories of Karl Marx (1818–1883)   The dominant intellectual influence on Karl Marx was the German philosopher G. W. F. Hegel (1770–1831).

Hegel   According to Ball, "it is difficult for us to appreciate the degree to which Hegel dominated German thought in the second quarter of the nineteenth century. It was largely within the framework of his philosophy that educated Germans—including the young Marx—discussed history, politics and culture" (1991:25). Marx's education at the University of Berlin was shaped by Hegel's ideas as well as by the split that developed among Hegel's followers after his death. The "Old Hegelians" continued to subscribe to the master's ideas, while the "Young Hegelians," although still working in the Hegelian tradition, were critical of many facets of his philosophical system.

Two concepts represent the essence of Hegel's philosophy—the dialectic and idealism (Hegel, 1807/1967, 1821/1967). The *dialectic* is both a way of thinking and an image of the world. On the one hand, it is a way of thinking that stresses the importance of processes, relations, dynamics, conflicts, and contradictions—a dynamic rather than a static way of thinking about the world. On the other hand, it is a view that the *world* is made up not of static structures but of processes, relationships, dynamics, conflicts, and contradictions. Although the dialectic is generally associated with Hegel, it certainly predates him in philosophy. Marx, trained in the Hegelian tradition, accepted the significance of the dialectic. However, he was critical of some aspects of the way Hegel used it. For example, Hegel tended to apply the dialectic only to ideas, whereas Marx felt that it applied as well to more material aspects of life, for example, the economy.

Hegel is also associated with the philosophy of *idealism,* which emphasizes the importance of the mind and mental products rather than the material world. It is the social definition of the physical and material worlds that matters most, not those worlds themselves. In its extreme form, idealism asserts that *only* the mind and psychological constructs exist. Some idealists believed that their mental processes would remain the same even if the physical and social worlds no longer existed. Idealists emphasize not only mental processes but also the ideas produced by these processes. Hegel paid a great deal of attention to the development of such ideas, especially to what he referred to as the "spirit" of society.

In fact, Hegel offered a kind of evolutionary theory of the world in idealistic terms. At first, people were endowed only with the ability to acquire a sensory understanding of the world around them. They could understand things like the sight, smell, and feel of the social and physical world. Later, people developed the ability to be conscious of, to understand, themselves. With self-knowledge and self-understanding, people began to understand that they could become more than they were. In terms of Hegel's dialectical approach, a contradiction developed between what people were and what they felt they could be. The resolution of this contradiction lay in the development of an individual's awareness of his or her place in the larger spirit of society. Individuals come to realize that their ultimate fulfillment lies in the development and the expansion of the spirit of society as a whole. Thus, individuals in Hegel's scheme evolve from an

KARL MARX: A Biographical Sketch

Karl Marx was born in Trier, Prussia, on May 5, 1818. His father, a lawyer, provided the family with a fairly typical middle-class existence. Both parents were from rabbinical families, but for business reasons the father had converted to Lutheranism when Karl was very young. In 1841 Marx received his doctorate in philosophy from the University of Berlin, a school heavily influenced by Hegel and the Young Hegelians, supportive, yet critical, of their master. Marx's doctorate was a dry philosophical treatise, but it did anticipate many of his later ideas. After graduation he became a writer for a liberal-radical newspaper and within ten months had become its editor-in-chief. However, because of its political positions, the paper was closed shortly thereafter by the government. The early essays published in this period began to reflect a number of the positions that would guide Marx throughout his life. They were liberally sprinkled with democratic principles, humanism, and youthful idealism. He rejected the abstractness of Hegelian philosophy, the naive dreaming of utopian communists, and those activists who were urging what he considered to be premature political action. In rejecting these activists, Marx laid the groundwork for his own life's work:

> Practical attempts, even by the masses, can be answered with a cannon as soon as they become dangerous, but ideas that have overcome our intellect and conquered our conviction, ideas to which reason has riveted our conscience, are chains from which one cannot break loose without breaking one's heart; they are demons that one can only overcome by submitting to them.

> (Marx, 1842/1977:20)

Marx married in 1843 and soon thereafter was forced to leave Germany for the more liberal atmosphere of Paris. There he continued to grapple with the ideas of Hegel and his supporters, but he also encountered two new sets of ideas—French socialism and English political economy. It was the unique way in which he combined Hegelianism, socialism, and political economy that shaped his intellectual orientation. Also of great importance at this point was his meeting the man who was to become his lifelong friend, benefactor, and collaborator—Friedrich Engels (Carver, 1983). The son of a textile manufacturer, Engels had become a socialist critical of the conditions facing the working class. Much of Marx's compassion for the misery of the working class came from his exposure to Engels and his ideas. In 1844 Engels and Marx had a lengthy conversation in a famous café in Paris and laid the groundwork for a lifelong association. Of that conversation Engels said, "Our complete agreement in all theoretical fields became obvious . . . and our joint work dates from that time" (McLellan, 1973:131). In the following year, Engels published a notable work, *The Condition of the Working Class in England*. During this period Marx wrote a number of abstruse works (many unpublished in his lifetime), including *The Holy Family* and *The German*

understanding of things to an understanding of self to an understanding of their place in the larger scheme of things.

Hegel, then, offered a general theory of the evolution of the world. It is a subjective theory in which change is held to occur at the level of consciousness. However, that change occurs largely beyond the control of actors. Actors are reduced to little more than vessels swept along by the inevitable evolution of consciousness.

Ideology (both coauthored with Engels), but he also produced *The Economic and Philosophic Manuscripts of 1844,* which better foreshadowed his increasing preoccupation with the economic domain.

While Marx and Engels shared a theoretical orientation, there were many differences between the two men. Marx tended to be theoretical, a disorderly intellectual, and very oriented to his family. Engels was a practical thinker, a neat and tidy businessman, and a person who did not believe in the institution of the family. In spite of their differences, Marx and Engels forged a close union in which they collaborated on books and articles and worked together in radical organizations, and Engels even helped support Marx throughout the rest of his life so that Marx could devote himself to his intellectual and political endeavors.

In spite of the close association of the names of Marx and Engels, Engels made it clear that he was the junior partner:

> Marx could very well have done without me. What Marx accomplished I would not have achieved. Marx stood higher, saw farther, and took a wider and quicker view than the rest of us. Marx was a genius.
>
> (Engels, cited in McLellan, 1973:131–132)

In fact, many believe that Engels failed to understand many of the subtleties of Marx's work (C. Smith, 1997). After Marx's death, Engels became the leading spokesperson for Marxian theory and in various ways distorted and oversimplified it, although he remained faithful to the political perspective he had forged with Marx.

Because some of his writings had upset the Prussian government, the French government (at the request of the Prussians) expelled Marx in 1845, and he moved to Brussels. His radicalism was growing, and he had become an active member of the international revolutionary movement. He also associated with the Communist League and was asked to write a document (with Engels) expounding its aims and beliefs. The result was the *Communist Manifesto* of 1848, a work that was characterized by ringing political slogans (for example, "Working men of all countries, unite!").

In 1849 Marx moved to London, and, in light of the failure of the political revolutions of 1848, he began to withdraw from active revolutionary activity and to move into more serious and detailed research on the workings of the capitalist system. In 1852, he began his famous studies in the British Museum of the working conditions in capitalism. These studies ultimately resulted in the three volumes of *Capital,* the first of which was published in 1867; the other two were published posthumously. He lived in poverty during these years, barely managing to survive on a small income from his writings and the support of Engels. In 1864 Marx became reinvolved in political activity by joining the *International,* an international movement of workers. He soon gained preeminence within the movement and devoted a number of years to it. He began to gain fame both as leader of the *International* and as the author of *Capital.* But the disintegration of the *International* by 1876, the failure of various revolutionary movements, and personal illness took their toll on Marx. His wife died in 1881, a daughter in 1882, and Marx himself on March 14, 1883.

Feuerbach Ludwig Feuerbach (1804–1872) was an important bridge between Hegel and Marx. As a Young Hegelian, Feuerbach was critical of Hegel for, among other things, his excessive emphasis on consciousness and the spirit of society. Feuerbach's adoption of a materialist philosophy led him to argue that what was needed was to move from Hegel's subjective idealism to a focus not on ideas but on the material reality of real human beings. In his critique of Hegel, Feuerbach focused on religion.

To Feuerbach, God is simply a projection by people of their human essence onto an impersonal force. People set God over and above themselves, with the result that they become alienated from God and project a series of positive characteristics onto God (that He is perfect, almighty, and holy), while they reduce themselves to being imperfect, powerless, and sinful. Feuerbach argued that this kind of religion must be overcome and that its defeat could be aided by a materialist philosophy in which people (not religion) became their own highest object, ends in themselves. Real people, not abstract ideas like religion, are deified by a materialist philosophy.

Marx, Hegel, and Feuerbach   Marx was simultaneously influenced by, and critical of, *both* Hegel and Feuerbach. Marx, following Feuerbach, was critical of Hegel's adherence to an idealist philosophy. Marx took this position not only because of his adoption of a materialist orientation but also because of his interest in practical activities. Social facts like wealth and the state are treated by Hegel as ideas rather than as real, material entities. Even when he examined a seemingly material process like labor, Hegel was looking only at abstract mental labor. This is very different from Marx's interest in the labor of real, sentient people. Thus Hegel was looking at the wrong issues as far as Marx was concerned. In addition, Marx felt that Hegel's idealism led to a very conservative political orientation. To Hegel, the process of evolution was occurring beyond the control of people and their activities. In any case, in that people seemed to be moving toward greater consciousness of the world as it could be, there seemed no need for any revolutionary change; the process was already moving in the "desired" direction. Whatever problems did exist lay in consciousness, and the answer therefore seemed to lie in changing thinking.

Marx took a very different position, arguing that the problems of modern life can be traced to real, material sources (for example, the structures of capitalism) and that the solutions, therefore, can be found *only* in the overturning of those structures by the collective action of large numbers of people (Marx and Engels, 1845/1956:254). Whereas Hegel "stood the world on its head" (that is, focused on consciousness, not the real material world), Marx firmly embedded his dialectic in a material base.

Marx applauded Feuerbach's critique of Hegel on a number of counts (for example, its materialism and its rejection of the abstractness of Hegel's theory), but he was far from fully satisfied with Feuerbach's own position (Thomson, 1994). For one thing, Feuerbach focused on the religious world, whereas Marx believed that it was the entire social world, and the economy in particular, that had to be analyzed. Although Marx accepted Feuerbach's materialism, he felt that Feuerbach had gone too far in focusing one-sidedly, nondialectically, on the material world. Feuerbach failed to include the most important of Hegel's contributions, the dialectic, in his materialist orientation, particularly the relationship between people and the material world. Finally, Marx argued that Feuerbach, like most philosophers, failed to emphasize praxis—practical activity—in particular, revolutionary activity. As Marx put it, "The philosophers have only *interpreted* the world, in various ways; the point, however, is to *change* it" (cited in Tucker, 1970:109).

Marx extracted what he considered to be the two most important elements from these two thinkers—Hegel's dialectic and Feuerbach's materialism—and fused them into his own distinctive orientation, *dialectical materialism,* which focuses on dialectical relationships within the material world.

Political Economy   Marx's materialism and his consequent focus on the economic sector led him rather naturally to the work of a group of *political economists* (for example, Adam Smith and David Ricardo). Marx was very attracted to a number of their positions. He lauded their basic premise that labor was the source of all wealth. This ultimately led Marx to his *labor theory of value,* in which he argued that the profit of the capitalist was based on the exploitation of the laborer. Capitalists performed the rather simple trick of paying the workers less than they deserved, because they received less pay than the value of what they actually produced in a work period. This *surplus value,* which was retained and reinvested by the capitalist, was the basis of the entire capitalist system. The capitalist system grew by continually increasing the level of exploitation of the workers (and therefore the amount of surplus value) and investing the profits for the expansion of the system.

Marx also was affected by the political economists' depiction of the horrors of the capitalist system and the exploitation of the workers. However, whereas they depicted the evils of capitalism, Marx criticized the political economists for seeing these evils as inevitable components of capitalism. Marx deplored their general acceptance of capitalism and the way they urged people to work for economic success within it. He also was critical of the political economists for failing to see the inherent conflict between capitalists and laborers and for denying the need for a radical change in the economic order. Such conservative economics was hard for Marx to accept, given his commitment to a radical change from capitalism to socialism.

Marx and Sociology   Marx was not a sociologist and did not consider himself to be one. Although his work is too broad to be encompassed by the term *sociology,* there is a sociological theory to be found in Marx's work. From the beginning, there were those who were heavily influenced by Marx, and there has been a continuous strand of Marxian sociology, primarily in Europe. But for the majority of early sociologists, his work was a negative force, something against which to shape their sociology. Until very recently, sociological theory, especially in America, has been characterized by either hostility to or ignorance of Marxian theory. This has, as we will see in Chapter 2, changed dramatically, but the negative reaction to Marx's work was a major force in the shaping of much of sociological theory (Gurney, 1981).

The basic reason for this rejection of Marx was ideological. Many of the early sociological theorists were inheritors of the conservative reaction to the disruptions of the Enlightenment and the French Revolution. Marx's radical ideas and the radical social changes he foretold and sought to bring to life were clearly feared and hated by such thinkers. Marx was dismissed as an ideologist. It was argued that he was not a serious sociological theorist. However, ideology per se could not have been the real reason for the rejection of Marx, because the work of Comte, Durkheim, and other conservative thinkers was also heavily ideological. It was the nature of the ideology, not the existence of ideology as such, that put off many sociological theorists. They were ready and eager to buy conservative ideology wrapped in a cloak of sociological theory, but not the radical ideology offered by Marx and his followers.

There were, of course, other reasons why Marx was not accepted by many early theorists. He seemed to be more an economist than a sociologist. Although the early sociologists would certainly admit the importance of the economy, they would also argue that it was only one of a number of components of social life.

Another reason for the early rejection of Marx was the nature of his interests. Whereas the early sociologists were reacting to the disorder created by the Enlightenment, the French Revolution, and later the Industrial Revolution, Marx was not upset by these disorders—or by disorder in general. Rather, what interested and concerned Marx most was the oppressiveness of the capitalist system that was emerging out of the Industrial Revolution. Marx wanted to develop a theory that explained this oppressiveness and that would help overthrow that system. Marx's interest was in revolution, which stood in contrast to the conservative concern for reform and orderly change.

Another difference worth noting is the difference in philosophical roots between Marxian and conservative sociological theory. Most of the conservative theorists were heavily influenced by the philosophy of Immanuel Kant. Among other things, this led them to think in linear, cause-and-effect terms. That is, they tended to argue that a change in A (say, the change in ideas during the Enlightenment) leads to a change in B (say, the political changes of the French Revolution). In contrast, Marx was most heavily influenced, as we have seen, by Hegel, who thought in dialectical rather than cause-and-effect terms. Among other things, the dialectic attunes us to the ongoing reciprocal effects of social forces. Thus, a dialectician would reconceptualize the example discussed above as a continual, ongoing interplay of ideas and politics.

Marx's Theory   To oversimplify enormously, Marx offered a theory of capitalist society based on his image of the basic nature of human beings. Marx believed that people are basically productive; that is, in order to survive, people need to work in, and with, nature. In so doing, they produce the food, clothing, tools, shelter, and other necessities that permit them to live. Their productivity is a perfectly natural way by which they express basic creative impulses. Furthermore, these impulses are expressed in concert with other people; in other words, people are inherently social. They need to work together to produce what they need to survive.

Throughout history this natural process has been subverted, at first by the mean conditions of primitive society and later by a variety of structural arrangements erected by societies in the course of history. In various ways, these structures interfered with the natural productive process. However, it is in capitalist society that this breakdown is most acute; the breakdown in the natural productive process reaches its culmination in capitalism.

Basically capitalism is a structure (or, more accurately, a series of structures) that erects barriers between an individual and the production process, the products of that process, and other people; ultimately, it even divides the individual himself or herself. This is the basic meaning of the concept of *alienation:* it is the breakdown of the natural interconnection between people and between people and what they produce. Alienation occurs because capitalism has evolved into a two-class system in which a few capitalists own the production process, the products, and the labor time of those who work for them. Instead of naturally producing for themselves, people produce unnaturally in capitalist society for a small group of capitalists. Intellectually, Marx was very concerned with the structures of capitalism and their oppressive impact on actors. Politically, he was led to an interest in emancipating people from the oppressive structures of capitalism.

Marx actually spent very little time dreaming about what a utopian socialist state would look like (Lovell, 1992). He was more concerned with helping to bring about the demise of capitalism. He believed that the contradictions and conflicts within capitalism would lead dialectically to its ultimate collapse, but he did not think that the process was inevitable. People had to act at the appropriate times and in the appropriate ways for socialism to come into being. The capitalists have great resources at their disposal to forestall the coming of socialism, but they could be overcome by the concerted action of a class-conscious proletariat. What would the proletariat create in the process? What is socialism? Most basically, it is a society in which, for the first time, people could approach Marx's ideal image of productivity. With the aid of modern technology, people could interact harmoniously with nature and other people to create what they needed to survive. To put it another way, in socialist society, people would no longer be alienated.

The Roots and Nature of the Theories of Max Weber (1864–1920) and Georg Simmel (1858–1918)   Although Marx and his followers in the late nineteenth and early twentieth centuries remained outside mainstream German sociology, to a considerable extent early German sociology can be seen as developing in opposition to Marxian theory.

Weber and Marx   Albert Salomon, for example, claimed that a large part of the theory of the early giant of German sociology, Max Weber, developed "in a long and intense debate with the ghost of Marx" (1945:596). This is probably an exaggeration, but in many ways Marxian theory did play a negative role in Weberian theory. In other ways, however, Weber was working *within* the Marxian tradition, trying to "round out" Marx's theory. Also, there were many inputs into Weberian theory other than Marxian theory (Burger, 1976). We can clarify a good deal about the sources of German sociology by outlining each of these views of the relationship between Marx and Weber (Antonio and Glassman, 1985; Schroeter, 1985). It should be borne in mind that Weber was not intimately familiar with Marx's work (much of it was not published until after Weber's death) and that Weber was reacting more to the work of the Marxists than to Marx's work itself (Antonio, 1985:29; Turner, 1981:19–20).

Weber *did* tend to view Marx and the Marxists of his day as economic determinists who offered single-cause theories of social life. That is, Marxian theory was seen as tracing all historical developments to economic bases and viewing all contemporaneous structures as erected on an economic base. Although this is not true of Marx's own theory, it was the position of many later Marxists.

One of the examples of economic determinism that seemed to rankle Weber most was the view that ideas are simply the reflections of material (especially economic) interests, that material interests determine ideology. From this point of view, Weber was supposed to have "turned Marx on his head" (much as Marx had inverted Hegel). Instead of focusing on economic factors and their effect on ideas, Weber devoted much of his attention to ideas and their effect on the economy. Rather than seeing ideas as simple reflections of economic factors, Weber saw them as fairly autonomous forces capable of profoundly affecting the economic world. Weber certainly devoted a lot of attention to ideas, particularly systems of religious ideas, and he was especially concerned with the impact of religious ideas on the economy. In *The Protestant Ethic and the Spirit of Capitalism* (1904–05/1958), he was concerned with Protestantism, mainly as a system of

MAX WEBER: A Biographical Sketch

Max Weber was born in Erfurt, Germany, on April 21, 1864, into a decidedly middle-class family. Important differences between his parents had a profound effect upon both his intellectual orientation and his psychological development. His father was a bureaucrat who rose to a relatively important political position. He was clearly a part of the political establishment and as a result eschewed any activity or idealism that would require personal sacrifice or threaten his position within the system. In addition, the senior Weber was a man who enjoyed earthly pleasures, and in this and many other ways he stood in sharp contrast to his wife. Max Weber's mother was a devout Calvinist, a woman who sought to lead an ascetic life largely devoid of the pleasures craved by her husband. Her concerns were more otherworldly; she was disturbed by the imperfections that were signs that she was not destined for salvation. These deep differences between the parents led to marital tension, and both the differences and the tension had an immense impact on Weber.

Because it was impossible to emulate both parents, Weber was presented with a clear choice as a child (Marianne Weber, 1975:62). He first seemed to opt for his father's orientation to life, but later he drew closer to his mother's approach. Whatever the choice, the tension produced by the need to choose between such polar opposites negatively affected Max Weber's psyche.

At age eighteen, Max Weber left home for a short time to attend the University of Heidelberg. Weber had already demonstrated intellectual precocity, but on a social level he entered Heidelberg shy and underdeveloped. However, that quickly changed after he gravitated toward his father's way of life and joined his father's old dueling fraternity. There he developed socially, at least in part because of the huge quantities of beer he consumed with his peers. In addition, he proudly displayed the dueling scars that were the trademarks of such fraternities. Weber not only manifested his identity with his father's way of life in these ways but also chose, at least for the time being, his father's career—the law.

After three terms, Weber left Heidelberg for military service, and in 1884 he returned to Berlin and to his parents' home to take courses at the University of Berlin. He remained there for most of the next eight years as he completed his studies, earned his Ph.D., became a lawyer (see Turner and Factor, 1994, for a discussion of the impact of legal thinking on Weber's theorizing) and started teaching at the University of Berlin. In the process, his

ideas, and its impact on the rise of another system of ideas, the "spirit of capitalism," and ultimately on a capitalist economic system. Weber had a similar interest in other world religions, looking at how their nature might have obstructed the development of capitalism in their respective societies. On the basis of this kind of work, some scholars came to the conclusion that Weber developed his ideas in opposition to those of Marx.

A second view of Weber's relationship to Marx, as mentioned earlier, is that he did not so much oppose Marx as try to round out his theoretical perspective. Here Weber is seen as working more within the Marxian tradition than in opposition to it. His work on religion, interpreted from this point of view, was simply an effort to show that not only do material factors affect ideas but ideas themselves affect material structures.

interests shifted more toward his lifelong concerns—economics, history, and sociology. During his eight years in Berlin, Weber was financially dependent on his father, a circumstance he progressively grew to dislike. At the same time, he moved closer to his mother's values, and his antipathy to his father increased. He adopted an ascetic life and plunged deeply into his work. For example, during one semester as a student, his work habits were described as follows: "He continues the rigid work discipline, regulates his life by the clock, divides the daily routine into exact sections for the various subjects, saves in his way, by feeding himself evenings in his room with a pound of raw chopped beef and four fried eggs" (Mitzman, 1969/1971:48; Marianne Weber, 1975:105). Thus Weber, following his mother, had become ascetic and diligent, a compulsive worker—in contemporary terms a "workaholic."

This compulsion for work led in 1896 to a position as professor of economics at Heidelberg. But in 1897, when Weber's academic career was blossoming, his father died following a violent argument between them. Shortly thereafter Weber began to manifest symptoms that were to culminate in a nervous breakdown. Often unable to sleep or to work, Weber spent the next six or seven years in near-total collapse. After a long hiatus, some of his powers began to return in 1903, but it was not until 1904, when he delivered (in the United States) his first lecture in six and a half years, that Weber was able to begin to return to active academic life. In 1904 and 1905, he published one of his best-known works, *The Protestant Ethic and the Spirit of Capitalism.* In this work, Weber announced the ascendance of his mother's religion on an academic level. Weber devoted much of his time to the study of religion, though he was not personally religious.

Although he continued to be plagued by psychological problems, after 1904 Weber was able to function, indeed to produce some of his most important work. In these years, Weber published his studies of the world's religions in world-historical perspective (for example, China, India, and ancient Judaism). At the time of his death (June 14, 1920), he was working on his most important work, *Economy and Society.* Although this book was published, and subsequently translated into many languages, it was unfinished.

In addition to producing voluminous writings in this period, Weber undertook a number of other activities. He helped found the German Sociological Society in 1910. His home became a center for a wide range of intellectuals, including sociologists such as Georg Simmel, Robert Michels and his brother Alfred, as well as the philosopher and literary critic Georg Lukács (Scaff, 1989:186–222). In addition, Weber was active politically and wrote essays on the issues of the day.

There was a tension in Weber's life and, more important, in his work, between the bureaucratic mind, as represented by his father, and his mother's religiosity. This unresolved tension permeates Weber's work as it permeated his personal life.

A good example of the view that Weber was engaged in a process of rounding out Marxian theory is in the area of stratification theory. In this work on stratification, Marx focused on social *class,* the economic dimension of stratification. Although Weber accepted the importance of this factor, he argued that other dimensions of stratification were also important. He argued that the notion of social stratification should be extended to include stratification on the basis of prestige (*status*) and *power.* The inclusion of these other dimensions does not constitute a refutation of Marx but is simply an extension of his ideas.

Both of the views outlined above accept the importance of Marxian theory for Weber. There are elements of truth in both positions; at some points Weber *was* working in opposition to Marx, while at other points he *was* extending Marx's ideas. However, a third view of this issue may best characterize the relationship between Marx and Weber. In this view, Marx is simply seen as only one of many influences on Weber's thought.

Other Influences on Weber We can identify a number of sources of Weberian theory, including German historians, philosophers, economists, and political theorists. Among those who influenced Weber, the philosopher Immanuel Kant (1724–1804) stands out above all the others. But we must not overlook the impact of Friedrich Nietzsche (1844–1900)—especially his emphasis on the hero—on Weber's work on the need for individuals to stand up to the impact of bureaucracies and other structures of modern society.

The influence of Immanuel Kant on Weber and on German sociology generally shows that German sociology and Marxism grew from different philosophical roots. As we have seen, it was Hegel, not Kant, who was the important philosophical influence on Marxian theory. Whereas Hegel's philosophy led Marx and the Marxists to look for relations, conflicts, and contradictions, Kantian philosophy led at least some German sociologists to take a more static perspective. To Kant the world was a buzzing confusion of events that could never be known directly. The world could only be known through thought processes that filter, select, and categorize these events. The content of the real world was differentiated by Kant from the forms through which that content can be comprehended. The emphasis on these forms gave the work of those sociologists within the Kantian tradition a more static quality than that of the Marxists within the Hegelian tradition.

Weber's Theory Whereas Karl Marx offered basically a theory of capitalism, Weber's work was fundamentally a theory of the process of rationalization (Brubaker, 1984; Kalberg, 1980, 1990, 1994). Weber was interested in the general issue of why institutions in the Western world had grown progressively more rational while powerful barriers seemed to prevent a similar development in the rest of the world.

Although rationality is used in many different ways in Weber's work, what interests us here is a process involving one of four types identified by Kalberg (1980, 1990, 1994; see also Brubaker, 1984; Levine, 1981a), *formal rationality.* Formal rationality involves, as was usually the case with Weber, a concern for the actor making choices of means and ends. However, in this case, that choice is made in reference to universally applied rules, regulations, and laws. These, in turn, are derived from various large-scale structures, especially bureaucracies and the economy. Weber developed his theories in the context of a large number of comparative historical studies of the West, China, India, and many other regions of the world. In these studies, he sought to delineate the factors that helped bring about or impede the development of rationalization.

Weber saw the bureaucracy (and the historical process of bureaucratization) as the classic example of rationalization, but rationalization is perhaps best illustrated today by the fast-food restaurant (Ritzer, 1996). The fast-food restaurant is a formally rational system in which people (both workers and customers) are led to seek the most rational means to ends. The drive-through window, for example, is a rational means by which workers can dispense, and customers can obtain, food quickly and efficiently. Speed and efficiency are dictated by the fast-food restaurants and the rules and regulations by which they operate.

Weber embedded his discussion of the process of bureaucratization in a broader discussion of the political institution. He differentiated among three types of authority systems—traditional, charismatic, and rational-legal. Only in the modern Western world can a rational-legal authority system develop, and only within that system does one find the full-scale development of the modern bureaucracy. The rest of the world remains dominated by traditional or charismatic authority systems, which generally impede the development of a rational-legal authority system and modern bureaucracies. Briefly, *traditional* authority stems from a long-lasting system of beliefs. An example would be a leader who comes to power because his or her family or clan has always provided the group's leadership. A *charismatic* leader derives his or her authority from extraordinary abilities or characteristics, or more likely simply from the *belief* on the part of followers that the leader has such traits. Although these two types of authority are of historical importance, Weber believed that the trend in the West, and ultimately in the rest of the world, is toward systems of *rational-legal* authority. In such systems, authority is derived from rules legally and rationally enacted. Thus, the president of the United States derives his authority ultimately from the laws of society. The evolution of rational-legal authority, with its accompanying bureaucracies, is only one part of Weber's general argument on the rationalization of the Western world.

Weber also did detailed and sophisticated analyses of the rationalization of such phenomena as religion, law, the city, and even music. But we can illustrate Weber's mode of thinking with one other example—the rationalization of the economic institution. This discussion is couched in Weber's broader analysis of the relationship between religion and capitalism. In a wide-ranging historical study, Weber sought to understand why a rational economic system (capitalism) had developed in the West and why it had failed to develop in the rest of the world. Weber accorded a central role to religion in this process. At one level, he was engaged in a dialogue with the Marxists in an effort to show that, contrary to what many Marxists of the day believed, religion was not merely an epiphenomenon. Instead, it had played a key role in the rise of capitalism in the West and in its failure to develop elsewhere in the world. Weber argued that it was a distinctively rational religious system (Calvinism) that played the central role in the rise of capitalism in the West. In contrast, in the other parts of the world that he studied, Weber found more irrational religious systems (for example, Confucianism, Taoism, Hinduism), which helped to inhibit the development of a rational economic system. However, in the end, one gets the feeling that these religions provided only temporary barriers, for the economic systems—indeed, the entire social structure—of these societies ultimately would become rationalized.

Although rationalization lies at the heart of Weberian theory, it is far from all there is to the theory. But this is not the place to go into that rich body of material. Instead, let us return to the development of sociological theory. A key issue in that development is: Why did Weber's theory prove more attractive to later sociological theorists than Marxian theory?

The Acceptance of Weber's Theory   One reason is that Weber proved to be more acceptable politically. Instead of espousing Marxian radicalism, Weber was more of a liberal on some issues and a conservative on others (for example, the role of the state). Although he was a severe critic of many aspects of modern capitalist society and came to many of the same critical conclusions as did Marx, he was not one to propose radical solutions to problems (Heins, 1993). In fact, he felt that the radical reforms offered by many Marxists and other socialists would do more harm than good.

Later sociological theorists, especially Americans, saw their society under attack by Marxian theory. Largely conservative in orientation, they cast about for theoretical alternatives to Marxism. One of those who proved attractive was Max Weber. (Durkheim and Vilfredo Pareto were others.) After all, rationalization affected not only capitalist but also socialist societies. Indeed, from Weber's point of view, rationalization constituted an even greater problem in socialist than in capitalist societies.

Also in Weber's favor was the form in which he presented his judgments. He spent most of his life doing detailed historical studies, and his political conclusions were often made within the context of his research. Thus they usually sounded very scientific and academic. Marx, although he did much serious research, also wrote a good deal of explicitly polemical material. Even his more academic work is laced with acid political judgments. For example, in *Capital* (1867/1967), he described capitalists as "vampires" and "werewolves." Weber's more academic style helped make him more acceptable to later sociologists.

Another reason for the greater acceptability of Weber was that he operated in a philosophical tradition that also helped shape the work of later sociologists. That is, Weber operated in the Kantian tradition, which meant, as we have seen, that he tended to think in cause-and-effect terms. This kind of thinking was more acceptable to later sociologists, who were largely unfamiliar and uncomfortable with the dialectical logic that informed Marx's work.

Finally, Weber appeared to offer a much more rounded approach to the social world than Marx. Whereas Marx appeared to be almost totally preoccupied with the economy, Weber was interested in a wide range of social phenomena. This diversity of focus seemed to give later sociologists more to work with than the apparently more single-minded concerns of Marx.

Weber produced most of his major works in the late 1800s and early 1900s. Early in his career, Weber was identified more as a historian who was concerned with sociological issues, but in the early 1900s his focus grew more and more sociological. Indeed, he became the dominant sociologist of his time in Germany. In 1910, he founded (with, among others, Georg Simmel, whom we discuss below) the German Sociological Society (Glatzer, 1998). His home in Heidelberg was an intellectual center not only for sociologists but for scholars from many fields. Although his work was broadly influential in Germany, it was to become even more influential in the United States, especially after Talcott Parsons introduced Weber's ideas (and those of other European theorists, especially Durkheim) to a large American audience. Although Marx's ideas did not have a significant positive effect on American sociological theorists until the 1960s, Weber was already highly influential by the late 1930s.

Simmel's Theory   Georg Simmel was Weber's contemporary and a cofounder of the German Sociological Society. Simmel was a somewhat atypical sociological theorist (Frisby, 1981; Levine, Carter, and Gorman, 1976a, 1976b). For one thing, he had an immediate and profound effect on the development of American sociological theory, whereas Marx and Weber were largely ignored for a number of years. Simmel's work helped shape the development of one of the early centers of American sociology—the University of Chicago—and its major theory, symbolic interactionism (Jaworski, 1995; 1997). The Chicago school and symbolic interactionism came, as we will see, to dominate American sociology in the 1920s and early 1930s (Bulmer, 1984). Simmel's ideas were influential at Chicago mainly because the dominant figures in the early years of Chicago, Albion Small and Robert Park, had been exposed to Simmel's theories in Berlin in the late 1800s. Park attended Simmel's lectures in 1899 and 1900, and Small carried on an extensive correspondence with Simmel during the 1890s. They were instrumental in bringing Simmel's ideas to students and faculty at Chicago, in translating some of his work, and in bringing it to the attention of a large-scale American audience (Frisby, 1984:29).

Another atypical aspect of Simmel's work is his "level" of analysis, or at least that level for which he became best known in America. Whereas Weber and Marx were preoccupied with large-scale issues like the rationalization of society and a capitalist economy, Simmel was best known for his work on smaller-scale issues, especially individual action and interaction. He became famous early for his thinking, derived from Kantian philosophy, on *forms* of interaction (for example, conflict) and *types* of interactants (for example, the stranger). Basically, Simmel saw that understanding interaction among people was one of the major tasks of sociology. However, it was impossible to study the massive number of interactions in social life without some conceptual tools. This is where forms of interaction and types of interactants came in. Simmel felt that he could isolate a limited number of forms of interaction that could be found in a large number of social settings. Thus equipped, one could analyze and understand these different interaction settings. The development of a limited number of types of interactants could be similarly useful in explaining interaction settings. This work had a profound effect on symbolic interactionism, which, as the name suggests, was focally concerned with interaction. One of the ironies, however, is that Simmel also was concerned with large-scale issues similar to those that obsessed Marx and Weber. However, this work was much less influential than his work on interaction, although there are contemporary signs of a growing interest in the large-scale aspects of Simmel's sociology.

It was partly Simmel's style in his work on interaction that made him accessible to early American sociological theorists. Although he wrote heavy tomes like those of Weber and Marx, he also wrote a set of deceptively simple essays on such interesting topics as poverty, the prostitute, the miser and the spendthrift, and the stranger. The brevity of such essays and the high interest level of the material made the dissemination of Simmel's ideas much easier. Unfortunately, the essays had the negative effect of obscuring Simmel's more massive works (for example, *Philosophy of Money*, translated in 1978; see Poggi, 1993), which were potentially as significant to sociology. Nevertheless, it was partly through the short and clever essays that Simmel had a much more significant effect on early American sociological theory than either Marx or Weber did.

We should not leave Simmel without saying something about *Philosophy of Money*, because its English translation made Simmel's work attractive to a whole new set of theorists interested in culture and society. Although a macro orientation is clearer in *Philosophy of Money*, it always existed in Simmel's work. For example, it is clear in his

GEORG SIMMEL: A Biographical Sketch

Georg Simmel was born in the heart of Berlin on March 1, 1858. He studied a wide range of subjects at the University of Berlin. However, his first effort to produce a dissertation was rejected, and one of his professors remarked, "We would do him a great service if we do not encourage him further in this direction" (Frisby, 1984:23). Despite this, Simmel persevered and received his doctorate in philosophy in 1881. He remained at the university in a teaching capacity until 1914, although he occupied a relatively unimportant position as *Privatdozent* from 1885 to 1900. In the latter position, Simmel served as an unpaid lecturer whose livelihood was dependent on student fees. Despite his marginality, Simmel did rather well in this position, largely because he was an excellent lecturer and attracted large numbers of (paying) students (Frisby, 1981:17; Salomon, 1963/1997). His style was so popular that even cultured members of Berlin society were drawn to his lectures, which became public events.

Simmel's marginality is paralleled by the fact that he was a somewhat contradictory and therefore bewildering person:

If we put together the testimonials left by relatives, friends, students, contemporaries, we find a number of sometimes contradictory indications concerning Georg Simmel. He is depicted by some as being tall and slender, by others as being short and as bearing a forlorn expression. His appearance is reported to be unattractive, typically Jewish, but also intensely intellectual and noble. He is reported to be hard-working, but also humorous and overarticulate as a lecturer. Finally we hear that he was intellectually brilliant [Lukács, 1991:145], friendly, well-disposed—but also that *inside* he was irrational, opaque, and wild.

(Schnabel, cited in Poggi, 1993:55)

Simmel wrote innumerable articles ("The Metropolis and Mental Life") and books (*The Philosophy of Money*). He was well known in German academic circles and even had an international following, especially in the United States, where his work was of great signifi-

famous work on the dyad and the triad. Simmel thought that some crucial sociological developments take place when a two-person group (or *dyad*) is transformed into a *triad* by the addition of a third party. Social possibilities emerge that simply could not exist in a dyad. For example, in a triad, one of the members can become an arbitrator or mediator of the differences between the other two. More important, two of the members can band together and dominate the other member. This represents on a small scale what can happen with the emergence of large-scale structures that become separate from individuals and begin to dominate them.

This theme lies at the base of *Philosophy of Money.* Simmel was concerned primarily with the emergence in the modern world of a money economy that becomes separate from the individual and predominant. This theme, in turn, is part of an even broader and more pervasive one in Simmel's work, the domination of the culture as a cance in the birth of sociology. Finally, in 1900, Simmel received official recognition, a purely honorary title at the University of Berlin, which did not give him full academic status. Simmel tried to obtain many academic positions, but he failed in spite of the support of such scholars as Max Weber.

One of the reasons for Simmel's failure was that he was a Jew in a nineteenth-century Germany rife with anti-Semitism (Kasler, 1985). Thus, in a report on Simmel written to a minister of education, Simmel was described as "an Israelite through and through, in his external appearance, in his bearing and in his mode of thought" (Frisby, 1981:25). Another reason was the kind of work that he did. Many of his articles appeared in newspapers and magazines; they were written for an audience more general than simply academic sociologists (Rammstedt, 1991). In addition, because he did not hold a regular academic appointment, he was forced to earn his living through public lectures. Simmel's audience, both for his writings and his lectures, was more the intellectual public than professional sociologists, and this tended to lead to derisive judgments from fellow professionals. For example, one of his contemporaries damned him because "his influence remained . . . upon the general atmosphere and affected, above all, the higher levels of journalism" (Troeltsch, cited in Frisby, 1981:13). Simmel's personal failures can also be linked to the low esteem that German academicians of the day had for sociology.

In 1914 Simmel finally obtained a regular academic appointment at a minor university (Strasbourg), but he once again felt estranged. On the one hand, he regretted leaving his audience of Berlin intellectuals. Thus his wife wrote to Max Weber's wife: "Georg has taken leave of the auditorium very badly. . . . The students were very affectionate and sympathetic. . . . It was a departure at the full height of life" (Frisby, 1981:29). On the other hand, Simmel did not feel a part of the life of his new university. Thus, he wrote to Mrs. Weber: "There is hardly anything to report from us. We live . . . a cloistered, closed-off, indifferent, desolate external existence. Academic activity is = 0, the people . . . alien and inwardly hostile" (Frisby, 1981:32).

World War I started soon after Simmel's appointment at Strasbourg; lecture halls were turned into military hospitals, and students went off to war. Thus, Simmel remained a marginal figure in German academia until his death in 1918. He never did have a normal academic career. Nevertheless, Simmel attracted a large academic following in his day, and his fame as a scholar has, if anything, grown over the years.

whole over the individual. As Simmel saw it, in the modern world, the larger culture and all its various components (including the money economy) expand, and as they expand, the importance of the individual decreases. Thus, for example, as the industrial technology associated with a modern economy expands and grows more sophisticated, the skills and abilities of the individual worker grow progressively less important. In the end, the worker is confronted with an industrial machine over which he or she can exert little, if any, control. More generally, Simmel thought that in the modern world, the expansion of the larger culture leads to the growing insignificance of the individual.

Although sociologists have become increasingly attuned to the broader implications of Simmel's work, his early influence was primarily through his studies of small-scale social phenomena, such as the forms of interaction and types of interactants.

The Origins of British Sociology

We have been examining the development of sociology in France (Comte, Durkheim) and Germany (Marx, Weber, and Simmel). We turn now to the parallel development of sociology in England. As we will see, Continental ideas had their impact on early British sociology, but more important were native influences.

Political Economy, Ameliorism, and Social Evolution Philip Abrams (1968) contended that British sociology was shaped in the nineteenth century by three often conflicting sources—political economy, ameliorism, and social evolution.[6] Thus when the Sociological Society of London was founded in 1903, there were strong differences over the definition of *sociology*. However, there were few who doubted the view that sociology could be a science. It was the differences that gave British sociology its distinctive character, and we will look at each of them briefly.

Political Economy We have already touched on *political economy,* which was a theory of industrial and capitalist society traceable in part to the work of Adam Smith (1723–1790).[7] As we saw, political economy had a profound effect on Karl Marx. Marx studied political economy closely, and he was critical of it. But that was not the direction taken by British economists and sociologists. They tended to accept Smith's idea that there was an "invisible hand" that shaped the market for labor and goods. The market was seen as an independent reality that stood above individuals and controlled their behavior. The British sociologists, like the political economists and unlike Marx, saw the market as a positive force, as a source of order, harmony, and integration in society. Because they saw the market, and more generally society, in a positive light, the task of the sociologist was not to criticize society but simply to gather data on the laws by which it operated. The goal was to provide the government with the facts it needed to understand the way the system worked and to direct its workings wisely.

The emphasis was on facts, but which facts? Whereas Marx, Weber, Durkheim, and Comte looked to the structures of society for their basic facts, the British thinkers tended to focus on the individuals who made up those structures. In dealing with large-scale structures, they tended to collect individual-level data and then combine them to form a collective portrait. In the mid-1800s it was the statisticians who dominated British social science, and this kind of data collection was deemed to be the major task of sociology. The objective was the accumulation of "pure" facts without theorizing or philosophizing. These empirical sociologists were detached from the concerns of social theorists. Instead of general theorizing, the "emphasis settled on the business of producing more exact indicators, better methods of classification and data collection, improved life tables, higher levels of comparability between discrete bodies of data, and the like" (Abrams, 1968:18).

It was almost in spite of themselves that these statistically oriented sociologists came to see some limitations in their approach. A few began to feel the need for broader theorizing. To them, a problem such as poverty pointed to failings in the market system as

[6]For more recent developments in British sociology, see Abrams et al. (1981).

[7]Smith is usually included as a leading member of the Scottish Enlightenment (Chitnis, 1976) and as one of the Scottish Moralists (Schneider, 1967:xi), who were seeking to establish the basis for sociology.

SIGMUND FREUD: A Biographical Sketch

Another leading figure in German social science in the late 1800s and early 1900s was Sigmund Freud. Although he was not a sociologist, Freud influenced the work of many sociologists (for example, Talcott Parsons and Norbert Elias) and continues to be of relevance to social theorists (Brennan, 1997; Carveth, 1982; Kaye, 1991; Kurzweil, 1995).

Sigmund Freud was born in the Austro-Hungarian city of Freiberg on May 6, 1856 (Puner, 1947). In 1859, his family moved to Vienna, and in 1873, Freud entered the medical school at the University of Vienna. Freud was more interested in science than in medicine and took a position in a physiology laboratory. He completed his degree in medicine, and after leaving the laboratory in 1882, he worked in a hospital and then set up a private medical practice with a specialty in nervous diseases.

Freud at first used hypnosis in an effort to deal with a type of neurosis known as *hysteria.* He had learned the technique in Paris from Jean Martin Charcot in 1885. Later he adopted a technique, pioneered by a fellow Viennese physician, Joseph Breuer, in which hysterical symptoms disappeared when the patient talked through the circumstances in which the symptoms first arose. By 1895, Freud had published a book with Breuer with a series of revolutionary implications: that the causes of neuroses like hysteria were psychological (not, as had been believed, physiological) and that the therapy involved talking through the original causes. Thus was born the practical and theoretical field of *psychoanalysis.* Freud began to part company with Breuer as he came to see sexual factors, or more generally the *libido,* at the root of neuroses. Over the next several years, Freud refined his therapeutic techniques and wrote a great deal about his new ideas.

By 1902, Freud began to gather a number of disciples around him, and they met weekly at his house. By 1903 or 1904, others (like Carl Jung) began to use Freud's ideas in their psychiatric practices. In 1908, the first Psychoanalytic Congress was held, and the next year a periodical for disseminating psychoanalytic knowledge was formed. As quickly as it had formed, the new field of psychoanalysis became splintered as Freud broke with people like Jung and they went off to develop their own ideas and found their own groups. World War I slowed the development of psychoanalysis, but it expanded and developed greatly in the 1920s. With the rise of Nazism, the center of psychoanalysis shifted to the United States, where it remains to this day. But Freud remained in Vienna until the Nazis took over in 1938, despite the fact that he was Jewish and the Nazis had burned his books as early as 1933. On June 4, 1938, only after a ransom had been paid and President Roosevelt had interceded, Sigmund Freud left Vienna. Freud had suffered from cancer of the jaw since 1923, and he died in London on September 23, 1939.

well as in the society as a whole. But most, focused as they were on individuals, did not question the larger system; they turned instead to more detailed field studies and to the development of more complicated and more exact statistical techniques. To them, the source of the problem had to lie in inadequate research methods, *not* in the system as a whole. As Philip Abrams noted, "Focusing persistently on the distribution of individual circumstances, the statisticians found it hard to break through to a perception of poverty as a product of social structure. . . . They did not and probably could not achieve the concept of structural victimization" (1968:27). In addition to their theoretical and methodological commitments to the study of individuals, the statisticians worked too closely with government policy makers to arrive at the conclusion that the larger political and economic system was the problem.

Ameliorism Related to, but separable from, political economy was the second defining characteristic of British sociology—*ameliorism,* or a desire to solve social problems by reforming individuals. Although British scholars began to recognize that there were problems in society (for example, poverty), they still believed in that society and wanted to preserve it. They desired to forestall violence and revolution and to reform the system so that it could continue essentially as it was. Above all, they wanted to prevent the coming of a socialist society. Thus, like French sociology and some branches of German sociology, British sociology was conservatively oriented.

Because the British sociologists could not, or would not, trace the source of problems such as poverty to the society as a whole, the source had to lie within the individuals themselves. This was an early form of what William Ryan (1971) later called "blaming the victim." Much attention was devoted to a long series of individual problems—"ignorance, spiritual destitution, impurity, bad sanitation, pauperism, crime, and intemperance—above all intemperance" (Abrams, 1968:39). Clearly, there was a tendency to look for a simple cause for all social ills, and the one that suggested itself before all others was alcoholism. What made this perfect to the ameliorist was that this was an individual pathology, not a social pathology. The ameliorists lacked a theory of social structure, a theory of the social causes of such individual problems.

Social Evolution But a stronger sense of social structure was lurking below the surface of British sociology, and it burst through in the latter part of the nineteenth century with the growth of interest in *social evolution.* One important influence was the work of Auguste Comte, part of which had been translated into English in the 1850s by Harriet Martineau (Hoecker-Drysdale, forthcoming). Although Comte's work did not inspire immediate interest, by the last quarter of the century, a number of thinkers had been attracted to it and to its concern for the larger structures of society, its scientific (positivistic) orientation, its comparative orientation, and its evolutionary theory. However, a number of British thinkers sharpened their own conception of the world in opposition to some of the excesses of Comtian theory (for example, the tendency to elevate sociology to the status of a religion).

In Abrams's view, the real importance of Comte lay in his providing one of the bases on which opposition could be mounted against the "oppressive genius of Herbert Spencer" (Abrams, 1968:58). In both a positive and a negative sense, Spencer was a dominant figure in British sociological theory, especially evolutionary theory (J. Turner, forthcoming).

Herbert Spencer (1820–1903) In attempting to understand Spencer's ideas, it is useful to compare and contrast them with Comtian theory.

Spencer and Comte Spencer is often categorized with Comte in terms of their influence on the development of sociological theory, but there are some important differences between them. For example, it is less easy to categorize Spencer as a conservative. In fact, in his early years, Spencer is better seen as a political liberal, and he retained elements of liberalism throughout his life. However, it is also true that Spencer grew more conservative during the course of his life and that his basic influence, as was true of Comte, was conservative.

One of his liberal views, which coexisted rather uncomfortably with his conservatism, was his acceptance of a laissez-faire doctrine: he felt that the state should not intervene in individual affairs, except in the rather passive function of protecting people. This meant that Spencer, unlike Comte, was not interested in social reforms; he wanted social life to evolve free of external control.

This difference points to Spencer as a *Social Darwinist* (G. Jones, 1980). As such, he held the evolutionary view that the world was growing progressively better. Therefore, it should be left alone; outside interference could only worsen the situation. He adopted the view that social institutions, like plants and animals, adapted progressively and positively to their social environment. He also accepted the Darwinian view that a process of natural selection, "survival of the fittest," occurred in the social world. (Interestingly, it was Spencer who coined the phrase "survival of the fittest" several years *before* Charles Darwin's work on natural selection.) That is, if unimpeded by external intervention, people who were "fit" would survive and proliferate whereas the "unfit" would eventually die out. Another difference was that Spencer emphasized the individual, whereas Comte focused on larger units such as the family.

Comte and Spencer shared with Durkheim and others a commitment to a science of sociology (Haines, 1992), which was a very attractive perspective to early theorists. Another influence of Spencer's work, shared with both Comte and Durkheim, was his tendency to see society as an *organism*. In this, Spencer borrowed his perspective and concepts from biology. He was concerned with the overall structure of society, the interrelationship of the *parts* of society, and the *functions* of the parts for each other as well as for the system as a whole.

Most important, Spencer, like Comte, had an evolutionary conception of historical development. However, Spencer was critical of Comte's evolutionary theory on several grounds. Specifically, he rejected Comte's law of the three stages. He argued that Comte was content to deal with evolution in the realm of ideas, in terms of intellectual development. Spencer, however, sought to develop an evolutionary theory in the real, material world.

Evolutionary Theory   It is possible to identify at least two major evolutionary perspectives in Spencer's work (Haines, 1988; Perrin, 1976).

The first relates primarily to the increasing *size* of society. Society grows through both the multiplication of individuals and the union of groups (compounding). The increasing size of society brings with it larger and more differentiated social structures, as well as the increasing differentiation of the functions they perform. In addition to their growth in terms of size, societies evolve through compounding, that is, by unifying more and more adjoining groups. Thus, Spencer talks of the evolutionary movement from simple to compound, doubly-compound, and trebly-compound societies.

Spencer also offers a theory of evolution from *militant* to *industrial* societies. Earlier, militant societies are defined by being structured for offensive and defensive warfare. While Spencer was critical of warfare, he felt that in an earlier stage it was functional in bringing societies together (for example, through military conquest) and in

HERBERT SPENCER: A Biographical Sketch

Herbert Spencer was born in Derby, England, on April 27, 1820. He was not schooled in the arts and humanities, but rather in technical and utilitarian matters. In 1837 he began work as a civil engineer for a railway, an occupation he held until 1846. During this period, Spencer continued to study on his own and began to publish scientific and political works.

In 1848 Spencer was appointed an editor of *The Economist,* and his intellectual ideas began to solidify. By 1850, he had completed his first major work, *Social Statics.* During the writing of this work, Spencer first began to experience insomnia, and over the years his mental and physical problems mounted. He was to suffer a series of nervous breakdowns throughout the rest of his life.

In 1853 Spencer received an inheritance that allowed him to quit his job and live for the rest of his life as a gentleman scholar. He never earned a university degree or held an academic position. As he grew more isolated, and physical and mental illness mounted, Spencer's productivity as a scholar increased. Eventually, Spencer began to achieve not only fame within England but also an international reputation. As Richard Hofstadter put it: "In the three decades after the Civil War it was impossible to be active in any field of intellectual work without mastering Spencer" (1959:33). Among his supporters was the important industrialist Andrew Carnegie, who wrote the following to Spencer during the latter's fatal illness of 1903:

> Dear Master Teacher . . . you come to me every day in thought, and the everlasting "why" intrudes—Why lies he? Why must he go? . . . The world jogs on unconscious of its greatest mind. . . . But it will wake some day to its teachings and decree Spencer's place is with the greatest.   (Carnegie, cited in Peel, 1971:2)

But that was not to be Spencer's fate.

creating the larger aggregates of people necessary for the development of industrial society. However, with the emergence of industrial society, warfare ceases to be functional and serves to impede further evolution. Industrial society is based on friendship, altruism, elaborate specialization, recognition for achievements rather than the characteristics one is born with, and voluntary cooperation among highly disciplined individuals. Such a society is held together by voluntary contractual relations and, more important, by a strong common morality. The government's role is restricted and focuses only on what people ought not to do. Obviously, modern industrial societies are less warlike than their militant predecessors. Although Spencer sees a general evolution in the direction of industrial societies, he also recognizes that it is possible that there will be periodic regressions to warfare and more militant societies.

In his ethical and political writings, Spencer offered other ideas on the evolution of society. For one thing, he saw society as progressing toward an ideal, or perfect, moral state. For another, he argued that the fittest societies survive, while unfit societies

One of Spencer's most interesting characteristics, one that was ultimately to be the cause of his intellectual undoing, was his unwillingness to read the work of other people. In this, he resembled another early giant of sociology, Auguste Comte, who practiced "cerebral hygiene." Of the need to read the works of others, Spencer said: "All my life I have been a thinker and not a reader, being able to say with Hobbes that 'if I had read as much as other men I would have known as little'" (Wiltshire, 1978:67). A friend asked Spencer's opinion of a book, and "his reply was that on looking into the book he saw that its fundamental assumption was erroneous, and therefore did not care to read it" (Wiltshire, 1978:67). One author wrote of Spencer's "incomprehensible way of absorbing knowledge through the powers of his skin . . . he never seemed to read books" (Wiltshire, 1978:67).

If he didn't read the work of other scholars, where, then, did Spencer's ideas and insights come from? According to Spencer, they emerged involuntarily and intuitively from his mind. He said that his ideas emerged "little by little, in unobtrusive ways, without conscious intention or appreciable effort" (Wiltshire, 1978:66). Such intuition was deemed by Spencer to be far more effective than careful study and thought: "A solution reached in the way described is more likely to be true than one reached in the pursuance of a determined effort [which] causes perversion of thought" (Wiltshire, 1978:66).

Spencer suffered because of his unwillingness to read seriously the works of other people. In fact, if he read other work, it was often only to find confirmation for his own, independently created ideas. He ignored those ideas that did not agree with his. Thus, his contemporary, Charles Darwin, said of Spencer: "If he had trained himself to observe more, even at the expense of . . . some loss of thinking power, he would have been a wonderful man" (Wiltshire, 1978:70). Spencer's disregard for the rules of scholarship led him to a series of outrageous ideas and unsubstantiated assertions about the evolution of the world. For these reasons, sociologists in the twentieth century came to reject Spencer's work and to substitute for it careful scholarship and empirical research.

Spencer died on December 8, 1903.

should be permitted to die off. The result of this process is adaptive upgrading for the world as a whole.

Thus Spencer offered a rich and complicated set of ideas on social evolution. His ideas first enjoyed great success, then were rejected for many years, and more recently have been revived with the rise of neoevolutionary sociological theories (Buttel, 1990).

The Reaction against Spencer in Britain   Despite his emphasis on the individual, Spencer was best known for his large-scale theory of social evolution. In this, he stood in stark contrast to the sociology that preceded him in Britain. However, the reaction against Spencer was based more on the threat that his idea of survival of the fittest posed to the ameliorism so dear to most early British sociologists. Although Spencer later repudiated some of his more outrageous ideas, he *did* argue for a survival-of-the-fittest philosophy and against government intervention and social reform:

Fostering the good-for-nothing at the expense of the good, is an extreme cruelty. It is a deliberate stirring-up of miseries for future generations. There is no greater curse to posterity than that of bequeathing to them an increasing population of imbeciles and idlers and criminals. . . . The whole effort of nature is to get rid of such, to clear the world of them, and make room for better. . . . If they are not sufficiently complete to live, they die, and it is best they should die.

(Spencer, cited in Abrams, 1968:74)

Such sentiments were clearly at odds with the ameliorative orientation of the British reformer-sociologists.

The Key Figure in Early Italian Sociology

We close this sketch of early, primarily conservative, European sociological theory with a brief mention of one Italian sociologist, Vilfredo Pareto (1848–1923). Pareto was influential in his time, but his contemporary relevance is minimal (for one exception, see Powers, 1986). There was a brief outburst of interest in Pareto's (1935) work in the 1930s, when the major American theorist, Talcott Parsons, devoted as much attention to him as he gave to Weber and Durkheim. However, in recent years, except for a few of his major concepts, Pareto also has receded in importance and contemporary relevance (Femia, 1995).

Zeitlin argued that Pareto developed his "major ideas as a refutation of Marx" (1981:171). In fact, Pareto was rejecting not only Marx but also a good portion of Enlightenment philosophy. For example, whereas the Enlightenment philosophers emphasized rationality, Pareto emphasized the role of nonrational factors such as human instincts. This emphasis also was tied to his rejection of Marxian theory. That is, because nonrational, instinctual factors were so important *and* so unchanging, it was unrealistic to hope to achieve dramatic social changes with an economic revolution.

Pareto also developed a theory of social change that stood in stark contrast to Marxian theory. Whereas Marx's theory focused on the role of the masses, Pareto offered an elite theory of social change, which held that society inevitably is dominated by a small elite that operates on the basis of enlightened self-interest. It rules over the masses of people, who are dominated by nonrational forces. Because they lack rational capacities, the masses, in Pareto's system, are unlikely to be a revolutionary force. Social change occurs when the elite begins to degenerate and is replaced by a new elite derived from the nongoverning elite or higher elements of the masses. Once the new elite is in power, the process begins anew. Thus, we have a cyclical theory of social change instead of the directional theories offered by Marx, Comte, Spencer, and others. In addition, Pareto's theory of change largely ignores the plight of the masses. Elites come and go, but the lot of the masses remains the same.

This theory, however, was not Pareto's lasting contribution to sociology. That lay in his scientific conception of sociology and the social world: "My wish is to construct a system of sociology on the model of celestial mechanics [astronomy], physics, chemistry" (cited in Hook, 1965:57). Briefly, Pareto conceived of society as a system in equilibrium, a whole consisting of interdependent parts. A change in one part was seen as leading to changes in other parts of the system. Pareto's systemic conception of society was the most important reason Parsons devoted so much attention to Pareto's work in his 1937 book, *The Structure of Social Action,* and it was Pareto's most important influence on Parsons's thinking. Fused with similar views held by those who had an organic image of society (Comte, Durkheim, and Spencer, for example), Pareto's theory played a central role in the development of Parsons's theory and, more generally, in structural functionalism.

Although few modern sociologists now read Pareto's work, it can be seen as a rejection of the Enlightenment and of Marxism and as offering an elite theory of social change that stands in opposition to the Marxian perspective.

Turn-of-the-Century Developments in European Marxism

While many nineteenth-century sociologists were developing their theories in opposition to Marx, there was a simultaneous effort by a number of Marxists to clarify and extend Marxian theory. Between roughly 1875 and 1925, there was little overlap between Marxism and sociology. (Weber is an exception to this.) The two schools of thought were developing in parallel fashion with little or no interchange between them.

After the death of Marx, Marxian theory was first dominated by those who saw in his theory scientific and economic determinism. Wallerstein calls this the era of "orthodox Marxism" (1986:1301). Friedrich Engels, Marx's benefactor and collaborator, lived on after Marx's death and can be seen as the first exponent of such a perspective. Basically, this view was that Marx's scientific theory had uncovered the economic laws that ruled the capitalist world. Such laws pointed to the inevitable collapse of the capitalist system. Early Marxian thinkers, like Karl Kautsky, sought to gain a better understanding of the operation of these laws. There were several problems with this perspective. For one thing, it seemed to rule out political action, a cornerstone of Marx's position. That is, there seemed no need for individuals, especially workers, to do anything. In that the system was inevitably crumbling, all they had to do was sit back and wait for its demise. On a theoretical level, deterministic Marxism seemed to rule out the dialectical relationship between individuals and larger social structures.

These problems led to a reaction among Marxian theorists and to the development of "Hegelian Marxism" in the early 1900s. The Hegelian Marxists refused to reduce Marxism to a scientific theory that ignored individual thought and action. They are labeled *Hegelian Marxists* because they sought to combine Hegel's interest in consciousness (which some, including the author of this text, view Marx as sharing) with the determinists' interest in the economic structures of society. The Hegelian theorists were significant for both theoretical and practical reasons. Theoretically, they reinstated the importance of the individual, consciousness, and the relationship between thought and action. Practically, they emphasized the importance of individual action in bringing about a social revolution.

The major exponent of this point of view was Georg Lukács (Fischer, 1984). According to Martin Jay, Lukács was "the founding father of Western Marxism" and his work *Class and Class Consciousness* is "generally acknowledged as the charter document of Hegelian Marxism" (1984:84). Lukács had begun in the early 1900s to integrate Marxism with sociology (in particular, Weberian and Simmelian theory). This integration was soon to accelerate with the development of critical theory in the 1920s and 1930s.

SUMMARY

This chapter sketches the early history of sociological theory. The first, and much briefer, section deals with the various social forces involved in the development of sociological theory. Although there were many such influences, we focus on how political revolution, the Industrial Revolution, and the rise of capitalism, socialism, urbanization, religious change, and the growth of science affected sociological theory. The second part of the chapter examines the influence of intellectual forces on the rise of sociological theory in various countries. We begin with France and the role played by the Enlightenment, stressing the conservative and romantic reaction to it. It is out of this interplay that French sociological theory developed. In this context, we examine the major figures in the early years of French sociology—Claude Henri Saint-Simon, Auguste Comte, and Emile Durkheim.

Next we turn to Germany and the role played by Karl Marx in the development of sociology in that country. We discuss the parallel development of Marxian theory and sociological theory and the ways in which Marxian theory influenced sociology, both positively and negatively. We begin with the roots of Marxian theory in Hegelianism, materialism, and political economy. Marx's theory itself is touched upon briefly. The discussion then shifts to the roots of German sociology. Max Weber's work is examined in order to show the diverse sources of German sociology. Also discussed are some of the reasons that Weber's theory proved more acceptable to later sociologists than did Marx's ideas. This section closes with a brief discussion of Georg Simmel's work.

The rise of sociological theory in Britain is considered next. The major sources of British sociology were political economy, ameliorism, and social evolution. In this context, we touch on the work of Herbert Spencer as well as on some of the controversy that surrounded it.

This chapter closes with a brief discussion of Italian sociological theory, in particular the work of Vilfredo Pareto, and the turn-of-the-century developments in European Marxian theory, primarily economic determinism and Hegelian Marxism.

2

A HISTORICAL SKETCH OF SOCIOLOGICAL THEORY: THE LATER YEARS

EARLY AMERICAN SOCIOLOGICAL THEORY
   Politics
   Social Change and Intellectual Currents
   The Chicago School
WOMEN IN EARLY SOCIOLOGY
SOCIOLOGICAL THEORY TO MID-CENTURY
   The Rise of Harvard, the Ivy League, and Structural Functionalism
   The Chicago School in Decline
   Developments in Marxian Theory
   Karl Mannheim and the Sociology of Knowledge
SOCIOLOGICAL THEORY FROM MID-CENTURY
   Structural Functionalism: Peak and Decline
   Radical Sociology in America: C. Wright Mills
   The Development of Conflict Theory
   The Birth of Exchange Theory
   Dramaturgical Analysis: The Work of Erving Goffman
   The Development of Sociologies of Everyday Life
   The Rise and Fall (?) of Marxian Sociology
   The Challenge of Feminist Theory
   Structuralism and Poststructuralism
RECENT DEVELOPMENTS IN SOCIOLOGICAL THEORY
   Micro-Macro Integration
   Agency-Structure Integration
   Theoretical Syntheses
THEORIES OF MODERNITY AND POSTMODERNITY
   The Defenders of Modernity
   The Proponents of Postmodernity
THEORIES TO WATCH IN THE EARLY TWENTY-FIRST CENTURY
   Multicultural Social Theory
   Postmodern and Post-Postmodern Social Theories
   Theories of Consumption
   Others

It is difficult to give a precise date for the founding of sociology in the United States. There was a course in social problems taught at Oberlin as early as 1858, Comte's term *sociology* was used by George Fitzhugh in 1854, and William Graham Sumner taught social science courses at Yale beginning in 1873. During the 1880s, courses specifically bearing the title "Sociology" began to appear. The first department with *sociology* in its title was founded at the University of Kansas in 1889. In 1892, Albion Small moved to the University of Chicago and set up the new department of sociology. The Chicago department became the first important center of American sociology in general and of sociological theory in particular (F. Matthews, 1977).

EARLY AMERICAN SOCIOLOGICAL THEORY

Politics

Schwendinger and Schwendinger (1974) argue that the early American sociologists are best described as political liberals and not, as was true of most early European theorists, as conservatives. The liberalism characteristic of early American sociology had basically two elements. First, it operated with a belief in the freedom and welfare of the individual. In this belief, it was influenced far more by Spencer's orientation than by Comte's more collective position. Second, many sociologists associated with this orientation adopted an evolutionary view of social progress (Fine, 1979). However, they split over how best to bring about this progress. Some argued that steps should be taken by the government to aid social reform, while others pushed a laissez-faire doctrine, arguing that the various components of society should be left to solve their own problems.

   Liberalism, taken to its extreme, comes very close to conservatism. The belief in social progress—in reform or a laissez-faire doctrine—and the belief in the importance of the individual both lead to positions supportive of the system as a whole. The overriding belief is that the social system works or can be reformed to work. There is little criticism of the system as a whole; in the American case this means, in particular, that there is little questioning of capitalism. Instead of imminent class struggle, the early sociologists saw a future of class harmony and class cooperation. Ultimately this meant that early American sociological theory helped to rationalize exploitation, domestic and international imperialism, and social inequality (Schwendinger and Schwendinger, 1974). In the end, the political liberalism of the early sociologists had enormously conservative implications.

Social Change and Intellectual Currents

In their analyses of the founding of American sociological theory, Roscoe Hinkle (1980) and Ellsworth Fuhrman (1980) outline several basic contexts from which that body of theory emerged. Of utmost importance are the social changes that occurred in American society after the Civil War (Bramson, 1961). In Chapter 1, we discussed an array of factors involved in the development of European sociological theory; several of these factors (such as industrialization and urbanization) were also intimately involved in the development of theory in America. In Fuhrman's view, the early American sociologists saw the positive possibilities of industrialization, but they were also well aware of its dangers. Although these early sociologists were attracted to the ideas generated by the labor movement and socialist groups about dealing with the dangers of industrialization, they were not in favor of radically overhauling society.

Arthur Vidich and Stanford Lyman (1985) make a strong case for the influence of Christianity, especially Protestantism, on the founding of American sociology. American sociologists retained the Protestant interest in saving the world and merely substituted one language (science) for another (religion). "From 1854, when the first works in sociology appeared in the United States, until the outbreak of World War I, sociology was a moral and intellectual response to the problems of American life and thought, institutions, and creeds" (Vidich and Lyman, 1985:1). Sociologists sought to define, study, and help solve these social problems. While the clergyman worked within religion to help improve it and people's lot within it, the sociologist did the same within society. Given their religious roots, and the religious parallels, the vast majority of sociologists did not challenge the basic legitimacy of society.

Another major factor in the founding of American sociology discussed by both Hinkle and Fuhrman is the simultaneous emergence in America, in the late 1800s, of academic professions (including sociology) and the modern university system. In Europe, in contrast, the university system was already well established *before* the emergence of sociology. Although sociology had a difficult time becoming established in Europe, it found the going easier in the more fluid setting of the new American university system.

Another characteristic of early American sociology (as well as other social science disciplines) was its turn away from a historical perspective and in the direction of a positivistic, or "scientistic," orientation. As Ross puts it, "The desire to achieve universalistic abstraction and quantitative methods turned American social scientists away from interpretive models available in history and cultural anthropology, and from the generalizing and interpretive model offered by Max Weber" (1991:473). Instead of interpreting long-term historical changes, sociology had turned in the direction of scientifically studying short-term processes.

Still another factor was the impact of established European theory on American sociological theory. European theorists largely created sociological theory, and the Americans were able to rely on this groundwork. The Europeans most important to the Americans were Spencer and Comte. Simmel was of some importance in the early years, but the influence of Durkheim, Weber, and Marx was not to have a dramatic effect for a number of years. As an illustration of the impact of early European theory on American sociology, the history of the ideas of Herbert Spencer is interesting and informative.

Herbert Spencer's Influence on Sociology   Why were Spencer's ideas so much more influential in the early years of American sociology than those of Comte, Durkheim, Marx, and Weber? Hofstadter (1959) offered several explanations. To take the easiest first, Spencer wrote in English, while the others did not. In addition, Spencer wrote in nontechnical terms, thereby making his work broadly accessible. Indeed, some

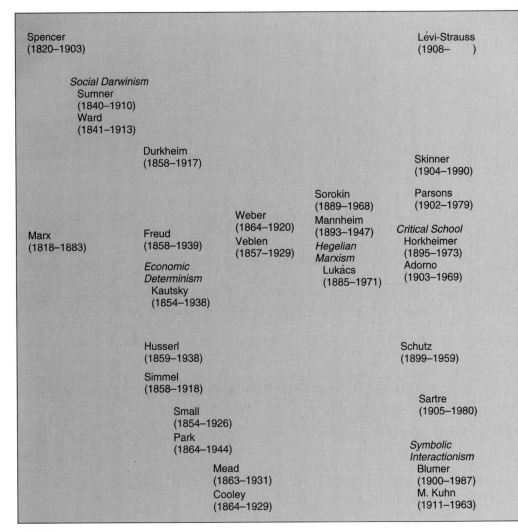

FIGURE 2.1
Sociological Theory: The Later Years

have argued that the lack of technicality is traceable to Spencer's *not* being a very sophisticated scholar. But there are other, more important reasons for Spencer's broad appeal. He offered a scientific orientation that was attractive to an audience becoming enamored of science and its technological products. He offered a comprehensive theory that seemed to deal with the entire sweep of human history. The breadth of his ideas, as well as the voluminous work he produced, allowed his theory to be many different things to many different people. Finally, and perhaps most important, his theory was soothing and reassuring to a society undergoing the wrenching process of industrialization—society was, according to Spencer, steadily moving in the direction of greater and greater progress.

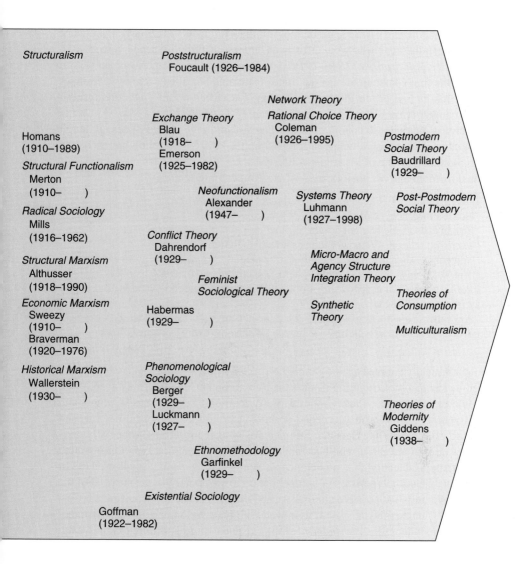

Spencer's most famous American disciple was William Graham Sumner, who accepted and expanded upon many of Spencer's Social Darwinist ideas. Spencer also influenced other early American sociologists, among them Lester Ward, Charles Horton Cooley, E. A. Ross, and Robert Park.

By the 1930s, however, Spencer was in eclipse in the intellectual world in general, as well as in sociology. His Social Darwinist, laissez-faire ideas seemed ridiculous in the light of massive social problems, a world war, and a major economic depression. In 1937 Talcott Parsons announced Spencer's intellectual death for sociology when he echoed historian Crane Brinton's words of a few years earlier, "Who now reads Spencer?" Today Spencer is of little more than historical interest, but his ideas *were* important in shaping early American sociological theory. Let us look briefly at the work of two American theorists who were influenced, at least in part, by Spencer's work.

William Graham Sumner (1840–1910) William Graham Sumner was the person who taught the first course in the United States that could be called sociology. Sumner contended that he had begun teaching sociology "years before any such attempt was made at any other university in the world" (Curtis, 1981:63).

Sumner was the major exponent of Social Darwinism in the United States, although he appeared to change his view late in life (N. Smith, 1979). The following exchange between Sumner and one of his students illustrates his "liberal" views on the need for individual freedom and his position against government interference:

> "Professor, don't you believe in any government aid to industries?"
> "No! It's root, hog, or die."
> "Yes, but hasn't the hog got a right to root?"
> "There are no rights. The world owes nobody a living."
> "You believe then, Professor, in only one system, the contract-competitive system?"
> "That's the only sound economic system. All others are fallacies."
> "Well, suppose some professor of political economy came along and took your job away from you. Wouldn't you be sore?"
> "Any other professor is welcome to try. If he gets my job, it is my fault. My business is to teach the subject so well that no one can take the job away from me."
>
> (Phelps, cited in Hofstadter, 1959:54)

Sumner basically adopted a survival-of-the-fittest approach to the social world. Like Spencer, he saw people struggling against their environment, and the fittest were those who would be successful. Thus Sumner was a supporter of human aggressiveness and competitiveness. Those who succeeded deserved it, and those who did not succeed deserved to fail. Again like Spencer, Sumner was opposed to efforts, especially government efforts, to aid those who had failed. In his view such intervention operated against the natural selection that, among people as among lower animals, allowed the fit to survive and the unfit to perish. As Sumner put it, "If we do not like the survival of the fittest, we have only one possible alternative, and that is survival of the unfittest" (Curtis, 1981:84). This theoretical system fit in well with the development of capitalism because it provided theoretical legitimacy for the existence of great differences in wealth and power.

Sumner is of little more than historical interest for two main reasons. First, his orientation and Social Darwinism in general have come to be regarded as little more than a crude legitimation of competitive capitalism and the status quo. Second, he failed to build a solid enough base at Yale to build a school of sociology with many disciples. That kind of success was to occur some years later at the University of Chicago (Heyl and Heyl, 1976). In spite of success in his time, "Sumner is remembered by few today" (Curtis, 1981:146).

Lester F. Ward (1841–1913) Lester Ward had an unusual career in that he spent most of it as a paleontologist working for the federal government. During that time, Ward read Spencer and Comte and developed a strong interest in sociology. He published a number of works in the late 1800s and early 1900s in which he expounded his sociological theory. As a result of the fame that this work achieved, in 1906 Ward was elected the first president of the American Sociological Society. It was only then that he took his first academic position, at Brown University, a position that he held until his death.

Ward, like Sumner, accepted the idea that people had evolved from lower forms to their present status. He believed that early society was characterized by its simplicity and its moral poverty, whereas modern society was more complex, happier, and offered greater freedom. One task of sociology, *pure sociology,* was to study the basic laws of social change and social structure. But Ward was not content simply to have sociology study social life. He believed that sociology should have a practical side; there should also be an *applied sociology.* This applied sociology involved the conscious use of scientific knowledge to attain a better society. Thus, Ward was not an extreme Social Darwinist; he believed in the need for and importance of social reform.

Although of historical importance, Sumner and Ward have not been of long-term significance to sociological theory. We turn now, however, first briefly to a theorist of the time, Thorstein Veblen, who has been of long-term significance and whose influence today in sociology is increasing, and then to a group of theorists, especially Mead, and to a school, the Chicago school, that came to dominate sociology in America. The Chicago school was unusual in the history of sociology in that it was one of the few (the Durkheimian school in Paris was another) "collective intellectual enterprises of an integrated kind" in the history of sociology (Bulmer, 1984:1). The tradition begun at the University of Chicago is of continuing importance to sociology and its theoretical (and empirical) status.

Thorstein Veblen (1857–1929)   Veblen, who was not a sociologist but mainly held positions in economics departments, and even in economics was a marginal figure, nonetheless produced a body of social theory that is of enduring significance to those in a number of disciplines, including sociology. The central problem for Veblen was the clash between "business" and "industry." By business, Veblen meant the owners, leaders, "captains" of industry who focused on the profits of their own companies, but to keep prices and profits high, often engaged in efforts to limit production. In so doing they obstructed the operation of the industrial system and adversely affected society as a whole (through higher rates of unemployment, for example), which is best served by the unimpeded operation of industry. Thus, business leaders were the source of many problems within society, which, Veblen felt, should be led by people (e.g., engineers) who understood the industrial system and its operation and were interested in the general welfare.

Most of Veblen's importance today is traceable to his book *The Theory of the Leisure Class* (1899/1994). Veblen is critical of the leisure class (which is closely tied to business) for its role in fostering wasteful consumption. To impress the rest of society, the leisure class engages in both "conspicuous leisure" (the nonproductive use of time) and "conspicuous consumption" (spending more money on goods than they are worth). Those in all other social classes are influenced by this example and seek, directly and indirectly, to emulate the leisure class. The result is a society characterized by the waste of time and money. What is of utmost importance about this work is that unlike most other sociological works of the time (as well as most of Veblen's other works), *The Theory of the Leisure Class* focuses on consumption rather than production. Thus, it anticipated the current shift in social theory away from a focus on production toward a focus on consumption (Slater, 1997; Ritzer, 1999).

The Chicago School[1]

The department of sociology at the University of Chicago was founded in 1892 by Albion Small. Small's intellectual work is of less contemporary significance than the key role he played in the institutionalization of sociology in the United States (Faris, 1970; Matthews, 1977). He was instrumental in creating a department at Chicago that was to become the center of the discipline in the United States for many years. Small collaborated on the first textbook in sociology in 1894. In 1895 he founded the *American Journal of Sociology,* a journal that to this day is a dominant force in the discipline. In 1905, Small cofounded the American Sociological Society, *the* major professional association of American sociologists to this date (Rhoades, 1981). (The embarrassment caused by the initials of the American Sociological Society, ASS, led to a name change in 1959 to the American Sociological Association—ASA.)

Early Chicago Sociology The early Chicago department had several distinctive characteristics. For one thing, it had a strong connection with religion. Some members were ministers themselves, and others were sons of ministers. Small, for example, believed that "the ultimate goal of sociology must be essentially Christian" (Matthews, 1977:95). This opinion led to a view that sociology must be interested in social reform, and this view was combined with a belief that sociology should be scientific.[2] Scientific sociology with an objective of social amelioration was to be practiced in the burgeoning city of Chicago, which was beset by the positive *and* negative effects of urbanization and industrialization.

W. I. Thomas (1863–1947) In 1895, W. I. Thomas became a fellow at the Chicago department, where he wrote his dissertation in 1896. Thomas's lasting significance was in his emphasis on the need to do scientific research on sociological issues (Lodge, 1986). Although he championed this position for many years, its major statement came in 1918 with the publication of *The Polish Peasant in Europe and America,* which Thomas coauthored with Florian Znaniecki. Martin Bulmer sees it as a "landmark" study because it moved sociology away from "abstract theory and library research and toward the study of the empirical world utilizing a theoretical framework" (1984:45). Norbert Wiley sees *The Polish Peasant* as crucial to the founding of sociology in the sense of "clarifying the unique intellectual space into which this discipline alone could see and explore" (1986:20). The book was the product of eight years of research in both Europe and the United States and was primarily a study of social disorganization among Polish

---

[1]See Bulmer (1985) for a discussion of what defines a school and why we can speak of the "Chicago school." Tiryakian (1979, 1986) also deals with schools in general, and the Chicago school in particular, and emphasizes the role played by charismatic leaders as well as methodological innovations. See also Amsterdamska (1985). For a discussion of this school within the broader context of developments within American sociological theory, see Hinkle (1994).

[2]As we will see, however, the Chicago school's conception of science was to become too "soft," at least in the eyes of the positivists who later came to dominate sociology.

migrants. The data were of little lasting importance. However, the methodology was significant. It involved a variety of data sources, including autobiographical material, paid writings, family letters, newspaper files, public documents, and institutional letters.

Although *The Polish Peasant* was primarily a macrosociological study of social institutions, over the course of his career Thomas gravitated toward a microscopic, social-psychological orientation. He is best known for the following social-psychological statement (made in a book coauthored by Dorothy Thomas): "If men define situations as real, they are real in their consequences" (Thomas and Thomas, 1928:572). The emphasis was on the importance of what people think and how this affects what they do. This microscopic, social-psychological focus stood in contrast to the macroscopic, social-structural and social-cultural perspectives of such European scholars as Marx, Weber, and Durkheim. It was to become one of the defining characteristics of Chicago's theoretical product—symbolic interactionism (Rock, 1979:5).

Robert Park (1864–1944)   Another figure of significance at Chicago was Robert Park (Shils, 1996). Park had come to Chicago as a part-time instructor in 1914 and quickly worked his way into a central role in the department. Park's importance for the development of sociology lay in several areas. First, he became the dominant figure in the Chicago department, which, in turn, dominated sociology into the 1930s. Second, Park had studied in Europe and was instrumental in bringing Continental thinkers to the attention of Chicago sociologists. Park had taken courses with Simmel, and Simmel's ideas, particularly his focus on action and interaction, were instrumental in the development of the Chicago school's theoretical orientation (Rock, 1979:36–48). Third, prior to becoming a sociologist, Park had been a reporter, and this experience gave him a sense of the importance of urban problems and of the need to go out into the field to collect data through personal observation (Lindner, 1996; Strauss, 1996). Out of this emerged the Chicago school's substantive interest in urban ecology (Gaziano, 1996; Maines, Bridger, and Ulmer, 1996; Perry, Abbott, and Hutter, 1997). Fourth, Park played a key role in guiding graduate students and helping develop "a cumulative program of graduate research" (Bulmer, 1984:13). Finally, in 1921, Park and Ernest W. Burgess published the first truly important sociology textbook, *An Introduction to the Science of Sociology*. It was to be an influential book for many years and was particularly notable for its commitments to science, to research, and to the study of a wide range of social phenomena.

Beginning in the late 1920s and early 1930s, Park began to spend less time in Chicago. Finally, his lifelong interest in race relations (he had been secretary to Booker T. Washington before becoming a sociologist) led him to take a position at Fisk University (a black university) in 1934. Although the decline of the Chicago department was not caused solely or even chiefly by Park's departure, its status began to wane in the 1930s. But before we can deal with the decline of Chicago sociology and the rise of other departments and theories, we need to return to the early days of the school and the two figures whose work was to be of the most lasting theoretical significance—Charles Horton Cooley and, most important, George Herbert Mead.[3]

---

[3]There were many other significant figures associated with the Chicago School, including Everett Hughes (Chapoulie, 1996; Strauss, 1996).

ROBERT PARK: A Biographical Sketch

Robert Park did not follow the typical career route of an academic sociologist—college, graduate school, professorship. Instead, he led a varied career before he became a sociologist late in life. Despite his late start, Park had a profound effect on sociology in general and on theory in particular. Park's varied experiences gave him an unusual orientation to life, and this view helped to shape the Chicago school, symbolic interactionism, and, ultimately, a good portion of sociology.

Park was born in Harveyville, Pennsylvania, on February 14, 1864 (Matthews, 1977). As a student at the University of Michigan, he was exposed to a number of great thinkers, such as John Dewey. Although he was excited by ideas, Park felt a strong need to work in the real world. As Park said, "I made up my mind to go in for experience for its own sake, to gather into my soul . . . 'all the joys and sorrows of the world'" (1927/1973:253). Upon graduation, he began a career as a journalist, which gave him this real-world opportunity. He particularly liked to explore ("hunting down gambling houses and opium dens" [Park, 1927/1973:254]). He wrote about city life in vivid detail. He would go into the field, observe and analyze, and finally write up his observations. In fact, he was already doing essentially the kind of research ("scientific reporting") that came to be one of the hallmarks of Chicago sociology—that is, urban ethnology using participant observation techniques (Lindner, 1996).

Although the accurate description of social life remained one of his passions, Park grew dissatisfied with newspaper work, because it did not fulfill his familial or, more important, his intellectual needs. Furthermore, it did not seem to contribute to the improvement of the world, and Park had a deep interest in social reform. In 1898, at age thirty-four, Park left newspaper work and enrolled in the philosophy department at Harvard. He remained there

Charles Horton Cooley (1864–1929)   The association of Cooley with the Chicago school is interesting in that he spent his career at the University of Michigan. But Cooley's theoretical perspective was in line with the theory of symbolic interactionism that was to become Chicago's most important product.

Cooley received his Ph.D. from the University of Michigan in 1894. He had developed a strong interest in sociology, but there was as yet no department of sociology at Michigan. As a result, the questions for his Ph.D. examination came from Columbia University, where sociology had been taught since 1889 under the leadership of Franklin Giddings. Cooley began his teaching career at Michigan in 1892 before completion of his doctorate.

Although Cooley had a wide range of views, he is remembered today mainly for his insights into the social-psychological aspects of social life. His work in this area is in line with that of George Herbert Mead, although Mead was to have a deeper and more lasting effect on sociology than Cooley had. Cooley had an interest in consciousness, but he refused (as did Mead) to separate consciousness from the social context. This is best exemplified by a concept of his that survives to this day—the *looking-glass self.*

for a year but then decided to move to Germany, at that time the heart of the world's intellectual life. In Berlin he encountered Georg Simmel, whose work was to have a profound influence on Park's sociology. In fact, Simmel's lectures were the *only* formal sociological training that Park received. As Park said, "I got most of my knowledge about society and human nature from my own observations" (1927/1973:257). In 1904, Park completed his doctoral dissertation at the University of Heidelberg. Characteristically, he was dissatisfied with his dissertation: "All I had to show was that little book and I was ashamed of it" (Matthews, 1977:57). He refused a summer teaching job at the University of Chicago and turned away from academe as he had earlier turned away from newspaper work.

His need to contribute to social betterment led him to become secretary and chief publicity officer for the Congo Reform Association, which was set up to help alleviate the brutality and exploitation then taking place in the Belgian Congo. During this period, he met Booker T. Washington, and he was attracted to the cause of improving the lot of black Americans. He became Washington's secretary and played a key role in the activities of the Tuskegee Institute. In 1912 he met W. I. Thomas, the Chicago sociologist, who was lecturing at Tuskegee. Thomas invited him to give a course on "the Negro in America" to a small group of graduate students at Chicago, and Park did so in 1914. The course was successful, and he gave it again the next year to an audience twice as large. At this time, he joined the American Sociological Society, and only a decade later he became its president. Park gradually worked his way into a full-time appointment at Chicago, although he did not get a full professorship until 1923, when he was fifty-nine years old. Over the approximately two decades that he was affiliated with the University of Chicago, he played a key role in shaping the intellectual orientation of the sociology department.

Park remained peripatetic even after his retirement from Chicago in the early 1930s. He taught courses and oversaw research at Fisk University until he was nearly eighty years old. He traveled extensively. He died on February 7, 1944, one week before his eightieth birthday.

By this concept, Cooley understood that people possess consciousness and that it is shaped in continuing social interaction.

A second basic concept that illustrates Cooley's social-psychological interests, and which is also of continuing interest and importance, is that of the primary group. *Primary groups* are intimate, face-to-face groups that play a key role in linking the actor to the larger society. Especially crucial are the primary groups of the young—mainly the family and the peer group. Within these groups, the individual grows into a social being. It is basically within the primary group that the looking-glass self emerges and that the ego-centered child learns to take others into account and, thereby, to become a contributing member of society.

Both Cooley (Winterer, 1994) and Mead rejected a *behavioristic* view of human beings, the view that people blindly and unconsciously respond to external stimuli. They believed that people had consciousness, a self, and that it was the responsibility of the sociologist to study this aspect of social reality. Cooley urged sociologists to try to put themselves in the place of the actors they were studying, to use the method of *sympathetic introspection*, in order to analyze consciousness. By analyzing what they as actors might do in various circumstances, sociologists could understand the meanings and motives that are at the base of social behavior. The method of sympathetic introspection seemed to many to be very unscientific. In this area, among others, Mead's work represents an advance over Cooley's. Nevertheless, there is a great deal of similarity in the interests of the two men, not the least of which is their shared view that sociology should focus on such social-psychological phenomena as consciousness, action, and interaction.

George Herbert Mead (1863–1931) The most important thinker associated with the Chicago school and symbolic interactionism was not a sociologist but a philosopher, George Herbert Mead.[4] Mead started teaching philosophy at the University of Chicago in 1894, and he taught there until his death in 1931 (G. Cook, 1993). He is something of a paradox, given his central importance in the history of sociological theory, both because he taught philosophy, not sociology, and because he published comparatively little during his lifetime. The paradox is, in part, resolved by two facts. First, Mead taught courses in social psychology in the philosophy department, and they were taken by many graduate students in sociology. His ideas had a profound effect on a number of them. These students combined Mead's ideas with those they were getting in the sociology department from people like Park and Thomas. Although at the time there was no theory known as symbolic interactionism, it was created by students out of these various inputs. Thus Mead had a deep, personal impact on the people who were later to develop symbolic interactionism. Second, these students put together their notes on Mead's courses and published a posthumous volume under his name. The work, *Mind, Self and Society* (Mead, 1934/1962), moved his ideas from the realm of oral to that of written tradition. Widely read to this day, this volume forms the main intellectual pillar of symbolic interactionism.

We deal with Mead's ideas in Chapter 6, but it is necessary at this point to underscore a few points in order to situate him historically. Mead's ideas need to be seen in the context of psychological behaviorism. Mead was quite impressed with this orientation and accepted many of its tenets. He adopted its focus on the actor and his behavior. He regarded as sensible the behaviorists' concern with the rewards and costs involved in the behaviors of the actors. What troubled Mead was that behaviorism did not seem to go far enough. That is, it excluded consciousness from serious consideration, arguing that it was not amenable to scientific study. Mead vehemently disagreed and sought to extend the principles of behaviorism to an analysis of the "mind." In so doing, Mead enunciated a focus similar to that of Cooley. But whereas Cooley's position seemed unscientific, Mead promised a more scientific conception of consciousness by extending the highly scientific principles and methods of psychological behaviorism.

Mead offered American sociology a social-psychological theory that stood in stark contrast to the primarily societal theories offered by most of the major European theorists. The most important exception was Simmel. Thus symbolic interactionism was developed, in large part, out of Simmel's interest in action and interaction and Mead's interest in consciousness. However, such a focus led to a weakness in Mead's work, as well as in symbolic interactionism in general, at the societal and cultural levels.

---

[4]For a dissenting view, see Lewis and Smith (1980).

The Waning of Chicago Sociology   Chicago sociology reached its peak in the 1920s, but by the 1930s, with the death of Mead and the departure of Park, the department had begun to lose its position of central importance in American sociology (Cortese, 1995). Fred Matthews (1977; see also Bulmer, 1984) pinpoints several reasons for the decline of Chicago sociology, two of which seem of utmost importance.

First, the discipline had grown increasingly preoccupied with being scientific—that is, using sophisticated methods and employing statistical analysis. However, the Chicago school was viewed as emphasizing descriptive, ethnographic studies (Prus, 1996), often focusing on their subjects' personal orientations (in Thomas's terms, their "definitions of the situation"). Park came progressively to despise statistics (he called it "parlor magic") because it seemed to prohibit the analysis of subjectivity, of the idiosyncratic, and of the peculiar. The fact that important work in quantitative methods was done at Chicago (Bulmer, 1984:151–189) tended to be ignored in the face of its overwhelming association with qualitative methods.

Second, more and more individuals outside Chicago grew increasingly resentful of Chicago's dominance of both the American Sociological Society and the *American Journal of Sociology*. The Eastern Sociological Society was founded in 1930, and eastern sociologists became more vocal about the dominance of the Midwest in general and Chicago in particular (Wiley, 1979:63). By 1935, the revolt against Chicago led to a non-Chicago secretary of the association and the establishment of a new official journal, the *American Sociological Review* (Lengermann, 1979). According to Wiley, "the Chicago school had fallen like a mighty oak" (1979:63). This signaled the growth of other power centers, most notably Harvard and the Ivy League in general. Symbolic interactionism was largely an indeterminate, oral tradition and as such eventually lost ground to more explicit and codified theoretical systems like the structural functionalism associated with the Ivy League (Rock, 1979:12).

WOMEN IN EARLY SOCIOLOGY

Simultaneously with the developments at the University of Chicago described in the previous section, even sometimes in concert with them, and at the same time that Durkheim, Weber, and Simmel were creating a European sociology, and sometimes in concert with them as well, a group of women who formed a broad and surprisingly connected network of social reformers were also developing pioneering sociological theories. These women included Jane Addams (1860–1935), Charlotte Perkins Gilman (1860–1935), Anna Julia Cooper (1858–1964), Ida Wells-Barnett (1862–1931), Marianne Weber (1870–1954), and Beatrice Potter Webb (1858–1943); with the possible exception of Cooper, they can all be connected through their relationship to Jane Addams. That they are not today known or recognized in conventional histories of the discipline as sociologists or as sociological theorists is a chilling testimony to the power of gender politics within the discipline of sociology and to sociology's essentially unreflective and uncritical interpretation of its own practices. While the sociological theory of each of these women is a product of individual theoretical effort, when they are read collectively they represent a coherent and complementary statement of early feminist sociological theory.

The chief hallmarks of their theories, hallmarks which may in part account for their being passed over in the development of professional sociology, include: (1) an emphasis on women's experience and women's lives and works' being equal in importance to men's; (2) an awareness that they spoke from a situated and embodied standpoint and therefore, for the most part, not with the tone of imperious objectivity that male sociological theory would come to associate with authoritative theory making; (3) the idea that the purpose of sociology and sociological theory is social reform—that is, the end is to improve people's lives through knowledge; and (4) the claim that the chief problem for amelioration in their time was inequality. What distinguishes these early women most from each other is the nature of and the remedy for the inequality on which they focused—gender, race, or class, or the intersection of these. But all these women translated their views into social and political activism that helped to shape and change the North Atlantic societies in which they lived, and this activism was as much a part of their sense of doing sociology as creating theory was. They believed in social science research as part of both their theoretical and activist enactments of sociology and were highly creative innovators of social science method.

As the developing discipline of sociology marginalized these women as sociologists and sociological theorists, it often incorporated their research methods into its own practices, while using their activism as an excuse to define these women as "not sociologists." Thus they are remembered as social activists and social workers rather than sociologists. Their heritage is a sociological theory that is a call to action as well as to thought.

SOCIOLOGICAL THEORY TO MID-CENTURY

The Rise of Harvard, the Ivy League, and Structural Functionalism

We can trace the rise of sociology at Harvard from the arrival of Pitirim Sorokin in 1930 (Johnston, 1995). When Sorokin arrived at Harvard, there was no sociology department, but by the end of his first year one had been organized, and he had been appointed its head. Although Sorokin was a sociological theorist, and he continued to publish into the 1960s, his work is surprisingly little cited today. His theorizing has not stood the test of time very well. Sorokin's long-term significance may well have been in the creation of the Harvard sociology department and the hiring of Talcott Parsons (who had been an instructor of economics at Harvard) for the position of instructor of sociology. Parsons became *the* dominant figure in American sociology for introducing European theorists to an American audience, for his own sociological theories, and for his many students who themselves became major sociological theorists.

Pitirim Sorokin (1889–1968)   Sorokin developed a theory that, if anything, surpassed Parsons's in scope and complexity. The most complete statement of this theory is contained in the four-volume *Social and Cultural Dynamics,* published between 1937 and 1941. In it, Sorokin drew on a wide range of empirical data to develop a general theory of social and cultural change. In contrast to those who sought to develop evolutionary theories of social change, Sorokin developed a cyclical theory. He saw societies as oscillating among three different types of mentalities—sensate, ideational, and idealistic. Societies dominated by *sensatism* emphasize the role of the senses in comprehending reality; those dominated by a more transcendental and highly religious way of understanding reality are *ideational;* and *idealistic* societies are transitional types balancing sensatism and religiosity.

The motor of social change is to be found in the internal logic of each of these systems. That is, they are pressed internally to extend their mode of thinking to its logical extreme. Thus a sensate society ultimately becomes so sensual that it provides the groundwork for its own demise. As sensatism reaches its logical end point, people turn to ideational systems as a refuge. But once such a system has gained ascendancy, it too is pushed to its end point, with the result that society becomes excessively religious. The stage is then set for the rise of an idealistic culture and, ultimately, for the cycle to repeat itself. Sorokin not only developed an elaborate theory of social change, but he also marshaled detailed evidence from art, philosophy, politics, and so forth to support his theory. It was clearly an impressive accomplishment.

There is much more to Sorokin's theorizing, but this introduction should give the reader a feeling for the breadth of his work. It is difficult to explain why Sorokin has fallen out of favor in sociological theory. Perhaps it is the result of one of the things that Sorokin loved to attack, and in fact wrote a book about, *Fads and Foibles in Modern Sociology and Related Sciences* (1956). It may be that Sorokin will be rediscovered by a future generation of sociological theorists. At the moment, his work remains outside the mainstream of modern sociological theorizing.

Talcott Parsons (1902–1979)   Although he published some early essays, Parsons's major contribution in the early years was in his influence on graduate students who themselves were to become notable sociological theorists. The most famous was Robert Merton, who received his Ph.D. in 1936 and soon became a major theorist and the heart of Parsonsian-style theorizing at Columbia University. In the same year (1936), Kingsley Davis received his Ph.D., and he, along with Wilbert Moore (who received his Harvard degree in 1940), wrote one of the central works in structural-functional theory, the theory that was to become the major product of Parsons and the Parsonsians. But Parsons's influence was not restricted to the 1930s. Remarkably, he produced graduate students of great influence well into the 1960s.

The pivotal year for Parsons and for American sociological theory was 1937, the year in which he published *The Structure of Social Action.* This book was of significance to sociological theory in America for four main reasons. First, it served to introduce grand European theorizing to a large American audience. The bulk of the book was devoted to Durkheim, Weber, and Pareto. His interpretations of these theorists shaped their images in American sociology for many years.

Second, Parsons devoted almost no attention to Marx (or to Simmel [Levine, 1991a]), although he emphasized the work of Durkheim and Weber and even Pareto. As a result, Marxian theory continued to be largely excluded from legitimate sociology.

Third, *The Structure of Social Action* made the case for sociological theorizing as a legitimate and significant sociological activity. The theorizing that has taken place in the United States since then owes a deep debt to Parsons's work.

Finally, Parsons argued for specific sociological theories that were to have a profound influence on sociology. At first, Parsons was thought of, and thought of himself, as an

PITIRIM A. SOROKIN: A Biographical Sketch

Pitirim Sorokin was born in a remote village in Russia on January 21, 1889 (Johnston, 1995). In his teenage years, and while a seminary student, Sorokin was arrested for revolutionary activities and spent four months in prison. Eventually, Sorokin made his way to St. Petersburg University and interspersed diligent studies, teaching responsibilities, and revolutionary activities that once again landed him in prison briefly. Sorokin's dissertation was scheduled to be defended in March 1917, but before his examination could take place, the Russian Revolution was under way. Sorokin was not able to earn his doctorate until 1922. Active in the revolution, but opposed to the Bolsheviks, Sorokin took a position in Kerensky's provisional government. But when the Bolsheviks emerged victorious, Sorokin once again found himself in prison, this time at the hands of the Bolsheviks. Eventually, under direct orders from Lenin, Sorokin was freed and allowed to return to the university and pick up where he had left off. However, his work was censored, and he was harassed by the secret police. Sorokin finally was allowed to leave Russia, and, after a stay in Czechoslovakia, he arrived in the United States in October 1923.

At first, Sorokin gave lectures at various universities, but eventually he obtained a position at the University of Minnesota. He soon became a full professor. Sorokin already had published several books in Russia, and he continued to turn them out at a prodigious rate in the United States. Of his productivity at Minnesota, Sorokin said, "I knew it exceeded the lifetime productivity of the average sociologist" (1963:224). Books such as *Social Mobility* and *Contemporary Sociological Theories* gave him a national reputation, and by 1929 he was offered (and accepted) the first chair at Harvard University in sociology. The position was placed in the department of economics because there was not yet a sociology department at Harvard.

Soon after his arrival at Harvard, a separate department of sociology was created, and Sorokin was named as its first chairman. In that position, Sorokin helped build the most important sociology department in the United States. During this period, Sorokin also completed what would become his best-known work, *Social and Cultural Dynamics* (1937–41).

Pitirim Sorokin has been described as "the Peck's bad boy and devil's advocate of American sociology" (R. Williams, 1980b:100). Blessed with an enormous ego, Sorokin seemed critical of almost everyone and everything. As a result, Sorokin and his work were the subject of much critical analysis. All of this is clear in an excerpt from a letter he wrote to the editor of the *American Journal of Sociology:*

action theorist. He seemed to focus on actors and their thoughts and actions. But by the close of his 1937 work and increasingly in his later work, Parsons sounded more like a structural-functional theorist focusing on large-scale social and cultural systems. Although Parsons argued that there was no contradiction between these theories, he became best known as a structural functionalist, and he was the primary exponent of this theory, which gained dominance within sociology and maintained that position until the 1960s. Parsons's theoretical strength, and that of structural functionalism, lay in delineating the relationships among large-scale social structures and institutions (see Chapter 3).

The strongly disparaging character of the reviews is a good omen for my books because of a high correlation between the damning of my books . . . and their subsequent career. The more strongly they have been damned (and practically all my books were damned by your reviewers), the more significant and successful were my damned works.

(Sorokin, 1963:229)

One of Sorokin's more interesting and long-running feuds was with Talcott Parsons. Parsons had been appointed at Harvard as an instructor of sociology when Sorokin was chairman of the department. Under Sorokin's leadership, Parsons made very slow career progress at Harvard. Eventually, however, he emerged as the dominant sociologist at Harvard and in the United States. The conflict between Sorokin and Parsons was heightened by the extensive overlap between their theories. Despite the similarities, Parsons's work attracted a far wider and far more enduring audience than did Sorokin's. As the years went by, Sorokin developed a rather interesting attitude toward Parsons's work, which was reflected in several of his books. On the one hand, he was inclined to criticize Parsons for stealing many of his best ideas. On the other hand, he was severely critical of Parsonsian theory.

Another tension in their relationship was over graduate students. One of the great achievements of the early Harvard department was its ability to attract talented graduate students like Robert Merton. Although these students were influenced by the ideas of both men, Parsons's influence proved more enduring than Sorokin's. Merton was Sorokin's graduate assistant, but he did not accept Sorokin's theoretical orientation. When Merton submitted a paper laying out his preliminary thoughts on his dissertation, Sorokin responded: "As a term paper—it is O.K. You will get something like A−. But, from a deeper and the only important standpoint, I have to make several—and sharp—criticisms of your paper" (cited in Merton, 1989:293).

Parsons replaced Sorokin as chairman of the sociology department and transformed it into the Department of Social Relations. Of that, Sorokin said:

So I am not responsible for whatever has happened to the department since, either for its merging with abnormal and social psychology and cultural anthropology to form a "Department of Social Relations," or for the drowning of sociology in an eclectic mass of the odds and ends of these disciplines. . . . The Department of Social Relations . . . has hardly produced as many distinguished sociologists as the Department of Sociology did . . . under my chairmanship.

(Sorokin, 1963:251)

Sorokin was eventually isolated in the Harvard department, relegated to a "desolate looking" office, and reduced to putting a mimeographed statement under the doors of departmental offices claiming that Parsons had stolen his ideas (Coser, 1977:490).

Sorokin died on February 11, 1968.

Parsons's major statements on his structural-functional theory came in the early 1950s in several works, most notably *The Social System* (1951 [Barber, 1994]). In that work and others, Parsons tended to concentrate on the structures of society and their relationship to each other. These structures were seen as mutually supportive and tending toward a dynamic equilibrium. The emphasis was on how order was maintained among the various elements of society (Wrong, 1994). Change was seen as an orderly process, and Parsons (1966, 1971) ultimately came to adopt a neoevolutionary view of social change. Parsons was concerned not only with the social system per se but also with its relationship to the other *action systems,* especially the cultural and personality systems. But his basic view on intersystemic relations was essentially the same as his view of intrasystemic relations, that is, that they were defined by cohesion, consensus, and order. In other words, the various *social structures* performed a variety of positive *functions* for each other.

It is clear, then, why Parsons came to be defined primarily as a *structural functionalist.* As his fame grew, so did the strength of structural-functional theory in the United States. His work lay at the core of this theory, but his students and disciples also concentrated on extending both the theory and its dominance in the United States.

Although Parsons played a number of important and positive roles in the history of sociological theory in the United States, his work also had negative consequences. First, he offered interpretations of European theorists that seemed to reflect his own theoretical orientation more than theirs. Many American sociologists were initially exposed to erroneous interpretations of the European masters. Second, as already pointed out, early in his career Parsons largely ignored Marx, with the result that Marx's ideas continued for many years on the periphery of sociology. Third, his own theory as it developed over the years had a number of serious weaknesses. However, Parsons's preeminence in American sociology served for many years to mute or overwhelm the critics. Not until much later did the weaknesses of Parsons's theory, and more generally of structural functionalism, receive a full airing.

But we are getting too far ahead of the story, and we need to return to the early 1930s and other developments at Harvard. We can gain a good deal of insight into the development of the Harvard department by looking at it through an account of its other major figure, George Homans.

George Homans (1910–1989)   A wealthy Bostonian, George Homans received his bachelor's degree from Harvard in 1932 (Homans, 1962, 1984; see also Bell, 1992). As a result of the Great Depression, he was unemployed but certainly not penniless. In the fall of 1932, L. J. Henderson, a physiologist, was offering a course in the theories of Vilfredo Pareto, and Homans was invited to attend and accepted. (Parsons also attended the Pareto seminars.) Homans's description of why he was drawn to and taken with Pareto says much about why American sociological theory was so highly conservative, so anti-Marxist:

> I took to Pareto because he made clear to me what I was already prepared to believe. . . Someone has said that much modern sociology is an effort to answer the arguments of the revolutionaries. As a Republican Bostonian who had not rejected his comparatively wealthy family, I felt during the thirties that I was under personal attack, above all from the Marxists. I was ready to believe Pareto because he provided me with a defense.
>
> (Homans, 1962:4)

Homans's exposure to Pareto led to a book, *An Introduction to Pareto* (coauthored with Charles Curtis), published in 1934. The publication of this book made Homans a sociologist even though Pareto's work was virtually the only sociology he had read up to that point.

In 1934 Homans was named a junior fellow at Harvard, a program started to avoid the problems associated with the Ph.D. program. In fact, Homans never did earn a Ph.D. even though he became one of the major sociological figures of his day. Homans was a junior fellow until 1939, and in those years he absorbed more and more sociology.

In 1939 Homans was affiliated with the sociology department, but the connection was broken by the war.

By the time Homans had returned from the war, the Department of Social Relations had been founded by Parsons at Harvard, and Homans joined it. Although Homans respected some aspects of Parsons's work, he was highly critical of Parsons's style of theorizing. A long-running exchange began between the two men that later manifested itself publicly in the pages of many books and journals. Basically, Homans argued that Parsons's theory was not a theory at all but rather a vast system of intellectual categories into which most aspects of the social world fit. Further, Homans believed that theory should be built from the ground up on the basis of careful observations of the social world. Parsons's theory, however, started on the general theoretical level and worked its way down to the empirical level.

In his own work, Homans amassed a large number of empirical observations over the years, but it was only in the 1950s that he hit upon a satisfactory theoretical approach with which to analyze these data. That theory was psychological behaviorism, as it was best expressed in the ideas of his colleague at Harvard, the psychologist B. F. Skinner. On the basis of this perspective, Homans developed his exchange theory. We will pick up the story of this theoretical development later in the chapter. The crucial point here is that Harvard and its major theoretical product, structural functionalism, became preeminent in sociology in the late 1930s, replacing the Chicago school and symbolic interactionism.

The Chicago School in Decline

We left the Chicago department in the mid-1930s on the wane with the death of Mead, the departure of Park, the revolt of eastern sociologists, and the founding of the *American Sociological Review*. But the Chicago school did not disappear. Into the early 1950s it continued to be an important force in sociology. Important Ph.D.s were still produced there, such as Anselm Strauss and Arnold Rose. Major figures remained at Chicago, such as Everett Hughes (Faught, 1980), who was of central importance to the development of the sociology of occupations.

However, the central figure in the Chicago department in this era was Herbert Blumer (1900–1987) (*Symbolic Interaction,* 1988). He was a major exponent of the theoretical approach developed at Chicago out of the work of Mead, Cooley, Simmel, Park, Thomas, and others. In fact, it was Blumer who coined the phrase *symbolic interactionism* in 1937. Blumer played a key role in keeping this tradition alive through his teaching at Chicago. He wrote a number of essays that were instrumental in keeping symbolic interactionism vital into the 1950s. Blumer was also important because of the organizational positions he held in sociology. From 1930 to 1935, he was the secretary-treasurer of the American Sociological Society, and in 1956 he became its president. More important, he held institutional positions that affected the nature of what was published in sociology. Between 1941 and 1952, he was editor of the *American Journal of Sociology* and was instrumental in keeping it one of the major outlets for work in the Chicago tradition in general and symbolic interactionism in particular.

While the East Coast universities were coming under the sway of structural function-alism, the Midwest remained (and to some degree to this day remains) a stronghold of symbolic interactionism. In the 1940s, major symbolic interactionists fanned out across the Midwest—Arnold Rose was at Minnesota, Robert Habenstein at Missouri, Gregory Stone at Michigan State, and, most important, Manford Kuhn (1911–1963) at Iowa.

A split developed between Blumer at Chicago and Kuhn at Iowa; in fact, people began to talk of the differences between the Chicago and the Iowa schools of symbolic interactionism. Basically, the split occurred over the issue of science and methodology. Kuhn accepted the symbolic-interactionist focus on actors and their thoughts and actions, but he argued that they should be studied more scientifically—for example, by using questionnaires. Blumer was in favor of "softer" methods such as sympathetic in-trospection and participant observation.

Despite this flurry of activity, the Chicago school was in decline, especially given the movement of Blumer in 1952 from Chicago to the University of California at Berkeley.

Gary Alan Fine (1995) has written of the development of a "second" Chicago school emerging in the post–World War II years, but while Chicago continued to have a strong department, it did not have the strong and coherent focus on interactionism and obser-vational research that had characterized the original Chicago School. Nonetheless, that focus was strong enough to have a profound effect on later work of this type. Whatever the state of the Chicago school, the Chicago tradition has remained alive to this day with major exponents dispersed throughout the country and the world. To take one recent ex-ample, Fine (1996) has done an observational study of restaurants from the point of view of the interaction that takes place in them and the order that is created.

Developments in Marxian Theory

From the early 1900s to the 1930s, Marxian theory had continued to develop largely independently of mainstream sociological theory. At least partially, the exception to this was the emergence of the critical, or Frankfurt, school out of the earlier Hegelian Marxism.

The idea of a school for the development of Marxian theory was the product of Felix J. Weil. The Institute of Social Research was officially founded in Frankfurt, Germany, on February 3, 1923 (Bottomore, 1984; Wiggershaus, 1994). Over the years, a number of the most famous thinkers in Marxian theory were associated with the critical school—Max Horkheimer, Theodor Adorno, Erich Fromm, Herbert Marcuse, and, more recently, Jurgen Habermas.

The Institute functioned in Germany until 1934, but by then things were growing in-creasingly uncomfortable under the Nazi regime. The Nazis had little use for the Marxian ideas that dominated the Institute, and their hostility was heightened because many of those associated with it were Jewish. In 1934 Horkheimer, as head of the In-stitute, came to New York to discuss its status with the president of Columbia Univer-sity. Much to Horkheimer's surprise, he was invited to affiliate the Institute with the university, and he was even offered a building on campus. And so *a* center of Marxian theory moved to *the* center of the capitalist world. The Institute stayed there until the end of the war, but after the war, pressure mounted to return it to Germany. In 1949,

Horkheimer did return to Germany, and he brought the Institute with him. Although the Institute itself moved to Germany, many of the figures associated with it took independent career directions.

It is important to underscore a few of the most important aspects of critical theory. In its early years, those associated with the Institute tended to be fairly traditional Marxists devoting a good portion of their attention to the economic domain. But around 1930, a major change took place as this group of thinkers began to shift its attention from the economy to the cultural system, which it came to see as the major force in modern capitalist society. This was consistent with, but an extension of, the position taken earlier by Hegelian Marxists like Georg Lukács. To help them understand the cultural domain, the critical theorists were attracted to the work of Max Weber. The effort to combine Marx and Weber and thereby create "Weberian Marxism"[5] (Dahms, 1997; Lowy, 1996) gave the critical school some of its distinctive orientations and served in later years to make it more legitimate to sociologists who began to grow interested in Marxian theory.

A second major step taken by at least some members of the critical school was to employ the rigorous social-scientific techniques developed by American sociologists to research issues of interest to Marxists. This, like the adoption of Weberian theory, made the critical school more acceptable to mainstream sociologists.

Third, critical theorists made an effort to integrate individually oriented Freudian theory with the societal- and cultural-level insights of Marx and Weber. This seemed to many sociologists to represent a more inclusive theory than that offered by either Marx or Weber alone. If nothing else, the effort to combine such disparate theories proved stimulating to sociologists and many other intellectuals.

The critical school has done much useful work since the 1920s, and a significant amount of it is of relevance to sociologists. However, the critical school had to await the late 1960s before it was "discovered" by large numbers of American theorists.

Karl Mannheim and the Sociology of Knowledge

Brief mention should be made at this point of the work of Karl Mannheim (1893–1947) (Kettler and Meja, 1995). Born in Hungary, Mannheim was forced to move first to Germany and later to England. Influenced by the work of Marx on ideology, as well as that of Weber, Simmel, and the neo-Marxist Georg Lukács, Mannheim is best known for his work on systems of knowledge (for example, conservatism). In fact, he is almost singlehandedly responsible for the creation of the contemporary field known as the sociology of knowledge. Also of significance is his thinking on rationality, which tends to pick up themes developed in Weber's work on this topic but deals with them in a far more concise and in a much clearer manner (Ritzer, 1998).

From a base in England starting in the 1930s, Karl Mannheim was busy creating a set of theoretical ideas that provided the foundation for an area of sociology—the sociology

---

[5]This label fits some critical theorists better than others and it also applies to a wide range of other thinkers (Agger, 1998).

of knowledge—that continues to be important to this day (McCarthy, 1996). Mannheim, of course, built on the work of many predecessors, most notably Karl Marx (although Mannheim was far from being a Marxist). Basically, the sociology of knowledge involves the systematic study of knowledge, ideas, or intellectual phenomena in general. To Mannheim, knowledge is determined by social existence. For example, Mannheim seeks to relate the ideas of a group to their position in the social structure. Marx did this by relating ideas to social classes, but Mannheim extends this perspective by linking ideas to a variety of different positions within society (for example, differences between generations).

In addition to playing a major role in creating the sociology of knowledge, Mannheim is perhaps best known for his distinction between two idea systems—*ideology* and *utopia* (B. Turner, 1995). An ideology is an idea system that seeks to conceal and conserve the present by interpreting it from the point of view of the past. A utopia, in contrast, is a system of ideas that seeks to transcend the present by focusing on the future. Conflict between ideologies and utopias is an ever-present reality in society.

SOCIOLOGICAL THEORY FROM MID-CENTURY

Structural Functionalism: Peak and Decline

The 1940s and 1950s were paradoxically the years of greatest dominance and the beginnings of the decline of structural functionalism. In these years, Parsons produced his major statements that clearly reflected his shift from action theory to structural functionalism. Parsons's students had fanned out across the country and occupied dominant positions in many of the major sociology departments (for example, Columbia and Cornell). These students were producing works of their own that were widely recognized contributions to structural-functional theory. For example, in 1945 Kingsley Davis and Wilbert Moore published an essay analyzing social stratification from a structural-functional perspective. It was one of the clearest statements ever made of the structural-functional view. In it, they argued that stratification was a structure that was functionally necessary for the existence of society. In other words, in ideological terms they came down on the side of inequality.

In 1949 Merton (1949/1968) published an essay that became *the* program statement of structural functionalism. In it, Merton carefully sought to delineate the essential elements of the theory and to extend it in some new directions. He made it clear that structural functionalism should deal not only with positive functions but also with negative consequences (dysfunctions). Moreover, it should focus on the net balance of functions and dysfunctions or whether a structure is overall more functional or more dysfunctional.

However, just as it was gaining theoretical hegemony, structural functionalism came under attack, and the attacks mounted until they reached a crescendo in the 1960s and 1970s. The Davis-Moore structural-functional theory of stratification was attacked from the start, and the criticisms persist to this day. Beyond that, a series of more general criticisms received even wider recognition in the discipline. There was an attack

C. WRIGHT MILLS: A Biographical Sketch

C. Wright Mills was born on August 28, 1916, in Waco, Texas. He came from a conventional middle-class background; his father was an insurance broker and his mother a housewife. He attended the University of Texas and by 1939 had obtained both a bachelor's and a master's degree. He was quite an unusual student who, by the time he left Texas, already had published articles in the two major sociology journals. Mills did his doctoral work at, and received a Ph.D. from, the University of Wisconsin (Scimecca, 1977). He took his first job at the University of Maryland but spent the bulk of his career, from 1945 until his death, at Columbia University.

Mills was a man in a hurry (Horowitz, 1983). By the time he died at forty-five from his fourth heart attack, Mills had made a number of important contributions to sociology.

One of the most striking things about C. Wright Mills was his combativeness; he seemed to be constantly at war. He had a tumultuous personal life, characterized by many affairs, three marriages, and a child from each marriage. He had an equally tumultuous professional life. He seemed to have fought with and against everyone and everything. As a graduate student at Wisconsin, he took on a number of his professors. Later, in one of his early essays, he engaged in a thinly disguised critique of the ex-chairman of the Wisconsin department. He called the senior theorist at Wisconsin, Howard Becker, a "real fool" (Horowitz, 1983). He eventually came into conflict with his coauthor, Hans Gerth, who called Mills "an excellent operator, whippersnapper, promising young man on the make, and Texas cowboy á la ride and shoot" (Horowitz, 1983:72). As a professor at Columbia, Mills was isolated and estranged from his colleagues. Said one of his Columbia colleagues:

> There was no estrangement between Wright and me. We began estranged. Indeed, at the memorial services or meeting that was organized at Columbia University at his death, I seemed to be the only person who could not say: 'I used to be his friend, but we became somewhat distant.' It was rather the reverse.
>
> (cited in Horowitz, 1983:83)

Mills was an outsider and he knew it: "I am an outlander, not only regionally, but down deep and for good" (Horowitz, 1983:84). In *The Sociological Imagination* (1959), Mills challenged not only the dominant theorist of his day, Talcott Parsons, but also the dominant methodologist, Paul Lazarsfeld, who also happened to be a colleague at Columbia.

Mills, of course, was at odds not only with people; he was also at odds with American society and challenged it on a variety of fronts. But perhaps most telling is the fact that when Mills visited the Soviet Union and was honored as a major critic of American society, he took the occasion to attack the censorship in the Soviet Union with a toast to an early Soviet leader who had been purged and murdered by the Stalinists: "To the day when the complete works of Leon Trotsky are published in the Soviet Union!" (Tilman, 1984:8)

C. Wright Mills died in Nyack, New York, on March 20, 1962.

by C. Wright Mills on Parsons in 1959, and other major criticisms were mounted by David Lockwood (1956), Alvin Gouldner (1959/1967, 1970), and Irving Horowitz (1962/1967). In the 1950s, these attacks were seen as little more than "guerrilla raids," but as sociology moved into the 1960s, the dominance of structural functionalism was clearly in jeopardy.

George Huaco (1986) linked the rise and decline of structural functionalism to the position of American society in the world order. As America rose to world dominance after 1945, structural functionalism achieved hegemony within sociology. Structural functionalism supported America's dominant position in the world in two ways. First, the structural-functional view that "every pattern has consequences which contribute to the preservation and survival of the larger system" was "nothing less than a celebration of the United States and its world hegemony" (Huaco, 1986:52). Second, the structural-functional emphasis on equilibrium (the best social change is no change) meshed well with the interests of the United States, then "the wealthiest and most powerful empire in the world." The decline of U.S. world dominance in the 1970s coincided with structural functionalism's loss of its preeminent position in sociological theory.

Radical Sociology in America: C. Wright Mills

As we have seen, although Marxian theory was largely ignored or reviled by mainstream American sociologists, there were exceptions, the most notable of which is C. Wright Mills (1916–1962). Mills is noteworthy for his almost single-handed effort to keep a Marxian tradition alive in sociological theory. Modern Marxian sociologists have far outstripped Mills in theoretical sophistication, but they owe him a deep debt nonetheless for the personal and professional activities that helped set the stage for their own work (Alt, 1985–86). Mills was not a Marxist, and he did not read Marx until the mid-1950s. Even then he was restricted to the few available English translations, because he could not read German. Because Mills had published most of his major works by then, his work was not informed by a very sophisticated Marxian theory.

Mills published two major works that reflected his radical politics as well as his weaknesses in Marxian theory. The first was *White Collar* (1951), an acid critique of the status of a growing occupational category, white-collar workers. The second was *The Power Elite* (1956), a book that sought to show how America was dominated by a small group of businessmen, politicians, and military leaders. Sandwiched in between was his most theoretically sophisticated work, *Character and Social Structure* (Gerth and Mills, 1953), coauthored with Hans Gerth (N. Gerth, 1993). Ironically, considering Mills's major role in the history of Marxian sociological theory, this book was stronger in Weberian and Freudian theory than in Marxian theory. Nevertheless, the book is a major theoretical contribution, though it is not widely read today—possibly because it did not seem to fit well with Mills's best-known radical works. In fact, it was heavily influenced by Hans Gerth, who had a keen interest in Weberian theory.

In the 1950s, Mills's interest moved more in the direction of Marxism and in the problems of the Third World. This interest resulted in a book on the communist revolution in Cuba, *Listen, Yankee: The Revolution in Cuba* (1960), and another book, entitled *The Marxists* (1962). Mills's radicalism put him on the periphery of American sociology. He was the object of much criticism, and he, in turn, became a severe critic

of sociology. The critical attitude culminated in *The Sociological Imagination* (1959).
Of particular note is Mills's severe criticism of Talcott Parsons and his practice of
grand theory. In fact, many sociologists were more familiar with Mills's critique than
they were with the details of Parsons's work.

The Sociological Imagination is also noted for its distinction between personal troubles and public issues, as well as the objective of linking the two. This approach is
reminiscent, within the realm of social problems, of the focus of *Character and Social
Structure:* the relationship between "the private and the public, the innermost acts of
the individual with the widest kinds of socio-historical phenomena" (Gerth and Mills,
1953:xvi). The issue of personal troubles and public issues, and their relationship, has
been extraordinarily influential in sociology (see, for example, Ritzer, 1995).

Mills died in 1962, an outcast in sociology. However, before the decade was out,
both radical sociology and Marxian theory were to begin to make important inroads
into the discipline.

The Development of Conflict Theory

Another precursor to a true union of Marxism and sociological theory was the development of a conflict-theory alternative to structural functionalism. As we have just
seen, structural functionalism had no sooner gained leadership in sociological theory
than it came under increasing attack. The attack was multifaceted: structural functionalism was accused of such things as being politically conservative, unable to deal with
social change because of its focus on static structures, and incapable of adequately analyzing social conflict.

One of the results of this criticism was an effort on the part of a number of sociologists to overcome the problems of structural functionalism by integrating a concern for
structure with an interest in conflict. This work constituted the development of *conflict
theory* as an alternative to structural-functional theory. Unfortunately, it often seemed
little more than a mirror image of structural functionalism with little intellectual integrity of its own.

The first effort of note was Lewis Coser's (1956) book on the functions of social
conflict (Jaworski, 1991). This work clearly tried to deal with social conflict from
within the framework of a structural-functional view of the world. Although it is useful to look at the functions of conflict, there is much more to the study of conflict than
an analysis of its positive functions.

Other people sought to reconcile the differences between structural functionalism
and conflict theory (Coleman, 1971; Himes, 1966; van den Berghe, 1963). Although
these efforts had some utility, the authors were generally guilty of papering over the
major differences between the two theoretical alternatives (A. Frank, 1966/1974).

The biggest problem with most of conflict theory was that it lacked what it needed
most—a sound basis in Marxian theory. After all, Marxian theory was well developed
outside of sociology and should have provided a base on which to develop a sophisticated sociological theory of conflict. The one exception here is the work of Ralf
Dahrendorf (born 1929).

Dahrendorf is a European scholar who is well versed in Marxian theory. He sought to embed his conflict theory in the Marxian tradition. However, in the end his conflict theory looked more like a mirror image of structural functionalism than like a Marxian theory of conflict. Dahrendorf's major work, *Class and Class Conflict in Industrial Society* (1959), was the most influential piece in conflict theory, but that was largely because it sounded so much like structural functionalism that it was palatable to mainstream sociologists. That is, Dahrendorf operated at the same level of analysis as the structural functionalists (structures and institutions) and looked at many of the same issues. (In other words, structural functionalism and conflict theory are part of the same paradigm; see Appendix.) Dahrendorf recognized that although aspects of the social system could fit together rather neatly, there also could be considerable conflict and tension among them.

In the end, conflict theory should be seen as little more than a transitional development in the history of sociological theory. It failed because it did not go far enough in the direction of Marxian theory. It was still too early in the 1950s and 1960s for American sociology to accept a full-fledged Marxian approach. But conflict theory was helpful in setting the stage for the beginning of that acceptance by the late 1960s.

We should note the contribution to conflict theory by Randall Collins (1975, 1990, 1993). On the one hand, Collins's effort suffers from the same weakness as the other works in the conflict tradition: it is relatively impoverished in terms of Marxian theory. On the other, Collins did identify another weakness in the conflict tradition, and he attempted to overcome it. The problem is that conflict theory generally focuses on social structures; it has little or nothing to say about actors and their thoughts and actions. Collins, schooled in the phenomenological-ethnomethodological tradition (which will be discussed shortly), attempted to move conflict theory in this direction.

The Birth of Exchange Theory

Another important theoretical development in the 1950s was the rise of exchange theory. The major figure in this development is George Homans, a sociologist whom we left earlier, just as he was being drawn to B. F. Skinner's psychological behaviorism. Skinner's behaviorism is a major source of Homans's, and sociology's, exchange theory.

Dissatisfied with Parsons's deductive strategy of developing theory, Homans was casting about for a workable alternative for handling sociological theory inductively. Further, Homans wanted to stay away from the cultural and structural foci of Parsonian theory and wanted to concentrate instead on people and their behavior. With this in mind, Homans turned to the work of his colleague at Harvard, B. F. Skinner. At first, Homans did not see how Skinner's propositions, developed to help explain the behavior of pigeons, might be useful for understanding human social behavior. But as Homans looked further at data from sociological studies of small groups and anthropological studies of primitive societies, he began to see that Skinner's behaviorism was applicable and that it provided a theoretical alternative to Parsonian-style structural functionalism. This realization led to an article entitled "Social Behavior as Exchange" in 1958 and in 1961 to a full-scale, book-length statement of Homans's theoretical position, *Social Behavior: Its Elementary Forms*. These works represented the birth of exchange theory as an important perspective in sociology. Since then exchange theory has attracted a good deal of attention, both positive and negative.

Homans's basic view was that the heart of sociology lies in the study of individual behavior and interaction. He was little interested in consciousness or in the various kinds of large-scale structures and institutions that were of concern to most sociologists. His main interest was rather in the reinforcement patterns, the history of rewards and costs, that lead people to do what they do. Basically, Homans argued that people continue to do what they have found to be rewarding in the past. Conversely, they cease doing what has proved to be costly in the past. In order to understand behavior, we need to understand an individual's history of rewards and costs. Thus, the focus of sociology should not be on consciousness or on social structures and institutions but on patterns of reinforcement.

As its name suggests, exchange theory is concerned not only with individual behavior but also with interaction between people involving an exchange of rewards and costs. The premise is that interactions are likely to continue when there is an exchange of rewards. Conversely, interactions that are costly to one or both parties are much less likely to continue.

Another major statement in exchange theory is Peter Blau's *Exchange and Power in Social Life,* published in 1964. Blau basically adopted Homans's perspective, but there was an important difference. Whereas Homans was content to deal mainly with elementary forms of social behavior, Blau wanted to integrate this with exchange at the structural and cultural levels, beginning with exchanges among actors, but quickly moving on to the larger structures that emerge out of this exchange. He ended by dealing with exchanges among large-scale structures. This approach is very different from the exchange theory envisioned by Homans. In some senses, it represents a return to the kind of Parsonsian-style theorizing that Homans found so objectionable. Nevertheless, the effort to deal with both small- and large-scale exchange in an integrated way proved a useful theoretical step.

Although he was eclipsed for many years by Homans and Blau, Richard Emerson (1981) has emerged as a central figure in exchange theory (Cook and Whitmeyer, forthcoming; Molm and Cook, 1995). He is noted particularly for his effort to develop a more integrated micro-macro approach to exchange theory. Exchange theory has now developed into a significant strand of sociological theory, and it continues to attract new adherents and to take new directions (Cook, O'Brien, and Kollock, 1990; Szmatka and Mazur, 1996; see also the ensuing discussion).

Dramaturgical Analysis: The Work of Erving Goffman

Erving Goffman (1922–1982) is often thought of as the last major thinker associated with the original Chicago school (Travers, 1992; Tseelon, 1992); Fine and Manning (forthcoming) see him as arguably the most influential twentieth-century American sociologist. He received his Ph.D. from Chicago in 1953, one year after Herbert Blumer (who had been Goffman's teacher) had left Chicago for Berkeley. Soon after, Goffman joined Blumer at Berkeley, where they were able to develop something of a center of symbolic interactionism. However, it never became anything like what Chicago had been. Blumer was past his organizational prime, and Goffman did not become a focus of graduate-student work. After 1952 the fortunes of symbolic interactionism declined, although it continues to be a prominent sociological theory.

In spite of the decline of symbolic interactionism in general, Goffman carved out a strong and distinctive place for himself in contemporary sociological theory (Manning, 1992). Between the 1950s and the 1970s, Goffman published a series of books and essays that gave birth to dramaturgical analysis as a variant of symbolic interactionism. Although Goffman shifted his attention in his later years, he remained best known for his *dramaturgical theory.*

Goffman's best-known statement of dramaturgical theory, *Presentation of Self in Everyday Life,* was published in 1959. To put it simply, Goffman saw much in common between theatrical performances and the kinds of "acts" we all put on in our day-to-day actions and interactions. Interaction is seen as very fragile, maintained by social performances. Poor performances or disruptions are seen as great threats to social interaction just as they are to theatrical performances.

Goffman went quite far in his analogy between the stage and social interaction. In all social interaction there is a *front region,* which is the parallel of the stage front in a theatrical performance. Actors both on the stage and in social life are seen as being interested in appearances, wearing costumes, and using props. Furthermore, in both there is a *back region,* a place to which the actors can retire to prepare themselves for their performance. Backstage or offstage, in theater terms, the actors can shed their roles and be themselves.

Dramaturgical analysis is clearly consistent with its symbolic-interactionist roots. It has a focus on actors, action, and interaction. Working in the same arena as traditional symbolic interactionism, Goffman found a brilliant metaphor in the theater to shed new light on small-scale social processes (Manning, 1991, 1992).

Goffman's work is widely read today and acknowledged for its originality and its profusion of insights (R. Collins, 1986b; Ditton, 1980). However, there are several general criticisms of this work. First, Goffman is seen as having been interested in somewhat esoteric topics rather than the truly essential aspects of social life. Second, he was a micro theorist in an era in which the great rewards have gone to macro theorists. As Randall Collins says, "The more we look at this [Goffman's] work . . . the more he emerges as the leading figure in the microsociology of our times" (1981c:6). Third, he attracted few students who were able to build theoretically upon his insights; indeed, some believe that it is impossible to build upon Goffman's work. It is seen as little more than a series of idiosyncratic bursts of brilliant insight. Finally, little theoretical work has been done by others in the dramaturgical tradition (one exception is Lyman and Scott [1970]).

The one area in which Goffman's work has proved fruitful is in empirical research utilizing his dramaturgical approach (Meyrowitz, 1995; Shirazi-Mahajan, 1995; Sijuwade, 1995).

The Development of Sociologies of Everyday Life

The 1960s and 1970s witnessed a boom (Ritzer, 1975a,b) in several theoretical perspectives that can be lumped together under the heading of sociologies of everyday life (J. Douglas, 1980; Weigert, 1981).

Phenomenological Sociology and the Work of Alfred Schutz (1899–1959)   The philosophy of phenomenology, with its focus on consciousness, has a long history, but the effort to develop a sociological variant of phenomenology can be traced to the publication of Alfred Schutz's *The Phenomenology of the Social World* in Germany in 1932. However, it was not translated into English until 1967, with the result that it has only recently had a dramatic effect on American sociological theory. Schutz arrived in the United States in 1939 after fleeing the Nazis in Austria. Shortly after, he took a position at the New School for Social Research in New York, from which he was able to influence the development of phenomenological, and later ethnomethodological, sociology in the United States.

Schutz took the phenomenological philosophy of Edmund Husserl, which was aimed inward toward an understanding of the transcendental ego, and turned it outward toward a concern for intersubjectivity (Rogers, forthcoming). Schutz was focally concerned with the way in which people grasp the consciousness of others while they live within their own stream of consciousness. Schutz also used intersubjectivity in a larger sense to mean a concern with the social world, especially the social nature of knowledge.

Much of Schutz's work focuses on an aspect of the social world called the *life-world,* or the world of everyday life. This is an intersubjective world in which people both create social reality and are constrained by the preexisting social and cultural structures created by their predecessors. While much of the life-world is shared, there are also private (biographically articulated) aspects of that world. Within the life-world, Schutz differentiated between intimate face-to-face relationships ("we-relations") and distant and impersonal relationships ("they-relations"). While face-to-face relations are of great importance in the life-world, it is far easier for the sociologist to study more impersonal relations scientifically. Although Schutz turned away from consciousness and to the intersubjective life-world, he did offer insights into consciousness, especially in his thoughts on meaning and people's motives.

Overall, Schutz was concerned with the dialectical relationship between the way people construct social reality and the obdurate social and cultural reality that they inherit from those who preceded them in the social world.

The mid-1960s were crucial in the development of phenomenological sociology. Not only was Alfred Schutz's major work translated and his collected essays published, but Peter Berger and Thomas Luckmann collaborated to publish a book, *The Social Construction of Reality* (1967), that became one of the most widely read theory books of the time. It made at least two important contributions. First, it constituted an introduction to Schutz's ideas that was written in such a way as to make it available to a large American audience. Second, it presented an effort to integrate Schutz's ideas with those of mainstream sociology.

Ethnomethodology   Although there are important differences between them, ethnomethodology and phenomenology are often seen as closely aligned (Langsdorf, 1995). One of the major reasons for this association is that the creator of this theoretical perspective, Harold Garfinkel, was a student of Alfred Schutz at the New School. Interestingly, Garfinkel had previously studied under Talcott Parsons, and it was the fusion of Parsonsian and Schutzian ideas that helped give ethnomethodology its distinctive orientation.

Hilbert (1992) has recently shed new light on the origins of Garfinkel's ideas and of ethnomethodology. While Garfinkel was a student of Parsons, he rejected the latter's structural-functional perspective and, in the process, rediscovered (accidentally) classical sociological ideas embedded in the work of Durkheim and Weber (Hilbert, 1992). Specifically, while he accepted basic themes in Parsons's work such as the importance of normative prescriptions and shared understandings, Garfinkel rejected Parsons's fundamental premise that the normative order is separate from and controls (through socialization) the behavioral order. Instead of Parsonsian theoretical abstractions, Garfinkel's focus was empirical studies of the everyday world. Thus, Garfinkel continued to work with the Parsonsian issues of order and society not theoretically, but rather in the "details of their workings . . . in their achievement" (Button, 1991:6–7). In these studies, Garfinkel discovered a variety of sociological principles that are consistent with the work of Durkheim and Weber. For one thing, Garfinkel found that the social world was not reified. This stood in contrast to Parsons's tendency to reify the cultural (and social) system but was consistent with Weber's refusal to reify social structure and with Durkheim's orientation to study, not reify, external and coercive social facts. For another, Garfinkel's commitment to empirical research stood in contrast to Parsons's propensity for grand theory and was more consistent with the empirical bent of both Weber and Durkheim.

After receiving his Ph.D. from Harvard in 1952, Garfinkel settled at the University of California at Los Angeles (Heritage, 1984; Rawls, forthcoming). It was there that ethnomethodology was developed by Garfinkel and his graduate students. Over the years a number of major ethnomethodologists emerged from this milieu. Geographically, ethnomethodology was the first distinctive theoretical product of the West Coast, and it remained centered there for a long time. Today, ethnomethodologists are also found throughout the rest of the United States, as well as in other parts of the world, especially Great Britain.

Ethnomethodology began to receive a wide national audience with the publication in 1967 of Garfinkel's *Studies in Ethnomethodology*. Although written in a difficult and obscure style, the book elicited a lot of interest. The fact that this book came out at the same time as the translation of Schutz's *The Phenomenology of the Social World* and the publication of Berger and Luckmann's *The Social Construction of Reality* seemed to indicate that sociologies of everyday life were coming of age.

Basically, *ethnomethodology* is the study of "the body of common-sense knowledge and the range of procedures and considerations [the methods] by means of which the ordinary members of society make sense of, find their way about in, and act on the circumstances in which they find themselves" (Heritage, 1984:4). Writers in this tradition are heavily tilted in the direction of the study of everyday life. While phenomenological sociologists tend to focus on what people think, ethnomethodologists are more concerned with what people actually do. Thus, ethnomethodologists devote a lot of attention to the detailed study of conversations. Such mundane concerns stand in stark contrast to the interest of many mainstream sociologists in such abstractions as bureaucracies, capitalism, the division of labor, and the social system. Ethnomethodologists might be interested in the way a sense of these structures is created in everyday life; they are not interested in such structures as phenomena in themselves.

Ethnomethodology is determinedly empirical in its orientation. Ethnomethodologists generally decline to theorize about the social world, preferring instead to go out and study it. This calls into question the inclusion of ethnomethodology in a book like this one. Says Button, "Ethnomethodology . . . never bought into the business of theorising," or "The idea that ethnomethodology is *theory* . . . would perplex many ethnomethodologists" (1991:4, 9). But ethnomethodology *is* treated in this book, and for at least two reasons. First, its basic premises constitute an attack on much of sociological theory, and we learn much about ethnomethodology (and traditional theory) from those attacks. Second, the findings of ethnomethodological studies are used to create theories of everyday life (as we will see in the work of Anthony Giddens, to take one example).

There was clearly something about ethnomethodology that was threatening to mainstream sociologists who were still in control of the discipline. In fact, both phenomenology and, more important, ethnomethodology have been subjected to some brutal attacks by mainstream sociologists. Here are two examples. The first is from a review of Garfinkel's *Studies in Ethnomethodology* by James Coleman:

> Garfinkel simply fails to generate any insights at all from the approach. . . .
>
> Perhaps the program would be more fertile in the hands of someone more carefully observant but it is strangely sterile here. . . .
>
> . . . this chapter is another major disaster, combining the rigidities of the most mathematically enraptured technicians with the technical confusions and errors of the soft clinician and without the insights or the technical competence of the creative and trained sociologist.
>
> Once again, Garfinkel elaborates very greatly points which are so commonplace that they would appear banal if stated in straightforward English. As it is, there is an extraordinarily high ratio of reading time to information transfer, so that the banality is not directly apparent upon a casual reading.
>
> (Coleman, 1968:126–130)

The second example is Lewis Coser's 1975 presidential address to the American Sociological Association. Coser saw few redeeming qualities in ethnomethodology and subjected it to a savage attack, engaging in a great deal of name-calling, labeling ethnomethodology "trivial," "a massive cop-out," "an orgy of subjectivism," and a "self-indulgent enterprise." The bitterness of these and other attacks is an indication of the degree to which they represented a threat to the establishment in sociology.

Today, ethnomethodology has overcome a significant part of the early opposition and has, to a large degree, become an accepted part of sociological theory. For example, it is now quite routine to see works by ethnomethodologists appearing in the major mainstream sociology journals such as the *American Sociological Review* (for example, Greatbatch and Dingwall, 1997). However, that acceptance is far from complete, as Pollner (1991:370) humorously points out: Few sociologists "want their children to marry an ethnomethodologist, much less to be one—and rarely to hire one. Nevertheless, the discipline recognizes and begins to incorporate the contributions of what was once regarded as a pariah." Other ethnomethodologists lament how their orientation is put upon, marginalized, and misunderstood (Button, 1991).

In the last few pages, we have dealt with several micro theories—exchange theory, phenomenological sociology, and ethnomethodology. Although the last two theories share a sense of a thoughtful and creative actor, such a view is not held by exchange theorists. Nevertheless, all three theories have a primarily micro orientation to actors and their actions and behavior. In the 1970s, such theories grew in strength in sociology and threatened to replace more macro-oriented theories (such as structural functionalism, conflict theory, neo-Marxian theories) as the dominant theories in sociology (Knorr-Cetina, 1981a; Ritzer, 1985).

The Rise and Fall (?) of Marxian Sociology

The late 1960s were the point at which Marxian theory finally began to make significant inroads into American sociological theory (Cerullo, 1994; Jay, 1984). There are a number of reasons for this. First, the dominant theory (structural functionalism) was under attack for a number of things, including being too conservative. Second, Mills's radical sociology and conflict theory, although not representing sophisticated Marxian theory, had laid the groundwork for an American theory that was true to the Marxian tradition. Third, the 1960s was the era of black protests, the reawakening of the women's movement, the student movement, and the anti–Vietnam War movement. Many of the young sociologists trained in this atmosphere were attracted to radical ideas. At first, this interest was manifest in what was called in those days "radical sociology" (Colfax and Roach, 1971). Radical sociology was useful as far as it went, but like Mills's work, it was rather weak on the details of Marxian theory.

It is hard to single out one work as essential to the development of Marxian sociology in America, but one that did play an important role was Henri Lefebvre's *The Sociology of Marx* (1968). It was important for its essential argument, which was that although Marx was not a sociologist, there was a sociology in Marx. An increasing number of sociologists turned to Marx's original work, as well as to that of many Marxists, for insights that would be useful in the development of a Marxian sociology. At first this simply meant that American theorists were finally reading Marx seriously, but later there emerged many significant pieces of Marxian scholarship by American sociologists.

American theorists were particularly attracted to the work of the critical school, especially because of its fusion of Marxian and Weberian theory. Many of the works have been translated into English, and a number of scholars have written books about the critical school (for example, Jay, 1973, 1986; Kellner, 1993).

Along with an increase in interest came institutional support for such an orientation. Several journals devoted considerable attention to Marxian sociological theory, including *Theory and Society, Telos,* and *Marxist Studies.* A section on Marxist sociology was created in the American Sociological Association in 1977. Not only did the first generation of critical theorists become well known in America, but second-generation thinkers, especially Jurgen Habermas, received wide recognition.

Of considerable importance was the development of significant pieces of American sociology done from a Marxian point of view. One very significant strand is a group of sociologists doing historical sociology from a Marxian perspective (for example, Skocpol, 1979; Wallerstein, 1974, 1980, 1989). Another is a group analyzing the economic realm from a sociological perspective (for example, Baran and Sweezy, 1966;

Braverman, 1974; Burawoy, 1979). Still others are doing fairly traditional empirical sociology, but work that is informed by a strong sense of Marxian theory (Kohn, 1976, for example).

However, with the disintegration of the Soviet Union and the fall of Marxist regimes around the world, Marxian theory fell on hard times in the 1990s. Some people remain unreconstructed Marxists; others have been forced to develop modified versions of Marxian theory (see the discussion below of the post-Marxists; there is also a journal entitled *Rethinking Marxism*). Still others have come to the conclusion that Marxian theory must be abandoned. Representative of the latter position is Ronald Aronson's book *After Marxism* (1995). The very first line of the book tells the story: "Marxism is over, and we are on our own" (Aronson, 1995:1). This from an avowed Marxist! While Aronson recognizes that some will continue to work with Marxian theory, he cautions that they must recognize that it is no longer part of the larger Marxian project of social transformation. That is, Marxian theory is no longer related, as Marx intended, to a program aimed at changing the basis of society; it is theory without practice. One-time Marxists are on their own in the sense that they can no longer rely on the Marxian project, but rather must grapple with modern society with their "own powers and energies" (Aronson, 1995:4).

Aronson is among the more extreme critics of Marxism from within the Marxian camp. Others recognize the difficulties, but seek in various ways to adapt some variety of Marxian theory to contemporary realities (Brugger, 1995; Kellner, 1995). Nevertheless, larger social changes have posed a grave challenge for Marxian theorists, who are desperately seeking to adapt to these changes in a variety of ways. Whatever else can be said, the "glory days" of Marxian social theory are over. Marxian social theorists of various types will survive, but they will not approach the status and power of their predecessors in the recent history of sociology.

The Challenge of Feminist Theory

Beginning in the late 1970s, precisely at the moment that Marxian sociology gained significant acceptance from American sociologists, a new theoretical outsider issued a challenge to established sociological theories—and even to Marxian sociology itself. This later brand of radical social thought is contemporary feminist theory, which has continued to grow in range and complexity and will influence sociology into the twenty-first century. The growth of contemporary feminist theory is based in the new activism of women for full civil equality—the so-called "second" wave of the women's movement which sprang into being in the 1960s. (The first stage or wave of the mobilization occurred in the early years of this century and the last decades of the last, and culminated in 1920 with women winning the right to vote.)

Three factors helped create this new wave of feminist activism: the general climate of critical thinking that characterized the period; the anger of women activists who flocked to the antiwar, civil rights, and student movements only to encounter the sexist attitudes of the liberal and radical men in those movements (Densimore, 1973; Evans, 1980; Morgan, 1970; Shreve, 1989; Snitow, Stansell, and Thompson, 1983); and women's experience of prejudice and discrimination as they moved in ever larger numbers into wage work and higher education (Bookman and Morgen, 1988; Caplan, 1993; Garland, 1988; MacKinnon, 1979). For these reasons, particularly the last, the women's movement continued into the 1990s, even though the activism of many other 1960s movements has faded. Moreover, during these years activism by and for women became an international phenomenon, drawing in women from many societies and from most stratificational locations in North America. Feminist writing has now entered its "third wave" in the writings of women who will spend most of their adult lives in the twenty-first century (C. Bailey, 1997; Orr, 1997).

A major feature of this international women's movement has been an explosively growing new literature on women that makes visible all aspects of women's hitherto unconsidered lives and experiences. This literature, which is popularly referred to as *women's studies* or the *new scholarship on women,* is the work of an international and interdisciplinary community of writers, located both within and outside universities and writing for both the general public and specialized academic audiences. In what must be one of the more impressive examples of sustained intellectual work in recent times, feminist scholars have launched a probing, multifaceted critique that makes visible the complexity of the system that subordinates women.

Feminist theory is the theoretical strand running through this literature: sometimes implicit in writings on such substantive issues as work (Daniels, 1988; DeVault, 1991; Hochschild, 1989, 1997; Kanter, 1977; Pierce, 1995; Rollins, 1985) or rape (Sanday, 1990, 1996; Scully, 1990) or popular culture (McCaughey, 1997; Radway, 1984); sometimes centrally and explicitly presented, as in the analyses of motherhood by Adrienne Rich (1976), Nancy Chodorow (1978), and Jessica Benjamin (1988); and increasingly the sole, systematic project of a piece of writing. Of this recent spate of wholly theoretical writing, certain statements have been particularly salient to sociology because they are directed to sociologists by people well versed in sociological theory (Chafetz, 1984; P. Collins, 1990, 1998; Lengermann and Niebrugge-Brantley, 1990; Lengermann and Niebrugge, 1995; D. Smith, 1979, 1987, 1990a, 1990b, 1992, 1993; Stacey and Thorne, 1985; Wallace, 1989). Journals that bring feminist theory to the attention of sociologists include *Signs, Feminist Studies, Sociological Inquiry,* and *Gender and Society,* as does the professional association Sociologists for Women in Society (SWS) and the National Women's Studies Association (NWSA).

Feminist theory looks at the world from the vantage points of a hitherto unrecognized and invisible minority, women, with an eye to discovering the significant but unacknowledged ways in which the activities of women—subordinated by gender and variously affected by other stratificational practices, such as class, race, age, enforced heterosexuality, and geosocial inequality—help to create our world. This viewpoint dramatically reworks our understanding of social life. From this base, feminist theorists have begun to challenge sociological theory.

Those issuing this challenge argue that sociologists have persistently refused to incorporate the insights of the new scholarship on women into their discipline's understanding of the social world. Instead, feminist sociologists have been segregated from the mainstream, and feminism's comprehensive theory of social organization has been reduced to a single research variable, sex, and a simple social role pattern, gender (Alway, 1995; Laslett and Thorne, 1992; Lemert, 1992b; D. Smith, 1990b; Stacey and

Thorne, 1985, 1996; R. Wallace, 1989; Yeatman, 1987). To date these charges seem valid. Reasons for sociology's avoidance of feminist theory may include deep anti-woman, antifeminist prejudices, suspicion of the scientific credentials of a theory so closely associated with political activism, and caution born of half-recognition of the profoundly radical implications of feminist theory for sociological theory and method. Yet these feminist writings now assume a critical mass in sociology. They offer an exciting paradigm for the study of social life. And those whose experiences and perceptions make them a receptive audience for this theory—women in general and both women and men affected by feminism in particular—may now constitute a numerical majority in the sociological community. For all these reasons, implications of feminist theory are moving increasingly into the mainstream of the discipline, engaging all its subspecialties, influencing many of its long-established theories, both macro and micro, and interacting with the new poststructuralist and postmodernist developments described below.

Structuralism and Poststructuralism

One development that we have said little about up to this point is the increase in interest in *structuralism* (Lemert, 1990). Usually traced to France (and often called *French structuralism* [Clark and Clark, 1982; Kurzweil, 1980]), structuralism has now become an international phenomenon. Although its roots lie outside sociology, structuralism clearly has made its way into sociology. The problem is that structuralism in sociology still is so undeveloped that it is difficult to define with any precision. The problem is exacerbated by structuralism's more or less simultaneous development in a number of fields; it is difficult to find one single coherent statement of structuralism. Indeed, there are significant differences among the various branches of structuralism.

We can get a preliminary feeling for structuralism by delineating the basic differences that exist among those who support a structuralist perspective. There are those who focus on what they call the "deep structures of the mind." It is their view that these unconscious structures lead people to think and act as people do. The work of the psychoanalyst Sigmund Freud might be seen as an example of this orientation. Then there are structuralists who focus on the invisible larger structures of society and see them as determinants of the actions of people as well as of society in general. Marx is sometimes thought of as someone who practiced such a brand of structuralism, with his focus on the unseen economic structure of capitalist society. Still another group sees structures as the models they construct of the social world. Finally, a number of structuralists are concerned with the dialectical relationship between individuals and social structures. They see a link between the structures of the mind and the structures of society. The anthropologist Claude Lévi-Strauss is most often associated with this view.

As structuralism grew within sociology, outside sociology a movement was developing beyond the early premises of structuralism: *poststructuralism* (Lemert, 1990). The major representative of poststructuralism is Michel Foucault (J. Miller, 1993). In his early work, Foucault focused on structures, but he later moved beyond structures to focus on power and the linkage between knowledge and power. More generally, poststructuralists accept the importance of structure but go beyond it to encompass a wide range of other concerns.

Poststructuralism is important not only in itself, but also because it is often seen as a precursor to postmodern social theory (to be discussed later in this chapter). In fact, it is difficult, if not impossible, to draw a clear line between poststructuralism and postmodern social theory. Thus Foucault, a poststructuralist, is often seen as a postmodernist, while Jean Baudrillard (1972/1981), who is usually labeled a postmodernist, certainly did work, especially early in his career, that is poststructuralist in character.

RECENT DEVELOPMENTS IN SOCIOLOGICAL THEORY

While many of the developments discussed in the preceding pages continued to be important in the late twentieth century, in this section we will deal with three broad movements that were of utmost importance—micro-macro integration, agency-structure integration, and theoretical syntheses.

Micro-Macro Integration

A good deal of the most recent work in American sociological theory has been concerned with the linkage between micro and macro theories and levels of analysis. In fact, I have argued that micro-macro linkage emerged as the central problematic in American sociological theory in the 1980s and it continued to be of focal concern in the 1990s (Ritzer, 1990a). (An important precursor to contemporary American work on the micro-macro linkage is the contribution of the European sociologist Norbert Elias [1939/1994] to our understanding of the relationship between micro-level manners and the macro-level state.)

There are a number of examples of efforts to link micro-macro levels of analysis and/or theories. In my own work (Ritzer, 1979, 1981a), I have sought to develop an integrated sociological paradigm that integrates micro and macro levels in both their objective and subjective forms. Thus, in my view, there are four major levels of social analysis that must be dealt with in an integrated manner—macro subjectivity, macro objectivity, micro subjectivity, and micro objectivity. Jeffrey Alexander (1982–83) has created a "multidimensional sociology" which deals, at least in part, with a model of levels of analysis that closely resembles my model. Alexander (1987) develops his model based on the problem of order, which is seen as having individual (micro) and collective (macro) levels, and on the problem of action, which is viewed as possessing materialist (objective) and idealist (subjective) levels. Out of these two continuua, Alexander develops four major levels of analysis—collective-idealist, collective-materialist, individual-idealist, individual-materialist. While the overall model developed by Alexander is strikingly similar to mine, Alexander accords priority to the collective-idealist level, while I insist that we be concerned with the dialectical relationship among all levels. Another kindred approach has been developed by Norbert Wiley (1988), who also delineates four very similar major levels of analysis—self or individual, interaction, social structure, and culture. However, while both Alexander and I focus on both objective and subjective levels, Wiley's levels are purely subjective.

James Coleman (1986) has concentrated on the micro-to-macro problem, while Allen Liska (1990) has extended Coleman's approach to deal with the macro-to-micro problem as well. Coleman (1990) has extended his micro-to-macro model and developed a much more elaborate theory of the micro-macro relationship based on a rational choice approach derived from economics (see below).

Agency-Structure Integration

Paralleling the growth in interest in the United States in micro-macro integration has been a concern in Europe for agency-structure integration (Sztompka, 1994). Just as I saw the micro-macro issue as the central problem in American theory, Margaret Archer (1988) sees the agency-structure topic as the basic concern in European social theory. While there are many similarities between the micro-macro and agency-structure literatures (Ritzer and Gindoff, 1992, 1994), there are also substantial differences. For example, while agents are usually micro-level actors, collectivities like labor unions can also be agents. And while structures are usually macro-level phenomena, we also find structures at the micro level. Thus, we must be careful in equating these two bodies of work, and much care needs to be taken in trying to interrelate them.

There are four major efforts in contemporary European social theory that can be included under the heading of agency-structure integration. The first is Anthony Giddens's (1984) structuration theory. The key to Giddens's approach is that he sees agency and structure as a "duality." That is, they cannot be separated from one another: agency is implicated in structure and structure is involved in agency. Giddens refuses to see structure as simply constraining (as, for example, does Durkheim), but sees structure as both constraining *and* enabling. Margaret Archer (1982) rejects the idea that agency and structure can be viewed as a duality, but rather sees them as a dualism. That is, agency and structure can and should be separated. In distinguishing them, we become better able to analyze their relationship to one another. Archer (1988) is also notable for extending the agency-structure literature to a concern for the relationship between culture and agency and more recently developing a more general agency-structure theory (Archer, 1995).

While both Giddens and Archer are British, the third major contemporary figure involved in the agency-structure literature is Pierre Bourdieu from France (Bourdieu, 1977; Bourdieu and Wacquant, 1992; Swartz, 1997). In Bourdieu's work, the agency-structure issue translates into a concern for the relationship between habitus and field. *Habitus* is an internalized mental, or cognitive, structure through which people deal with the social world. The habitus both produces, and is produced by, the society. The *field* is a network of relations among objective positions. The structure of the field serves to constrain agents, be they individuals or collectivities. Overall, Bourdieu is concerned with the relationship between habitus and field. While the field conditions the habitus, the habitus constitutes the field. Thus, there is a dialectical relationship between habitus and field.

The final major theorist of the agency-structure linkage is the German social thinker Jurgen Habermas. We have already mentioned Habermas as a significant contemporary contributor to critical theory. Habermas (1987a) has also dealt with the agency-structure issue under the heading of "the colonization of the life-world." The life-world is a micro world where people interact and communicate. The system has its roots in the life-world, but it ultimately comes to develop its own structural characteristics. As these structures grow in independence and power, they come to exert more and more control over the life-world. In the modern world, the system has come to "colonize" the life-world, that is, to exert control over it.

The theorists discussed in this section not only are the leading theorists on the agency-structure issue, but they are arguably (especially Bourdieu, Giddens, and Habermas) the leading theorists in the world today. After a long period of dominance by American theorists (Mead, Parsons, Merton, Homans, and others), the center of social theory seems to be returning to its birthplace—Europe. Furthermore, Nedelmann and Sztompka have argued that with the end of the Cold War and the fall of communism, we are about to "witness another Golden Era of European Sociology" (1993:1). This seems to be supported by the fact that today the works that catch the attention of large numbers of the world's theorists are European in origin. One example is Ulrich Beck's *Risk Society: Towards a New Modernity* (1992), in which he discusses the unprecedented risks facing society today. It is clear that, at least for now, the center of sociological theory *has* shifted back to Europe.

Theoretical Syntheses

The movements toward micro-macro and agency-structure integration began in the 1980s, and both continued to be strong in the 1990s. They set the stage for the broader movement toward theoretical syntheses which began at about the beginning of the 1990s. Lewis (1991) has suggested that the relatively low status of sociology may be the result of excessive fragmentation and that the movement toward greater integration may enhance the status of the discipline. What is involved here is a wide-ranging effort to synthesize two or more different theories (for example, structural functionalism and symbolic interactionism). Such efforts have occurred throughout the history of sociological theory (Holmwood and Stewart, 1994). However, there are two distinctive aspects of the new synthetic work in sociological theory. First, it is very widespread and not restricted to isolated attempts at synthesis. Second, the goal is generally a relatively narrow synthesis of theoretical ideas, and not the development of a grand synthetic theory that encompasses all of sociological theory.

These synthetic works are occurring within and among many of the theories (and theorists; see, for example, Levine's [1991a] call for a synthesis of the ideas of Simmel and Parsons) discussed in this chapter as well as in and among some theories we have yet to mention. Examples include neofunctionalism (Alexander, 1998a; Alexander and Colomy, 1985, 1990a) which seeks to overcome many of the limitations of structural-functionalism by integrating ideas from a wide range of theories; symbolic interactionism which has "cobbled a new theory from the shards of other theoretical approaches [e.g. feminist and exchange theory]" (Fine, 1990:136–137); exchange theory which has sought to synthesize ideas derived from such sources as symbolic interactionism and network theory (Cook, O'Brien, and Kollock, 1990); post-Marxists who have sought to integrate mainstream ideas into Marxian theory (Elster, 1985; Mayer, 1994; Roemer, 1986c); and postmodern Marxists who, as the name suggests, have attempted to bring postmodern ideas into Marxian theory (Harvey, 1989; Jameson, 1984; Laclau and Mouffe, 1985).

Then there are efforts to bring perspectives from outside sociology into sociological theory. There have been works oriented to bringing biological ideas into sociology in an effort to create sociobiology (Crippen, 1994; Maryanski and Turner, 1992). Rational choice theory is based in economics, but it has made inroads into a number of fields including sociology (Coleman, 1990). Systems theory has its roots in the hard sciences, but in the late twentieth century Niklas Luhmann (1982) made a powerful effort to develop a system theory that could be applied to the social world.

THEORIES OF MODERNITY AND POSTMODERNITY

As we begin the twenty-first century, social theorists[6] have become increasingly preoccupied with whether society, as well as theories about it, has undergone a dramatic transformation. On one side is a group of theorists (for example, Jurgen Habermas and Anthony Giddens) who believe that we continue to live in a society that can still best be described as modern and about which we can theorize in much the same way that social thinkers have long contemplated society. On the other side is a group of thinkers (for example, Jean Baudrillard, Jean-François Lyotard, and Fredric Jameson) who contend that society has changed so dramatically that we now live in a qualitatively different, postmodern society. Furthermore, they argue that this new society needs to be thought about in new and different ways.

The Defenders of Modernity

All the great classical sociological theorists (Marx, Weber, Durkheim, and Simmel) were concerned, in one way or another, with the modern world and its advantages and disadvantages. Of course, the last of these (Weber) died in 1920, and the world has changed dramatically since then. While all contemporary theorists recognize these dramatic changes, there are some who believe that there is more continuity than discontinuity between the world today and the world that existed around the last *fin de siecle.*

Mestrovic (1998:2) has labeled Anthony Giddens "the high priest of modernity." Giddens (1990, 1991, 1992) uses terms like "radical," "high," or "late" modernity to describe society today and to indicate that while it is not the same society as the one described by the classical theorists, it is continuous with that society. Giddens sees modernity today as a "juggernaut" that is, at least to some degree, out of control. Ulrich Beck (1992) contends that while the classical stage of modernity was associated with industrial society, the emerging new modernity is best described as a "risk society." While the central dilemma in classical modernity was wealth and how it ought to be distributed, the central problem in new modernity is the prevention, minimization, and channeling of risk (from, for example, a nuclear accident). Jurgen Habermas (1981, 1987b) sees modernity as an "unfinished project." That is, the central issue in the modern world

---

[6]I am using the term "social" rather than "sociological" theorist here to reflect the fact that many contributors to the recent literature are not sociologists, although they are theorizing about the social world.

continues, as it was in Weber's day, to be rationality. The utopian goal is still the max-imization of the rationality of both the "system" and the "life-world." I (Ritzer, 1996) also see rationality as the key process in the world today. However, I pick up on Weber's focus on the problem of the increase in formal rationality and the danger of an "iron cage" of rationality. While Weber focused on the bureaucracy, today I see the paradigm of this process as the fast-food restaurant, and I describe the increase in formal rationality as the McDonaldization of society.

Not only do these and other theorists (for example, Touraine, 1995; Wagner, 1994) persist in seeing the world in modern terms, but they continue to think about it using modern tools. Basically, they are standing back and apart from society, rationally and systematically analyzing and describing it, and portraying it using grand narratives, al-beit in more self-conscious ways than their forebears did. Modernity as a juggernaut, the transition from industrial to risk society, the rationalization of life-world and system, and the McDonaldization of society are far more similar to the grand narratives of the classical theorists of modernity than they are at variance with them.

The Proponents of Postmodernity

Postmodernism is hot (Kellner, 1989a; Ritzer, 1997; Seidman, 1994a), indeed it is so hot, it is discussed so endlessly in many fields including sociology, that it may already be in the process of burning out (Lemert, 1994b). We need to differentiate, at least ini-tially, between postmodernity and postmodern social theory (Best and Kellner, 1991). *Postmodernity* is a new historical epoch that is supposed to have succeeded the modern era, or modernity. *Postmodern social theory* is a new way of thinking about post-modernity; the world is so different that it requires entirely new ways of thinking. Post-modernists would tend to reject the theoretical perspectives outlined in the previous section, as well as the ways in which the thinkers involved created their theories.

There are probably as many portrayals of postmodernity as there are postmodern so-cial theorists. To simplify things, we will summarize some of the key elements of a de-piction offered by one of the most prominent postmodernists, Fredric Jameson (1984, 1991). First, postmodernity is a depthless, superficial world; it is a world of simulation (for example, a jungle cruise at Disneyland rather than the real thing). Second, it is a world that is lacking in affect and emotion. Third, there is a loss of a sense of one's place in history; it is hard to distinguish past, present, and future. Fourth, instead of the explosive, expanding, productive technologies of modernity (for example, automobile assembly lines), postmodern society is dominated by implosive, flattening, reproductive technologies (television, for example). In these and other ways, postmodern society is very different from modern society.

Such a different world requires a different way of thinking. Rosenau (1992; Ritzer, 1997) defines the postmodern mode of thought in terms of the things that it opposes, largely characteristics of the modern way of thinking. First, postmodernists reject the kind of grand narratives that characterize much of classical sociological theory. Instead, postmodernists prefer more limited explanations, or even no explanations at all. Sec-ond, there is a rejection of the tendency to put boundaries between disciplines—to en-gage in something called sociological (or social) theory that is distinct from, say, philosophical thinking or even novelistic storytelling. Third, postmodernists are often more interested in shocking or startling the reader than they are in engaging in careful, reasoned academic discourse. Finally, instead of looking for the core of society (say rationality, or capitalistic exploitation), postmodernists are more inclined to focus on more peripheral aspects of society.

Clearly, much is at stake in the debate between the modernists and the postmodernists, including the future of sociological theory. If the modernists win out, sociological theory in the first decade of the twenty-first century will look much like it always has, but if the postmodernists emerge victorious, the world, and social theories of that world, will be very different. The most likely scenario, however, is that the world will be composed of some combination of modern and postmodern elements and the social theorists of each persuasion will continue to battle it out for hegemony.

THEORIES TO WATCH IN THE EARLY TWENTY-FIRST CENTURY

It is impossible to predict the directions that sociological theory will take, but in this section we discuss several approaches that are likely to attract considerable attention and undergo substantial development.

Multicultural Social Theory

A recent development, closely tied to postmodernism—especially its emphasis on the periphery and its tendency to level the intellectual playing field—is the rise of multicultural social theory (Lemert, 1993; Rogers, 1996a). This rise of multicultural theory was foreshadowed by the emergence of feminist sociological theory in the 1970s. The feminists complained that sociological theory had been largely closed to women's voices; in the ensuing years many minority groups echoed the feminists' complaints. In fact, minority women (for example, African Americans and Latinas) began to complain that feminist theory was restricted to white, middle-class females and had to be more receptive to many other voices. Today, feminist theory has become far more diverse, as has sociological theory.

A good example of the increasing diversity of sociological theory is the rise of "queer" sociological theory (Morton, 1996; Warner, 1993). Seidman (1994b) documents the silence of classical sociological theory on sexuality in general and homosexuality in particular. He finds it striking that while the classical theorists were dealing with a wide range of issues relating to modernity, they had nothing to say about the making of modern bodies and modern sexuality. While the silence was soon to be broken, it was not until the work of Michel Foucault (1980) on the relationships among power, knowledge, and sexuality that the postmodern study of sexuality in general, and homosexuality in particular, began. What emerged was the sense of homosexuality as both a subject and an identity paralleling the heterosexual self and identity.

Seidman has argued, however, that what distinguishes queer theory is a rejection of any single identity, including homosexuality, and the argument that all identities are multiple or composite, unstable and exclusionary. Thus, at any given time each of us is a composite of a series of identity components (for example, "sexual orientation, race, class, nationality, gender, age, ableness" [Seidman, 1994b:173]), and these components can be combined and recombined in many different ways. As a result, Seidman rejects the homosexual-heterosexual dichotomy and seeks to move queer theory in the direction of a more general social theory:

> Queer theorists shift their focus from an exclusive preoccupation with the oppression and liberation of the homosexual subject to an analysis of the institutional practices and discourses producing sexual knowledges and how they organize social life, with particular attention to the way in which these knowledges and social practices repress differences. In this regard, queer theory is suggesting . . . the study . . . of those knowledges and social practices which organize "society" as a whole by sexualizing—heterosexualizing or homosexualizing—bodies, desires, acts, identities, social relations, knowledges, cultures, and social institutions. Queer theory aspires to transform homosexual theory into a general social theory or one standpoint from which to analyze whole societies.
>
> (Seidman, 1994b:174)

Thus, queer theory is put forth as but one of what have been called "standpoint theories," that is, theories that view the social world from a specific vantage point (much as Marx viewed capitalism from the standpoint of the proletariat). We can expect to see a burgeoning of such multicultural, standpoint theories as the twenty-first century unfolds.

Multicultural theory has taken a series of diverse forms beyond that of queer theory. Examples include Afrocentric theory (Asante, 1996), Appalachian studies (Banks, Billings, and Tice, 1996), Native American theory (Buffalohead, 1996), and even theories of masculinity (Connell, 1996; Kimmel, 1996). Among the things that characterize multicultural theory are the following:

- A rejection of universalistic theories that tend to support those in power; multicultural theories seek to empower those who lack clout.
- Multicultural theory seeks to be inclusive, to offer theory on the behalf of many disempowered groups.
- Multicultural theorists are not value free; they often theorize on behalf of those without power and to work in the social world to change social structure, culture, and the prospects for individuals.
- Multicultural theorists seek to disrupt not only the social world but the intellectual world; they seek to make it far more open and diverse.
- There is no effort to draw a clear line between theory and other types of narratives.
- There is ordinarily a critical edge to multicultural theory; it is both self-critical and critical of other theories and, most importantly, of the social world.
- Multicultural theorists recognize that their work is limited by the particular historical, social, and cultural context in which they happen to live (Rogers, 1996b:11–16).

Postmodern and Post-Postmodern Social Theories

It is safe to assume that postmodern social theories will continue to be important in sociology and many other fields. In fact, sociology has been slow to pick up on postmodern theory and there continues to be considerable hostility toward it in the discipline. However, the theory is too powerful and too well entrenched in many other fields to be largely ignored in sociology. Thus, postmodern social theory will attract more adherents (and detractors) in sociology in the years to come.

At the same time, there is already well established, primarily in France (the center of theoretical movements like postmodernism), a body of work that can best be thought of as post-postmodernism. For example, postmodern social theory is associated with a critique of a liberal, humanistic perspective and a shift away from a concern with the human subject. However, Ferry and Renaut (1985/1990) seek to rescue humanism and subjectivity and Lilla (1994:20) offers a defense of human rights. Manent (1994/1998) self-consciously analyzes modernity and the human subject. Lipovetsky (1987/1994) attacks the tendency of postmodern social theorists to be hypercritical of the contemporary world by defending the importance of fashion. He argues, for example, that fashion enhances rather than detracts from individuality. Thus, just as postmodern social theory is likely to thrive in the coming years, so too are theories that constitute a reaction against it and a return to more modern concerns. Postmodern social theory is not only important in itself, but also for its stimulation of reactions against it. Sociology, and sociological theory in particular, is likely to be revived by postmodern social theory and the challenges it poses (Owen, 1997).

Theories of Consumption

Coming of age during the Industrial Revolution, and animated by its problems and prospects, sociological theory has long had a "productivist bias." That is, theories have tended to focus on industry, industrial organizations, work, and workers. This is most obvious in Marxian and neo-Marxian theory, but it is found in many other theories such as Durkheim's thinking on the division of labor, Weber's work on the rise of capitalism in the West and the failure to develop it in other parts of the world, Simmel's analysis of the tragedy of culture produced by the proliferation of human products, the interest of the Chicago school in work, the concern in conflict theory with relations between employers and employees, leaders and followers, and so on. Much less attention has been devoted to consumption and the consumer. There are exceptions such as Thorstein Veblen's (1899/1994) famous work on "conspicuous consumption" and Simmel's thinking on money and fashion, but in the main social theorists have had far less to say about consumption than production.

Postmodern social theory has tended to define postmodern society as a consumer society with the result that consumption plays a central role in that theory. Most notable is Jean Baudrillard's (1970/1998) *Consumer Society*. Lipovetsky's post-postmodern work on fashion is reflective of the growing interest in and out of postmodern social theory in consumption. Since consumption is likely to continue to grow in importance, especially in the West, and production is likely to decline, it is safe to assume that we will see a dramatic increase in theoretical (and empirical) work on consumption (for an overview of extant theories of consumption, see Slater, 1997). To take one example, we are witnessing something of an outpouring of theoretically based work on the settings in which we consume, such as *Consuming Places* (Urry, 1995), *Enchanting a Disenchanted World: Revolutionizing the Means of Consumption* (Ritzer, 1999), and *Shelf Life: Supermarkets and the Changing Cultures of Consumption* (Humphery,

1998). We are likely to see much more work on such settings, as well as on consumers, consumer goods, and the process of consumption.

Others

Beyond the previous generalizations, it is difficult to foresee the future of sociological theory. For one thing, it is possible that new theories will burst upon the scene and attract adherents. It is also possible that what is today a minor theory will vault to prominence. Some of today's most important theories may grow less attractive. However, it is safe to assume that most, if not all, the theories singled out for discussion in this book will continue to be important. It is likely that some (feminist, multicultural, rational choice) will increase in importance while others (neofunctionalism) will experience a decline. One things seems sure—the landscape of social theory is likely to be dotted with more theories, none of which is likely to gain hegemony in the field. Postmodernists have criticized the idea of "totalizations," or overarching theoretical frameworks. It seems unlikely that social theory will come to be dominated by a single totalization. Rather, we are likely to see a field with a proliferating number of perspectives that have some supporters and that help us to understand part of the social world. Sociological theory will not be a simple world to understand and to use, but it will be an exciting world that offers a plethora of old and new ideas.

SUMMARY

This chapter picks up where Chapter 1 left off and deals with the history of sociological theory since the beginning of the twentieth century. We begin with the early history of American sociological theory, which was characterized by its liberalism, by its interest in Social Darwinism, and consequently by the influence of Herbert Spencer. In this context, the work of the two early sociological theorists, Sumner and Ward, is discussed. However, they did not leave a lasting imprint on American sociological theory. In contrast, the Chicago school, as embodied in the work of people like Small, Park, Thomas, Cooley, and especially Mead, did leave a strong mark on sociological theory, especially on symbolic interactionism.

While the Chicago school was still predominant, a different form of sociological theory began to develop at Harvard. Pitirim Sorokin played a key role in the founding of sociology at Harvard, but it was Talcott Parsons who was to lead Harvard to a position of preeminence in American theory, replacing Chicago's symbolic interactionism. Parsons was important not only for legitimizing "grand theory" in the United States and for introducing European theorists to an American audience but also for his role in the development of action theory and, more important, structural functionalism. In the 1940s and 1950s, structural functionalism was furthered by the disintegration of the Chicago school that began in the 1930s and was largely complete by the 1950s.

The major development in Marxian theory in the early years of the twentieth century was the creation of the Frankfurt, or critical, school. This Hegelianized form of Marxism also showed the influence of sociologists like Weber and of the psychoanalyst Sigmund Freud. Marxism did not gain a widespread following among sociologists in the early part of the century.

Structural functionalism's dominance within American theory in mid-century was rather short-lived. Although traceable to a much earlier date, phenomenological sociology, especially the work of Alfred Schutz, began to attract significant attention in the 1960s. Marxian theory was still largely excluded from American theory, but C. Wright Mills kept a radical tradition alive in America in the 1940s and 1950s. Mills also was one of the leaders of the attacks on structural functionalism, attacks that mounted in intensity in the 1950s and 1960s. In light of some of these attacks, a conflict-theory alternative to structural functionalism emerged in this period. Although influenced by Marxian theory, conflict theory suffered from an inadequate integration of Marxism. Still another alternative born in the 1950s was exchange theory, and it continues to attract a small but steady number of followers. Although symbolic interactionism lost some of its steam, the work of Erving Goffman on dramaturgical analysis in this period gained a following.

Important developments took place in other sociologies of everyday life (symbolic interactionism can be included under this heading) in the 1960s and 1970s, including some increase in interest in phenomenological sociology and, more important, an outburst of work in ethnomethodology. During this period Marxian theories of various types came into their own in sociology, although those theories have been seriously compromised by the fall of the Soviet Union and other communist regimes in the late 1980s and early 1990s. Also of note during this period was the growing importance of structuralism and then poststructuralism, especially in the work of Michel Foucault. Of overwhelming significance was the explosion of interest in feminist theory, an outpouring of work that continues apace as we move beyond the year 2000.

In addition to those just mentioned, three other notable developments occurred in the 1980s and continued into the 1990s. First was the rise in interest in the United States in the micro-macro link. Second was the parallel increase in attention in Europe to the relationship between agency and structure. Third was the growth, especially in the 1990s, of a wide range of synthetic efforts.

The chapter concludes with a discussion of some theories to watch as we enter the twenty-first century. Multicultural theories of various types are likely to flourish. Postmodern social theories will continue to develop, but so will reactions against them, including those we can think of as post-postmodern social theories. Relating to postmodern theory, but also a reflection of changes in society and a reaction against the productivist bias that has dominated sociological theory since its inception, theories of consumption will attract attention. Whatever theories come to flower, it seems clear that a single theoretical perspective will be unlikely to dominate the discipline.

From the point of view of the remainder of this book, this chapter has played two major roles. First, it demonstrated that the classical theorists introduced in Chapter 1—Comte, Spencer, Marx, Durkheim, Weber, and Simmel—influenced the later development of sociological theory in a variety of direct and indirect ways. Second, it allowed us to introduce, within their historical context, the other classical theorists who will be discussed in detail later in this book—the founding "mothers," Veblen, Mannheim, Mead, Schutz, and Parsons.

PART TWO

MODERN SOCIOLOGICAL THEORY: THE MAJOR SCHOOLS

STRUCTURAL FUNCTIONALISM, NEOFUNCTIONALISM, AND CONFLICT THEORY

STRUCTURAL FUNCTIONALISM
    The Functional Theory of Stratification and Its Critics
    Talcott Parsons's Structural Functionalism
    Robert Merton's Structural Functionalism
    The Major Criticisms
NEOFUNCTIONALISM
CONFLICT THEORY
    The Work of Ralf Dahrendorf
    The Major Criticisms and Efforts to Deal with Them
    A More Integrative Conflict Theory

Structural functionalism, especially in the work of Talcott Parsons, Robert Merton, and their students and followers, was for many years *the* dominant sociological theory. However, in the last three decades it has declined dramatically in importance (Chriss, 1995) and, in at least some senses, has receded into the recent history of sociological theory. This decline is reflected in Colomy's (1990a) description of structural functionalism as a theoretical "tradition." Structural functionalism is now mainly of historical significance, although it is also notable for the role it played in the emergence of neofunctionalism in the 1980s. After offering an overview of structural functionalism, we will discuss neofunctionalism as a possible successor to it as well as an example of the recent movement toward synthesis within sociological theory. However, the future of neofunctionalism itself has been cast into doubt by the fact that its founder, Jeffrey Alexander (personal communication, October 17, 1994), has arrived at the conclusion that neofunctionalism "is no longer satisfactory to me." He states, "I am now separating myself from the movement I started."

For many years, the major alternative to structural functionalism was conflict theory. We will discuss Ralf Dahrendorf's traditional version of conflict theory, as well as a more recent integrative and synthetic effort by Randall Collins.

Before turning to the specifics of structural functionalism and conflict theory, we need, following Thomas Bernard (1983), to place these theories in the broader context of the debate between consensus theories (one of which is structural functionalism) and conflict theories (one of which is the sociological conflict theory to be discussed in this chapter). *Consensus theories* see shared norms and values as fundamental to society, focus on social order based on tacit agreements, and view social change as occurring in a slow and orderly fashion. In contrast, *conflict theories* emphasize the dominance of some social groups by others, see social order as based on manipulation and control by dominant groups, and view social change as occurring rapidly and in a disorderly fashion as subordinate groups overthrow dominant groups.

Although these criteria broadly define the essential differences between the sociological theories of structural functionalism and conflict theory, Bernard's view is that the disagreement is far broader and has "been a recurring debate that has taken a variety of different forms throughout the history of Western thought" (1983:6). Bernard traced the debate back to ancient Greece (and the differences between Plato [consensus] and Aristotle [conflict]) and through the history of philosophy. Later, in sociology the debate was joined by (the conflict theorist is listed first) Marx and Comte, Simmel and Durkheim, and Dahrendorf and Parsons. We already have examined briefly the ideas of the first two pairs of sociologists (although, as we have seen, their work is far broader than is implied by the label of "conflict" or "consensus" theorist); in this chapter we examine Dahrendorf's conflict theory and Parsons's consensus theory, among others.

Although we emphasize the differences between structural functionalism and conflict theory, we should not forget that they have important similarities. In fact, Bernard argues that "the areas of agreement among them are more extensive than the areas of disagreement" (1983:214). For example, they are both macro-level theories focally concerned with large-scale social structures and social institutions. As a result, in my (Ritzer, 1980) terms, both theories exist within the same sociological ("social facts") paradigm (see the Appendix).

STRUCTURAL FUNCTIONALISM

Robert Nisbet argued that structural functionalism was "without any doubt, the single most significant body of theory in the social sciences in the present century" (cited in Turner and Maryanski, 1979:xi). Kingsley Davis (1959) took the position that structural functionalism was, for all intents and purposes, synonymous with sociology. Alvin Gouldner (1970) implicitly took a similar position when he attacked Western sociology largely through a critical analysis of the structural-functional theories of Talcott Parsons.

Despite its undoubted hegemony in the two decades after World War II, structural functionalism has declined in importance as a sociological theory. Even Wilbert Moore, a man who was intimately associated with this theory, argued that it had "become an embarrassment in contemporary theoretical sociology" (1978:321). Two observers even stated: "Thus, functionalism as an explanatory theory is, we feel, 'dead' and continued efforts to use functionalism as a theoretical explanation should be abandoned in favor of more promising theoretical perspectives" (Turner and Maryanski, 1979:141).[1] Nicholas Demerath and Richard Peterson (1967) took a more positive view, arguing that structural functionalism is not a passing fad. However, they admitted that it is likely to evolve into another sociological theory, just as this theory itself evolved out of the earlier organicism (see the following section). The rise of neofunctionalism (which we will

---

[1]Despite this statement, Jonathan Turner and Alexandra Maryanski (1979) are willing to argue that functionalism can continue to be useful as a method.

discuss later in this chapter) seems to support Demerath and Peterson's position rather than the more negative perspective of Turner and Maryanski.

In structural functionalism, the terms *structural* and *functional* need not be used in conjunction, although they are typically conjoined. We could study the structures of society without being concerned with their functions (or consequences) for other structures. Similarly, we could examine the functions of a variety of social processes that may not take a structural form. Still, the concern for both elements characterizes structural functionalism. Although structural functionalism takes various forms (Abrahamson, 1978), *societal functionalism* is the dominant approach among sociological structural functionalists (Sztompka, 1974) and as such will be the focus of this chapter. The primary concern of societal functionalism is the large-scale social structures and institutions of society, their interrelationships, and their constraining effects on actors.

The Functional Theory of Stratification and Its Critics

The functional theory of stratification as articulated by Kingsley Davis and Wilbert Moore (1945) is perhaps the best-known single piece of work in structural-functional theory. Davis and Moore made it clear that they regarded social stratification as both universal and necessary. They argued that no society is ever unstratified, or totally classless. Stratification is, in their view, a *functional* necessity. All societies need such a system, and this need brings into existence a system of stratification.[2] They also viewed a stratification system as a structure, pointing out that stratification refers not to the individuals in the stratification system but rather to a system of *positions.* They focused on how certain positions come to carry with them different degrees of prestige and not on how individuals come to occupy certain positions.

Given this focus, the major functional issue is how a society motivates and places people in their "proper" positions in the stratification system. This is reducible to two problems. First, how does a society instill in the "proper" individuals the desire to fill certain positions? Second, once people are in the right positions, how does society then instill in them the desire to fulfill the requirements of those positions?

Proper social placement in society is a problem for three basic reasons. First, some positions are more pleasant to occupy than others. Second, some positions are more important to the survival of society than others. Third, different social positions require different abilities and talents.

Although these issues apply to all social positions, Davis and Moore were concerned with the functionally more important positions in society. The positions that rank high within the stratification system are presumed to be those that are *less* pleasant to occupy but *more* important to the survival of society and that require the greatest ability and talent. In addition, society must attach sufficient rewards to these positions so that enough people will seek to occupy them and the individuals who do

---

[2]This is an example of a teleological argument. We will have occasion to discuss this issue later in the chapter, but for now we can define a *teleological argument* as one that sees the social world as having purposes, or goals, which bring needed structures or events into being. In this case society "needs" stratification, so it brings such a system into existence.

come to occupy them will work diligently. The converse was implied by Davis and Moore but not discussed. That is, low-ranking positions in the stratification system are presumed to be *more* pleasant and *less* important and to require less ability and talent. Also, society has less need to be sure that individuals occupy these positions and perform their duties with diligence.

Davis and Moore did not argue that a society consciously develops a stratification system in order to be sure that the high-level positions are filled, and filled adequately. Rather, they made it clear that stratification is an "unconsciously evolved device." However, it is a device that every society does, and *must,* develop if it is to survive.

In order to be sure that people occupy the higher-ranking positions, society must, in Davis and Moore's view, provide these individuals with various rewards, including great prestige, high salary, and sufficient leisure. For example, to ensure enough doctors for our society, we need to offer them these and other rewards. Davis and Moore implied that we could not expect people to undertake the "burdensome" and "expensive" process of medical education if we did not offer such rewards. The implication seems to be that people at the top must receive the rewards that they do. If they did not, those positions would remain understaffed or unfilled and society would crumble.

The structural-functional theory of stratification has been subject to much criticism since its publication in 1945 (see Tumin, 1953, for the first important criticism; Huaco, 1966, for a good summary of the main criticisms to that date).

One basic criticism is that the functional theory of stratification simply perpetuates the privileged position of those people who already have power, prestige, and money. It does this by arguing that such people deserve their rewards; indeed they need to be offered such rewards for the good of society.

The functional theory also can be criticized for assuming that simply because a stratified social structure has existed in the past, it must continue to exist in the future. It is possible that future societies will be organized in other, nonstratified ways.

In addition, it has been argued that the idea of functional positions varying in their importance to society is difficult to support. Are garbage collectors really any less important to the survival of society than advertising executives? Despite the lower pay and prestige of the garbage collectors, they actually may be *more* important to the survival of the society. Even in cases where it could be said that one position serves a more important function for society, the greater rewards do not necessarily accrue to the more important position. Nurses may be much more important to society than movie stars are, but nurses have far less power, prestige, and income than movie stars have.

Is there really a scarcity of people capable of filling high-level positions? In fact, many people are prevented from obtaining the training they need to achieve prestigious positions, even though they have the ability. In the medical profession, for example, there is a persistent effort to limit the number of practicing doctors. In general, many able people never get a chance to show that they can handle high-ranking positions, even though there is a clear need for them and their contributions. Those in high-ranking positions have a vested interest in keeping their own numbers small and their power and income high.

Finally, it can be argued that we do not have to offer people power, prestige, and income to get them to want to occupy high-level positions. People can be equally motivated by the satisfaction of doing a job well or by the opportunity to be of service to others.

Talcott Parsons's Structural Functionalism

Over the course of his life, Talcott Parsons did a great deal of theoretical work (Holmwood, 1996). There are important differences between his early work and his later work. In this section we deal with his later, structural-functional theorizing. We begin this discussion of Parsons's structural functionalism with the four functional imperatives for all "action" systems, his famous AGIL scheme. After this discussion of the four functions, we will turn to an analysis of Parsons's ideas on structures and systems.

AGIL A *function* is "a complex of activities directed towards meeting a need or needs of the system" (Rocher, 1975:40). Using this definition, Parsons believes that there are four functional imperatives that are necessary for (characteristic of) all systems—adaptation (A), goal attainment (G), integration (I), and latency (L), or pattern maintenance. Together, these four functional imperatives are known as the AGIL scheme. In order to survive, a system must perform these four functions:

1 *Adaptation:* A system must cope with external situational exigencies. It must adapt to its environment and adapt the environment to its needs.

2 *Goal attainment:* A system must define and achieve its primary goals.

3 *Integration:* A system must regulate the interrelationship of its component parts. It also must manage the relationship among the other three functional imperatives (A, G, L).

4 *Latency (pattern maintenance):* A system must furnish, maintain, and renew both the motivation of individuals and the cultural patterns that create and sustain the motivation.

Parsons designed the AGIL scheme to be used at *all* levels in his theoretical system (for one example, see Paulsen and Feldman, 1995). In the discussion below on the four action systems, we will illustrate how Parsons uses AGIL.

The *behavioral organism* is the action system that handles the adaptation function by adjusting to and transforming the external world. The *personality system* performs the goal-attainment function by defining system goals and mobilizing resources to attain them. The *social system* copes with the integration function by controlling its component parts. Finally, the *cultural system* performs the latency function by providing actors with the norms and values that motivate them for action. Figure 3.1 (on page 100) summarizes the structure of the action system in terms of the AGIL schema.

The Action System We are now ready to discuss the overall shape of Parsons's action system. Figure 3.2 (on page 101) is an outline of the major levels in Parsons's schema.

It is obvious that Parsons had a clear notion of "levels" of social analysis as well as their interrelationship. The hierarchical arrangement is clear, and the levels are integrated in Parsons's system in two ways. First, each of the lower levels provides the conditions, the energy, needed for the higher levels. Second, the higher levels control those below them in the hierarchy.

In terms of the environments of the action system, the lowest level, the physical and organic environment, involves the nonsymbolic aspects of the human body, its anatomy and physiology. The highest level, ultimate reality, has, as Jackson Toby suggests "a metaphysical flavor," but Toby also argues that Parsons "is not referring to the

TALCOTT PARSONS: A Biographical Sketch

Talcott Parsons was born in 1902 in Colorado Springs, Colorado. He came from a religious and intellectual background; his father was a Congregational minister, a professor, and ultimately president of a small college. Parsons got an undergraduate degree from Amherst College in 1924 and set out to do graduate work at the London School of Economics. In the next year, he moved on to Heidelberg, Germany. Max Weber had spent a large portion of his career at Heidelberg, and although he had died five years before Parsons arrived, Weber's influence survived and his widow continued to hold meetings in her home, meetings that Parsons attended. Parsons was greatly affected by Weber's work and ultimately wrote his doctoral thesis at Heidelberg, dealing, in part, with Weber's work.

Parsons became an instructor at Harvard in 1927, and although he switched departments several times, Parsons remained at Harvard until his death in 1979. His career progress was not rapid; he did not obtain a tenured position until 1939. Two years previously, he had published *The Structure of Social Action,* a book that not only introduced major sociological theorists like Weber to large numbers of sociologists but also laid the groundwork for Parsons's own developing theory.

After that, Parsons made rapid academic progress. He was made chairman of the Harvard sociology department in 1944 and two years later set up and chaired the innovative Department of Social Relations, which included not only sociologists but a variety of other social scientists. By 1949 he had been elected president of the American Sociological Association. In the 1950s and into the 1960s, with the publication of such books as *The Social System* (1951), Parsons became the dominant figure in American sociology.

However, by the late 1960s, Parsons came under attack from the emerging radical wing of American sociology. Parsons was seen as being a political conservative, and his theory was considered highly conservative and little more than an elaborate categorization scheme. But in the 1980s, there was a resurgence in interest in Parsonian theory not only in the United States but around the world (Alexander, 1982–83; Buxton, 1985; Camic, 1990; Holton and Turner, 1986; Sciulli and Gerstein, 1985). Holton and Turner have perhaps gone the farthest, arguing that "Parsons' work . . . represents a more powerful contribution to sociological theory than that of Marx, Weber, Durkheim or any of their contemporary followers" (1986:13). Furthermore, Parsons's ideas influenced not only conservative thinkers but neo-Marxian theorists as well, especially Jurgen Habermas.

supernatural so much as to the universal tendency for societies to address symbolically the uncertainties, concerns, and tragedies of human existence that challenge the meaningfulness of social organization" (1977:3).

The heart of Parsons's work is found in his four action systems. In the assumptions that Parsons made regarding his action systems we encounter the problem of order that was his overwhelming concern and that has become a major source of criticism of his work (Schwanenberg, 1971). The Hobbesian problem of order—what prevents a social war of all against all—was not answered to Parsons's (1937) satisfaction by the earlier philosophers. Parsons found his answer to the problem of order in structural functionalism, which operates in his view with the following set of assumptions:

Upon Parsons's death, a number of his former students, themselves sociologists of considerable note, reflected on his theory, as well as on the man behind the theory (for a more recent, and highly personal, reminiscence, see Fox, 1997). In their musings, these sociologists offered some interesting insights into Parsons and his work. The few glimpses of Parsons reproduced here do not add up to a coherent picture, but they do offer some provocative glimpses of the man and his work.

Robert Merton was one of his students when Parsons was just beginning his teaching career at Harvard. Merton, who became a noted theorist in his own right, makes it clear that graduate students came to Harvard in those years to study not with Parsons but rather with Pitirim Sorokin, the senior member of the department, who was to become Parsons's archenemy:

> Of the very first generation of graduate students coming to Harvard . . . precisely none came to study with Talcott. They could scarcely have done so for the simplest of reasons: in 1931, he had no public identity whatever as a sociologist.
>
> Although we students came to study with the renowned Sorokin, a subset of us stayed to work with the unknown Parsons.
>
> (Merton, 1980:69)

Merton's reflections on Parsons's first course in theory are interesting too, especially because the material provided the basis for one of the most influential theory books in the history of sociology:

> Long before Talcott Parsons became one of the Grand Old Men of world sociology, he was for an early few of us its Grand Young Man. This began with his first course in theory. . . . [It] would provide him with the core of his masterwork, *The Structure of Social Action* which . . . did not appear in print until five years after its first oral publication.
>
> (Merton, 1980;69–70)

Although all would not share Merton's positive evaluation of Parsons, they would acknowledge the following:

> The death of Talcott Parsons marks the end of an era in sociology. When [a new era] does begin . . . it will surely be fortified by the great tradition of sociological thought which he has left to us.
>
> (Merton, 1980:71)

1 Systems have the property of order and interdependence of parts.

2 Systems tend toward self-maintaining order, or equilibrium.[3]

3 The system may be static or involved in an ordered process of change.

4 The nature of one part of the system has an impact on the form that the other parts can take.

5 Systems maintain boundaries with their environments.

---

[3]Most often, to Parsons, the problem of order related to the issue of why action was nonrandom or patterned. The issue of equilibrium was a more empirical question to Parsons. Nonetheless, Parsons himself often conflated the issues of order and equilibrium.

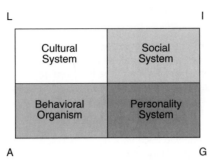

FIGURE 3.1
Structure of the General Action System

6 Allocation and integration are two fundamental processes necessary for a given state of equilibrium of a system.

7 Systems tend toward self-maintenance involving the maintenance of boundaries and of the relationships of parts to the whole, control of environmental variations, and control of tendencies to change the system from within.

These assumptions led Parsons to make the analysis of the *ordered* structure of society his first priority. In so doing, he did little with the issue of social change, at least until later in his career:

> We feel that it is uneconomical to describe changes in systems of variables before the variables themselves have been isolated and described; therefore, we have chosen to begin by studying particular combinations of variables and to move toward description of how these combinations change only when a firm foundation for such has been laid.
>
> (Parsons and Shils, 1951:6)

Parsons was so heavily criticized for his static orientation that he devoted more and more attention to change; in fact, as we will see, he eventually focused on the evolution of societies. However, in the view of most observers, even his work on social change tended to be highly static and structured.

In reading about the four action systems, the reader should keep in mind that they do not exist in the real world but are, rather, analytical tools for analyzing the real world.

Social System   Parsons's conception of the social system begins at the micro level with interaction between ego and alter ego, defined as the most elementary form of the social system. He spent little time analyzing this level, although he did argue that features of this interaction system are present in the more complex forms taken by the social system. Parsons defined a *social system* thus:

> A social system consists in a plurality of individual actors *interacting* with each other in a situation which has at least a physical or environmental aspect, actors who are motivated in terms of a tendency to the "optimization of gratification" and whose relation to their situations, including each other, is defined and mediated in terms of a system of culturally structured and shared symbols.
>
> (Parsons, 1951:5–6)

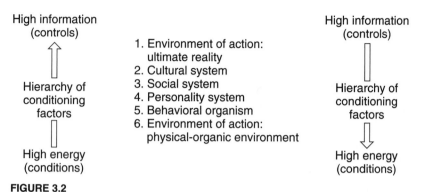

FIGURE 3.2
Parsons's Action Schema

This definition seeks to define a social system in terms of many of the key concepts in Parsons's work—actors, interaction, environment, optimization of gratification, and culture.

Despite his commitment to viewing the social system as a system of interaction, Parsons did not take interaction as his fundamental unit in the study of the social system. Rather, he used the *status-role* complex as the basic unit of the system. This is neither an aspect of actors nor an aspect of interaction, but rather a *structural* component of the social system. *Status* refers to a structural position within the social system, and *role* is what the actor does in such a position, seen in the context of its functional significance for the larger system. The actor is viewed not in terms of thoughts and actions but instead (at least in terms of position in the social system) as nothing more than a bundle of statuses and roles.

In his analysis of the social system, Parsons was interested primarily in its structural components. In addition to a concern with the status-role, Parsons (1966:11) was interested in such large-scale components of social systems as collectivities, norms, and values. In his analysis of the social system, however, Parsons was not simply a structuralist but also a functionalist. He thus delineated a number of the functional prerequisites of a social system. First, social systems must be structured so that they operate compatibly with other systems. Second, to survive, the social system must have the requisite support from other systems. Third, the system must meet a significant proportion of the needs of its actors. Fourth, the system must elicit adequate participation from its members. Fifth, it must have at least a minimum of control over potentially disruptive behavior. Sixth, if conflict becomes sufficiently disruptive, it must be controlled. Finally, a social system requires a language in order to survive.

It is clear in Parsons's discussion of the functional prerequisites of the social system that his focus was large-scale systems and their relationship to one another (societal functionalism). Even when he talked about actors, it was from the point of view of the system. Also, the discussion reflects Parsons's concern with the maintenance of order within the social system.

Actors and the Social System   However, Parsons did not completely ignore the issue of the relationship between actors and social structures in his discussion of the social system. In fact, he called the integration of value patterns and need-dispositions "the fundamental dynamic theorem of sociology" (Parsons, 1951:42). Given his central concern with the social system, of key importance in this integration are the processes of internalization and socialization. That is, Parsons was interested in the ways that the norms and values of a system are transferred to the actors within the system. In a successful socialization process these norms and values are internalized; that is, they become part of the actors' "consciences." As a result, in pursuing their own interests, the actors are in fact serving the interests of the system as a whole. As Parsons put it, "The combination of value-orientation patterns which is acquired [by the actor in socialization] *must in a very important degree be a function of the fundamental role structure and dominant values of the social system"* (1951:227).

In general, Parsons assumed that actors usually are passive recipients in the socialization process.[4] Children learn not only how to act but also the norms and values, the morality, of society. Socialization is conceptualized as a conservative process in which need-dispositions (which are themselves largely molded by society) bind children to the social system, and it provides the means by which the need-dispositions can be satisfied. There is little or no room for creativity; the need for gratification ties children to the system as it exists. Parsons sees socialization as a lifelong experience. Because the norms and values inculcated in childhood tend to be very general, they do not prepare children for the various specific situations that they encounter in adulthood. Thus socialization must be supplemented throughout the life cycle with a series of more specific socializing experiences. Despite this need later in life, the norms and values learned in childhood tend to be stable and, with a little gentle reinforcement, tend to remain in force throughout life.

Despite the conformity induced by lifelong socialization, there is a wide range of individual variation in the system. The question is: Why is this normally not a major problem for the social system, given its need for order? For one thing, a number of social control mechanisms can be employed to induce conformity. However, as far as Parsons was concerned, social control is strictly a second line of defense. A system runs best when social control is used only sparingly. For another thing, the system must be able to tolerate some variation, some deviance. A flexible social system is stronger than a brittle one that accepts no deviation. Finally, the social system should provide a wide range of role opportunities that allow different personalities to express themselves without threatening the integrity of the system.

Socialization and social control are the main mechanisms that allow the social system to maintain its equilibrium. Modest amounts of individuality and deviance are accommodated, but more extreme forms must be met by reequilibrating mechanisms. Thus, social order is built into the structure of Parsons's social system:

> Without deliberate planning on anyone's part there have developed in our type of social system, and correspondingly in others, mechanisms which, within limits, are capable of forestalling and reversing the deep-lying tendencies for deviance to get into the vicious

---

[4]This is a controversial interpretation of Parsons's work with which many disagree. François Bourricaud, for example, talks of "the dialectics of socialization" (1981:108) in Parsons's work and not of passive recipients of socialization.

circle phase which puts it beyond the control of ordinary approval-disapproval and reward-punishment sanctions.

(Parsons, 1951:319)

Again, Parsons's main interest was the system as a whole rather than the actor in the system—how the system controls the actor, not how the actor creates and maintains the system. This reflects Parsons's commitment on this issue to a structural-functional orientation.

Society   Although the idea of a social system encompasses all types of collectivities, one specific and particularly important social system is *society*, "a relatively self-sufficient collectivity the members of which are able to satisfy all their individual and collective needs and to live entirely within its framework" (Rocher, 1975:60).[5] As a structural functionalist, Parsons distinguished among four structures, or subsystems, in society in terms of the functions (AGIL) they perform (see Figure 3.3). The *economy* is the subsystem that performs the function for society of adapting to the environment through labor, production, and allocation. Through such work, the economy adapts the environment to society's needs, and it helps society adapt to these external realities. The *polity* (or political system) performs the function of goal attainment by pursuing societal objectives and mobilizing actors and resources to that end. The *fiduciary system* (for example, in the schools, the family) handles the latency function by transmitting culture (norms and values) to actors and allowing it to be internalized by them. Finally, the integration function is performed by the *societal community* (for example, the law), which coordinates the various components of society (Parsons and Platt, 1973).

As important as the structures of the social system were to Parsons, the cultural system was more important. In fact, as we saw earlier, the cultural system stood at the top of Parsons's action system, and Parsons (1966) labeled himself a "cultural determinist."

Cultural System   Parsons conceived of culture as the major force binding the various elements of the social world, or, in his terms, the action system. Culture mediates interaction among actors and integrates the personality and the social systems. Culture has the peculiar capacity to become, at least in part, a component of the other systems. Thus, in the social system culture is embodied in norms and values, and in the personality system it is internalized by the actor. But the cultural system is not simply a part of other systems; it also has a separate existence in the form of the social stock of knowledge, symbols, and ideas. These aspects of the cultural system are available to the social and personality systems, but they do not become part of them (Morse, 1961:105; Parsons and Shils, 1951:6).

Parsons defined the cultural system, as he did his other systems, in terms of its relationship to the other action systems. Thus *culture* is seen as a patterned, ordered system of symbols that are objects of orientation to actors, internalized aspects of the personality system, and institutionalized patterns (Parsons, 1990) in the social system. Because it is largely symbolic and subjective, culture is readily transmitted from one system to another. Culture can move from one social system to another through diffusion and

---

[5]Barber (1993, 1994) argues that while there is considerable terminological confusion in Parsons's work, the idea of a social system should be restricted to inclusive, total systems like societies.

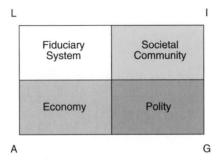

FIGURE 3.3
Society, Its Subsystems, and the Functional Imperatives

from one personality system to another through learning and socialization. However, the symbolic (subjective) character of culture also gives it another characteristic, the ability to control Parsons's other action systems. This is one of the reasons that Parsons came to view himself as a cultural determinist.

However, if the cultural system is preeminent in Parsonsian theory, then we must question whether he offers a genuinely integrative theory. As pointed out in the Appendix, a truly integrative theory gives rough equivalency to all major levels of analysis. Cultural determinism, indeed any kind of determinism, is highly suspect from the point of view of an integrated sociology. (For a more integrated conception of Parsons's work, see Camic, 1990.) This problem is exacerbated when we look at the personality system and see how weakly it is developed in Parsons's work.

Personality System   The personality system is controlled not only by the cultural system but also by the social system. That is not to say that Parsons did not accord some independence to the personality system:

> My view will be that, while the main content of the structure of the personality is derived from social systems and culture through socialization, the personality becomes an independent system through its relations to its own organism and through the uniqueness of its own life experience; it is not a mere epiphenomenon.
>
> (Parsons, 1970a:82)

We get the feeling here that Parsons is protesting too much. If the personality system is not an epiphenomenon, it is certainly reduced to secondary or dependent status in his theoretical system.

The *personality* is defined as the organized system of orientation and motivation of action of the individual actor. The basic component of the personality is the "need-disposition." Parsons and Shils defined *need-dispositions* as the "most significant units of motivation of action" (1951:113). They differentiated need-dispositions from drives, which are innate tendencies—"physiological energy that makes action possible" (Parsons and Shils, 1951:111). In other words, drives are better seen as part of the biological organism. Need-dispositions are then defined as "these same tendencies when they are not innate but acquired through the process of action itself" (Parsons and Shils, 1951:111). In other words, need-dispositions are drives that are shaped by the social setting.

Need-dispositions impel actors to accept or reject objects presented in the environment or to seek out new objects if the ones that are available do not adequately satisfy need-dispositions. Parsons differentiated among three basic types of need-dispositions. The first type impels actors to seek love, approval, and so forth from their social relationships. The second type includes internalized values that lead actors to observe various cultural standards. Finally, there are the role expectations that lead actors to give and get appropriate responses.

This gives a very passive image of actors. They seem to be either impelled by drives, dominated by the culture, or, more usually, shaped by a combination of drives and culture (that is, by need-dispositions). A passive personality system is clearly a weak link in an integrated theory, and Parsons seemed to be aware of it. On various occasions, he tried to endow the personality with some creativity. For example, he said: "We do not mean . . . to imply that a person's values are entirely 'internalized culture' or mere adherence to rules and laws. The person makes creative modifications as he internalizes culture; but the novel aspect is not the culture aspect" (Parsons and Shils, 1951:72). Despite claims such as these, the dominant impression that emerges from Parsons's work is one of a passive personality system.

Parsons's emphasis on need-dispositions creates other problems. Because it leaves out so many other important aspects of personality, his system becomes a largely impoverished one. Alfred Baldwin, a psychologist, makes precisely this point:

> It seems fair to say that Parsons fails in his theory to provide the personality with a reasonable set of properties or mechanisms aside from need-dispositions, and gets himself into trouble by not endowing the personality with enough characteristics and enough different kinds of mechanisms for it to be able to function.
>
> (A. Baldwin, 1961:186)

Baldwin makes another telling point about Parsons's personality system, arguing that even when Parsons analyzed the personality system, he was really not focally interested in it: "Even when he is writing chapters on personality structure, Parsons spends many more pages talking about social systems than he does about personality" (1961:180). This is reflected in the various ways that Parsons linked the personality to the social system. First, actors must learn to see themselves in a way that fits with the place they occupy in society (Parsons and Shils, 1951:147). Second, role expectations are attached to each of the roles occupied by individual actors. Then there is the learning of self-discipline, internalization of value orientations, identification, and so forth. All these forces point toward the integration of the personality system with the social system, which Parsons emphasized. However, he also pointed out the possible malintegration, which is a problem for the system that needs to be overcome.

Another aspect of Parsons's work—his interest in internalization as the personality system's side of the socialization process—reflects the passivity of the personality system. Parsons (1970a:2) derived this interest from Durkheim's work on internalization, as well as from Freud's work, primarily that on the superego. In emphasizing internalization and the superego, Parsons once again manifested his conception of the personality system as passive and externally controlled.

Although Parsons was willing to talk about the subjective aspects of personality in his early work, he progressively abandoned that perspective. In so doing, he limited his possible insights into the personality system. Parsons at one point stated clearly that he was shifting his attention away from the internal meanings that the actions of people may have: "The organization of observational data in terms of the theory of action is quite possible and fruitful in modified behavioristic terms, and such formulation avoids many of the difficult questions of introspection or empathy" (Parsons and Shils, 1951:64).

Behavioral Organism   Though he included the behavioral organism as one of the four action systems, Parsons had very little to say about it. It is included because it is the source of energy for the rest of the systems. Although it is based on genetic constitution, its organization is affected by the processes of conditioning and learning that occur during the individual's life.[6] The behavioral organism is clearly a residual system in Parsons's work, but at the minimum Parsons is to be lauded for including it as a part of his sociology, if for no other reason than that he anticipated the interest in sociobiology and the sociology of the body (B. Turner, 1985) by some sociologists.

Change and Dynamism in Parsonsian Theory   Parsons's work with conceptual tools such as the four action systems and the functional imperatives led to the accusation that he offered a structural theory that was unable to deal with social change. Parsons had long been sensitive to this charge, arguing that although a study of change was necessary, it must be preceded by a study of structure. But by the 1960s he could resist the attacks no longer and made a major shift in his work to the study of social change,[7] particularly the study of social evolution (Parsons, 1977b:50).

Evolutionary Theory   Parsons's (1966) general orientation to the study of social change was shaped by biology. To deal with this process, Parsons developed what he called "a paradigm of evolutionary change."

The first component of that paradigm is the process of *differentiation*. Parsons assumed that any society is composed of a series of subsystems that differ in terms of both their *structure* and their *functional* significance for the larger society. As society evolves, new subsystems are differentiated. This is not enough, however; they also must be more adaptive than earlier subsystems. Thus, the essential aspect of Parsons's evolutionary paradigm was the idea of *adaptive upgrading*. Parsons described this process:

> If differentiation is to yield a balanced, more evolved system, each newly differentiated substructure . . . must have increased adaptive capacity for performing its *primary* function, as compared to the performance of *that* function in the previous, more diffuse structure. . . . We may call this process the *adaptive upgrading* aspect of the evolutionary change cycle.
>
> (Parsons, 1966:22)

This is a highly positive model of social change (although Parsons certainly had a sense of its darker side). It assumes that as society evolves, it grows generally better

---

[6]Because of this social element, in his later work Parsons dropped the word *organism* and labeled this the "behavioral system" (1975:104).

[7]To be fair, we must report that Parsons had done some earlier work on social change (see Parsons, 1942, 1947; see also Alexander, 1981; Baum and Lechner, 1981).

able to cope with its problems. In contrast, in Marxian theory social change leads to the eventual destruction of capitalist society. For this reason, among others, Parsons is often thought of as a very conservative sociological theorist. In addition, while he did deal with change, he tended to focus on the positive aspects of social change in the modern world rather than on its negative side.

Next, Parsons argued that the process of differentiation leads to a new set of problems of *integration* for society. As subsystems proliferate, the society is confronted with new problems in coordinating the operations of these units.

A society undergoing evolution must move from a system of ascription to one of achievement. A wider array of skills and abilities is needed to handle the more diffuse subsystems. The generalized abilities of people must be freed from their ascriptive bonds so that they can be utilized by society. Most generally, this means that groups formerly excluded from contributing to the system must be freed for inclusion as full members of the society.

Finally, the *value* system of the society as a whole must undergo change as social structures and functions grow increasingly differentiated. However, since the new system is more diverse, it is harder for the value system to encompass it. Thus a more differentiated society requires a value system that is "couched at a higher level of generality in order to legitimize the wider variety of goals and functions of its subunits" (Parsons, 1966:23). However, this process of generalization of values often does not proceed smoothly as it meets resistance from groups committed to their own narrow value systems.

Evolution proceeds through a variety of cycles, but no general process affects all societies equally. Some societies may foster evolution, whereas others may "be so beset with internal conflicts or other handicaps" that they impede the process of evolution, or they may even "deteriorate" (Parsons, 1966:23). What most interested Parsons were those societies in which developmental "breakthroughs" occur, since he believed that once they occurred, the process of evolution would follow his general evolutionary model.

Although Parsons conceived of evolution as occurring in stages, he was careful to avoid a unilinear evolutionary theory: "We do not conceive societal evolution to be either a continuous or a simple linear process, but we can distinguish between broad levels of advancement without overlooking the considerable variability found in each" (1966:26). Making it clear that he was simplifying matters, Parsons distinguished three broad evolutionary stages—primitive, intermediate, and modern. Characteristically, he differentiated among these stages primarily on the basis of cultural dimensions. The crucial development in the transition from primitive to intermediate is the development of language, primarily written language. The key development in the shift from intermediate to modern is "the institutionalized codes of normative order," or law (Parsons, 1966:26).

Parsons next proceeded to analyze a series of specific societies in the context of the evolution from primitive to modern society. One particular point is worth underscoring here: Parsons turned to evolutionary theory, at least in part, because he was accused of being unable to deal with social change. However, his analysis of evolution is *not* in terms of process; rather, it is an attempt to "order structural types and relate them sequentially" (Parsons, 1966:111). This is comparative *structural* analysis, not really a study of the processes of social change. Thus, even when he was supposed to be looking at change, Parsons remained committed to the study of structures and functions.

Generalized Media of Interchange   One of the ways in which Parsons introduces some dynamism, some fluidity (Alexander, 1983:115) into his theoretical system is through his ideas on the generalized media of interchange within and among the four action systems (especially within the social system) discussed above. The model for the generalized media of interchange is money, which operates as such a medium within the economy. But instead of focusing on material phenomena such as money, Parsons focuses on *symbolic* media of exchange. Even when Parsons does discuss money as a medium of interchange within the social system, he focuses on its symbolic rather than its material qualities. In addition to money, and more clearly symbolic, are other generalized media of interchange—political power, influence, and value commitments. Parsons makes it quite clear why he is focusing on symbolic media of interchange: "The introduction of a theory of media into the kind of structural perspective I have in mind goes far, it seems to me, to refute the frequent allegations that this type of structural analysis is inherently plagued with a static bias, which makes it impossible to do justice to dynamic problems" (1975:98–99).

Symbolic media of interchange have the capacity, like money, to be created and to circulate in the larger society. Thus, within the social system, those in the political system are able to create political power. More importantly, they can expend that power, thereby allowing it to circulate freely in, and have influence over, the social system. Through such an expenditure of power, leaders presumably strengthen the political system as well as the society as a whole. More generally, it is the generalized media that circulate between the four action systems and within the structures of each of those systems. It is their existence and movement that gives dynamism to Parsons's largely structural analyses.

As Alexander (1983:115) points out, generalized media of interchange lend dynamism to Parsons's theory in another sense. They allow for the existence of "media entrepreneurs" (for example, politicians) who do not simply accept the system of exchange as it is. That is, they can be creative and resourceful and in this way alter not only the quantity of the generalized media but also the manner and direction in which the media flow.

Robert Merton's Structural Functionalism

While Talcott Parsons is the most important structural-functional theorist, his student Robert Merton authored some of the most important statements on structural functionalism in sociology (Sztompka, forthcoming; Tiryakian, 1991). Merton criticized some of the more extreme and indefensible aspects of structural functionalism. But equally important, his new conceptual insights helped to give structural functionalism a continuing usefulness.

Although both Merton and Parsons are associated with structural functionalism, there are important differences between them. For one thing, while Parsons advocated the creation of grand, overarching theories, Merton favored more limited, middle-range theories. For another, Merton was more favorable toward Marxian theories than Parsons was. In fact, Merton and some of his students (especially Alvin Gouldner) can be seen as having pushed structural functionalism more to the left politically.

A Structural-Functional Model   Merton criticized what he saw as the three basic postulates of functional analysis as it was developed by anthropologists such as Malinowski and Radcliffe-Brown. The first is the postulate of the functional unity of society. This postulate holds that all standardized social and cultural beliefs and practices are functional for society as a whole as well as for individuals in society. This view implies that the various parts of a social system must show a high level of integration. However, Merton maintained that although it may be true of small, primitive societies, the generalization cannot be extended to larger, more complex societies.

Universal functionalism is the second postulate. That is, it is argued that *all* standardized social and cultural forms and structures have positive functions. Merton argued that this contradicts what we find in the real world. It is clear that not every structure, custom, idea, belief, and so forth has positive functions. For example, rabid nationalism can be highly dysfunctional in a world of proliferating nuclear arms.

Third is the postulate of indispensability. The argument here is that all standardized aspects of society not only have positive functions but also represent indispensable parts of the working whole. This postulate leads to the idea that all structures and functions are functionally necessary for society. No other structures and functions could work quite as well as those that are currently found within society. Merton's criticism, following Parsons, was that we must at least be willing to admit that there are various structural and functional alternatives to be found within society.

Merton's position was that all these functional postulates rely on nonempirical assertions based on abstract, theoretical systems. At a minimum, it is the responsibility of the sociologist to examine each empirically. Merton's belief that empirical tests, not theoretical assertions, are crucial to functional analysis led him to develop his "paradigm" of functional analysis as a guide to the integration of theory and research.

Merton made it clear from the outset that structural-functional analysis focuses on groups, organizations, societies, and cultures. He stated that any object that can be subjected to structural-functional analysis must "represent a standardized (that is, patterned and repetitive) item" (Merton, 1949/1968:104). He had in mind such things as "social roles, institutional patterns, social processes, cultural patterns, culturally patterned emotions, social norms, group organization, social structure, devices for social control, etc." (Merton, 1949/1968:104).

Early structural functionalists tended to focus almost entirely on the *functions* of one social structure or institution for another. However, in Merton's view, early analysts tended to confuse the subjective motives of individuals with the functions of structures or institutions. The focus of the structural functionalist should be on social functions rather than on individual motives. *Functions,* according to Merton, are defined as "those observed consequences which make for the adaptation or adjustment of a given system" (1949/1968:105). However, there is a clear ideological bias when one focuses only on adaptation or adjustment, for they are always positive consequences. It is important to note that one social fact can have negative consequences for another social fact. To rectify this serious omission in early structural functionalism, Merton developed the idea of a *dysfunction*. Just as structures or institutions could contribute to the maintenance of other parts of the social system, they also could have negative consequences for them. Slavery in the southern United States, for example, clearly had positive consequences for white southerners, such as supplying cheap labor, support for the cotton economy, and social status. It also had dysfunctions, such as making southerners overly dependent on an agrarian economy and therefore unprepared for industrialization. The lingering disparity between the North and the South in industrialization can be traced, at least in part, to the dysfunctions of the institution of slavery in the South.

Merton also posited the idea of *nonfunctions,* which he defined as consequences that are simply irrelevant to the system under consideration. Included here might be social forms that are "survivals" from earlier historical times. Although they may have had positive or negative consequences in the past, they have no significant effect on contemporary society. One example, although a few might disagree, is the Women's Christian Temperance Movement.

To help answer the question of whether positive functions outweigh dysfunctions, or vice versa, Merton developed the concept of *net balance.* However, we never can simply add up positive functions and dysfunctions and objectively determine which outweighs the other, because the issues are so complex and based on so much subjective judgment that they cannot easily be calculated and weighed. The usefulness of Merton's concept comes from the way it orients the sociologist to the question of relative significance. To return to the example of slavery, the question becomes whether, on balance, slavery was more functional or dysfunctional to the South. Still, this question is too broad and obscures a number of issues (for example, that slavery was functional for groups like white slaveholders).

To cope with problems like these, Merton added the idea that there must be *levels of functional analysis.* Functionalists had generally restricted themselves to analysis of the society as a whole, but Merton made it clear that analysis also could be done on an organization, institution, or group. Returning to the issue of the functions of slavery for the South, it would be necessary to differentiate several levels of analysis and ask about the functions and dysfunctions of slavery for black families, white families, black political organizations, white political organizations, and so forth. In terms of net balance, slavery was probably more functional for certain social units and more dysfunctional for other social units. Addressing the issue at these more specific levels helps in analyzing the functionality of slavery for the South as a whole.

Merton also introduced the concepts of *manifest* and *latent* functions. These two terms have also been important additions to functional analysis.[8] In simple terms,

---

[8]Colin Campbell (1982) has criticized Merton's distinction between manifest and latent functions. Among other things, he points out that Merton is vague about these terms and uses them in various ways (for example, as intended versus actual consequences and as surface meanings versus underlying realities). More important, he feels that Merton (like Parsons) never adequately integrated action theory and structural functionalism. The result is that we have an uncomfortable mixture of the intentionality ("manifest") of action theory and the structural consequences ("functions") of structural functionalism. Because of these and other confusions, Campbell believes, Merton's distinction between manifest and latent functions is little used in contemporary sociology.

manifest functions are those that are intended, whereas *latent functions* are unintended. The manifest function of slavery, for example, was to increase the economic productivity of the South, but it had the latent function of providing a vast underclass that served to increase the social status of southern whites, both rich and poor. This idea is related to another of Merton's concepts— *unanticipated consequences.* Actions have both intended and unintended consequences. Although everyone is aware of the intended consequences, sociological analysis is required to uncover the unintended consequences; indeed, to some this is the very essence of sociology. Peter Berger (1963) has called this "debunking," or looking beyond stated intentions to real effects.

Merton made it clear that unanticipated consequences and latent functions are not the same. A latent function is one type of unanticipated consequence, one that is functional for the designated system. But there are two other types of unanticipated consequences: "those that are dysfunctional for a designated system, and these comprise the latent dysfunctions," and "those which are irrelevant to the system which they affect neither functionally or dysfunctionally . . . non-functional consequences" (Merton, 1949/1968:105).

As further clarification of functional theory, Merton pointed out that a structure may be dysfunctional for the system as a whole and yet may continue to exist. One might make a good case that discrimination against blacks, females, and other minority groups is dysfunctional for American society, yet it continues to exist because it is functional for a part of the social system; for example, discrimination against females is generally functional for males. However, these forms of discrimination are not without some dysfunctions, even for the group for which they are functional. Males do suffer from their discrimination against females; similarly, whites are hurt by their discriminatory behavior toward blacks. One could argue that these forms of discrimination adversely affect those who discriminate by keeping vast numbers of people underproductive and by increasing the likelihood of social conflict.

Merton contended that not all structures are indispensable to the workings of the social system. Some parts of our social system *can* be eliminated. This helps functional theory overcome another of its conservative biases. By recognizing that some structures are expendable, functionalism opens the way for meaningful social change. Our society, for example, could continue to exist (and even be improved) by the elimination of discrimination against various minority groups.

Merton's clarifications are of great utility to sociologists (for example, Gans, 1972, 1994) who wish to perform structural-functional analyses.

Social Structure and Anomie   Before leaving this section, we must devote some attention to one of the best-known contributions to structural functionalism, indeed all of sociology (Adler and Laufer, 1995; Merton, 1995; Menard, 1995)—Merton's (1968) analysis of the relationship between culture, structure, and anomie. Merton defines *culture* as "that organized set of *normative values* governing behavior which is common to members of a designated society or group" and *social structure* as "that organized set of *social relationships* in which members of the society or group are variously implicated" (1968:216; italics added). Anomie occurs "when there is an acute disjunction between the cultural norms and goals and the socially structured capacities of members of the group to act in accord with them" (Merton, 1968:216). That is, because of their position

ROBERT K. MERTON: An Autobiographical Sketch*

It is easy enough to identify the principal teachers, both close at hand and at a distance, who taught me most. During my graduate studies, they were: P. A. Sorokin, who oriented me more widely to European social thought and with whom, unlike some other students of the time, I never broke although I could not follow him in the directions of inquiry he began to pursue in the late 1930s; the then quite young Talcott Parsons, engaged in thinking through the ideas which first culminated in his magisterial *Structure of Social Action;* the biochemist and sometime sociologist L. J. Henderson, who taught me something about the disciplined investigation of what is first entertained as an interesting idea; the economic historian E. F. Gay, who taught me about the workings of economic development as reconstructible from archival sources; and, quite consequentially, the then dean of the history of science, George Sarton, who allowed me to work under his guidance for several years in his famed (not to say, hallowed) workshop in the Widener Library of Harvard.   Beyond these teachers with whom I studied directly, I learned most from two sociologists: Emile Durkheim, above all others, and Georg Simmel, who could teach me only through the powerful works they left behind, and from that sociologically sensitive humanist, Gilbert Murray.   During the latter period of my life, I learned most from my colleague, Paul F. Lazarsfeld, who probably had no idea of how much he taught me during our uncountable conversations and collaborations during more than a third of a century.

Looking back over my work through the years, I find more of a pattern in it than I had supposed was there.   For almost from the beginning of my own work, after those apprenticeship years as a graduate student, I was determined to follow my intellectual interests as they evolved rather than pursue a predetermined lifelong plan.   I chose to adopt the practice of my master-at-a-distance, Durkheim, rather than the practice of my master-at-close-range, Sarton.   Durkheim repeatedly changed the subjects he chose to investigate.   Starting with his study of the social division of labor, he examined methods of sociological inquiry and then turned successively to the seemingly unrelated subjects of suicide, religion, moral education, and socialism, all the while developing a theoretical orientation which, to his mind, could be effectively developed by attending to such varied aspects of life in society.   Sarton had proceeded quite the other way: in his earliest years as a scholar, he had worked out a program of research in the history of science that was to culminate in his monumental five-volume *Introduction* [sic] *to the History of Science* (which carried the story through to the close of the fourteenth century!).

The first of these patterns seemed more suitable for me.   I wanted and still want to advance sociological theories of social structure and cultural change that will help us understand how social institutions and the character of life in society come to be as they are.   That concern with theoretical sociology has led me to avoid the kind of subject specialization that

in the social structure of society, some people are unable to act in accord with normative values.   The culture calls for some type of behavior that the social structure prevents from occurring.

For example, in American society, the culture places great emphasis on material success.   However, by their position within the social structure, many people are prevented has become (and, in my opinion, has for the most part rightly become) the order of the day in sociology, as in other evolving disciplines. For my purposes, study of a variety of sociological subjects was essential.

In that variety, only one special field—the sociology of science—has persistently engaged my interest. During the 1930s, I devoted myself almost entirely to the social contexts of science and technology, especially in seventeenth-century England, and focused on the unanticipated consequences of purposive social action. As my theoretical interests broadened, I turned, during the 1940s and afterward, to studies of the social sources of nonconforming and deviant behavior, of the workings of bureaucracy, mass persuasion, and communication in modern complex society, and to the role of the intellectual, both within bureaucracies and outside them. In the 1950s, I centered on developing a sociological theory of basic units of social structure: the role-set and status-set and the role models people select not only for emulation but also as a source of values adopted as a basis for self-appraisal (this latter being "the theory of reference groups"). I also undertook, with George Reader and Patricia Kendall, the first large-scale sociological study of medical education, aiming to find out how, all apart from explicit plan, different kinds of physicians are socialized in the same schools of medicine, this being linked with the distinctive character of professions as a type of occupational activity. In the 1960s and 1970s, I returned to an intensive study of the social structure of science and its interaction with cognitive structure, these two decades being the time in which the sociology of science finally came of age, with what's past being only prologue. Throughout these studies, my primary orientation was toward the connections between sociological theory, methods of inquiry, and substantive empirical research.

I group these developing interests by decades only for convenience. Of course, they did not neatly come and go in accord with such conventional divisions of the calendar. Nor did all of them go, after the first period of intensive work on them. I am at work on a volume centered on the unanticipated consequences of purposive social action, thus following up a paper first published almost half a century ago and intermittently developed since. Another volume in the stocks, entitled *The Self-Fulfilling Prophecy,* follows out in a half-dozen spheres of social life the workings of this pattern as first noted in my paper by the same title, a mere third of a century ago. And should time, patience, and capacity allow, there remains the summation of work on the analysis of social structure, with special reference to status-sets, role-sets, and structural contexts on the structural side, and manifest and latent functions, dysfunctions, functional alternatives, and social mechanisms on the functional side.

Mortality being the rule and painfully slow composition being my practice, there seems small point in looking beyond this series of works in progress.

(For more on Merton, see Schultz, 1995.)

from achieving such success. If one is born into the lower socioeconomic classes and as a result is able to acquire, at best, only a high school degree, then one's chances of achieving economic success in the generally accepted way (for example, through succeeding in the conventional work world) are slim or nonexistent. Under such circumstances (and they are widespread in contemporary American society) anomie can be said to exist, and as a result, there is a tendency toward deviant behavior. In this context, deviance often takes the form of alternative, unacceptable, and sometimes illegal means of achieving economic success. Thus, becoming a drug dealer or a prostitute in order to achieve economic success is an example of deviance generated by the disjunction between cultural values and social-structural means of attaining those values. This is one way in which the structural functionalist would seek to explain crime and deviance.

Thus, in this example of structural functionalism, Merton is looking at social (and cultural) structures, but he is not focally concerned with the functions of those structures. Rather, consistent with his functional paradigm, he is mainly concerned with dysfunctions, in this case anomie. More specifically, as we have seen, Merton links anomie with deviance and thereby is arguing that disjunctions between culture and structure have the dysfunctional consequence of leading to deviance within society.

It is worth noting that implied in Merton's work on anomie is a critical attitude toward social stratification (for example, for blocking the means of some to socially desirable goals). Thus, while Davis and Moore wrote approvingly of a stratified society, Merton's work indicates that structural functionalists can be critical of social stratification.

The Major Criticisms

No single sociological theory in the history of the discipline has been the focus of as much interest as structural functionalism. From the late 1930s to early 1960s, it was virtually unchallenged as the dominant sociological theory in the United States. By the 1960s, however, criticisms of the theory had increased dramatically and ultimately became more prevalent than praise. Mark Abrahamson depicted this situation quite vividly: "Thus, metaphorically, functionalism has ambled along like a giant elephant, ignoring the stings of gnats, even as the swarm of attackers takes its toll" (1978:37).

Substantive Criticisms   One major criticism is that structural functionalism does not deal adequately with history—that it is inherently ahistorical. In fact, structural functionalism was developed, at least in part, in reaction to the historical evolutionary approach of certain anthropologists. Many of the early anthropologists were seen as describing the various stages in the evolution of a given society or society in general. Frequently, depictions of the early stages were highly speculative. Furthermore, the later stages were often little more than idealizations of the society in which the anthropologist lived. Early structural functionalists were seeking to overcome the speculative character and ethnocentric biases of these works. In its early years in particular, structural functionalism went too far in its criticism of evolutionary theory and came to focus on either contemporary or abstract societies. However, structural functionalism need not be ahistorical (Turner and Maryanski, 1979). Although practitioners have tended to operate as if it were ahistorical, nothing in the theory prevents them from dealing with historical issues. In fact, Parsons's (1966, 1971) work on social change, as we have seen, reflects the ability of structural functionalists to deal with change if they so wish.

Structural functionalists also are attacked for being unable to deal effectively with the *process* of social change (Abrahamson, 1978; P. Cohen, 1968; Mills, 1959; Turner and Maryanski, 1979). Whereas the preceding criticism deals with the seeming inability of structural functionalism to deal with the past, this one is concerned with the parallel incapacity of the approach to deal with the contemporary process of social change. Structural functionalism is far more likely to deal with static structures than with change processes. Percy Cohen (1968) sees the problem as lying in structural-functional theory, in which all the elements of a society are seen as reinforcing one another as well as the system as a whole. This makes it difficult to see how these elements can also contribute to change. While Cohen sees the problem as inherent in the theory, Turner and Maryanski believe, again, that the problem lies with the practitioners and not with the theory.

In the view of Turner and Maryanski, structural functionalists frequently do not address the issue of change, and even when they do, it is in developmental rather than revolutionary terms. However, according to them, there is no reason why structural functionalists could not deal with social change. Whether the problem has to do with the theory or with the theorists, the fact remains that the main contributions of structural functionalists lie in the study of static, not changing, social structures.[9]

Perhaps the most often voiced criticism of structural functionalism is that it is unable to deal effectively with conflict (Abrahamson, 1978; P. Cohen, 1968; Gouldner, 1970; Horowitz, 1962/1967; Mills, 1959; Turner and Maryanski, 1979).[10] This criticism takes a variety of forms. Alvin Gouldner argues that Parsons, as the main representative of structural functionalism, tended to overemphasize harmonious relationships. Irving Louis Horowitz contends that structural functionalists tend to see conflict as necessarily destructive and as occurring outside the framework of society. Most generally, Abrahamson argues that structural functionalism exaggerates societal consensus, stability, and integration and, conversely, tends to disregard conflict, disorder, and change. The issue once again is whether this is inherent in the theory or in the way that practitioners have interpreted and used it (P. Cohen, 1968; Turner and Maryanski, 1979). Whatever one's position, it is clear that structural functionalism has had relatively little to offer on the issue of social conflict.

The overall criticisms that structural functionalism is unable to deal with history, change, and conflict have led many (for example, P. Cohen, 1968; Gouldner, 1970) to argue that structural functionalism has a conservative bias. As Gouldner vividly puts it in his criticism of Parsons's structural functionalism: "Parsons persistently sees the partly filled glass of water as half *full* rather than half *empty*" (1970:290). One who sees a glass as half full is emphasizing the positive aspects of a situation, whereas one who sees it as half empty is focusing on the negative side. To put this in social terms, a conservative structural functionalist would emphasize the economic advantages of living in our society rather than its disadvantages.

It may indeed be true that there is a conservative bias in structural functionalism that is attributable not only to what it ignores (change, history, conflict) but also to what it chooses to focus on. For one thing, structural functionalists have tended to focus on

---

[9]However, there are some important works on social change by structural functionalists (C. Johnson, 1966; Smelser, 1959, 1962).

[10]Again, there are important exceptions—see Coser (1956, 1967), Goode (1960), and Merton (1975).

culture, norms, and values (P. Cohen, 1968; Mills, 1959; Lockwood, 1956). David Lockwood (1956), for example, is critical of Parsons for his preoccupation with the normative order of society. More generally, Percy Cohen (1968) argues that structural functionalists focus on normative elements, although this focus is not inherent in the theory. Crucial to structural functionalism's focus on cultural and societal factors and what leads to the theory's conservative orientation is a passive sense of the individual actor. People are seen as constrained by cultural and social forces. Structural functionalists (for example, Parsons) lack a dynamic, creative sense of the actor. As Gouldner says, to emphasize his criticism of structural functionalism, "Human beings are as much engaged in using social systems as in being used by them" (1970:220).

Related to their cultural focus is the tendency of structural functionalists to mistake the legitimizations employed by elites in society for social reality (Gouldner, 1970; Horowitz, 1962/1967; Mills, 1959). The normative system is interpreted as reflective of the society as a whole, when it may in fact be better viewed as an ideological system promulgated by, and existing for, the elite members of society. Horowitz enunciates this position quite explicitly: "Consensus theory . . . tends to become a metaphysical representation of the dominant ideological matrix" (1962/1967:270).

These substantive criticisms point in two basic directions. First, it seems clear that structural functionalism has a rather narrow focus that prevents it from addressing a number of important issues and aspects of the social world. Second, its focus tends to give it a very conservative flavor; in practice in the past, and to some degree still, structural functionalism has operated in support of the status quo and dominant elites (Huaco, 1986).

Methodological and Logical Criticisms   One of the often expressed criticisms (see, for example, Abrahamson, 1978; Mills, 1959) is that structural functionalism is basically vague, unclear, and ambiguous. For example: What exactly is a structure? A function? A social system? How are parts of social systems related to each other as well as to the larger social system? Part of the ambiguity is traceable to the fact that structural functionalists choose to deal with abstract social systems instead of real societies.

A related criticism is that, although no single grand scheme ever can be used to analyze all societies throughout history (Mills, 1959), structural functionalists have been motivated by the belief that there is a single theory or at least a set of conceptual categories that could be used to do this. Many critics regard this grand theory as an illusion, believing that the best sociology can hope for is more historically specific, "middle-range" (Merton, 1968) theories.

Among the other specific methodological criticisms is the issue of whether there exist adequate methods to study the questions of concern to structural functionalists. Percy Cohen (1968), for instance, wonders what tools can be used to study the contribution of one part of a system to the system as a whole. Another methodological criticism is that structural functionalism makes comparative analysis difficult. If the assumption is that part of a system makes sense only in the context of the social system in which it exists, how can we compare it with a similar part in another system? Cohen asks, for example: If the English family makes sense only in the context of English society, how can we compare it to the French family?

Teleology and Tautology   Percy Cohen (1968) and Turner and Maryanski (1979) see teleology and tautology as the two most important logical problems confronting structural functionalism. Some tend to see teleology as an inherent problem (Abrahamson, 1978; P. Cohen, 1968), but I believe that Turner and Maryanski (1979) are correct when they argue that the problem with structural functionalism is not teleology per se, but *illegitimate* teleology. In this context, *teleology* is defined as the view that society (or other social structures) has purposes or goals. In order to achieve these goals, society creates, or causes to be created, specific social structures and social institutions. Turner and Maryanski do not see this view as necessarily illegitimate; in fact, they argue that social theory *should* take into account the teleological relationship between society and its component parts.

The problem, to Turner and Maryanski, is the extension of teleology to unacceptable lengths. An illegitimate teleology is one that implies "that purpose or end states guide human affairs when such is not the case" (Turner and Maryanski, 1979:118). For example, it is illegitimate to assume that because society needs procreation and socialization it will create the family institution. A variety of alternative structures could meet these needs; society does not "need" to create the family. The structural functionalist must define and document the various ways in which the goals do, in fact, lead to the creation of specific substructures. It also would be useful to be able to show why other substructures could not meet the same needs. A legitimate teleology would be able to define and demonstrate *empirically* and *theoretically* the links between society's goals and the various substructures that exist within society. An illegitimate teleology would be satisfied with a blind assertion that a link between a societal end and a specific substructure must exist. Turner and Maryanski admit that functionalism is often guilty of presenting illegitimate teleologies: "We can conclude that functional explanations often become illegitimate teleologies—a fact which seriously hampers functionalism's utility for understanding patterns of human organization" (1979:124).

The other major criticism of the logic of structural functionalism is that it is tautological. A *tautological* argument is one in which the conclusion merely makes explicit what is implicit in the premise or is simply a restatement of the premise. In structural functionalism, this circular reasoning often takes the form of defining the whole in terms of its parts and then defining the parts in terms of the whole. Thus, it would be argued that a social system is defined by the relationship among its component parts and that the component parts of the system are defined by their place in the larger social system. Because each is defined in terms of the other, neither the social system nor its parts are in fact defined at all. We really learn nothing about either the system or its parts. Structural functionalism has been particularly prone to tautologies, although there is some question about whether this propensity is inherent in the theory or simply characteristic of the way most structural functionalists have used, or misused, the theory.

NEOFUNCTIONALISM

Under the barrage of criticisms, structural functionalism declined in significance from the mid-1960s to the present day. However, by the mid-1980s, a major effort was undertaken to revive the theory under the heading "neofunctionalism." The term *neofunctionalism* was used to indicate continuity with structural functionalism but also to demonstrate that an effort was being made to extend structural functionalism and overcome its major difficulties. Jeffrey Alexander and Paul Colomy define *neofunctionalism* as "a self-critical strand of functional theory that seeks to broaden functionalism's intellectual scope while retaining its theoretical core" (1985:11). Thus, it seems clear that Alexander and Colomy see structural functionalism as overly narrow and that their goal is the creation of a more synthetic theory, which they prefer to label "neofunctionalism."[11]

It should be noted that while structural functionalism in general, and Talcott Parsons's theories in particular, did become extremist, there was a strong synthetic core in the theory from its beginnings. On the one hand, throughout his intellectual life Parsons sought to integrate a wide range of theoretical inputs. On the other, he was interested in the interrelationship of the major domains of the social world, most notably the cultural, social, and personality systems. However, in the end, Parsons adopted a narrow structural-functionalist orientation and came to see the cultural system as determining the other systems. Thus, Parsons abandoned his synthetic orientation, and neofunctionalism can be viewed as an effort to recapture such an orientation.

Alexander (1985a:10) has enumerated the problems associated with structural functionalism that neofunctionalism needs to surmount, including "anti-individualism," "antagonism to change," "conservatism," "idealism," and an "antiempirical bias." Efforts were made to overcome these problems programmatically (Alexander, 1985a) and at more specific theoretical levels, for example Colomy's (1986; Alexander and Colomy, 1990b; Colomy and Rhoades, 1994) attempt to refine differentiation theory.

Despite his enthusiasm for neofunctionalism, in the mid-1980s Alexander was forced to conclude that "neofunctionalism is a tendency rather than a developed theory" (1985a:16). Only five years after Alexander's confession of the weakness of neofunctionalism, Colomy sought to consolidate the general theoretical position of neofunctionalism and argued that it had already made enormous strides:

> In the ensuing five years that tendency has crystallized into a self-conscious intellectual movement. It has generated significant advances at the level of general theory and played a leading part in pushing sociological metatheory in a synthetic direction . . . neofunctionalism is delivering on its promissory notes. Today, neofunctionalism is more than a promise; it has become a field of intense theoretical discourse and growing empirical investigation.
>
> (Colomy, 1990b:xxx)

While there is no question that neofunctionalism had made some strides, it is doubtful that it was quite as far advanced as Colomy would have had us believe.

Although neofunctionalism may not be a developed theory, Alexander (1985a; see also Colomy, 1990b) has outlined some of its basic orientations. First, neofunctionalism operates with a descriptive model of society that sees society as composed of elements which, in interaction with one another, form a pattern. This pattern allows the system to be differentiated from its environment. Parts of the system are "symbiotically con-

---

[11]Turner and Maryanski (1988a) have challenged neofunctionalism by arguing that it is not really functional in its orientation, since it has abandoned many of the basic tenets of structural functionalism.

nected," and their interaction is not determined by some overarching force. Thus, neofunctionalism rejects any monocausal determinism and is open-ended and pluralistic.

Second, Alexander argues that neofunctionalism devotes roughly equal attention to action and order. It thus avoids the tendency of structural functionalism to focus almost exclusively on the macro-level sources of order in social structures and culture and to give little attention to more micro-level action patterns (Schwinn, 1998). Neofunctionalism also purports to have a broad sense of action, including not only rational but also expressive action.

Third, neofunctionalism retains the structural-functional interest in integration, *not* as an accomplished fact but rather as a social *possibility!* It recognizes that deviance and social control are realities within social systems. There is concern for equilibrium within neofunctionalism, but it is broader than the structural-functional concern encompassing both moving and partial equilibrium. There is a disinclination to see social systems as characterized by static equilibrium. *Equilibrium,* broadly defined, is seen as a reference point for functional analysis but not as descriptive of the lives of individuals in actual social systems.

Fourth, neofunctionalism accepts the traditional Parsonsian emphasis on personality, culture, and social system. In addition to being vital to social structure, the interpenetration of these systems also produces tension that is an ongoing source of both change and control.

Fifth, neofunctionalism focuses on social change in the processes of differentiation within the social, cultural, and personality systems. Thus, change is not productive of conformity and harmony but rather "individuation and institutional strains" (Alexander, 1985a:10).

Finally, Alexander argues that neofunctionalism "implies the commitment to the independence of conceptualization and theorizing from other levels of sociological analysis" (1985a:10).

Alexander and Colomy (1990a) staked out a very ambitious claim for neofunctionalism. They did not see neofunctionalism as, in their terms, a mere modest "elaboration," or "revision," of structural functionalism but rather as a much more dramatic "reconstruction" of it in which differences with the founder (Parsons) are clearly acknowledged and explicit openings are made to other theorists and theories.[12] Efforts were made to integrate into neofunctionalism insights from the masters, such as Marx's work on material structures and Durkheim's on symbolism. In an attempt to overcome the idealist bias of Parsonsian structural functionalism, especially its emphasis on macrosubjective phenomena like culture, more materialist approaches were encouraged. The structural-functional tendency to emphasize order was countered by a call for rapprochement with theories of social change. Most important, to compensate for the macro-level biases of traditional structural functionalism, efforts were made to integrate ideas from exchange theory, symbolic interactionism, pragmatism, phenomenology, and so on. In other words, Alexander and Colomy endeavored to synthesize structural functionalism with a number of other theoretical traditions. Such a reconstruction was

---

[12]This view seems to be in accord, at least partially, with Turner and Maryanski's (1988a) claim that neofunctionalism has little in common with structural functionalism.

JEFFREY C. ALEXANDER: An Autobiographical Sketch

Since my earliest days as an intellectual I have been preoccupied with the problems of social action and social order and with the possibilities of developing approaches to these problems that avoid the extremes of one-dimensional thought. I have always been convinced that tense dichotomies, while vital as ideological currents in a democratic society, can be overcome in the theoretical realm.

My theoretical concerns first took form during the late 1960s and early 1970s, when I participated in the student protest movements as an undergraduate at Harvard College and as a graduate student at the University of California, Berkeley. New Left Marxism represented a sophisticated effort to overcome the economism of vulgar Marxism, as it tried to reinsert the actor into history. Because it described how material structures are interpenetrated with culture, personality, and everyday life, New Left Marxism—which for better or worse we largely taught ourselves—provided my first important training in the path to theoretical synthesis, which has marked my intellectual career.

In the early 1970s, I became dissatisfied with New Left Marxism, in part for political and empirical reasons. The New Left's turn toward sectarianism and violence frightened and depressed me, whereas the Watergate crisis demonstrated America's capacity for self-criticism. I decided that capitalist democratic societies provided opportunities for inclusion, pluralism, and reform that could not be envisioned even within the New Left version of Marxian thought.

Yet there were also more abstract theoretical reasons for leaving the Marxian approach to synthesis behind. As I more fully engaged classical and contemporary theory, I realized that this synthesis was achieved more by hyphenating—psychoanalytic-Marxism, cultural-Marxism, phenomenological-Marxism—than by opening up the central categories of action and order. In fact, the neo-Marxist categories of consciousness, action, community, and culture were black boxes. This recognition led me to the traditions which supplied the theoretical resources upon which New Left Marxism had drawn. I was fortunate in this graduate student effort to be guided by Robert Bellah and Neil Smelser, whose ideas about culture, social structure, and sociological theory made an indelible impression upon me and continue to be intellectual resources today.

In *Theoretical Logic in Sociology* (1982–83), I published the results of this effort. The idea for this multivolume work began germinating in 1972, after an extraordinary encounter with Talcott Parsons's masterpiece, *The Structure of Social Action,* allowed me to see my problems with Marxism in a new way. Later, under the supervision of Bellah, Smelser, and Leo Lowenthal, I worked through classical and contemporary theory with this new framework in mind.

supposed to both revive structural functionalism and provide the base for the development of a new theoretical tradition.

Alexander and Colomy recognized an important difference between neofunctionalism and structural functionalism:

Earlier functional research was guided by . . . envisioning a single, all embracing conceptual scheme that tied areas of specialized research into a tightly wrought package. What neofunctionalist empirical work points to, by contrast, is a loosely organized

My ambition in *Theoretical Logic* was to show that Durkheim and Weber supplied extensive theories of the culture that Marx had neglected and that Weber actually developed the first real sociological synthesis. I concluded, however, that Durkheim ultimately moved in an idealistic direction and that Weber developed a mechanistic view of modern society. I suggested that Parsons's work should be seen as a masterly modern effort at synthesis rather than as theory in the functionalist mode. Yet Parsons, too, failed to pursue synthesis in a truly determined way, allowing his theory to become overly formal and normatively based.

In my work over the last decade I have tried to re-create the framework for synthesis which I take to be the unfulfilled promise of earlier work. In *Twenty Lectures: Sociological Theory Since World War II* (1987), I argued that the divisions in post-Parsonsian sociology—between conflict and order theories, micro and macro approaches, structural and cultural views—were not fruitful. These groupings obscured basic social processes, like the continuing play of order and conflict and the dichotomized dimensions of society, that are always intertwined.

My response to this dead end has been to return to the original concerns of Parsons (Alexander, 1985b; Alexander and Colomy, 1990a) and to the earlier classics (Alexander, 1988a).

Yet, in trying to push theory into a new, "post-Parsonsian" phase, I have also tried to go beyond classical and modern theory. My encounters with the powerful group of phenomenologists in my home department at UCLA, particularly those with Harold Garfinkel, were an important stimulus. In "Action and Its Environments" (1987), which I still regard as my most important piece of theoretical work, I laid out the framework for a new articulation of the micro-macro link.

I have also concentrated on developing a new cultural theory. An early reading of Clifford Geertz convinced me that traditional social-science approaches to culture are too limited. Since that time, my approach has been powerfully affected by semiotics, hermeneutics, and poststructuralist thought. Incorporating theories from outside of sociology, I have tried to theorize the manifold ways in which social structure is permeated by symbolic codes and meanings (see Alexander, 1988a).

I believe this movement toward theoretical synthesis is being pushed forward by events in the world at large. In the postcommunist world, it seems important to develop models that help us understand our complex and inclusive, yet very fragile, democracies. I am presently at work on a theory of democracy that emphasizes the communal dimension which I call "civil society." I am also publishing a collection of essays which I have written criticizing the growing relativism in the human studies. I would like to believe, despite a great deal of evidence to the contrary, that progress is possible not only in society but in sociology as well. It is only through a multidimensional and synthetic view of society that such progress can be achieved.

package, one organized around a general logic and possessing a number of rather autonomous "proliferations" and "variations" at different levels and in different empirical domains.

(Alexander and Colomy, 1990a:52)

The thoughts of Alexander and Colomy indicate movement away from the Parsonsian tendency to see structural functionalism as a grand overarching theory. Instead, they offer a more limited, a more synthetic, but still a holistic theory.

However, as pointed out in the beginning of this chapter, the future of neofunction-alism has been cast into doubt by the fact that its founder and leading exponent, Jeffrey Alexander, has made it clear that he has outgrown a neofunctionalist orientation. This shift in thinking is apparent in the title of his recent book, *Neofunctionalism and After* (Alexander, 1998a). Alexander argues in that work that one of his major goals was the (re)establishment of the legitimacy and importance of Parsonsian theory. To the degree that neofunctionalism has succeeded in this effort, Alexander regards the neofunction-alist project as completed. Thus, he is ready to move beyond Parsons, beyond neo-functionalism, although he makes it plain that his future theoretical directions will be deeply indebted to both. Neofunctionalism has grown too confining for Alexander, and he now sees it, as well as his own work, as part of what he has called "the new theo-retical movement." As he puts it, "I am pointing to a new wave of theory creation that goes beyond the important achievements of neofunctionalism" (Alexander, 1998a:228). Such a theoretical perspective would be even more synthetic than neo-functionalism, and more eclectic, drawing upon a wide range of theoretical resources, and it would use those synthetic and eclectic resources in more opportunistic ways. Specifically, Alexander is seeking to do much more with developments in microsocio-logical and cultural theory.

It is worth noting that Alexander (1998) has grown increasingly concerned with the issue of "civil society," even though this issue does not fall within the confines of neo-functionalism. Alexander's interest is important in itself, as well as for the fact that this issue is of growing concern in sociology in general (for example, see Cohen and Arato, 1992; Hearn, 1997; Seligman, 1993b). For our purposes, we can work with Alexander's (1993:797) definition of civil society as "the realm of interaction, institutions, and soli-darity that sustains the public life of societies outside the worlds of economy and state." Unlike most concerns of sociologists, the focus here is not on social institutions, but on what goes on outside these institutions. Civil society, for Alexander, encompasses an in-terest in both individual voluntarism and collective solidarity. Given the threats to both within the contemporary world, as well as the widespread failure of various institutions, the focus of many sociological theorists has shifted to a concern for civil society.

Although in its early stages, Alexander's thinking on civil society represents a sub-stantive focus beyond neofunctionalism. While he is clearly drawing on the structural-functional and neofunctional traditions, Alexander is also moving into new theoretical ground with his work on civil society. Whatever the fate of that work, Alexander's shift in direction leads one to question the future of neofunctionalism. Things move swiftly in contemporary sociology and it may be that what was a dramatic new movement only a decade ago is today becoming part of our near-history.

CONFLICT THEORY

Conflict theory can be seen as a development that took place, at least in part, in reaction to structural functionalism and as a result of many of the criticisms discussed earlier. However, it should be noted that conflict theory has various other roots, such as Marx-ian theory and Simmel's work on social conflict. In the 1950s and 1960s, conflict the-ory provided an alternative to structural functionalism, but it was superseded by a variety of neo-Marxian theories (see Chapter 4). Indeed, one of the major contributions of conflict theory was the way it laid the groundwork for theories more faithful to Marx's work, theories that came to attract a wide audience in sociology. The basic problem with conflict theory is that it never succeeded in divorcing itself sufficiently from its structural-functional roots. It was more a kind of structural functionalism turned on its head than a truly critical theory of society.

The Work of Ralf Dahrendorf

Like functionalists, conflict theorists are oriented toward the study of social structures and institutions. In the main, this theory is little more than a series of contentions that are often the direct opposites of functionalist positions. This antithesis is best exemplified by the work of Ralf Dahrendorf (1958, 1959), in which the tenets of conflict and functional theory are juxtaposed. To the functionalists, society is static or, at best, in a state of moving equilibrium, but to Dahrendorf and the conflict theorists, every society at every point is subject to processes of change. Where functionalists emphasize the orderliness of society, conflict theorists see dissension and conflict at every point in the social system. Functionalists (or at least early functionalists) argue that every element in society contributes to stability; the exponents of conflict theory see many societal elements contributing to disintegration and change.

Functionalists tend to see society as being held together informally by norms, values, and a common morality. Conflict theorists see whatever order there is in society as stemming from the coercion of some members by those at the top. Where functionalists focus on the cohesion created by shared societal values, conflict theorists emphasize the role of power in maintaining order in society.

Dahrendorf (1959, 1968) is the major exponent of the position that society has two faces (conflict and consensus) and that sociological theory therefore should be divided into two parts, conflict theory and consensus theory. Consensus theorists should examine value integration in society, and conflict theorists should examine conflicts of interest and the coercion that holds society together in the face of these stresses. Dahrendorf recognized that society could not exist without both conflict and consensus, which are prerequisites for each other. Thus, we cannot have conflict unless there is some prior consensus. For example, French housewives are highly unlikely to conflict with Chilean chess players because there is no contact between them, no prior integration to serve as a basis for a conflict. Conversely, conflict can lead to consensus and integration. An example is the alliance between the United States and Japan that developed after World War II.

Despite the interrelationship between consensus and conflict, Dahrendorf was not optimistic about developing a single sociological theory encompassing both processes: "It seems at least conceivable that unification of theory is not feasible at a point which has puzzled thinkers ever since the beginning of Western philosophy" (1959:164). Eschewing a singular theory, Dahrendorf set out to construct a conflict theory of society.[13]

---

[13]Dahrendorf called conflict and coercion "the ugly face of society" (1959:164). We can ponder whether a person who regards them as "ugly" can develop an adequate theory of conflict and coercion.

Dahrendorf began with, and was heavily influenced by, structural functionalism. He noted that to the functionalist, the social system is held together by voluntary cooperation or general consensus or both. However, to the conflict (or coercion) theorist, society is held together by "enforced constraint"; thus, some positions in society are delegated power and authority over others. This fact of social life led Dahrendorf to his central thesis that the differential distribution of authority "invariably becomes the determining factor of systematic social conflicts" (1959:165).

Authority   Dahrendorf concentrated on larger social structures.[14]   Central to his thesis is the idea that various positions within society have different amounts of authority. Authority does not reside in individuals but in positions. Dahrendorf was interested not only in the structure of these positions but also in the conflict among them: "The *structural* origin of such conflicts must be sought in the arrangement of social roles endowed with expectations of domination or subjection" (1959:165; italics added). The first task of conflict analysis, to Dahrendorf, was to identify various authority roles within society. In addition to making the case for the study of large-scale structures like authority roles, Dahrendorf was opposed to those who focus on the individual level. For example, he was critical of those who focus on the psychological or behavioral characteristics of the individuals who occupy such positions. He went so far as to say that those who adopted such an approach were not sociologists.

The authority attached to positions is the key element in Dahrendorf's analysis. Authority always implies both superordination and subordination. Those who occupy positions of authority are expected to control subordinates; that is, they dominate because of the expectations of those who surround them, not because of their own psychological characteristics. Like authority, these expectations are attached to positions, not people. Authority is not a generalized social phenomenon; those who are subject to control, as well as permissible spheres of control, are specified in society. Finally, because authority is legitimate, sanctions can be brought to bear against those who do not comply.

Authority is not a constant as far as Dahrendorf was concerned, because authority resides in positions and not persons. Thus, a person of authority in one setting does not necessarily hold a position of authority in another setting. Similarly, a person in a subordinate position in one group may be in a superordinate position in another. This follows from Dahrendorf's argument that society is composed of a number of units that he called *imperatively coordinated associations*. These may be seen as associations of people controlled by a hierarchy of authority positions. Since society contains many such associations, an individual can occupy a position of authority in one and a subordinate position in another.

Authority within each association is dichotomous; thus two, and only two, conflict groups can be formed within any association. Those in positions of authority and those in positions of subordination hold certain interests that are "contradictory in substance and direction." Here we encounter another key term in Dahrendorf's theory of

---

[14]In his other work, Dahrendorf (1968) continued to focus on social facts (for example, positions and roles), but he also manifested a concern for the dangers of reification endemic to such an approach.

conflict—*interests.* Groups on top and at the bottom are defined by common interests. Dahrendorf continued to be firm in his thinking that even these interests, which sound so psychological, are basically large-scale phenomena:

> For purposes of the sociological analysis of conflict groups and group conflicts, it is necessary to assume certain *structurally generated* orientations of the actions of incumbents of defined *positions.* By analogy to conscious ("subjective") orientations of action, it appears justifiable to describe these as interests. . . . The assumption of "objective" interests associated with social positions has *no psychological implications* or ramifications; it belongs to the level of sociological analysis proper.
>
> (Dahrendorf, 1959:175; italics added)

Within every association, those in dominant positions seek to maintain the status quo while those in subordinate positions seek change. A conflict of interest within any association is at least latent at all times, which means that the legitimacy of authority is *always* precarious. This conflict of interest need not be conscious in order for superordinates or subordinates to act. The interests of superordinates and subordinates are objective in the sense that they are reflected in the expectations (roles) attached to positions. Individuals do not have to internalize these expectations or even be conscious of them in order to act in accord with them. If they occupy given positions, then they will behave in the expected manner. Individuals are "adjusted" or "adapted" to their roles when they contribute to conflict between superordinates and subordinates. Dahrendorf called these unconscious role expectations *latent interests. Manifest interests* are latent interests that have become conscious. Dahrendorf saw the analysis of the connection between latent and manifest interests as a major task of conflict theory. Nevertheless, actors need not be conscious of their interests in order to act in accord with them.

Groups, Conflict, and Change   Next, Dahrendorf distinguished three broad types of groups. The first is the *quasi group,* or "aggregates of incumbents of positions with identical role interests" (Dahrendorf, 1959:180). These are the recruiting grounds for the second type of group—the *interest group.* Dahrendorf described the two groups:

> Common modes of behavior are characteristic of *interest groups* recruited from larger quasi-groups. Interest groups are groups in the strict sense of the sociological term; and they are the real agents of group conflict. They have a structure, a form of organization, a program or goal, and a personnel of members.
>
> (Dahrendorf, 1959:180)

Out of all the many interest groups emerge *conflict groups,* or those that actually engage in group conflict.

Dahrendorf felt that the concepts of latent and manifest interests, of quasi groups, interest groups, and conflict groups, were basic to an explanation of social conflict. Under *ideal* conditions no other variables would be needed. However, because conditions are never ideal, many different factors do intervene in the process. Dahrendorf mentioned technical conditions such as adequate personnel, political conditions such as the overall political climate, and social conditions such as the existence of communication links. The way people are recruited into the quasi group was another social condition important to Dahrendorf. He felt that if the recruitment is random and deter-mined by chance, then an interest group, and ultimately a conflict group, is unlikely to emerge. In contrast to Marx, Dahrendorf did not feel that the *lumpenproletariat*[15] would ultimately form a conflict group, because people are recruited to it by chance. However, when recruitment to quasi groups is structurally determined, these groups provide fertile recruiting grounds for interest groups and, in some cases, conflict groups.

The final aspect of Dahrendorf's conflict theory is the relationship of conflict to change. Here Dahrendorf recognized the importance of Lewis Coser's work (see the next section), which focused on the functions of conflict in maintaining the status quo. Dahrendorf felt, however, that the conservative function of conflict is only one part of social reality; conflict also leads to change and development.

Briefly, Dahrendorf argued that once conflict groups emerge, they engage in actions that lead to changes in social structure. When the conflict is intense, the changes that occur are radical. When it is accompanied by violence, structural change will be sud-den. Whatever the nature of conflict, sociologists must be attuned to the relationship be-tween conflict and change as well as that between conflict and the status quo.

The Major Criticisms and Efforts to Deal with Them

Conflict theory has been criticized on a variety of grounds. For example, it has been attacked for ignoring order and stability, whereas structural functionalism has been criticized for ignoring conflict and change. Conflict theory has also been criticized for being ideologically radical, whereas functionalism was criticized for its conservative ideology. In comparison to structural functionalism, conflict theory is rather underde-veloped. It is not nearly as sophisticated as functionalism, perhaps because it is a more derivative theory.

Dahrendorf's conflict theory has been subjected to a number of critical analyses (for example, Hazelrigg, 1972; J. Turner, 1973; Weingart, 1969), including some critical re-flections by Dahrendorf (1968) himself. First, Dahrendorf's model is not so clear a re-flection of Marxian ideas as he claimed. In fact, as we will see shortly, it constitutes an inadequate translation of Marxian theory into sociology. Second, as has been noted, conflict theory has more in common with structural functionalism than with Marxian theory. Dahrendorf's emphasis on such things as systems (imperatively coordinated as-sociations), positions, and roles links him directly to structural functionalism. As a re-sult, his theory suffers from many of the same inadequacies as structural functionalism. For example, conflict seems to emerge mysteriously from legitimate systems (just as it does in structural functionalism). Further, conflict theory seems to suffer from many of the same conceptual and logical problems (for example, vague concepts, tautologies) as structural functionalism (J. Turner, 1975, 1982). Finally, like structural functionalism, conflict theory is almost wholly macroscopic and as a result has little to offer to our un-derstanding of individual thought and action.

Both functionalism and Dahrendorf's conflict theory are inadequate, because each is itself useful for explaining only a *portion* of social life. Sociology must be able to

---

[15]This is Marx's term for the mass of people at the bottom of the economic system, those who stand below even the proletariat.

explain order as well as conflict, structure as well as change. This last fact has motivated several efforts to reconcile conflict and functional theory. Although none has been totally satisfactory, these efforts suggest at least some agreement among sociologists that what is needed is a theory explaining *both* consensus and dissension. Still, not all theorists seek to reconcile these conflicting perspectives. Dahrendorf, for example, saw them as alternative perspectives to be used situationally. According to Dahrendorf, when we are interested in conflict we should use conflict theory; when we wish to examine order, we should take a functional perspective. This position seems unsatisfactory, because there is a strong need for a theoretical perspective that enables us to deal with conflict and order *simultaneously*.

The criticisms of conflict theory and structural functionalism, as well as the inherent limitations in each, led to many efforts to cope with the problems by reconciling or integrating the two theories (Bailey, 1997; Chapin, 1994; van den Berghe, 1963; Himes, 1966). The assumption was that some combination of the two theories would be more powerful than either one alone. The best known of these works was Lewis Coser's *The Functions of Social Conflict* (1956).

The early seminal work on the functions of social conflict was done by Georg Simmel, but it has been expanded by Coser (Jaworski, 1991), who argued that conflict may serve to solidify a loosely structured group. In a society that seems to be disintegrating, conflict with another society may restore the integrative core. The cohesiveness of Israeli Jews might be attributed, at least in part, to the long-standing conflict with the Arab nations in the Middle East. The possible end of the conflict might well exacerbate underlying strains in Israeli society. Conflict as an agent for solidifying a society is an idea that has long been recognized by propagandists, who may construct an enemy where none exists or seek to fan antagonisms toward an inactive opponent.

Conflict with one group may serve to produce cohesion by leading to a series of alliances with other groups. For example, conflict with the Arabs has led to an alliance between the United States and Israel. Continued lessening of the Israeli-Arab conflict might weaken the bonds between Israel and the United States.

Within a society, conflict can bring some ordinarily isolated individuals into an active role. The protests over the Vietnam War motivated many young people to take vigorous roles in American political life for the first time. With the end of that conflict, a more apathetic spirit emerged again among American youth.

Conflict also serves a communication function. Prior to conflict, groups may be unsure of their adversary's position, but as a result of conflict, positions and boundaries between groups often become clarified. Individuals therefore are better able to decide on a proper course of action in relation to their adversary. Conflict also allows the parties to get a better idea of their relative strengths and may well increase the possibility of rapprochement, or peaceful accommodation.

From a theoretical perspective, it is possible to wed functionalism and conflict theory by looking at the functions of social conflict. Still, it must be recognized that conflict also has dysfunctions.

While a number of theorists sought to integrate conflict theory with structural functionalism, others wanted no part of conflict theory (or structural functionalism). For example, the Marxist André Gunder Frank (1966/1974) rejected conflict theory because it represented an inadequate form of Marxian theory. Although conflict theory has some

Marxian elements, it is not the true heir of Marx's original theory. In the next chapter we will examine an array of theories that are more legitimate heirs. Before we do, however, we must deal with a more successfully integrative type of conflict theory.

A More Integrative Conflict Theory

Randall Collins's *Conflict Sociology* (1975) was highly integrative because it moved in a much more micro-oriented direction than the macro conflict theory of Dahrendorf and others. Collins himself says of his early work, "My own main contribution to conflict theory . . . was to add a micro level to these macro-level theories. I especially tried to show that stratification and organization are grounded in the interactions of everyday life" (1990:72).[16]

Collins made it clear that his focus on conflict would not be ideological; that is, he did not begin with the political view that conflict is either good or bad. Rather, he claimed, he chose conflict as a focus on the realistic ground that conflict is a—perhaps *the*—central process in social life.

Unlike others who started, and stayed, at the societal level, Collins approached conflict from an individual point of view, because his theoretical roots lie in phenomenology and ethnomethodology. Despite his preference for individual-level and small-scale theories, Collins was aware that "sociology cannot be successful on the microlevel alone" (1975:11); conflict theory cannot do without the societal level of analysis. However, whereas most conflict theorists believed that social structures are external to, and coercive of, the actor, Collins saw social structures as inseparable from the actors who construct them and whose interaction patterns are their essence. Collins was inclined to see social structures as interaction patterns rather than as external and coercive entities. In addition, whereas most conflict theorists saw the actor as constrained by external forces, Collins viewed the actor as constantly creating and re-creating social organization.

Collins saw Marxian theory as the "starting point" for conflict theory, but it is, in his view, laden with problems. For one thing, he saw it (like structural functionalism) as heavily ideological, a characteristic he wanted to avoid. For another, he tended to see Marx's orientation as reducible to an analysis of the economic domain, although this is an unwarranted criticism of Marx's theory. Actually, although Collins invoked Marx frequently, his conflict theory shows relatively little Marxian influence. It is far more influenced by Weber, Durkheim, and above all phenomenology and ethnomethodology.

Social Stratification   Collins chose to focus on social stratification because it is an institution that touches so many features of life, including "wealth, politics, careers, families, clubs, communities, lifestyles" (1975:49). In Collins's view, the great theories of stratification are "failures." He criticized Marxian theory as "a monocausal explanation for a multicausal world" (Collins, 1975:49). He viewed Weber's theory as little more than an "antisystem" with which to view the features of the two great theories. Weber's work was of some use to Collins, but "the efforts of phenomenological

---

[16]Collins also stresses that conflict theory, more than other sociological theories, has been open to the integration of the findings of empirical research.

sociology to ground all concepts in the observables of every life" (Collins, 1975:53) were the most important to him because his major focus in the study of social stratification was small-scale, not large-scale. In his view, social stratification, like all other social structures, is reducible to people in everyday life encountering each other in patterned ways.

Despite his ultimate commitment to a microsociology of stratification, Collins began (even though he had some reservations about them) with the large-scale theories of Marx and Weber as underpinnings for his own work. He started with Marxian principles, arguing that they, "with certain modifications, provide the basis for a conflict theory of stratification" (Collins, 1975:58).

First, Collins contended that it was Marx's view that the material conditions involved in earning a living in modern society are the major determinants of a person's lifestyle. The basis of earning a living for Marx is a person's relationship to private property. Those who own or control property are able to earn their livings in a much more satisfactory way than those who do not and who must sell their labor time to gain access to the means of production.

Second, from a Marxian perspective, material conditions affect not only how individuals earn a living but also the nature of social groups in the different social classes. The dominant social class is better able to develop more coherent social groups, tied together by intricate communication networks, than is the subordinate social class.

Finally, Collins argued that Marx also pointed out the vast differences among the social classes in their access to, and control over, the cultural system. That is, the upper social classes are able to develop highly articulated symbol and ideological systems, systems that they are often able to impose on the lower social classes. The lower social classes have less-developed symbol systems, many of which are likely to have been imposed on them by those in power.

Collins viewed Weber as working within and developing further Marx's theory of stratification. For one thing, Weber was said to have recognized the existence of different forms of conflict that lead to a multifaceted stratification system (for example, class, status, and power). For another, Weber developed the theory of organizations to a high degree, which Collins saw as still another arena of conflict of interest. Weber was also important to Collins for his emphasis on the state as the agency that controls the means of violence, which shifted attention from conflict over the economy (means of production) to conflict over the state. Finally, Weber was recognized by Collins for his understanding of the social arena of emotional products, particularly religion. Conflict clearly can occur in this arena, and these emotional products, like other products, can be used as weapons in social conflict.

A Conflict Theory of Stratification   With this background, Collins turned to his own conflict approach to stratification, which has more in common with phenomenological and ethnomethodological theories than with Marxian or Weberian theory. Collins opened with several assumptions. People are seen as inherently sociable but also as particularly conflict-prone in their social relations. Conflict is likely to occur in social relations because "violent coercion" can always be used by one person or many people in an interaction setting. Collins believed that people seek to maximize their "subjective status" and that their ability to do this depends on their resources as well as the resources of those with whom they are dealing. He saw people as self-interested; thus, clashes are possible because sets of interests may be inherently antagonistic.

This conflict approach to stratification can be reduced to three basic principles. First, Collins believed that people live in self-constructed subjective worlds. Second, other people may have the power to affect, or even control, an individual's subjective experience. Third, other people frequently try to control the individual, who opposes them. The result is likely to be interpersonal conflict.

On the basis of this approach, Collins developed five principles of conflict analysis that he applied to social stratification, although he believed that they could be applied to any area of social life. First, Collins believed that conflict theory must focus on real life rather than on abstract formulations. This belief seems to reflect a preference for a Marxian-style material analysis over the abstraction of structural functionalism. Collins urged us to think of people as animals whose actions, motivated by self-interest, can be seen as maneuvers to obtain various advantages so that they can achieve satisfaction and avoid dissatisfaction. However, unlike exchange and rational choice theorists, Collins did not see people as wholly rational. He recognized that they are vulnerable to emotional appeals in their efforts to find satisfaction.

Second, Collins believed that a conflict theory of stratification must examine the material arrangements that affect interaction. Although the actors are likely to be affected by such material factors as "the physical places, the modes of communication, the supply of weapons, devices for staging one's public impression, tools, goods" (Collins, 1975:60), not all actors are affected in the same way. A major variable is the resources that the different actors possess. Actors with considerable material resources can resist or even modify these material constraints, whereas those with fewer resources are more likely to have their thoughts and actions determined by their material setting.

Third, Collins argued that in a situation of inequality, those groups that control resources are likely to try to exploit those that lack resources. He was careful to point out that such exploitation need not involve conscious calculation on the part of those who gain from the situation; rather, the exploiters are merely pursuing what they perceive to be their best interests. In the process they may be taking advantage of those who lack resources.

Fourth, Collins wanted the conflict theorist to look at such cultural phenomena as beliefs and ideals from the point of view of interests, resources, and power. It is likely that those groups with resources and, therefore, power can impose their idea systems on the entire society; those without resources have an idea system imposed on them.

Finally, Collins made a firm commitment to the scientific study of stratification and every other aspect of the social world. Thus, he prescribed several things: Sociologists should not simply theorize about stratification but should study it empirically, if possible, in a comparative way. Hypotheses should be formulated and tested empirically through comparative studies. Last, the sociologist should look for the causes of social phenomena, particularly the multiple causes of any form of social behavior.

This kind of scientific commitment led Collins to develop a wide array of propositions about the relationship between conflict and various specific aspects of social life. We can present only a few here, but they should allow readers to get a feel for Collins's type of conflict sociology.

1.0 Experiences of giving and taking orders are the main determinants of individual outlooks and behaviors.
1.1 The more one gives orders, the more he is proud, self-assured, formal, and identifies with organizational ideals in whose names he justifies the orders.
1.2 The more one takes orders, the more he is subservient, fatalistic, alienated from organizational ideals, externally conforming, distrustful of others, concerned with extrinsic rewards, and amoral.

(Collins, 1975:73–74)

Among other things, these propositions all reflect Collins's commitment to the *scientific study* of the small-scale social manifestations of social conflicts.

Other Social Domains   Collins was not content to deal with conflict within the stratification system but sought to extend it to various other social domains. For example, he extended his analysis of stratification to relationships between the sexes as well as among age groups. He took the view that the family is an arena of sexual conflict, in which males have been the victors, with the result that women are dominated by men and subject to various kinds of unequal treatment. Similarly, he saw the relationship between age groups—in particular, between young and old—as one of conflict. This idea contrasts with the view of structural functionalists, who saw harmonious socialization and internalization in this relationship. Collins looked at the resources possessed by the various age groups. Adults have a variety of resources, including experience, size, strength, and the ability to satisfy the physical needs of the young. In contrast, one of the few resources young children have is physical attractiveness. This means that young children are likely to be dominated by adults. However, as children mature, they acquire more resources and are better able to resist, with the result of increasing social conflict between the generations.

Collins also looked at formal organizations from a conflict perspective. He saw them as networks of interpersonal influences and as the arenas in which conflicting interests are played out. In short, "Organizations are arenas for struggle" (Collins, 1975:295). Collins again couched his argument in propositional form. For example, he argued that "coercion leads to strong efforts to avoid being coerced" (Collins, 1975:298). In contrast, he felt that the offering of rewards is a preferable strategy: "Control by material rewards leads to compliance to the extent that rewards are directly linked to the desired behavior" (Collins, 1975:299). These propositions and others all point to Collins's commitment to a scientific, largely micro-oriented study of conflict.

General Perspective   In sum, Collins is, like Dahrendorf, not a true exponent of Marxian conflict theory, although for different reasons. Although Collins used Marx as a starting point, Weber, Durkheim, and particularly ethnomethodology were much more important influences on his work. Collins's small-scale orientation is a helpful beginning toward the development of a more integrated conflict theory. However, despite his stated intentions of integrating large- and small-scale theory, he did not accomplish the task fully.

In his later work, Collins takes the general view that conflict theory is preferable to most other theories because of its willingness to be synthetic: "Conflict theory . . .

engages freely in what may be called intellectual piracy: it is quite willing to incorporate . . . elements . . . of micro-sociologies" (1990:72). While little overt conflict theorizing was done between 1975 and 1990, Collins believes that conflict theory, in spite of the appearances, had not been moribund for a decade and a half but had been developing quietly under a variety of different guises in a number of areas within sociology.

First, Collins sees a conflict approach as lying at the heart of much historical-comparative research, especially the work of Michael Mann (1986). Thus, conflict theory stands to be enriched by the integration of a wide range of insights that can be derived from historical-comparative research. Furthermore, Collins sees Mann as utilizing a kind of network theory, and this leads to an interest in synthesizing Mann's approach with mainstream work in network theory. Second, there is the possibility of integrating network theory and conflict theory. In fact, as we will see, network theory plays a prominent role in contemporary efforts at synthesis, since there are those from other theoretical perspectives, especially exchange theory, who see possibilities of integration with it. Curiously, Collins does not address the possibility of integration with his own theory of interaction ritual chains (see Chapter 10). This is surprising, since that theory's micro-level insights would mesh well with the traditional macro-level concerns of conflict theory. Perhaps Collins did not suggest such an integration because his own variety of conflict theory is itself highly microscopic and already encompasses interaction ritual chains.

More generally, Collins defines conflict theory in such a sweeping way that it seems open to insights from all theories and seems capable of covering all levels of social reality. Specifically, Collins seeks to differentiate between narrow *theories of conflict* (for example, those of Simmel and Coser) and *conflict theory,* which he defines as "a theory about the organization of society, the behavior of people and groups, it explains why structures take the forms that they do . . . and how and what kinds of changes occur. . . . Conflict theory is a general approach to the entire field of sociology" (1990:70). Thus, Collins is after more than a series of specific syntheses; he is interested in pushing conflict theory in the direction of a more holistic perspective. One must be wary of the theoretical imperialism implied by this approach.

SUMMARY

Not too many years ago, structural functionalism was *the* dominant theory in sociology. Conflict theory was its major challenger and was the likely alternative to replace it in that position. However, dramatic changes have taken place in recent years. Both theories have been the subject of intense criticism, whereas a series of alternative theories (to be discussed throughout the rest of this book) developed that have attracted ever greater interest and ever larger followings.

Although several varieties of structural functionalism exist, our focus here is on societal functionalism and its large-scale focus, its concern with interrelationships at the societal level and with the constraining effects of social structures and institutions on actors. Structural functionalists developed a series of large-scale concerns in social systems, subsystems, relationships among subsystems and systems, equilibrium, and orderly change.

We examine three bodies of work by structural functionalists (Davis and Moore, Parsons, and Merton). Davis and Moore, in one of the best-known and most criticized pieces in the history of sociology, examined social stratification as a social system and the various positive functions it performs. We also discuss in some detail Talcott Parsons's structural-functional theory and his ideas on the four functional imperatives of all action systems—adaptation, goal attainment, integration, and latency (AGIL). We also analyze his structural-functional approach to the four action systems—the social system, cultural system, personality system, and behavioral organism. Finally, we deal with his structural-functional approach to dynamism and social change—his evolutionary theory and his ideas on the generalized media of interchange.

Merton's effort to develop a "paradigm" for functional analysis is the most important single piece in modern structural functionalism. Merton began by criticizing some of the more naive positions of structural functionalism. He then sought to develop a more adequate model of structural-functional analysis. On one point Merton agreed with his predecessors—the need to focus on large-scale social phenomena. But, Merton argued, in addition to focusing on positive functions, structural functionalism should be concerned with dysfunctions and even nonfunctions. Given these additions, Merton urged that analysts concern themselves with the net balance of functions and dysfunctions. Further, he argued, in performing structural-functional analysis, we must move away from global analyses and specify the *levels* on which we are working. Merton also added the idea that structural functionalists should be concerned not only with manifest (intended) but also with latent (unintended) functions. This section concludes with a discussion of Merton's application of his functional paradigm to the issue of the relationship of social structure and culture to anomie and deviance.

Next, we discuss the numerous criticisms of structural functionalism that have succeeded in damaging its credibility and popularity. We discuss the criticisms that structural functionalism is ahistorical, unable to deal with conflict and change, highly conservative, preoccupied with societal constraints on actors, accepting of elite legitimations, teleological, and tautological.

The criticisms of structural functionalism led to an effort to respond to them—the development of an orientation known as neofunctionalism. Neofunctionalism sought to buttress structural functionalism by synthesizing it with a wide array of other theoretical perspectives. A fair amount of work was done under the rubric of neofunctionalism in the late 1980s and early 1990s, and it attracted considerable attention. However, its future is questionable, especially since its founder, Jeffrey Alexander, has moved beyond it theoretically.

The last part of this chapter is devoted to the major alternative to structural functionalism in the 1950s and 1960s—conflict theory. The best-known work in this tradition is by Ralf Dahrendorf, who, although he consciously tried to follow the Marxian tradition, is best seen as having inverted structural functionalism. Dahrendorf looked at change rather than equilibrium, conflict rather than order, how the parts of society contribute to change rather than to stability, and conflict and coercion rather than normative constraint. Dahrendorf offered a large-scale theory of conflict that parallels the structural functionalist's large-scale theory of order. His focus on authority, positions, imperatively coordinated associations, interests, quasi groups, interest groups, and conflict groups reflects this orientation. Dahrendorf's theory suffers from some of the same problems as structural functionalism; in addition, it represents a rather impoverished effort to incorporate Marxian theory. Dahrendorf also can be criticized for being satisfied with alternative theories of order and conflict rather than seeking a theoretical integration of the two.

The chapter concludes with a discussion of Randall Collins's effort to develop a more integrative conflict theory, especially one that integrates micro and macro concerns.

4

VARIETIES OF
NEO-MARXIAN THEORY

ECONOMIC DETERMINISM
HEGELIAN MARXISM
   Georg Lukács
   Antonio Gramsci
CRITICAL THEORY
   The Major Critiques of Social and Intellectual Life
   The Major Contributions
   Criticisms of Critical Theory
   The Ideas of Jurgen Habermas
   Critical Theory Today
NEO-MARXIAN ECONOMIC SOCIOLOGY
   Capital and Labor
   Fordism and Post-Fordism
HISTORICALLY ORIENTED MARXISM
   The Modern World-System
POST-MARXIST THEORY
   Analytical Marxism
   Postmodern Marxian Theory
   After Marxism
   Criticisms of Post-Marxism

In this chapter we deal with a variety of theories that are better reflections of Marx's ideas than the conflict theories discussed at the close of the preceding chapter. Although each of the theories discussed here is derived from Marx's theory, there are many important differences among them.

ECONOMIC DETERMINISM

Marx often sounded like an economic determinist; that is, he seemed to consider the economic system of paramount importance and to argue that it determined all other sectors of society—politics, religion, idea systems, and so forth. Although Marx did see the economic sector as preeminent, at least in capitalist society, as a dialectician he could not have taken a deterministic position, because the dialectic is characterized by the notion that there is continual feedback and mutual interaction among the various sectors of society. Politics, religion, and so on cannot be reduced to epiphenomena determined by the economy, because they affect the economy just as they are affected by it. Despite the nature of the dialectic, Marx still is being interpreted as an economic determinist. Although some aspects of Marx's work would lead to this conclusion, adopting it means ignoring the overall dialectical thrust of his theory.

Agger (1978) argued that economic determinism reached its peak as an interpretation of Marxian theory during the period of the Second Communist International, between 1889 and 1914. This historical period is often seen as the apex of early market capitalism, and its booms and busts led to many predictions about its imminent demise. Those Marxists who believed in economic determinism saw the breakdown of capitalism as inevitable. In their view, Marxism was capable of producing a scientific theory of this breakdown (as well as other aspects of capitalist society) with the predictive reliability of the physical and natural sciences. All an analyst had to do was examine the structures of capitalism, especially the economic structures. Built into these structures was a series of processes that would inevitably bring down capitalism, so it was up to the economic determinist to discover how these processes worked.

Friedrich Engels, Marx's collaborator and benefactor, led the way in this interpretation of Marxian theory, as did Karl Kautsky and Eduard Bernstein. Kautsky, for example, discussed the inevitable decline of capitalism as

> unavoidable in the sense that the inventors improve technic and the capitalists in their desire for profit revolutionize the whole economic life, as it is also inevitable that the workers aim for shorter hours of labor and higher wages, that they organize themselves, that they fight the capitalist class and its state, as it is inevitable that they aim for the conquest of political power and the overthrow of capitalist rule. Socialism is inevitable because the class struggle and the victory of the proletariat is inevitable.
>
> (Kautsky, cited in Agger, 1978:94)

The imagery here is of actors impelled by the structures of capitalism into a series of actions.

It was this imagery that led to the major criticism of scientifically oriented economic determinism—that it was untrue to the dialectical thrust of Marx's theory. Specifically, the theory seemed to short-circuit the dialectic by making individual thought and action insignificant. The economic structures of capitalism that determined individual thought and action were the crucial element. This interpretation also led to political quietism and therefore was inconsistent with Marx's thinking. Why should individuals act if the capitalist system was going to crumble under its own structural contradictions? Clearly, given Marx's desire to integrate theory and practice, a perspective that omits action and even reduces it to insignificance would not be in the tradition of his thinking.

HEGELIAN MARXISM

As a result of the criticisms just discussed, economic determinism began to fade in importance, and a number of theorists developed other varieties of Marxian theory. One group of Marxists returned to the Hegelian roots of Marx's theory in search of a subjective orientation to complement the strength of the early Marxists at the objective, material level. The early Hegelian Marxists sought to restore the dialectic between the subjective and the objective aspects of social life. Their interest in subjective factors laid the basis for the later development of critical theory, which came to focus almost exclusively on subjective factors. A number of thinkers (for example, Karl Korsch) could be taken as illustrative of Hegelian Marxism, but we will focus on the work of one who has gained great prominence, Georg Lukács, especially his book *History and Class Consciousness* (1922/1968). We also give brief attention to the ideas of Antonio Gramsci.

Georg Lukács

The attention of Marxian scholars of the early twentieth century was limited mainly to Marx's later, largely economic works, such as *Capital* (1867/1967). The early work, especially *The Economic and Philosophic Manuscripts of 1844* (1932/1964), which was more heavily influenced by Hegelian subjectivism, was largely unknown to Marxian thinkers. The rediscovery of the *Manuscripts* and their publication in 1932 was a major turning point. However, by the 1920s, Lukács already had written his major work, in which he emphasized the subjective side of Marxian theory. As Martin Jay puts it, "*History and Class Consciousness* anticipated in several fundamental ways the philosophical implications of Marx's *1844 Manuscripts,* whose publication it antedated by almost a decade" (1984:102). Lukács' major contribution to Marxian theory lies in his work on two major ideas—reification (Dahms, 1998) and class consciousness.

Reification   Lukács made it clear from the beginning that he was not totally rejecting the work of the economic Marxists on reification, but simply seeking to broaden and extend their ideas. Lukács commenced with the Marxian concept of commodities, which he characterized as "the central, structural problem of capitalist society" (1922/1968:83). A *commodity* is at base a relation among people that, they come to believe, takes on the character of a thing and develops an objective form. People in their interaction with nature in capitalist society produce various products, or commodities (for example, bread, automobiles, motion pictures). However, people tend to lose sight of the fact that they produce these commodities and give them their value. Value comes to be seen as produced by a market that is independent of the actors. The *fetishism of commodities* is the process by which commodities and the market for them are granted independent objective existence by the actors in capitalist society. Marx's concept of the fetishism of commodities was the basis for Lukács's concept of reification.

The crucial difference between the fetishism of commodities and reification is in the extensiveness of the two concepts. Whereas the former is restricted to the economic institution, the latter is applied by Lukács to all society—the state, the law, *and* the economic sector. The same dynamic applies in all sectors of capitalist society: people come to believe that social structures have a life of their own, and as a result they do come to have an objective character. Lukács delineated this process:

> Man in capitalist society confronts a reality "made" by himself (as a class) which appears to him to be a natural phenomenon alien to himself; he is wholly at the mercy of its "laws"; his activity is confined to the exploitation of the inexorable fulfillment of certain individual laws for his own (egoistic) interests. But even while "acting" he remains, in the nature of the case, the object and not the subject of events.
>
> (Lukács, 1922/1968:135)

In developing his ideas on reification, Lukács integrated insights from Weber and Simmel. However, because reification was embedded in Marxian theory, it was seen as a problem limited to capitalism and not, as it was to Weber and Simmel, the inevitable fate of humankind.

Class and False Consciousness   *Class consciousness* refers to the belief systems shared by those who occupy the same class position within society. Lukács made it clear that class consciousness is neither the sum nor the average of individual consciousnesses; rather, it is a property of a group of people who share a similar place in the productive system. This view leads to a focus on the class consciousness of the bourgeoisie and especially of the proletariat. In Lukács's work, there is a clear link between objective economic position, class consciousness, and the "real, psychological thoughts of men about their lives" (1922/1968:51).

The concept of class consciousness necessarily implies, at least in capitalism, the prior state of *false consciousness.* That is, classes in capitalism generally do not have a clear sense of their true class interests. For example, until the revolutionary stage, members of the proletariat do not fully realize the nature and extent of their exploitation in capitalism. The falsity of class consciousness is derived from the class's position within the economic structure of society: "Class consciousness implies a class-conditioned *unconsciousness* of one's own socio-historical and economic condition. . . . The 'falseness,' the illusion implicit in this situation, is in no sense arbitrary" (Lukács, 1922/1968:52). Most social classes throughout history have been unable to overcome false consciousness and thereby achieve class consciousness. The structural position of the proletariat within capitalism, however, gives it the unique ability to achieve class consciousness.

The ability to achieve class consciousness is peculiar to capitalist societies. In precapitalist societies, a variety of factors prevented the development of class consciousness. For one thing, the state, independent of the economy, affected social strata; for another, status (prestige) consciousness tended to mask class (economic) consciousness. As a result, Lukács concluded, "There is therefore no possible position within such a society from which the economic basis of all social relations could be made conscious" (1922/1968:57). In contrast, the economic base of capitalism is clearer and simpler. People may not be conscious of its effects, but they are at least unconsciously aware of them. As a result, "class consciousness arrived at the point where *it could become conscious*" (Lukács, 1922/1968:59). At this stage, society turns into an ideological battleground in which those who seek to conceal the class character of society are pitted against those who seek to expose it.

Lukács compared the various classes in capitalism on the issue of class consciousness. He argued that the petty bourgeoisie and the peasants cannot develop class consciousness because of the ambiguity of their structural position within capitalism. Because these two classes represent vestiges of society in the feudal era, they are not able to develop a clear sense of the nature of capitalism. The bourgeoisie can develop class consciousness, but at best it understands the development of capitalism as something external, subject to objective laws, that it can experience only passively.

The proletariat has the capacity to develop true class consciousness, and as it does, the bourgeoisie is thrown on the defensive. Lukács refused to see the proletariat as simply driven by external forces but viewed it instead as an active creator of its own fate. In the confrontation between the bourgeoisie and the proletariat, the former class has all the intellectual and organizational weapons, whereas all the latter has, at least at first, is the ability to see society for what it is. As the battle proceeds, the proletariat moves from being a "class in itself," that is, a structurally created entity, to a "class for itself," a class conscious of its position and its mission. In other words, "the class struggle must be raised from the level of economic necessity to the level of conscious aim and effective class consciousness" (Lukács, 1922/1968:76). When the struggle reaches this point, the proletariat is capable of the action that can overthrow the capitalist system.

Lukács had a rich sociological theory, although it is embedded in Marxian terms. He was concerned with the dialectical relationship among the structures (primarily economic) of capitalism, the idea systems (especially class consciousness), individual thought, and, ultimately, individual action. His theoretical perspective provides an important bridge between the economic determinists and more modern Marxists.

Antonio Gramsci

The Italian Marxist Antonio Gramsci also played a key role in the transition from economic determinism to more modern Marxian positions (Salamini, 1981). Gramsci was critical of Marxists who are "deterministic, fatalistic and mechanistic" (1971:336). In fact, he wrote an essay entitled "The Revolution against *'Capital'*" (Gramsci, 1917/1977) in which he celebrated "the resurrection of political will against the economic determinism of those who reduced Marxism to the historical laws of Marx's best-known work [*Capital*]" (Jay, 1984:155). Although he recognized that there were historical regularities, he rejected the idea of automatic or inevitable historical developments. Thus, the masses had to act in order to bring about a social revolution. But to act, the masses had to become conscious of their situation and the nature of the system in which they lived. Thus, although Gramsci recognized the importance of structural factors, especially the economy, he did not believe that these structural factors led the masses to revolt. The masses needed to develop a revolutionary ideology, but they could not do so on their own. Gramsci operated with a rather elitist conception in which ideas were generated by intellectuals and then extended to the masses and put into practice by them. The masses could not generate such ideas, and they could experience them, once in existence, only on faith. The masses could not become self-conscious on their own; they needed the help of social elites. However, once the masses had been influenced by these ideas, they would take the actions that lead to social revolution. Gramsci, like Lukács, focused on collective ideas rather than on social structures like the economy, and both operated within traditional Marxian theory.

Gramsci's central concept, and one that reflects his Hegelianism, is hegemony (for a contemporary use of the concept of hegemony, see the discussion of the work of Laclau and Mouffe later in this chapter; Abrahamsen, 1997). According to Gramsci, "the essential ingredient of the most modern philosophy of praxis [the linking of thought and action] is the historical-philosophical concept of 'hegemony'" (1932/1975:235). *Hegemony* is defined by Gramsci as cultural leadership exercised by the ruling class. He contrasts hegemony to coercion that is "exercised by legislative or executive powers, or expressed through police intervention" (Gramsci, 1932/1975:235). Whereas economic Marxists tended to emphasize the economy and the coercive aspects of state domination, Gramsci emphasized "'hegemony' and cultural leadership" (1932/1975:235). In an analysis of capitalism, Gramsci wanted to know how some intellectuals, working on behalf of the capitalists, achieved cultural leadership and the assent of the masses.

Not only does the concept of hegemony help us to understand domination within capitalism, but it also serves to orient Gramsci's thoughts on revolution. That is, through revolution, it is not enough to gain control of the economy and the state apparatus; it is also necessary to gain cultural leadership over the rest of society. It is here that Gramsci sees a key role for communist intellectuals and the communist party.

We turn now to critical theory, which grew out of the work of Hegelian Marxists like Lukács and Gramsci, and which has moved even further from the traditional Marxian roots of economic determinism.

CRITICAL THEORY

Critical theory is the product of a group of German neo-Marxists who were dissatisfied with the state of Marxian theory (Bernstein, 1995; Kellner, 1993; for a broader view of critical theory, see Agger, 1998), particularly its tendency toward economic determinism. The organization associated with critical theory, the Institute of Social Research, was officially founded in Frankfurt, Germany, on February 23, 1923 (Wiggershaus, 1994). Critical theory has spread beyond the confines of the Frankfurt school (*Telos*, 1989–90). Critical theory was and is largely a European orientation, although its influence in American sociology has grown (van den Berg, 1980).

The Major Critiques of Social and Intellectual Life

Critical theory is composed largely of criticisms of various aspects of social and intellectual life, but its ultimate goal is to reveal more accurately the nature of society (Bleich, 1977). First we focus on the major criticisms offered by the school, all of which manifest a preference for oppositional thinking and for unveiling and debunking various aspects of social reality (Connerton, 1976).

Criticisms of Marxian Theory   Critical theory takes as its starting point a critique of Marxian theories. The critical theorists are most disturbed by the economic determinists—the mechanistic, or mechanical, Marxists (Antonio, 1981; Schroyer, 1973; Sewart, 1978). Some (for example, Habermas, 1971) criticize the determinism implicit in parts of Marx's original work, but most focus their criticisms on the neo-Marxists, primarily because they had interpreted Marx's work too mechanistically. The critical theorists do not say that economic determinists were wrong in focusing on the economic realm but that they should have been concerned with other aspects of social life as well. As we will see, the critical school seeks to rectify this imbalance by focusing its attention on the cultural realm (Schroyer, 1973:33). In addition to attacking other Marxian theories, the critical school critiqued societies, like the former Soviet Union, built ostensibly on Marxian theory (Marcuse, 1958).

Criticisms of Positivism   Critical theorists also focus on the philosophical under-pinnings of scientific inquiry, especially positivism (Bottomore, 1984; Morrow, 1994). The criticism of positivism is related, at least in part, to the criticism of economic deter-minism, because some of those who were determinists accepted part or all of the posi-tivistic theory of knowledge. Positivism is depicted as accepting the idea that a single scientific method is applicable to all fields of study. It takes the physical sciences as the standard of certainty and exactness for all disciplines. Positivists believe that knowl-edge is inherently neutral. They feel that they can keep human values out of their work. This belief, in turn, leads to the view that science is not in the position of advocating any specific form of social action. (See Chapter 1 for more discussion of positivism.)

Positivism is opposed by the critical school on various grounds (Sewart, 1978). For one thing, positivism tends to reify the social world and see it as a natural process. The critical theorists prefer to focus on human activity as well as on the ways in which such activity affects larger social structures. In short, positivism loses sight of the actors (Habermas, 1971), reducing them to passive entities determined by "natural forces." Given their belief in the distinctiveness of the actor, the critical theorists would not ac-cept the idea that the general laws of science can be applied without question to human action. Positivism is assailed for being content to judge the adequacy of means toward given ends and for not making a similar judgment about ends. This critique leads to the view that positivism is inherently conservative, incapable of challenging the existing system. As Martin Jay says of positivism, "The result was the absolutizing of 'facts' and the reification of the existing order" (1973:62). Positivism leads the actor and the social scientist to passivity. Few Marxists of any type would support a perspective that does not relate theory and practice. Despite these criticisms of positivism, some Marxists (for example, some structuralists, analytic Marxists) espouse positivism, and Marx him-self was often guilty of being overly positivistic (Habermas, 1971).

Criticisms of Sociology   Sociology is attacked for its "scientism," that is, for mak-ing the scientific method an end in itself. In addition, sociology is accused of accepting the status quo. The critical school maintains that sociology does not seriously criticize society, nor does it seek to transcend the contemporary social structure. Sociology, the critical school contends, has surrendered its obligation to help people oppressed by con-temporary society.

Members of this school are critical of sociologists' focus on society as a whole rather than on individuals in society; sociologists are accused of ignoring the interaction of the individual and society. Although most sociological perspectives are *not* guilty of ignor-ing this interaction, this view is a cornerstone of the critical school's attacks on sociolo-gists. Because they ignore the individual, sociologists are seen as being unable to say anything meaningful about political changes that could lead to a "just and humane soci-ety" (Frankfurt Institute for Social Research, 1973:46). As Zoltan Tar put it, sociology becomes "an integral part of the existing society instead of being a means of critique and a ferment of renewal" (1977:x).

Critique of Modern Society   Most of the critical school's work is aimed at a critique of modern society and a variety of its components. Whereas much of early

Marxian theory aimed specifically at the economy, the critical school shifted its orientation to the cultural level in light of what it considers the realities of modern capitalist society. That is, the locus of domination in the modern world shifted from the economy to the cultural realm. Still, the critical school retains its interest in domination,[1] although in the modern world it is likely to be domination by cultural rather than economic elements. The critical school thus seeks to focus on the cultural repression of the individual in modern society.

The critical thinkers have been shaped not only by Marxian theory but also by Weberian theory, as reflected in their focus on rationality as the dominant development within the modern world. In fact, supporters of this approach are often labeled "Weberian Marxists" (Dahms, 1997; Lowy, 1996). As Trent Schroyer (1970) made clear, the view of the critical school is that in modern society the repression produced by rationality has replaced economic exploitation as the dominant social problem. The critical school clearly has adopted Weber's differentiation between *formal rationality* and *substantive rationality,* or what the critical theorists think of as *reason.* To the critical theorists, formal rationality is concerned unreflectively with the question of the most effective means for achieving any given purpose (Tar, 1977). This is viewed as "technocratic thinking," in which the objective is to serve the forces of domination, not to emancipate people from domination. The goal is simply to find the most efficient means to whatever ends are defined as important by those in power. Technocratic thinking is contrasted to reason, which is, in the minds of critical theorists, the hope for society. Reason involves the assessment of means in terms of the ultimate human values of justice, peace, and happiness. Critical theorists identified Nazism in general, and its concentration camps more specifically, as examples of formal rationality in mortal combat with reason. Thus, as George Friedman puts it, "Auschwitz was a rational place, but it was not a reasonable one" (1981:15; see also Chapter 12 and the discussion of Bauman, 1989).

Despite the seeming rationality of modern life, the critical school views the modern world as rife with irrationality (Crook, 1995). This idea can be labeled the "irrationality of rationality," or more specifically the irrationality of formal rationality. In Herbert Marcuse's view, although it appears to be the embodiment of rationality, "this society is irrational as a whole" (1964:ix; see also Farganis, 1975). It is irrational that the rational world is destructive of individuals and their needs and abilities; that peace is maintained through a constant threat of war; and that despite the existence of sufficient means, people remain impoverished, repressed, exploited, and unable to fulfill themselves.

The critical school focuses primarily on one form of formal rationality—modern technology (Feenberg, 1996). Marcuse (1964), for example, was a severe critic of modern technology, at least as it is employed in capitalism. He saw technology in modern capitalist society as leading to totalitarianism. In fact, he viewed it as leading to new, more effective, and even more "pleasant" methods of external control over individuals. The prime example is the use of television to socialize and pacify the population (other examples are mass sports, and pervasive exploitation of sex). Marcuse rejected the idea

---

[1]This is made abundantly clear by Trent Schroyer (1973), who entitled his book on the critical school *The Critique of Domination.*

that technology is neutral in the modern world and saw it instead as a means to dominate people. It is effective because it is made to seem neutral when it is in fact enslaving. It serves to suppress individuality. The actor's inner freedom has been "invaded and whittled down" by modern technology. The result is what Marcuse called "one-dimensional society," in which individuals lose the ability to think critically and negatively about society. Marcuse did not see technology per se as the enemy, but rather technology as it is employed in modern capitalist society: "Technology, no matter how 'pure,' sustains and streamlines the continuum of domination. This fatal link can be cut only by a revolution which makes technology and technique subservient to the needs and goals of free men" (1969:56). Marcuse retained Marx's original view that technology is not inherently a problem and that it can be used to develop a "better" society.

Critique of Culture   The critical theorists level significant criticisms at what they call the "culture industry," the rationalized, bureaucratized structures (for example, the television networks) that control modern culture. Interest in the culture industry reflects their concern with the Marxian concept of "superstructure" rather than with the economic base. The *culture industry,* producing what is conventionally called "mass culture," is defined as the "administered . . . nonspontaneous, reified, phony culture rather than the real thing" (Jay, 1973:216). Two things worry the critical thinkers most about this industry. First, they are concerned about its falseness. They think of it as a prepackaged set of ideas mass-produced and disseminated to the masses by the media. Second, the critical theorists are disturbed by its pacifying, repressive, and stupefying effect on people (D. Cook, 1996; Friedman, 1981; Tar, 1977:83; Zipes, 1994).

Douglas Kellner (1990b) has self-consciously offered a critical theory of television. While he embeds his work in the cultural concerns of the Frankfurt school, Kellner draws on other Marxian traditions to present a more rounded conception of the television industry. He critiques the critical school because it "neglects detailed analysis of the political economy of the media, conceptualizing mass culture merely as an instrument of capitalist ideology" (Kellner, 1990b:14). Thus, in addition to looking at television as part of the culture industry, Kellner connects it to both corporate capitalism and the political system. Furthermore, Kellner does not see television as monolithic or as controlled by coherent corporate forces, but rather as a "highly conflictual mass medium in which competing economic, political, social and cultural forces intersect" (1990b:14). Thus, while working within the tradition of critical theory, Kellner rejects the view that capitalism is a totally administered world. Nevertheless, Kellner sees television as a threat to democracy, individuality, and freedom and offers suggestions (for example, more democratic accountability, greater citizen access and participation, greater diversity on television) to deal with the threat. Thus, Kellner goes beyond a mere critique to offer proposals for dealing with the dangers posed by television.

The critical school is also interested in and critical of what it calls the "knowledge industry," which refers to entities concerned with knowledge production (for example, universities and research institutes) that have become autonomous structures in our society. Their autonomy has allowed them to extend themselves beyond their original mandate (Schroyer, 1970). They have become oppressive structures interested in expanding their influence throughout society.

Marx's critical analysis of capitalism led him to have hope for the future, but many critical theorists have come to a position of despair and hopelessness. They see the problems of the modern world not as specific to capitalism but as endemic to a rationalized world. They see the future, in Weberian terms, as an "iron cage" of increasingly rational structures from which hope for escape lessens all the time.

Much of critical theory (like the bulk of Marx's original formulation) is in the form of critical analyses. Even though the critical theorists also have a number of positive interests, one of the basic criticisms made of critical theory is that it offers more criticisms than it does positive contributions. This incessant negativity galls many, and for this reason they feel that critical theory has little to offer sociological theory.

The Major Contributions

Subjectivity   The great contribution of the critical school has been its effort to reorient Marxian theory in a subjective direction. Although this constitutes a critique of Marx's materialism and his dogged focus on economic structures, it also represents a strong contribution to our understanding of the subjective elements of social life at both the individual and the cultural levels.

The Hegelian roots of Marxian theory are the major source of interest in subjectivity. Many of the critical thinkers see themselves as returning to those roots, as expressed in Marx's early works. In doing so, they are following up on the work of the early twentieth-century Marxian revisionists, such as Georg Lukács, who sought not to focus on subjectivity but simply to integrate such an interest with the traditional Marxian concern with objective structures (Agger, 1978). Lukács did not seek a fundamental restructuring of Marxian theory, although the later critical theorists do have this broader and more ambitious objective.

We begin with the critical school's interest in culture. As pointed out above, the critical school has shifted to a concern with the cultural "superstructure" rather than with the economic "base." One factor motivating this shift is that the critical school feels that Marxists have overemphasized economic structures and that this emphasis has served to overwhelm their interest in the other aspects of social reality, especially the culture. In addition to this factor, a series of external changes in the society point to such a shift (Agger, 1978). In particular, the prosperity of the post–World War II period in America *seems* to have led to a disappearance of internal economic contradictions in general and class conflict in particular. False consciousness *seems* to be nearly universal: all social classes, including the working class, appear to be beneficiaries and ardent supporters of the capitalist system. In addition, the former Soviet Union, despite its socialist economy, was at least as oppressive as capitalist society. Because the two societies had different economies, the critical thinkers had to look elsewhere for the major source of oppression. What they looked toward initially was culture.

To the previously discussed aspects of the Frankfurt school's concerns—rationality, the culture industry, and the knowledge industry—can be added an additional set of concerns, the most notable of which is an interest in ideology. By *ideology* the critical theorists mean the idea systems, often false and obfuscating, produced by societal elites. All these specific aspects of the superstructure and the critical school's orientation to them can be subsumed under the heading "critique of domination" (Agger, 1978;

Schroyer, 1973). This interest in domination was at first stimulated by fascism in the 1930s and 1940s, but it has shifted to a concern with domination in capitalist society. The modern world has reached a stage of unsurpassed domination of individuals. In fact, the control is so complete that it no longer requires deliberate actions on the part of the leaders. The control pervades all aspects of the cultural world and, more important, is internalized in the actor. In effect, actors have come to dominate themselves in the name of the larger social structure. Domination has reached such a complete stage that it no longer appears to be domination at all. Because domination is no longer perceived as personally damaging and alienating, it often seems as if the world is the way it is supposed to be. It is no longer clear to actors what the world *ought* to be like. Thus, the pessimism of the critical thinkers is buttressed, because they no longer can see how rational analysis can help alter the situation.

One of the critical school's concerns at the cultural level is with what Habermas (1975) called *legitimations.* These can be defined as systems of ideas generated by the political system, and theoretically by any other system, to support the existence of the system. They are designed to "mystify" the political system, to make it unclear exactly what is happening.

In addition to such cultural interests, the critical school is also concerned with actors and their consciousness and what happens to them in the modern world. The consciousness of the masses came to be controlled by external forces (such as the culture industry). As a result, the masses failed to develop a revolutionary consciousness. Unfortunately, the critical theorists, like most Marxists and most sociologists, often fail to differentiate clearly between individual consciousness and culture, nor do they specify the many links between them. In much of their work, they move freely back and forth between consciousness and culture with little or no sense that they are changing levels.

Of great importance here is the effort by critical theorists, most notably Marcuse (1969), to integrate Freud's insights at the level of consciousness (and unconsciousness) into the critical theorists' interpretation of the culture. Critical theorists derive three things from Freud's work: (1) a psychological structure to work with in developing their theories; (2) a sense of psychopathology that allows them to understand both the negative impact of modern society and the failure to develop revolutionary consciousness; and (3) the possibilities of psychic liberation (Friedman, 1981). One of the benefits of this interest in individual consciousness is that it offers a useful corrective to the pessimism of the critical school and its focus on cultural constraints. Although people are controlled, imbued with false needs, and anesthetized, in Freudian terms they are also endowed with a libido (broadly conceived as sexual energy), which provides the basic source of energy for creative action oriented toward the overthrow of the major forms of domination.

Dialectics   The second main positive focus of critical theory is an interest in dialectics (this idea is critiqued from the viewpoint of analytical Marxism later in this chapter). At the most general level, a dialectical approach means a focus on the social *totality.*[2] "No partial aspect of social life and no isolated phenomenon may be comprehended unless it is related to the historical whole, to the social structure conceived as a global

---

[2]Jay (1984) sees "totality" as the heart of Marxian theory in general, not just of critical theory. On the other hand, this idea is rejected by postmodern Marxists (see the discussion later in this chapter).

entity" (Connerton, 1976:12). This approach involves rejection of a focus on any *specific* aspect of social life, especially the economic system, outside of its broader context. This approach also means a concern with the interrelation of the various levels of social reality—most important, individual consciousness, the cultural superstructure, and the economic structure. Dialectics also carries with it a methodological prescription: One component of social life cannot be studied in isolation from the rest.

This idea has both diachronic and synchronic components. A *synchronic* view leads us to be concerned with the interrelationship of components of society within a contemporary totality. A *diachronic* view carries with it a concern for the historical roots of today's society as well as for where it might be going in the future (Bauman, 1976). The domination of people by social and cultural structures—the "one-dimensional" society, to use Marcuse's phrase—is the result of a specific historical development and is not a universal characteristic of humankind. This historical perspective counteracts the common-sense view that emerges in capitalism that the system is a natural and inevitable phenomenon. In the view of the critical theorists (and other Marxists), people have come to see society as "second nature"; it is "perceived by common-sensical wisdom as an alien, uncompromising, demanding and high-handed power—exactly like non-human nature. To abide by the rules of reason, to behave rationally, to achieve success, to be free, man now had to accommodate himself to the 'second nature' " (Bauman, 1976:6).

The critical theorists also are oriented to thinking about the future, but following Marx's lead, they refuse to be utopian; rather, they focus on criticizing and changing contemporary society (Alway, 1995). However, instead of directing their attention to society's economic structure as Marx had done, they concentrate on its cultural superstructure. Their dialectical approach commits them to work in the real world. This means that they are not satisfied with seeking truth in scientific laboratories. The ultimate test of their ideas is the degree to which they are accepted and used in practice. This process they call *authentication,* which occurs when the people who have been the victims of distorted communication take up the ideas of critical theory and use them to free themselves from that system (Bauman, 1976:104). Thus we arrive at another aspect of the concerns of the critical thinkers—the *liberation* of humankind (Marcuse, 1964:222).

In more abstract terms, critical thinkers can be said to be preoccupied with the interplay and relationship between theory and practice. The view of the Frankfurt school was that the two have been severed in capitalist society (Schroyer, 1973:28). That is, theorizing is done by one group, which is delegated, or more likely takes, that right, whereas practice is relegated to another, less powerful group. In many cases, the theorist's work is uninformed by what went on in the real world, leading to an impoverished and largely irrelevant body of Marxian and sociological theory. The point is to unify theory and practice so as to restore the relationship between them. Theory thus would be informed by practice, whereas practice would be shaped by theory. In the process, both theory and practice would be enriched.

Despite this avowed goal, most of critical theory has failed abysmally to integrate theory and practice. In fact, one of the most often voiced criticisms of critical theory is that it is usually written in such a way as to be totally inaccessible to the mass of people. Furthermore, in its commitment to studying culture and superstructure, critical theory addresses a number of very esoteric topics and has little to say about the pragmatic, day-to-day concerns of most people.

Knowledge and Human Interests One of the best-known dialectical concerns of the critical school is Jurgen Habermas's (1970, 1971) interest in the relationship between knowledge and human interests—an example of a broader dialectical concern with the relationship between subjective and objective factors. But Habermas has been careful to point out that subjective and objective factors cannot be dealt with in isolation from one another. To him, knowledge systems exist at the objective level whereas human interests are more subjective phenomena.

Habermas differentiated among three knowledge systems and their corresponding interests. The interests that lie behind and guide each system of knowledge are generally unknown to laypeople, and it is the task of the critical theorists to uncover them. The first type of knowledge is *analytic science,* or *classical positivistic scientific systems.* In Habermas's view, the underlying interest of such a knowledge system is technical prediction and control, which can be applied to the environment, other societies, or people within society. In Habermas's view, analytic science lends itself quite easily to enhancing oppressive control. The second type of knowledge system is *humanistic knowledge,* and its interest is in *understanding* the world. It operates from the general view that understanding our past generally helps us to understand what is transpiring today. It has a practical interest in mutual and self-understanding. It is neither oppressive nor liberating. The third type is *critical knowledge,* which Habermas, and the Frankfurt school in general, espoused. The interest attached to this type of knowledge is *human emancipation.* It was hoped that the critical knowledge generated by Habermas and others would raise the self-consciousness of the masses (through mechanisms articulated by the Freudians) and lead to a social movement that would result in the hoped-for emancipation.

Criticisms of Critical Theory

A number of criticisms have been leveled at critical theory (Bottomore, 1984). First, critical theory has been accused of being largely ahistorical, of examining a variety of events without paying much attention to their historical and comparative contexts (for example, Nazism in the 1930s, anti-Semitism in the 1940s, student revolts in the 1960s). This is a damning criticism of any Marxian theory, which should be inherently historical and comparative. Second, the critical school, as we have seen already, generally has ignored the economy. Finally, and relatedly, critical theorists have tended to argue that the working class has disappeared as a revolutionary force, a position decidedly in opposition to traditional Marxian analysis.

Criticisms such as these led such traditional Marxists as Bottomore to conclude, "The Frankfurt School, in its original form, and as a school of Marxism or sociology, is dead" (1984:76). Similar sentiments have been expressed by Greisman, who labels critical theory "the paradigm that failed" (1986:273). If it is dead as a distinctive school, it is because many of its basic ideas have found their way into Marxism, neo-Marxian sociology, and even mainstream sociology. Thus, as Bottomore himself concludes in the case of Habermas, the critical school has undergone a rapprochement with Marxism and sociology, and "at the same time some of the distinctive ideas of the Frankfurt School are conserved and developed" (1984:76).

The Ideas of Jurgen Habermas

Although critical theory *may* be on the decline, Jurgen Habermas[3] and his theories are very much alive (Bernstein, 1995; Carleheden and Gabriels, 1996; Morrow and Brown, 1994; Outhwaite, 1994). We touched on a few of his ideas earlier in this chapter, but we close this section on critical theory with a more detailed look at his theory (still other aspects of his thinking will be covered in Chapters 11 and 12).

Differences with Marx   Habermas contends that his goal has been "to develop a theoretical program that I understand as a reconstruction of historical materialism" (1979:95). Habermas takes Marx's starting point (human potential, species-being, "sensuous human activity") as his own. However, Habermas (1971) argues that Marx failed to distinguish between two analytically distinct components of species-being—work (or labor, purposive-rational action) and social (or symbolic) interaction (or communicative action). In Habermas's view, Marx tended to ignore the latter and to reduce it to work. As Habermas put it, the problem in Marx's work is the *"reduction of the self-generative act of the human species* to labor" (1971:42). Thus, Habermas says: "I take as my starting point the fundamental distinction between *work* and *interaction*" (1970:91). Throughout his writings, Habermas's work is informed by this distinction, although he is most prone to use the terms *purposive-rational action* (work) and *communicative action* (interaction).

Under the heading "purposive-rational action," Habermas distinguishes between instrumental action and strategic action. Both involve the calculated pursuit of self-interest. *Instrumental action* involves a single actor rationally calculating the best means to a given goal. *Strategic action* involves two or more individuals coordinating purposive-rational action in the pursuit of a goal. The objective of *both* instrumental and strategic action is instrumental mastery.

Habermas is most interested in *communicative action,* in which

> the actions of the agents involved are coordinated not through egocentric calculations of success but through acts of *reaching understanding*. In communicative action participants are not primarily oriented to their own successes; they pursue their individual goals under the condition that they can *harmonize* their plans of action on the basis of *common situation definitions.*
>
> (Habermas, 1984:286; italics added)

Whereas the end of purposive-rational action is to achieve a goal, the objective of communicative action is to achieve communicative understanding (Stryker, 1998).

Clearly, there is an important speech component in communicative action. However, such action is broader than that encompassing "speech acts or equivalent nonverbal expressions" (Habermas, 1984:278).

Habermas's key point of departure from Marx is to argue that communicative action, *not* purposive-rational action (work), is the most distinctive and most pervasive human phenomenon. It (not work) is the foundation of all sociocultural life as well as all the

---

[3]Habermas began as Theodor Adorno's research assistant in 1955 (Wiggershaus, 1994:537).

human sciences. Whereas Marx was led to focus on work, Habermas is led to focus on communication.

Not only did Marx focus on work, but he took free and creative work (species-being) as his baseline for critically analyzing work in various historical epochs, especially capitalism. Habermas, too, adopts a baseline, but in the realm of communicative rather than purposive-rational action. Habermas's baseline is undistorted communication, communication without compulsion. With this baseline, Habermas is able to critically analyze distorted communication. Habermas is concerned with those social structures that distort communication, just as Marx examined the structural sources of the distortion of work. Although they have different baselines, both Habermas and Marx *have* baselines, and these permit them to escape relativism and render judgments about various historical phenomena. Habermas is critical of those theorists, especially Weber and previous critical theorists, for their lack of such a baseline and their lapse into relativism.

There is still another parallel between Marx and Habermas and their baselines. For both, these baselines represent not only their analytical starting points but also their political objectives. That is, whereas for Marx the goal was a communist society in which undistorted work (species-being) would exist for the first time, for Habermas the political goal is a society of undistorted communication (communicative action). In terms of immediate goals, Marx seeks the elimination of (capitalist) barriers to undistorted work, and Habermas is interested in the elimination of barriers to free communication.

Here Habermas (1973; see also, Habermas, 1994:101), like other critical theorists, draws on Freud and sees many parallels between what psychoanalysts do at the individual level and what he thinks needs to be done at the societal level. Habermas sees psychoanalysis as a theory of distorted communication and as preoccupied with allowing individuals to communicate in an undistorted way. The psychoanalyst seeks to find the sources of distortions in individual communication, that is, repressed blocks to communication. Through reflection, the psychoanalyst attempts to help the individual overcome these blocks. Similarly, through *therapeutic critique,* "a form of argumentation that serves to clarify systematic self-deception" (Habermas, 1984:21), the critical theorist attempts to aid people in general to overcome social barriers to undistorted communication. There is, then, an analogy (many critics think an illegitimate analogy) between psychoanalysis and critical theory. The psychoanalyst aids the patient in much the same way that the social critic helps those unable to communicate adequately to become "undisabled" (Habermas, 1994:112).

As for Marx, the basis of Habermas's ideal future society exists in the contemporary world. That is, for Marx elements of species-being are found in work in capitalist society. For Habermas, elements of undistorted communication are to be found in every act of contemporary communication.

Rationalization   This brings us to the central issue of rationalization in Habermas's work. Here Habermas is influenced not only by Marx's work but by Weber's as well. Most prior work, in Habermas's view, has focused on the rationalization of purposive-rational action, which has led to a growth of productive forces and an increase in technological control over life (Habermas, 1970). This form of rationalization, as it was to Weber and Marx, is a major, perhaps *the* major, problem in the modern world. However, the problem is rationalization of purposive-rational action, *not* rationalization in general. In fact, for Habermas, the antidote to the problem of the rationalization of purposive-rational action lies in the rationalization of communicative action. The rationalization of communicative action leads to communication free from domination, free and open communication. Rationalization here involves emancipation, *"removing restrictions on communication"* (Habermas, 1970:118; see also Habermas, 1979). This is where Habermas's previously mentioned work on *legitimations* and, more generally, *ideology* fits in. That is, these are two of the main causes of distorted communication, causes that must be eliminated if we are to have free and open communication.

At the level of social norms, such rationalization would involve decreases in normative repressiveness and rigidity leading to increases in individual flexibility and reflectivity. The development of this new, less-restrictive or nonrestrictive normative system lies at the heart of Habermas's theory of social evolution. Instead of a new productive system, rationalization for Habermas (1979) leads to a new, less-distorting normative system. Although he regards it as a misunderstanding of his position, many have accused Habermas of cutting his Marxian roots in this shift from the material to the normative level.

The end point of this evolution for Habermas is a rational society (Delanty, 1997). *Rationality* here means removal of the barriers that distort communication, but more generally it means a communication system in which ideas are openly presented and defended against criticism; unconstrained agreement develops during argumentation. To understand this better, we need more details of Habermas's communication theory.

Communication   Habermas distinguishes between the previously discussed communicative action and discourse. Whereas communicative action occurs in everyday life, *discourse* is

> that form of communication that is removed from contexts of experience and action and whose structure assures us: that the bracketed validity claims of assertions, recommendations, or warnings are the exclusive object of discussion; that participants, themes, and contributions are not restricted except with reference to the goal of testing the validity claims in questions; that no force except that of the better argument is exercised; and that all motives except that of the cooperative search for truth are excluded.
>
> (Habermas, 1975:107–108)

In the theoretical world of discourse, but also hidden and underlying the world of communicative actions, is the "ideal speech situation," in which force or power does not determine which arguments win out; instead the better argument emerges victorious. The weight of evidence and argumentation determine what is considered to be valid or true. The arguments that emerge from such a discourse (and that the participants agree on) are true (Hesse, 1995). Thus Habermas adopts a consensus theory of truth (rather than a copy [or "reality"] theory of truth [Outhwaite, 1994:41]). This truth is part of all communication, and its full expression is the goal of Habermas's evolutionary theory. As Thomas McCarthy says, "The idea of truth points ultimately to a form of interaction that is free from all distorting influences. The 'good and true life' that is the goal of critical theory is inherent in the notion of truth; it is anticipated in every act of speech" (1982:308).

Consensus arises theoretically in discourse (and pretheoretically in communicative action) when four types of validity claims are raised and recognized by interactants. First, the speaker's utterances are seen as understandable, comprehensible. Second, the propositions offered by the speaker are true; that is, the speaker is offering reliable knowledge. Third, the speaker is being truthful (veracious) and sincere in offering the propositions; the speaker is reliable. Fourth, it is right and proper for the speaker to utter such propositions; he or she has the normative basis to do so. Consensus arises when all these validity claims are raised and accepted; it breaks down when one or more are questioned. Returning to an earlier point, there are forces in the modern world that distort this process, prevent the emergence of a consensus, and would have to be overcome for Habermas's ideal society to come about.

Critical Theory Today

While Habermas is the most prominent of today's social thinkers, he is not alone in struggling to develop a critical theory that is better adapted to contemporary realities (see, for example, the various essays in Wexler, 1991; Antonio and Kellner, 1994). Castells (1996b) has made the case for the need for a critical theory of the new "information society." To illustrate these continuing efforts, a brief discussion follows of Kellner's (1989c) effort to develop a critical theory of what he labels "techno-capitalism."

Techno-Capitalism   Kellner's theory is based on the premise that we have not moved into a postmodern, or postindustrial, age, but rather that capitalism continues to reign supreme, as it did in the heyday of critical theory. Thus, he feels that the basic concepts developed to analyze capitalism (for example, reification, alienation) continue to be relevant in the analysis of techno-capitalism. Kellner defines techno-capitalism as

> a configuration of capitalist society in which technical and scientific knowledge, automation, computers and advanced technology play a role in the process of production parallel to the role of human labor power, mechanization and machines in earlier eras of capitalism, while producing as well new modes of societal organization and forms of culture and everyday life.
>
> (Kellner, 1989c:178)

In technical Marxian terms, in techno-capitalism "constant capital progressively comes to replace variable capital, as the ratio between technology and labor increases at the expense of the input of human labor power" (Kellner, 1989c:179). Yet, we should not lose sight of the fact that techno-capitalism remains a form of capitalism, albeit one in which technology is of far greater importance than ever before.

Kellner has learned from the failures of other Marxists. Thus, for example, he resists the idea that technology determines the "superstructure" of society. The state and culture are seen as at least partially autonomous in techno-capitalism. He also refuses to see techno-capitalism as a new stage in history, but views it rather as a new configuration, or constellation, within capitalism. Kellner also does not simply focus on the problems caused by techno-capitalism, but also sees in it new possibilities for social progress and the emancipation of society. In fact, a key role for critical theory, in Kellner's view, is not just to criticize it, but to "attempt to analyze the emancipatory possibilities unleashed by techno-capitalism" (1989c:215). Kellner also refuses to return to the old class politics, but sees great potential in the various social movements (women, the environment) that have arisen in the last few decades.

Kellner does not endeavor to develop a full-scale theory of techno-capitalism. His main point is that although it has changed dramatically, capitalism remains predominant in the contemporary world. Thus, the tools provided by the critical school, and Marxian theory more generally, continue to be relevant in today's world. We close this section with Kellner's description of "techno-culture," since a concern with culture was so central to critical theory in its prime:

> Techno-culture represents a configuration of mass culture and the consumer society in which consumer goods, film, television, mass images and computerized information become a dominant form of culture throughout the developed world [and] which increasingly penetrate developing countries as well. In this techno-culture, image, spectacle, and aestheticized commodification, or "commodity aesthetics," come to constitute new forms of culture which colonize everyday life and transform politics, economics and social relations. In all these domains, *technology* plays an increasingly fundamental role.
>
> (Kellner, 1989c:181)

There is much here to be explored by future critical theorists, such as the nature of techno-culture itself, its commodification, its colonization of the life-world, and its dialectical impact on the economy and other sectors of society. There is much that is new here, but there is also much that is based on the fundamental ideas of critical theory.

NEO-MARXIAN ECONOMIC SOCIOLOGY

Many neo-Marxists (for example, critical theorists) have made relatively few comments on the economic institution, at least in part as a reaction against the excesses of the economic determinists. However, these reactions have themselves set in motion a series of counterreactions. In this section we will deal with the work of some of those Marxists who have returned to a focus on the economic realm. Their work constitutes an effort to adapt Marxian theory to the realities of modern capitalist society (Lash and Urry, 1987; Mészáros, 1995).

We will deal with two bodies of work in this section. The first focuses on the broad issue of capital and labor. The second comprises the narrower, and more contemporary, work on the transition from Fordism to post-Fordism.

Capital and Labor

Marx's original insights into economic structures and processes were based on his analysis of the capitalism of his time—what we can think of as competitive capitalism. Capitalist industries were comparatively small, with the result that no single industry, or small group of industries, could gain complete and uncontested control over a market. Much of Marx's economic work was based on the premise, accurate for his time, that capitalism was a competitive system. To be sure, Marx foresaw the possibility of future monopolies, but he commented only briefly on them. Many later

Marxian theorists continued to operate as if capitalism remained much as it had been in Marx's time.

Monopoly Capital   It is in this context that we must examine the work of Paul Baran and Paul Sweezy (1966). They began with a criticism of Marxian social science for repeating familiar formulations and for failing to explain important recent developments in capitalistic society. They accused Marxian theory of stagnating because it continued to rest on the assumption of a competitive economy. A modern Marxian theory must, in their view, recognize that competitive capitalism has been largely replaced by monopoly capitalism.

In *monopoly capitalism* one, or a few, capitalists control a given sector of the economy. Clearly, there is far less competition in monopoly capitalism than in competitive capitalism. In competitive capitalism, organizations competed on a price basis; that is, capitalists tried to sell more goods by offering lower prices. In monopoly capitalism, firms no longer have to compete in this way because one or a few firms control a market; competition shifts to the sales domain. Advertising, packaging, and other methods of appealing to potential consumers are the main areas of competition.

The movement from price to sales competition is part of another process characteristic of monopoly capitalism—*progressive rationalization.* Price competition comes to be seen as highly irrational. That is, from the monopoly capitalist's point of view, offering lower and lower prices can lead only to chaos in the marketplace, to say nothing of lower profits and perhaps even bankruptcy. Sales competition, in contrast, is not a cutthroat system; in fact, it even provides work for the advertising industry. Furthermore, prices can be kept high, with the costs of the sales and promotion simply added to the price. Thus sales competition is also far less risky than price competition.

Another crucial aspect of monopoly capitalism is the rise of the giant corporation, with a few large corporations controlling most sectors of the economy. In competitive capitalism, the organization was controlled almost single-handedly by an entrepreneur. The modern corporation is owned by a large number of stockholders, but a few large stockholders own most of the stock. Although stockholders "own" the corporation, managers exercise the actual day-to-day control. The managers are crucial in monopoly capitalism, whereas the entrepreneurs were central in competitive capitalism. Managers have considerable power, which they seek to maintain. They even seek financial independence for their firms by trying, as much as possible, to generate whatever funds they need internally rather than relying on external sources of funding.

Baran and Sweezy commented extensively on the central position of the corporate manager in modern capitalist society. Managers are viewed as a highly rational group oriented to maximizing the profits of the organization. Therefore they are not inclined to take the risks that were characteristic of the early entrepreneurs. They have a longer time perspective than the entrepreneur. Whereas the early capitalist was interested in maximizing profits in the short run, modern managers are aware that such efforts may well lead to chaotic price competition that might adversely affect the long-term profitability of the firm. The manager will thus forgo *some* profits in the short run to maximize long-term profitability.

Baran and Sweezy have been criticized on various grounds. For example, they overemphasize the rationality of managers. Herbert Simon (1957), for example, would argue that managers are more interested in finding (and are only able to find) minimally satisfactory solutions than they are in finding the most rational and most profitable solutions. Another issue is whether managers are, in fact, the pivotal figures in modern capitalism. Many would argue that it is the large stockholders who really control the capitalistic system.

Dealing with Surplus   The central issue in monopoly capitalism is the ability of the system to generate and use economic surplus. *Economic surplus* is defined as the difference between the value of what a society produces and the costs of producing it. Because of their concern with the surplus issue, Baran and Sweezy moved away from Marx's interest in the exploitation of labor and stressed instead the links between the economy and other social institutions, in particular in the absorption of economic surplus by these other institutions.

Modern capitalistic managers are victims of their own success. On the one hand, they are able to set prices arbitrarily because of their monopolistic position in the economy. On the other hand, they seek to cut costs within the organization, particularly the costs associated with blue-collar work. The ability to set high prices and to cut costs leads to the rising level of economic surplus.

The issue that then confronts the capitalist is what to do with the surplus. One possibility is to consume it—to pay managers huge salaries and stockholders huge dividends that are turned into yachts, Rolls-Royces, jewelry, and caviar. This *is* done to some extent, but the surplus is so huge that elites could never consume even a small part of it. In any case, conspicuous consumption (Veblen, 1899/1994) was more characteristic of the early entrepreneurs than of the modern manager and stockholder.

A second alternative is to invest the surplus in such things as improved technology and foreign ventures. This seemingly reasonable action, which is taken by managers to some extent, has the major drawback that such investments, if made wisely, generate even more surplus. This only exacerbates the problem of using economic surplus.

Increasing sales efforts also may absorb some of the surplus. Modern capitalists can stimulate the demand for their products by advertising; by creating and expanding the markets for their products; and by such devices as model changes, planned obsolescence, and readily available consumer credit. However, this alternative also has problems. First, it cannot absorb enough surplus. Second, it is likely to stimulate even further expansion of the corporation, which, in turn, leads to still greater levels of surplus.

According to Baran and Sweezy, the only choice remaining is *waste*. The surplus needs to be squandered, and there are two ways of so doing. The first is nonmilitary government spending through keeping millions of workers in government jobs and supporting myriad government programs. The second is military spending, including the military's vast payroll and its budget of billions of dollars for expensive hardware that rapidly becomes obsolete.

It seems as if there is really *no good way* of getting rid of surplus, and perhaps that is the view Baran and Sweezy wish communicated. It leaves us with the clear impression that this is an irresolvable contradiction within capitalism. Virtually all the capitalists' expenditures lead to greater demand and ultimately to greater surpluses. Government and military employees spend their money on more goods; as some military equipment is consumed (for example, in the 1991 war with, and the 1998 bombing of, Iraq), there is a demand for new and better equipment.

In sum, Baran and Sweezy accepted the traditional economic focus of Marxian theory, but shifted from the labor process to economic structures of modern capitalistic society.

Labor and Monopoly Capital Harry Braverman (1974) considered the labor process and the exploitation of the worker to be the heart of Marxian theory. Although his emphasis is different from that of Baran and Sweezy, he saw his work as tied closely to theirs (Braverman, 1974). The title of his book, *Labor and Monopoly Capital,* reflects his main focus, and its subtitle, *The Degradation of Work in the Twentieth Century,* shows his interest in adapting Marx's perspective to the realities of work in the twentieth century.

Braverman intended not only to update Marx's interest in manual workers but also to examine what has happened to white-collar and service workers. Marx paid little attention to these two groups, but they have become major occupational categories that need to be subjected to serious scrutiny. In relation to Baran and Sweezy's work, it could be said that one of the major developments in monopoly capitalism has been the relative decline in blue-collar workers and the simultaneous increases in white-collar and service workers to staff the large organizations characteristic of monopoly capitalism.

Like Marx, Braverman made it quite clear that his criticisms of the contemporary work world do not reflect a yearning for an era now past. He said that he was not romanticizing the old-time crafts and "the outworn conditions of now archaic modes of labor" (Braverman, 1974:6). Also like Marx (and Marcuse), Braverman was a critic not of science and technology per se but simply of the way that they are used in capitalism "as weapons of domination in the creation, perpetuation and deepening of a gulf between classes in society" (1974:6). In the employ of the capitalist, science and technology have been used systematically to rob work of its craft heritage without providing anything to take its place. Braverman believed that in different (that is, socialist) hands, science and technology could be used differently to produce

> an age that has not yet come into being, in which, for the worker, the craft satisfaction that arises from conscious and purposeful mastery of the labor process will be combined with the marvel of science and the ingenuity of engineering, an age in which everyone will be able to benefit, in some degree, from this combination.
>
> (Braverman, 1974:7)

Toward the goal of extending Marx's analysis of blue-collar workers to white-collar and service workers, Braverman argued that the concept "working class" does not describe a specific group of people or occupations but is rather an expression of a process of buying and selling labor power. In terms of that process, Braverman argued that in modern capitalism virtually no one owns the means of production; therefore the many, including most white-collar and service workers, are forced to sell their labor power to the few who do. In his view, capitalist control and exploitation, as well as the derivative processes of mechanization and rationalization, are being extended to white-collar and service occupations, although their impact is not yet as great as it has been on blue-collar occupations.

Braverman based his analysis on Marx's anthropology, specifically his concept of human potential (species-being). Braverman argued that all forms of life need to sustain themselves in their natural environment; that is, they need to appropriate nature for their own use. Work is the process by which nature is altered in order to enhance its usefulness. In that sense, animals work, too, but what is distinctive about humans is their consciousness. People have a set of mental capacities that other animals lack. Human work is thus characterized by a unity of conception (thought) and execution (action). This unity can be dissolved, and capitalism is a crucial stage in the destruction of the unity of thought and execution in the working world.

A key ingredient in this breakdown in capitalism is the sale and purchase of labor power. Capitalists can purchase certain kinds of labor power and not others. For instance, they can purchase manual labor and insist that mental labor be kept out of the process. Although the opposite can also occur, it is less likely. As a result, capitalism is characterized by an increasing number of manual workers and fewer and fewer mental workers. This seems to contradict the statistics, which reflect a massive growth in white-collar, presumably mental, occupations. However, as we will see, Braverman believed that many white-collar occupations are being *proletarianized,* made indistinguishable in many ways from manual work.

Managerial Control Braverman recognized economic exploitation, which was Marx's focus, but concentrated on the issue of *control.* He asked the question: How do the capitalists control the labor power that they employ? One answer is that they exercise such control through managers. In fact, Braverman defined *management* as *"a labor process conducted for the purpose of control within the corporation"* (1974:267).

Braverman concentrated on the more impersonal means employed by managers to control workers. One of his central concerns was the utilization of specialization to control workers. Here he carefully differentiated between the division of labor in society as a whole and specialization of work within the organization. All known societies have had a division of labor (for example, between men and women, farmers and artisans, and so forth), but the specialization of work within the organization is a special development of capitalism. Braverman believed that the division of labor at the societal level may enhance the individual, whereas specialization in the workplace has the disastrous effect of subdividing human capabilities: "The subdivision of the individual, when carried on without regard to human capabilities and needs, is a crime against the person and against humanity" (1974:73).

Specialization in the workplace involves the continual division and subdivision of tasks or operations into minute and highly specialized activities, each of which is then likely to be assigned to a *different* worker. This process constitutes the creation of what Braverman calls "detail workers." Out of the range of abilities any individual possesses, capitalists select a small number that the worker is to use on the job. As Braverman put it, the capitalist first breaks down the work process and then "dismembers the worker as well" (1974:78) by requiring the worker to use only a small proportion of his or her skills and abilities. In Braverman's terms, the worker "never voluntarily converts himself into a lifelong detail worker. This is the contribution of the capitalist" (1974:78).

Why does the capitalist do this? First, it increases the control of management. It is easier to control a worker doing a specified task than it is one employing a wide range of skills. Second, it increases productivity. That is, a group of workers performing highly specialized tasks can produce more than the same number of craftspeople, each of whom has all the skills and performs all the production activities. For instance, workers on an automobile assembly line produce more cars than would a corresponding number of skilled craftspeople, each of whom produces his or her own car. Third, specialization allows the capitalist to pay the least for the labor power needed. Instead of highly paid, skilled craftspeople, the capitalist can employ lower-paid, unskilled workers. Following the logic of capitalism, employers seek to progressively cheapen the labor of workers, which results in a virtually undifferentiated mass of what Braverman called "simple labor."

Specialization is not a sufficient means of control for capitalists and the managers in their employ. Another important means is scientific technique, including such efforts as scientific management, which is an attempt to apply science to the control of labor on the behalf of management. To Braverman, scientific management is the science of "how best to control alienated labor" (1974:90). Scientific management is found in a series of stages aimed at the control of labor—gathering many workers in one workshop, dictating the length of the workday, supervising workers directly to ensure diligence, enforcing rules against distractions (for example, talking), and setting minimum acceptable production levels. Overall scientific management contributed to control by *"the dictation to the worker of the precise manner in which work is to be performed"* (Braverman, 1974:90). For example, Braverman discussed F. W. Taylor's (Kanigel, 1997) early work on the shoveling of coal, which led him to develop rules about the kind of shovel to use, the way to stand, the angle at which the shovel should enter the coal pile, and how much coal to pick up in each motion. In other words, Taylor developed methods that ensured almost total control over the labor process. Workers were to be left with as few independent decisions as possible; thus, a separation of the mental and manual was accomplished. Management used its monopoly over work-related knowledge to control each step of the labor process. In the end, the work itself was left without any meaningful skill, content, or knowledge. Craftsmanship was utterly destroyed.

Braverman also saw machinery as a means of control over workers. Modern machinery comes into existence "when the tool and/or the work are given a fixed motion path by the structure of the machine itself" (Braverman, 1974:188). The skill is built into the machine rather than left for the worker to acquire. Instead of controlling the work process, workers come to be controlled by the machine. Furthermore, it is far easier for management to control machines than to control workers.

Braverman argued that through such mechanisms as the specialization of work, scientific management, and machines, management has been able to extend its control over its manual workers. Although this is a useful insight, especially the emphasis on control, Braverman's distinctive contribution has been his effort to extend this kind of analysis to sectors of the labor force that were not analyzed in Marx's original analysis of the labor process. Braverman argued that white-collar and service workers are now being subjected to the same processes of control that were used on manual workers in the last century (Schmutz, 1996).

One of Braverman's examples is white-collar clerical workers. At one time such workers were considered to be a group distinguished from manual workers by such things as their dress, skills, training, and career prospects (Lockwood, 1956). However, today both groups are being subjected to the same means of control. Thus it has become more difficult to differentiate between the factory and the modern factorylike office, as the workers in the latter are progressively proletarianized. For one thing, the work of the clerical worker has grown more and more specialized. This means, among other things, that the mental and manual aspects of office work have been separated. Office managers, engineers, and technicians now perform the mental work, whereas the "line" clerical workers do little more than manual tasks such as keypunching. As a result, the level of skills needed for these jobs has been lowered, and the jobs require little or no special training.

Scientific management also is now seen as invading the office. Clerical tasks have been scientifically studied, and as a result of that research, they have been simplified, routinized, and standardized. Finally, mechanization has made significant inroads into the office, primarily through the computer and computer-related equipment.

By applying these mechanisms to clerical work, managers find it much easier to control such workers. It is unlikely that such control mechanisms are as strong and effective in the office as in the factory; still, the trend is toward the development of the white-collar "factory."[4]

Several obvious criticisms can be leveled at Braverman. For one thing, he has probably overestimated the degree of similarity between manual and clerical work. For another, his preoccupation with control has led him to devote relatively little attention to the dynamics of economic exploitation in capitalism. Nonetheless, he has enriched our understanding of the labor process in modern capitalist society (Foster, 1994; Meiksins, 1994).

Other Work on Labor and Capital   The issue of control is even more central to Richard Edwards (1979). To Edwards, control lies at the heart of the twentieth-century transformation of the workplace. Following Marx, Edwards sees the workplace, both past and present, as an arena of class conflict, in his terms a "contested terrain." Within this arena, dramatic changes have taken place in the way in which those at the top control those at the bottom. During nineteenth-century competitive capitalism, "simple" control was used, in which "bosses exercised power personally, intervening in the labor process often to exhort workers, bully and threaten them, reward good performance, hire and fire on the spot, favor loyal employees, and generally act as despots, benevolent or otherwise" (Edwards, 1979:19). Although this system of control continues in many small businesses, it has proven too crude for modern, large-scale organizations. In such organizations, simple control has tended to be replaced by impersonal and more sophisticated technical and bureaucratic control. Modern workers can be controlled by the technologies with which they work. The classic example of this is the automobile assembly line, in which the workers' actions are determined by the incessant demands of the line. Another example is the modern computer, which can keep careful track of how much work an employee does and how many mistakes he or she makes. Modern

---

[4]It is important to note that Braverman's book was written before the boom in computer technology in the office, especially the now-widespread use of the word processor. It may be that such technology, requiring greater skill and training than older office technologies, will increase worker autonomy (Zuboff, 1988).

workers also are controlled by the impersonal rules of bureaucracies rather than the personal control of supervisors. Capitalism is constantly changing and with it the means by which workers are controlled.

Also of note is the work of Michael Burawoy (1979) and its interest in why workers in a capitalist system work so hard. He rejects Marx's explanation that such hard work is a result of coercion. The advent of labor unions and other changes largely eliminated the arbitrary power of management. "Coercion alone could no longer explain what workers did once they arrived on the shop floor" (Burawoy, 1979:xii). To Burawoy, workers, at least in part, consent to work hard in the capitalist system, and at least part of that consent is produced in the workplace.

We can illustrate Burawoy's approach with one aspect of his research, the games that workers play on the job and, more generally, the informal practices that they develop. Most analysts see these as workers' efforts to reduce alienation and other job-related discontent. In addition, they usually have been seen as social mechanisms that workers develop to oppose management. In contrast, Burawoy concludes that these games "are usually neither independent nor in opposition to management" (1979:80). In fact, "management, at least at the lower levels, actually participates not only in the organization of the game but in the enforcement of its rules" (1979:80). Rather than challenging management, the organization, or, ultimately, the capitalist system, these games actually support them. For one thing, playing the game creates consent among the workers about the rules on which the game is based and, more generally, about the system of social relations (owner-manager-worker) that defines the rules of the game. For another, because managers and workers both are involved in the game, the system of antagonistic social relations to which the game was supposed to respond is obscured.

Burawoy argues that such methods of generating active cooperation and consent are far more effective in getting workers to cooperate in the pursuit of profit than coercion (such as firing those who do not cooperate). In the end, Burawoy believes that games and other informal practices are all methods of getting workers to accept the system and of eliciting their contributions to ever higher profits.

Fordism and Post-Fordism

One of the most recent concerns of economically oriented Marxists is the issue of whether we have witnessed, or are witnessing, a transition from "Fordism" to "post-Fordism" (Amin, 1994; Kiely, 1998). This is related to the broader issue of whether we have undergone a transition from a modern to a postmodern society (Gartman, 1998). We will discuss this larger issue in general (Chapter 13), as well as the way in which it is addressed by contemporary Marxian theorists (later in this chapter). In general, *Fordism* is associated with the modern era, while *post-Fordism* is linked to the more recent, postmodern epoch. (The Marxian interest in Fordism is not new; Gramsci [1971] published an essay on it in 1931.)

Fordism, of course, refers to the ideas, principles, and systems spawned by Henry Ford. Ford is generally credited with the development of the modern mass-production system, primarily through the creation of the automobile assembly line. The following characteristics may be associated with Fordism:

- The mass production of homogeneous products.
- The use of inflexible technologies such as the assembly line.
- The adoption of standardized work routines (Taylorism).
- Increases in productivity derived from "economies of scale as well as the deskilling, intensification and homogenization of labor" (Clarke, 1990:73).
- The resulting rise of the mass worker and bureaucratized unions.
- The negotiation by the unions of uniform wages tied to increases in profits and productivity.
- The growth of a market for the homogenized products of mass-production industries and the resulting homogenization of consumption patterns.
- A rise in wages, caused by unionization, leading to a growing demand for the increasing supply of mass-produced products.
- A market for products that is governed by Keynesian macroeconomic policies, and a market for labor that is handled by collective bargaining overseen by the state.
- Mass educational institutions providing the mass workers required by industry (Clarke, 1990:73).

While Fordism has grown throughout the twentieth century, especially in the United States, it reached its peak and began to decline in the 1970s, especially after the oil crisis of 1973 and the subsequent decline of the American automobile industry and rise of its Japanese counterpart. As a result, it is argued that we are witnessing the decline of Fordism and the rise of post-Fordism, characterized by the following:

- A decline of interest in mass products is accompanied by a growth of interest in more specialized products, especially those high in style and quality.
- More specialized products require shorter production runs, resulting in smaller and more productive systems.
- More flexible production is made profitable by the advent of new technologies.
- New technologies require that workers, in turn, have more diverse skills and better training, more responsibility and greater autonomy.
- Production must be controlled through more flexible systems.
- Huge, inflexible bureaucracies need to be altered dramatically in order to operate more flexibly.
- Bureaucratized unions (and political parties) no longer adequately represent the interests of the new, highly differentiated labor force.
- Decentralized collective bargaining replaces centralized negotiations.
- The workers become more differentiated as people and require more differentiated commodities, lifestyles, and cultural outlets.
- The centralized welfare state can no longer meet the needs (for example, health, welfare, education) of a diverse population, and differentiated, more flexible institutions are required (Clarke, 1990:73–74).

If one needed to sum up the shift from Fordism to post-Fordism, it would be described as the transition from homogeneity to heterogeneity. There are two general issues involved here. First, has a transition from Fordism to post-Fordism actually occurred (Pelaez and Holloway, 1990)? Second, does post-Fordism hold out the hope of solving the problems associated with Fordism?

First, of course, there has been *no* clear historical break between Fordism and post-Fordism (S. Hall, 1988). Even if we are willing to acknowledge that elements of post-Fordism have emerged in the modern world, it is equally clear that elements of Fordism persist and show no signs of disappearing. For example, something we might call "McDonaldism," a phenomenon that has many things in common with Fordism, is growing at an astounding pace in contemporary society. On the basis of the model of the fast-food restaurant, more and more sectors of society are coming to utilize the principles of McDonaldism (Ritzer, 1996). McDonaldism shares many characteristics with Fordism—homogeneous products, rigid technologies, standardized work routines, deskilling, homogenization of labor (and customer), the mass worker, homogenization of consumption, and so on. Thus, Fordism is alive and well in the modern world, although it has been transmogrified into McDonaldism. Furthermore, classic Fordism—for example, in the form of the assembly line—remains a significant presence in the American economy.

Second, even if we accept the idea that post-Fordism is with us, does it represent a solution to the problems of modern capitalist society? Some neo-Marxists (and many supporters of the capitalist system [Womack, Jones, and Roos, 1990]) hold out great hope for it: "Post-Fordism is mainly an expression of hope that future capitalist development will be the salvation of social democracy" (Clarke, 1990:75). However, this is merely a hope, and in any case, there is already evidence that post-Fordism may not be the nirvana hoped for by some observers.

The Japanese model (tarnished by the precipitous decline of Japanese industry in the 1990s) is widely believed to be the basis of post-Fordism. However, research on Japanese industry (Satoshi, 1982) and on American industries utilizing Japanese management techniques (Parker and Slaughter, 1990) indicates that there are great problems with these systems and that they may even serve to *heighten* the level of exploitation of the worker. Parker and Slaughter label the Japanese system as it is employed in the United States (and it is probably worse in Japan) "management by stress": "The goal is to stretch the system like a rubber band on the point of breaking" (1990:33). Among other things, work is speeded up even further than on the traditional American assembly lines, putting enormous strain on the workers, who need to labor heroically just to keep up with the line. More generally, Levidow describes the new, post-Fordist workers as "relentlessly pressurized to increase their productivity, often in return for lower real wages—be they factory workers, homeworkers in the rag trade, privatized service workers or even polytechnic lecturers" (1990:59). Thus, it may well be that rather than representing a solution to the problems of capitalism, post-Fordism may simply be merely a new, more insidious phase in the heightening of the exploitation of workers by capitalists.

HISTORICALLY ORIENTED MARXISM

Marxists oriented toward historical research argue that they are being true to the Marxian concern for historicity. The most notable of Marx's historical research was his study of precapitalist economic formations (1857–58/1964). There is a good deal of subsequent historical work from a Marxian perspective (for example, Amin, 1977; Dobb, 1964; Hobsbawm, 1965). In this section, we deal with a body of work that

IMMANUEL WALLERSTEIN: A Biographical Sketch

Although Immanuel Wallerstein achieved recognition in the 1960s as an expert on Africa, his most important contribution to sociology is his 1974 book, *The Modern World-System*. That book was an instant success. It has received worldwide recognition and has been translated into ten languages and Braille.

Born on September 28, 1930, Wallerstein received all his degrees from Columbia University, including a doctorate in 1959. He next assumed a position on the faculty at Columbia; after many years there, and a five-year stint at McGill University in Montreal, Wallerstein became, in 1976, distinguished professor of sociology at the State University of New York at Binghamton.

Wallerstein was awarded the prestigious Sorokin Award for the first volume of *The Modern World-System* in 1975. Since that time, he has continued to work on the topic and has produced a number of articles as well as two additional volumes, in which he takes his analysis of the world-system up to the 1840s. We can anticipate more work from Wallerstein on this issue in the coming years. He is in the process of producing a body of work that will attract attention for years to come.

In fact, in many ways the attention it has already attracted and will continue to attract is more important than the body of work itself. The concept of the world-system has become the focus of thought and research in sociology, an accomplishment to which few scholars can lay claim. Many of the sociologists now doing research and theorizing about the world-system are critical of Wallerstein in one way or another, but they all clearly recognize the important role he played in the genesis of their ideas.

Although the concept of the world-system is an important contribution, at least as significant has been the role Wallerstein played in the revival of theoretically informed historical research. The most important work in the early years of sociology, by people like Marx, Weber, and Durkheim, was largely of this variety. However, in more recent years, most sociologists have turned away from doing this kind of research and toward using such ahistorical methods as questionnaires and interviews. These methods are quicker and easier to use than historical methods, and the data produced are easier to analyze with a computer. Use of such methods tends to require a narrow range of technical knowledge rather than a wide range of historically oriented knowledge. Furthermore, theory plays a comparatively minor role in research utilizing questionnaires and interviews. Wallerstein has been in the forefront of those involved in a revival of interest in historical research with a strong theoretical base.

reflects a historical orientation—Immanuel Wallerstein's (1974, 1980, 1989, 1992, 1995) research on the modern world-system.

The Modern World-System

Wallerstein chose a unit of analysis unlike those used by most Marxian thinkers. He did not look at workers, classes, or even states, because he found most of these too narrow for his purposes. Instead, he looked at a broad economic entity with a division of labor that is not circumscribed by political or cultural boundaries. He found that unit in his concept of the *world-system,* which is a largely self-contained social system with a set of boundaries and a definable life span; that is, it does not last forever. It is composed internally of a variety of social structures and member groups. However, Wallerstein was not inclined to define the system in terms of a consensus that holds it together. Rather, he saw the system as held together by a variety of forces that are in inherent tension. These forces always have the potential for tearing the system apart.

Wallerstein argued that thus far we have had only two types of world-systems. One is the world empire, of which ancient Rome is an example. The other is the modern capitalist world-economy. A world empire is based on political (and military) domination, whereas a capitalist world-economy relies on economic domination. A capitalist world-economy is seen as more stable than a world empire for several reasons. For one thing, it has a broader base, because it encompasses many states. For another, it has a built-in process of economic stabilization. The separate political entities within the capitalist world-economy absorb whatever losses occur, while economic gain is distributed to private hands. Wallerstein foresaw the *possibility* of still a third world-system, a *socialist world government.* Whereas the capitalist world-economy separates the political from the economic sector, a socialist world-economy would reintegrate them.

The *core* geographical area dominates the capitalist world-economy and exploits the rest of the system. The *periphery* consists of those areas that provide raw materials to the core and are heavily exploited by it. The *semiperiphery* is a residual category that encompasses a set of regions somewhere between the exploiting and the exploited. The key point is that to Wallerstein the international division of exploitation is defined not by state borders but by the economic division of labor in the world.

In the first volume on the world-system, Wallerstein (1974) dealt with the origin of the world-system roughly between the years 1450 and 1640. The significance of this development was the shift from political (and thus military) to economic dominance. Wallerstein saw economics as a far more efficient and less primitive means of domination than politics. Political structures are very cumbersome, whereas economic exploitation "makes it possible to increase the flow of the surplus from the lower strata to the upper strata, from the periphery to the center, from the majority to the minority" (Wallerstein, 1974:15). In the modern era, capitalism provided a basis for the growth and development of a world-economy; this has been accomplished without the aid of a unified political structure. Capitalism can be seen as an economic alternative to political domination. It is better able to produce economic surpluses than the more primitive techniques employed in political exploitation.

Wallerstein argued that three things were necessary for the rise of the capitalist world-economy out of the "ruins" of feudalism: geographical expansion through exploration and colonization, development of different methods of labor control for zones (for example, core, periphery) of the world-economy, and development of strong states that were to become the core states of the emerging capitalist world-economy. Let us look at each of these in turn.

Geographical Expansion   Wallerstein argued that geographical expansion by nations is a prerequisite for the other two stages. Portugal took the lead in overseas exploration, and other European nations followed. Wallerstein was wary of talking about specific countries or about Europe in general terms. He preferred to see overseas expansion as caused by a group of people acting in their immediate interests. Elite groups, such as nobles, needed overseas expansion for various reasons. For one thing, they were confronted with a nascent class war brought on by the crumbling of the feudal economy. The slave trade provided them with a tractable labor force on which to build the capitalist economy. The expansion also provided them with various commodities needed to develop it—gold bullion, food, and raw materials of various types.

Worldwide Division of Labor   Once the world had undergone geographical expansion, it was prepared for the next stage, the development of a worldwide division of labor. In the sixteenth century, capitalism replaced statism as the major mode of dominating the world, but capitalism did not develop uniformly around the world. In fact, Wallerstein argued, the solidarity of the capitalist system was ultimately based on its unequal development. Given his Marxian orientation, Wallerstein did not think of this as a consensual equilibrium but rather as one that was laden with conflict from the beginning. Different parts of the capitalist world-system came to specialize in specific functions—breeding labor power, growing food, providing raw materials, and organizing industry. Furthermore, different areas came to specialize in producing particular types of workers. For example, Africa produced slaves; western and southern Europe had many peasant tenant-farmers; western Europe was also the center of wage workers, the ruling classes, and other skilled and supervisory personnel.

More generally, each of the three parts of the international division of labor tended to differ in terms of mode of labor control. The core had free labor; the periphery was characterized by forced labor; and the semiperiphery was the heart of sharecropping. In fact, Wallerstein argued that the key to capitalism lies in a core dominated by a free labor market for skilled workers and a coercive labor market for less skilled workers in peripheral areas. Such a combination is the essence of capitalism. If a free labor market should develop throughout the world, we would have socialism.

Some regions of the world begin with small initial advantages, which are used as the basis for developing greater advantages later on. The core area in the sixteenth century, primarily western Europe, rapidly extended its advantages as towns flourished, industries developed, and merchants became important. It also moved to extend its domain by developing a wider variety of activities. At the same time, each of its activities became more specialized in order to produce more efficiently. In contrast, the periphery stagnated and moved more toward what Wallerstein called a "monoculture," or an undifferentiated, single-focus society.

Development of Core States   The third stage of the development of the world-system involved the political sector and how various economic groups used state structures to protect and advance their interests. Absolute monarchies arose in western Europe at about the same time as capitalism developed. From the sixteenth to the eighteenth centuries, the states were the central economic actors in Europe, although the center later shifted to economic enterprises. The strong states in the core areas played a key role in the development of capitalism and ultimately provided the economic base for their own demise. The European states strengthened themselves in the sixteenth century by, among other things, developing and enlarging bureaucratic systems and creating a monopoly of force in society, primarily by developing armies and legitimizing their activities so that they were assured of internal stability. Whereas the states of the core zone developed strong political systems, the periphery developed correspondingly weak states.

Later Developments   In *The Modern World-System II,* Wallerstein (1980) picked up the story of the consolidation of the world-economy between 1600 and 1750. This was not a period of a significant expansion of the European world-economy, but there were a number of significant changes within that system. For example, Wallerstein discussed the rise and subsequent decline in the core of the Netherlands. Later, he analyzed the conflict between two core states, England and France, as well as the ultimate victory of England. In the periphery, Wallerstein's detailed descriptions include the cyclical fortunes of Hispanic America. In the semiperiphery we witness, among other things, the decline of Spain and the rise of Sweden. Wallerstein continued his historical analysis from a Marxian viewpoint of the various roles played by different societies within the division of labor of the world-economy. Although Wallerstein paid close attention to political and social factors, his main focus remained the role of economic factors in world history.

In a later work, Wallerstein (1989) brings his historical analysis up to the 1840s. Wallerstein looks at three great developments during the period from 1730 to the 1840s—the Industrial Revolution (primarily in England), the French Revolution, and the independence of the once-European colonies in America. In his view, none of these were fundamental challenges to the world capitalist system; instead, they represented its "further consolidation and entrenchment" (Wallerstein, 1989:256).

Wallerstein continues the story of the struggle between England and France for dominance of the core. Whereas the world-economy had been stagnant during the prior period of analysis, it was now expanding, and Great Britain was able to industrialize more rapidly and come to dominate large-scale industries. This shift in domination to England occurred in spite of the fact that in the eighteenth century France had dominated in the industrial realm. The French Revolution played an important role in the development of the world capitalist system, especially by helping to bring the lingering cultural vestiges of feudalism to an end and by bringing the cultural-ideological system into line with economic and political realities. However, the revolution served to inhibit the industrial development of France, as did the ensuing Napoleonic rules and wars. By the end of this period, "Britain was finally truly hegemonic in the world-system" (Wallerstein, 1989:122).

The period between 1750 and 1850 was marked by the incorporation of vast new zones (the subcontinent of India, the Ottoman and Russian empires, and West Africa) into the periphery of the world-economy. These zones had been part of what Wallerstein calls the "external area" of the world-system and thus had been linked to, but were not in, that system. *External zones* are those from which the capitalist world-economy wanted goods but which were able to resist the reciprocal importation of manufactured goods from the core nations. As a result of the incorporation of these external zones, countries adjacent to the once-external nations were also drawn into the world-system. Thus, the incorporation of India contributed to China's becoming part of the periphery. By the end of the nineteenth century and the beginning of the twentieth, the pace of incorporation had quickened, and "the entire globe, even those regions that had never been part even of the external area of the capitalist world-economy were pulled inside" (Wallerstein, 1989:129).

The pressure for incorporation into the world-economy comes not from the nations being incorporated but "rather from the need of the world-economy to expand its boundaries, a need which was itself the outcome of pressures internal to the world-economy" (Wallerstein, 1989:129). Furthermore, the process of incorporation is not an abrupt process but one which occurs gradually.

Reflecting his Marxian focus on economics, Wallerstein (1989:170) argues that becoming part of the world-economy "necessarily" means that the political structures of the involved nations must become part of the interstate system. Thus, states in incorporated zones must either transform themselves into part of that interstate political system, be replaced by new political forms willing to accept this role, or be taken over by states that already are part of that political system. The states that emerge at the end of the process of incorporation must not only be part of the interstate system but also must be strong enough to protect their economies from external interference. However, they must not be too strong; that is, they must not become powerful enough to be able to refuse to act in accord with the dictates of the capitalist world-economy.

Finally, Wallerstein examines the decolonization of the Americas between 1750 and 1850. That is, he details the fact that the Americas freed themselves from the control of Great Britain, France, Spain, and Portugal. This decolonization, especially in the United States, was, of course, to have great consequences for later developments in the world capitalist system.

World-System Theory Today   Marxists have criticized the world-system perspective for its failure to adequately emphasize relations between social classes (Bergesen, 1984). From their point of view, Wallerstein focuses on the wrong issue. To Marxists the key is not the core-periphery international division of labor, but rather class relationships *within* given societies. Bergesen seeks to reconcile these positions by arguing that there are strengths and weaknesses on both sides. His middle-ground position is that core-periphery relations are not only unequal exchange relations but also global *class* relations. His key point is that core-periphery relations *are* important, not only as exchange relations, as Wallerstein argues, but also, and more important, as power-dependence relationships, that is, class relationships.

More recently, world-system theorists have pushed the theory forward to deal with the world today and in the coming years (Wallerstein, 1992) as well as backward to before the modern era (Chase-Dunn and Hall, 1994). Let us close this section with some of Wallerstein's thoughts on the recent past and near future.

Wallerstein argued that the United States was the hegemonic power in the world-system from 1945 through 1990. The United States achieved hegemony with the end of World War II generally, and more specifically with the Yalta Conference and the policy of containment of the Soviet Union. While containment policy led to a military status quo for the next forty-five years, it also had implications for the world-economy. The Soviet Union accepted the idea that it was not to ask for, nor would it receive, economic assistance from the United States. Thus, the Soviet Union became a second-rate economic power and, in the process, aided the economic position of the United States in various ways (for example, the United States did not have to funnel money to the Soviet Union).

Another implication of the deal between the United States and the Soviet Union was that both sides were allowed to condemn each other loudly. This mutual condemnation, in turn, permitted both sides to exert strong internal control, especially of the "left," or "all those who wished to put into question radically the existing world order, the capitalist world economy that was reviving and flourishing under U.S. hegemony with the collusion of what may be called its subimperialist agent, the Soviet Union" (Wallerstein, 1992:6).

A third implication of the "deal" between these two superpowers was that events in the Third World were not to be allowed to upset the world political and economic status quo.

By 1960, the United States seemed to have achieved its objectives and was astride the world-system, but signs of trouble were beginning to mount—growing realization of the gap between the rich and poor both in the United States and in the rest of the world, the early signs that Western Europe and Japan were catching up economically with the United States, increasing (and increasingly costly) uprisings in the Third World, the economic costs of the Vietnam War, and so on.

Wallerstein sees this set of changes as culminating in 1968 in a series of uprisings around the world: "The worldwide explosion of 1968 . . . went on for three years more or less until the raging fires were brought under control by the forces sustaining the world-system" (Wallerstein, 1992:11). But this was a costly victory, and its costs were exacerbated by a prolonged stagnation of the world-economy. The United States embarked on a twenty-year decline that it was only partially able to stem. For its part, the Soviet Union found itself no longer able to sustain its "pseudo-empire" and was forced to begin dismantling it. Thus, Wallerstein concludes, "The heyday of U.S. prosperity is over. The scaffolding is being dismantled" (1992:16).

What of the future? While the U.S. economy is faltering, "there is a lot of fat in a hegemonic power, and one can live off that fat for 50–100 years" (Wallerstein, 1992:22). Wallerstein sees the emergence of a Japan-America economic cartel, questionably, given the recent decline of the Japanese economy, in which America will be the junior partner. The United States will retain its military and political power, but "psychologically the decline will be terrible" (Wallerstein, 1992:22). That is, Americans have grown accustomed to being atop the world-system, and they will have a difficult time adjusting to a less exalted position.

Looking ahead, Wallerstein sees a fundamental restructuring of the world-system in the next fifty years. The tension will be between the well-to-do Northern hemisphere and the increasingly disadvantaged Southern hemisphere, and the choice will be repressive restructuring or egalitarian restructuring (which will require a major redistribution of the world's wealth away from the United States). In either case the result will be a fundamentally different world-system.

POST-MARXIST THEORY

Dramatic changes have taken place in recent years in neo-Marxian theory (Aronson, 1995; Grossberg and Nelson, 1988; Jay, 1988). The most recent varieties of neo-Marxian theory are rejecting many of the basic premises of Marx's original theory as well as those of the neo-Marxian theories discussed earlier in this chapter. Hence these new approaches have come to be thought of as post-Marxist theories (Dandaneau, 1992; Wright, 1987). While these theories reject the basic elements of Marxian theory, they still have sufficient affinities with it for them to be considered part of neo-Marxian theory. Post-Marxist theories are discussed here because they often involve the synthesis of Marxian theories with other theories, ideas, methods, and so on. How can we account for these dramatic changes in neo-Marxian theory? Two sets of factors are involved, one external to theory and involving changes in the social world and the other internal to theory itself (P. Anderson, 1984; Ritzer, 1991a).

First, and external to Marxian theory, is the end of the Cold War (Halliday, 1990) and the collapse of world communism. The Soviet Union is gone, and Russia has moved toward a market economy resembling, at least in part, a capitalist economy (Piccone, 1990; Zaslavsky, 1988). Eastern Europe has shifted, often even more rapidly than Russia, in the direction of a capitalist-style economy (Kaldor, 1990). China clings to communism, but capitalism flourishes throughout the nation. Cuba is isolated, awaiting only the death or overthrow of Fidel Castro to move in the direction of capitalism. Thus, the failure of communism on a worldwide scale made it necessary for Marxists to reconsider and reconstruct their theories (Burawoy, 1990; Aronson, 1995).

These changes in the world were related to a second set of changes, internal to theory itself, the series of intellectual changes that, in turn, affected neo-Marxian theory (P. Anderson, 1990a, 1990b). New theoretical currents such as poststructuralism and postmodernism (see Chapter 13) had a profound impact on neo-Marxian theory. In addition, a movement known as *analytical Marxism* gained ground; it was premised on the belief that Marxian theories needed to employ the same methods as any other scientific enterprise. This approach led to reinterpretations of Marx in more conventional intellectual terms, efforts to apply rational choice theory to Marxian issues, and attempts to study Marxian topics utilizing the methods and techniques of positivistic science. As Mayer puts it more specifically, "Increased humility toward the conventional norms of science coincides with diminished piety toward Marxist theory itself" (1994:296).

Thus, a combination of social and intellectual changes dramatically altered the landscape of neo-Marxian theory in the 1990s. While the theories discussed earlier remain important, much of the energy in neo-Marxian theory as we enter the twenty-first century is focused on the theories to be discussed in this section.

Analytical Marxism

Here is the way one of the leaders of analytical Marxism, John Roemer, defines it:

> During the past decade, what now appears as a new species in social theory has been forming: analytically sophisticated Marxism. Its practitioners are largely inspired by Marxian questions, which they pursue with contemporary tools of logic, mathematics

and model building. Their methodological posture is conventional. These writers are, self-consciously, products of both the Marxian and neo-Marxian traditions.

(Roemer, 1986a:1)

Thus, analytical Marxists bring mainstream, "state-of-the-art" methods of analytical philosophy and social science to bear on Marxian substantive issues (Mayer, 1994:22). Analytical Marxism is discussed in this chapter because it "explicitly proposes to synthesize *non-Marxist* methods and Marxist theory" (Weldes, 1989:371).

Analytical Marxism adopts a nondogmatic approach to Marx's theory. It does not blindly and unthinkingly support Marx's theory, it does not deny historical facts in order to support Marx's theory, nor does it totally reject Marx's theory as fundamentally wrong. Rather, it views Marx's theory as a form of nineteenth-century social science with great power and with a valid core but also with substantial weaknesses. Marx's theory should be drawn upon, but it requires the utilization of methods and techniques appropriate to the twenty-first century. It rejects the idea that there is a distinctive Marxian methodology and criticizes those who think that such a methodology exists and is valid:

I do not think there is a specific form of Marxist logic or explanation. Too often, obscurantism protects itself behind a yoga of special terms and privileged logic. The yoga of Marxism is "dialectics." Dialectical logic is based on several propositions which may have a certain inductive appeal, but are far from being rules of inference: that things turn into their opposites, and quantity turns into quality. In Marxian social science, dialectics is often used to justify a lazy kind of teleological reasoning. Developments occur because they must in order for history to be played out as it was intended.

(Roemer, 1986b:191)

Similarly, Elster says: "There is no specifically Marxist form of analysis . . . there is no commitment to any specific method of analysis, beyond those that characterize good social science generally" (1986:220). Along the same lines, analytical Marxists reject the idea that fact and value cannot be separated, that they are dialectically related. They seek, following the canons of mainstream philosophic and social-scientific thinking, to separate fact and value and to deal with facts dispassionately through theoretical, conceptual, and empirical analysis.

One might ask why analytical Marxism should be called Marxist. Roemer in reply to this question, says "I am not sure that it should" (1986a:2). However, he does offer several reasons why we can consider it a (neo-) Marxian theory. First, it deals with traditional Marxian topics like exploitation and class. Second, it continues to regard socialism as preferable to capitalism. Third, it seeks to understand and explain the problems associated with capitalism. However, while it is Marxist in these senses, it also "borrows willingly and easily from other viewpoints" (Roemer, 1986a:7). Again, analytical Marxism is very much in line with the move toward theoretical syntheses discussed throughout this book.

Three varieties of analytical Marxism will be discussed, at least briefly, in this section. First, we will discuss the effort to reanalyze Marx's work by utilizing mainstream intellectual tools. Second, we will deal with rational choice and game-theoretic Marxism. Finally, we will touch on empirical research from a Marxian perspective that utilizes state-of-the-art methodological tools.

Reanalyzing Marx   As pointed out above, analytical Marxists reject the use of such idiosyncratic concepts as the dialectic and seek instead to analyze Marx (as well as the social world) using concepts that are part of the broader intellectual tradition. The major example of this, and one of the key documents in analytical Marxism, is G. A. Cohen's *Karl Marx's Theory of History: A Defence* (1978). Instead of interpreting Marx as an exotic dialectician, Cohen argues that he employs the much more prosaic functional form of explanation in his work. He offers the following examples of functional explanation in Marx's work:

- Relations of production *correspond* to productive forces.
- The legal and political superstructure *rises on* a real foundation.
- The social, political, and intellectual process *is conditioned by* the mode of production of material life.
- Consciousness is determined by social being.

(Cohen, 1978/1986:221)

In each of these examples, the second concept *explains* the first concept. The nature of the explanation is functional, in Cohen's view, because "the character of what is explained is determined by its effect on what explains it" (1978/1986:221). Thus, in the case of the last example, the character of consciousness is explained by its effect on, more specifically its propensity to sustain, social being. More generally, social phenomena are explained in terms of their consequences for other social phenomena. It is Cohen's view that Marx practices functional thinking in the examples above, and throughout his work, because he seeks to explain social and economic phenomena in this manner. Thus, Marx is not a dialectician; he is a functional thinker. In adopting such a perspective, Cohen is reinterpreting Marx using mainstream philosophic ideas *and* viewing Marx as part of that mainstream.

Cohen takes pains to differentiate functional thinking from the sociological variety of (structural) functional*ism* discussed in Chapter 3. Cohen sees (structural) functionalism as composed of three theses. First, all elements of the social world are interconnected. Second, all components of society reinforce one another, as well as the society as a whole. Third, each aspect of society is as it is because of its contribution to the larger society. These theses are objectionable to Marxists for a variety of reasons, especially because of their conservatism. However, the functional explanations mentioned previously can be employed by Marxists without their accepting any of the tenets of functionalism. Thus, functional explanation is not necessarily conservative; indeed it can be quite revolutionary.

Rational Choice Marxism   Many analytical Marxists have drawn on neoclassical economics, especially rational choice theory and game theory (see Chapter 8 for a discussion of the use of rational choice theory in mainstream sociological theory). Roemer argues that "Marxian analysis requires micro-foundations," especially rational choice and game theory as well as "the arsenal of modelling techniques developed by neoclassical economics" (1986b:192). In drawing on such approaches, Marxian theory is giving up its pretensions of being different and is utilizing approaches widely used throughout the social sciences. But while neo-Marxian theory can and should draw upon neoclassical economics, it remains different from the latter. For example, it retains an interest in collective action for changing society and accepts the idea that capitalism is an unjust system.

Jon Elster (1982, 1986) is a major proponent, along with John Roemer, of analytical Marxism. Elster believes that neo-Marxian theory has been impeded by its adoption of the kind of functional theorizing discussed by Cohen. He also believes that Marxian theory ought to be making greater use of game theory, a variant of rational choice theory. Game theory, like other types of rational choice theory, assumes that actors are rational and that they seek to maximize their gains. Although it recognizes structural constraints, it does not suggest that they completely determine actors' choices. What is distinctive about game theory as a type of rational choice theory is that it permits the analyst to go beyond the rational choices of a single actor and to deal with the interdependence of the decisions and actions of a number of actors. Elster (1982) identifies three interdependencies among actors involved in a game. First, the reward for each actor depends on the choices made by all actors. Second, the reward for each actor depends on the reward for all. Finally, the choice made by each actor depends on the choices made by all. The analysis of "games" (such as the famous "prisoner's dilemma" game, in which actors end up worse off if they follow their own self-interests than if they sacrifice those interests) helps explain the strategies of the various actors and the emergence of such collectivities as social class. Thus, rational choice Marxism searches for the micro-foundations of Marxist theory, although the rational actor of this theory is very different from critical theory's actor (discussed earlier in this chapter), who is largely derived from Freudian theory.

Elster's rational choice orientation is also manifest in *Making Sense of Marx* (1985). Elster argues that Marx's basic method for explaining social phenomena was a concern for the unintended consequences of human action. To Elster, and in contrast with most other Marxists, who see Marx as a "methodological holist" concerned with macro structures, Marx practiced "methodological individualism," or "the doctrine that all social phenomena—their structure and their change—are in principle explicable in ways that only involve individuals—their properties, their goals, their beliefs and their actions" (1985:5). To Elster, Marx *was* concerned with actors, their goals, their intentions, and their rational choices. Elster uses such a rational choice perspective to critique the orientation of the structural Marxists: "Capitalist entrepreneurs are *agents* in the genuinely active sense. They cannot be reduced to mere place-holders in the capitalist system of production" (1985:13). Rational choice Marxism focuses on these rational agents (capitalist and proletariat) and their interrelationships.

Roemer (1982) has been in the forefront of the development of an approach within analytical Marxism toward exploitation (for a critique, see Schwartz, 1995). Roemer has moved away from thinking of exploitation as occurring at the point of production (and therefore from the highly dubious labor theory of value) and toward thinking of exploitation as relating to coercion associated with differential ownership of property. As Mayer puts it, "exploitation can arise from unequal possession of productive resources even without a coercive production process" (1994:62). Among other things, this perspective allows us to conceive of exploitation in socialist as well as capitalist societies. This view of exploitation also relates to rational choice theory in the sense, for example, that those whose exploitation arises from the unequal distribution of property can join social movements designed to redistribute property more equally. This kind of orientation also allows analytical Marxism to retain its ethical and political goals while buying into a mainstream orientation like rational choice theory.

Empirically Oriented Marxism   The leading figure associated with the importation and application of rigorous methods to the empirical study of Marxian concepts is Erik Olin Wright (1985). Wright explicitly associates himself with analytical Marxism in general and the work of John Roemer in particular. Wright's work involves three basic components: first, the clarification of basic Marxian concepts such as class; second, empirical studies of those concepts; third, the development of a more coherent theory based on those concepts (especially class).

In his book, *Classes* (1985), Wright seeks to answer the question posed by Marx, but never answered by him: "What constitutes class?" He makes it clear that his answer will be true to Marx's original theoretical agenda. However, it will not be the same as the answer Marx might have offered, because since Marx's day there has been over 100 years of both theoretical work and history. Thus, we are more sophisticated theoretically, *and* times have changed. As a result, Wright, like the other analytical Marxists, starts with Marx but does not accept his position as dogma or try to divine how he might have defined *class*. Because of Marx and the theoretical work done since his time, contemporary Marxists are in a better position to come up with such definitions. In any case, we live in very different times, and Marx's definition, even if we could divine it, might well not be appropriate for modern society.

Since this is a book on theory, we need not go into detail about Wright's research or that of any of the other empirically oriented Marxists. However, it would be useful to say something about his best-known conceptual contribution—the idea of "contradictory locations within class relations" (Wright, 1985:43). His basic premise is that a given position need not, as is commonly assumed, be located within a given class; it may be in more than one class simultaneously. Thus, a position may be simultaneously proletarian and bourgeois. For example, managers are bourgeois in the sense that they supervise subordinates, but they are also proletarian in that they are supervised by others. The idea of contradictory class locations is derived through careful conceptual analysis and then is studied empirically (see Gubbay, 1997, for a critique of Wright's approach to social class).

Analytical Marxism Today   While, as we have seen, analytical Marxists consider themselves to be Marxists, there are those (for example, Callinicos, 1989) who wonder whether their attraction to mainstream concepts and methods makes this designation meaningless or subversive of a Marxian orientation (Kirkpatrick, 1994). In response, Elster asserts: "Most of the views that *I* hold to be true and important, I can trace back to Marx" (1985:531).

Mayer (1994) has offered an overview of analytical Marxism that attempts, among other things, to review and rebut what he sees as the six major criticisms of the approach. However, before we discuss those criticisms, there is one critique that emanates from Mayer's work itself: "Analytical Marxism is not a unified or even an internally consistent body of thought" (1994:300). The differences among the three major practitioners discussed here (Cohen, Roemer, and Wright), to say nothing of the others who can be included under this heading (especially Adam Przeworski [1985] and his work on the state), are enormous and make it difficult to discuss these individuals in the same context. Those differences may splinter analytical Marxism before it has an opportunity to develop into a coherent perspective.

The first criticism reviewed by Mayer is that analytical Marxism is atomistic and focuses on rational actors. He responds that analytical Marxists do not conceive of society as composed of isolated individuals and that they do recognize that people do not always behave rationally. Second, analytical Marxists are accused of economic determinism, but the response is that the predominant position is that economic factors are primary, not that they are deterministic. The third critique is that analytical Marxists are ahistorical, but Mayer does not see this characteristic as inherent in the approach. Rather, it is traceable to its newness and to the fact that there has not been time to deal with historical issues. Fourth, and relatedly, analytical Marxists are accused of offering static approaches that have difficulty dealing with change. While Mayer recognizes this problem, he argues that virtually all social scientists have this predicament. Fifth, there is the accusation of tautology—"assuming what needs to be proven" (Mayer, 1994:305). Mayer sees this as a problem inherent in all deductive approaches. Finally, analytical Marxism is seen as lacking in moral fervor, but Mayer counters, "Analytical Marxists are quite capable of moral passion, and what their moral critique of capitalism lacks in fervor it more than gains in accuracy and insight" (1994:315).

Mayer concludes with a discussion of six challenges facing analytical Marxism, challenges that must be met if analytical Marxism is to be a significant force in the social sciences. First, analytical Marxism must develop a more dynamic approach. As Mayer puts it, "Any version of Marxism unable to account for social dynamics cannot expect to flourish" (1994:317). Second, the theories of the analytical Marxists must do a better job of relating to specific events and situations. Third, practitioners of this approach must right the current imbalance in the direction of theory and do more empirical research. Fourth, analytical Marxists must expand from their base in economic factors and deal with a wider range of social factors. Fifth, they must also move away from a focus on advanced capitalist nations and deal with less developed nations. Finally, analytical Marxists must demonstrate the existence of viable alternatives to capitalism.

Postmodern Marxian Theory

Marxian theory has been profoundly affected by theoretical developments in structuralism, poststructuralism (Anderson, 1984:33), and, of particular interest here, postmodernism (Wood and Foster, 1997; see Chapter 13).

Hegemony and Radical Democracy   A major representative work of postmodern Marxism is Ernesto Laclau and Chantal Mouffe's *Hegemony and Socialist Strategy* (1985). In Ellen Wood's view, this work, accepting the focus on linguistics, texts, and discourse in postmodernism, detaches ideology from its material base and ultimately dissolves "the social altogether into ideology or 'discourse' " (1986:47). The concept of hegemony, which is of central importance to Laclau and Mouffe, was developed by Gramsci to focus on cultural leadership rather than on the coercive effect of state domination. This shift in focus, of course, leads us away from the traditional Marxian concern with the material world and in the direction of ideas and discourse. As Wood puts it, "In short, the Laclau-Mouffe argument is that there *are* no such things as material interests but only discursively constructed *ideas* about them" (1986:61).

In addition to substituting ideas for material interests, Laclau and Mouffe also displace the proletariat from its privileged position at the center of Marxian theory. As Wood argues, Laclau and Mouffe are part of a movement involved in the "declassing of the socialist project" (1986:4). Laclau and Mouffe put the issue of class in subjective, discursive terms. The social world is characterized by diverse positions and antagonisms. As a result, it is impossible to come up with the kind of "unified discourse" that Marx envisioned surrounding the proletariat. The universal discourse of the proletariat "has been replaced by a polyphony of voices, each of which constructs its own irreducible discursive identity" (Laclau and Mouffe, 1985:191). Thus, instead of focusing on the single discourse of the proletariat, Marxian theorists are urged to focus on a multitude of diverse discourses emanating from a wide range of dispossessed voices, such as those of women, blacks, ecologists, immigrants, consumers, and the like. Marxian theory has, as a result, been *decentered* and *detotalized* because it no longer focuses only on the proletariat and no longer sees the problems of the proletariat as *the* problem in society.

Having rejected a focus on material factors and a focal concern for the proletariat, Laclau and Mouffe proceed to reject, as the goal of Marxian theory, communism involving the emancipation of the proletariat. Alternatively, they propose a system labeled "radical democracy." Instead of focusing, as the political right does, on individual democratic rights, they propose to "create a new hegemony, which will be the outcome of the articulation of the greatest number of democratic struggles" (Mouffe, 1988:41). What is needed in this new hegemony is a "hegemony of democratic values, and this requires a multiplication of democratic practices, institutionalizing them into even more diverse social relations" (Mouffe, 1988:41). Radical democracy seeks to bring together under a broad umbrella a wide range of democratic struggles—antiracist, antisexist, anticapitalist, antiexploitation of nature (Eder, 1990), and many others. Thus, this is a "radical and plural democracy" (Laclau, 1990:27). The struggle of one group must not be waged at the expense of the others; all democratic struggles must be seen as equivalent struggles. Thus, it is necessary to bring these struggles together by modifying their identity so that the groups see themselves as part of the larger struggle for radical democracy. As Laclau and Mouffe argue:

> The alternative of the Left should consist of locating itself fully in the field of the democratic revolution and expanding the chains of equivalents between different struggles against oppression. *The task of the Left therefore cannot be to renounce liberal-democratic ideology, but on the contrary, to deepen and expand it in the direction of a radical and plural democracy.* . . . . It is not in the abandonment of the democratic

terrain but, on the contrary, in the extension of the field of democratic struggles to the whole of civil society and the state, that the possibility resides for a hegemonic strategy of the Left.

(Laclau and Mouffe, 1985:176)

While radical democracy retains the objective of the abolition of capitalism, it recognizes that such abolition will not eliminate the other inequalities within society. Dealing with all social inequalities requires a far broader movement than that anticipated by traditional Marxists.

Continuities and Time-Space Compression   Another Marxian foray into postmodernist theory (see Chapter 13 for a discussion of yet another, the work of Fredric Jameson) is David Harvey's *The Condition of Postmodernity* (1989). While Harvey sees much of merit in postmodern thinking, he sees serious weaknesses in it from a Marxian viewpoint. Postmodernist theory is accused of overemphasizing the problems of the modern world and of underemphasizing its material achievements. Most important, it seems to accept postmodernity and its associated problems rather than suggesting ways of overcoming these difficulties: "The rhetoric of postmodernism is dangerous for it avoids confronting the realities of political economy and the circumstances of global power" (Harvey, 1989:117). What postmodernist theory needs to confront is the source of its ideas—the political and economic transformation of early twenty-first-century capitalism.

Central to the political economic system is control over markets and the labor process (these two arenas involve the issue of *accumulation* in capitalism). While the postwar period between 1945 and 1973 was characterized by an inflexible process of accumulation, since 1973 we have moved to a more flexible process. Harvey associates the earlier period with Fordism (as well as Keynesian economics) and the later period with post-Fordism (for a critique of this, see Gartman, 1998), but we need not discuss these issues here, since they have already been covered in this chapter. While Fordism is inflexible, Harvey sees post-Fordism as associated with flexible accumulation resting "on flexibility with respect to labour processes, labour markets, products, and patterns of consumption. It is characterized by the emergence of entirely new sectors of production, new ways of providing financial services, new markets, and, above all, greatly intensified rates of commercial, technological, and organizational innovation" (1989:147).

While Harvey sees great changes, and argues that it is these changes that lie at the base of postmodern thinking, he believes that there are many *continuities* between the Fordist and post-Fordist eras. His major conclusion is that while "there has certainly been a sea-change in the surface appearance of capitalism since 1973 . . . the underlying logic of capitalist accumulation and its crisis tendencies remain the same" (Harvey, 1989:189).

Central to Harvey's approach is the idea of time-space compression. He believes that modernism served to compress both time and space and that that process has accelerated in the postmodern era, leading to "an intense phase of time-space compression that has a disorienting and disruptive impact upon political-economic practices, the balance of class power, as well as upon cultural and social life" (Harvey, 1989:284). But this time-space compression is *not* essentially different from earlier epochs in capitalism: "We have, in short, witnessed another fierce round in that process of annihilation of space through time that has always lain at the center of capitalism's dynamic" (Harvey, 1989:293). To give an example of the annihilation of space through time, cheeses once available only in France are now widely sold throughout the United States because of rapid, low-cost transportation. Or, in the 1991 war with Iraq, television transported us instantaneously from air raids in Baghdad to "scud" attacks on Tel Aviv to military briefings in Riyadh.

Thus, to Harvey, postmodernism is *not* discontinuous with modernism; they are reflections of the same underlying capitalist dynamic.[5] Both modernism and postmodernism, Fordism and post-Fordism, coexist in today's world. The emphasis on Fordism and post-Fordism will "vary from time to time and place to place, depending on which configuration is profitable and which is not" (Harvey, 1989:344). Such a viewpoint serves to bring the issue of postmodernity under the umbrella of neo-Marxian theory, although it is, in turn, modified by developments in postmodern thinking.

Finally, Harvey discerns changes and cracks in postmodernity, indicating that we may already be moving into a new era, an era that neo-Marxian theory must be prepared to theorize, perhaps by integrating still other idea systems.

After Marxism

There are innumerable post-Marxist positions that *could* be discussed in this section, but I will close with one of the more extreme positions taken on this issue.

The title of Ronald Aronson's (1995) book, *After Marxism,* tells much of the story. Aronson, a self-avowed Marxist, makes it clear that Marxism is over and that Marxist theorists are now on their own in dealing with the social world and its problems. This position is based on the idea that the "Marxian project" involved the integration of theory and practice. While some Marxists may continue to buy into parts of Marxian theory, the Marxian project of the transformation from capitalism to socialism is dead, since it has clearly failed in its objectives. It is history, not Aronson, that has rendered the judgment that the Marxian project has failed. Thus, those Marxists who continue to buy into the theory are destroying the dialectical whole of theory and practice that constituted the Marxian project. This splintering is disastrous because what gave Marxism its compelling power is the fact that it represented "a single coherent theoretical and practical project" (Aronson, 1995:52).

But how can the Marxian project be over if capitalism continues to exist and may, with the death of communism, be more powerful than ever? In fact, Aronson recognizes that there are a variety of arguments to be made on behalf of the idea that Marxism is still relevant. For example, he recognizes that most people around the world are worse off today than they were at the dawn of capitalism and that in spite of a number of changes, the fundamental exploitative structure of capitalism is unaltered. In spite of

---

[5]Bauman (1990) contends that capitalism and socialism are simply mirror images of modernity.

such realities, Aronson argues that a variety of transformations must lead us to the conclusion that crucial aspects of Marxian theory are obsolete:

- The working class has *not* become increasingly impoverished.
- The class structure has *not* simplified to two polarized classes (bourgeoisie and proletariat).
- Because of the transformation of manufacturing processes, the number of industrial workers has declined, the working class has become more fragmented, and their consciousness of their situation has eroded.
- The overall shrinkage of the working class has led to a decline in its strength, its class consciousness, and its ability to engage in class struggle.
- Workers are increasingly less likely to identify themselves as workers; they have multiple and competing identities, so being a worker is now just one of many identities.

While Marxism is over as far as Aronson is concerned, he argues that we should not regret its existence, even with the excesses (for example, Stalinism) that were committed in its name. Marxism

> gave hope, it made sense of the world; it gave direction and meaning to many and countless lives. As the twentieth century's greatest call to arms, it inspired millions to stand up and fight, to believe that humans could one day shape their lives and their world to meet their needs.

> (Aronson, 1995:85)

In addition to the failures of Marxism in the real world, Aronson traces the demise of Marxism to problems within the theory itself. Those problems he traces to the fact that Marx's original theory was created during the early days of the modern world and, as a result, contains an uncomfortable mixture of modern and premodern ideas. This problem has plagued Marxian theory throughout its history. For example, the premodern, prophetic belief in emancipation coexisted with a modern belief in science and the search for facts: "Beneath its veneer of science, such dogmatic prophecy reveals its deeper and premodern kinship with religious anticipations of a world redeemed by a divine power beyond our control" (Aronson, 1995:97). To take one other example, Marxism tended to emphasize objective processes and to de-emphasize subjective processes.

Aronson begins one of his chapters with the provocative statement: "Feminism destroyed Marxism" (1995:124). He quickly makes it clear that feminism did not accomplish this feat on its own. However, feminism did contribute to the destruction of Marxism by demanding a theory that focuses on the "oppression of women *as women*" (Aronson, 1995:126). This focus clearly undermined Marxian theory, which purported to offer a theory applicable to all human beings. Feminism also set the stage for the development of other groups demanding that theories focus on their specific plight rather than on the universal problems of humanity.

Aronson describes post-Marxist theories like the analytical Marxism discussed earlier as Marxism without Marxism. That is, they are pure theories, lacking in practice, and therefore, in his view, should not be called Marxism:

They may claim the name, as does analytical Marxism, but they do so as so many Marxisms without Marxism. They have become so transformed, so limited, so narrowly theoretical that even when their words and commitments ring true they only invoke Marxism's aura, but no more. However evocative, the ideas cannot conjure the fading reality.

(Aronson, 1995:149)

Such Marxian theories will survive, but they will occupy a far humbler place in the world. They will represent just one theoretical voice in a sea of such voices.

Given all of this, Aronson concludes that critical analysts of the modern world are on their own without a Marxian project to build upon. However, this is a mixed blessing. While the Marxian project had enormous strengths, it was also an albatross around the necks of critical analysts. Should former Marxists search for a new Marx? or a new Marxian project? In light of developments in society and in theory, Aronson feels that the answer to these questions is no, because we have moved "beyond the possibility of the kind of holism, integration, coherence and confidence that Marxism embodied" (1995:168). Thus, for example, instead of a single radical movement, what we must seek today is a radical coalition of groups and ideas. The goal of such a coalition is the emancipation of modernity from its explosive inner tensions and its various forms of oppressiveness.

One problem facing such a new radical movement is that it can no longer hope to be driven by a compelling vision of some future utopia. Yet, it must have some sort of emotional cement to hold it together and to keep it moving ahead. The movement must have a moral base, a sense of what is right and what is wrong. It must also have hope, albeit a far more modest hope than that which characterized the Marxian project. Although modest, such hopes are also less likely to lead to the profound disenchantment that characterized the Marxian project when it failed to achieve its social objectives.

Criticisms of Post-Marxism

Many Marxian theorists are unhappy with post-Marxist developments (for example, Burawoy, 1990; Wood, 1986; Wood and Foster, 1997). Burawoy, for instance, attacks the analytical Marxists for eliminating the issue of history and for making a fetish of clarity and rigor. Weldes criticizes analytical Marxism for allowing itself to be colonized by mainstream economics, adopting a purely "technical, problem-solving approach," becoming increasingly academic and less political, and growing more conservative (1989:354). Wood picks up on the political issue and criticizes analytical Marxism (as well as postmodern Marxism) for its political quietism and its "cynical defeatism, where every radical programme of change is doomed to failure" (1989:88). Even supporters of one branch of analytical Marxism, the rigorous empirical study of Marxian ideas, have been critical of their brethren in rational choice theory who, mistakenly in their view, adopt a position of methodological individualism (Levine, Sober, and Wright, 1987).

The work of Laclau and Mouffe has come under particularly heavy attack. For example, Allen Hunter criticizes them for their overall commitment to idealism and, more specifically, for situating "themselves at the extreme end of discourse analysis, viewing *everything* as discourse" (1988:892). Similarly, Geras (1987) attacks Laclau and Mouffe for their idealism, but he also sees them as profligate, dissolute, illogical, and obscurantist. The tenor of Laclau and Mouffe's reply to Geras is caught by its title "Post-Marxism without Apologies" (1987). Burawoy attacks Laclau and Mouffe for getting "lost in the web of history where everything is important and explanation is therefore impossible" (1990:790).

Finally, in contrast to Aronson, Burawoy believes that Marxism remains useful in understanding capitalism's dynamics and contradictions (see also, Wood, 1995). Thus, with the demise of communism and the ascendancy of worldwide capitalism, "Marxism will . . . , once more, come into its own" (Burawoy, 1990:792). More recently, and in light of developments in the 1990s, Wood and Foster (1997:67) argue that Marxism is more necessary than ever because "humanity is more and more connected in the global dimensions of exploitation and oppression."

SUMMARY

In this chapter we examine a wide range of approaches that can be categorized as neo-Marxian sociological theories. All of them take Marx's work as their point of departure, but they often go in very different directions. Although these diverse developments give neo-Marxian theory considerable vitality, they also create at least some unnecessary and largely dysfunctional differentiation and controversy. Thus, one task for the modern Marxian sociological theorist is to integrate this broad array of theories while recognizing the value of various specific pieces of work.

The first neo-Marxian theory historically, but the least important at present, especially to the sociologically oriented thinker, is economic determinism. It was against this limited view of Marxian theory that other varieties developed. Hegelian Marxism, especially in the work of Georg Lukács, was one such reaction. This approach sought to overcome the limitations in economic determinism by returning to the subjective, Hegelian roots of Marxian theory. Hegelian Marxism is also of little contemporary relevance; its significance lies largely in its impact on later neo-Marxian theories.

The critical school, which was the inheritor of the tradition of Hegelian Marxism, *is* of contemporary importance to sociology. The great contributions of the critical theorists (Marcuse, Habermas, and so forth) are the insights offered into culture, consciousness, and their interrelationships. These theorists have enhanced our understanding of such cultural phenomena as instrumental rationality, the "culture industry," the "knowledge industry," communicative action, domination, and legitimations. To this they add a concern with consciousness, primarily in the form of an integration of Freudian theory in their work. However, critical theory has gone too far in its efforts to compensate for the limitations of economic determinism; it needs to reintegrate a concern for economics, indeed, for large-scale social forces in general.

Next we offer discussions of two lines of work in neo-Marxian economic sociology. The first deals with the relationship between capital and labor, especially in the works of Baran and Sweezy and of Braverman. The second is concerned with the transition from Fordism to post-Fordism. Both sets of work represent efforts to return to some of the traditional economic concerns of Marxian sociology. This work is significant for its effort to update Marxian economic sociology by taking into account the emerging realities of contemporary capitalist society.

Another concern is historically oriented Marxism, specifically the work of Immanuel Wallerstein and his supporters on the modern world-system. The chapter closes with a section devoted to what, in light of the demise of communism, have come to be called post-Marxist theories. Included under this heading are several types of analytical Marxism and postmodern Marxian theory. Also included in this section is a discussion of an example of the kind of position taken by Marxists who have been forced to give up on the Marxian project in light of developments in the world.

5

SYSTEMS THEORY

SOCIOLOGY AND MODERN SYSTEMS THEORY
   Gains from Systems Theory
   Some General Principles
   Applications to the Social World
NIKLAS LUHMANN'S GENERAL SYSTEM THEORY
   Autopoietic Systems
   Society and Psychic Systems
   Double Contingency
   Evolution of Social Systems
   Differentiation
   Luhmann's Sociology of Knowledge
   Criticisms

While it has adherents in many different fields, systems theory has had a checkered history in sociology. As a result, were it not for the work of the German social thinker, Niklas Luhmann, this chapter would not be here. Over more than two decades until his death in 1998, Luhmann doggedly pursued the development of systems theory (he preferred "system theory"). (Although his work is not nearly as well known or influential, Kenneth Bailey [1990, 1994, 1997] has also been a notable contributor to the development of this theory.) For years Luhmann labored in virtual anonymity, but more recently his work has gained increasing worldwide recognition. As a result, this chapter is largely devoted to his thinking. However, before we get to his work, we will discuss some early insights and conceptual ideas from the work of Walter Buckley (1967), especially his *Sociology and Modern Systems Theory.*

SOCIOLOGY AND MODERN SYSTEMS THEORY

Gains from Systems Theory

A central issue addressed by Buckley is what sociology has to gain from systems theory. First, because systems theory is derived from the hard sciences and because it is, at least in the eyes of its proponents, applicable to *all* behavioral and social sciences, it promises a common vocabulary to unify them. Second, systems theory is multi-leveled and can be applied equally well to the largest-scale and the smallest-scale, to the most objective and the most subjective, aspects of the social world. Third, systems theory is interested in the varied relationships of the many aspects of the social world and thus operates against piecemeal analyses of the social world. The argument of systems theory is that the intricate relationship of parts cannot be treated out of the context of the whole. Systems theorists reject the idea that society or other large-scale components of society should be treated as unified social facts. Instead, the focus is on relationships or processes at various levels within the social system. Buckley described the focus:

> The kind of system we are interested in may be described generally as a complex of elements or components directly or indirectly related in a causal network, such that each component is related to at least some others in a more or less stable way within any particular period of time.
>
> (Buckley, 1967:41)

Richard A. Ball offers a clear conception of the relational orientation of systems theory, or what he calls General Systems Theory (GST):

> GST begins with a processual conception of reality as consisting fundamentally of relationships among relationships, as illustrated in the concept of "gravity" as used in modern physics. The term "gravity" does not describe an entity at all. There is no such "thing" as gravity. It is a *set of relationships.* To think of these relationships as entities is to fall into reification. . . . The GST approach demands that sociologists develop the logic of relationships and conceptualize social reality in relational terms.
>
> (Ball, 1978:66)

Fourth, the systems approach tends to see all aspects of sociocultural systems in process terms, especially as networks of information and communication. Fifth, and perhaps most important, systems theory is inherently integrative. Buckley, in his definition of the perspective, saw it involving the integration of large-scale objective structures, symbol systems, action and interaction, and "consciousness and self-awareness." Ball also accepted the idea of integration of levels: "The individual and society are treated equally, not as separate entities but as mutually constitutive fields, related through various 'feedback' processes" (1978:68). In fact, systems theory is so attuned to integration that Buckley criticized the tendency of other sociologists to make analytical distinctions among levels:

> We note the tendency in much of sociology to insist on what is called an "analytical distinction" between "personality" (presumably intracranial), symbol systems (culture), and matrices of social relations (social systems), though the actual work of the proponents of the distinctions shows it to be misleading or often untenable in practice.
>
> (Buckley, 1967:101)

(Buckley was somewhat unfair here, because he did much the same thing throughout his own work. Making analytical distinctions is apparently acceptable to systems theorists as long as one is making such distinctions in order to make better sense out of the interrelationships among the various aspects of social life.) Finally, systems theory tends to see the social world in dynamic terms, with an overriding concern for "sociocultural emergence and dynamics in general" (Buckley, 1967:39).

Some General Principles

Buckley discussed the relationship among sociocultural systems, mechanical systems, and organic systems. Buckley focused on delineating the essential differences among these systems. On a number of dimensions a continuum runs from the mechanical systems to organic systems to sociocultural systems—going from least to most complexity of the parts, from least to most instability of the parts, and from lowest to highest degree to which the parts are attributable to the system as a whole.

On other dimensions, the systems differ qualitatively rather than simply quantitatively. In mechanical systems, the interrelationships of the parts are based on transfers of energy. In organic systems, the interrelationships of the parts are based more on exchange of information than on energy. In sociocultural systems, the interrelationships are based even more on information exchange.

The three types of systems also differ in the degree to which they are open or closed—that is, in the degree of interchange with aspects of the larger environment. A more open system is better able to respond selectively to a greater range and detail of the endless variety of the environment. In these terms, mechanical systems tend to be closed; organic systems more open; and sociocultural systems the most open of the three (as we will see, Luhmann disagrees with this last point). The degree of openness of a system is related to two crucial concepts in systems theory: *entropy,* or the tendency of systems to run down; and *negentropy,* or the tendency of systems to elaborate structures (Bailey, 1990). Closed systems tend to be entropic, whereas open systems tend to be negentropic. Sociocultural systems also tend to have more tension built into them than the other two. Finally, sociocultural systems can be purposive and goal-seeking because they receive feedback from the environment that allows them to keep moving toward their goals.

Feedback is an essential aspect of the cybernetic approach that systems theorists take to the social system. This is in contrast to the equilibrium approach, which is characteristic of many sociologists (for instance, Parsons) who purportedly operate from a systems approach. Using feedback enables cybernetic systems theorists to deal with friction, growth, evolution, and sudden changes. The openness of a social system to its environment and the impact of environmental factors on the system are important concerns to these systems theorists.

A variety of internal processes also affect social systems. Two other concepts are critical here. *Morphostasis* refers to those processes that help the system maintain itself, whereas *morphogenesis* refers to those processes that help the system change, grow more elaborate (for more on these two processes, see the discussion of Archer's work in Chapter 11). Social systems develop more and more complex "mediating systems" that intervene between external forces and the action of the system. Some of these mediating systems help the system to maintain itself, and others help it to change. These mediating systems grow more and more independent, autonomous, and determinative of the actions of the system. In other words, these mediating systems permit the social system to grow less dependent on the environment.

These complex mediating systems perform a variety of functions in the social system. For example, they allow the system to adjust itself temporarily to external conditions. They can direct the system from harsh to more congenial environments. They can also allow the system to reorganize its parts in order to deal with the environment more effectively.

Applications to the Social World

Buckley (1967) moved from a discussion of general principles to the specifics of the social world to show the applicability of systems theory. He began at the individual level, where he was very impressed by Mead's work, in which consciousness and action are interrelated. In fact, Buckley recast the Meadian problematic in systems-theory terms. Action begins with a *signal* from the environment, which is transmitted to the actor. However, the transmission may be complicated by *noise* in the environment. When it gets through, the signal provides the actor with *information*. On the basis of this information, the actor is allowed to *select* a response. The key here is the actor's possession of a mediating mechanism—self-consciousness. Buckley discussed self-consciousness in the terminology of systems theory:

> In the language of cybernetics, such self-consciousness is a mechanism of internal feedback of the system's own states which may be mapped or compared with other information from the situation and from memory, permitting a selection from a repertoire of actions in a goal-directed manner that takes one's own self and behavior implicitly into account.
>
> (Buckley, 1967:100)

To Mead and the symbolic interactionists and systems theorists, consciousness is not separated from action and interaction but rather is an integral part of both.

Despite his views that consciousness and interaction are interrelated and that levels should not be separated, Buckley did move from consciousness to the interactional domain. Patterns of interaction—namely, imitation and response—clearly fit into a systemic view of the world. More important, Buckley tied the interpersonal realm directly to the personality system; indeed, he saw the two as mutually determinative. Finally, Buckley turned to the large-scale organization of society, especially roles and institutions, which he saw in systemic terms and as related to, if not indistinguishable from, the other levels of social reality.

Buckley concluded by discussing some of the general principles of systems theory as they apply to the sociocultural domain. First, the systems theorist accepts the idea that tension is a normal, ever-present, and necessary reality of the social system. Second, there is a focus on the nature and sources of variety in the social system. The emphasis on both tension and variety makes the systems perspective a dynamic one. Third, there is a concern for the selection process at both the individual and the interpersonal levels, whereby the various alternatives open to the system are sorted and sifted. This lends further dynamism. Fourth, the interpersonal level is seen as the basis of the development of larger structures. The transactional processes of exchange, negotiation, and bargaining are the processes out of which emerge relatively stable social and cultural structures. Finally, despite the inherent dynamism of the systems approach, there is a recognition of the processes of perpetuation and transmission. As Buckley put it, "Out of the continuous transactions emerge some relatively stable accommodations and adjustments" (1967:160).

An interesting note: There are a number of rather striking similarities between systems theory and the dialectical approach, even though they are derived from extremely different sources (one scientific, the other philosophical) and have very different vocabularies (Ball, 1978). Similarities between them include a focus on relations, process, creativity, and tension.

NIKLAS LUHMANN'S GENERAL SYSTEM THEORY[1]

The most prominent systems theorist in sociology is Niklas Luhmann (1927–1998). Luhmann developed a sociological approach that combined elements of Talcott Parsons's structural functionalism (see Chapter 3) with general systems theory and introduced concepts from cognitive biology and cybernetics. Luhmann sees Parsons's later ideas as the only general theory that is complex enough to form the basis for a new sociological approach that reflects the latest findings in biological and cybernetic systems. However, he sees two problems with Parsons's approach. First it has no place for *self-reference* and, according to Luhmann, society's ability to refer to itself is central to our understanding of it as a system. Second, Parsons does not recognize *contingency*. As a result, Parsons cannot adequately analyze modern society as it is because he does not see that it could be otherwise. Thus, to take one example from Parsons's work, the AGIL scheme (see p. 97) should not be seen as a fact, but instead as a model of possibilities. For example, the AGIL scheme shows that the adaptive and the goal attainment subsystems can be related in various ways; therefore the aim of analysis should be to understand why the system produced a particular relationship between these two subsystems at any given time. Luhmann addresses these two problems in Parsons's work by developing a theory that takes self-reference as central to systems and that focuses on contingency, the fact that things could be different.

The key to understanding what Luhmann means by a system can be found in the distinction between a system and its environment. Basically, the difference between the two is one of *complexity*. The system is always less complex than its environment. For example, a business, such as an automobile manufacturer, can be seen as a system that deals with a highly complex environment which includes many different types of people, a constantly changing physical environment, and many other diverse systems.[2] However, this complexity is represented in a much simplified form within the system. When the manufacturer needs raw materials (steel, rubber, etc.), it doesn't normally care

---

[1]This section was coauthored with Douglas Goodman and Matthias Jonge.

[2]Strictly speaking, the automobile industry is not an autopoietic system in Luhmann's sense, since it is not producing its own basic elements. However, we will use this example to explain the general idea of systems theory because it is more concrete than the abstractions of the economic system or the law system. Later, when we define an autopoietic system, we will need to use a more abstract example.

where they come from, how they are produced, and the nature of their suppliers. All of this complexity is reduced to information about the price and the quality of the raw materials. Similarly, all the diverse practices of its customers are reduced to those that directly impact on whether or not they buy a car.

Simplifying complexity means being forced to select (the manufacturer cares about how raw materials are produced, but may not pay attention to the political situation in the nation in which they are produced). Being forced to select means contingency since one could always select differently (the manufacturer *could* monitor the political situation). And contingency means *risk*. Thus, if the manufacturer chooses not to monitor the political situation in the nation producing the raw material, the production process might be severely disrupted by a rebellion that shuts off the supply of such material.

A system simply cannot be as complex as its environment. A system that tried would bring to mind the Borges (1964) story of the king who ordered a cartographer to create a completely accurate map of his country. When the cartographer was done, the map was as big as the country and was therefore useless as a map. Maps, like systems, must reduce complexity. The cartographer must select what features are important. Different maps of the same area can be made because the selection is contingent. This is always necessary, but it is also risky since the map maker can never be sure that what is left out will not be important to the user.

While they can never be as complex as their environment, systems develop new subsystems and establish various relations between these subsystems in order to deal effectively with their environment. If they did not, they would be overwhelmed by the complexity of the environment. For example, an automobile manufacturer could create a department of international affairs charged with monitoring political conditions in supplying nations. This new department would be responsible for keeping manufacturing apprised of potential disruptions in the supply of raw materials and for finding alternative sources in case of a disruption. Thus, paradoxically, "Only complexity can reduce complexity" (Luhmann, 1995:26).

Autopoietic Systems

Luhmann is best known for his thinking on autopoiesis.[3] The concept of autopoiesis refers to a diversity of systems from biological cells to the entire world society. Luhmann uses the term to refer to such systems as the economy, the political system, the legal system, the scientific system, and bureaucracies, among others. In the description below, we will try to provide a variety of examples to give a sense of the scope of the concept. Autopoietic systems have the following four characteristics.

1 An autopoietic system produces the basic elements that make up the system. This may seem paradoxical. How can a system produce its own elements, the very things out of which it is made? Think of a modern economic system and its basic element, money. We say money is a basic element because the value of things in the economic system

---

[3]On the significance of this concept, see Bailey, 1998.

can be given in terms of money, but it is very difficult to say what money itself is worth. The meaning of money, what it is worth, what it can be used for, are determined by the economic system itself. Money, as we understand that term today, did not exist before the economic system. Both the modern form of money and the economic system emerged together and they depend on each other. A modern economic system without money is difficult to imagine. Money without an economic system is just a piece of paper or metal.

2 Autopoietic systems are self-organizing in two ways—they organize their own boundaries and they organize their internal structures. They organize their own boundaries by distinguishing between what is in the system and what is in the environment. For example, the economic system counts anything that is scarce and on which a price can be set as part of the economic system. Air is everywhere in abundant supply, therefore no price is set on it and it is not part of the economic system. Air is, however, a necessary part of the environment. What is inside or outside an autopoietic system is determined by the self-organization of the system, not, as a structural functionalist would have us believe, the functional necessities of the system.

Other forces may try to limit the scope of autopoietic systems. For example, capitalist economic systems have always expanded their boundaries in order to include sex and illicit drugs. This occurs even though the political system passes laws aimed at keeping sex or illicit drugs from becoming economic commodities. Rather than keeping them out of the economic system, such laws instead affect the prices of sex and illicit drugs *within* the economic system. Their illegality makes their prices higher thereby discouraging their purchase. But within the economic system, the high prices that discourage purchases also encourage sales. If a great deal of money can be made from selling sex and drugs, they will remain in the economic system. Therefore laws that try to keep a commodity out of the economic system, simply affect the way they are priced within the economic system.

Within its boundaries, an autopoietic system produces its own structures. For example, because of the existence of money, the market is structured in an impersonal way, banks are established to store and lend money, the concept of interest has developed, and so on. If the economic system did not have as its basic element such an abstract and portable entity, the internal structure would be entirely different. For example, if the economy were based on barter instead of money, there would be no banks, no concept of interest, and the market where goods are bought and sold would be structured in an entirely different way.

3 Autopoietic systems are self-referential (Esposito, 1996). For example, the economic system uses price as a way of referring to itself. By attaching a fluctuating monetary value to shares in a company, the stock market exemplifies such self-reference within the economic system. The prices in the stock market are determined not by any individual, but by the economy itself. Similarly, the legal system has laws that refer to the legal system: laws about how laws can be enacted, applied, interpreted, and so on.

4 An autopoietic system is a closed system. This means that there is no direct connection between a system and its environment. Instead, a system deals with its representations of the environment. For example, the economic system supposedly responds to the material needs and desires of people; however, those needs and desires affect the economic system only to the extent that they can be represented in terms of money. Consequently, the economic system responds well to the material needs and desires of rich people but very poorly to the needs and desires of poor people.

Another example would be a bureaucracy, such as the Internal Revenue Service. The IRS never really deals with its clients; it deals solely with representations of the clients. Taxpayers are represented by the forms that they file and that are filed about them. The real taxpayer has an effect on the bureaucracy only by causing a disturbance in the bureaucracy's representations. Those who cause disturbances (misfiled forms, contradictory forms, false forms) often are dealt with very harshly since they threaten the system.

Even though an autopoietic system is closed with no direct connection to the environment, the environment must be allowed to disturb its inner representations. Without such disturbances, the system would be destroyed by environmental forces that would overwhelm it. For example, the prices of stocks in the stock market fluctuate daily. The difference between the price of a company's stock from one day to the next has little to do with the real value of the company—that is, its assets or profits—and everything to do with the state of the stock market. That is, the market may be in a boom period (a "bull" market) in which the prices of stocks are far higher than they should be given the state of the companies involved. However, over the long run the price of stocks needs to reflect the actual status of the companies involved or the system will fall apart. This is what happened in the stock market crash of 1929. The prices of stocks had no relation to real value and so the system reached a state of crisis. To function properly, the stock market as a system must, at least at times, be disturbed by the actual condition of the companies that are part of its environment.

A closed social system is distinct from the individuals that appear to be part of it. According to Luhmann, in such systems, the individual is part of the environment. To take the example of a bureaucracy again, this means that not only are the clients part of the environment, but so are the people who work in the bureaucracy. From the perspective of the bureaucracy, the people who work in it are external sources of complexity and unpredictability. In order to be a closed system, the bureaucracy must find a way to represent even its own workers in a simplified way. Thus, instead of being seen as full-fledged human beings, one worker is seen as a "manager," another as an "accountant," and so on. The real, fully human worker affects the bureaucracy only as a disturbance to the bureaucracy's representations.

Society and Psychic Systems

Luhmann argues that society is an autopoietic system. It fulfills the four characteristics listed above—society produces its own basic elements; it establishes its own boundaries and structures; it is self-referential; and it is closed.

The basic element of society is communication and communication is produced by society. Participants in society refer to society through communication. In fact, that is what we are doing right now! The individual is relevant to society only to the extent that he or she participates in communication or can be interpreted as participating in a

communication. Those secret parts of you that are never communicated, or not understood as a communication by others, are not part of society. They are, instead, part of the
environment which may disturb society. According to Luhmann's conception, whatever
is not communication is part of society's environment. This includes the biological systems of human beings and even their psychic systems. The individual as a biological
organism and the individual as consciousness are not part of society but are external to it.
This leads to the strange idea that the individual is *not* part of society.

By the psychic system, Luhmann means the consciousness of the individual. The
psychic system and society—the system of all communications—have a property in
common. They both rely on *meaning*. Meaning is closely related to the choices that a
system makes. The meaning of a particular action (or object) is its difference from other
possible actions (or objects). Meaning appears only against the backdrop of contingency.
If there is no possibility of being different, then there is no meaning. Action has meaning only to the extent that a selection is made from among a range of possible actions.
For example, our clothing means something only because we could have chosen to wear
something else.

Systems such as the psychic and social systems that rely on meaning are closed
because (1) meaning always refers to other meaning; (2) only meaning can change
meaning; and (3) meaning usually produces more meaning. Meaning forms the boundary to each of these systems. For example, in the psychic system, what is not meaningful is seen as outside the system, as a "cause" of our action, while what is
meaningful is inside the system as a "motivation" for our action. Events enter our psychic system only as meaning. Even our own bodies are simply environments for this
meaning system. Our bodies can be seen only as disturbances to our psychic systems.
The body enters our consciousness by becoming meaningful, so that, for example, a
physical agitation enters consciousness as an emotion. Similarly, in the social system,
meaning is the difference between a communication within the system and noise from
outside the system.

Psychic systems and social systems have evolved together. Each is a necessary environment for the other. The elements of the psychic meaning system are conceptual
representations; the elements of the social meaning system are communications. It
would be wrong to think that meaning in the psychic system has priority over meaning
in the social system. Because both are autopoietic systems, they both produce their
own meanings out of their own processes. In the psychic system, meaning is bound to
consciousness, while in the social system it is bound to communication. Meaning in
the social system cannot be ascribed to an individual's intention, nor is it a property of
the particular elements of the social system; instead it refers to a selection from among
the elements. The meaning of what is communicated is derived from its difference
from what could be communicated. For example, "Hello," "What's up?" "How ya
doin'," "Good day," "Hey!" may all come from the same intention, that is to greet
someone, but if a friend says "Good day" when she usually says "Hey!" some meaning
would be communicated. The meaning is not necessarily intended, nor is it connected
to the particular words. The meaning comes from the selection of *those particular
words* in comparison to the words that could have been selected. The meaning comes
from the contingency of those selected words.

Double Contingency

The social system based on communication creates social structures in order to solve what Luhmann calls the problem of double contingency.[4] Double contingency refers to the fact that every communication must take into consideration the way that it is received. But we also know that the way that it is received will depend on the receiver's estimation of the communicator. This forms an impossible circle: the receiver depends on the communicator and the communicator depends on the receiver. For example, a professor, in choosing how to greet a student, might use the informal "Hey!" if she thinks it will appear more friendly (the communicator takes into account the receiver). But if the student being greeted thinks the professor is talking down to him, he will not see it as a friendly gesture (the receiver takes into account the communicator). The less we know about each other's expectations, the greater the problem of double contingency.

Fortunately, we almost always know a great deal about others' expectations because of social structures. In the example above, we know that the people involved are a professor and a student. Based on this alone, we expect that they will have a certain type of relationship conforming to institutional rules and traditions. We will have other expectations by knowing their genders, their ethnicities, their ages, their dress, and so on. Because of these expectations, norms and role expectations develop for interpreting people's communications. Either people fit the norms and role expectations or they do not. If we find a number of examples that do not fit our expectations, our expectations might change, but society can never do without these expectations because of the problem of double contingency.

It is because each of us has a different set of norms that communication becomes necessary, and it is because communication has the problem of double contingency that we develop sets of norms. This shows how society as an autopoietic system works: the structure (roles, institutional and traditional norms) of society creates the elements (communication) of society and those elements create the structure, so that, as in all autopoietic systems, the system constitutes its own elements.

Because of double contingency, any given communication is improbable. First it is improbable that we would have something we want to communicate to a particular person. Second, since the information can be communicated in a number of ways, it is improbable that we will choose any one particular way. Third, it is improbable that the person we are addressing will understand us correctly. Social structures have developed in order to make improbable communications more probable. For example, to say "Good day" to a particular person at any particular time is an improbable thing, but social structures make a greeting normative in certain circumstances, they provide us with a limited number of acceptable ways to greet people, and they make sure that the addressee will understand the greeting in approximately the same way that the addressor intends it.

The improbabilities that we've discussed so far refer only to interactions, but society is more than a collection of independent interactions. Interactions last only as long as

---

[4]Parsons (1951) also dealt with the problem of double contingency, but he limits its solution to a preexisting value consensus. Luhmann acknowledges the possibility that a new value consensus can be created on the spot.

the people involved in the communication are present, but, from the viewpoint of society, interactions are episodes in ongoing social processes. Every social system is faced with a problem: it will cease to exist if there is no guarantee of further communications, that is, no possibility of connecting previous communications to future communications. To avoid a breakdown of communication, structures must be developed to permit earlier communications to connect with later communications. The selections made in one communication are restricted by the selections made in previous communications and the present communication also restricts future communications. This is another way in which the improbabilities of the communicative process are overcome and transformed into probabilities by the social system. It is this need to overcome double contingency and make improbable communications more probable that regulates the evolution of social systems.

Evolution of Social Systems

Evolution is, roughly speaking, a process of trial-and-error. Evolution is not teleological. Its outcomes are not governed by a predefined goal. One implication is that, in Luhmann's theory, the idea of progress makes no sense. This differentiates it from Parsons's idea of evolutionary universals in modern societies (see pp. 106–108). To assume a necessary path of societal development is teleological and ignores the fact that there are a variety of ways of dealing with a given problem.

On the general level, evolution makes improbability more probable. For example, it is improbable that a random set of biological mutations will produce a given animal such as a human. Natural selection and the inheritance of stable characteristics make it more probable that an ape will evolve into something like a human rather than something like a squid.

Strictly speaking, evolution is not a process, but a set of processes that can be described as performing three functions: variation, selection, and stabilization of reproducible characteristics. These represent the concrete mechanisms by which evolution operates. *Variation* is a process of trial-and-error. If a system faces a unique problem, a variety of solutions may develop to deal with the environmental disturbance. Some of these solutions will work, others will not. The *selection* of a particular solution does not imply that the "best" solution is chosen. It may simply be that the particular solution is the easiest to stabilize, in other words, the easiest to reproduce as a stable and enduring structure. In a social system, this *stabilization* usually involves a new kind of differentiation that requires the adjustment of all parts of the system to the new solution. The evolutionary process will have achieved a temporary end only when the stabilization phase is complete.

Let us take an example from the economy. One problem that economic systems have faced is how to exchange goods in an equitable way with other economic systems—that is, how can an economy that uses dollars exchange goods with an economy that uses yen? A variety of different solutions have developed (evolutionary variation). Some early systems initiated "gift" exchanges that eliminated a concern for the exact equality of the goods exchanged. Others have used a stable commodity such as gold to regulate the interchange. Both of these proved difficult to reproduce on a global scale. For the first solution, only so much can be exchanged as gifts and, for the second, the value of commodities such as gold do not remain stable because more or less gold is available at any given time. Instead, a more reproducible form has been the establishment of a new structure, a currency exchange market, that operates at the global level and allows the exchange rate of currencies to float (evolutionary selection). This may not be the best solution since it is susceptible to wild fluctuations caused by speculators, as seen in the "Asian" financial crisis of 1998. However, it is the only solution that appears to be reproducible on a global scale (evolutionary stabilization). Of course, the reproducibility of this solution does not mean that the other solutions have disappeared. States still exchange gifts, especially with heads of states through diplomats, and many countries try to fix their exchange rate by tying it to a commodity such as gold or even another currency such as the U.S. dollar.

Differentiation

From the viewpoint of Luhmann's system theory, the principal feature of modern society is the increased process of system differentiation as a way of dealing with the complexity of its environment. Differentiation is the "replication, within a system of the difference between a system and its environment" (1982b:230).[5] This means that in a differentiated system there are two kinds of environments: one common to all subsystems and a different *internal environment* for each subsystem. For example, an automobile manufacturer, such as Ford, sees other manufacturers, General Motors and Daimler-Chrysler, for instance, as part of its environment. The international relations department (a subsystem) of Ford also sees General Motors and Chrysler as outside it and part of its environment. However, the international relations department also sees other subsystems within Ford (such as the human relations department [subsystem]) as outside the international relations subsystem and therefore part of its environment. Other subsystems such as the human relations department are internal to the organizational system as a whole, but are in the environment of the international relations subsystem, hence an internal environment. Similarly, the human relations subsystem sees other manufacturers as part of its environment, but in addition sees other subsystems (this time including the international relations subsystem) as part of its environment. Therefore each of the subsystems has a different view of the internal environment of the system. This creates a highly complex and dynamic internal environment.

Differentiation within a system is a way of dealing with changes in the environment. As we have seen, each system must maintain its boundary in relation to the environment. Otherwise it would be overwhelmed by the complexity of its environment, break down, and cease to exist. In order to survive, the system must be able to deal with environmental variations. For instance, it is well known that any large-scale organization as a system adjusts slowly to alterations in its environment (e.g., concrete demands by the public, political changes, or even technological changes such as the availability of personal computers). However, organizations do develop; they evolve by creating

---

[5]For a general discussion of differentiation and the limits of the concept, see Wagner, 1998.

differentiation within the system. That is, an environmental change will be "translated" into the structure of the organization. An example would be the creation by the automobile manufacturer of a new department to deal with a new situation such as the presence of personal computers in the workplace. New workers would be hired; they would be trained to handle the new technology; a manager would be selected; and so forth.

The differentiation process is a means of increasing the complexity of the system, since each subsystem can make different connections with other subsystems. It allows for more variation within the system in order to respond to variation in the environment. In the above example, the new department is, like every other department of the bureaucratic system, an environment for other departments, but the new one increases organizational complexity because new and additional relations between departments are made possible. A new department created to service workers' computers will be better able to respond to further changes in computer technologies and help the entire organization to integrate these new capabilities. In addition, it may provide for new connections between existing departments, such as allowing general accounting to be centralized or salespeople to access inventory directly.

Not only does more variation caused by differentiation allow for better responses to the environment, it also allows for faster evolution. Remember that evolution is a process of selection from variation. The more variation that is available, the better the selection. However, Luhmann argues that only a few forms of internal differentiation have developed. He calls these segmentation, stratification, center-periphery, and functional differentiation. These differentiations increase the complexity of the system through the repetition of the differentiation between system and environment within the system. In terms of their evolutionary potential, these forms of differentiation have a different ability to produce variability and therefore provide for more selectivity for evolutionary processes. The more complex forms of differentiation therefore have the potential to accelerate the evolution of the system.

Segmentary Differentiation   Segmentary differentiation divides parts of the system on the basis of the need to fulfill identical functions over and over. For instance, our automobile manufacturer has functionally similar factories for the production of cars at many different locations. Every location is organized in much the same way; each has the same structure and fulfills the same function—producing cars.

Stratificatory Differentiation   Stratificatory differentiation is a vertical differentiation according to rank or status in a system conceived as a hierarchy. Every rank fulfills a particular and distinct function in the system. In the automobile firm, we find different ranks. For example, the manager of the new department of international relations occupies the top rank within the hierarchy of that department. The manager has the function of using power to direct the operations of that department. Then, there are a variety of lower-ranking workers within the department who handle a variety of specific functions (e.g., word processing). In addition, the manager of the department of international relations has a position within the stratificatory system of the automobile manufacturer. Thus, the president of the company has a higher-ranking position than that of the manager of international relations and is in a position to issue orders to the latter.

In segmentary differentiation, inequality results from accidental variations in environments (such as more cars being sold in one geographic area than another), but it has no systemic function. In stratificatory differentiation, however, inequality is essential to the system. More correctly, we see the interplay of equality and inequality. All members in the same ranks (e.g., all the word processors) are basically equal, while different ranks are distinguished by their inequality. The higher ranks (e.g., department managers) have more access to resources and greater ability to become the subject of influential communications. Consequently, a stratified system is more concerned with the well-being of those in the upper ranks and generally is concerned about the lower ranks only if they threaten the higher ranks. However, both ranks depend on one another and the social system can survive only if all ranks, including the lowest, successfully realize their functions.

The importance of the lower ranks and yet their difficulty in becoming the subject of influential communication create a structural problem that limits the complexity of the system. When those directing the system become too removed from the lowest ranks, the system tends to collapse because the important functions of the lowest ranks are not being properly performed. In order to have an effect on the system, the lower ranks must resort to conflict.

Center-Periphery Differentiation   The third type of differentiation, that between *center and periphery,* is a link between segmentary and stratificatory differentiation (Luhmann, 1997:663–678). For instance, some automobile firms have built factories in other countries; nevertheless, the headquarters of the company remains the center, ruling and, to some extent, controlling the peripheral factories.[6]

Differentiations of Functional Systems   *Functional differentiation* is the most complex form of differentiation and the form that dominates modern society. Every function within a system is ascribed to a particular unit. For instance, an automobile manufacturer has functionally differentiated departments such as production, administration, accounting, planning, and personnel.

Functional differentiation is more flexible than stratificatory differentiation, but, if one system fails to fulfill its task, the whole system will have great trouble surviving.[7] However, so long as each unit fulfills its function, the different units can attain a high degree of independence. In fact, functionally differentiated systems are a complex mixture of interdependence and independence. For instance, while the planning division is dependent upon the accounting division for economic data, as long as the figures are accurate the planning division can be blissfully ignorant of exactly how the accountants produced the data.

---

[6]It has been objected (Schimank, 1996) that this distinction does not fit Luhmann's general argument. The differentiation between center and periphery does not refer to the social system as a whole. Rather, in the above example it refers to a differentiation of functions within the industrial system. Thus it refers to a specific system within the social system and does not refer to the social system as a whole.

[7]Most of the systems discussed here can also be called subsystems of the world social system. However, we will use the term system rather than subsystem except when it is necessary to distinguish between the subsystem and the overarching system that contains it.

This indicates a further difference between the forms of differentiation. In the case of segmentary differentiation, if a segment fails to fulfill its function (e.g., one of the automobile manufacturer's factories cannot produce cars because of a labor strike), it does not threaten the system. However, in the case of the more complex forms of differentiation such as functional differentiation, failure will cause a problem for the social system, possibly leading to its breakdown. Thus, on the one hand, the growth of complexity increases the abilities of a system to deal with its environment. On the other hand, complexity increases the risk of a system breakdown if a function is not properly fulfilled.

However, in most cases, this increased vulnerability is a necessary price to pay for the increase in possible relations between different subsystems. More types of possible relations between the subsystems means more variation to use to select structural responses to changes in the environment. In a segmentary system, the relations between different subsystems are not structurally different. For example, the relations that any two factories have with each other are all basically the same. In a stratified system, the relations between ranks are basically different from those within the rank. For example, the relations that a factory has with headquarters is different from that which it has with another factory. In functionally differentiated systems, the different relations multiply. The accounting and production departments have a different relationship with each other than that between accounting and research, which is, in turn, different from the relationship between production and research. Functional differentiation gives the automobile manufacturer greater flexibility. Thus, for example, in an environment in which technical advances are providing opportunities for economic advantage, the company can be led by research, but in an environment in which economic advantage is found in doing the same old thing only cheaper, the company can be led by accounting.

We should note that the more complex forms of differentiation do not exclude the less complex forms, and, in fact, they may require the less complex forms. For example, an automobile manufacturer is stratified, but it still contains individual factories that are a segmentary form. This is important, since we usually speak of functionally differentiated systems within modern society to describe its dominant mode of differentiation; nevertheless, the other forms continue to exist.

Code   A code is a way to distinguish elements of a system from elements that do not belong to the system. A code is the basic "language" of a functional system. Codes are, for instance, truth (versus nontruth) for the science system, payment (versus nonpayment) for the economic system, and legal (versus illegal) for the legal system. Every communication using a particular code is a part of the system whose code reference is being used.

A code is used to limit the kind of permissible communication. Every communication that does not use the code is not a communication belonging to the system under consideration. Thus, within the scientific system we will usually find only communications with reference to the code of truth. For instance, if the head of NASA (National Aeronautics and Space Administration) and the head of NIH (National Institutes of Health) met to discuss what facts had been discovered about aging in John Glenn's 1998 space flight, it would be part of the scientific system using the code of truth or nontruth.

If these same people met to discuss who will pay for what part of the research conducted on that space flight, it would be in the economic system using the code of payment or nonpayment.

In Luhmann's system theory, no system uses and understands the code of another system. There is no way to translate the code of one system into the code of another system. Because the systems are closed, they can react only to things happening in their environment (if what happens makes enough "noise" to be noticed by the system). But the system must describe the noise in the environment in relation to its own code. This is the only way to make sense of what is happening, the only way to give it meaning. For example, an economic system will "see" a scientific system only in terms of what makes money (makes future payments possible) or requires investments (requires initial payments before it can be repaid).

Problems of Functional Differentiation   Functional differentiation causes at least one central problem for modern society. What is necessary for society as a whole may not be dealt with by any functional system. There may not be a functional system that has a code that can adequately represent the problem. For instance, the economic system cannot adequately represent ecological problems, since much pollution looks economically rational. The legal system may have laws aimed at restricting air pollution, but those laws are interpreted within the economic system of the polluters. This is demonstrated by an example from the former Czechoslovakia where there were legally prescribed limitations on air pollution. Industries reacted to these laws by building higher smokestacks leading to a wider dispersion of pollution and thus a decreasing level of air pollution near the measurement points. This reaction contradicted the intention of the law, but it was a reaction in accord with the code of the economic system; it was a way to minimize costs. Better protection against air pollution would have cost much more than building higher smokestacks.

Such problems generally are caused by functional differentiation. Functional differentiation requires a displacement of problems from the level of society to the level of subsystems. Every subsystem has gained independence and flexibility in making decisions using its own codes. However, each is dependent on other subsystems to move the social system as a whole. In short, the result of greater independence of functional systems is greater vulnerability of the social system as a whole.

Luhmann has investigated the problematic relationship between the functional differentiation of modern society and its efforts to deal with the problems of ecology (1986/1989). Modern society has no specific differentiated system to deal with ecological problems. Everything that happens in its environment (note the double meaning of the term: environment of a system and natural environment) must be treated within the existing functional systems and their codes. That means, every problem in the environment is a problem for a system only if it can be represented in the system's code. For example, the law can move against polluters only if what they do can be represented as illegal. Thus, it is possible that ecological problems will not be dealt with sufficiently. Of greater importance is a general conclusion: functional differentiation can be conceived of as a causative factor of ecological crisis (Luhmann, 1986/1989:42).

Functional systems produce both too much and too little *resonance* to problems in their environment. Too little resonance means that a system does not react well to problems that cannot be represented by its codes. For instance, environmental groups may confront the automobile industry with a demand for cars that produce less air pollution; however, the automobile industry is unlikely to react to these demands unless the protests start to affect their profits. Too much resonance means that the treatment of ecological problems within a functional system may lead to reactions in other functional systems because the systems are interdependent. For instance, the automobile industry may produce cars that pollute less by making them smaller, lighter, and, consequently, cheaper. This can have the consequence that the development of the public transportation system will slow down since now everyone can buy a car. In addition, it is likely that this will also increase the number of traffic accidents and thus the cost within the health system. The reaction to the demand of the environmental groups has unpredictable consequences within complex interdependent functional systems.

Luhmann's Sociology of Knowledge

For Luhmann, the principal question for sociology is: What is society? This was the starting point of Luhmann's attempt to develop a system theory (1987). Sociology, as a science of society, is possible only with a clearly defined concept of society. Luhmann's system theory defines *society* as the "all encompassing social system including all other societal systems" (1997:78; translated by one of the authors). This implies that the concept of *society* is identical with the concept of a *world society;* there can be only one society. A *social system* is every system producing communication as its basic element to reproduce itself. A *societal system* is a functional system like the economy, science, and law within the all-encompassing system of society.[8]

An all-encompassing world society has no boundaries in time and space; in a sense, a world society has no "address" and no other societies in the environment. How, then, can society be observed? There is only one answer, a society can be observed only from a perspective within society, that is, through a functional system of society. However, no functional system has the "right" perspective for the observation of society. Every perspective is a legitimate one. How can we then arrive at a single way of gaining information about the social world? In fact, there is no way to create such a simple perspective. No point of view is superior to any others. Therefore, a commonly shared perspective can never be achieved since there is no possibility of evaluating competing views. For instance, if we as sociologists want to know something about society, we are accustomed to searching for sociological knowledge. According to Luhmann's argument, it would also be possible to read a newspaper, read a book, watch television, or speak with a friend. Any of these ways is a legitimate way of obtaining information

---

[8]Since the original publication of *Social Systems* (1984/1995), Luhmann has deepened and applied his approach to various functional systems within the system of society, such as the economy (Luhmann, 1988), science (Luhmann, 1990a), law (Luhmann, 1993), and art (Luhmann, 1995). He has attempted to demonstrate the usefulness of his general theory for the analysis of any functionally differentiated system. He has also discussed issues which cut across functional systems, especially the communication of ecological risks (Luhmann, 1986/1989) and the use of the general concept of risk (Luhmann, 1991).

about society. Neither science, nor any other system, has a privileged position. If no functional system has a superior position from which to observe and thus to describe society as a system, then we have the problem of an unlimited variety of equally valid observations of society.

Luhmann has tried to work out a way in which we can nevertheless arrive at knowledge of society. Society describes itself through, for instance, legends and myths in ancient times and scientific knowledge in modern times. However, sociologists are able to observe these observations. And because sociologists are able to observe as second-order observers the first-order observations of society, they can draw conclusions about the relations between society and its semantics, that is, the self-descriptions of society. This is the key to knowledge about a society—to observe the semantics of society, that is, the "communication about the communications" constituting the system of society.

Luhmann has attempted to demonstrate that the observation of society is not arbitrary because "there are structural conditions for the soundness of representation; and there are historical trends in the evolution of semantics strongly limiting the range of variation. Sociological theory is able to recognize connections of the kind of correlations between social structures and semantics" (1997:89; translated by one of the authors). Luhmann's studies reconstruct the historical usage and meaning of terms in relation to changing social structures, taking semantics as an expression of the interpretation of social structures. Thus, the proper way of observing society sociologically is an investigation of changing semantics in relation to changing social structures.[9] Luhmann has done a great deal of work outlining the development, for instance, of the semantics of morality, individuality, law, knowledge (1980/1981/1989/1995), and love (1982/1986). This method is part of a sociology of knowledge and can be used in the general task of the development of a theory of society.

Criticisms

In sum, Luhmann's theory of modern society and his concept of society are highly developed analytical tools that allow sociology to obtain a fresh perspective on current social problems in society (and in sociology). The general theory of evolution and differentiation, as well as Luhmann's thinking on specific systems like science and the economy, open up new avenues of theory and research. The basic distinction between system and environment opens up the possibility of a new kind of interdisciplinary research based on the assumption that complexity is the overarching problem connecting the apparently separated realms of the natural and the human sciences (Luhmann, 1985).

There are a number of criticisms of Luhmann's system theory, but we will briefly mention only four of them:

First, many theorists, including Jurgen Habermas, have argued that what Luhmann sees as a necessary evolutionary development is, in fact, regressive and unnecessary. Society may in fact be developing into a closed system of functionally differentiated

---

[9]This argumentation indicates an inconsistency in Luhmann's idea that we discuss in the concluding section.

realms unable to act in the name of the social whole, but this is something to resist. Theories should be developed to help counter this trend not, as Luhmann does, to make it appear inevitable.

Second, in Luhmann's theory, differentiation is the key to describing the development of society and the increasing complexity of social systems in dealing with their environments. But we can also find two counterprocesses in contemporary society. One is de-differentiation (Lash, 1988), that is, a process of dissolving boundaries between social systems, for example, between high and popular culture. The other is interpenetration (R. Münch, 1987), that is, a process of building institutions to mediate between social systems. Luhmann's system theory tends to see these processes as antievolutionary since evolution is defined as increased differentiation. It is possible that Luhmann's theory could recognize de-differentiation and interpenetration as valid sources of evolutionary variability, but this would mean dropping the single-minded focus on differentiation that has proved so theoretically rewarding.

Third, Luhmann's theory seems limited in its ability to describe relations between systems. Not all systems appear to be as closed and autonomous as Luhmann assumes. Not only do some systems appear to translate each other's codes, but they sometimes incorporate other systems as their elements. Most obvious is the way in which the social system incorporates the psychic system. The meaning of a communication within the social system is not completely determined by the social system itself. Psychic systems (individuals) protest and restrict the meanings that are assigned to a particular communication. Luhmann is correct that the meaning of a communication is not simply the intention of the individual, but certainly the intention has some, albeit complex, effect on the social meaning. The social system is not simply closed to the psychic system. Similarly, it is possible that an apparently autonomous system such as the political system can be reduced to the status of a subsystem of another system such as the economy. In that case, the code of the political system may be simply a variation on the code of the economic system.

Finally, Luhmann's system theory assumes a variety of equally valid views of society without the possibility of giving one priority over the others. (This resembles the position taken by the postmodern social theorist, Lyotard [1984].) Nevertheless, Luhmann claims that we are able to develop a secure knowledge of society observing the semantics of the self-descriptions of society. This standpoint is inconsistent since it is not possible to claim both positions at once.

In spite of these and other weaknesses, Luhmann's systems theory has emerged as one of the leading social theories as we move into the twenty-first century and it has sparked a resurgence of interest in systems theory.

SUMMARY

This chapter began with some of Walter Buckley's early thoughts on the nature of systems theory. There are various gains to be derived from a sociological system theory including a common vocabulary across hard sciences and various social sciences, applicability at both the micro and macro levels, analysis of the social world as a whole, a focus on processes, an integrative perspective, and a dynamic orientation. A variety of principles of systems theory are discussed including the degree to which systems are open or closed, tend to run down (entropy), tend to elaborate structures (negentropy), are characterized by feedback, and feature processes that help the system to maintain itself (morphostasis) and to grow (morphogenesis). Buckley applied systems theory to consciousness, interaction, and the sociocultural domain.

Today's most important systems theorist is Niklas Luhmann. Among other things, Luhmann sees systems as self-referencing, contingent, and as always *less* complex than the environment. Systems must reduce complexity; they cannot be as complex as their environment or they would be overwhelmed and unable to function. Luhmann's most important contribution is his sense of systems as being autopoietic. That is, systems produce their own basic elements, they organize their own boundaries and the relationships among their internal structures, they are self-referential, and they are closed. It is the view of systems as autopoietic and closed to their environments that differentiates Luhmann's approach from earlier systems theorists. Two of the systems singled out for analysis by Luhmann are the social and the psychic systems. Social systems are plagued by the problem of double contingency—every communication must take into account how it is received, but how it is received depends on the receiver's estimation of the communicator. Because of this, communication is improbable, but social structures have developed to make communication more probable.

Luhmann is concerned with evolution involving three mechanisms—variation, selection, and stabilization. Modern society deals with the increasing complexity of its environment through a process of differentiation. Differentiation leads to increasing complexity of the system and allows for a greater ability to respond to the environment, as well as to faster evolution. Luhmann identifies four forms of differentiation—segmentary, stratificatory, center-periphery, and functional. It is the latter that is the most complex form of differentiation and the one that dominates modern society. It allows for greater system flexibility, but if one functionally differentiated system fails to perform its function, the system as a whole may fail. Furthermore, it is possible that society will not have a functionally differentiated subsystem capable of handling an important problem.

Since Luhmann conceives of society as an all-encompassing system, a world system, it can be observed only from within the system. No functional system has the right perspective; all perspectives are legitimate. Nonetheless, Luhmann seeks to accord priority to sociological knowledge by arguing that its task is the study of first-order observations of society (legends, myths, and so on).

Luhmann's theory has been subjected to a number of major criticisms, but it remains a powerful perspective as we enter the twenty-first century.

6

SYMBOLIC
INTERACTIONISM

THE MAJOR HISTORICAL ROOTS
  Pragmatism
  Behaviorism
  Between Reductionism and Sociologism
THE IDEAS OF GEORGE HERBERT MEAD
  The Priority of the Social
  The Act
  Gestures
  Significant Symbols
  Mental Processes and the Mind
  Self
  Society
SYMBOLIC INTERACTIONISM: THE BASIC PRINCIPLES
  Capacity for Thought
  Thinking and Interaction
  Learning Meanings and Symbols
  Action and Interaction
  Making Choices
  The Self and the Work of Erving Goffman
  Groups and Societies
CRITICISMS
TOWARD A MORE SYNTHETIC AND INTEGRATIVE
SYMBOLIC INTERACTIONISM
  Redefining Mead and Blumer
  Micro-Macro Integration
  Symbolic Interactionism and Cultural Studies
THE FUTURE OF SYMBOLIC INTERACTIONISM

Symbolic interactionism offers a wide range of interesting and important ideas, and a number of major thinkers have been associated with the approach, including George Herbert Mead, Charles Horton Cooley, W. I. Thomas, Herbert Blumer, and Erving Goffman.

THE MAJOR HISTORICAL ROOTS

We begin our discussion of symbolic interactionism with Mead. The two most significant intellectual roots of Mead's work in particular, and of symbolic interactionism in general, are the philosophy of pragmatism and psychological behaviorism (Joas, 1985; Rock, 1979).

Pragmatism

Pragmatism is a wide-ranging philosophical position,[1] from which we can identify several aspects that influenced Mead's developing sociological orientation (Charon, 1998; Joas, 1993). First, to pragmatists true reality does not exist "out there" in the real world; it "is actively created as we act in and toward the world" (J. Hewitt, 1984:8; see also Shalin, 1986). Second, people remember and base their knowledge of the world on what has proven useful to them. They are likely to alter what no longer "works." Third, people define the social and physical "objects" that they encounter in the world according to their use for them. Finally, if we want to understand actors, we must base that understanding on what they actually do in the world. Three points are critical for symbolic interactionism: (1) a focus on the interaction between the actor and the world, (2) a view of both the actor and the world as dynamic processes and not static structures, and (3) the great importance attributed to the actor's ability to interpret the social world.

The last point is most pronounced in the work of the philosophical pragmatist John Dewey (Sjoberg et al., 1997). Dewey did not conceive of the mind as a thing or a structure but rather as a thinking process that involves a series of stages. These stages include defining objects in the social world, outlining possible modes of conduct, imagining the consequences of alternative courses of action, eliminating unlikely possibilities, and finally selecting the optimal mode of action (Stryker, 1980). This focus on the thinking process was enormously influential in the development of symbolic interactionism.

In fact, David Lewis and Richard Smith argue that Dewey (along with William James; see Musolf, 1994) was more influential in the development of symbolic interactionism than was Mead. They go so far as to say that "Mead's work was peripheral to the mainstream of early Chicago sociology" (Lewis and Smith, 1980:xix). In making this argument, they distinguish between two branches of pragmatism—"philosophical realism" (associated with Mead) and "nominalist pragmatism" (associated with Dewey and James). In their view, symbolic interactionism was influenced more by the nominalist approach and was even inconsistent with philosophical realism. The nominalist position is that although macro-level phenomena exist, they do not have "independent and determining effects upon the consciousness of and behavior of individuals" (Lewis and Smith, 1980:24). More positively, this view "conceives of the individuals themselves as existentially free agents who accept, reject, modify, or otherwise 'define' the community's norms, roles, beliefs, and so forth, according to their own personal interests and plans of the moment" (Lewis and Smith, 1980:24). In

---

[1]See Joas (1996) for an effort to develop a theory of creative action based, at least in part, on pragmatism.

contrast, to social realists the emphasis is on society and how it constitutes and controls individual mental processes. Rather than being free agents, actors and their cognitions and behaviors are controlled by the larger community.[2]

Given this distinction, Mead fits better into the realist camp and therefore did not mesh well with the nominalist direction taken by symbolic interactionism. The key figure in the latter development is Herbert Blumer, who, while claiming to operate with a Meadian approach, was in fact himself better thought of as a nominalist. Theoretically, Lewis and Smith catch the essence of their differences:

> Blumer . . . moved completely toward psychical interactionism. . . . Unlike the Meadian social behaviorist, the psychical interactionist holds that the meanings of symbols are not universal and objective; rather meanings are individual and subjective in that they are "attached" to the symbols by the receiver according to however he or she chooses to "interpret" them.
>
> (Lewis and Smith, 1980:172)

Behaviorism

Buttressing the Lewis and Smith interpretation of Mead is the fact that Mead was influenced by psychological behaviorism (J. Baldwin, 1986, 1988a, 1988b), a perspective which also led him in a realist and an empirical direction. In fact, Mead called his basic concern *social behaviorism* to differentiate it from the *radical behaviorism* of John B. Watson (who was one of Mead's students).

Radical behaviorists of Watson's persuasion (K. Buckley, 1989) were concerned with the *observable* behaviors of individuals. Their focus was on the stimuli that elicited the responses, or behaviors, in question. They either denied or were disinclined to attribute much importance to the covert mental process that occurred between the time that a stimulus was applied and a response emitted. Mead recognized the importance of observable behavior, but he also felt that there were *covert* aspects of behavior that the radical behaviorists had ignored. But because he accepted the empiricism that was basic to behaviorism, Mead did not simply want to philosophize about these covert phenomena. Rather, he sought to extend the empirical science of behaviorism to them—that is, to what goes on between stimulus and response. Bernard Meltzer summarized Mead's position:

> For Mead, the unit of study is "the act," which comprises both overt and covert aspects of human action. Within the act, all the separated categories of the traditional, orthodox psychologies find a place. Attention, perception, imagination, reasoning, emotion, and so forth, are seen as parts of the act . . . the act, then, encompasses the total process involved in human activity.
>
> (Meltzer, 1964/1978:23)

Mead and the radical behaviorists also differed in their views on the relationship between human and animal behavior. Whereas radical behaviorists tended to see no difference between humans and animals, Mead argued that there was a significant,

---

[2]For a criticism of the distinctions made here, see D. Miller (1982b, 1985).

qualitative difference. The key to this difference was seen as the human possession of mental capacities that allowed people to use language between stimulus and response in order to decide how to respond.

Mead simultaneously demonstrated his debt to Watsonian behaviorism and dissociated himself from it. Mead made this clear when he said, on the one hand, that "we shall approach this latter field [social psychology] from a behavioristic point of view." On the other hand, Mead criticized Watson's position when he said, "The behaviorism which we shall make use of is *more adequate* than that of which Watson makes use" (1934/1962:2; italics added).

Charles Morris, in his introduction to *Mind, Self and Society,* enumerated three basic differences between Mead and Watson. First, Mead considered Watson's exclusive focus on behavior too simplistic. In effect, he accused Watson of wrenching behavior out of its broader social context. Mead wanted to deal with behavior as a small part of the broader social world.

Second, Mead accused Watson of an unwillingness to extend behaviorism into mental processes. Watson had no sense of the actor's consciousness and mental processes, as Mead made vividly clear: "John B. Watson's attitude was that of the Queen in *Alice in Wonderland*—'Off with their heads!'—there were no such things. There was no . . . consciousness" (1934/1962:2–3). Mead contrasted his perspective with Watson's: "It is behavioristic, but unlike Watsonian behaviorism it recognizes the parts of the act which do not come to external observation" (1934/1962:8). More concretely, Mead saw his mission as extending the principles of Watsonian behaviorism to include mental processes.

Finally, because Watson rejected the mind, Mead saw him as having a passive image of the actor as puppet. Mead, on the other hand, subscribed to a much more dynamic and creative image of the actor, and it was this that made him attractive to later symbolic interactionists.

Pragmatism and behaviorism, especially in the theories of Dewey and Mead, were transmitted to many graduate students at the University of Chicago, primarily in the 1920s. These students, among them Herbert Blumer, established symbolic interactionism. Of course, other important theorists influenced these students, the most important of whom was Georg Simmel (see Chapter 1). Simmel's interest in forms of action and interaction was both compatible with and an extension of Meadian theory.

Between Reductionism and Sociologism

Blumer coined the term *symbolic interactionism* in 1937 and wrote several essays that were instrumental in its development. Whereas Mead sought to differentiate the nascent symbolic interactionism from behaviorism, Blumer saw symbolic interactionism as embattled on two fronts. First was the reductionist behaviorism that had worried Mead. To this was added the serious threat from larger-scale sociologistic theories, especially structural functionalism. To Blumer, behaviorism and structural functionalism both tended to focus on factors (for example, external stimuli and norms) that cause human behavior. As far as Blumer was concerned, both theories ignored the crucial process by which actors endow the forces acting upon them and their own behaviors with meaning (Morrione, 1988).

To Blumer, behaviorists, with their emphasis on the impact of external stimuli on individual behavior, were clearly psychological reductionists. In addition to behaviorism, several other types of psychological reductionism troubled Blumer. For example, he criticized those who seek to explain human action by relying on conventional notions of the concept of "attitude" (Blumer, 1955/1969:94). In his view, most of those who use the concept think of an attitude as an "already organized tendency" within the actor; they tend to think of actions as being impelled by attitudes. In Blumer's view, this is very mechanistic thinking; what is important is not the attitude as an internalized tendency "but the defining process through which the actor comes to forge his act" (Blumer, 1955/1969:97). Blumer also singled out for criticism those who focus on conscious and unconscious motives. He was particularly irked by their view that actors are impelled by independent, mentalistic impulses over which they are supposed to have no control. Freudian theory, which sees actors as impelled by such forces as the id or libido, is an example of the kind of psychological theory to which Blumer was opposed. In short, Blumer was opposed to any psychological theory that ignores the process by which actors construct meaning—the fact that actors have selves and relate to themselves. Blumer's general criticisms were similar to Mead's, but he extended them beyond behaviorism to include other forms of psychological reductionism as well.

Blumer also was opposed to sociologistic theories (especially structural functionalism) that view individual behavior as determined by large-scale external forces. In this category Blumer included theories that focus on such social-structural and social-cultural factors as "'social system,' 'social structure,' 'culture,' 'status position,' 'social role,' 'custom,' 'institution,' 'collective representation,' 'social situation,' 'social norm,' and 'values'" (Blumer, 1962/1969:83). Both sociologistic theories and psychological theories ignore the importance of meaning and the social construction of reality:

> In both such typical psychological and sociological explanations the meanings of things for the human beings who are acting are either bypassed or swallowed up in the factors used to account for their behavior. If one declares that the given kinds of behavior are the result of the particular factors regarded as producing them, there is no need to concern oneself with the meaning of the things towards which human beings act.
>
> (Blumer, 1969b:3)

THE IDEAS OF GEORGE HERBERT MEAD

Mead is the most important thinker in the history of symbolic interactionism, and his book *Mind, Self and Society* is the most important single work in that tradition.

The Priority of the Social

In his review of *Mind, Self and Society,* Ellsworth Faris argued that "not mind and then society; but society first and then minds arising within that society . . . would probably have been [Mead's] preference" (cited in Miller, 1982a:2). Faris's inversion of the title of this book reflects the widely acknowledged fact, recognized by Mead himself, that society, or more broadly the social, is accorded priority in Mead's analysis.

GEORGE HERBERT MEAD: A Biographical Sketch

Most of the important theorists discussed throughout this book achieved their greatest recognition in their lifetimes for their published work. George Herbert Mead, however, was at least as important, at least during his lifetime, for his teaching as for his writing. His words had a powerful impact on many people who were to become important sociologists in the twentieth century. As one of his students said, "Conversation was his best medium; writing was a poor second" (T. V. Smith, 1931:369). Let us have another of his students, himself a well-known sociologist—Leonard Cottrell—describe what Mead was like as a teacher:

For me, the course with Professor Mead was a unique and unforgettable experience. . . . Professor Mead was a large, amiable-looking man who wore a magnificent mustache and a Vandyke beard. He characteristically had a benign, rather shy smile matched with a twinkle in his eyes as if he were enjoying a secret joke he was playing on the audience. . . .

As he lectured—always without notes—Professor Mead would manipulate the piece of chalk and watch it intently. . . . When he made a particularly subtle point in his lecture he would glance up and throw a shy, almost apologetic smile over our heads—never looking directly at anyone. His lecture flowed and we soon learned that questions or comments from the class were not welcome. Indeed, when someone was bold enough to raise a question there was a murmur of disapproval from the students. They objected to any interruption of the golden flow. . . .

His expectations of students were modest. He never gave exams. The main task for each of us students was to write as learned a paper as one could. These Professor Mead read with great care, and what he thought of your paper was your grade in the course. One might suppose that students would read materials for the paper rather than attend his lectures but that was not the case. Students always came. They couldn't get enough of Mead.

(Cottrell, 1980:49–50)

Mead had enormous difficulty writing and this troubled him a great deal. "'I am vastly depressed by my inability to write what I want to'" (cited in G. Cook, 1993:xiii). However, over the years many of Mead's ideas came to be published, especially in *Mind, Self and Society* (a book based on students' notes from a course taught by Mead). This book and others of Mead's works had a powerful influence on the development of contemporary sociology, especially symbolic interactionism.

In Mead's view, traditional social psychology began with the psychology of the individual in an effort to explain social experience; in contrast, Mead always gives priority to the social world in understanding social experience. Mead explains his focus in this way:

We are not, in social psychology, building up the behavior of the social group in terms of the behavior of separate individuals composing it; rather, we are *starting out with a given social whole* of complex group activity, into which we analyze (as elements) the behavior of each of the separate individuals composing it. . . . We attempt, that is, to explain the conduct of the social group, rather than to account for the organized conduct of the social

Born in South Hadley, Massachusetts, on February 27, 1863, Mead was trained mainly in philosophy and its application to social psychology. He received a bachelor's degree from Oberlin College (where his father was a professor) in 1883, and after a few years as a secondary-school teacher, surveyor for railroad companies, and private tutor, Mead began graduate study at Harvard in 1887. After a few years of study at Harvard, as well as at the Universities of Leipzig and Berlin, Mead was offered an instructorship at the University of Michigan in 1891. It is interesting to note that Mead *never* received any graduate degrees. In 1894, at the invitation of John Dewey, he moved to the University of Chicago and remained there for the rest of his life.

As Mead makes clear in the following excerpt from a letter, he was heavily influenced by Dewey: " 'Mr. Dewey is a man of not only great originality and profound thought but the most appreciative thinker I ever met. I have gained more from him than from any one man I ever met' " (cited in G. Cook, 1993:32). This was especially true of Mead's early work at Chicago and he even followed Dewey into educational theory (Dewey left Chicago in 1904). However, Mead's thinking quickly diverged from Dewey's and led him in the direction of his famous social psychological theories of mind, self, and society. He began teaching a course on social psychology in 1900. In 1916–1917 it was transformed into an advanced course (the stenographic student notes from the 1928 course became the basis of *Mind, Self and Society*) that followed a course in elementary social psychology that was taught after 1919 by Ellsworth Faris of the sociology department. It was through this course that Mead had such a powerful influence on students in sociology (as well as psychology and education).

In addition to his scholarly pursuits, Mead became involved in social reform. He believed that science could be used to deal with social problems. For example, he was heavily involved as a fund raiser and policy maker at the University of Chicago Settlement House which had been inspired by Jane Addams's Hull House. Perhaps most importantly, he played a key role in social research conducted by the settlement house.

Although eligible for retirement in 1928, he continued to teach at the invitation of the university and in the summer of 1930 became chair of the philosophy department. Unfortunately, he became embroiled in a bitter conflict between the department and the president of the university. This led in early 1931 to a letter of resignation from Mead written from his hospital bed. He was released from the hospital in late April, but died from heart failure the following day. Of him, John Dewey said he was " 'the most original mind in philosophy in the America of the last generations' " (G. Cook, 1993:194).

group in terms of the conduct of the separate individuals belonging to it. For social psychology, the *whole (society) is prior to the part (the individual),* not the part to the whole; and the part is explained in terms of the whole, not the whole in terms of the part or parts.

(Mead, 1934/1962:7; italics added)

To Mead, the social whole precedes the individual mind both logically and temporally. A thinking, self-conscious individual is, as we will see later, logically impossible in Mead's theory without a prior social group. The social group comes first, and it leads to the development of self-conscious mental states.

The Act

Mead considers the act to be the most "primitive unit" in his theory (1982:27). In analyzing the act, Mead comes closest to the behaviorist's approach and focuses on stimulus and response. However, even here the stimulus does not elicit an automatic, unthinking response from the human actor. As Mead says, "We conceive of the stimulus as an occasion or opportunity for the act, not as a compulsion or a mandate" (1982:28).

Mead (1938/1972) identified four basic and interrelated stages in the act (Schmitt and Schmitt, 1996); the four stages represent an organic whole (in other words, they are dialectically interrelated). Both lower animals and humans act, and Mead is interested in the similarities, and especially the differences, between the two.

Impulse   The first stage is that of the *impulse,* which involves an "immediate sensuous stimulation" and the actor's reaction to the stimulation, the need to do something about it. Hunger is a good example of an impulse. The actor (both nonhuman and human) may respond immediately and unthinkingly to the impulse, but more likely the human actor will think about the appropriate response (for example, eat now or later). In thinking about a response, the person will consider not only the immediate situation but also past experiences and anticipated future results of the act.

Hunger may come from an inner state of the actor or may be elicited by the presence of food in the environment, or, most likely, it may arise from some combination of the two. Furthermore, the hungry person must find a way of satisfying the impulse in an environment in which food may not be immediately available or plentiful. This impulse, like all others, may be related to a problem in the environment (that is, the lack of immediately available food), a problem that must be overcome by the actor. Indeed, while an impulse like hunger may come largely from the individual (although even here hunger can be induced by an external stimulus, and there are also social definitions of when it is appropriate to be hungry), it is usually related to the existence of a problem in the environment (for example, the lack of food). Overall, the impulse, like all other elements of Mead's theory, involves both the actor and the environment.

Perception   The second stage of the act is *perception,* in which the actor searches for, and reacts to, stimuli that relate to the impulse, in this case hunger as well as the various means available to satisfy it. People have the capacity to sense or perceive stimuli through hearing, smell, taste, and so on. Perception involves incoming stimuli, as well as the mental images they create. People do not simply respond immediately to external stimuli but rather think about, and assess, them through mental imagery. People are not simply subject to external stimulation; they also actively select characteristics of a stimulus and choose among sets of stimuli. That is, a stimulus may have several dimensions, and the actor is able to select among them. Furthermore, people are usually confronted with many different stimuli, and they have the capacity to choose which to attend to and which to ignore. Mead refuses to separate people from the objects that they perceive. It is the act of perceiving an object that makes it an object to a person; perception and object cannot be separated from (are dialectically related to) one another.

Manipulation   The third stage is *manipulation.* Once the impulse has manifested itself and the object has been perceived, the next step is manipulating the object or, more generally, taking action with regard to it. In addition to their mental advantages, people have another advantage over lower animals. People have hands (with opposable thumbs) that allow them to manipulate objects far more subtly than can lower animals. The manipulation phase constitutes, for Mead, an important temporary pause in the process so that a response is not manifested immediately. A hungry human being sees a mushroom, but before eating it, he or she is likely to pick it up first, examine it, and perhaps check in a guidebook to see whether that particular variety is edible. The lower animal, on the other hand, is likely to eat the mushroom without handling and examining it (and certainly without reading about it). The pause afforded by handling the object allows humans to contemplate various responses. In thinking about whether to eat the mushroom, both the past and the future are involved. People may think about past experiences in which they ate certain mushrooms that made them ill, and they may think about the future sickness, or even death, that might accompany eating a poisonous mushroom. The manipulation of the mushroom becomes a kind of experimental method in which the actor mentally tries out various hypotheses about what would happen if the mushroom were consumed.

Consummation   On the basis of these deliberations, the actor may decide to eat the mushroom (or not), and this constitutes the last phase of the act, *consummation,* or more generally the taking of action which satisfies the original impulse. Both humans and lower animals may consume the mushroom, but the human is less likely to eat a bad mushroom because of his or her ability to manipulate the mushroom and to think (and read) about the implications of eating it. The lower animal must rely on a trial-and-error method, and this is a less-efficient technique than the capacity of humans to think through their actions.[3] Trial-and-error in this situation is quite dangerous; as a result, it seems likely that lower animals are more prone to die from consuming poisonous mushrooms than are humans.

While, for ease of discussion, the four stages of the act have been separated from one another in sequential order, the fact is that Mead sees a dialectical relationship among the four stages. John Baldwin expresses this idea in the following way: "Although the four parts of the act sometimes *appear* to be linked in linear order, they actually interpenetrate to form one organic process: Facets of each part are present at all times from the beginning of the act to the end, such that each part affects the other" (1986:55–56). Thus, the later stages of the act may lead to the emergence of earlier stages. For example, manipulating food may lead the individual to the impulse of hunger and the perception that one is hungry and that food is available to satisfy the need.

---

[3]For a critique of Mead's thinking on the differences between humans and lower animals, see Alger and Alger, 1997.

Gestures

While the act involves only one person, the *social act* involves two or more persons. The *gesture* is in Mead's view the basic mechanism in the social act and in the social process more generally. As he defines them, "gestures are movements of the first organism which act as specific stimuli calling forth the (socially) appropriate responses of the second organism" (Mead, 1934/1962:14; see also Mead, 1959:187). Both lower animals and humans are capable of gestures in the sense that the action of one individual mindlessly and automatically elicits a reaction by another individual. The following is Mead's famous example of a dog fight in terms of gestures:

> The act of each dog becomes the stimulus to the other dog for his response. . . . The very fact that the dog is ready to attack another becomes a stimulus to the other dog to change his own position or his own attitude. He has no sooner done this than the change of attitude in the second dog in turn causes the first dog to change his attitude.
>
> (Mead, 1934/1962:42–43)

Mead labels what is taking place in this situation a "conversation of gestures." One dog's gesture automatically elicits a gesture from the second; there are no thought processes taking place on the part of the dogs.

Humans sometimes engage in mindless conversations of gestures. Mead gives as examples many of the actions and reactions that take place in boxing and fencing matches, when one combatant adjusts "instinctively" to the actions of the second. Mead labels such unconscious actions "nonsignificant" gestures; what distinguishes humans is their ability to employ "significant" gestures, or those that require thought on the part of the actor before a reaction.

The vocal gesture is particularly important in the development of significant gestures. However, not all vocal gestures are significant. The bark of one dog to another is not significant; even some human vocal gestures (for example, a mindless grunt) may not be significant. However, it is the development of vocal gestures, especially in the form of language, which is the most important factor in making possible the distinctive development of human life: "The specialization of the human animal within this field of the gesture has been responsible, ultimately, for the origin and growth of present human society and knowledge, with all the control over nature and over the human environment which science makes possible" (Mead, 1934/1962:14).

This development is related to a distinctive characteristic of the vocal gesture. When we make a physical gesture, such as a facial grimace, we cannot see what we are doing (unless we happen to be looking in the mirror). On the other hand, when we utter a vocal gesture, we hear ourselves just as others do. One result is that the vocal gesture can affect the speaker in much the same way that it affects the listeners. Another is that we are far better able to stop ourselves in vocal gestures than we are able to in physical gestures. In other words, we have far better control over vocal gestures than physical ones. This ability to control oneself and one's reactions is critical, as we will see, to the other distinctive capabilities of humans. More generally, "it has been the vocal gesture that has preeminently provided the medium of social organization in human society" (Mead, 1959:188).

Significant Symbols

A significant symbol is a kind of gesture, one which only humans can make. Gestures become *significant symbols* when they arouse in the individual who is making them the same kind of response (it need not be identical) as they are supposed to elicit from those to whom the gestures are addressed. Only when we have significant symbols can we truly have communication; communication in the full sense of the term is not possible among ants, bees, and so on. Physical gestures can be significant symbols, but as we have seen, they are not ideally suited to be significant symbols because people cannot easily see or hear their own physical gestures. Thus, it is vocal utterances that are most likely to become significant symbols, although not all vocalizations are such symbols. The set of vocal gestures most likely to become significant symbols is *language:* "a symbol which answers to a meaning in that experience of the first individual and which also calls out the meaning in the second individual. Where the gesture reaches that situation it has become what we call 'language.' It is now a significant symbol and it signifies a certain meaning" (Mead, 1934/1962:46). In a conversation of gestures, only the gestures themselves are communicated. However, with language the gestures and their meanings are communicated.

One of the things that language, or significant symbols more generally, does is call out the same response in the individual who is speaking as it does in others. The word *dog* or *cat* elicits the same mental image in the person uttering the word as it does in those to whom it is addressed. Another effect of language is that it stimulates the person speaking as it does others. The person yelling "fire" in a crowded theater is at least as motivated to leave the theater as are those to whom the shout is addressed. Thus, significant symbols allow people to be the stimulators of their own actions.

Adopting his pragmatist orientation, Mead also looks at the "functions" of gestures in general and of significant symbols in particular. The function of the gesture "is to make adjustment possible among the individuals implicated in any given social act with reference to the object or objects with which that act is concerned" (Mead, 1934/1962:46). Thus, an involuntary facial grimace may be made in order to prevent a child from going too close to the edge of a precipice and thereby prevent him or her from being in a potentially dangerous situation. While the nonsignificant gesture works, the "significant symbol affords far greater facilities for such adjustment and readjustment than does the nonsignificant gesture, because it calls out in the individual making it the same attitude toward it . . . and enables him to adjust his subsequent behavior to theirs in the light of that attitude" (Mead, 1934/1962:46). From a pragmatic point of view, a significant symbol works better in the social world than does a nonsignificant gesture. In other words, in communicating our displeasure to others, an angry verbal rebuke works far better than contorted body language. The individual who is manifesting displeasure is not usually conscious of body language and therefore is unlikely to be able to consciously adjust later actions in light of how the other person reacts to the body language. On the other hand, a speaker is conscious of uttering an angry rebuke and reacts to it in much the same way (and at about the same time) as the person to whom it is aimed reacts. Thus, the speaker can think about how the other person might react and can prepare his or her reaction to that reaction.

Of crucial importance in Mead's theory is another function of significant symbols—that they make the mind, mental processes, and so on, possible. It is only through significant symbols, especially language, that human *thinking* is possible (lower animals cannot think, in Mead's terms). Mead defines *thinking* as "simply an internalized or implicit conversation of the individual with himself by means of such gestures" (1934/1962:47). Even more strongly, Mead argues: "Thinking is the same as talking to other people" (1982:155). In other words, thinking involves talking to oneself. Thus, we can see clearly here how Mead defines thinking in behaviorist terms. Conversations involve behavior (talking), and that behavior also occurs within the individual; when it does, thinking is taking place. This is not a mentalistic definition of thinking; it is decidedly behavioristic.

Significant symbols also make possible *symbolic interaction.* That is, people can interact with one another not just through gestures but also through significant symbols. This ability, of course, makes a world of difference and makes possible much more complex interaction patterns and forms of social organization than would be possible through gestures alone.

The significant symbol obviously plays a central role in Mead's thinking. In fact, David Miller (1982a:10–11) accords the significant symbol *the* central role in Mead's theory.

Mental Processes and the Mind

Mead uses a number of similar-sounding concepts when discussing mental *processes,* and it is important to sort them out. Before we do, the point should be made that Mead is always inclined to think in terms of processes rather than structures or contents. In fact, Mead is often labeled a "process philosopher" (Cronk, 1987; D. Miller, 1982a).

Intelligence   One term that sounds as though it belongs under the heading of "mental processes" but actually does not in Mead's thinking is *intelligence.*[4] Mead defines *intelligence* most broadly as the mutual adjustment of the acts of organisms. By this definition, lower animals clearly have "intelligence," because in a conversation of gestures they adapt to one another. Similarly, humans can adapt to one another through the use of nonsignificant symbols (for example, involuntary grimaces). However, what distinguishes humans is that they can also exhibit intelligence, or mutual adaptation, through the use of significant symbols. Thus, a bloodhound has intelligence, but the intelligence of the detective is distinguished from that of the bloodhound by the capacity to use significant symbols.

Mead argues that animals have "unreasoning intelligence." In contrast, humans have "reason," which Mead defines in a characteristically behavioristic manner: "When you are reasoning you are indicating to yourself the characters that call out certain responses—and that is all you are doing" (1934/1962:93). In other words, individuals are carrying on conversations with themselves.

---

[4]However, as we will see later, Mead uses this term inconsistently; sometimes it includes mental processes.

What is crucial to the reflective intelligence of humans is their ability to inhibit action temporarily, to delay their reactions to a stimulus (Mead, 1959:84). In the case of lower animals, a stimulus leads immediately and inevitably to a reaction; lower animals lack the capacity to inhibit their reactions temporarily. As Mead puts it, "Delayed reaction is necessary to intelligent[5] conduct. The organization, implicit testing, and final selection . . . would be impossible if his overt responses or reactions could not in such situations be delayed" (1934/1962:99). There are three components here. First, humans, because of their ability to delay reactions, are able to organize in their own minds the array of possible responses to a situation. Humans possess in their minds the alternative ways of completing a social act in which they are involved. Second, people are able to test out mentally, again through an internal conversation with themselves, the various courses of action. In contrast, lower animals lack this capacity and therefore must try out reactions in the real world in trial-and-error fashion. The ability to try out responses mentally, as we saw in the case of the poison mushroom, is much more effective than the trial-and-error method. There is no social cost involved in mentally trying out a poorly adapted response. However, when a lower animal actually uses such a response in the real world (for example, when a dog approaches a poisonous snake), the results can be costly, even disastrous. Finally, humans are able to pick out one stimulus among a set of stimuli rather than simply reacting to the first or strongest stimulus. In addition, humans can select among a range of alternative actions, whereas lower animals simply act. As Mead says:

> It is the entrance of the alternative possibilities of future response into the determination of present conduct in any given environmental situation, and their operation, through the mechanism of the central nervous system, as part of the factors or conditions determining present behavior, which *decisively* contrasts intelligent conduct or behavior with reflex, instinctive, and habitual conduct or behavior-delayed reaction with immediate reaction.
> (Mead, 1934/1962:98; italics added)

The ability to choose among a range of actions means that the choices of humans are likely to be better adapted to the situation than are the immediate and mindless reactions of lower animals. As Mead contends, "Intelligence is largely a matter of selectivity" (1934/1962:99).

Consciousness Mead also discusses *consciousness,* which he sees as having two distinguishable meanings (1938/1972:75). The first is that to which the actor alone has access, that which is entirely subjective. Mead is less interested in this sense of consciousness than the second, which basically involves reflective intelligence. Thus, Mead is less interested in the way in which we experience immediate pain or pleasure than he is in the way in which we think about the social world.

Consciousness is to be explained or accounted for within the social process. That is, in contrast to most analysts, Mead believes that consciousness is *not* lodged in the brain: "Consciousness is functional not substantive; and in either of the main senses of the

---

[5]Here is one place where Mead is using *intelligence* in a different sense from that employed in the previous discussion.

term it must be located in the objective world rather than in the brain—it belongs to, or is a characteristic of, the environment in which we find ourselves. What is located, what does take place, in the brain, however, is the physiological process whereby we lose and regain consciousness" (1934/1962:112).

In a similar manner, Mead (1934/1962:332) refuses to position *mental images* in the brain but sees them as social phenomena: "What we term 'mental images' . . . can exist in their relation to the organism without being lodged in a substantial consciousness. The mental image is a memory image. Such images which, as symbols, play so large a part in thinking, belong to the environment."

Meaning   Meaning is yet another related concept that Mead addresses behavioristically. Characteristically, Mead rejects the idea that meaning lies in consciousness: "Awareness or consciousness is not necessary to the presence of meaning in the process of social experience" (1934/1962:77). Similarly, Mead rejects the idea that meaning is a "psychical" phenomenon or an "idea." Rather, *meaning* lies squarely within the social act: "Meaning arises and lies within the field of the relation between the gesture of a given human organism and the subsequent behavior of this organism as indicated to another human organism by that gesture. If that gesture does so indicate to another organism the subsequent (or resultant) behavior of the given organism, then it has meaning" (Mead, 1934/1962:75–76). It is the adjustive response of the second organism that gives meaning to the gesture of the first organism. The meaning of a gesture can be seen as the "ability to predict the behavior that is likely to occur next" (Baldwin, 1986:72).

While meaning is to be found in behavior, it becomes conscious when meaning is associated with symbols. However, although meaning can become conscious among humans, it is present in the social act *prior* to the emergence of consciousness and the awareness of meaning. Thus, in these terms, lower animals (and humans) can engage in meaningful behavior even though they are not aware of the meaning.

Mind   Like consciousness, the *mind,* which is defined by Mead as a process and not a thing, as an inner conversation with one's self, is not found within the individual; it is not intracranial but is a social phenomenon. It arises and develops within the social process and is an integral part of that process. The social process precedes the mind; it is not, as many believe, a product of the mind. Thus, the mind, too, is defined functionally rather than substantively. Given these similarities to ideas like consciousness, is there anything distinctive about the mind? We have already seen that humans have the peculiar capacity to call out in themselves the response they are seeking to elicit from others. A distinctive characteristic of the mind is the ability of the individual "to call out in himself not simply a single response of the other but the response, so to speak, of the community as a whole. That is what gives to an individual what we term 'mind.' To do anything now means a certain organized response; and if one has in himself that response, he has what we term 'mind'" (Mead, 1934/1962:267). Thus, the mind can be distinguished from other like-sounding concepts in Mead's work by its ability to respond to the overall community and put forth an organized response.

Mead also looks at the mind in another, pragmatic way. That is, the mind involves thought processes oriented toward problem solving. The real world is rife with problems, and it is the function of the mind to try to solve those problems and permit people to operate more effectively in the world.

Self

Much of Mead's thinking in general, and especially on the mind, involves his ideas on the critically important concept of the *self,* basically the ability to take oneself as an object; the self is the peculiar ability to be both subject and object. As is true of all Mead's major concepts, the self presupposes a social process: communication among humans. Lower animals do not have selves, nor do human infants at birth. The self arises with development and through social activity and social relationships. To Mead, it is impossible to imagine a self arising in the absence of social experiences. However, once a self has developed, it is possible for it to continue to exist without social contact. Thus, Robinson Crusoe developed a self while he was in civilization, and he continued to have it when he was living alone on what he thought for awhile was a deserted island. In other words, he continued to have the ability to take himself as an object. Once a self is developed, people usually, but not always, manifest it. For example, the self is not involved in habitual actions or in immediate physiological experiences of pleasure or pain.

The self is dialectically related to the mind. That is, on the one hand, Mead argues that the body is not a self and becomes a self only when a mind has developed. On the other hand, the self, and its reflexiveness, is essential to the development of the mind. Of course, it is impossible to separate mind and self, because the self is a mental process. However, even though we may think of it as a mental process, the self is a social process. In his discussion of the self, as we have seen in regard to all other mental phenomena, Mead resists the idea of lodging it in consciousness and instead embeds it in social experience and social processes. In this way, Mead seeks to give a behavioristic sense of the self: "But it is where one does respond to that which he addresses to another and where that response of his own becomes a part of his conduct, where he not only hears himself but responds to himself, talks and replies to himself as truly as the other person replies to him, that we have *behavior* in which the individuals become objects to themselves" (1934/1962:139; italics added). The self, then, is simply another aspect of the overall social process of which the individual is a part.

The general mechanism for the development of the self is reflexivity, or the ability to put ourselves unconsciously into others' places and to act as they act. As a result, people are able to examine themselves as others would examine them. As Mead says:

> It is by means of reflexiveness—the turning-back of the experience of the individual upon himself—that the whole social process is thus brought into the experience of the individuals involved in it; it is by such means, which enable the individual to take the attitude of the other toward himself, that the individual is able consciously to adjust himself to that process, and to modify the resultant process in any given social act in terms of his adjustment to it.
>
> (Mead, 1934/1962:134)

The self also allows people to take part in their conversations with others. That is, one is aware of what one is saying and as a result is able to monitor what is being said and to determine what is going to be said next.

In order to have selves, individuals must be able to get "outside themselves" so that they can evaluate themselves, so that they can become objects to themselves. To do this, people basically put themselves in the same experiential field as they put everyone else. Everyone is an important part of that experiential situation, and people must take themselves into account if they are to be able to act rationally in a given situation. Having done this, they seek to examine themselves impersonally, objectively, and without emotion.

However, people cannot experience themselves directly. They can do so only indirectly by putting themselves in the position of others and viewing themselves from that standpoint. The standpoint from which one views one's self can be that of a particular individual or that of the social group as a whole. As Mead puts it, most generally, "It is only by taking the roles of others that we have been able to come back to ourselves" (1959:184–185).

Child Development   Mead is very interested in the genesis of the self. He sees the conversation of gestures as the background for the self, but it does not involve a self, since in such a conversation the people are not taking themselves as objects. Mead traces the genesis of the self through two stages in childhood development.

Play Stage   The first stage is the *play stage;* it is during this stage that children learn to take the attitude of particular others to themselves. While lower animals also play, only human beings "play at being someone else" (Aboulafia, 1986:9). Mead gives the example of a child playing (American) "Indian": "This means that the child has a certain set of stimuli which call out in itself the responses they would call out in others, and which answer to an Indian" (Mead, 1934/1962:150). As a result of such play, the child learns to become both subject and object and begins to become able to build a self. However, it is a limited self because the child can take only the role of distinct and separate others. Children may play at being "mommy" and "daddy" and in the process develop the ability to evaluate themselves as their parents, and other specific individuals, do. However, they lack a more general and organized sense of themselves.

Game Stage   It is the next stage, the *game stage,* that is required if the person is to develop a self in the full sense of the term. Whereas in the play stage the child takes the role of discrete others, in the game stage the child must take the role of everyone else involved in the game. Furthermore, these different roles must have a definite relationship to one another. In illustrating the game stage, Mead gives his famous example of a baseball (or, as he calls it, "ball nine") game:

> But in a game where a number of individuals are involved, then the child taking one role must be ready to take the role of everyone else. If he gets in a ball nine he must have the responses of each position involved in his own position. He must know what everyone else is going to do in order to carry out his own play. He has to take all of these roles. They do not all have to be present in consciousness at the same time, but at some moments he has to have three or four individuals present in his own attitude, such as the one who is going to throw the ball, the one who is going to catch it, and so on. These

responses must be, in some degree, present in his own make-up. In the game, then, there is a set of responses of such others so organized that the attitude of one calls out the appropriate attitudes of the other.

(Mead, 1934/1962:151)

In the play stage, children are not organized wholes because they play at a series of discrete roles. As a result, in Mead's view they lack definite personalities. However, in the game stage,[6] such organization begins and a definite personality starts to emerge. Children begin to become able to function in organized groups and, most important, to determine what they will do within a specific group.

Generalized Other   The game stage yields one of Mead's (1959:87) best-known concepts, the *generalized other*. The generalized other is the attitude of the entire community or, in the example of the baseball game, the attitude of the entire team. The ability to take the role of the generalized other is essential to the self: "Only in so far as he takes the attitudes of the organized social group to which he belongs toward the organized, co-operative social activity or set of such activities in which that group is engaged, does he develop a complete self" (Mead, 1934/1962:155). It is also crucial that people be able to evaluate themselves from the point of view of the generalized other and not merely from the viewpoint of discrete others. Taking the role of the generalized other, rather than that of discrete others, allows for the possibility of abstract thinking and objectivity (Mead, 1959:190). Here is the way Mead describes the full development of the self:

> So the self reaches its full development by organizing these individual attitudes of others into the organized social or group attitudes, and by thus becoming an individual reflection of the general systematic pattern of social or group behavior in which it and others are involved—a pattern which enters as a whole into the individual's experience in terms of these organized group attitudes which, through the mechanism of the central nervous system, he takes toward himself, just as he takes the individual attitudes of others.

(Mead, 1934/1962:158)

In other words, to have a self, one must be a member of a community and be directed by the attitudes common to the community. While play requires only pieces of selves, the game requires a coherent self.

Not only is taking the role of the generalized other essential to the self, but it is also crucial for the development of organized group activities. A group requires that individuals direct their activities in accord with the attitudes of the generalized other. The generalized other also represents Mead's familiar propensity to give priority to the social, since it is through the generalized other that the group influences the behavior of individuals.

Mead also looks at the self from a pragmatic point of view. At the individual level, the self allows the individual to be a more efficient member of the larger society. Because of the self, people are more likely to do what is expected of them in a given

---

[6]Although Mead uses the term "games," it is clear, as Aboulafia (1986:198) points out, that he means any system of organized responses (for example, the family).

situation. Since people often try to live up to group expectations, they are more likely to avoid the inefficiencies that come from failing to do what the group expects. Furthermore, the self allows for greater coordination in society as a whole. Because individuals can be counted on to do what is expected of them, the group can operate more effectively.

The preceding, as well as the overall discussion of the self, might lead us to believe that Mead's actors are little more than conformists and that there is little individuality, since everyone is busy conforming to the expectations of the generalized other. But Mead is clear that each self is different from all others. Selves share a common structure, but each self receives unique biographical articulation. In addition, it is clear that there is not simply one grand generalized other but that there are many generalized others in society, because there are many groups in society. People, therefore, have multiple generalized others and, as a result, multiple selves. Each person's unique set of selves makes him or her different from everyone else. Furthermore, people need not accept the community as it is; they can reform things and seek to make them better. We are able to change the community because of our capacity to think. But Mead is forced to put this issue of individual creativity in familiar, behavioristic terms: "The only way in which we can react against the disapproval of the entire community is by setting up a higher sort of community which in a certain sense out-votes the one we find . . . he may stand out by himself over against it. But to do that he has to comprehend the voices of the past and of the future. That is the only way the self can get a voice which is more than the voice of the community" (1934/1962:167–168). In other words, to stand up to the generalized other, the individual must construct a still larger generalized other, composed not only from the present but also from the past and the future, and then respond to it.

Mead identifies two aspects, or phases, of the self, which he labels the "I" and the "me" (for a critique of this distinction, see Athens, 1995). As Mead puts it, "The self is essentially a social process going on with these two distinguishable phases" (1934/1962:178). It is important to bear in mind that the "I" and "me" are processes within the larger process of the self; they are not "things."

"I" and "Me"   The "I" is the immediate response of an individual to others. It is the incalculable, unpredictable, and creative aspect of the self. People do not know in advance what the action of the "I" will be: "But what that response will be he does not know and nobody else knows. Perhaps he will make a brilliant play or an error. The response to that situation as it appears in his immediate experience is uncertain" (Mead, 1934/1962:175). We are never totally aware of the "I," and through it we surprise ourselves with our actions. We know the "I" only after the act has been carried out. Thus, we know the "I" only in our memories. Mead lays great stress on the "I" for four reasons. First, it is a key source of novelty in the social process. Second, Mead believes that it is in the "I" that our most important values are located. Third, the "I" constitutes something that we all seek—the realization of the self. It is the "I" that permits us to develop a "definite personality." Finally, Mead sees an evolutionary process in history in which people in primitive societies are dominated more by "me" while in modern societies there is a greater component of "I."

The "I" gives Mead's theoretical system some much-needed dynamism and creativity. Without it, Mead's actors would be totally dominated by external and internal controls. With it, Mead is able to deal with the changes brought about not only by the great figures in history (for example, Einstein) but also by individuals on a day-to-day basis. It is the "I" that makes these changes possible. Since every personality is a mix of "I" and "me," the great historical figures are seen as having a larger proportion of "I" than most others have. But in day-to-day situations, anyone's "I" may assert itself and lead to change in the social situation. Uniqueness is also brought into Mead's system through the biographical articulation of each individual's "I" and "me." That is, the specific exigencies of each person's life give him or her a unique mix of "I" and "me."

The "I" reacts against the "me," which is the "organized set of attitudes of others which one himself assumes" (Mead, 1934/1962:175). In other words, the "me" is the adoption of the generalized other. In contrast to the "I," people are conscious of the "me"; the "me" involves conscious responsibility. As Mead says, "The 'me' is a conventional, habitual individual" (1934/1962:197). Conformists are dominated by "me," although everyone—whatever his or her degree of conformity—has, and must have, substantial "me." It is through the "me" that society dominates the individual. Indeed, Mead defines the idea of *social control* as the dominance of the expression of the "me" over the expression of the "I." Later in *Mind, Self and Society,* Mead elaborates on his ideas on social control:

> Social control, as operating in terms of self-criticism, exerts itself so intimately and extensively over individual behavior or conduct, serving to integrate the individual and his actions with reference to the organized social process of experience and behavior in which he is implicated. . . . Social control over individual behavior or conduct operates by virtue of the social origin and basis of such [self-] criticism. That is to say, self-criticism is essentially social criticism, and behavior controlled socially. Hence social control, so far from tending to crush out the human individual or to obliterate his self-conscious individuality, is, on the contrary, actually constitutive of and inextricably associated with that individuality.
>
> (Mead, 1934/1962:255)

Mead also looks at the "I" and "me" in pragmatic terms. The "me" allows the individual to live comfortably in the social world, while the "I" makes the change of society possible. Society gets enough conformity to allow it to function, and it gets a steady infusion of new developments to prevent it from stagnating. The "I" and the "me" are thus part of the whole social process and allow both individuals and society to function more effectively.

Society

At the most general level, Mead uses the term *society* to mean the ongoing social process that precedes both the mind and the self. Given its importance in shaping the mind and self, society is clearly of central importance to Mead. At another level, society to Mead represents the organized set of responses that are taken over by the individual in the form of the "me." Thus, in this sense individuals carry society around with them, giving them the ability through self-criticism, to control themselves. Mead also deals with the evolution of society. But Mead has relatively little to say explicitly about society, in spite of its centrality in his theoretical system. His most important contributions lie in his thoughts on mind and self. Even John Baldwin, who sees a much more societal (macro) component in Mead's thinking, is forced to admit: "The macro components of Mead's theoretical system are not as well developed as the micro" (1986:123).

At a more specific societal level Mead does have a number of things to say about social *institutions*. Mead broadly defines an *institution* as the "common response in the community" or "the life habits of the community" (1934/1962:261, 264; see also Mead, 1936:376). More specifically, he says that "the whole community acts toward the individual under certain circumstances in an identical way . . . there is an identical response on the part of the whole community under these conditions. We call that the formation of the institution" (Mead, 1934/1962:167). We carry this organized set of attitudes around with us, and they serve to control our actions, largely through the "me."

Education is the process by which the common habits of the community (the institution) are "internalized" in the actor. This is an essential process, since, in Mead's view, people neither have selves nor are genuine members of the community until they can respond to themselves as the larger community does. To do so, people must have internalized the common attitudes of the community.

But again Mead is careful to point out that institutions need not destroy individuality or stifle creativity. Mead recognizes that there are "oppressive, stereotyped, and ultraconservative social institutions—like the church—which by their more or less rigid and inflexible unprogressiveness crush or blot out individuality" (1934/1962:262). However, he is quick to add: "There is no necessary or inevitable reason why social institutions should be oppressive or rigidly conservative, or why they should not rather be, as many are, flexible and progressive, fostering individuality rather than discouraging it" (Mead, 1934/1962:262). To Mead, institutions should define what people ought to do only in a very broad and general sense and should allow plenty of room for individuality and creativity. Mead here demonstrates a very modern conception of social institutions as both constraining individuals *and* enabling them to be creative individuals (see Giddens, 1984).

What Mead lacks in his analysis of society in general, and institutions in particular,[7] is a true macro sense of them in the way that theorists like Marx, Weber, and Durkheim dealt with this level of analysis. This is true in spite of the fact that Mead does have a notion of *emergence* in the sense that the whole is seen as more than the sum of its parts. More specifically, "Emergence involves a reorganization, but the reorganization brings in something that was not there before. The first time oxygen and hydrogen come together, water appears. Now water is a combination of hydrogen and oxygen, but water was not there before in the separate elements" (Mead, 1934/1962:198). However, Mead is much more prone to apply the idea of emergence to consciousness than to apply it to the larger society. That is, mind and self are seen as emergent from

---

[7]There are at least two places where Mead offers a more macro sense of society. At one point he defines *social institutions* as "organized forms of group or social activity" (Mead, 1934/1962:261). Earlier, in an argument reminiscent of Comte, he offers a view of the family as the fundamental unit within society and as the base of such larger units as the clan and state.

the social process. Moreover, Mead is inclined to use the term *emergence* merely to mean the coming into existence of something new or novel (D. Miller, 1973:41).

SYMBOLIC INTERACTIONISM: THE BASIC PRINCIPLES

The heart of this chapter is our discussion of the basic principles of symbolic interaction theory. Although we try to characterize the theory in general terms, this is not easy to do, for as Paul Rock says, it has a "deliberately constructed vagueness" and a "resistance to systematisation" (1979:18–19). There are significant differences within symbolic interactionism, some of which are discussed as we proceed.

Some symbolic interactionists (Blumer, 1969a; Manis and Meltzer, 1978; A. Rose, 1962) have tried to enumerate the basic principles of the theory. These principles include the following:

1 Human beings, unlike lower animals, are endowed with the capacity for thought.
2 The capacity for thought is shaped by social interaction.
3 In social interaction people learn the meanings and the symbols that allow them to exercise their distinctively human capacity for thought.
4 Meanings and symbols allow people to carry on distinctively human action and interaction.
5 People are able to modify or alter the meanings and symbols that they use in action and interaction on the basis of their interpretation of the situation.
6 People are able to make these modifications and alterations because, in part, of their ability to interact with themselves, which allows them to examine possible courses of action, assess their relative advantages and disadvantages, and then choose one.
7 The intertwined patterns of action and interaction make up groups and societies.

Capacity for Thought

The crucial assumption that human beings possess the ability to think differentiates symbolic interactionism from its behaviorist roots. This assumption also provides the basis for the entire theoretical orientation of symbolic interactionism. Bernard Meltzer, James Petras, and Larry Reynolds stated that the assumption of the human capacity for thought is one of the major contributions of early symbolic interactionists, such as James, Dewey, Thomas, Cooley, and of course Mead: "Individuals in human society were not seen as units that are motivated by external or internal forces beyond their control, or within the confines of a more or less fixed structure. Rather, they were viewed as reflective or interacting units which comprise the societal entity" (1975:42). The ability to think enables people to act reflectively rather than just behave unreflectively. People must often construct and guide what they do, rather than just release it.

The ability to think is embedded in the mind, but the symbolic interactionists have a somewhat unusual conception of the mind as originating in the socialization of consciousness. They distinguish it from the physiological brain. People must have brains in order to develop minds, but a brain does not inevitably produce a mind, as is clear in the case of lower animals (Troyer, 1946). Also, symbolic interactionists do not conceive of the mind as a thing, a physical structure, but rather as a continuing process. It is a process that is itself part of the larger process of stimulus and response. The mind is related to virtually every other aspect of symbolic interactionism, including socialization, meanings, symbols, the self, interaction, and even society.

Thinking and Interaction

People possess only a general capacity for thought. This capacity must be shaped and refined in the process of social interaction. Such a view leads the symbolic interactionist to focus on a specific form of social interaction—*socialization.* The human ability to think is developed early in childhood socialization and is refined during adult socialization. Symbolic interactionists have a view of the socialization process that is different from that of most other sociologists. To symbolic interactionists, conventional sociologists are likely to see socialization as simply a process by which people learn the things that they need to survive in society (for instance, culture, role expectations). To the symbolic interactionists, socialization is a more dynamic process that allows people to develop the ability to think, to develop in distinctively human ways. Furthermore, socialization is not simply a one-way process in which the actor receives information, but is a dynamic process in which the actor shapes and adapts the information to his or her own needs (Manis and Meltzer, 1978:6).

Symbolic interactionists are, of course, interested not simply in socialization but in interaction in general, which is of "vital importance in its own right" (Blumer, 1969b:8). *Interaction* is the process in which the ability to think is both developed and expressed. All types of interaction, not just interaction during socialization, refine our ability to think. Beyond that, thinking shapes the interaction process. In most interaction, actors must take account of others and decide if and how to fit their activities to others. However, not all interaction involves thinking. The differentiation made by Blumer (following Mead) between two basic forms of social interaction is relevant here. The first, nonsymbolic interaction—Mead's conversation of gestures—does not involve thinking. The second, symbolic interaction, does require mental processes.

The importance of thinking to symbolic interactionists is reflected in their views on *objects.* Blumer differentiates among three types of objects: *physical objects,* such as a chair or a tree; *social objects,* such as a student or a mother; and *abstract objects,* such as an idea or a moral principle. Objects are seen simply as things "out there" in the real world; what is of greatest significance is the way that they are defined by actors. The latter leads to the relativistic view that different objects have different meanings for different individuals: "A tree will be a different object to a botanist, a lumberman, a poet, and a home gardener" (Blumer, 1969b:11).

Individuals learn the meanings of objects during the socialization process. Most of us learn a common set of meanings, but in many cases, as with the tree mentioned above, we have different definitions of the same objects. Although this definitional view can be taken to an extreme, symbolic interactionists need not deny the existence of objects in the real world. All they need do is point out the crucial nature of the definition of those objects as well as the possibility that actors may have different definitions of the same object. As Herbert Blumer said: "The nature of an object . . . consists of the meaning that it has for the person for whom it is an object" (1969b:11).

Learning Meanings and Symbols

Symbolic interactionists, following Mead, tend to accord causal significance to social interaction. Thus, meaning stems not from solitary mental processes but from interaction. This focus derives from Mead's pragmatism: he focused on human action and interaction, not on isolated mental processes. Symbolic interactionists have in general continued in this direction. Among other things, the central concern is not how people mentally create meanings and symbols but how they learn them during interaction in general and socialization in particular.

People learn symbols as well as meanings in social interaction. Whereas people respond to signs unthinkingly, they respond to symbols in a thoughtful manner. Signs stand for themselves (for example, the gestures of angry dogs, or water to a person dying of thirst). "*Symbols are social objects used to represent* (or 'stand in for,' 'take the place of') whatever people agree they shall represent" (Charon, 1998:47). Not all social objects stand for other things, but those that do are symbols. Words, physical artifacts, and physical actions (for example, the word *boat,* a cross or a Star of David, and a clenched fist) all can be symbols. People often use symbols to communicate something about themselves: they drive Rolls-Royces, for instance, to communicate a certain style of life.

Symbolic interactionists conceive of language as a vast system of symbols. Words are symbols because they are used to stand for things. Words make all other symbols possible. Acts, objects, and other words exist and have meaning only because they have been and can be described through the use of words.

Symbols are crucial in allowing people to act in distinctively human ways. Because of the symbol, the human being "does not respond passively to a reality that imposes itself but actively creates and re-creates the world acted in" (Charon, 1998:69). In addition to this general utility, symbols in general and language in particular have a number of specific functions for the actor.

First, symbols enable people to deal with the material and social world by allowing them to name, categorize, and remember the objects that they encounter there. In this way, people are able to order a world that otherwise would be confusing. Language allows people to name, categorize, and especially remember much more efficiently than they could with other kinds of symbols, such as pictorial images.

Second, symbols improve people's ability to perceive the environment. Instead of being flooded by a mass of indistinguishable stimuli, the actor can be alerted to some parts of the environment rather than others.

Third, symbols improve the ability to think. Although a set of pictorial symbols would allow a limited ability to think, language greatly expands this ability. Thinking, in these terms, can be conceived of as symbolic interaction with one's self.

Fourth, symbols greatly increase the ability to solve various problems. Lower animals must use trial and error, but human beings can think through symbolically a variety of alternative actions before actually taking one. This ability reduces the chance of making costly mistakes.

Fifth, the use of symbols allows actors to transcend time, space, and even their own persons. Through the use of symbols, actors can imagine what it was like to live in the past or might be like to live in the future. In addition, actors can transcend their own persons symbolically and imagine what the world is like from another person's point of view. This is the well-known symbolic-interactionist concept of *taking the role of the other* (D. Miller, 1981).

Sixth, symbols allow us to imagine a metaphysical reality, such as heaven or hell. Seventh, and most generally, symbols allow people to avoid being enslaved by their environment. They can be active rather than passive—that is, self-directed in what they do.

Action and Interaction

Symbolic interactionists' primary concern is with the impact of meanings and symbols on human action and interaction. Here it is useful to employ Mead's differentiation between covert and overt behavior. *Covert behavior* is the thinking process, involving symbols and meanings. *Overt behavior* is the actual behavior performed by an actor. Some overt behavior does not involve covert behavior (habitual behavior or mindless responses to external stimuli). However, most human action involves both kinds. Covert behavior is of greatest concern to symbolic interactionists, whereas overt behavior is of greatest concern to exchange theorists or to traditional behaviorists in general.

Meanings and symbols give human social action (which involves a single actor) and social interaction (which involves two or more actors engaged in mutual social action) distinctive characteristics. Social action is that in which the individuals are acting with others in mind. In other words, in undertaking an action, people simultaneously try to gauge its impact on the other actors involved. Although they often engage in mindless, habitual behavior, people have the capacity to engage in social action.

In the process of social interaction, people symbolically communicate meanings to the others involved. The others interpret those symbols and orient their responding action on the basis of their interpretation. In other words, in social interaction, actors engage in a process of mutual influence.

Making Choices

Partly because of the ability to handle meanings and symbols, people, unlike lower animals, can make choices in the actions in which they engage. People need not accept the meanings and symbols that are imposed on them from without. On the basis of their own interpretation of the situation, "humans are capable of forming new meanings and new lines of meaning" (Manis and Meltzer, 1978:7). Thus, to the symbolic interactionist, actors have at least some autonomy. They are not simply constrained or determined; they are capable of making unique and independent choices. Furthermore, they are able to develop a life that has a unique style (Perinbanayagam, 1985:53).

W. I. Thomas and Dorothy Thomas were instrumental in underscoring this creative capacity in their concept of *definition of the situation* : "If men define situations as real, they are real in their consequences" (Thomas and Thomas, 1928:572). The Thomases knew that most of our definitions of situations have been provided for us by society. In fact, they emphasized this point, identifying especially the family and the community as sources of our social definitions. However, the Thomases' position is distinctive for its emphasis on the possibility of "spontaneous" individual definitions of situations, which allow people to alter and modify meanings and symbols.

This ability of actors to make a difference is reflected in an essay by Gary Fine and Sherryl Kleinman (1983) in which they look at the phenomenon of a "social network." Instead of viewing a social network as an unconscious and/or constraining social structure, Fine and Kleinman see a network as a set of social relationships that people endow with meaning and use for personal and/or collective purposes.

The Self and the Work of Erving Goffman

The self is a concept of enormous importance to symbolic interactionists (Bruder, 1998). In fact, Rock argues that the self "constitutes the very hub of the interactionists' intellectual scheme. All other sociological processes and events revolve around that hub, taking from it their analytic meaning and organization" (1979:102). In attempting to understand this concept beyond its initial Meadian formulation, we must first understand the idea of the *looking-glass self* developed by Charles Horton Cooley (Franks and Gecas, 1992). Cooley defined this concept as

> a somewhat definite imagination of how one's self—that is, any idea he appropriates—appears in a particular mind, and the kind of self-feeling one has is determined by the attitude toward this attributed to that other mind. . . . So in imagination we perceive in another's mind some thought of our appearance, manners, aims, deeds, character, friends, and so on, and are variously affected by it.
>
> (Cooley, 1902/1964:169)

The idea of a looking-glass self can be broken down into three components. First, we imagine how we appear to others. Second, we imagine what their judgment of that appearance must be. Third, we develop some self-feeling, such as pride or mortification, as a result of our imagining others' judgments.

Cooley's concept of the looking-glass self and Mead's concept of the self were important in the development of the modern symbolic-interactionist conception of the self. Blumer defined the *self* in extremely simple terms: "Nothing esoteric is meant by this expression [self]. It means merely that a human being can be an object of his own action . . . he acts toward himself and guides himself in his actions toward others on the basis of the kind of object he is to himself" (1969b:12). The self is a process, not a thing (Perinbanayagam, 1985). As Blumer made clear, the self helps allow human beings to act rather than simply respond to external stimuli:

> The process [interpretation] has two distinct steps. First, the actor indicates to himself the things toward which he is acting; he has to point out in himself the things that have meaning. . . . This interaction with himself is something other than an interplay of psychological elements; it is an instance of the person engaging in a process of communicating with himself. . . . Second, by virtue of this process of communicating with himself, interpretation becomes a matter of handling meanings. The actor selects, checks, suspends, regroups, and transforms the meanings in the light of the situation in which he is placed and the direction of his action.
>
> (Blumer, 1969b:5)

Although this description of interpretation underscores the part played by the self in the process of choosing how to act, Blumer has really not gone much beyond the early formulations of Cooley and Mead. However, other modern thinkers and researchers have refined the concept of the self.

The Work of Erving Goffman   The most important work on the self in symbolic interactionism is *Presentation of Self in Everyday Life* (1959) by Erving Goffman (J. Dowd, 1996; Schwalbe, 1993; Travers, 1992; Tseelon, 1992). Goffman's conception of the self is deeply indebted to Mead's ideas, in particular his discussion of the tension between *I,* the spontaneous self, and *me,* social constraints within the self. This tension is mirrored in Goffman's work on what he called the "crucial discrepancy between our all-too-human selves and our socialized selves" (1959:56). The tension results from the difference between what people expect us to do and what we may want to do spontaneously. We are confronted with the demand to do what is expected of us; moreover, we are not supposed to waver. As Goffman put it, "We must not be subject to ups and downs" (1959:56). In order to maintain a stable self-image, people perform for their social audiences. As a result of this interest in performance, Goffman focused on *dramaturgy,* or a view of social life as a series of dramatic performances akin to those performed on the stage.

Dramaturgy   Goffman's sense of the self was shaped by his dramaturgical approach. To Goffman (as to Mead and most other symbolic interactionists), the self is

> not an organic thing that has a specific location. . . . In analyzing the self then we are drawn from its possessor, from the person who will profit or lose most by it, for he and his body merely provide the peg on which something of collaborative manufacture will be hung for a time. . . . The means of producing and maintaining selves do not reside inside the peg.
>
> (Goffman, 1959:252–253)

Goffman perceived the self not as a possession of the actor but rather as the product of the dramatic interaction between actor and audience. The self "is a dramatic effect arising . . . from a scene that is presented" (Goffman, 1959:253). Because the self is a product of dramatic interaction, it is vulnerable to disruption during the performance. Goffman's dramaturgy is concerned with the processes by which such disturbances are prevented or dealt with. Although the bulk of his discussion focuses on these dramaturgical contingencies, Goffman pointed out that most performances are successful. The result is that in ordinary circumstances a firm self is accorded to performers, and it "appears" to emanate from the performer.

Goffman assumed that when individuals interact, they want to present a certain sense of self that will be accepted by others. However, even as they present that self, actors are aware that members of the audience can disturb their performance. For that reason actors are attuned to the need to control the audience, especially those elements of it that might be disruptive. The actors hope that the sense of self that they present to the audience will be strong enough for the audience to define the actors as the actors want. The actors also hope that this will cause the audience to act voluntarily as the actors want them to. Goffman characterized this central interest as "impression management." It involves techniques actors use to maintain certain impressions in the face of problems they are likely to encounter, and methods they use to cope with these problems.

Following this theatrical analogy, Goffman spoke of a front stage. The *front* is that part of the performance that generally functions in rather fixed and general ways to define the situation for those who observe the performance. Within the front stage, Goffman further differentiated between the setting and the personal front. The *setting* refers to the physical scene that ordinarily must be there if the actors are to perform. Without it, the actors usually cannot perform. For example, a surgeon generally requires an operating room, a taxi driver a cab, and an ice skater ice. The *personal front* consists of those items of expressive equipment that the audience identifies with the performers and expects them to carry with them into the setting. A surgeon, for instance, is expected to dress in a medical gown, have certain instruments, and so on.

Goffman then subdivided the personal front into appearance and manner. *Appearance* includes those items that tell us the performer's social status (for instance, the surgeon's medical gown). *Manner* tells the audience what sort of role the performer expects to play in the situation (for example, the use of physical mannerisms, demeanor). A brusque manner and a meek manner indicate quite different kinds of performances. In general, we expect appearance and manner to be consistent.

Although Goffman approached the front and other aspects of his system as a symbolic interactionist, he did discuss their structural character. For example, he argued that fronts tend to become institutionalized, so "collective representations" arise about what is to go on in a certain front. Very often when actors take on established roles, they find particular fronts already established for such performances. The result, Goffman argued, is that fronts tend to be selected, not created. This idea conveys a much more structural image than we would receive from most symbolic interactionists.

Despite such a structural view, Goffman's most interesting insights lie in the domain of interaction. He argued that because people generally[8] try to present an idealized picture of themselves in their front-stage performances, inevitably they feel that they must hide things in their performances. First, actors may want to conceal secret pleasures (for instance, drinking alcohol) engaged in prior to the performance or in past lives (for instance, as drug addicts) that are incompatible with their performance. Second, actors may want to conceal errors that have been made in the preparation of the performance as well as steps that have been taken to correct these errors. For example, a taxi driver may seek to hide the fact that he started in the wrong direction. Third, actors may find it necessary to show only end products and to conceal the process involved in producing them. For example, professors may spend several hours preparing a lecture, but they may want to act as if they have always known the material. Fourth, it may be necessary for actors to conceal from the audience that "dirty work" was involved in the making of the end products. Dirty work may include tasks that "were physically unclean, semi-legal, cruel, and degrading in other ways" (Goffman, 1959:44). Fifth, in giving a certain performance, actors may have to let other standards slide. Finally,

---

[8]But not always—see Ungar (1984) on self-mockery as a way of presenting the self.

ERVING GOFFMAN: A Biographical Sketch

Erving Goffman died in 1982 at the peak of his fame. He had long been regarded as a "cult" figure in sociological theory. This status was achieved in spite of the fact that he had been professor in the prestigious sociology department at the University of California, Berkeley, and later held an endowed chair at the Ivy League's University of Pennsylvania.

By the 1980s he had emerged as a centrally important theorist. In fact, he had been elected president of the American Sociological Association in the year he died but was unable to give his presidential address because of advanced illness. Given Goffman's maverick status, Randall Collins says of his address: "Everyone wondered what he would do for his Presidential address: a straight, traditional presentation seemed unthinkable for Goffman

with his reputation as an iconoclast . . . we got a far more dramatic message: Presidential address cancelled, Goffman dying. It was an appropriately Goffmanian way to go out" (1986b:112).

Goffman was born in Alberta, Canada, on June 11, 1922 (S. Williams, 1986). He earned his advanced degrees from the University of Chicago and is most often thought of as a member of the Chicago school and as a symbolic interactionist. However, when he was asked shortly before his death whether he was a symbolic interactionist, he replied that the label was too vague to allow him to put himself in that category (Manning, 1992). In fact, it is hard to squeeze his work into any single category. In creating his theoretical perspective, Goffman drew on many sources and created a distinctive orientation.

Collins (1986b; Williams, 1986) links Goffman more to social anthropology than to symbolic interactionism. As an undergraduate at the University of Toronto, Goffman had studied with an anthropologist, and at Chicago "his main contacts were not with Symbolic Interactionists, but with W. Lloyd Warner [an anthropologist]" (Collins, 1986b:109). In Collins's view, an examination of the citations in Goffman's early work indicates that he was influenced by social anthropologists and rarely cited symbolic interactionists, and when he did, it was to be critical of them. However, Goffman was influenced by the descriptive studies produced at Chicago and integrated their outlook with that of social anthropology to produce his distinctive perspective. Thus, whereas a symbolic interactionist would look at how people create or negotiate their self-image, Goffman was concerned with how "society . . . forces people to present a certain image of themselves . . . because it forces us to switch back and forth between many complicated roles, is also making us always somewhat untruthful, inconsistent, and dishonorable" (Collins, 1986a:107).

Despite the distinctiveness of his perspective, Goffman had a powerful influence on symbolic interactionism. In addition, it could be argued that he had a hand in shaping another sociology of everyday life, ethnomethodology. In fact, Collins sees Goffman as a key figure in the formation not only of ethnomethodology, but of conversation analysis as well: "It was Goffman who pioneered the close empirical study of everyday life, although he had done it with his bare eyes, before the days of tape recorders and video recorders" (1986b:111). (See Chapter 7 for a discussion of the relationship between ethnomethodology and conversation analysis.) In fact, a number of important ethnomethodologists (Sacks, Schegloff) studied with Goffman at Berkeley and not with the founder of ethnomethodology, Harold Garfinkel.

Given their influence on symbolic interactionism, structuralism, and ethnomethodology, Goffman's theories are likely to be influential for a long time.

actors probably find it necessary to hide any insults, humiliations, or deals made so that the performance could go on. Generally, actors have a vested interest in hiding all such facts from their audience.

Another aspect of dramaturgy in the front stage is that actors often try to convey the impression that they are closer to the audience than they actually are. For example, actors may try to foster the impression that the performance in which they are engaged at the moment is their only performance or at least their most important one. To do this, actors have to be sure that their audiences are segregated so that the falsity of the performance is not discovered. Even if it is discovered, Goffman argued, the audiences themselves may try to cope with the falsity, so as not to shatter their idealized image of the actor. This reveals the interactional character of performances. A successful performance depends on the involvement of all the parties. Another example of this kind of impression management is an actor's attempt to convey the idea that there is something unique about this performance as well as his or her relationship to the audience. The audience, too, wants to feel that it is the recipient of a unique performance.

Actors try to make sure that all the parts of any performance blend together. In some cases, a single discordant aspect can disrupt a performance. However, performances vary in the amount of consistency required. A slip by a priest on a sacred occasion would be terribly disruptive, but if a taxi driver made one wrong turn, it would not be likely to damage the overall performance greatly.

Another technique employed by performers is *mystification.* Actors often tend to mystify their performance by restricting the contact between themselves and the audience. By generating "social distance" between themselves and the audience, they try to create a sense of awe in the audience. This, in turn, keeps the audience from questioning the performance. Again Goffman pointed out that the audience is involved in this process and often itself seeks to maintain the credibility of the performance by keeping its distance from the performer.

This leads us to Goffman's interest in teams. To Goffman, as a symbolic interactionist, a focus on individual actors obscured important facts about interaction. Goffman's basic unit of analysis was thus not the individual but the team. A *team* is any set of individuals who cooperate in staging a single routine. Thus, the preceding discussion of the relationship between the performer and audience is really about teams.[9] Each member is reliant on the others, because all can disrupt the performance and all are aware that they are putting on an act. Goffman concluded that a team is a kind of "secret society."

Goffman also discussed a *back stage* where facts suppressed in the front or various kinds of informal actions may appear. A back stage is usually adjacent to the front stage, but it is also cut off from it. Performers can reliably expect no members of their front audience to appear in the back. Furthermore, they engage in various types of impression management to make sure of this. A performance is likely to become difficult when

---

[9]A performer and the audience are one kind of team, but Goffman also talked of a group of performers as one team and the audience as another. Interestingly, Goffman argued that a team can also be a single individual. His logic, following classic symbolic interactionism, was that an individual can be his or her own audience—can *imagine* an audience to be present.

actors are unable to prevent the audience from entering the back stage. There is also a third, residual domain, the *outside,* which is neither front nor back.

No area is *always* one of these three domains. Also, a given area can occupy all three domains at different times. A professor's office is front stage when a student visits, back stage when the student leaves, and outside when the professor is at a university basketball game.

Impression Management   In general, *impression management* is oriented to guarding against a series of unexpected actions, such as unintended gestures, inopportune intrusions, and faux pas, as well as intended actions, such as making a scene. Goffman was interested in the various methods of dealing with such problems. First, there is a set of methods involving actions aimed at producing dramaturgical loyalty by, for example, fostering high in-group loyalty, preventing team members from identifying with the audience, and changing audiences periodically so that they do not become too knowledgeable about the performers. Second, Goffman suggested various forms of dramaturgical discipline, such as having the presence of mind to avoid slips, maintaining self-control, and managing the facial expressions and verbal tone of one's performance. Third, he identified various types of dramaturgical circumspection, such as determining in advance how a performance should go, planning for emergencies, selecting loyal teammates, selecting good audiences, being involved in small teams where dissension is less likely, making only brief appearances, preventing audience access to private information, and settling on a complete agenda to prevent unforeseen occurrences.

The audience also has a stake in successful impression management by the actor or team of actors. The audience often acts to save the show through such devices as giving great interest and attention to it, avoiding emotional outbursts, not noticing slips, and giving special consideration to a neophyte performer.

Manning points not only to the centrality of the self, but also to Goffman's *cynical* view of people in this work:

> The overall tenor of *The Presentation of Self* is to a world in which people, whether individually or in groups, pursue their own ends in cynical disregard for others. . . . The view here is of the individual as a set of performance masks hiding a manipulative and cynical self.
>
> (Manning, 1992:44)

Manning puts forth a "two selves thesis" to describe this aspect of Goffman's thinking; that is, people have both a performance self and a hidden, cynical self.

Role Distance   Goffman (1961) was interested in the degree to which an individual embraces a given role. In his view, because of the large number of roles, few people get completely involved in any given role. *Role distance* deals with the degree to which individuals separate themselves from the roles they are in. For example, if older children ride on a merry-go-round, they are likely to be aware that they are really too old to enjoy such an experience. One way of coping with this feeling is to demonstrate distance from the role by doing it in a careless, lackadaisical way of performing seemingly dangerous acts while on the merry-go-round. In performing such acts, the older children are really explaining to the audience that they are not as immersed in the activity as small children might be or that if they are, it is because of the special things they are doing.

One of Goffman's key insights is that role distance is a function of one's social status. High-status people often manifest role distance for reasons other than those of people in low-status positions. For example, a high-status surgeon may manifest role distance in the operating room to relieve the tension of the operating team. People in low-status positions usually manifest more defensiveness in exhibiting role distance. For instance, people who clean toilets may do so in a lackadaisical and uninterested manner. They may be trying to tell their audience that they are too good for such work.

Stigma   Goffman (1963b) was interested in the gap between what a person ought to be, *"virtual social identity,"* and what a person actually is, *"actual social identity."* Anyone who has a gap between these two identities is stigmatized. *Stigma* focuses on the dramaturgical interaction between stigmatized people and normals. The nature of that interaction depends on which of the two types of stigma an individual has. In the case of *discredited* stigma, the actor assumes that the differences are known by the audience members or are evident to them (for example, a paraplegic or someone who has lost a limb). A *discreditable* stigma is one in which the differences are neither known by audience members nor perceivable by them (for example, a person who has had a colostomy or a homosexual passing as straight). For someone with a discredited stigma, the basic dramaturgical problem is managing the tension produced by the fact that people know of the problem. For someone with a discreditable stigma, the dramaturgical problem is managing information so that the problem remains unknown to the audience. (For a discussion of how the homeless deal with stigma, see Anderson, Snow, and Cress, 1994.)

Most of the text of Goffman's *Stigma* is devoted to people with obvious, often grotesque stigmas (for instance, the loss of a nose). However, as the book unfolds, the reader realizes that Goffman is really saying that we are all stigmatized at some time or other, or in one setting or other. His examples include the Jew "passing" in a predominantly Christian community, the fat person in a group of people of normal weight, and the individual who has lied about his past and must be constantly sure that the audience does not learn of this deception.

Basic Presuppositions   In an overview of much of Goffman's work on interaction, Manning identifies four "interactional principles that constrain face-to-face interaction" (1992:78):

1 "[I]nteractants must display *situational propriety,*" or "the practical knowledge of how to carry on in social situations" (Manning, 1992:78–79). Involved here are things like observing the etiquette in specific social situations—in other words, doing what is considered appropriate. However, it should be made clear that what is considered appropriate may vary from situation to situation.

2 People must show the appropriate level of *involvement* in a given social situation. For example, people cannot generally appear to be preoccupied when engaged in social interaction.

3 People must display appropriate levels of *civil inattention* when interacting with strangers. That is, in anonymous situations there are various things that it is incumbent on us to ignore. Civil inattention "displays a delicate balance between the recognition of those around us and a studied deference to them. We respect their right to unaccosted anonymity" (Manning, 1992:85).

4 Interactants must be *accessible* to others, or else social interaction will break down altogether.

At the base of these four presuppositions is the even more basic presupposition that Goffman called "Felicity's Condition," or "any arrangement which leads us to judge an individual's verbal acts to be not a manifestation of strangeness" (Goffman, cited in Manning, 1992:88).

Frame Analysis In *Frame Analysis* (1974), Goffman moved away from his classic symbolic-interactionist roots and toward the study of the small-scale structures of social life (for a study employing the idea of frames, see McLean, 1998). Although he still felt that people define situations in the sense meant by W. I. Thomas, he now thought that such definitions were less important: "Defining situations as real certainly has consequences, but these may contribute very marginally to the events in progress" (Goffman, 1974:1). Furthermore, even when people define situations, they do not ordinarily create those definitions. Action is defined more by mechanical adherence to rules than through an active, creative, and negotiated process. Goffman enunciated his goal: "to try to isolate some of the basic frameworks of understanding available in our society for making sense out of events and to analyze the special vulnerabilities to which these frames of reference are subject" (1974:10).

Goffman looked beyond and behind everyday situations in a search for the structures that invisibly govern them. These are "'schemata of interpretation' that enable individuals 'to locate, perceive, identify, and label' occurrences within their life space and the world at large. By rendering events or occurrences meaningful, frames function to organize experience and guide action, whether individual or collective" (Snow, 1986:464). Frames are principles of organization that define our experiences. They are assumptions about what we are seeing in the social world. Without frames, our world would be little more than a number of chaotic individual and unrelated events and facts. Gonos provided other structural characteristics of frames:

> From Goffman's analyses of particular framed activities, we can derive certain principal characteristics of frames. A frame is not conceived as a loose, somewhat accidental amalgamation of elements put together over a short time-span. Rather, it is constituted of a set number of essential components, having a definite arrangement and stable relations. These components are not gathered from here and there, as are the elements of a situation, but are always found together as a system. The standard components cohere and are complete. . . . Other less essential elements are present in any empirical instance and lend some of their character to the whole. . . . In all this, frames are very close in conception to "structures."
>
> (Gonos, 1977:860)

To Gonos, frames are largely rules or laws that fix interaction. The rules are usually unconscious and ordinarily nonnegotiable. Among the rules identified by Gonos are those that define "how signs are to be 'interpreted,' how outward indications are to be related to 'selves,' and what 'experience' will accompany activity" (1980:160). Gonos concludes, "Goffman's problematic thus promotes the study not of observable interaction of 'everyday life' as such, but its eternal structure and ideology; not of situations, but of their frames" (1980:160).

Manning (1992:119) gives the following examples of how different frames applied to the same set of events serve to give those same events very different meaning. For example, what are we to make of the sight of a woman putting two watches in her pocket and leaving a shop without paying? Seen through the frame of a store detective, this appears to be a clear case of shoplifting. However, the legal frame leads her lawyer to see this as the act of an absentminded woman who was out shopping for gifts for her daughters. To take another example, a medical frame may lead a woman to see the actions of her gynecologist in one way, but if she uses a frame of sexuality and sexual harassment, she may see those same actions in a very different way.

Another change that Manning argues is clear in *Frame Analysis,* and that was foreshadowed in other works by Goffman, is a shift away from the cynical view of life that lay at the heart of *Presentation of Self in Everyday Life.* In fact, on the first page of *Frame Analysis,* Goffman says, "All the world is not a stage—certainly the theater isn't entirely" (1974:1). Goffman clearly came to recognize the limitations of the theater as a metaphor for everyday life. While still useful in some ways, this metaphor conceals some aspects of life just as it illuminates others. One of the things that is concealed is the importance of ritual in everyday life. Here is the way Manning describes one of the roles played by ritual in everyday life:

> For Goffman, ritual is essential because it maintains our confidence in basic social relationships. It provides others with opportunities to affirm the legitimacy of our position in the social structure while obliging us to do the same. Ritual is a placement mechanism in which, for the most part, social inferiors affirm the higher positions of their superiors. The degree of ritual in a society reflects the legitimacy of its social structure, because the ritual respect paid to individuals is also a sign of respect for the roles they occupy.
>
> (Manning, 1992:133)

More generally, we can say that rituals are one of the key mechanisms by which everyday life, and the social world in general, is made orderly and given solidity.

Goffman's interest in rituals brought him close to the later work of Emile Durkheim, especially *The Elementary Forms of Religious Life.* More generally, in accord with Durkheim's sense of social facts, Goffman came to focus on rules and to see them as external constraints on social behavior. However, rules are generally only partial, indeterminate guides to conduct. Furthermore, while people are constrained, such constraint does not rule out the possibility of individual variation, even imaginative use by individuals of those rules. As Manning puts it, "For the most part, Goffman assumed that rules are primarily constraints. . . . However, at other times Goffman emphasized the limitations of the Durkheimian idea that rules are constraints governing behavior, and argued instead that we frequently ignore or abuse rules intended to limit our actions" (1992:158). In fact, in line with modern thinking, to Goffman rules could be both constraints and resources to be used by us in social interaction.

Groups and Societies

Symbolic interactionists are generally highly critical of the tendency of other sociologists to focus on macro structures. As Rock says, "Interactionism discards most macrosociological thought as an unsure and overambitious metaphysics . . . not accessible to intelligent examination" (1979:238). Dmitri Shalin points to "interactionist criticism aimed at the classical view of social order as external, atemporal, determinate at any given moment and resistant to change" (1986:14). Rock also says, "Whilst it [symbolic interactionism] does not wholly shun the idea of social structure, its stress upon activity and process relegates structural metaphors to a most minor place" (1979:50).

Blumer is in the forefront of those who are critical of this "sociological determinism [in which] the social action of people is treated as an outward flow or expression of forces playing on them rather than as acts which are built up by people through their interpretation of the situations in which they are placed" (1962/1969:84). This focus on the constraining effects of large-scale social structures leads traditional sociologists to a set of assumptions about the actor and action different from those held by symbolic interactionists. Instead of seeing actors as those who actively define their situations, traditional sociologists tend to reduce actors to "mindless robots on the societal or aggregate level" (Manis and Meltzer, 1978:7). In an effort to stay away from determinism and a robotlike view of actors, symbolic interactionists take a very different view of large-scale social structures, a view that is ably presented by Blumer.[10]

To Blumer, society is not made up of macro structures. The essence of society is to be found in actors and action: "Human society is to be seen as consisting of acting people, and the life of the society is to be seen as consisting of their actions" (Blumer, 1962/1969:85). Human society is action; group life is a "complex of ongoing activity." However, society is not made up of an array of isolated acts. There is collective action as well, which involves "individuals fitting their lines of action to one another . . . participants making indications to one another, not merely each to himself" (Blumer, 1969b:16). This gives rise to what Mead called the *social act* and Blumer, *joint action.*

Blumer accepted the idea of emergence, that large-scale structures emerge from micro processes (Morrione, 1988). According to Maines, "The key to understanding Blumer's treatment of large-scale organizations rests on his conception of joint action" (1988:46). A joint action is not simply the sum total of individual acts—it comes to have a character of its own. A joint action thus is not external to or coercive of actors and their actions; rather, it is created by actors and their actions. The study of joint action is, in Blumer's view, the domain of the sociologist.

From this discussion one gets the sense that the joint act is almost totally flexible— that is, that society can become almost anything that the actors want it to be. However, Blumer was not prepared to go as far as that. He argued that each instance of joint action must be formed anew, but he did recognize that joint action is likely to have a "well-established and repetitive form" (Blumer, 1969b:17). Not only does most joint action recur in patterns, but Blumer was also willing to admit that such action is guided by systems of preestablished meanings, such as culture and social order.

It would appear that Blumer admitted that there are large-scale structures and that they are important. Here Blumer followed Mead (1934/1962), who admitted that such structures are very important. However, such structures have an extremely limited role in

---

[10]Although they recognize that Blumer takes this view, Wood and Wardell (1983) argue that Mead did *not* have an "astructural bias." See also Joas (1981).

symbolic interactionism.[11]   For one thing, Blumer most often argued that large-scale structures are little more than "frameworks" within which the really important aspects of social life, action and interaction, take place (1962/1969:87).   Large-scale structures do set the conditions and limitations on human action, but they do not determine it.   In his view, people do not act within the context of such structures as society; rather, they act in situations.   Large-scale structures are important in that they shape the situations in which individuals act and supply to actors the fixed set of symbols that enable them to act.

Even when Blumer discussed such preestablished patterns, he hastened to make it clear that "areas of unprescribed conduct are just as natural, indigenous, and recurrent in human group life as those areas covered by preestablished and faithfully followed prescriptions of joint action" (1969b:18).   Not only are there many unprescribed areas, but even in prescribed areas joint action has to be consistently created and re-created. Actors are guided by generally accepted meanings in this creation and re-creation, but they are not determined by them.   They may accept them as is, but they also can make minor and even major alterations in them.   In Blumer's words, "It is the social process in group life that creates and upholds the rules, not the rules that create and uphold group life" (1969b:19).

Clearly, Blumer was not inclined to accord culture independent and coercive status in his theoretical system.   Nor was he about to accord this status to the extended connections of group life, or what is generally called "social structure," for example, the division of labor.   "A network or an institution does not function automatically because of some inner dynamics or system requirements; it functions because people at different points do something, and what they do is a result of how they define the situation in which they are called on to act" (Blumer, 1969b:19).

CRITICISMS

Having analyzed the ideas of symbolic interactionism, particularly those of the Chicago school of Mead, Blumer, and Goffman, we will now enumerate some of the major criticisms of this perspective.

The first criticism is that the mainstream of symbolic interactionism has too readily given up on conventional scientific techniques.   Eugene Weinstein and Judith Tanur expressed this point well: "Just because the contents of consciousness are qualitative, does not mean that their exterior expression cannot be coded, classified, even counted" (1976:105).   Science and subjectivism are *not* mutually exclusive.

Second, Manford Kuhn (1964), William Kolb (1944), Bernard Meltzer, James Petras, and Larry Reynolds (1975), and many others have criticized the vagueness of essential Meadian concepts such as mind, self, I, and me.   Most generally, Kuhn (1964) spoke of the ambiguities and contradictions in Mead's theory.   Beyond Meadian theory, they have criticized many of the basic symbolic-interactionist concepts for being confused and imprecise and therefore incapable of providing a firm basis for theory and research.

[11]Later we will discuss some more recent perspectives in symbolic interactionism which accord a greater role to large-scale structures and which argue, more specifically, that Blumer adopted such a position (Blumer, 1990; Maines, 1989a, 1989b; Maines and Morrione, 1990).

Because these concepts are imprecise, it is difficult, if not impossible, to operationalize them; the result is that testable propositions cannot be generated (Stryker, 1980).

The third major criticism of symbolic interactionism has been of its tendency to downplay or ignore large-scale social structures. This criticism has been expressed in various ways. For example, Weinstein and Tanur argued that symbolic interactionism ignores the connectedness of outcomes to each other: *"It is the aggregated outcomes that form the linkages among episodes of interaction that are the concern of sociology qua sociology. . . .* The concept of social structure is necessary to deal with the incredible density and complexity of relations through which episodes of interaction are interconnected" (1976:106). Sheldon Stryker argued that the micro focus of symbolic interactionism serves "to minimize or deny the facts of social structure and the impact of the macro-organizational features of society on behavior" (1980:146).

Somewhat less predictable is the fourth criticism, that symbolic interactionism is not sufficiently microscopic, that it ignores the importance of such factors as the unconscious and emotions (Meltzer, Petras, and Reynolds, 1975; Stryker, 1980). Similarly, symbolic interactionism has been criticized for ignoring such psychological factors as needs, motives, intentions, and aspirations. In their effort to deny that there are immutable forces impelling the actor to act, symbolic interactionists have focused instead on meanings, symbols, action, and interaction. They ignore psychological factors that might impel the actor, an action which parallels their neglect of the larger societal constraints on the actor. In both cases, symbolic interactionists are accused of making a "fetish" out of everyday life (Meltzer, Petras, and Reynolds, 1975:85). This focus on everyday life, in turn, leads to a marked overemphasis on the immediate situation and an "obsessive concern with the transient, episodic, and fleeting" (Meltzer, Petras, and Reynolds, 1975:85).

TOWARD A MORE SYNTHETIC AND INTEGRATIVE SYMBOLIC INTERACTIONISM

It may have been out of self-defense, but symbolic interactionism, as it evolved primarily under the stewardship of Herbert Blumer, moved in a decidedly micro direction. This micro focus stood in contrast to at least the implications of the more integrative title of George Herbert Mead's *Mind, Self and Society.* However, symbolic interactionism has entered a new, "post-Blumerian" age (Fine, 1990, 1992). On one front, there are efforts to reconstruct Blumerian theory and argue that it always had an interest in macro-level phenomena (discussed later in this chapter) (Anderson, 1994).[12] More important, there are ongoing efforts to synthesize symbolic interactionism with ideas derived from a number of other theories. This "new" symbolic interactionism has, in Fine's terms, "cobbled a new theory from the shards of other theoretical approaches" (1990:136–137; Fine, 1992). Symbolic interactionism now combines indigenous insights with those from other micro theories like exchange theory, ethnomethodology and conversation analysis, and phenomenology. More surprising is the integration of ideas from macro

---

[12]For a critique of efforts by symbolic interactionists to integrate macro-level phenomena, see J. Turner 1995.

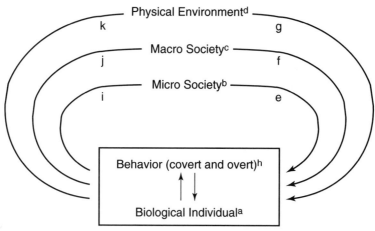

FIGURE 6.1
An Overview of the Components of Mead's Theoretical System

theories (for example, structural functionalism) as well as of the ideas of macro theorists like Parsons, Durkheim, Simmel, Weber, and Marx. Symbolic interactionists are also endeavoring to integrate insights from poststructuralism, postmodernism, and radical feminism. Post-Blumerian symbolic interactionism is becoming a much more synthetic perspective than it was in Blumer's heyday.

Redefining Mead and Blumer

In addition to ongoing synthetic work in symbolic interactionism, there is an effort to redefine the major thinkers associated with it, especially Mead and Blumer, as having more integrative orientations than is usually thought to be the case.

Mead   As we saw earlier, despite Mead's lack of interest in macro-level phenomena, there is much in his ideas on mind, self, and society that suggests an integrated sociological theory. In this context, it is useful to look at John Baldwin's (1986) analysis of Mead. Baldwin notes the fragmentation of the social sciences in general, and sociological theory in particular, and argues that such fragmentation is serving to prevent the development of a general "unifying" sociological theory and, more generally, a science of the social world. He makes the case for the need for such a theory and for Meadian theory as a model for that theory (Baldwin, 1986:156). While Baldwin is proposing the kind of grand synthesis that is being rejected in this postmodern era, we can welcome his effort to see a more integrative approach in Meadian theory.

Baldwin makes the case for Mead on several grounds. First, he argues that Mead's theoretical system covers the full range of social phenomena from micro to macro levels—"physiology, social psychology, language, cognition, behavior, society, social change and ecology" (Baldwin, 1986:156). Along these lines, Baldwin offers a model of Mead's theoretical orientation, as shown in Figure 6.1.

Second, Baldwin argues that not only does Mead have an integrated, micro-macro sense of the social world, but he also offers "a flexible system for interweaving contributions from all schools of contemporary social science" (1986:156). Thus, Mead's theory provides a base not only for micro-macro integration but for theoretical synthesis as well. Finally, Baldwin contends that Mead's "commitment to scientific methods helps ensure that data and theories on all components of the social system can be integrated in a balanced manner, with their relative importance established in an empirically defensible manner" (1986:156).

Blumer   Recall that we depicted Blumer as offering a very limited conception of macro and objective phenomena. However, several symbolic interactionists have sought to demonstrate that Blumer had a stronger sense of macro structures and objectivity and that this, along with the obvious strength of his theory at the micro levels and on subjectivity, gives his theory an integrative orientation (Maines, 1989a, 1989b; Maines and Morrione, 1990; Morrione, 1988).

Maines (1989a) has attacked three "myths" associated with Blumer's theory—that it is unscientific, subjectivistic, and astructural. It is the latter two myths that concern us here because they go to the heart of creating a more integrated conception of Blumer's ideas. That is, if Blumer can be shown to offer a more objectivist position to supplement his clear interest in subjectivity *and* a macro sense to complement his obvious micro orientation, he could then be seen as offering a fully integrated sociological theory (see Appendix).

On the issue of subjectivity, Maines argues that Blumer is merely adopting a position that is in line with contemporary thinking on human agency (see Chapter 11). Agency implies a concern with *both* the subjective manner in which people construct social reality and the resulting objective action, interaction, and their patterns. Furthermore, Maines sees Blumer adopting the position of some, but *not* all, agency theorists that collective entities such as "organizations, institutions, social movements, social classes, nations, interest groups, or races" act and are characterized by subjective processes (1989a:389).

In fleshing out Blumer's thoughts on macro-level phenomena, Maines discusses three implications of Blumer's conception of joint action. First, joint action involves social organization, since action occurs in recurrent patterns. Second, actions tend to be interconnected; that is, they tend to be institutionalized. Finally, social action has continuity; that is, it has history. A concern with organization, institutionalization, and history would clearly associate Blumer with a macro orientation, and Maines proceeds to demonstrate Blumer's macro concerns in a series of substantive areas (for example, race relations and industrialization).

Maines and Morrione have posthumously published Blumer's book, *Industrialization as an Agent of Social Change*. The book was originally written in the early 1960s, but it was never published, because Blumer was not satisfied with it. The publication of this book points to Blumer's macro and objectivistic side. The industrialization process clearly occurs at the macro level, and it involves such objective structures as production systems based on mechanization, procurement, and distribution systems and a service structure (Maines and Morrione, 1990:xviii). Blumer may not be fully satisfactory as an integrative theorist, but recent interpretations of his work demonstrate that his thinking is more in line with contemporary developments than is often believed.

Micro-Macro Integration

Stryker enunciated an integrative goal for symbolic interactionism: "A satisfactory theoretical framework must bridge social structure and person, must be able to move from the level of the person to that of large-scale social structure and back again. . . . There must exist a conceptual framework facilitating movement across the levels of organization and person" (1980:53). (Perinbanayagam articulated a similar goal for symbolic interactionism: "the existence of structure *and* meaning, self *and* others, the dialectic of being and emergence, leading to a dialectical interactionism" [1985:xv].) Stryker embedded his orientation in Meadian symbolic interactionism but sought to extend it to the societal level, primarily through the use of role theory:

> This version begins with Mead, but goes beyond Mead to introduce role theoretic concepts and principles, in order to adequately deal with the reciprocal impact of social person and social structure. The nexus in this reciprocal impact is interaction. It is in the context of the social process—the ongoing patterns of interaction joining individual actors—that social structure operates to constrain the conceptions of self, the definitions of the situation, and the behavioral opportunities and repertoires that bound and guide the interaction that takes place.
>
> (Stryker, 1980:52)

Stryker developed his orientation in terms of eight general principles:

1 Human action is dependent on a named and classified world in which the names and classifications have meaning for actors. People learn through interaction with others how to classify the world, as well as how they are expected to behave toward it.

2 Among the most important things that people learn are the symbols used to designate social *positions*. A critical point here is that Stryker conceived of positions in structural terms: "the relatively stable, morphological components of social structure" (Stryker, 1980:54). Stryker also accorded *roles* central importance, conceiving of them as the shared behavioral expectations attached to social positions.

3 Stryker also recognized the importance of larger social structures, although he was inclined, like other symbolic interactionists, to conceive of them in terms of organized patterns of behavior. In addition, his discussion treated social structure as simply the "framework" within which people act. Within these structures, people name one another, that is, recognize one another as occupants of positions. In so doing, people evoke reciprocal expectations of what each is expected to do.

4 Furthermore, in acting in this context, people name not only each other but also themselves; that is, they apply positional designations to themselves. These self-designations become part of the self, internalized expectations with regard to their own behavior.

5 When interacting, people define the situation by applying names to it, to other participants, to themselves, and to particular features of the situation. These definitions are then used by the actors to organize their behavior.

6 Social behavior is not determined by social meanings, although it is constrained by them. Stryker is a strong believer in the idea of *role making*. People do not simply take roles; rather, they take an active, creative orientation to their roles.

7 Social structures also serve to limit the degree to which roles are "made" rather than just "taken." Some structures permit more creativity than others.

8 The possibilities of role making make various social changes possible. Changes can occur in social definitions—in names, symbols, and classifications—and in the possibilities for interaction. The cumulative effect of these changes can be alterations in the larger social structures.

Although Stryker offered a useful beginning toward a more adequate symbolic interactionism, his work has a number of limitations. The most notable is that he said little about larger social structures per se. Stryker saw the need to integrate these larger structures in his work, but he recognized that a "full-fledged development of how such incorporation could proceed is beyond the scope of the present work" (1980:69). Stryker saw only a limited future role for large-scale structural variables in symbolic interactionism. He hoped ultimately to incorporate such structural factors as class, status, and power as variables constraining interaction, but he was disinclined to see symbolic interactionism deal with the interrelationships among these structural variables. Presumably, this kind of issue is to be left to other theories that focus more on large-scale social phenomena.

Symbolic Interactionism and Cultural Studies

A number of thinkers have addressed, in whole or in part, the relationship between symbolic interactionism and a number of the newer theoretical movements, including poststructuralism, postmodernism, and cultural studies (Farberman, 1991; Schwalbe, 1993; Shalin, 1993). In this section we will focus on Norman Denzin's effort of this type, *Symbolic Interactionism and Cultural Studies* (1992; see also, Becker and McCall, 1990).

The study of culture in the form of the sociology of culture, or more generally cultural studies, has grown enormously in recent years. These recent studies of culture have been heavily influenced by a number of theoretical perspectives, including poststructuralism and postmodernism (see Chapter 13). Denzin defines cultural studies as

> that interdisciplinary project . . . which . . . directs itself always to the problem of how the history that human beings make and live spontaneously is determined by structures of meaning that they have not chosen for themselves. . . . Culture, in its meaning-making and interactional forms, becomes a site of political struggle. . . . A central problem becomes examination of how interacting individuals connect lived experiences to the cultural representations of those experiences.
>
> (Denzin, 1992:74)

Cultural studies focuses on three interrelated problems—"the production of cultural meanings, the textual analysis of these meanings, and the study of lived cultures and lived experiences" (Denzin, 1992:34). Work in this area is directed at the full array of cultural forms, including "artworks, popular music, popular literature, the news, television, and the mass media" (Denzin, 1992:76). Studies of these cultural forms have come to be heavily influenced by theories such as poststructuralism and postmodernism, and Denzin seeks to associate symbolic interactionism with these studies and theories.

In Denzin's view, symbolic interactionism should have played a bigger role in cultural studies than it has. One basic problem is that symbolic interactionism has tended to neglect the idea that connects "symbolic" and "interaction" (and is a focal concern in cultural studies)—"communication." Denzin seeks to correct this problem:

> In seeking to reorient symbolic interactionists towards a cultural studies perspective, I chose, then, to focus on this missing, undertheorized term in their perspective. There is a paradox here, of course; for communication is interaction and for interaction to unfold, interactants must communicate.
>
> (Denzin, 1992:97–98)

Interactionists are urged, more specifically, to focus on communication technologies and technological apparatuses and the ways in which they produce reality and representations of that reality.

In fact, Denzin shows that symbolic interactionists have, in the past, focused on the kinds of communication of interest to cultural studies (for example, the movies). However, those involved in the field have tended to lose sight of this focus, and Denzin is interested in having them return to their cultural roots.

Denzin wants the studies of interactionists to focus on culture, especially popular culture, but he wants symbolic interactionism to take a *critical* approach to culture. Such a critical orientation is consistent with a tradition within interactionism to focus on the underdog, as well as its relationship to those in power.

To move in this direction requires a change in the theoretical orientation of symbolic interactionism. On the one hand, symbolic interactionism must abandon its traditional modern orientation (see Chapter 12). More specifically, what must be abandoned are the canonical reading of the classic texts in symbolic interactionism discussed throughout this chapter, the sense that it is a science of social totality, and the historical myths that have dominated the field and kept it from moving in new theoretical directions. In addition to abandoning certain orientations, symbolic interactionism is urged to move in other directions:

> The interactionist tradition must confront, absorb, debate, and be in conflict with the new terrains of theory which continue to appear in the postmodern era (e.g. hermeneutics, phenomenology, structuralism, poststructuralism, postmodern theory, psychoanalysis, semiotics, post-Marxism, cultural studies, feminist theory, film theory, etc.).
>
> (Denzin, 1992:169)

Thus, Denzin recommends a similar, albeit more specific, direction for symbolic interactionism than the one outlined by Fine.

As pointed out previously, Denzin's program for symbolic interactionism draws heavily on poststructuralism (Dunn, 1997) and postmodernism (see Chapter 13; for a critique of this view, see Maines, 1996). For example, because it focuses on ever-changing emergent phenomena, symbolic interactionism is comfortable with the postmodern rejection of grand theories (for example, Marx's theory of capitalism), or as they call them, grand narratives. If they focus more on communication, symbolic interactionists will be in tune with the postmodern concern with it, especially the video images from television and the movies. There is much to be gained from the study of texts in general, and their deconstruction in particular. Denzin argues that there is a great deal to be learned from feminism in general, and poststructural and postmodern feminism in particular. And, more in line with the feminists, Denzin wants symbolic interactionism to be more political. Clearly, Denzin is charting a new, synthetic direction for symbolic interactionism.

THE FUTURE OF SYMBOLIC INTERACTIONISM

Gary Fine (1993) has offered an interesting portrait of symbolic interactionism in the 1990s. His fundamental point is that symbolic interactionism has changed dramatically in recent years. Four terms describe symbolic interactionism. First, it has undergone considerable *fragmentation* since its heyday at the University of Chicago in the 1920s and 1930s. A great diversity of work is now included under the broad heading of symbolic interactionism. Second, symbolic interactionism has undergone *expansion* and has extended far beyond its traditional concern with micro relations. Third, symbolic interactionism has *incorporated* ideas from many other theoretical perspectives. Finally, the ideas of symbolic interactionists have, in turn, been *adopted* by sociologists who are focally committed to other theoretical perspectives. Further, symbolic interactionists are deeply involved in some of the major issues confronting sociological theory in the 1990s—micro-macro, agency-structure, and so on.

Thus, lines dividing symbolic interactionism and other sociological theories have blurred considerably. While symbolic interactionism will survive, it is increasingly unclear what it means to be a symbolic interactionist (and every other type of sociological theorist for that matter). Here is the way Fine puts it:

> Predicting the future is dangerous, but it is evident that the label symbolic interaction will abide. . . . Yet, we will find more intermarriage, more interchange, and more interaction. Symbolic interaction will serve as a label of convenience for the future, but will it serve as a label of thought?
>
> (Fine, 1993:81–82)

Throughout this book we are dealing with ongoing syntheses among many sociological theories. All these syntheses lead to the more general question of whether *any* of the familiar theoretical labels will describe distinctive modes of thought in the future.

SUMMARY

This chapter begins with a brief discussion of the roots of symbolic interactionism in philosophical pragmatism (the work of John Dewey) and psychological behaviorism (the work of John B. Watson). Out of the confluence of pragmatism, behaviorism, and other influences, such as Simmelian sociology, symbolic interactionism developed at the University of Chicago in the 1920s.

The symbolic interactionism that developed stood in contrast to the psychological reductionism of behaviorism and the structural determinism of more macro-oriented sociological theories, such as structural functionalism. Its distinctive orientation was toward the mental capacities of actors and their relationship to action and interaction. All this was conceived in terms of process; there was a disinclination to see the actor impelled by either internal psychological states or large-scale structural forces.

The single most important theory in symbolic interactionism is that of George Herbert Mead. Substantively, Mead's theory accorded primacy and priority to the social world. That is, it is out of the social world that consciousness, the mind, the self, and so on emerge. The most basic unit in his social theory is the act, which includes four dialectically related stages—impulse, perception, manipulation, and consummation. A *social* act involves two or more persons, and the basic mechanism of the social act is the gesture. While lower animals and humans are capable of having a conversation of gestures, only humans can communicate the conscious meaning of their gestures. Humans are peculiarly able to create vocal gestures, and this leads to the distinctive human ability to develop and use significant symbols. Significant symbols lead to the development of language and the distinctive capacity of humans to communicate, in the full sense of the term, with one another. Significant symbols also make possible thinking, as well as symbolic interaction.

Mead looks at an array of mental processes as part of the larger social process, including reflective intelligence, consciousness, mental images, meaning, and, most generally, the mind. Humans have the distinctive capacity to carry on an inner conversation with themselves. All the mental processes are, in Mead's view, lodged not in the brain but rather in the social process.

The self is the ability to take oneself as an object. Again, the self arises within the social process. The general mechanism of the self is the ability of people to put themselves in the place of others, to act as they act and to see themselves as others see them. Mead traces the genesis of the self through the play and game stages of childhood. Especially important in the latter stage is the emergence of the generalized other. The ability to view oneself from the point of view of the community is essential to the emergence of the self as well as of organized group activities. The self also has two phases—the "I," which is the unpredictable and creative aspect of the self, and the "me," which is the organized set of attitudes of others assumed by the actor. Social control is manifest through the "me," while the "I" is the source of innovation in society.

Mead has relatively little to say about society, which he views most generally as the ongoing social processes that precede mind and self. Mead largely lacks a macro sense of society. Institutions are defined as little more than collective habits.

Symbolic interactionism may be summarized by the following basic principles:

1 Human beings, unlike lower animals, are endowed with a capacity for thought.

2 The capacity for thought is shaped by social interaction.

3 In social interaction, people learn the meanings and the symbols that allow them to exercise their distinctively human capacity for thought.

4 Meanings and symbols allow people to carry on distinctively human action and interaction.

5 People are able to modify or alter the meanings and symbols that they use in action and interaction on the basis of their interpretation of the situation.

6 People are able to make these modifications and alterations because, in part, of their ability to interact with themselves, which allows them to examine possible courses of action, assess their relative advantages and disadvantages, and then choose one.

7 The intertwined patterns of action and interaction make up groups and societies.

In the context of these general principles, we seek to clarify the nature of the work of several important thinkers in the symbolic-interactionist tradition, including Charles Horton Cooley, Herbert Blumer, and, most important, Erving Goffman. We present in detail Goffman's dramaturgical analysis of the self and his related works on role distance, stigma, and frame analysis. However, we also note that Goffman's work on frames has exaggerated a tendency in his earlier work and moved further in the direction of a structuralist analysis.

We also review some of the major criticisms of symbolic interactionism, as well as three efforts to move it in more integrative and synthetic directions—the redefinition of the approaches of Mead and Blumer in more integrative terms, the effort by Stryker to develop an approach that better deals with macro-level phenomena, and Denzin's attempt to reorient symbolic interactionism in the direction of cultural studies, post-structuralism, and postmodernism. The chapter closes with one image of symbolic interactionism's future.

7

ETHNOMETHODOLOGY

DEFINING ETHNOMETHODOLOGY

THE DIVERSIFICATION OF ETHNOMETHODOLOGY

SOME EARLY EXAMPLES
    Breaching Experiments
    Accomplishing Gender

CONVERSATION ANALYSIS
    Telephone Conversations: Identification and Recognition
    Initiating Laughter
    Generating Applause
    Booing
    The Interactive Emergence of Sentences and Stories
    Formulations
    Integration of Talk and Nonvocal Activities
    Doing Shyness (and Self-Confidence)

STUDIES OF INSTITUTIONS
    Job Interviews
    Executive Negotiations
    Calls to Emergency Centers
    Dispute Resolution in Mediation Hearings

CRITICISMS OF TRADITIONAL SOCIOLOGY

STRESSES AND STRAINS IN ETHNOMETHODOLOGY

SYNTHESIS AND INTEGRATION
    Ethnomethodology and Symbolic Interactionism
    Ethnomethodology and the Micro-Macro Order

Given its Greek roots, the term *ethnomethodology* literally means the "methods" that people use on a daily basis to accomplish their everyday lives. To put it slightly differently, the world is seen as an ongoing practical accomplishment. People are viewed as rational, but they use "practical reasoning," not formal logic, in accomplishing their everyday lives.

DEFINING ETHNOMETHODOLOGY

We begin with the definition of *ethnomethodology* offered in Chapter 2: the study of "the body of common-sense knowledge and the range of procedures and considerations by means of which the ordinary members of society make sense of, find their way about in, and act on the circumstances in which they find themselves" (Heritage, 1984:4).

HAROLD GARFINKEL: A Biographical Sketch*

Like many who came of age during the Depression and later WW II, Harold Garfinkel took a convoluted path into sociology. Garfinkel was born in Newark, New Jersey on October 29, 1917. His father was a small businessman who sold household goods on installment to immigrant families. While his father was eager for him to learn a trade, Harold wanted to go to college. He did go into his father's business, but also began taking business courses at the then-unaccredited University of Newark. Because the courses tended to be taught by graduate students from Columbia, they were both high in quality and, because the students lacked practical experience, highly theoretical. His later theoretical orientation, and his specific orientation to "accounts," are traceable, at least in part, to these courses in general, and particularly to an accounting course, "theory of accounts." "'How do you make the columns and figures accountable [to superiors]?'" was the big question according to Garfinkel'" (Rawls, forthcoming). Also of importance was the fact that Garfinkel encountered other Jewish students at Newark who were taking courses in sociology and were later themselves to become social scientists.

Graduating in 1939, Garfinkel spent a summer in a Quaker work camp in rural Georgia. There he learned that the University of North Carolina had a sociology program that was also oriented to the furtherance of public works projects like the one in which he was involved. Admitted to the program with a fellowship, Garfinkel chose Guy Johnson as his thesis advisor and the latter's interest in race relations led Garfinkel to do his Master's thesis on interracial homicide. He was also exposed to a wide range of social theory, most notably the works of phenomenologists and the recently published (in 1937), *The Structure of Social Action,* by Talcott Parsons. While the vast majority of graduate students at North Carolina at the time were drawn toward statistics and "scientific sociology," Garfinkel was attracted to theory, especially Florian Znaniecki's now almost forgotten work on social action and the importance of the actor's point of view.

Garfinkel was drafted in 1942 and entered the airforce. He eventually was given the task of training troops in tank warfare on a golf course on Miami beach in the complete absence of tanks. Garfinkel had only pictures of tanks from Life Magazine. The real tanks

We can gain further insight into the nature of ethnomethodology by examining efforts by its founder, Harold Garfinkel (1988, 1991), to define it. Like Durkheim, Garfinkel considers "social facts" to be the fundamental sociological phenomenon. However, Garfinkel's social facts are very different from Durkheim's social facts. For Durkheim, social facts are external to and coercive of individuals. Those who adopt such a focus tend to see actors as constrained or determined by social structures and institutions and able to exercise little or no independent judgment. In the acerbic terms of the ethnomethodologists, such sociologists tended to treat actors like "judgmental dopes."

In contrast, ethnomethodology treats the objectivity of social facts as the accomplishment of members (a definition of "members" follows shortly)—as a product of members' methodological activities. Garfinkel, in his inimitable and nearly impenetrable style, describes the focus of ethnomethodology as follows:

were all in combat. The man who would insist on concrete empirical detail in lieu of theo-rized accounts was teaching real troops who were about to enter live combat to fight against only imagined tanks in situations where things like the proximity of the troops to the imagined tank could make the difference between life and death. The impact of this on the development of his views can only be imagined. He had to train troops to throw ex-plosives into the tracks of imaginary tanks; to keep imaginary tanks from seeing them by directing fire at imaginary tank ports. This task posed in a new and very concrete way the problems of the adequate description of action and accountability that Garfinkel had taken up at North Carolina as theoretical issues   (Rawls, forthcoming).

When the war ended, Garfinkel proceeded to Harvard and studied with Talcott Parsons. While Parsons stressed the importance of abstract categories and generalizations, Garfinkel was interested in detailed description. When Garfinkel achieved prominence within the disci-pline, this became a focal debate within sociology. However, he soon became more inter-ested in the empirical demonstration of the importance of his theoretical orientation than in debating it in the abstract. While still a student at Harvard, Garfinkel taught for two years at Princeton and after obtaining his doctorate, moved on to Ohio State where he had a two-year position involved in a "soft money" project studying leadership on airplanes and submarines. That research as cut short by cuts in funding, but Garfinkel then joined a project researching juries in Wichita, Kansas. In preparing for a talk on the project at the 1954 American Socio-logical Association meetings, Garfinkel came up with the term "ethnomethodology" to de-scribe what fascinated him about the jury deliberations and social life more generally.

In the fall of 1954 Garfinkel took a position at UCLA; a position he held until he retired in 1987. From the beginning, he used the term ethnomethodology in his seminars. A number of notable students were taken by Garfinkel's approach and disseminated it around the United States and eventually the world. Most notable were a group of sociologists, especially Har-vey Sacks, Emmanuel Schegloff and Gail Jefferson, who, inspired by Garfinkel's approach, developed what is, at least at the moment, the most important variety of ethnomethodology—conversation analysis.

*This biographical sketch is based on Anne Rawls, "Harold Garfinkel," in George Ritzer, ed., *The Black-well Companion to Major Social Theorists*. Cambridge, MA and Oxford, England: Blackwell, forthcoming.

For ethnomethodology the objective reality of social facts, in that, and just how, it is every society's locally, endogenously produced, naturally organized, reflexively accountable, ongoing, practical achievement, being everywhere, always, only, exactly and entirely, members' work, with no time out, and with no possibility of evasion, hiding out, passing, postponement, or buy-outs, is *thereby* sociology's fundamental phenomenon.

(Garfinkel, 1991:11)

To put it another way, ethnomethodology is concerned with the organization of every-day life, or as Garfinkel (1988:104) describes it, "immortal, ordinary society." In Pollner's terms, this is "the extraordinary organization of the ordinary" (1987:xvii).

Ethnomethodology is certainly not a macrosociology in the sense intended by Durkheim and his concept of a social fact, but its adherents do not see it as a microso-ciology either. Thus, while ethnomethodologists refuse to treat actors as judgmental dopes, they do not believe that people are "almost endlessly reflexive, self-conscious and calculative" (Heritage, 1984:118). Rather, following Alfred Schutz, they recognize that most often action is routine and relatively unreflective. Hilbert (1992) argues that ethnomethodologists do not focus on actors or individuals, but rather on "members." However, members are viewed not as individuals, but rather "strictly and solely, [as] membership activities—the artful practices whereby they produce what are *for them* large-scale organization structure and small-scale interactional or personal structure" (Hilbert, 1992:193). In sum, ethnomethodologists are interested in *neither* micro structures *nor* macro structures; they are concerned with the artful practices that produce *both* types of structures. Thus, what Garfinkel and the ethnomethodologists have sought is a new way of getting at the traditional concern of sociology with objective structures, both micro and macro (Maynard and Clayman, 1991).

One of Garfinkel's key points about ethnomethods is that they are "reflexively accountable." *Accounts* are the ways in which actors explain (describe, criticize, and idealize specific) situations (Bittner, 1973; Orbuch, 1997). *Accounting* is the process by which people offer accounts in order to make sense of the world. Ethnomethodologists devote a lot of attention to analyzing people's accounts, as well as to the ways in which accounts are offered and accepted (or rejected) by others. This is one of the reasons that ethnomethodologists are preoccupied with analyzing conversations. To take an example, when a student explains to her professor why she failed to take an examination, she is offering an account. The student is trying to make sense out of an event for her professor. Ethnomethodologists are interested in the nature of that account but more generally in the *accounting practices* (Sharrock and Anderson, 1986) by which the student offers the account and the professor accepts or rejects it. In analyzing accounts, ethnomethodologists adopt a stance of "ethnomethodological indifference." That is, they do not judge the nature of the accounts but rather analyze them in terms of how they are used in practical action. They are concerned with the accounts as well as the methods needed by both speaker and listener to proffer, understand, and accept or reject accounts (for more on this, see Young, 1997).

Extending the idea of accounts, ethnomethodologists take great pains to point out that sociologists, like everyone else, offer accounts. Thus, reports of sociological studies can be seen as accounts and analyzed in the same way that all other accounts can be studied. This perspective on sociology serves to disenchant the work of sociologists, indeed all scientists. A good deal of sociology (indeed all sciences) involves commonsense interpretations. Ethnomethodologists can study the accounts of the sociologist in the same way that they can study the accounts of the layperson. Thus, the everyday practices of sociologists and all scientists come under the scrutiny of the ethnomethodologist.

We can say that accounts are reflexive in the sense that they enter into the constitution of the state of affairs they make observable and are intended to deal with. Thus, in trying to describe what people are doing, we are altering the nature of what they are doing. This is as true for sociologists as it is for laypeople. In studying and reporting on social life, sociologists are, in the process, changing what they are studying. That is, subjects alter their behavior as a result of being the subject of scrutiny and in response to descriptions of that behavior (for a similar idea, see the discussion of Giddens's "double hermeneutic" in Chapter 11).

THE DIVERSIFICATION OF ETHNOMETHODOLOGY

Ethnomethodology was "invented" by Garfinkel beginning in the late 1940s, but it was first systematized with the publication of his *Studies in Ethnomethodology* in 1967. Over the years, ethnomethodology has grown enormously and expanded in a number of different directions. Only a decade after the publication of *Studies in Ethnomethodology,* Don Zimmerman concluded that there already were several varieties of ethnomethodology. As Zimmerman put it, ethnomethodology encompassed "a number of more or less distinct and sometimes incompatible lines of inquiry" (1978:6). Ten years later, Paul Atkinson (1988) underscored the lack of coherence in ethnomethodology and argued further that at least some ethnomethodologists had strayed too far from the underlying premises of the approach. Thus, while it is a very vibrant type of sociological theory, ethnomethodology has experienced some increasing "growing pains" in recent years. It is safe to say that ethnomethodology, its diversity, and its problems are likely to proliferate in coming years. After all, the subject matter of ethnomethodology is the infinite variety of everyday life. As a result, there will be many more studies, more diversification, and further "growing pains."

Studies of Institutional Settings Maynard and Clayman (1991) describe a number of varieties of work in ethnomethodology, but two stand out from our point of view.[1] The first type is ethnomethodological *studies of institutional settings.* Early ethnomethodological studies carried on by Garfinkel and his associates (which are discussed below) took place in casual, noninstitutionalized settings like the home. Later, there was a move toward studying everyday practices in a wide variety of institutional settings—courtrooms, medical settings (Ten Have, 1995), and police departments. The goal of such studies is an understanding of the way people perform their official tasks and, in the process, constitute the institution in which the tasks take place.

Conventional sociological studies of such institutional settings focus on their structure, formal rules, and official procedures to explain what people do within them. To the ethnomethodologists, such external constraints are inadequate for explaining what really goes on in these institutions. People are not determined by these external forces; rather, they use them to accomplish their tasks and to create the institution in which they exist. People employ their practical procedures not only to make their daily lives but also to manufacture the institutions' products. For example, the crime rates compiled by the police department are not merely the result of officials' following clearly defined rules in their production. Rather, officials utilize a range of common-sense procedures to decide, for example, whether victims should be classified as homicides. Thus, such rates are based on the interpretive work of professionals, and this kind of record keeping is a practical activity worthy of study in its own right.

---

[1]Another body of ethnomethodological work deals with the *study of science,* particularly in fields like mathematics, astronomy, biology, and optics (for example, Lynch, 1985; 1993). In common with the rest of ethnomethodology, studies in this area concentrate on the common-sense procedures, the practical reasoning employed by scientists even in some of the greatest discoveries in the history of mathematics and science. The focus is on the work that scientists do as well as the conversations in which they engage. The ethno-methodologist is concerned with the "workbench practices" employed by scientists on a day-to-day basis.

Conversation Analysis   The second variety of ethnomethodology is *conversation analysis.*[2] The goal of conversation analysis is "the detailed understanding of the fundamental structures of conversational interaction" (Zimmerman, 1988:429). *Conversation* is defined in terms that are in line with the basic elements of the ethnomethodological perspective: "Conversation is an *interactional activity* exhibiting *stable, orderly* properties that are the analyzable *achievements* of the conversants" (Zimmerman, 1988:406; italics added). While there are rules and procedures for conversations, they do not determine what is said but rather are used to "accomplish" a conversation. The focus of conversational analysis is the constraints on what is said that are internal to the conversation itself and not external forces that constrain talk. Conversations are seen as internally, sequentially ordered.

Zimmerman details five basic working principles of conversation analysis. First, conversation analysis requires the collection and analysis of highly detailed data on conversations. This data includes not only words but also "the hesitations, cut-offs, restarts, silences, breathing noises, throat clearings, sniffles, laughter, and laughterlike noises, prosody, and the like, not to mention the 'nonverbal' behaviors available on video records that are usually closely integrated with the stream of activity captured on the audiotape" (Zimmerman, 1988:413). All these things are part of most conversations, and they are seen as methodic devices in the making of a conversation by the actors involved.

Second, even the finest detail of a conversation must be presumed to be an orderly accomplishment. Such minute aspects of a conversation are not ordered just by the ethnomethodologist; they are first "ordered by the methodical activities of the social actors themselves" (Zimmerman, 1988:415).

Third, interaction in general and conversation in particular have stable, orderly properties that are the achievements of the actors involved. In looking at conversations, ethnomethodologists treat them as if they were autonomous, separable from the cognitive processes of the actors as well as the larger context in which they take place.

Fourth, "the fundamental framework of conversation is sequential organization" (Zimmerman, 1988:422). Finally, and relatedly, "the course of conversational interaction is managed on a turn-by-turn or local basis" (Zimmerman, 1988:423). Here Zimmerman invokes Heritage's (1984) distinction between "context-shaped" and "context-renewing" conversation. Conversations are context-shaped in the sense that what is said at any given moment is shaped by the preceding sequential context of the conversation. Conversations are context-shaping in that what is being said in the present turn becomes part of the context for future turns.

Methodologically, conversation analysts are led to study conversations in naturally occurring situations, often using audiotape or videotape. This method allows information to flow from the everyday world rather than being imposed on it by the researcher. The researcher can examine and reexamine an actual conversation in minute detail instead of relying on his or her notes. This technique also allows the researcher to do highly detailed analyses of conversations.

Conversation analysis is based on the assumption that conversations are the bedrock of other forms of interpersonal relations. They are the most pervasive form of interac-

---

[2]While I am treating conversation analysis as a variety of ethnomethodology, it should be noted that conversation analysis has distinctive roots in the work of Harvey Sacks (who was a student of Erving Goffman, not Harold Garfinkel) and has over the years developed a distinctive set of interests.

tion, and a conversation "consists of the fullest matrix of socially organized communicative practices and procedures" (Heritage and Atkinson, 1984:13).

We have tried to give some general sense of ethnomethodology in the preceding pages. However, the heart of ethnomethodology lies not in its theoretical statements but in its empirical studies. What we know theoretically is derived from those studies. Thus, we turn now to a series of those studies in the hope of giving the reader a better feel for ethnomethodology.

SOME EARLY EXAMPLES

We begin with some of the early research in ethnomethodology that gained for it much early notoriety. While some of the early methods are rarely, if ever, used today, they tell us a good deal about ethnomethodological research.

Breaching Experiments

In breaching experiments, social reality is violated in order to shed light on the methods by which people construct social reality. The assumption behind this research is not only that the methodical production of social life occurs all the time but also that the participants are unaware that they are engaging in such actions. The objective of the breaching experiment is to disrupt normal procedures so that the process by which the everyday world is constructed or reconstructed can be observed and studied. In his work, Garfinkel (1967) offered a number of examples of breaching experiments, most of which were undertaken by his students in casual settings to illustrate the basic principles of ethnomethodology.

Lynch (1991:15) offers the following example of breaching, derived from earlier work by Garfinkel (1963):

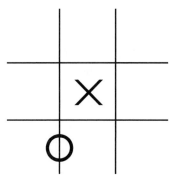

FIGURE 7.1
Breaching In Tic-Tac-Toe. (*Source:* Michael Lynch, 1991. "Pictures of Nothing? Visual Constructs in Social Theory." *Sociological Theory* 9:15.)

This, of course, is a game of tic-tac-toe. The well-known rules allow participants in the game to place a mark *within* each of the cells, but the rules have been breached in this case and a mark has been placed *between* two cells. If this breach were to occur in a real game of tic-tac-toe, the other player (player 2) would likely insist on a correct placement. If such a placement was not to occur, player 2 would try to explain why player 1 had taken such an extraordinary action. The actions of player 2 would be studied by the ethnomethodologist to see how the everyday world of tic-tac-toe is reconstructed.

To take one other example, Garfinkel asked his students to spend between fifteen minutes and an hour in their homes imagining that they were boarders and then acting on the basis of that assumption. "They were instructed to conduct themselves in a circumspect and polite fashion. They were to avoid getting personal, to use formal address, to speak only when spoken to" (Garfinkel, 1967:47). In the vast majority of cases, family members were dumbfounded by such behavior: "Reports were filled with accounts of astonishment, bewilderment, shock, anxiety, embarrassment, and anger, and with charges by various family members that the student was mean, inconsiderate, selfish, nasty, or impolite" (Garfinkel, 1967:47). These reactions indicate how important it is that people act in accord with the common-sense assumptions about how they are supposed to behave.

What most interested Garfinkel was how the family members sought in common-sense ways to cope with such a breach. They demanded explanations from the students for their behavior. In their questions, they often implied an explanation of the aberrant behavior:

"Did you get fired?"
"Are you sick?"
"Are you out of your mind or are you just stupid?"

(Garfinkel, 1967:47)

Family members also sought to explain the behaviors to themselves in terms of previously understood motives. For example, a student was thought to be behaving oddly because she was working too hard or had had a fight with her fiancé. Such explanations are important to participants—the other family members, in this case—because the explanations help them feel that under normal circumstances interaction would occur as it always had.

If the student did not acknowledge the validity of such explanations, family members were likely to withdraw and to seek to isolate, denounce, or retaliate against the culprit. Deep emotions were aroused because the effort to restore order through explanation was rejected by the student. The other family members felt that more intense statements and actions were necessary to restore the equilibrium:

"Don't bother with him, he's in one of his moods again."
"Why must you always create friction in our family harmony?"
"I don't want any more of *that* out of *you* and if you can't treat your mother decently you'd better move out!"

(Garfinkel, 1967:48)

In the end, the students explained the experiment to their families, and in most situations harmony was restored. However, in some instances hard feelings lingered.

Breaching experiments are undertaken to illustrate the way people order their everyday lives. These experiments reveal the resilience of social reality, since the subjects (or victims) move quickly to normalize the breach—that is, to render the situation accountable in familiar terms. It is assumed that the way people handle these breaches tells us much about how they handle their everyday lives (Handel, 1982). Although these experiments seem innocent enough, they often lead to highly emotional reactions. These extreme reactions reflect how important it is to people to engage in routine, common-sense activities. The reactions to breaches are sometimes so extreme that Hugh Mehan and Houston Wood have cautioned about their use: *"Interested persons are strongly advised not to undertake any new breaching studies"* (1975:113).

Accomplishing Gender

It seems incontrovertible that one's gender—male or female—is biologically based. People are seen as simply manifesting the behaviors that are an outgrowth of their biological makeup. People are not usually thought of as *accomplishing* their gender. In contrast, sexiness is clearly an accomplishment; people need to speak and act in certain ways in order to be seen as sexy. However, it is generally assumed that one does not have to do or say *anything* to be seen as a man or a woman. Ethnomethodology has investigated the issue of gender, with some very unusual results.

The ethnomethodological view is traceable to one of Harold Garfinkel's (1967) now classic demonstrations of the utility of this orientation. In the 1950s Garfinkel met a person named Agnes, who seemed unquestionably a woman.[3] Not only did she have the figure of a woman, but it was virtually a "perfect" figure with an ideal set of measurements. She also had a pretty face, a good complexion, no facial hair, and plucked eyebrows—and she wore lipstick. This was clearly a woman, or was it? Garfinkel discovered that Agnes had not always appeared to be a woman. In fact, at the time he met her, Agnes was trying, eventually successfully, to convince physicians that she needed an operation to remove her male genitalia and create a vagina.

Agnes was defined as a male at birth. In fact, she was by all accounts a boy until she was sixteen years of age. At that age, sensing something was awry, Agnes ran away from home and started to dress like a girl. She soon discovered that dressing like a woman was not enough; she had to *learn to act* like (to "pass" as) a woman if she was to be accepted as one. She did learn the accepted practices and as a result came to be defined, and to define herself, as a woman. Garfinkel was interested in the passing practices that allowed Agnes to function like a woman in society. The more general point here is that we are not simply born men or women; we all also learn and routinely use the commonplace practices that allow us to pass as men or women. It is only in learning these practices that we come to be, in a sociological sense, a man or a woman. Thus, even a category like gender, which is thought to be an ascribed status, can be understood as an accomplishment of a set of situated practices.

CONVERSATION ANALYSIS

We now turn to what has become the major type of research within ethnomethodology—conversation analysis. The goal of conversation analysis is to study the taken-for-granted ways in which conversation is organized. Conversation analysts are concerned

---

[3]For an interesting debate over Garfinkel's interpretation of Agnes, see Denzin, 1990a, 1991; Hilbert, 1991; Lynch and Bogen, 1991; and Maynard, 1991b.

with the relationships among utterances in a conversation rather than in the relationships between speakers and hearers (Sharrock and Anderson, 1986:68).

Telephone Conversations: Identification and Recognition

Emanuel A. Schegloff (1979) viewed his examination of the way in which telephone conversations are opened as part of a larger effort to understand the orderly character of social interaction:

> The work in which my colleagues and I have been engaged is concerned with the *organization of social interaction.* We bring to the materials with which we work—audio and videotapes of *naturally occurring* interaction, and transcripts of those tapes—an interest in *detecting* and *describing* the *orderly* phenomena of which conversation and interaction are composed, and an interest in depicting the *systematic organizations* by reference to which those phenomena are produced.
>
> (Schegloff, 1979:24, italics added)

This interest extends to various orderly phenomena within interaction, such as the organization of turn taking in conversations and the ways in which people seek to repair breaches in normal conversational procedure. In addition, there is interest in the overall structure of a conversation, including openings, closings, and regularly recurring internal sequences.

In this context Schegloff looked at the opening of a phone conversation, which he defined as "a place where the type of conversation being opened can be proffered, displayed, accepted, rejected, modified—in short, incipiently constituted by the parties to it" (1979:25). Although the talk one hears on the phone is no different from that in face-to-face conversations, the participants lack visual contact. Schegloff focused on one element of phone conversations not found in face-to-face conversations, the sequence by which the parties who have no visual contact identify and recognize each other.

Schegloff found that telephone openings are often quite straightforward and standardized:

A. Hello?
B. Shar'n?
A. Hi!

(Schegloff, 1979:52)

But some openings "look and sound idiosyncratic—almost virtuoso performances" (Schegloff, 1979:68):

A. Hello.
B. Hello Margie?
A. Yes.
B. hhh We do painting, antiquing,
A. is that right.
B. eh, hh—hhh
A. hnh, hnh, hnh
B. nhh, hnh, hnh! hh
A. hh
B. keep people's pa'r tools

A. y(hhh)! hnh, hnh
B. I'm sorry about that—that—I din' see that.

(adapted from Schegloff, 1979:68)

Although such openings may be different from the usual openings, they are not without their organization. They are "engendered by a systemic sequential organization adapted and fitted by the parties to some particular circumstances" (Schegloff, 1979:68). For example, the preceding conversation is almost incomprehensible until we understand that *B* is calling to apologize for keeping some borrowed power tools too long. *B* makes a joke out of it by building it into a list (painting, antiquing), and it is only at the end when both are laughing that the apology comes.

Schegloff's conclusion was that even very idiosyncratic cases are to be examined for their organizational pattern:

> Particular cases can, therefore, be examined for their local, interactional, biographical, ethnographic, or other idiosyncratic interest. The same materials can be inspected so as to extract from their local particularities the formal organization into which their particularities are infused. For students of interaction, the organizations through which the work of social life gets accomplished occupy the center of attention.

(Schegloff, 1979:71)

Initiating Laughter

Gail Jefferson (1979; see also Jefferson, 1984) looked at the question of how one knows when to laugh in the course of a conversation. The lay view is that laughter is a totally free event in the course of a conversation or interaction. However, Jefferson found that several basic structural characteristics of an utterance are designed to induce the other party to laugh. The first is the placement, by the speaker, of a laugh at the end of his utterance:

Dan. I thought that was pretty out of sight. Did you hear me say you're a
junkie . . . heh, heh
Dolly. heh, heh, heh.

(adapted from Jefferson, 1979:80)

The second device reported by Jefferson is within-speech laughter—for example, in mid-sentence:

A. You know I didn't . . . you know
B. Hell, *you* know I'm on ret (haha);
A. ehh, yeh, ha ha.

(adapted from Jefferson, 1979:83)

Jefferson concluded from these examples that the occurrence of laughter is more organized than we realize:

> It appears, then, that the order of alternative responses to a candidate laughable is not organized as freely as one might suppose; i.e., the issue is not that *something* should occur, laughter *or* whatever else, but that *laughter* should occur, on a volunteer basis *or* by invitation.

(Jefferson, 1979:83)

Jefferson was interested not only in the decision to laugh but also in the declining of an invitation to laugh. She found that silence after an invitation is not enough, that a clear signal is required indicating refusal of the invitation. If, for example, someone refuses to laugh, a strategy would be to commence, just after the onset of the speaker's laugh, a serious pursuit of the topic.

Glenn (1989) has examined the initiation of shared laughter in a multiparty conversation. Glenn argues that whereas in two-party interactions the speaker ordinarily laughs first, in multiparty interactions someone other than the speaker usually provides the first laugh. In a two-party interaction, the speaker is virtually forced to laugh at his or her own material because there is only one other person present who can perform that function. However, in a multiparty interaction, the fact that there are many other people who can laugh first means that the speaker can better afford the risk of not taking the initiative of being the first to laugh.

Generating Applause

John Heritage and David Greatbatch (1986) have studied the rhetoric of British political speeches (derived from a body of work developed by J. Maxwell Atkinson [1984a, 1984b]) and uncovered basic devices by which speakers generate applause from their audiences. They argue that applause is generated by "statements that are verbally constructed (a) to *emphasize* and thus highlight their contents against a surrounding background of speech materials and (b) to *project a clear completion point* for the message in question" (Heritage and Greatbatch, 1986:116). Emphasis tells the audience that applause is appropriate, and advance notice of a clear completion point allows the audience to begin applauding more or less in unison. In their analysis of British political speeches, Heritage and Greatbatch uncovered seven basic rhetorical devices:

1 *Contrast:* For example, a politician might argue: "Too much is spent on war . . . too little is spent on peace." Such a statement generates applause because, for emphasis, the same point is made first in negative and then in positive terms. The audience is also able to anticipate when to applaud by matching the unfolding of the second half of the statement with the already completed first half.

2 *List:* A list of political issues, especially the often used three-part list, provides emphasis as well as a completion point that can be anticipated by the audience.

3 *Puzzle solution:* Here the politician first poses a puzzle for the audience and then offers a solution. This double presentation of the issue provides emphasis, and the audience can anticipate the completion of the statement at the end of the solution.

4 *Headline—punch line:* Here the politician proposes to make a statement and then makes it.

5 *Combination:* This involves use of two or more of the devices just listed.

6 *Position taking:* This involves an initial description of a state of affairs that the speaker would be expected to feel strongly about. However, at first it is presented nonevaluatively. Only at the end does the speaker offer his or her own position.

7 *Pursuit:* This occurs when an audience fails to respond to a particular message. The speaker may actively pursue applause by, for example, restating the central point.

In the political party conferences studied by Heritage and Greatbatch, these seven devices accounted for slightly more than two-thirds of the total applause. Of the seven, the *contrast* (accounting for almost a quarter of applause events) was by far the most commonly applauded format. The speaker's manner of delivering the message ("intonation, timing, and gesture") also is important (Heritage and Greatbatch, 1986:143). Finally, Heritage and Greatbatch note that the seven devices are not restricted to political speech making, but also are found in advertising slogans, newspaper editorials, scientific texts, and so forth. In fact, they conclude that these devices have their roots and are found in everyday, natural, conversational interaction. The implication is that we all use these devices daily to generate positive reactions from those with whom we interact.

Booing

In a later and parallel piece of research, Steven Clayman (1993) studied booing as an expression of disapproval in the context of public speaking. While applause allows the audience to affiliate with the speaker, booing is an act of disaffiliation.

There are two fundamental ways in which responses such as applause and booing begin—as a result of independent individual decision making or as a product of the mutual monitoring of the behavior of members of an audience. Previous research has demonstrated that individual decision making predominates in the onset of applause. Because the decision is made largely alone, applause occurs almost immediately after a popular remark is made. Also consistent with individual decision making is the fact that applause occurs in a burst that reaches its peak in the first second or two. Further, as demonstrated in the preceding section, a series of well-known devices are employed by speakers to lead audience members to the decision to applaud and then to the applause itself.

Booing, however, is a result more of mutual monitoring than of individual decision making. There is usually a significant time lag between the utterance of the objectionable words and the onset of booing. If booing were the result of a number of individuals making independent decisions, it would occur about as quickly as applause. The time lag tends to indicate that audience members are monitoring the behavior of others before deciding whether or not booing is appropriate. In addition, the onset of booing is often preceded by displays by the audience. For example, the audience may engage in incipient displays of their disaffiliation[4] from the speaker by "a variety of vocalizations—whispering or talking among themselves, talking, shouting, or jeering at the speaker . . . the resulting sound can be characterized as a 'murmur,' 'buzz,' or 'roar'" (Clayman, 1993:117). Audience members monitor these sounds; they indicate to the members that the audience is predisposed to disapprove of the utterance in question. A given audience member feels freer to boo because she has reason to believe that she will not be alone and therefore suffer the disapproval of other audience members.

Of course, one might ask where the incipient displays come from, if not from independent decision making? Clayman believes that some degree of independent decision making is involved here. Individual decision making occurs in the case of incipient displays because the resulting behaviors (for example, private whispering with neighbors, self-talk [for example, "yikes"]) are more private and less likely to be disapproved of by the rest of the audience than is booing. Thus, there is little or no need to monitor the audience in order to determine the appropriateness of such behaviors.

---

[4]Booing is also likely to occur after displays of affiliation such as applause, but a different process is involved and we will not deal with it here.

Clayman is also interested in the methods speakers use to deal with booing. For example, the speaker may interpret the reason for the booing and attempt to offer a counterposition that, it is hoped, will lead to an affiliative response by the audience. Or the speaker may joke about the booing. However, Clayman finds that such explicit techniques are used infrequently, often to deal with particularly intense episodes of booing. Speakers generally do not deal with booing explicitly because such actions call attention to the booing, halt the forward progress of the speech, and may lead to further acts of booing, which are made more likely by the recognition that previous incidents received from the speaker.

The speaker is more likely to use implicit defenses such as talking right through the booing. Such action serves to make the booing less clear, less conspicuous, and may cut it short. Interestingly, this is the opposite of the case of applause, where the speaker tries to avoid speaking until the applause has died down or disappeared altogether. This is because the speaker wishes applause to last as long as possible and talking during applause would tend to cut it short.

Clayman concludes that collectively produced applause and booing are very much like individually produced agreement and disagreement in everyday behavior. In both cases, "Agreements tend to be produced promptly, in an unqualified manner, and are treated as requiring no special explanation or account. Disagreements, by contrast, typically are delayed, qualified, and accountable" (Clayman, 1993:125). This similarity leads to the conclusion that applause and booing may be explained by general interactional principles that cut across all sectors of life and not just by the organizational and institutional structures and norms involved in public speaking. Those "general principles of human conduct" are part of the interaction order which "is a species of social institution in its own right, one that predates and is constitutive of most other societal institutions, and possesses its own indigenous organizational properties and conventional practices" (Clayman, 1993:127). In other words, the fundamental principles being uncovered by conversation analysts allow us to understand the positive (applause) and negative (booing) responses to public speeches.

The Interactive Emergence of Sentences and Stories

Charles Goodwin (1979) challenged the traditional linguistic assumption that sentences can be examined in isolation from the process of interaction in which they occur. His view was that "sentences emerge with conversation" (Goodwin, 1979:97). The fact is that the "speaker can reconstruct the meaning of his sentence *as he is producing it* in order to maintain its appropriateness to its recipient of the moment" (Goodwin, 1979:98; italics added).

Speakers pay acute attention to listeners as they are speaking. As the listeners react verbally, facially, or with body language, the speaker—on the basis of these reactions—adjusts the sentence as it is emerging. The reactions allow the speaker to decide whether his or her point is being made, and if not, to alter the structure of the sentence. Goodwin described some of the alterations that took place in a particular sentence sequence:

> In the course of its production the unfolding meaning of John's sentence is reconstructed twice, a new segment is added to it, and another is deleted prior to its production but replaced with a different segment. The sentence eventually produced emerges as the prod-

uct of a dynamic process of interaction between speaker and hearer as they mutually constructed the turn of talk.

(Goodwin, 1979:112)

In other words, sentences are the products of collaborative processes.

Mandelbaum (1989) has examined the interactive emergence of stories. Her key point is that the audience is not passive, as is conventionally assumed, but rather can be seen as the "co-author" of the story. Paralleling Goodwin's analysis of the interactive emergence of sentences, Mandelbaum shows that the audience members have resources that allow them to work with the author to alter a story while the storytelling is in process. The audience participates by allowing the suspension of turn-by-turn talk so that the storyteller may dominate the conversation. The audience members also help the story along by displaying their understanding through the use of such expressions as "uh huh" and "mm hm." The audience may also "repair" some problem in the story, thereby permitting it to proceed more smoothly. Most important, for the purposes of this discussion, the audience may intervene in the story and cause it to move off in a new direction. Thus, in a very real sense, stories, like sentences and conversations in general, are interactional products.

Formulations

Heritage and Watson (1979) were interested in orderliness within conversations. They placed this issue within the general context of ethnomethodological concerns:

> A central focus of ethnomethodological work is the analysis of the practical sociological reasoning through which social activity is rendered accountable and orderly. Assumed by this concern is the notion that all scenic features of social interaction [for example, biographies, events, personalities, locations] are occasioned and established as a concerted practical accomplishment, in and through which the parties display for one another their competence in the practical management of social order. As analysts, our interest is to explicate, in respect of naturally occurring occasions of use, the methods by which such orderliness can be displayed, managed, and recognized by members.

> (Heritage and Watson, 1979:123–124)

Their specific concern was the issue of when conversational order itself becomes a topic of conversation for the participants. Specifically, they looked at *formulations,* which they defined as a part of a conversation used to describe that conversation. In particular, their concern was a specific type of formulation, one in which an actor seeks to "characterize states of affairs already described or negotiated (in whole or in part) in the preceding talk" (Heritage and Watson, 1979:126).

The conversations that Heritage and Watson used are too lengthy to include here, but the following gives a sense of what they meant by formulations:

A. I was so depressed that . . .
B. Yes
A. . . . that I climbed on the railing of the bridge
B. *You were prepared to commit suicide because . . .*
A. Yes, I am so overweight.

In this example, in saying that *A* was prepared to commit suicide, *B* is formulating what *A* was trying to say in his previous two statements.

Such formulations illustrate the practical management of conversations. A formulation is a part of a conversation in which the objective "is manifestly and specifically to exhibit participants' understanding" (Heritage and Watson, 1979:129). A formulation is one example of how members demonstrate their understanding of what is occurring.

Integration of Talk and Nonvocal Activities

Conversation analysts have focused on talk, and other ethnomethodologists on nonvocal activities. Some researchers are using videotapes and films to analyze the integration of vocal and nonvocal activities. Goodwin (1984), for example, examined a videotape of a dinner party involving two couples. One issue in the relationship between vocal and nonvocal activities is the body posture of a person (in this case Ann) who tells a story at the party:

> Ann clasps her hands together, places both elbows on the table, and leans forward while gazing toward her addressed recipient, Beth. With this posture the speaker displays full orientation toward her addressed recipient, complete engagement in telling her story, and lack of involvement in any activities other than conversation. The posture appears to . . . constitute a visual display that a telling is in progress.
>
> (Goodwin, 1984:228)

More generally, Goodwin concludes, "Ann's telling is thus made visible not only in her talk but also in the way in which she organizes her body and activities during the telling" (1984:229).

Another nonvocal activity examined by Goodwin is the gaze, which he relates to talk:

> When a speaker gazes at a recipient that recipient should be gazing at him. When speakers gaze at nongazing recipients, and thus locate violations of the rule, they frequently produce phrasal breaks such as restarts and pauses, in their talk. These phrasal breaks both orient to the event as a violation by locating the talk in progress at that point as impaired in some fashion and provide a remedy by functioning as requests for the gaze of the hearer. Thus just after phrasal breaks nongazing recipients frequently begin to move their gaze to the speaker.
>
> (Goodwin, 1984:230)

Body posture and gaze are only two of many nonvocal activities that are intimately related to vocal activities.

Doing Shyness (and Self-Confidence)

We tend to think of shyness and self-confidence as psychological traits, but Manning and Ray (1993) have attempted to show that they are things that we "do" as we are managing conversational encounters. There are a range of typical procedures that we all use to get acquainted with those we do not know, and the shy and self-confident modify these procedures, albeit in different ways, in order to deal with social situations distinctively. Thus, the shy and the self-confident employ different conversational strategies.

Manning and Ray conducted a laboratory study with college students involving the videotaping and transcribing of the interaction of ten shy and ten self-confident dyads. While we all engage in "setting-talk"—that is, talk about our immediate environment— shy people do this much more than those who are self-confident. Take the following example:

A. (nervous laughter) A microphone
B. We're being tape recorded
A. I know probably
B. Huh
A. Okay
B. I guess they're going to observe how nervous we are (laughs)
A. I know

(Manning and Ray, 1993:182)

Manning and Ray found that shy participants were more than two and a half times as likely to engage in setting-talk at the beginning of a conversation than those who are self-confident. Further, those who are shy were eight times more likely to return to setting-talk later, whenever the conversation flagged. Manning and Ray conclude, "We believe that shy participants used setting-talk as a 'safe' topic, comparable to discussions about the weather. By contrast . . . self-confident participants viewed setting-talk as a dead end to be avoided" (1993:183). Instead, those high in self-confidence were more likely to exchange names and move immediately into the introduction of a topic for conversation (a "pretopical sequence"). While shy participants tend to reject these pretopical sequences, those who are self-confident are likely to respond to them, and in depth.

One key issue is whether these and other differences in conversation are symptoms of underlying psychological differences, or whether shyness and self-confidence *are* the different conversational procedures. Needless to say, Manning and Ray, adopting the ethnomethodological perspective, tend to prefer the latter view:

> It is possible that the symptoms of shyness and the "state" these symptoms indicate are one and the same . . . "shy" people probably are shy only at certain times and under certain circumstances. Therefore it is reasonable to assume that there is an interactional mechanism for doing shyness, which can be either "activated" or "deactivated" through collaborative efforts to maintain topical talk.
>
> (Manning and Ray, 1993:189)

STUDIES OF INSTITUTIONS

As pointed out earlier in this chapter, a number of ethnomethodologists have grown interested in the study of conversation and interaction in various social institutions. In this section we will examine a few examples of this kind of work.

Job Interviews

Some ethnomethodologists have turned their attention to the work world. For example, Button (1987) has looked at the job interview. Not surprisingly, he sees the interview as a sequential, turn-taking conversation and as the "situated practical accomplishment of the parties to that setting" (Button, 1987:160). One issue addressed in this study involves the things that interviewers can do, after an answer has been given, to move on to something else, thereby preventing the interviewee from returning to, and perhaps correcting, his or her answer. First, the interviewer may indicate that the interview as a whole is over. Second, the interviewer may ask another question that moves the discussion off in a different direction. Third, the interviewer may assess the answer given in such a way that the interviewee is precluded from returning to it.

Button wonders what it is that makes a job interview an interview. He argues that it is not the sign on the door or the gathering together of people. Rather, it is "what those people do, and how they structure and organize their interactions with one another, that achieves for some social settings its characterizability as an interview. This integrally involves the way in which the participants organize their speech exchange with one another" (Button, 1987:170). Thus it is the nature of the interaction, of the conversation, that defines a job interview.

Executive Negotiations

Anderson, Hughes, and Sharrock (1987) have examined the nature of negotiations among business executives. One of their findings about such negotiations is how reasonable, detached, and impersonal they are:

> Everything is carried out in a considered, measured, reasonable way. No personal animus is involved or intended in their maneuverings. It is simply what they do; part of their working day . . . Animosities, disagreements and disputes are always contained, in hand, controlled. If a deal cannot be made this time, so be it.
>
> (Anderson, Hughes, and Sharrock, 1987:155)

This kind of interaction tells us a great deal about the business world.

Interestingly, Anderson, Hughes, and Sharrock go on to argue that what takes place in the business world is no different from what takes place in everyday life. In most of our social relationships we behave the way the business executives described above behaved. "Business life does not take place in a sealed compartment, set off from the rest of social life. It is continuous with and interwoven with it" (Anderson, Hughes, and Sharrock, 1987:155).

Calls to Emergency Centers

Whalen and Zimmerman (1987) have examined telephone calls to emergency communications centers. The context of such calls leads to a reduction of the opening of telephone conversations. In normal telephone conversations we usually find summons-answer, identification-recognition, greeting, and "howareyou" sequences. In emergency calls, however, the opening sequences are reduced and recognitions, greetings, and "howareyou" are routinely absent.

Another interesting aspect of emergency phone calls is that certain opening events that would be ignored in a normal conversation are treated quite seriously:

> . . . those situations in which caller hangs up after dispatcher answers, or there is silence on the line or sounds such as dogs barking, arguing and screaming in the background, or a smoke alarm ringing. Despite the lack of direct conversational engagement on the line, dispatchers initially treat these events as possible indicators of a need for assistance, and thus as functional or *virtual* requests.
>
> (Whalen and Zimmerman, 1987:178)

The peculiar nature of the emergency telephone conversation leads to these and other adaptations to the structure of the normal conversation.

In a related study, Whalen, Zimmerman, and Whalen (1988) looked at a specific emergency telephone conversation that failed, leading to the delayed dispatch of an ambulance and the death of a woman. While the media tended to blame the dispatcher for this incident, Whalen, Zimmerman, and Whalen trace the problem to the nature of the specific emergency phone conversation:

> Our investigation revealed that the participants had rather different understandings of what was happening and different expectations of what was supposed to happen in this conversation. Over the course of the interaction the talk of both caller and nurse-dispatcher (and her supervisor) operated to extend and deepen this misalignment. This misalignment contributed in a fundamental way to a dispute that contaminated and transformed the participants' activity.
>
> (Whalen, Zimmerman, and Whalen, 1988:358)

Thus, it was the nature of the specific conversation, not the abilities of the dispatcher, that "caused" the mishap.

Dispute Resolution in Mediation Hearings

Angela Garcia (1991) analyzed conflict resolution in a California program designed to mediate a variety of disputes—between landlord and tenant, over small sums of money, and among family members or friends. Her ultimate goal is to compare institutional conflict resolution to that which takes place in ordinary conversations. Garcia's key point is that institutional mediation makes conflict resolution easier by eliminating processes that lead to escalating levels of strife in ordinary conversation. Further, when arguments do occur in mediation, procedures exist that do not exist in ordinary conversation that make termination of the conflict possible.

Garcia begins with the familiar concern of conversation analysts with turn taking. Mediation stipulates who is allowed to speak at any given time and what form responses may take. For example, complainants speak first and they may not be interrupted by disputants during their presentations. These constraints on interruptions greatly restrict the amount of conflict in mediated disputes. In contrast, the ability to interrupt in normal conversations greatly escalates the likelihood and amount of conflict. Also reducing the possibility of conflict is the fact that disputants must ask the mediators' permission to speak or to use sanctions. The request may be denied and even if it isn't, the fact that a request has been made serves to mitigate the possibility of direct conflict between disputants. Another key factor in reducing the possibility of conflict is the fact that disputants address their remarks to the mediator rather than to each other. During periods when an issue is under joint discussion, the mediator, not the participants, controls both the topic and who participates by asking disputants directed questions. The mediator therefore serves as both a buffer and a controller and in both roles operates to limit the possibility of conflict.

The mediator seeks especially to limit the possibility of direct and adjacent accusations and denials by the disputants. Such "cross talk" is highly likely to lead to conflict, and mediators seek to prevent it from occurring and are quick to act once it begins. To halt cross talk, the mediator may try to change topics, redirect a question, or sanction the disputants.

In sum, "in mediation, the adjacent and directly addressed oppositional utterances that constitute argument do not occur" (Garcia, 1991:827). Garcia summarizes her conclusions by offering four characteristics of mediation that allow disputants to reduce or eliminate arguments while at the same time saving face:

1 Accusations and denials are not adjacent to one another in the turn-taking system of a mediated dispute, thereby reducing the possibility of escalation into an argument.

2 Denials are made not directly to accusations, but to queries by the mediator. As a result, since they are separated from responses, denials are less likely to provoke disputational responses.

3 Because there is a delay between accusation and response, disputants are permitted not to respond to certain accusations without their lack of response implying that they are guilty of those accusations. The delay allows the disputant to "bypass some accusations, focus on the more important accusations, or ignore accusations she or he cannot credibly deny" (Garcia, 1991:830). The result is that there generally end up being fewer issues on the table about which arguments can occur.

4 Accusations and denials are mitigated by the mediation system. For example, the agent being accused may be referred to implicitly rather than explicitly, may be referred to collectively as "we" with the result that the complainant is including himself as the blamed party, or the accusations themselves can be downgraded by the use of words and phrases like "I would imagine" or "maybe."

Unlike Clayman in his study of booing, Garcia does not argue that the structure of interaction in mediation is similar to the interactional organization of everyday life. In fact, her point is that they are very different interactional orders. However, like Clayman and other conversation analysts, Garcia (1991:833) does see the key to understanding what goes on in interaction, specifically in this case in mediation, in "the interactional order of mediation itself," rather than in the social or normative structure of mediation.

More recently, Greatbatch and Dingwall (1997) examined divorce mediation sessions conducted in ten agencies in England. In contrast to Garcia's study, disputants do talk directly to one another and often become involved in arguments. Given this, Greatbatch and Dingwall are interested in the ways in which such arguments are exited. While mediators can take various actions, the focus in this study is on things that the disputants can do to exit an argument such as one party passing on the opportunity to speak leaving only the other party talking, taking the initiative and addressing the mediator rather than the other disputant, announcing that one is withdrawing from the argument, and offering conciliatory accounts (e.g. "I'm to blame"). In spite of these important differences, in most instances in the British case disputants do not talk directly to one another; they do address mediators. Perhaps of greater importance than the specific differences between the two studies is the fact that Greatbatch and Dingwall (1997:164) also take issue with Garcia's argument that what takes place in such settings is not similar to everyday life: "The deescalatory practices described here are not unique to mediation; they are generic speaking practices deriving from ordinary conversation." In other words, the things that disputants do to exit arguments are similar to the ways in which we extricate ourselves from arguments on a daily basis.

CRITICISMS OF TRADITIONAL SOCIOLOGY

Ethnomethodologists criticize traditional sociologists for imposing *their* sense of social reality on the social world (Mehan and Wood, 1975). They believe that sociology has not been attentive enough to, or respectful enough of, the everyday world that should be its ultimate source of knowledge (Sharrock and Anderson, 1986). More extremely, sociology has rendered the most essential aspects of the social world (ethnomethods) unavailable and focuses instead on a constructed world that conceals everyday practices. Enamored of their own view of the social world, sociologists have tended not to share the same social reality as those they study. As Mehan and Wood put it, "In attempting to do a social *science,* sociology has become alienated from the social" (1975:63).

Within this general orientation, Mehan and Wood (see also Sharrock and Anderson, 1986) leveled a number of specific criticisms at sociology. The concepts used by sociologists are said to distort the social world, to destroy its ebb and flow. Further distortion is caused by sociology's reliance on scientific techniques and statistical analyses of data. Statistics simply do not usually do justice to the elegance and sophistication of the real world. The coding techniques used by sociologists, when they translate human behavior into their preconceived categories, distort the social world. Furthermore, the seeming simplicity of the codes conceals the complicated and distorting work involved in turning aspects of the social world into the sociologist's preconceived categories. Sociologists are also seen as tending to accept unquestioningly a respondent's description of a phenomenon rather than looking at the phenomenon itself. Thus, a description of a social setting is taken to *be* that setting rather than one conception of that setting. Finally, Mehan and Wood argued that sociologists are prone to offer abstractions of the social world that are increasingly removed from the reality of everyday life.

Confusing Topic and Resource   Taking a slightly different approach, Don Zimmerman and Melvin Pollner (1970) argued that conventional sociology has suffered from a confusion of *topic* and *resource.* That is, the everyday social world is a resource for the favorite topics of sociology, but it is rarely a topic in its own right. This can be illustrated in a variety of ways. For example, Roy Turner (1970; see also Sharrock and Anderson, 1986) argued that sociologists usually look at everyday speech not as a topic in itself but as a resource with which to study hidden realities such as norms, values, attitudes, and so on. However, instead of being a resource, everyday speech can be seen as one of the ways in which the business of social life is carried on—a topic in itself. Matthew Speier (1970) argued that when sociologists look at childhood socialization, they look not at the processes themselves but at a series of abstract "stages" generalized from those processes. Speier argued that *"socialization is the acquisition of interactional competencies"* (1970:189). Thus, the ethnomethodologist must look at the way these competencies are acquired and used in the everyday reality of the real world.

Another analysis of childhood socialization, by Robert W. Mackay (1974), is even more useful as a critique of traditional sociology and the confusion of topic and resource. Mackay contrasted the "normative" approach of traditional sociology with the interpretive approach of ethnomethodology. The normative approach is seen as arguing that socialization is merely a series of stages in which "complete" adults teach "incomplete" children the ways of society. Mackay viewed this as a "gloss" that ignores the reality that socialization involves an interaction between children and adults. Children are not passive, incomplete receptacles; rather, they are active participants in the socialization process, because they have the ability to reason, invent, and acquire knowledge. Socialization is a two-sided process. Mackay believed that the ethnomethodological orientation "restores the interaction between adults and children based on interpretive competencies as the phenomenon of study" (1974:183).

Zimmerman and Pollner (1970) cited other examples of the confusion of topic and resource. For example, they argued that sociologists normally explain action in bureaucracies by the rules, norms, and values of the organization. However, had they looked at organizations as topics, they would have seen that actors often simply make it *appear* through their actions that those actions can be explained by the rules. It is not the rules but the actors' *use* of the rules that should be the topic of sociological research. Zimmerman and Pollner then cited the example of a code of behavior among prison convicts. Whereas traditional sociology would look at the ways in which actors are constrained by a convict code, ethnomethodologists would examine how the convicts use the code as an explanatory and persuasive device. Don Zimmerman and Lawrence Wieder offered the following generalization on the confusion of topic and resource:

> The ethnomethodologist is *not* concerned with providing casual explanations of observably regular, patterned, repetitive actions by some kind of analysis of the actor's point of view. He *is* concerned with how members of society go about the task of *seeing, describing,* and *explaining* order in the world in which they live.
>
> (Zimmerman and Wieder, 1970:289)

Social order is not a reality in itself to the ethnomethodologist but an accomplishment of social actors.

STRESSES AND STRAINS IN ETHNOMETHODOLOGY

While ethnomethodology has made enormous strides in sociology and has demonstrated, especially in the area of conversation analysis, some capacity to cumulate knowledge of the world of everyday life, there are some problems worth noting.

First, while ethnomethodology is far more accepted today than it was a decade or two ago, it is still regarded with considerable suspicion by many sociologists (Pollner, 1991). They view it as focusing on trivial matters and ignoring the crucially important issues confronting society today. The ethnomethodologists' response is that they *are* dealing with the crucial issues because it is everyday life that matters most. Paul Atkinson sums up the situation: "Ethnomethodology continues to be greeted with mixtures of incomprehension and hostility in some quarters, but it is unquestionably a force to be reckoned with when it comes to the theory, methods, and empirical conduct of sociological inquiry" (1988:442).

Second, there are those (for example, Atkinson, 1988) who believe that ethnomethodology has lost sight of its phenomenological roots and its concern for conscious, cognitive processes (exceptions are Cicourel [1974] and Coulter [1983, 1989], although the latter is inclined to embed cognition within the everyday world). Instead of focusing on such conscious processes, ethnomethodologists, especially conversation analysts, have come to focus on the "structural properties of the talk itself" (Atkinson, 1988:449). Ignored in the process are motives and the internal motivations for action. In Atkinson's view, ethnomethodology has grown "unduly restricted" and come to be "behaviorist and empiricist" (1988:441). In moving in this direction, ethnomethodology is seen as having gone back on some of its basic principles, including its desire not to treat the actor as a judgmental dope:

> Garfinkel's early inspiration was to reject the judgmental dope image in order to focus attention on the skillful and artful, methodical work put into the production of social order.

In the intervening years, however, some versions of ethnomethodology have returned to the judgmental dope as their model actor. Intentionality and meaning have been all but eliminated.

(Atkinson, 1988:449)

Third, some ethnomethodologists have worried about the link between the concerns in their work (for example, conversations) and the larger social structure. This concern exists even though, as we discussed earlier in the chapter and will return to toward the end, ethnomethodologists tend to see themselves as bridging the micro-macro divide. For example, some years ago, Zimmerman viewed cross-fertilization with macrosociology as "an open question, and an intriguing possibility" (1978:12). Later, Pollner urged ethnomethodology to "return to sociology to understand those [taken-for-granted] practices in their larger social context . . . mundane reason in terms of structural and historical processes. Mundane reason, it is suggested is not simply the product of local work of mundane reasoners, for it is also shaped by longer term and larger scale dynamics" (1987:xvi). Some such cross-fertilization has been undertaken by people like Giddens (1984), who has integrated ethnomethodological ideas into his structuration theory. More generally, Boden (1990a; see the next section) has outlined what ethnomethodology has to offer to the issue of the relationship between structure and agency. She argues that the findings of ethnomethodological studies are relevant not only to micro structures but to macro structures as well. There is hope that institutional studies will shed more light on the macro structure and its relationship to micro-level phenomena.

Fourth, and from within the field, Pollner (1991) has criticized ethnomethodology for losing sight of its original radical reflexivity. Radical reflexivity leads to the view that all social activity is accomplished, including the activities of ethnomethodologists. However, ethnomethodology has come to be more accepted by mainstream sociologists. As Pollner puts it, "Ethnomethodology is settling down in the suburbs of sociology" (1991:370). As they have come to be more accepted, ethnomethodologists have tended to lose sight of the need to analyze their own work. As a result, in Pollner's view, ethnomethodology is in danger of losing its self-analytical and critical edge and becoming just another establishment theoretical specialty.

Finally, it should be noted that although they are discussed under the same heading, there is a growing uneasiness in the relationship between ethnomethodology and conversation analysis (Lynch, 1993:203–264). As mentioned earlier, they have somewhat different roots. More important, in recent years it is conversation analysis that has made the greatest headway in sociology as a whole. Its tendency to study conversations empirically makes it quite acceptable to the discipline's mainstream. The tension between the two is likely to increase if conversation analysis continues to settle into the mainstream while ethnomethodological studies of institutions remain more on the periphery.

SYNTHESIS AND INTEGRATION

Even ethnomethodology, one of the most determinedly micro-extremist perspectives in sociological theory, has shown some signs of openness to synthesis and integration. For example, ethnomethodology seems to be expanding into domains that appear more in line with mainstream sociology. Good examples are Heritage and Greatbatch's (1986) analysis of the methods used to generate applause from audiences and Clayman's (1993) study of booing. Typologies developed by such ethnomethodologists seem little different from the kinds of typologies employed by various other types of sociological theorists.

However, ethnomethodology remains embattled and insecure and thus, in some ways, seems to run counter to the trend toward theoretical synthesis. Seemingly rejecting the idea of synthesis, Garfinkel sees ethnomethodology as an "incommensurably alternate sociology" (1988:108). Boden (1990a) finds it necessary to make a strong, albeit somewhat self-conscious, case *for* ethnomethodology and conversation analysis. It is certainly true, as Boden suggests, that ethnomethodology has widened and deepened its support in sociology. However, one wonders whether it, or any other sociological theory for that matter, is, as Boden contends, "here to stay." In any case, such an argument contradicts the idea that theoretical boundaries are weakening and new synthetic perspectives are emerging. It may be that ethnomethodology is still too new and too insecure to consider an erosion of its boundaries.

Nevertheless, much of Boden's (1990a) essay deals with synthetic efforts *within* ethnomethodology, especially regarding integrative issues such as the relationship between agency and structure, the embeddedness of action, and fleeting events within the course of history. Boden also deals with the extent to which an array of European and American theorists have begun to integrate ethnomethodology and conversation analysis into their orientations. Unfortunately, what is lacking is a discussion of the degree to which ethnomethodologists are integrating the ideas of other sociological theories into their perspective. Ethnomethodologists seem quite willing to have other theorists integrate ethnomethodological perspectives, but they seem far less eager to reciprocate.

Ethnomethodology and Symbolic Interactionism

Boden (1990b) has also contributed to the slight movement within ethnomethodology toward synthesis in her discussion of its linkages to symbolic interactionism. Conversation analysis is, as we saw earlier, focally concerned with talk. As Boden puts it, "Talk is the stuff, the very sinew, of social interaction. The mundane of momentous talk of people in their everyday work is what conversation analysis studies" (1990b:244). While symbolic interactionists are interested in talk, their main concern is with action and interaction. Boden (1990b:244) provides the linkage here by defining *talk* as "language-in-action" and arguing that "it is here, as thought becomes action through language, that conversation analysis meets symbolic interaction (and vice versa)." She goes further to note that the social world needs "to be studied in situ, and the combined creative forces of symbolic interaction and conversation analysis can expose just that momentary yet recurrent and patterned quality of the world" (Boden, 1990b:246).

To further solidify the linkage between symbolic interactionism and conversation analysis, Boden suggests redefining conversation analysis. She argues that the term *conversation analysis* is, in fact, too narrow because researchers are interested, as we saw earlier, in far more than the exchange of words. She suggests, instead, that such work be called "interactional analysis" because researchers are interested in "everything in the interaction, from a quiet in-breath to the entire spatial and temporal organization of the scene" (Boden, 1990b:248). By using the term *interactional analysis* to describe the interest in both verbal and nonverbal phenomena, Boden clearly aligns conversation analysis with symbolic interactionism.

As we saw in Chapter 6, Mead was interested in mental processes but saw them as forms of action and interaction. This is part of Mead's effort to extend behaviorism into the mind. Boden contends that "the symbolic interaction that is *thought,* in Mead's sense, becomes quite concretely available, both for analysis and further theorizing, through the fine-grained activities of talk in interaction" (1990b:253). Thus, in studying talk, conversation analysts (and symbolic interactionists) are shedding light on mental processes. Similarly, Boden seeks to link conversation analysis with Blumer's interest in "joint action." Her point here is that conversation is joint action not just in the sense that it is negotiated locally but also in the sense that "talk and tasks are mutually elaborative in a turn-by-turn manner" (Boden, 1990b:255).

In her conclusion, Boden offers some broad linkages between conversation analysis and symbolic interactionism: "Symbolic interactionists and conversation analysts travel together more broadly along a route that examines the intertwining of meaning, shared symbols, joint action, and social order" (1990b:265). Furthermore, she explicitly links the two theories to the integrative concerns discussed in the previous chapter: "Thus, at the larger intersection of *agency and structure,* sociologists generally may expect to find both symbolic interactionists and conversation analysts" (Boden, 1990b:265; italics added).

Ethnomethodology and the Micro-Macro Order

Boden's effort to tie the relationship between conversation analysis and symbolic interactionism to agency and structure brings us to Hilbert's (1990) work on the relationship between ethnomethodology and the micro-macro order. As we saw earlier, Hilbert rejects the conventional idea that ethnomethodology is a microsociology, but it is not, in his view, to be seen as a macrosociology either. Rather, Hilbert argues that ethnomethodology "transcends" the micro-macro issue because it is concerned "with social practices [membership practices] which are the methods of producing *both* microstructure and macrostructure as well as any presumed 'linkage' between these two" (1990:794).

Hilbert, somewhat erroneously (see Chapter 10), reduces the micro-macro linkage issue to a set of structural concerns. That is, it involves a focus on micro structures, macro structures, and the linkage between them. In Hilbert's view, ethnomethodologists are "indifferent" to structures *at any level.* Instead of being concerned with either micro or macro structures, ethnomethodologists are interested in the membership practices, the "ethnomethods," "the artful production," of structure in general. That is, ethnomethodologists are interested in the "methods of producing, maintaining, sustaining, and reproducing social structure by and for the membership, whether oriented to large scale institutional (macro) structure or smaller, more intimate (micro) structure" (Hilbert, 1990:799).

Hilbert offers what he calls the "radical thesis" of ethnomethodology, which serves to transcend the issue of micro-macro linkage:

> The empirical phenomena that conversation analysts witness but which members cannot possibly know about, and . . . the structural phenomena that members orient to and take

for granted but which nevertheless are nonempirical and unavailable for social science are (in a subtle way) . . . *the same phenomena.*

(Hilbert, 1990:801)

In other words, to the ethnomethodologist there is no distinction to be made between micro and macro structures because they are simultaneously generated. However, neither ethnomethodologists nor any other sociological theorists have offered the ultimate solution to the micro-macro issue. Hilbert's effort is marred by his reduction of this issue to a concern for the linkage of micro and macro *structures.* As we will see in Chapter 10, there is far more to this issue than such a linkage. Nevertheless, the ethnomethodologists do offer an interesting, indeed radical, approach to this question, dissolving it and arguing that the micro and the macro are the same thing! Certainly one way to deal with the micro-macro issue is to refuse to separate the two levels, seeing them instead as part of the same general process.

SUMMARY

This chapter has been devoted to a very distinctive kind of sociology and sociological theory—ethnomethodology. Ethnomethodology is the study of the everyday practices used by the ordinary members of society in order to deal with their day-to-day lives. People are seen as accomplishing their everyday lives through a variety of artful practices. Over the years, ethnomethodology has grown increasingly diverse. However, the two main varieties of ethnomethodology are institutional studies and conversation analysis.

We examined several early examples of ethnomethodology including "breaching experiments," as well as Garfinkel's famous study of Agnes and the ways in which "she" accomplished being a female (even though "she" was actually a he). The bulk of the chapter is devoted to a discussion of the heart of ethnomethodology—studies of conversations and institutions. Included in the discussion of studies of conversations are reviews of work on such things as how people know when it is appropriate to laugh, applaud, and boo. We also discussed several institutional studies, including one that dealt with the way disputes are resolved in mediation hearings.

Ethnomethodologists tend to be highly critical of mainstream sociology. For example, mainstream sociologists are seen as imposing their sense of social reality on people rather than studying what people actually do. Sociologists distort the social world in various ways through imposing their concepts, utilizing statistics, and so on. Sociologists are also accused of confusing topic and resource—that is, using the everyday world as a resource rather than as a topic in its own right.

There are a variety of stresses and strains within ethnomethodology, including its continued exclusion from the mainstream of sociology, the accusation that it has lost sight of cognitive processes, the inability to deal adequately with social structures, the loss of its original radical quality, and the tension between ethnomethodologists and conversation analysts. The chapter closes with a discussion of some work within ethnomethodology on integration and synthesis. However, there are those who regard ethnomethodology as incompatible with other sociological theories.

8

EXCHANGE, NETWORK, AND RATIONAL CHOICE THEORIES

EXCHANGE THEORY
  Behaviorism
  Rational Choice Theory
  The Social Psychology of Groups
  The Exchange Theory of George Homans
  Peter Blau's Exchange Theory
  The Work of Richard Emerson and His Disciples
NETWORK THEORY
RATIONAL CHOICE THEORY
  Foundations of Social Theory

In this chapter we will focus on three related theories—exchange theory, rational choice theory, and network theory. Rational choice theory was one of the intellectual influences that helped shape the development of exchange theory, especially its tendency to assume a rational actor. However, while contemporary exchange theory continues to demonstrate the influence of rational choice theory, it has been affected by other intellectual currents and has gone off in a series of unique directions. Thus, contemporary exchange and rational choice theories are far from coterminous. One fundamental difference is that while rational choice theorists focus on individual decision making, the basic unit of analysis to the exchange theorist is the social relationship. Recently, exchange theorists have been devoting more attention to networks of social relationships, and this focus tends to connect them with network theory itself. Network theory has much in common with rational choice theory, although it rejects the assumption of the rationality of human actors (Mizruchi, 1994). Overall, and unlike the theories discussed in the preceding two chapters, these theories share a positivistic orientation.

EXCHANGE THEORY

We begin, following Molm and Cook (1995), with an overview of the history of the development of exchange theory, beginning with its roots in behaviorism.

Behaviorism

Behaviorism is best known in psychology, but in sociology it had both direct effects on behavioral sociology (Bushell and Burgess, 1969; Baldwin and Baldwin, 1986) and indirect effects, especially on exchange theory. The behavioral sociologist is concerned with the relationship between the effects of an actor's behavior on the environment and their impact on the actor's later behavior. This relationship is basic to *operant conditioning,* or the learning process by which "behavior is modified by its consequences" (Baldwin and Baldwin, 1986:6). One might almost think of this behavior, at least initially in the infant, as a random behavior. The environment in which the behavior exists, be it social or physical, is affected by the behavior and in turn "acts" back in various ways. That reaction—positive, negative, or neutral—affects the actor's later behavior. If the reaction has been rewarding to the actor, the same behavior is likely to be emitted in the future in similar situations. If the reaction has been painful or punishing, the behavior is less likely to occur in the future. The behavioral sociologist is interested in the relationship between the *history* of environmental reactions or consequences and the nature of present behavior. Past consequences of a given behavior govern its present state. By knowing what elicited a certain behavior in the past, we can predict whether an actor will produce the same behavior in the present situation.

Of great interest to behaviorists are rewards (or reinforcers) and costs (or punishments). Rewards are defined by their ability to strengthen (that is, reinforce) behavior, while costs reduce the likelihood of behavior. As we will see, behaviorism in general, and the ideas of rewards and costs in particular, had a powerful impact on early exchange theory.

Rational Choice Theory

The basic principles of rational choice theory are derived from neoclassical economics (as well as utilitarianism and game theory; Levi et al., 1990). Based on a variety of different models, Friedman and Hechter (1988) have put together what they describe as a "skeletal" model of rational choice theory.

The focus in rational choice theory is on actors. Actors are seen as being purposive, or as having intentionality. That is, actors have ends or goals toward which their actions are aimed. Actors are also seen as having preferences (or values, utilities). Rational choice theory is unconcerned with what these preferences, or their sources, are. Of importance is the fact that action is undertaken to achieve objectives that are consistent with an actor's preference hierarchy.

Although rational choice theory starts with actors' purposes or intentions, it must take into consideration at least two major constraints on action. The first is the scarcity of resources. Actors have different resources as well as differential access to other resources. For those with lots of resources, the achievement of ends may be relatively easy. However, for those with few, if any, resources, the attainment of ends may be difficult or impossible.

Related to scarcity of resources is the idea of *opportunity costs* (Friedman and Hechter, 1988:202). In pursuing a given end, actors must keep an eye on the costs of forgoing their next-most-attractive action. An actor may choose not to pursue the most highly valued end if her resources are negligible, if as a result the chances of achieving that end are slim, and if in striving to achieve that end she jeopardizes her chances of achieving her next-most-valued end. Actors are seen as trying to maximize their bene-fits,[1] and that goal may involve assessing the relationship between the chances of achieving a primary end and what that achievement does for chances for attaining the second-most-valuable objective.

A second source of constraints on individual action is social institutions. As Fried-man and Hechter put it, an individual will typically

> find his or her actions checked from birth to death by familial and school rules; laws and ordinances; firm policies; churches, synagogues and mosques; and hospitals and funeral parlors. By restricting the feasible set of courses of action available to individuals, en-forceable rules of the game—including norms, laws, agendas, and voting rules—system-atically affect social outcomes.
>
> (Friedman and Hechter, 1988:202)

These institutional constraints provide both positive and negative sanctions that serve to encourage certain actions and to discourage others.

Friedman and Hechter enumerate two other ideas that they see as basic to rational choice theory. The first is an aggregation mechanism, or the process by which "the sep-arate individual actions are combined to produce the social outcome" (Friedman and Hechter, 1988:203). The second is the importance of information in making rational choices. At one time, it was assumed that actors had perfect, or at least sufficient, in-formation to make purposive choices among the alternative courses of action open to them. However, there is a growing recognition that the quantity or quality of available information is highly variable and that variability has a profound effect on actors' choices (Heckathorn, 1997).

At least in its early formation, exchange theory was affected by a rudimentary theory of rationality. Later in this chapter, when we deal with rational choice theory itself, we will deal with some of the greater complexity associated with it.

The Social Psychology of Groups

The bulk of *The Social Psychology of Groups* (Thibaut and Kelley, 1959) is devoted to dyadic relationships. Thibaut and Kelley are focally interested in interaction and its consequences for the members of the dyad. As in behaviorism (although their work shows little direct influence of behaviorism) and in exchange theory, rewards and costs are central to Thibaut and Kelley's analysis of dyadic relationships:

> The reward-cost positions the members of a dyad may achieve in the relationship will be better (1) the more rewarding to the other is the behavior each can produce and (2) the lower the cost at which such behavior can be produced. If both persons are able to pro-duce their maximum rewards for the other at minimum cost to themselves, the relation-ship will not only provide each with excellent reward-cost positions but will have the additional advantage that both persons will be able to achieve their best reward-cost po-sitions at the same time.
>
> (Thibaut and Kelley, 1959:31)

---

[1]Although contemporary rational choice theorists recognize that there are limits on the desire and ability to maximize (Heckathorn, 1997).

Molm and Cook (1995) argue that three aspects of Thibaut and Kelley's theory were of particular importance to the development of exchange theory. The first is their interest in power and dependence, an issue that became central to Richard Emerson and his followers (see below). Thibaut and Kelley see power as deriving from the ability of one actor in a dyad to affect the quality of outcomes attained by the other actor. They differentiate between two types of power. The first is *fate control,* which occurs when actor A can affect the outcomes of actor B *"regardless of what B does"* (Thibaut and Kelley, 1959:102). The second is *behavior control:* "If, by varying his behavior, A can make it desirable for B to vary his behavior too, then A has behavior control over B" (Thibaut and Kelley, 1959:103). In a dyad, both participants are dependent on the relationship. As a result, each has power over the other to some degree. This mutual dependency limits the amount of power one can exercise over the other.

The second key concern of Thibaut and Kelley involves the ideas of *comparison level* (CL) and *comparison level for alternatives* (CL_{alt}). Both are standards for the evaluation of outcomes of relationships. CL is the standard by which an actor determines whether a relationship is attractive or satisfactory. This standard is usually based on what the actor thinks she deserves from the relationship. Relationships which stand above the CL are deemed satisfying; those that fall below are considered unsatisfying. The determination of the location of CL is based on personal or symbolic experience with the totality of outcomes known to the actor. CL_{alt} is the standard used by an actor to decide whether or not to remain in a relationship. When outcomes drop below the CL_{alt}, the actor will leave a relationship. The determination of the level of CL_{alt} is based on the best—that is, most rewarding and least costly—alternatives available to an actor. Molm and Cook argue that this kind of thinking provided the base for some of Emerson's ideas on social networks: "Although Thibaut and Kelley focused primarily on the dyad and never developed the concept of alternatives into the idea of social networks, in which actors have alternative exchange partners, the concept of CL_{alt} laid the foundation for Emerson to do so later" (1995:213).

The third significant contribution by Thibaut and Kelley to exchange theory is their notion of the "outcome matrix," a way of visually depicting "all of the possible events that may occur in the interaction between A and B" (Thibaut and Kelley, 1959:13). The two axes of the matrix are all items in the behavior repertoires of A and B. Within each cell of the matrix is entered "the outcomes, in terms of rewards gained and costs incurred, to each person of that particular portion of the interaction" (Thibaut and Kelley, 1959:13). This matrix was used during the 1960s and 1970s in research on things like bargaining and cooperating to deal with patterns of interdependence, and this research, in turn, "provided the impetus for later, more sophisticated studies of social exchange" (Molm and Cook, 1995:214).

The Exchange Theory of George Homans

The heart of George Homans's exchange theory lies in a set of fundamental propositions. Although some of Homans's propositions deal with at least two interacting individuals, he was careful to point out that these propositions are based on psychological principles. According to Homans, they are psychological for two reasons. First, "they are usually stated and empirically tested by persons who call themselves psychologists" (Homans, 1967:39–40). Second, and more important, they are psychological because of the level at which they deal with the individual in society: "They are propositions about the behavior of individual human beings, rather than propositions about groups or societies as such; and *the behavior of men, as men,* is generally considered the province of psychology" (Homans, 1967:40; italics added). As a result of this position, Homans admitted to being "what has been called—and it is a horrid phrase—a psychological reductionist" (1974:12). Reductionism, to Homans is "the process of showing how the propositions of one named science [in this case, sociology] follow in logic from the more general propositions of another named science [in this case, psychology]" (1984:338).

Although Homans made the case for psychological principles, he did not think of individuals as isolated. He recognized that people are social and spend a considerable portion of their time interacting with other people. He attempted to explain social behavior with psychological principles: "What the position [Homans's] does assume is that the general propositions of psychology, which are propositions about the effects on human behavior of the results thereof, do not change when the results come from other men rather than from the physical environment" (Homans, 1967:59). Homans did not deny the Durkheimian position that something new emerges from interaction. Instead, he argued that those emergent properties can be explained by psychological principles; there is no need for new sociological propositions to explain social facts. He used the basic sociological concept of a norm as illustration:

> The great example of a social fact is a social norm, and the norms of the groups to which they belong certainly constrain towards conformity the behavior of many more individuals. The question is not that of the existence of constraint, but of its explanation. . . . The norm does not constrain automatically: individuals conform, when they do so, because they perceive it is to their net advantage to conform, and it is psychology that deals with the effect on behavior of perceived advantage.
>
> (Homans, 1967:60)

Homans detailed a program to "bring men back in[to]" sociology, but he also tried to develop a theory that focuses on psychology, people, and the "elementary forms of social life." According to Homans, this theory "envisages social *behavior* as an exchange of activity, tangible or intangible, and more or less rewarding or costly, between at least two persons" (1961:13; italics added).

For example, Homans sought to explain the development of power-driven machinery in the textile industry, and thereby the Industrial Revolution, through the psychological principle that people are likely to act in such a way as to increase their rewards. More generally, in his version of exchange theory, he sought to explain elementary social behavior in terms of rewards and costs. He was motivated in part by the structural-functional theories of his acknowledged "colleague and friend" Talcott Parsons. He argued that such theories "possess every virtue except that of explaining anything" (Homans, 1961:10). To Homans, the structural functionalists did little more than create conceptual categories and schemes. Homans admitted that a scientific sociology needs such categories, but sociology "also needs a set of general propositions about the relations among the categories, for without such propositions explanation is impossible. No explanation without propositions!" (1974:10). Homans, therefore, set for himself the task of developing those propositions that focus on the psychological level; these form the groundwork of exchange theory.

In *Social Behavior: Its Elementary Forms* (1961, 1974),[2] Homans acknowledged that his exchange theory is derived from both behavioral psychology and elementary economics (rational choice theory). In fact, Homans (1984) regrets that his theory was labeled "exchange theory" because he sees it as a behavioral psychology applied to specific situations. Homans began with a discussion of the exemplar of the behaviorist paradigm, B. F. Skinner, in particular of Skinner's study of pigeons:[3]

> Suppose, then, that a fresh or naive pigeon is in its cage in the laboratory. One of the items in its inborn repertory of behavior which it uses to explore its environment is the peck. As the pigeon wanders around the cage pecking away, it happens to hit a round red target, at which point the waiting psychologists or, it may be, an automatic machine feeds it grain. The evidence is that the probability of the pigeon's emitting the behavior again—the probability, that is, of its not just pecking but pecking on the target—has increased. In Skinner's language the pigeon's behavior in pecking the target is an *operant;* the operant has been *reinforced;* grain is the *reinforcer;* and the pigeon has undergone *operant conditioning.* Should we prefer our language to be ordinary English, we may say that the pigeon has learned to peck the target by being rewarded for doing so.
>
> (Homans, 1961:18)

Skinner was interested in this instance in pigeons; Homans's concern was humans. According to Homans, Skinner's pigeons are not engaged in a true exchange relationship with the psychologist. The pigeon is engaged in a one-sided exchange relationship, whereas human exchanges are at least two-sided. The pigeon is being reinforced by the grain, but the psychologist is not truly being reinforced by the pecks of the pigeon. The pigeon is carrying on the same sort of relationship with the psychologist as it would with the physical environment. Because there is no reciprocity, Homans defined this as *individual behavior.* Homans seemed to relegate the study of this sort of behavior to the psychologist, whereas he urged the sociologist to study social behavior "where the activity of each of at least two animals reinforces (or punishes) the activity of the other, and where accordingly each influences the other" (1961:30). However, it is significant that, according to Homans, *no new propositions* are needed to explain social behavior as opposed to individual behavior. The laws of individual behavior as developed by Skinner in his study of pigeons explain social behavior as long as we take into account the complications of mutual reinforcement. Homans admitted that he might ultimately have to go beyond the principles derived by Skinner, but only reluctantly.

In his theoretical work, Homans restricted himself to everyday social interaction. It is clear, however, that he believed that a sociology built on his principles would ulti-

---

[2]In the following discussion we move back and forth between the two editions of Homans's book. We do not restrict ourselves to the revised edition because many aspects of the first edition more clearly reflect Homans's position. In the preface to the revised edition, he said that although it was a thorough revision, he had not "altered the substance of the underlying argument" (Homans, 1974:v). Thus we feel safe in dealing simultaneously with both volumes.

[3]Skinner also studied other species, including humans.

mately be able to explain all social behavior. Here is the case Homans used to exemplify the kind of exchange relationship he was interested in:

> Suppose that two men are doing paperwork jobs in an office. According to the office rules, each should do his job by himself, or, if he needs help, he should consult the supervisor. One of the men, whom we shall call Person, is not skillful at the work and would get it done better and faster if he got help from time to time. In spite of the rules he is reluctant to go to the supervisor, for to confess his incompetence might hurt his chances for promotion. Instead he seeks out the other man, whom we shall call Other for short, and asks him for help. Other is more experienced at the work than is Person; he can do his work well and quickly and be left with time to spare, and he has reason to suppose that the supervisor will not go out of his way to look for a breach of rules. Other gives Person help and in return Person gives Other thanks and expressions of approval. The two men have exchanged help and approval.
>
> (Homans, 1961:31–32)

Focusing on this sort of situation, and basing his ideas on Skinner's findings, Homans developed several propositions.

The Success Proposition

> For all actions taken by persons, the more often a particular action of a person is rewarded, the more likely the person is to perform that action.
>
> (Homans, 1974:16)

In terms of Homans's Person-Other example in an office situation, this proposition means that a person is more likely to ask others for advice if he or she has been rewarded in the past with useful advice. Furthermore, the more often a person received useful advice in the past, the more often he or she will request more advice. Similarly, the other person will be more willing to give advice and give it more frequently if he or she often has been rewarded with approval in the past. Generally, behavior in accord with the success proposition involves three stages: first, a person's action; next, a rewarded result; and finally, a repetition of the original action or at minimum one similar in at least some respects.

Homans specified a number of things about the success proposition. First, although it is generally true that increasingly frequent rewards lead to increasingly frequent actions, this reciprocation cannot go on indefinitely. At some point individuals simply cannot act that way as frequently. Second, the shorter the interval between behavior and reward, the more likely a person is to repeat the behavior. Conversely, long intervals between behavior and reward lower the likelihood of repeat behavior. Finally, it was Homans's view that intermittent rewards are more likely to elicit repeat behavior than regular rewards. Regular rewards lead to boredom and satiation, whereas rewards at irregular intervals (as in gambling) are very likely to elicit repeat behaviors.

The Stimulus Proposition

> If in the past the occurrence of a particular stimulus, or set of stimuli, has been the occasion on which a person's action has been rewarded, then the more similar the present stimuli are to the past ones, the more likely the person is to perform the action, or some similar action.
>
> (Homans, 1974:23)

Again we look at Homans's office example: If, in the past, Person and Other found the giving and getting of advice rewarding, then they are likely to engage in similar actions in similar situations in the future. Homans offered an even more down-to-earth example: "A fisherman who has cast his line into a dark pool and has caught a fish becomes more apt to fish in dark pools again" (1974:23).

Homans was interested in the process of *generalization,* that is, the tendency to extend behavior to similar circumstances. In the fishing example, one aspect of generalization would be to move from fishing in dark pools to fishing in any pool with any degree of shadiness. Similarly, success in catching fish is likely to lead from one kind of fishing to another (for instance, freshwater to saltwater) or even from fishing to hunting. However, the process of *discrimination* is also of importance. That is, the actor may fish only under the specific circumstances that proved successful in the past. For one thing, if the conditions under which success occurred were too complicated, then similar conditions may not stimulate behavior. If the crucial stimulus occurs too long before behavior is required, then it may not actually stimulate that behavior. An actor can become oversensitized to stimuli, especially if they are very valuable to the actor. In fact, the actor could respond to irrelevant stimuli, at least until the situation is corrected by repeated failures. All this is affected by the individual's alertness or attentiveness to stimuli.

The Value Proposition

The more valuable to a person is the result of his action, the more likely he is to perform the action.

(Homans, 1974:25)

In the office example, if the rewards each offers to the other are considered valuable, then the actors are more likely to perform the desired behaviors than if the rewards are not valuable. At this point, Homans introduced the concepts of rewards and punishments. Rewards are actions with positive values; an increase in rewards is more likely to elicit the desired behavior. Punishments are actions with negative values; an increase in punishment means that the actor is less likely to manifest undesired behaviors. Homans found punishments to be an inefficient means of getting people to change their behavior, because people may react in undesirable ways to the punishment. It is preferable simply not to reward undesirable behavior; then such behavior eventually becomes extinguished. Rewards are clearly to be preferred, but they may be in short supply. Homans did make it clear that his is not simply a hedonistic theory; rewards can be either materialistic (for example, money) or altruistic (helping others).

The Deprivation-Satiation Proposition

The more often in the recent past a person has received a particular reward, the less valuable any further unit of that reward becomes for him.

(Homans, 1974:29)

In the office, Person and Other may reward each other so often for giving and getting advice that the rewards cease to be valuable to each other. Time is crucial here; people are less likely to become satiated if particular rewards are stretched over a long period of time.

At this point, Homans defined two other critical concepts: cost and profit. The *cost* of any behavior is defined as the rewards lost in forgoing alternative lines of action. *Profit* in social exchange is seen as the greater number of rewards gained over costs incurred. The latter led Homans to recast the deprivation-satiation proposition as "the greater the profit a person receives as a result of his action, the more likely he is to perform the action" (1974:31).

The Aggression-Approval Propositions

Proposition A: When a person's action does not receive the reward he expected, or receives punishment he did not expect, he will be angry; he becomes more likely to perform aggressive behavior, and the results of such behavior become more valuable to him.

(Homans, 1974:37)

In the office case, if Person does not get the advice he or she expected and Other does not receive the praise he or she anticipated, then both are likely to be angry.[4] We are surprised to find the concepts of frustration and anger in Homans's work, because they would seem to refer to mental states. In fact, Homans admitted as much: "When a person does not get what he expected, he is said to be frustrated. A purist in behaviorism would not refer to the expectation at all, because the word seems to refer . . . to a state of mind" (1974:31). Homans went on to argue that frustration of such expectations need *not* refer "only" to an internal state. It can also refer to "wholly external events," observable not just by Person but also by outsiders.

Proposition A on aggression-approval refers only to negative emotions, whereas Proposition B deals with more positive emotions:

Proposition B: When a person's action receives the reward he expected, especially a greater reward than he expected, or does not receive punishment he expected, he will be pleased; he becomes more likely to perform approving behavior, and the results of such behavior become more valuable to him.

(Homans, 1974:39)

For example, in the office, when Person gets the advice that he or she expects and Other gets the praise that he or she expects, both are pleased and more likely to get or give advice. Advice and praise become more valuable to each.

The Rationality Proposition

In choosing between alternative actions, a person will choose that one for which, as perceived by him at the time, the value, V, of the result, multiplied by the probability, p, of getting the result, is the greater.

(Homans, 1974:43)

---

[4]Although Homans still called this the "law of distributive justice" in the revised later edition, he developed the concept more extensively in the first edition. *Distributive justice* refers to whether the rewards and costs are distributed fairly among the individuals involved. In fact, Homans originally stated it as a proposition: "The more to a man's disadvantage the rule of distributive justice fails of realization, the more likely he is to display the emotional behavior we call anger" (1961:75).

GEORGE CASPAR HOMANS: An Autobiographical Sketch

How I became a sociologist, which was largely a matter of accident, I have described in other publications. [For a full autobiography, see Homans, 1984.] My sustained work in sociology began with my association, beginning in 1933, with Professors Lawrence Henderson and Elton Mayo at the Harvard Business School. Henderson, a biochemist, was studying the physiological characteristics of industrial work, Mayo, a psychologist, the human factors. Mayo was then and later the director of the famous researches at the Hawthorne Plant of the Western Electric Company in Chicago.

I took part in a course of readings and discussions under Mayo's direction. Among other books, Mayo asked his students to read several books by prominent social anthropologists, particularly Malinowski, Radcliffe-Brown, and Firth. Mayo wanted us to read these books so that we should understand how in aboriginal, in contrast to modern, societies social rituals supported productive work.

I became interested in them for a wholly different reason. In those days the cultural anthropologists were intellectually dominant, and friends of mine in this group, such as Clyde Kluckhohn, insisted that every culture was unique. Instead I began to perceive from my reading that certain institutions of aboriginal societies repeated themselves in places so far separated in time and space that the societies could not have borrowed them from one another. Cultures were not unique and, what was more, their similarities could only be explained on the assumption that human nature was the same the world over. Members of the human species working in similar circumstances had independently created the similar institutions. This was not a popular view at the time. I am not sure it is now.

By this time I had also been exposed to a number of concrete or "field" studies of small human groups both modern and aboriginal. When I was called to active duty in the Navy in World War II, I reflected on this material during long watches at sea. Quite suddenly, I conceived that a number of these studies might be described in concepts common to them all. In a few days I had sketched out such a conceptual scheme.

Back at Harvard with a tenured position after the war, I began working on a book, later entitled *The Human Group,* which was intended to apply my conceptual scheme to the studies in question. In the course of this work it occurred to me that a conceptual scheme was

While the earlier propositions rely heavily on behaviorism, the rationality proposition demonstrates most clearly the influence of rational choice theory on Homans's approach. In economic terms, actors who act in accord with the rationality proposition are maximizing their utilities.

Basically, people examine and make calculations about the various alternative actions open to them. They compare the amount of rewards associated with each course of action. They also calculate the likelihood that they will actually receive the rewards. Highly valued rewards will be devalued if the actors think it unlikely that they will obtain them. On the other hand, lesser-valued rewards will be enhanced if they are seen as highly attainable. Thus, there is an interaction between the value of the reward and the likelihood of attainment. The most desirable rewards are those that are *both* very valuable *and* highly attainable. The least desirable rewards are those that are not very valuable and are unlikely to be attained.

useful only as the starting point of a science. What was next required were propositions re-lating the concepts to one another. In *The Human Group,* I stated a number of such propo-sitions, which seemed to hold good for the groups I had chosen.

I had long known Professor Talcott Parsons and was now closely associated with him in the Department of Social Relations. The sociological profession looked upon him as its lead-ing theorist. I decided that what he called theories were only conceptual schemes, and that a theory was not a theory unless it contained at least a few propositions. I became confident that this view was correct by reading several books on the philosophy of science.

Nor was it enough that a theory should contain propositions. A theory of a phenomenon was an explanation of it. Explanation consisted in showing that one or more propositions of a low order of generality followed in logic from more general propositions applied to what were variously called given or boundary conditions or parameters. I stated my position on this issue in my little book *The Nature of Social Science* (1967).

I then asked myself what general propositions I could use in this way to explain the em-pirical propositions I had stated in *The Human Group* and other propositions brought to my attention by later reading of field and experimental studies in social psychology. The general propositions would have to meet only one condition: in accordance with my original insight, they should apply to individual human beings as members of a species.

Such propositions were already at hand—luckily, for I could not have invented them for myself. They were the propositions of behavioral psychology as stated by my old friend B. F. Skinner and others. They held good of persons both when acting alone in the physical envi-ronment and when in interaction with other persons. In the two editions of my book *Social Behavior* (1961 and revised in 1974), I used these propositions to try to explain how, under appropriate given conditions, relatively enduring social structures could arise from, and be maintained by, the actions of individuals, who need not have intended to create the struc-tures. This I conceive to be the central intellectual problem of sociology.

Once the structures have been created, they have further effects on the behavior of per-sons who take part in them or come into contact with them. But these further effects are ex-plained by the same propositions as those used to explain the creation and maintenance of the structures in the first place. The structures only provide new given conditions to which the propositions are to be applied. My sociology remains fundamentally individualistic and not collectivistic.

[George Homans died in 1989; see Bell, 1992, for a biographical sketch of Homans.]

Homans relates the rationality proposition to the success, stimulus, and value propo-sitions. The rationality proposition tells us that whether or not people will perform an action depends on their perceptions of the probability of success. But what determines this perception? Homans argues that perceptions of whether chances of success are high or low are shaped by past successes and the similarity of the present situation to past successful situations. The rationality proposition also does not tell us why an actor val-ues one reward more than another; for this we need the value proposition. In these ways, Homans links his rationality principle to his more behavioristic propositions.

In the end, Homans's theory can be condensed to a view of the actor as a rational profit seeker. However, Homans's theory was weak on mental states (Abrahamsson, 1970; J. N. Mitchell, 1978) and large-scale structures (Ekeh, 1974). For example, on consciousness Homans admitted the need for a "more fully developed psychology" (1974:45).

Despite such weaknesses, Homans remained a behaviorist who worked resolutely at the level of individual behavior. He argued that large-scale structures can be understood if we adequately understand elementary social behavior. He contended that exchange processes are "identical" at the individual and societal levels, although he granted that at the societal level, "the way the fundamental processes are combined is more complex" (Homans, 1974:358).

Peter Blau's Exchange Theory

Peter Blau's (1964) goal was "an understanding of social structure on the basis of an analysis of the social processes that govern the relations between individuals and groups. The basic question . . . is how social life becomes organized into increasingly complex structures of associations among men" (1964:2). Blau's intention was to go beyond Homans's concern with elementary forms of social life and into an analysis of complex structures: "The main sociological purpose of studying processes of face-to-face interaction is to lay the foundation for an understanding of the social structures that evolve and the emergent social forces that characterize their development" (1964:13).[5]

Blau focused on the process of exchange, which, in his view, directs much of human behavior and underlies relationships among individuals as well as among groups. In effect, Blau envisioned a four-stage sequence leading from interpersonal exchange to social structure to social change:

Step 1: Personal exchange transactions between people give rise to . . .
Step 2: Differentiation of status and power, which leads to . . .
Step 3: Legitimization and organization, which sow the seeds of . . .
Step 4: Opposition and change

Micro to Macro   On the individual level, Blau and Homans were interested in similar processes. However, Blau's concept of social exchange is limited to actions that are contingent, that depend, on rewarding reactions from others—actions that cease when expected reactions are not forthcoming. People are attracted to each other for a variety of reasons that induce them to establish social associations. Once initial ties are forged, the rewards that they provide to each other serve to maintain and enhance the bonds. The opposite situation is also possible: with insufficient rewards, an association will weaken or break. Rewards that are exchanged can be either intrinsic (for instance, love, affection, respect) or extrinsic (for instance, money, physical labor). The parties cannot always reward each other equally; when there is inequality in the exchange, a difference of power will emerge within an association.

When one party needs something from another but has nothing comparable to offer in return, four alternatives are available. First, people can force other people to help them. Second, they can find another source to obtain what they need. Third, they can attempt to get along without what they need from the others. Finally, and most

---

[5]It is interesting to note that Blau (1987b) no longer accepts the idea of building macro theory on a micro base.

important, they can subordinate themselves to the others, thereby giving the others "generalized credit" in their relationship; the others then can draw on this credit when they want them to do something. (This latter alternative is, of course, the essential characteristic of power.)

Up to this point, Blau's position is similar to Homans's position, but Blau extended his theory to the level of social facts. He noted, for example, that we cannot analyze processes of social interaction apart from the social structure that surrounds them. Social structure emerges from social interaction, but once this occurs, social structures have a separate existence that affects the process of interaction.

Social interaction exists first within social groups. People are attracted to a group when they feel that the relationships offer more rewards than those in other groups. Because they are attracted to the group, they want to be accepted. To be accepted, they must offer group members rewards. This involves impressing the group members by showing the members that associating with the new people will be rewarding. The relationship with the group members will be solidified when the newcomers have impressed the group—when members have received the rewards they expected. Newcomers' efforts to impress group members generally lead to group cohesion, but competition and, ultimately, social differentiation can occur when too many people actively seek to impress each other with their abilities to reward.

The paradox here is that although group members with the ability to impress can be attractive associates, their impressive characteristics also can arouse fears of dependence in other group members and cause them to acknowledge their attraction only reluctantly. In the early stages of group formation, competition for social recognition among group members actually acts as a screening test for potential leaders of the group. Those best able to reward are most likely to end up in leadership positions. Those group members with less ability to reward want to continue to receive the rewards offered by the potential leaders, and this usually more than compensates for their fears of becoming dependent on them. Ultimately, those individuals with the greater ability to reward emerge as leaders, and the group is differentiated.

The inevitable differentiation of the group into leaders and followers creates a renewed need for integration. Once they have acknowledged the leader's status, followers have an even greater need for integration. Earlier, followers flaunted their most impressive qualities. Now, to achieve integration with fellow followers, they display their weaknesses. This is, in effect, a public declaration that they no longer want to be leaders. This self-deprecation leads to sympathy and social acceptance from the other also-rans. The leader (or leaders) also engages in some self-deprecation at this point, in order to improve overall group integration. By admitting that subordinates are superior in some areas, the leader reduces the pain associated with subordination and demonstrates that he or she does not seek control over every area of group life. These types of forces serve to reintegrate the group despite its new, differentiated status.

All this is reminiscent of Homans's discussion of exchange theory. Blau, however, moved to the societal level and differentiated between two types of social organization. Exchange theorists and behavioral sociologists also recognize the emergence of social organization, but there is, as we will see, a basic difference between Blau and "purer" social behaviorists on this issue. The first type, in which Blau recognized the emergent properties of social groups, emerges from the processes of exchange and competition discussed earlier. The second type of social organization is not emergent but is explicitly established to achieve specified objectives—for example, manufacturing goods that can be sold for a profit, participating in bowling tournaments, engaging in collective bargaining, and winning political victories. In discussing these two types of organization, Blau clearly moved beyond the "elementary forms of social behavior" that are typically of interest to social behaviorists.

In addition to being concerned with these organizations, Blau was interested in the subgroups within them. For example, he argued that leadership and opposition groups are found in both types of organization. In the first type, these two groups emerge out of the process of interaction. In the second, leadership and opposition groups are built into the structure of the organization. In either case, differentiation between the groups is inevitable and lays the groundwork for opposition and conflict within the organization between leaders and followers.

Having moved beyond Homans's elementary forms of behavior and into complex social structures, Blau knew that he must adapt exchange theory to the societal level. Blau recognized the essential difference between small groups and large collectivities, whereas Homans minimized this difference in his effort to explain all social behavior in terms of basic psychological principles.

> The complex social structures that characterize large collectives differ fundamentally from the simpler structures of small groups. A structure of social relations develops in a small group in the course of social interaction among its members. Since there is no direct social interaction among most members of a large community or entire society, some other mechanism must mediate the structure of social relations among them.
>
> (Blau, 1964:253)

This statement requires scrutiny. On the one hand, Blau clearly ruled out social behaviorism as an adequate paradigm for dealing with complex social structures (see Appendix). On the other, he ruled out the social-definitionist paradigm, because he argued that social interaction and the social definitions that accompany it do not occur directly in a large-scale organization. Thus, starting from the social-behavior paradigm, Blau aligned himself with the social-facts paradigm in dealing with more complex social structures.

Norms and Values   For Blau, the mechanisms that mediate among the complex social structures are the norms and values (the value consensus) that exist within society:

> Commonly agreed upon values and norms serve as media of social life and as mediating links for social transactions. They make indirect social exchange possible, and they govern the processes of social integration and differentiation in complex social structures as well as the development of social organization and reorganization in them.
>
> (Blau, 1964:255)

Other mechanisms mediate among social structures, but Blau focused upon value consensus. Looking first at social norms, Blau argued that they substitute indirect exchange for direct exchange. One member conforms to the group norm and receives approval for that conformity and implicit approval for the fact that conformity contributes to the group's maintenance and stability. In other words, the group or collectivity engages in an exchange relationship with the individual. This is in contrast to Homans's simpler notion, which focused on interpersonal exchange. Blau offered a number of examples of collectivity-individual exchanges replacing individual-individual exchanges:

> Staff officials do not assist line officials in their work in exchange for rewards received from them, but furnishing this assistance is the official obligation of staff members, and in return for discharging these obligations they receive financial rewards from the company.
>
> Organized philanthropy provides another example of indirect social exchange. In contrast to the old-fashioned lady bountiful who brought her baskets to the poor and received their gratitude and appreciation, there is no direct contact and no exchange between individual donors and recipients in contemporary organized charity. Wealthy businessmen and members of the upper class make philanthropic contributions to conform with the normative expectations that prevail in their social class and to earn the social approval of their peers, not in order to earn the gratitude of the individuals who benefit from their charity.
>
> (Blau, 1964:260)

The concept of norm in Blau's formulation moves Blau to the level of exchange between individual and collectivity, but the concept of values moves him to the largest-scale societal level and to the analysis of the relationship *among collectivities.* Blau said:

> Common values of various types can be conceived of as media of social transactions that expand the compass of social interaction and the structure of social relations through social space and time. Consensus on social values serves as the basis for extending the range of social transactions beyond the limits of direct social contacts and for perpetuating social structures beyond the life span of human beings. Value standards can be considered media of social life in two senses of the term; the value context is the medium that molds the form of social relationships; and common values are the mediating links for social associations and transactions on a broad scale.
>
> (Blau, 1964:263–264)

For example, *particularistic* values are the media of integration and solidarity. These values serve to unite the members of a group around such things as patriotism, or the good of the school, or the company. These are seen as similar at the collective level to sentiments of personal attraction that unite individuals on a face-to-face basis. However, they extend integrative bonds beyond mere personal attraction. Particularistic values also differentiate the in-group from the out-group, thereby enhancing their unifying function.

Blau's analysis carries us far from Homans's version of exchange theory. The individual and individual behavior, paramount for Homans, have almost disappeared in Blau's conception. Taking the place of the individual are a wide variety of *social facts.* For example, Blau discussed groups, organizations, collectivities, societies, norms, and values. Blau's analysis is concerned with what holds large-scale social units together and what tears them apart, clearly traditional concerns of the social factist.

Although Blau argued that he was simply extending exchange theory to the societal level, in so doing he twisted exchange theory beyond recognition. He was even forced to admit that processes at the societal level are fundamentally different from those at the

PETER M. BLAU: A Biographical Sketch

Peter Blau was born in Vienna, Austria, on February 7, 1918. He emigrated to the United States in 1939 and became a United States citizen in 1943. In 1942 he received his bachelor's degree from the relatively little known Elmhurst College in Elmhurst, Illinois. His schooling was interrupted by World War II, and he served in the United States Army and was awarded the Bronze Star. After the war, he returned to school and completed his education, receiving his Ph.D. from Columbia University in 1952.

Blau first received wide recognition in sociology for his contributions to the study of formal organizations. His empirical studies of organizations as well as his textbooks on formal organizations are still widely cited in that subfield, and he continues to be a regular contributor to it. He is also noted for a book he coauthored with Otis Dudley Duncan, *The American Occupational Structure,* which won the prestigious Sorokin Award from the American Sociological Association in 1968. That work constitutes a very important contribution to the sociological study of social stratification.

Although he is well known for a range of work, what interests us here is Blau's contribution to sociological theory. What is distinctive about it is that Blau has made important contributions to two distinct theoretical orientations. His 1964 book *Exchange and Power in Social Life* is a major component of contemporary exchange theory. Blau's chief contribution there was to take the primarily small-scale exchange theory and try to apply it to larger-scale issues. Although it has some notable weaknesses, it constitutes an important effort to theoretically integrate large- and small-scale sociological issues. Blau has also been in the forefront of structural theory. During his term as president of the American Sociological Association (1973–1974), he made this the theme of the annual meeting of the association. Since then he has published a number of books and articles designed to clarify and to extend structural theory. His latest work in this area is *Structural Contexts of Opportunities* (1994) and the second edition of *Crosscutting Social Circles* (Blau and Schwartz, 1997).

individual level. In his effort to extend exchange theory, Blau managed only to transform it into another macro-level theory. Blau seemed to recognize that exchange theory is concerned primarily with face-to-face relations. As a result, it needs to be complemented by other theoretical orientations that focus mainly on macro structures. Blau (1987b; 1994) has now come to recognize this explicitly, and his more recent work focuses on macro-level, structural phenomena.

The Work of Richard Emerson and His Disciples

While Richard Emerson had published an important paper on power-dependence relations a decade earlier (1962), it was two related essays written in 1972 (Emerson, 1972a, 1972b) that "marked the beginning of a new stage in the development of social exchange theory" (Molm and Cook, 1995:215; Cook and Whitmeyer, forthcoming). Molm and Cook see three basic factors as the impetus for this new body of work. First,

Emerson was interested in exchange theory as a broader framework for his earlier interest in power dependence. It seemed clear to Emerson that power was central to the exchange theory perspective. Second, Emerson felt that he could use behaviorism (operant psychology) as the base of his exchange theory but avoid some of the problems that had befallen Homans. For one thing, Homans and other exchange theorists had been accused of assuming an overly rational image of human beings, but Emerson felt he could use behaviorism without assuming a rational actor. For another, Emerson believed he could avoid the problem of tautology that ensnared Homans:

> Homans predicted individual exchange behavior from the reinforcement provided by another actor, but behavioral responses and reinforcement do not have independent meaning in operant psychology. A reinforcer is, by definition, a stimulus consequence that increases or maintains response frequency.
>
> (Molm and Cook, 1995:214)

In addition, Emerson felt he could avoid the charge of reductionism (one that Homans reveled in) by being able to develop an exchange perspective capable of explaining macro-level phenomena. Third, unlike Blau, who resorted to an explanation reliant on normative phenomena, Emerson wanted to deal with social structure and social change using "social relations and social networks as building blocks that spanned different levels of analysis" (Molm and Cook, 1995:215). In addition, the actors in Emerson's system could be either individuals or larger corporate structures (albeit, structures working through agents). Thus, Emerson used the principles of operant psychology to develop a theory of social structure.

In the two essays published in 1972, Emerson developed the basis of his integrative exchange theory. In the first of those essays (1972a) Emerson dealt with the psychological basis for social exchange, while in the second (1972b) he turned to the macro-level and exchange relations and network structures. Later, Emerson made the micro-macro linkage more explicit: "I am attempting to extend exchange theory and research from *micro* to more *macro* levels of analysis through the study of *exchange network structures*" (cited in Cook, 1987b:212). As Karen Cook, Emerson's most important disciple, points out, it is the idea of exchange network structures that is central to the micro-macro linkage: "The use of the notion, exchange networks, allows for the development of theory that bridges the conceptual gap between isolated individuals or dyads and larger aggregates or collections of individuals (e.g., formal groups or associations, organizations, neighborhoods, political parties, etc.)" (1987b:219).[6]

Both Emerson and Cook accept and begin with the basic, micro-level premises of exchange theory. Emerson, for example, says, "The exchange approach takes as its first focus of attention the benefits people obtain from, and contribute to, the process of social interaction" (1981:31). More specifically, Emerson accepts behavioristic principles as his starting point. Emerson (1981:33) outlines three core assumptions of exchange theory:

---

[6]Emerson and Cook (as well as Blau) are not the only ones to have developed integrative exchange theories. See also Uehara (1990) and Willer, Markovsky, and Patton (1989).

1 People for whom events are beneficial tend to act "rationally," so such events occur.

2 Because people eventually become satiated with behavioral events, such events come to be of diminishing utility.

3 The benefits that people obtain through social processes are dependent on the benefits that they are able to provide in exchange, giving exchange theory "its focus [on] the flow of *benefits through social interaction.*"

All this is quite familiar, but Emerson begins to point behavioristically oriented exchange theory in a different direction at the close of his first, micro-oriented 1972 essay: "Our main purpose in this chapter is to incorporate operant principles into a framework which can handle more complex situations than operant psychology confronts" (1972a:48).

This theme opens the second 1972 essay: "The purpose of this essay is to begin construction of a theory of social exchange in which *social structure* is taken as the dependent variable" (Emerson, 1972b:58). Whereas in the first 1972 essay Emerson was concerned with a single actor involved in an exchange relation with his or her environment (for example, a person fishing in a lake), in the second essay Emerson turns to social-exchange relationships as well as to exchange networks.

The actors in Emerson's macro-level exchange theory can be either individuals or collectivities. Emerson is concerned with the exchange relationship among actors. An *exchange network* has the following components (Cook et al., 1983:277):

1 There is a set of either individual or collective actors.
2 Valued resources are distributed among the actors.
3 There is a set of exchange opportunities among all actors in the network.
4 Exchange relations, or exchange opportunities, exist among the actors.
5 Exchange relations are connected to one another in a single network structure.

In sum: "An 'exchange network' is a specific social structure formed by two or more connected exchange relations between actors" (Cook et al., 1983:277).

The connection between exchange *relations* is of great importance and is critical to linking exchange between two actors (dyadic exchange) to more macro-level phenomena (Yamagishi, Gillmore, and Cook, 1988:835). What is crucial is the contingent relationship between dyadic exchanges. Thus, we may say that two dyadic-exchange relations, *A-B* and *A-C,* form a minimal network *(A-B-C)* when exchange in one is contingent on exchange (or nonexchange) in the other. It is *not* enough for *A, B,* and *C* to have a common membership for an exchange network to develop; there must be a contingent relationship between exchanges in *A-B* and *B-C.*

Each exchange relation is embedded within a larger exchange network consisting of two or more such relationships. If the exchange in one relationship affects exchange in another, they can be said to be connected. That connection can be *positive,* where the exchange in one positively affects the exchange in another (for example, the money obtained from one is used to gain social status in another); *negative,* where one serves to inhibit the exchange in the other (for example, time spent earning money in one relationship reduces the ability to spend time with friends in another) (Molm, 1991), or *mixed.*

Power-Dependence Emerson defined *power* as "the level of potential *cost* which one actor can induce another to 'accept,'" while *dependence* involves "the level of potential cost an actor will accept within a relation" (1972b:64). These definitions lead to Emerson's power-dependence theory, which Yamagishi, Gillmore, and Cook summarize in the following way: "The power of one party over another in an exchange relation is an inverse function of his or her dependence on the other party" (1988:837). Unequal power and dependency lead to imbalances in relationships, but over time these move toward a more balanced power-dependence relationship.

Molm and Cook (1995) regard dependence as the critical concept in Emerson's work. As Molm puts it, "The actors' *dependencies* on each other are the major structural determinants of their interaction and of their power over each other" (1988:109). Here is the way Emerson originally dealt with the issue: "The dependence of actor A upon actor B is (1) directly proportional to A's *motivational investment* in goals mediated by B, and (2) inversely proportional to the *availability* of those goals to A outside of the A-B relation" (1962:32). Thus, a sense of dependence is linked to Emerson's definition of power, "the power of A over B is equal to, and based upon, the dependence of B upon A" (1962:33). There is balance in the relationship between A and B when the dependence of A on B equals the dependence of B on A. Where there is an imbalance in the dependencies, the actor with less dependence has an advantage in terms of power. Thus, power is a potential built into the structure of the *relationship* between A and B. Power can also be used to acquire rewards from the relationship. Even in balanced relationships, power exists, albeit in a kind of equilibrium.

Power-dependence studies have focused on positive outcomes—the ability to reward others. However, in a series of studies, Molm (1988, 1989, 1994) has emphasized the role of negative outcomes—punishment power—in power-dependence relationships. That is, power can be derived from both the ability to reward and the ability to punish others. In general, Molm has found that punishment power is weaker than reward power, in part because acts of punishment are likely to elicit negative reactions. However, in one of her recent studies, Molm (1994) has suggested that the relative weakness of punishment power may arise because it is not widely used, and not because it is inherently less effective than reward power. Molm, Quist, and Wisely (1994) found that the use of punishment power is more likely to be perceived as fair when it is used by those who also have the power to reward.

A More Integrative Exchange Theory In explaining power dependence, network theory (see below) looks at things such as structural centrality, while exchange theory focuses on the dyadic relation between actors. The research by Cook et al. (1983) tends to find support for the importance of the exchange relationship and identifies weaknesses in the network approach. However, Cook et al. (1983:298) are well aware of the micro biases of exchange theory and the need to integrate it with, to raise it to, the macroscopic level.

In order to move away from the dyadic approach of exchange theory and toward a focus on the power of a position within a structure, Cook and Emerson argue that the determination of the power of a position is based on the amount of dependence of the entire structure on that position. Such systemwide dependence will, in their view, be a function of *both* the structural centrality of the position and the nature of power-dependence relationships. They argue that they are adopting a "'vulnerability' approach to the problem of raising power-dependence theory from a dyadic to a more macrostructural level of analysis" (Cook et al., 1983:301). Vulnerability involves the networkwide dependence on a particular structural position. Cook et al. conclude:

> It is clear that the integration of structural network principles with exchange network theory provides useful insights into the dynamics of power in networks of connected exchange relations. . . . This theoretical formulation offers an explicit procedure for linking actors' exchange behavior to network properties . . . and suggests mechanisms which may yield "possible transformations" of these networks as a result of power dynamics or changes in the nature of the exchange connections.
>
> (Cook et al., 1983:303)

Yamagishi, Gillmore, and Cook (1988) go further in linking exchange theory and network theory. They argue that power (and dependence) are central to exchange theory but that power cannot be studied meaningfully in the dyad. Rather, power "is fundamentally a social structural phenomenon" (Yamagishi, Gillmore, and Cook, 1988:834). They are able to generate predictions about the distribution of power in all three types of exchange networks—positive, negative, and mixed—and support their predictions with experiments and computer simulations. Fully adequate analysis must involve the traditional exchange-theory concerns with processes within exchange relations as well as the traditional network-theory concern with the linkages between exchange relations.

A central issue emerges here: What is the difference, if any, between an exchange network and the kind of network of interest to network theorists? According to Cook and Whitmeyer, "Exchange networks are viewed as connected sets of exchange relations" (1992:113). The exchange theorist is, by definition, interested in "the exchange aspects of all ties and contends that the appropriate network in any analysis is one that contains all relevant exchange relations" (Cook and Whitmeyer, 1992:109). In contrast, network theorists are described as being more "catholic" in their approach to the content of such ties. While exchange theorists accept many of the types of ties dealt with by network theorists, they reject others. For example, on network studies that focus on "centrality," or "'network position-conferred advantage'" Cook and Whitmeyer argue that when exchange is ignored or obscured, "the causal processes involved in centrality will likewise be hidden. When the exchange relations are excluded, the results are likely to be spurious if not in error" (1992:120–121). In spite of such differences, Cook and Whitmeyer (1992) regard exchange and network theory as compatible, and they argue that a synthesis of the two approaches is likely to be more powerful than either one alone.

Cook, O'Brien, and Kollock (1990) define *exchange theory* in inherently integrative terms as being concerned with exchanges at various levels of analysis, including those among interconnected individuals, corporations, and nation-states. They identify two strands of work in the history of exchange—one at the micro level, focusing on social behavior as exchange, and the other at the more macro level, viewing social structure as exchange. They see the strength of exchange theory in micro-macro integration, since "it includes within a single theoretical framework propositions that apply to individual actors as well as to the macro level (or systemic level) and it attempts to formulate explicitly the consequences of changes at one level for other levels of analysis" (Cook, O'Brien, and Kollock, 1990:175).

Cook, O'Brien, and Kollock identify three contemporary trends, all of which point toward a more integrative exchange theory. The first is the increasing use of field research focusing on more macroscopic issues, which can complement the traditional use of the laboratory experiment to study microscopic issues. Second, they note the shift, discussed earlier, in substantive work away from a focus on dyads and toward larger networks of exchange. Third, and most important, is the ongoing effort, also discussed earlier, to synthesize exchange theory and structural sociologies, especially network theory. (We will say more about network theory shortly.)

Along the way, Cook, O'Brien, and Kollock discuss the gains to be made from integrating insights from a variety of other micro theories. Decision theory offers "a better understanding of the way actors make choices relevant to transactions" (Cook, O'Brien, and Kollock, 1990:168). More generally, cognitive science (which includes cognitive anthropology and artificial intelligence) sheds "more light on the way in which actors perceive, process, and retrieve information" (Cook, O'Brien, and Kollock, 1990:168). Symbolic interactionism offers knowledge about how actors signal their intentions to one another, and this is important in the development of trust and commitment in exchange relationships. Most generally, they see their synthetic version of exchange theory as being well equipped to deal with the centrally important issue of the agency-structure relationship. In their view, "Exchange theory is one of a limited number of theoretical orientations in the social sciences that explicitly conceptualize purposeful actors in relation to structures" (Cook, O'Brien, and Kollock, 1990:172).

There are a number of recent examples of efforts by exchange theorists to synthesize their approach with other theoretical orientations. For example, Yamagishi and Cook (1993) have sought to integrate exchange theory with social dilemma theory (Yamagishi, 1995), a variant of rational choice theory. The social dilemma approach is derived from the famous dyadic concept of the prisoner's dilemma and the research on it. "A social dilemma is defined as a situation involving a particular type of incentive structure, such that 1) if all group members cooperate, all gain, whereas 2) for each individual it is more beneficial not to cooperate" (Yamagishi and Cook, 1993:236). Without going into the details of their study, Yamagishi and Cook find that the nature of the exchange relationship and structure affects the way people deal with social dilemmas.

In another effort, Hegtvedt, Thompson, and Cook (1993) sought to integrate exchange theory and one approach that deals with cognitive processes, attribution theory. The integration with this theory gives exchange theory a mechanism to deal with the way people perceive and make attributions, while exchange theory compensates for the weakness in attribution theory in dealing with "the social structural antecedents and the behavioral consequences of attribution" (Hegtvedt, Thompson, and Cook, 1993:100). Thus, for example, the authors found support for the hypotheses that perceived power is related to one's structural power position and that those "who perceive themselves to have greater power are more likely to attribute their exchange outcomes to personal actions or interactions" (Hegtvedt, Thompson, and Cook, 1993:104). While not fully

RICHARD EMERSON: A Biographical Sketch

Richard Emerson was born in Salt Lake City, Utah, in 1925. Raised near mountains, he  never seemed to stray too far away from rivers, mountain peaks, and glaciers. One of his most prized personal accomplishments was his participation in the successful ascent of Mt. Everest in 1963. Aspects of this experience are captured in his publication "Everest Traverse" in the December 1963 edition of the *Sierra Club Annual Bulletin* and in an article published in *Sociometry* in 1966. He received a grant from the National Science Foundation to study group performance under prolonged stress on this climb. This project earned him the Hubbard Medal, presented to him by President Kennedy on behalf of the National Geographic Society in July 1963.

His love of mountains and the rural social life of the mountain villages of Pakistan became a constant source of sociological inspiration for Richard Emerson during his career. His studies of interpersonal behavior, group performance, power, and social influence were often driven by his close personal encounters with expedition teams for which the intensity of cooperation and competition were exacerbated by environmental stress.

After World War II and a tour of duty with the Army in Western Europe, he completed his B.A. in 1950 at the University of Utah and then went on to earn an M.A. (1952) and a Ph.D. (1955) from the University of Minnesota, where his major field was sociology and his minor field, psychology. His doctoral dissertation was titled "The Determinants of Influence in Face to Face Groups."

Emerson's first academic post was at the University of Cincinnati (1955–1964). Upon leaving Cincinnati Emerson wrote, "A recurring theme in my work was crystallized in the article on power-dependence relations. However, this theory is clearly a springboard for the future rather than a summary of the past. I have rather specific plans for both theoretical and empirical extensions into stratification and community power structure." He was still engaged in this work when he died unexpectedly in December 1982. His work on power-dependence relations (1962) is now a citation classic and has influenced much of the current work on power in American sociology.

Two other pieces have been highly influential. These are his two chapters on social exchange theory which were written in 1967 and subsequently published in 1972. This work was completed at the University of Washington, where he joined the faculty in 1965. He was drawn to the Northwest, I am sure, by the lure of the Olympics and Cascades.

Emerson's influence on sociological theory crystallized while he was at the University of Washington, where he collaborated with Karen Cook for a ten-year period (1972–1982) on the empirical development of social exchange theory. They carried out a program of research in the first computerized laboratory for conducting research of this type in the United States. This work was funded by three successive grants from the National Science Foundation.

Emerson is remembered by former colleagues and students as a "thinker." This aspect of his personality is best captured in a quote from an article he wrote in 1960 in Bowen's book, *The New Professors:* "So, what is there of value in the academic (that is, 'nonpractical, removed-from-life') study of a topic? People ask this question, too. Such questions are difficult to answer because those who ask have never climbed a mountain and have no interest in a topic. I say they are far removed from life."

*This biographical sketch was written by Karen Cook.

supportive of the authors' hypotheses, this study points to the importance of studying the relationship between social structure, cognitive processes (perception and attribution), and behavior.

In recent years, exchange theory has begun to move in a variety of new directions (Molm, forthcoming). First, there is increasing attention to the risk and uncertainty involved in exchange relationships (Kollock, 1994). For example, one actor may provide valuable outcomes for the other without receiving anything of value in return. Second, an interest in risk leads to a concern for trust in exchange relations. The issue is: Can one actor trust another to reciprocate when valued outcomes have been provided? Third, there is the related issue of actors reducing risk and increasing trust by developing a set of mutual commitments to one another (Molm, 1997). This, in turn, is linked to a fourth issue—increasing attention to affect and emotions in a theory which has been dominated by a focus on self-interested actors. Finally, while much of recent exchange theory has focused on structure, there is increasing interest in fleshing out the nature and role of the actor in exchange relationships. In terms of issues in need of greater attention, Molm argues that exchange theory has tended to focus on exchange structures, but needs to do more with change, or exchange dynamics.

NETWORK THEORY

Network analysts (for example, Harrison White, 1992; Wasserman and Faust, 1994; Wellman and Berkowitz, 1988/1997) take pains to differentiate their approach from what Ronald Burt calls "atomistic" and "normative" sociological approaches (Burt, 1982; see also Granovetter, 1985). Atomistic sociological orientations focus on actors making decisions in isolation from other actors. More generally, they focus on the "personal attributes" of actors (B. Wellman, 1983). Atomistic approaches are rejected because they are too microscopic and ignore relationships among actors. As Barry Wellman puts it, "Accounting for individual motives is a job better left to psychologists" (1983:163). This, of course, constitutes a rejection of a number of sociological theories that are in one way or another deeply concerned with motives.

In the view of network theorists, normative approaches focus on culture and the socialization process through which norms and values are internalized in actors. In the normative orientation, what holds people together is sets of shared ideas. Network theorists reject such a view and argue that one should focus on the objective pattern of ties linking the members of society (Mizruchi, 1994). Here is how Wellman articulates this view:

> Network analysts want to study regularities in how people and collectivities behave rather than regularities in beliefs about how they ought to behave. Hence network analysts try to avoid normative explanations of social behavior. They dismiss as non-structural any explanation that treats social process as the sum of individual actors' personal attributes and internalized norms.
>
> (B. Wellman, 1983:162)

Having made clear what it is not, network theory then clarifies its major concern—social relationships, or the objective pattern of ties linking the members (individual and collective) of society (Burt, 1992). Let us look at how Wellman articulates this focus:

Network analysts start with the simple, but powerful, notion that the primary business of sociologists is to study social structure. . . . The most direct way to study a social structure is to analyze the pattern of ties linking its members. Network analysts search for *deep* structures—regular network patterns beneath the often complex surface of social systems. . . . Actors and their behavior are seen as constrained by these structures. Thus, the focus is not on voluntaristic actors, but on structural constraint.

(B. Wellman, 1983:156–157)

One distinctive aspect of network theory is that it focuses on a wide range of micro to macro structures. That is, to network theory the actors may be people (Wellman and Wortley, 1990), but they also may be groups, corporations (W. Baker, 1990; Clawson, Neustadtl, and Bearden, 1986; Mizruchi and Koenig, 1986), and societies. Links occur at the large-scale, social-structural level as well as at more microscopic levels. Mark Granovetter describes such micro-level links as action "embedded" in "the concrete personal relations and structures (or 'networks') of such relations" (1985:490). Basic to any of these links is the idea that any "actor" (individual or collective) may have differential access to valued resources (wealth, power, information). The result is that structured systems tend to be stratified, with some components dependent on others.

One key aspect of network analysis is that it tends to move sociologists away from the study of social groups and social categories and toward the study of ties among and between actors that are not "sufficiently bounded and densely knit to be termed groups" (B. Wellman, 1983:169). A good example of this is Granovetter's (1973, 1983) work on "the strength of weak ties." Granovetter differentiates between "strong ties," for example, links between people and their close friends, and "weak ties," for example, links between people and mere acquaintances. Sociologists have tended to focus on people with strong ties or social groups. They have tended to regard strong ties as crucial, whereas weak ties have been thought of as being of trivial sociological importance. Granovetter's contribution is to make it clear that weak ties can be very important. For example, weak ties between two actors can serve as a bridge between two groups with strong internal ties. Without such a weak tie, the two groups might be totally isolated. This isolation, in turn, could lead to a more fragmented social system. An individual without weak ties would find himself or herself isolated in a tightly knit group and would lack information about what is going on in other groups as well as in the larger society. Weak ties therefore prevent isolation and allow for individuals to be better integrated into the larger society. Although Granovetter emphasizes the importance of weak ties, he hastens to make it clear "that strong ties can also have value" (1983:209; see Bian, 1997). For example, people with strong ties have greater motivation to help one another and are more readily available to one another.

Network theory is relatively new and undeveloped. As Burt says, "There is currently a loose federation of approaches referenced as network analysis" (1982:20). But it is growing, as evidenced by the number of papers and books being published from a network perspective and the fact that there is now a journal (*Social Networks*) devoted to it. Although it may be a loose conglomeration of work, network theory does seem to rest on a coherent set of principles (B. Wellman, 1983).

First, ties among actors usually are symmetrical in both content and intensity. Actors supply each other with different things, and they do so with greater or lesser intensity.

Second, the ties among individuals must be analyzed within the context of the structure of larger networks. Third, the structuring of social ties leads to various kinds of non-random networks. On the one hand, networks are transitive: if there is a tie between *A* and *B* and *B* and *C,* there is likely to be a tie between *A* and *C.* The result is that there is more likely to be a network involving *A, B,* and *C.* On the other hand, there are limits to how many links can exist and how intense they can be. The result is that there are also likely to develop network clusters with distinct boundaries separating one cluster from another. Fourth, the existence of clusters leads to the fact that there can be cross-linkages between clusters as well as between individuals. Fifth, there are asymmetric ties among elements in a system, with the result that scarce resources are differentially distributed. Finally, the unequal distribution of scarce resources leads to both collaboration and competition. Some groups band together to acquire scarce resources collaboratively, whereas others compete and conflict over resources. Thus, network theory has a dynamic quality (Rosenthal et al., 1985), with the structure of the system changing with shifting patterns of coalition and conflict.

To take one example, Mizruchi (1990) is interested in the issue of the cohesion of corporations and its relationship to power. He argues that historically *cohesion* has been defined in two different ways. The first, or subjective view, is that "cohesion is a function of group members' feelings of identification with the group, in particular their feeling that their individual interests are bound up with the interests of the group" (Mizruchi, 1990:21). The emphasis here is on the normative system, and cohesion is produced either by the internalization of the normative system or by group pressure. The second, or objective view, is that "solidarity can be viewed as an objective, observable process independent of the sentiments of individuals" (Mizruchi, 1990:22). Needless to say, given his alignment with network theory, Mizruchi comes down on the side of the objective approach to cohesion.

Mizruchi sees similarity of behavior as a result of not only cohesion but also what he calls *structural equivalence:* "Structurally equivalent actors are those with identical relations with other actors in the social structure" (1990:25). Thus, structural equivalence exists among, say, corporations, even though there may be no communication among them. They behave in the same way because they stand in the same relationship to some other entity in the social structure. Mizruchi concludes that structural equivalence plays at least as strong a role as cohesion in explaining similarity of behavior. Mizruchi accords great importance to structural equivalence, which, after all, implies a network of social relations.

A More Integrative Network Theory   Ronald Burt (1982) has been in the forefront of network theorists who have sought to develop an integrated approach instead of another form of structural determinism. Burt begins by articulating a schism within action theory between the "atomistic" and "normative" orientations. The atomistic orientation "assumes that alternative actions are evaluated independently by separate actors so that evaluations are made without reference to other actors," whereas the "normative perspective is defined by separate actors within a system having interdependent interests as social norms generated by actors socializing one another" (Burt, 1982:5).

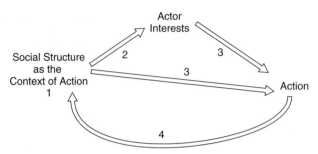

FIGURE 8.1
Ronald Burt's Integrative Model

Burt develops a perspective that "circumvents the schism between atomistic and normative action," one that "is less a synthesis of the existing two perspectives on action than it is a third view intellectually bridging the two views" (1982:8). Although he admittedly borrows from the other two perspectives, Burt develops what he calls a *structural perspective* that differs from the other two "in the criterion for the postulate of marginal evaluation. The criterion assumed by the proposed structural perspective is an actor's status/role-set as generated by the division of labor. An actor evaluates the utility of alternative actions partly in regard to his personal conditions and partly in regard to the conditions of others" (1982:8). He sees his approach as a logical extension of the atomistic approach and an "empirically accurate restriction" on normative theory.

Figure 8.1 depicts Burt's structural theory of action. According to Burt's description of the premise of a structural theory of action, "actors are purposive under social structural constraints" (1982:9; see also, Mizruchi, 1994). In his view:

> Actors find themselves in a social structure. That social structure defines their social similarities, which in turn pattern their perceptions of the advantages to be had by taking each of several alternative actions. At the same time, social structure differentially constrains actors in their ability to take actions. Actions eventually taken are therefore a joint function of actors pursuing their interests to the limit of their ability where both interests and ability are patterned by social structure. Finally, actions taken under social structural constraint can modify social structure itself, and these modifications have the potential to create new constraints to be faced by actors within the structure.
>
> (Burt, 1982:9)

RATIONAL CHOICE THEORY

Although it influenced the development of exchange theory, rational choice theory was generally marginal to mainstream sociological theory (Hechter and Kanazawa, 1997). It is largely through the efforts of one man, James S. Coleman, that rational choice theory has become one of the "hot" theories in contemporary sociology (Chriss, 1995; Tilly, 1997). For one thing, in 1989 Coleman founded a journal, *Rationality and Society,* devoted to the dissemination of work from a rational choice perspective. For another, Coleman (1990) published an enormously influential book, *Foundations of*

Social Theory, based on this perspective. Finally, Coleman became president of the American Sociological Association in 1992 and used that forum to push rational choice theory and to present an address entitled "The Rational Reconstruction of Society" (Coleman, 1993b).

Since we have previously outlined the basic tenets of rational choice theory, it would be useful to begin with Coleman's (1989) introductory comments to the first issue of *Rationality and Society*. The journal was to be interdisciplinary because rational choice theory (or, as Coleman calls it, "the paradigm of rational action" [1989:5]) is the only theory with the possibility of producing paradigmatic integration. Coleman does not hesitate to argue that the approach operates from a base in methodological individualism and to use rational choice theory as the micro-level base for the explanation of macro-level phenomena. Even more interesting is what Coleman's approach does *not* find "congenial":

> work that is methodologically holistic, floating at the system level without recourse to the actors whose actions generate that system . . . the view of action as purely expressive, the view of action as irrational, and also the view of action as something wholly caused by outside forces without the intermediation of intention or purpose. It excludes that empirical work widely carried out in social science in which individual behavior is "explained" by certain factors or determinants without any model of action whatsoever.
>
> (Coleman, 1989:6)

Thus, a large portion of work in sociology is excluded from the pages of *Rationality and Society*. Not to be excluded, however, are macro-level concerns and their linkage to rational action. Beyond such academic concerns, Coleman wants work done from a rational choice perspective to have practical relevance to our changing social world. For example, Heckathorn and Broadhead (1996) have examined the issue of public policies aimed at AIDS prevention from a rational choice perspective.

Foundations of Social Theory

Coleman argues that sociology should focus on social systems, but that such macro phenomena must be explained by factors internal to them, prototypically individuals. He favors working at this level for several reasons, including the fact that data are usually gathered at the individual level and then aggregated or composed to yield the system level. Among the other reasons for favoring a focus on the individual level is that this is where "interventions" are ordinarily made to create social changes. As we will see, central to Coleman's perspective is the idea that social theory is not merely an academic exercise but should affect the social world through such "interventions."

Given his focus on the individual, Coleman recognizes that he is a methodological individualist, although he sees his particular perspective as a "special variant" of that orientation. His view is special in the sense that it accepts the idea of emergence and that while it focuses on factors internal to the system, those factors are not necessarily individual actions and orientations. That is, micro-level phenomena other than individuals can be the focus of his analysis.

Coleman's rational choice orientation is clear in his basic idea that "persons act purposively toward a goal, with the goal (and thus the actions) shaped by values or preferences" (1990:13).   But Coleman (1990:14) then goes on to argue that for most theoretical purposes, he will need a more precise conceptualization of the rational actor derived from economics, one that sees the actors choosing those actions that will maximize utility, or the satisfaction of their needs and wants.

There are two key elements in his theory—actors and resources.   Resources are those things over which actors have control and in which they have some interest.   Given these two elements, Coleman details how their interaction leads to the system level:

> A minimal basis for a social system of action is two actors, each having control over resources of interest to the other.   It is each one's interest in resources under the other's control that leads the two, as purposive actors, to engage in actions that involve each other . . . a system of action. . . . It is this structure, together with the fact that the actors are purposive, each having the goal of maximizing the realization of his interests, that gives the interdependence, or systemic character, to their actions.
>
> (Coleman, 1990:29)

Although he has faith in rational choice theory, Coleman does not believe that this perspective, at least as yet, has all the answers.   But it is clear that he believes that it can move in that direction, since he argues that the "success of a social theory based on rationality lies in successively diminishing that domain of social activity that cannot be accounted for by the theory" (Coleman, 1990:18).

Coleman recognizes that in the real world people do not always behave rationally, but he feels that this makes little difference in his theory: "My implicit assumption is that the theoretical predictions made here will be substantively the same whether the actors act precisely according to rationality as commonly conceived or deviate in the ways that have been observed" (1990:506; Inbar, 1996).

Given his orientation to individual rational action, it follows that Coleman's focus in terms of the micro-macro issue is the micro-to-macro linkage, or how the combination of individual actions brings about the behavior of the system.   While he accords priority to this issue, Coleman is here also interested in the macro-to-micro linkage, or how the system constrains the orientations of actors.   Finally, he evinces an interest in the micro-micro aspect of the relationship, or the impact of individual actions on other individual actions.

In spite of this seeming balance, there are at least three major weaknesses in Coleman's approach.   First, he accords overwhelming priority to the micro-to-macro issue, thereby giving short shrift to the other relationships.   Second, he ignores the macro-macro issue.   Finally, his causal arrows go in only one direction; in other words, he ignores the dialectical relationship among and between micro and macro phenomena.

Utilizing his rational choice approach, Coleman explains a series of macro-level phenomena.   His basic position is that theorists need to keep their conceptions of the actor constant and generate from those micro-constants various images of macro-level phenomena.   In this way, differences in macro phenomena can be traced to different structures of relations at the macro level and not to variations at the micro level.

A key step in the micro-to-macro movement is the granting of the authority and rights possessed by one individual to another.   This action tends to lead to the subordination of one actor to another.   More important, it creates the most basic macro phenomenon—an acting unit consisting of two people, rather than two independent actors. The resulting structure functions independently of the actors. Instead of maximizing his or her own interests, in this instance an actor seeks to realize the interests of another actor, or of the independent collective unit. Not only is this a different social reality, but it is one that "has special deficiencies and generates special problems" (Coleman, 1990:145). Given his applied orientation, Coleman is interested in the diagnosis and solution of these problems.

Collective Behavior   One example of Coleman's approach to dealing with macro phenomena is the case of collective behavior (Zablocki, 1996). He chooses to deal with collective behavior because its often disorderly and unstable character is thought to be hard to analyze from a rational choice perspective. But Coleman's view is that rational choice theory can explain all types of macro phenomena, not just those that are orderly and stable. What is involved in moving from the rational actor to "the wild and turbulent systemic functioning called collective behavior is a simple (and rational) transfer of control over one's actions to another actor . . . made unilaterally, not as part of an exchange" (Coleman, 1990:198).

Why do people unilaterally transfer control over their actions to others? The answer, from a rational choice perspective, is that they are doing so in an attempt to maximize their utility. Normally, individual maximization involves a balancing of control among several actors, and this produces equilibrium within society. However, in the case of collective behavior, because there is a unilateral transfer of control, individual maximization does not necessarily lead to system equilibrium. Instead, there is the disequilibrium characteristic of collective behavior.

Norms   Another macro-level phenomenon that comes under Coleman's scrutiny is norms. While most sociologists take norms as given and invoke them to explain individual behavior, they do not explain why and how norms come into existence. Coleman wonders how, in a group of rational actors, norms can emerge and be maintained. Coleman argues that norms are initiated and maintained by some people who see benefits resulting from the observation of norms and harm stemming from the violation of those norms. People are willing to give up some control over their own behavior, but in the process they gain some control (through norms) over the behavior of others. Coleman summarizes his position on norms:

> The central element of this explanation . . . is the giving up of partial rights of control over one's own action and the receiving of partial rights of control over the actions of others, that is, the emergence of a norm. The end result is that control . . . which was held by each alone, becomes widely distributed over the whole set of actors, who exercise that control.
> (Coleman, 1990:292)

Once again, people are seen as maximizing their utility by partially surrendering rights of control over themselves and gaining partial control over others. Because the transfer of control is not unilateral, there is equilibrium in the case of norms.

But there are also circumstances in which norms act to the advantage of some people and the disadvantage of others. In some cases, actors surrender the right to control their

JAMES S. COLEMAN: A Biographical Sketch

James S. Coleman had a remarkably varied career in sociology; the label "theorist" is only one of several that can be applied to him. He received his Ph.D. from Columbia University in 1955 (on the importance of the Columbia "school" to his work, see Swedberg, 1996), and a year later he began his academic career as Assistant Professor at the University of Chicago (to which he returned in 1973, after a fourteen-year stay at Johns Hopkins University, and where he remained until his death). In the same year that he began teaching at Chicago, Coleman was the junior author (with Seymour Martin Lipset and Martin A. Trow) of one of the landmark studies in the history of industrial sociology, if not sociology as a whole, *Union Democracy*. (Coleman's doctoral dissertation at Columbia, directed by Lipset, dealt with some of the issues examined in *Union Democracy*.) Coleman then turned his attention to research on youth and education, the culmination of which was a landmark federal government report (it came to be widely known as the "Coleman Report") that helped lead to the highly controversial policy of busing as a method for achieving racial equality in America's schools. It is through this work that Coleman has had a greater practical impact than any other American sociologist. Next, Coleman turned his attention from the practical world to the rarefied atmosphere of mathematical sociology (especially *Introduction to Mathematical Sociology* [1964] and *The Mathematics of Collective Action* [1973]). In later years, Coleman turned to sociological theory, especially rational choice theory, in the publication of the book *Foundations of Social Theory* (1990) and the founding in 1989 of the journal *Rationality and Society*. The body of work mentioned here reflects almost unbelievable diversity, and it does not even begin to scratch the surface of the 28 books and 301 articles listed on Coleman's resume.

Coleman received a B.S. from Purdue University in 1949 and worked as a chemist for Eastman Kodak before he entered the famous department of sociology at Columbia University in 1951. One key influence on Coleman was the theorist Robert Merton (see Chapter 3), especially his lectures on Durkheim and the social determinants of individual behavior. Another influence was the famous methodologist Paul Lazarsfeld, from whom Coleman derived his lifelong interests in quantitative methods and mathematical sociology. The third important influence was Seymour Martin Lipset, whose research team Coleman joined, thereby ultimately participating in the production of the landmark study, *Union Democracy*. Thus, Coleman's graduate training gave him a powerful introduction to theory, methods, and their linkage in empirical research. This was, and is, the model for all aspiring sociologists.

On the basis of these experiences, Coleman describes his "vision" for sociology when he left graduate school and embarked on his professional career:

own actions to those who initiate and maintain the norms. Such norms become effective when a consensus emerges that some people have the right to control (through norms) the actions of other people. Furthermore, the effectiveness of norms depends on the ability to enforce that consensus. It is consensus and enforcement that prevent the kind of disequilibrium characteristic of collective behavior.

Coleman recognizes that norms become interrelated, but he sees such a macro issue as beyond the scope of his work on the foundations of social systems. On the other

Sociology . . . should have the social system (whether a small system or a large one) as its unit of analysis, rather than the individual; but it should use quantitative methods, leaving behind the unsystematic techniques which lend themselves to investigator bias, fail to lend themselves to replication, and often lack an explanatory or causation focus. Why did I, and other students at Columbia at the time, have this vision? I believe it was the unique combination of Robert K. Merton and Paul Lazarsfeld.

(Coleman, 1994:30–31)

Looking back from the vantage point of the mid-1990s, Coleman found that his approach had changed, but not as much as he had assumed. For example, with respect to his work on social simulation games at Johns Hopkins in the 1960s he says, They "led me to change my theoretical orientation from one in which properties of the system are not only determinants of action (à la Emile Durkheim's *Suicide* study), to one in which they are also consequences of actions sometimes intended, sometimes unintended" (Coleman, 1994:33). Thus, Coleman needed a theory of action, and he chose, in common with most economists,

the simplest such foundation, that of rational, or if you prefer, purposive action. The most formidable task of sociology is the development of a theory that will move from the micro level of action to the macro level of norms, social values, status distribution, and social conflict.

(Coleman, 1994:33)

It is this interest that explains why Coleman is drawn to economics:

What distinguishes economics from the other social sciences is not its use of "rational choice" but its use of a mode of analysis that allows moving between the level of individual action and the level of system functioning. By making two assumptions, that persons act rationally and that markets are perfect with full communication, economic analysis is able to link the macro level of system functioning with the micro level of individual actions.

(Coleman, 1994:32)

Another aspect of Coleman's vision for sociology, consistent with his early work on schools, is that it be applicable to social policy. Of theory he says, "One of the criteria for judging work in social theory is its potential usefulness for informing social policy" (Coleman, 1994:33). Few sociologists would disagree with Coleman's goal of linking theory, methods, and social policy, although many would disagree with at least some of the ways in which Coleman chose to link them. Whether or not they agree with the specifics, future sociologists will continue to be challenged by the need to do a better job of linking these three key aspects of sociological practice, and at least some of them will find in the work of James Coleman a useful model.

James Coleman died on March 25, 1995 (J. Clark, 1996).

hand, he is willing to take on the micro issue of the internalization of norms. He recognizes that in discussing internalization he is entering "waters that are treacherous for a theory grounded in rational choice" (Coleman, 1990:292). He sees the internalization of norms as the establishment of an internal sanctioning system; people sanction themselves when they violate a norm. Coleman looks at this in terms of the idea of one actor or set of actors endeavoring to control others by having norms internalized in them. Thus, it is in the interests of one set of actors to have another set internalize norms and be controlled by them. He feels that this is rational "when such attempts can be effective at reasonable cost" (Coleman, 1990:294).

Coleman looks at norms from the point of view of the three key elements of his theory—micro to macro, purposive action at the micro level, and macro to micro. Norms are macro-level phenomena that come into existence on the basis of micro-level purposive action. Once in existence, norms, through sanctions or the threat of sanctions, affect the actions of individuals. Certain actions may be encouraged, while others are discouraged.

The Corporate Actor   With the case of norms, Coleman has moved to the macro level, and he continues his analysis at this level in a discussion of the corporate actor (J. Clark, 1996). Within such a collectivity, actors may not act in terms of their self-interest but must act in the interest of the collectivity.

There are various rules and mechanisms for moving from individual choice to collective (social) choice. The simplest is the case of voting and the procedures for tabulating the individual votes and coming up with a collective decision. This is the micro-to-macro dimension, while such things as the slate of candidates proposed by the collectivity involves the macro-to-micro linkage.

Coleman argues that both corporate actors and human actors have purposes. Furthermore, within a corporate structure such as an organization, human actors may pursue purposes of their own that are at variance with corporate purposes. This conflict of interest helps us understand the sources of revolts against corporate authority. The micro-to-macro linkage here involves the ways in which people divest authority from the corporate structure and vest legitimacy in those engaged in the revolt. But there is also a macro-to-micro linkage in that certain macro-level conditions lead people to such acts of divestment and investment.

As a rational choice theorist, Coleman starts with the individual and with the idea that all rights and resources exist at this level. The interests of individuals determine the course of events. However, this is untrue, especially in modern society, where "a large fraction of rights and resources, and therefore sovereignty, may reside in corporate actors" (Coleman, 1990:531). In the modern world corporate actors have taken on increasing importance. The corporate actor may act to the benefit or the harm of the individual. How are we to judge the corporate actor in this regard? Coleman contends that "only by starting conceptually from a point where all sovereignty rests with individual persons is it possible to see just how well their ultimate interests are realized by any existing social system. The postulate that individual persons are sovereign provides a way in which sociologists may evaluate the functioning of social systems" (1990:531–532).

To Coleman, the key social change has been the emergence of corporate actors to complement "natural person" actors. Both may be considered actors because they have "control over resources and events, interests in resources and events, and the capability of taking actions to realize those interests through that control" (Coleman, 1990:542). Of course, there have always been corporate actors, but the old ones, like the family, are steadily being replaced by new, purposively constructed, freestanding corporate actors. The existence of these new corporate actors raises the issue of how to ensure their social responsibility. Coleman suggests that we can do this by instituting internal reforms or by changing the external structure such as the laws affecting such corporate actors or the agencies that regulate them.

Coleman differentiates between primordial structures based on the family, such as neighborhoods and religious groups, and purposive structures, such as economic organizations and the government. He sees a progressive "unbundling" of the activities that were once tied together within the family. The primordial structures are "unraveling" as their functions are being dispersed and being taken over by a range of corporate actors. Coleman is concerned about this unraveling as well as about the fact that we are now forced to deal with positions in purposive structures rather than with the people who populated primordial structures. He thus concludes that the goal of his work is "providing the foundation for constructing a viable social structure, as the primordial structure on which persons have depended vanishes" (Coleman, 1990:652).

Coleman is critical of most of social theory for adopting a view that he labels *homo sociologicus*. This perspective emphasizes the socialization process and the close fit between the individual and society. Therefore, *homo sociologicus* is unable to deal with the freedom of individuals to act as they will in spite of the constraints placed upon them. Furthermore, this perspective lacks the ability to evaluate the actions of the social system. In contrast, *homo economicus,* in Coleman's view, possesses all these capacities. In addition, Coleman attacks traditional social theory for doing little more than chanting old theoretical mantras and for being irrelevant to the changes taking place in society and incapable of helping us know where society is headed. Sociological theory (as well as sociological research) must have a purpose, a role in the functioning of society. Coleman is in favor of social theory that is interested not just in knowledge for the sake of knowledge but also in "a search for knowledge for the reconstruction of society" (1990:651).

Coleman's views on social theory are closely linked to his views on the changing nature of society. The passing of primordial structures and their replacement by purposive structures has left a series of voids that have not been filled adequately by the new social organizations. Social theory, and the social sciences more generally, are made necessary by the need to reconstruct a new society (Coleman, 1993a, 1993b; Bulmer, 1996). The goal is not to destroy purposive structures but rather to realize the opportunities and avoid the problems of such structures. The new society requires a new social science. The linkages among institutional areas have changed, and as a result the social sciences must be willing to cut across traditional disciplinary boundaries.

Criticisms   Needless to say, rational choice theory in general (Goldfield and Gilbert, 1997; Green and Shapiro, 1994; Imber, 1997) has come under heavy fire in sociology. In fact, as Heckathorn (1997:15) points out, there is a kind of "hysteria" in some quarters of sociology about rational choice theory. James Coleman's work has been attacked from many quarters (Alexander, 1992; Rambo, 1995). For example, Tilly (1997:83) offers the following basic criticisms of Coleman's theory:

1 Neglected to specify causal mechanisms.
2 Promoted an incomplete and therefore misleading psychological reductionism.

3 Advocated a form of general theory—rational choice analysis—that has for some time been enticing social scientists into blind alleys, where they have wandered aimlessly, falling victim to local thugs and confidence men selling various brands of individual reductionism.

More generally, some researchers have found rational choice theory wanting (Weakliem and Heath, 1994), but the vast majority of the criticisms have come from supporters of alternative positions within sociology (Wrong, 1997). For example, given his macro-structural position, Blau (1997) argues that sociology should focus on macro-level phenomena and, as a result, the explanation of individual behavior that is the metier of rational choice theory falls outside of the bounds of sociology.

Rational choice theory has been criticized from many quarters for being overly ambitious, for seeking to replace all other theoretical perspectives. Thus, Green and Shapiro (1994:203) argue that rational choice theory would do well "to probe the limits of what rational choice can explain" and to "relinquish the . . . tendency to ignore, absorb, or discredit competing theoretical accounts."

From a feminist point of view, England and Kilbourne (1990) have criticized the assumption of selfishness in rational choice theory; from their perspective selfishness-altruism should be considered as a variable. The assumption of selfishness represents a masculine bias. They recognize that rejecting this assumption, and looking at it as a variable, would reduce the "deductive determinacy" of rational choice theory, but they think the benefits of such a more realistic, less-biased theoretical orientation outweigh the costs.

From a symbolic-interactionist perspective, Denzin (1990b; see also Chapter 6 of this book) offers just the critique one might expect from such a diametrically opposed theoretical orientation:

> Rational choice theory . . . fails to offer a convincing answer to the question: How is society possible? . . . its ideal norms of rationality do not fit everyday life and the norms of rationality and emotionality that organize the actual activities of interacting individuals.
>
> Rational choice theory has limited utility for contemporary social theory. Its scheme of group life and its picture of the human being, of action, interaction, the self, gender, emotionality, power, language, the political economy of everyday life, and of history, are woefully narrow and completely inadequate *for interpretive purposes.*
>
> (Denzin, 1990a:182–183; italics added)

Most of those operating from a broadly interpretive perspective would accept Denzin's strong criticisms of rational choice theory.

In addition to general criticisms, rational choice theory has been attacked for underplaying or ignoring things like culture (Fararo, 1996) and chance events (G. Hill, 1997).

Finally, although many other criticisms could be delineated, we might mention Smelser's (1992) argument that like many other theoretical perspectives, rational choice theory has degenerated as a result of internal evolution or responses to external criticisms. Thus, rational choice theory has become tautological and invulnerable to falsifiability, and most important, it has developed the "capacity to explain everything and hence nothing" (Smelser, 1992:400).

Rational choice theory has many supporters (Hedstrom and Swedberg, 1996). We will see many efforts to legitimize it further as a sociological theory and even more attempts to apply and extend the theory. We are also likely to see a further escalation of the criticisms leveled at rational choice theory.

SUMMARY

This chapter deals with three interrelated theories which, among other things, share a positivistic orientation. Modern exchange theory has evolved out of a series of intellectual influences, especially behaviorism and rational choice theory. Thibaut and Kelley's work, *The Social Psychology of Groups,* while lying outside sociology, was an important precursor to developments within sociology. The founder of modern exchange theory was George Homans. His reductionistic, determinedly micro-oriented exchange theory is summarized in a small number of propositions. Blau sought to extend exchange theory to the macro level, primarily by emphasizing the importance of norms. Much of the contemporary work in exchange theory has been influenced by Richard Emerson's more structural effort to develop an integrative, micro-macro approach to exchange. Emerson's disciples, and others, are busy extending his theoretical perspective into a variety of new domains.

One of Emerson's concerns is with networks, a concern also of those associated with network theory. While there are many overlaps between exchange theory and network theory, many network theorists operate outside an exchange framework. Network theory is distinguished by its focus on the objective pattern of ties within and between micro and macro levels of social reality.

Thanks largely to the efforts of James Coleman, rational choice theory, which had played a role in the development of exchange theory, has come into its own as a theoretical perspective. Utilizing a few basic principles derived largely from economics, rational choice theory purports to be able to deal with micro- and macro-level issues, as well as the role played by micro-level factors in the formation of macro-level phenomena. The number of supporters of rational choice theory is increasing in sociology, but so is the resistance to it by those who support other theoretical perspectives.

9

CONTEMPORARY
FEMINIST THEORY

Patricia Madoo Lengermann
The George Washington University

Jill Niebrugge-Brantley
Gettysburg College

THE BASIC THEORETICAL QUESTIONS
SOCIOLOGICAL THEORIES OF GENDER: 1960–PRESENT
  Macro-Social Theories of Gender
  Micro-Social Theories of Gender
VARIETIES OF CONTEMPORARY FEMINIST THEORY
  Gender Difference
  Gender Inequality
  Gender Oppression
  Structural Oppression
  Feminism and Postmodernism
A FEMINIST SOCIOLOGICAL THEORY
  A Feminist Sociology of Knowledge
  The Macro-Social Order
  The Micro-Social Order
  Subjectivity
TOWARD AN INTEGRATIVE THEORY

Feminist theory is a generalized, wide-ranging system of ideas about social life and human experience developed from a woman-centered perspective. Feminist theory is woman-centered—or women-centered—in three ways. First, its major "object" for investigation, the starting point of all its investigation, is the situation (or the situations) and experiences of women in society. Second, it treats women as the central "subjects" in the investigative process; that is, it seeks to see the world from the distinctive vantage points of women in the social world. Third, feminist theory is critical and activist on behalf of women, seeking to produce a better world for women—and thus, it argues, for humankind.

Feminist theory differs from most sociological theories in two key ways. First, it is the work of an interdisciplinary community, which includes not only sociologists but also scholars from other disciplines, such as anthropology, biology, economics, history, law, literature, philosophy, political science, psychology, and theology; people best recognized as creative writers; people who see themselves primarily as political activists; spokespersons for women of color; and writers from various European or Third World intellectual communities.[1] Second, feminist sociologists, like other feminist academics, work with a double agenda: to broaden and deepen their discipline of origin—sociology, in this case—by reworking disciplinary knowledge to take account of discoveries being made by feminist scholars; and to develop a critical understanding of society in order to change the world in directions deemed more just and humane. A double agenda of this type is the hallmark of any critical theory.

THE BASIC THEORETICAL QUESTIONS

The impetus for contemporary feminist theory begins in a deceptively simple question: *"And what about the women?"* In other words, where are the women in any situation being investigated? If they are not present, why? If they are present, what exactly are they doing? How do they experience the situation? What do they contribute to it? What does it mean to them?

Thirty years of posing this question has produced some generalizable conclusions. Women are present in most social situations. Where they are not, it is not because they lack ability or interest but because there have been deliberate efforts to exclude them. Where they are present, women have played roles very different from the popular conception of them (as, for example, passive wives and mothers). Indeed, as wives and as mothers and in a series of other roles, women have, along with men, actively created the situations being studied. Yet though women are actively present in most social situations, scholars, publics, and social actors themselves, both male and female, have been blind to their presence. Moreover, women's roles in most social situations, although essential, have been different from, less privileged than, and subordinate to those of men. Their invisibility is only one indicator of this inequality.

Feminism's second basic question is: *"Why then is all this as it is?"* As the first question calls for a description of the social world, this second question requires an explanation of that world. Description and explanation of the social world are two faces of any sociological theory. Feminism's attempts to answer these questions have therefore produced a theory of universal importance for sociology.

The third question for all feminists is *"How can we change and improve the social world so as to make it a more just place for women and for all people?"* This commitment to social transformation in the interest of justice is the distinctive characteristic of critical social theory, a commitment shared in sociology by feminism, Marxism, neo-Marxism, and social theories being developed by racial and ethnic minorities and in postcolonial societies. Patricia Hill Collins (1998:xiv) forcefully states the importance of this commitment to seeking justice and confronting injustice: "Critical social theory

[1]This chapter, however, draws primarily on the English-language contribution to this international effort.

encompasses bodies of knowledge . . . that actively grapple with the central questions facing groups of people differently placed in specific political, social, and historic contexts characterized by injustice." This commitment to critical theory requires that feminist theorists ask of their work, "What are the consequences of this way of thinking for transforming the inequities in women's lives? How is this way of explaining the world going to improve life for all women?" (Hennessy and Ingraham, 1997:5).

Over the thirty-year period the circle of feminists exploring these questions has become steadily larger and more inclusive of people from diverse backgrounds, both in the United States and internationally. This has led to an intense focus on the qualifying question guiding feminist theoretical work today: *"And what about the differences among women?"* We call this question feminism's qualifying question because it leads to a general conclusion that the invisibility, inequality, and role differences in relation to men which generally characterize women's lives are profoundly affected by a woman's social location—that is, by her class, race, age, affectional preference, marital status, religion, ethnicity, and global location.

How general is feminist theory? Some might argue that because the questions are particular to the situation of women, the theory that is produced will also be particular and restricted in scope, equivalent to sociology's theories of deviance or small-group processes. But in fact feminism's basic questions have produced a theory of social life universal in its applicability. The appropriate parallels to feminist theory are not theories of small groups or deviance, each of which is created when sociologists turn their attention away from the "whole picture" and to the details of a feature of that picture. Rather, the appropriate parallel is to one of Marx's epistemological accomplishments. Marx helped social scientists discover that the knowledge people had of society, what they assumed to be an absolute and universal statement about reality, in fact reflected the experience of those who economically and politically ruled the social world. Marxian theory effectively demonstrated that one could also view the world from the vantage point of the world's workers, those who, though economically and politically subordinate, were nevertheless indispensable producers of our world. This new vantage point relativized ruling-class knowledge and, in allowing us to juxtapose that knowledge with knowledge gained from taking the workers' perspective, vastly expanded our ability to analyze social reality. A century after Marx's death we are assimilating the implications of this discovery.

Feminism's basic theoretical questions similarly produce a revolutionary switch in our understanding of the world. These questions, too, lead us to discover that what we have taken as universal and absolute knowledge of the world is, in fact, knowledge derived from the experiences of a powerful section of society, men as "masters." That knowledge is relativized if we rediscover the world from the vantage point of a hitherto invisible, unacknowledged "underside": women, who in subordinated but indispensable "serving" roles have worked to sustain and re-create the society that we live in. This discovery raises questions about everything that we thought we knew about society. This discovery and its implications constitute the essence of contemporary feminist theory's significance for sociological theory.

Feminism's radical challenge to established systems of knowledge, by contrasting them with women-centered understandings of reality, not only relativizes established knowledge, but also "deconstructs" such knowledge. To say that knowledge is "deconstructed" is to say that we discover what was hitherto hidden behind the presentation of the knowledge as established, singular, and natural—namely, that that presentation is a construction resting on social, relational, and power arrangements. Feminism deconstructs established systems of knowledge by showing their masculinist bias and the gender politics framing and informing them. But feminism itself has become the subject of relativizing and deconstructionist pressures from within its own theoretical boundaries especially in the last decade. The first and the more powerful of these pressures comes from women confronting the white, privileged-class, heterosexual status of many leading feminists—that is, from women of color, women in postcolonial societies, working-class women, lesbians. These women, speaking from "margin to center" (hooks, 1984), show that there are many differently situated women, and there are many women-centered knowledge systems which oppose both established, male-stream knowledge claims and any hegemonic feminist claims about a unitary woman's standpoint. The second deconstructionist pressure within feminism comes from a growing postmodernist literature, which raises questions about gender as an undifferentiated concept and about the individual self as a stable locus of consciousness and personhood from which gender and the world are experienced. The potential impact of these questions falls primarily on feminist epistemology—its system for making truth claims—and is explored more fully below.

SOCIOLOGICAL THEORIES OF GENDER: 1960–PRESENT

The relation between feminist theory and existing sociology can be traced in at least two key areas of scholarship. One meeting place feminism and sociology, and an increasingly important area in the last five years, is in the impact of feminist theory on sociology's substantive fields—deviance (Barry, 1995; Bergen, 1996; Stiglmayer, 1994), family (McMahon, 1995; Stacey, 1996), occupations and professions (Pierce, 1995; Williams, 1995), political sociology (Fraser, 1997; Jackman, 1994; Stetson and Masur, 1995), social movements (Ferree and Martin, 1995; Taylor, 1989; Whittier, 1995; *Gender & Society* 12:6, 1998 and 13:1, 1999), and stratification (Ferree and Hall, 1996; Ridgeway, 1997). A second meeting place, and the focus of this section, is the work of OSC sociological theories (see the collection edited by England [1993] for extended critical discussions of the relations between feminism and sociological theories; see also, Chafetz, 1997). Most of the work done linking feminism to existing social theories focuses on gender, and we organize our discussion of this work into macro-social theories of gender, and micro-social theories of gender.

Macro-Social Theories of Gender

Feminism's first question, "And what about the women?" has produced significant responses from theorists working out of three major macro-social perspectives that are more fully presented elsewhere in this book—structural-functionalism (Chapter 3), conflict theory (Chapter 3), and neo-Marxian world-systems theory (Chapter 4). These theorists all use the same analytic process in placing gender in their generalized theoretical account of large-scale social phenomena. First, they define those phenomena as a system of interrelated and interacting structures, which are understood as "patterned regularities in people's behavior" (Chafetz, 1984:23). Functionalists and analytic conflict theorists focus on nation-states or, on occasion, especially within analytic conflict theory, on premodern cultural groupings; world-systems theory treats global capitalism as a transnational system within which nation-states are important structures. The variations between these theories center on the particular structures and systemic processes they see as important. Second, these theorists move to situate women within the system described. All three theories arrive at the same conclusion: women's primary location—in the sense that it is a location seen within all cultures as the distinctive "sphere" for women—is the household/family. From that primary location, and always with it as a framing condition, women may have other significant structural sites for activity, most notably in the market economy. The issue then becomes that of understanding the functions of the household/family in the social system and of charting the relationship between household and economy. Third, each of these groups of gender theorists seeks to explain gender stratification—viewed as the near universal social disadvantage of women—in terms of the triangulated structural alignment of household/family, economy, and general social-system needs and processes.

Functionalism   The major proponent of a functionalist theory of gender is Miriam Johnson (1988, 1989, 1993). Speaking as a functionalist and a feminist, Johnson first acknowledges the failure of functionalism to adequately explore women's disadvantage in society. She accepts that there is an unintentional sexist bias in Talcott Parsons's theory of the family and that functionalism marginalizes issues of social inequality, domination, and oppression—a tendency originating in functionalism's primary concern with social order. Yet Johnson cogently demonstrates that the analytic variety and complexity of Parsonsian functionalism should be retained in analyses of gender because of the tremendous analytic range and flexibility of such a multifaceted theory—reiterating the position of many neofunctionalists (see Chapter 3). Johnson's work explores the relevance for gender of many of Parsons's key typologies: role as the basic unit in the social system, expressive versus instrumental role orientations, family as an institution in relation to other institutions, the functional prerequisites of the social system (adaptation, goal attainment, integration, and latency), the analytic levels of social action (social, cultural, personality, and behavioral), the stages of societal change (differentiation, adaptive upgrading, integration, and value generalization).

Most significant for a functionalist understanding of gender is Johnson's application of Parsons's concepts of expressive versus instrumental roles, his thesis of the family's relationship to other institutions, and his model of the functional prerequisites. Johnson locates much of the origin of gender inequality in the structure of the patriarchal family, in place in almost all known societies. The family has functions distinct from those of the economy and other "public" institutions: it socializes children and emotionally renews its adult members, activities essential to social cohesion and value reproduction (integration and latency). Women's primary social location in the structure of the family is as the principal producer of those essential functions. In these activities she must orient expressively, that is, with emotional attunement and relational responsiveness. Women's functions in the family and orientation toward expressiveness affect their functions in all other social structures, especially the economy. Women, for example, are channeled toward occupations typed as expressive; in male-dominated occupations they are expected to be expressive but are simultaneously sanctioned for this orientation; and always the responsibility toward family frames and intrudes upon economic participation.

None of the functions described above would, however, necessarily result in a gender stratification system which devalues and disadvantages women. To understand why gender stratification is produced we must return to the patriarchal family. Here in their expressively oriented care of children, women act with strength and authority, giving both boys and girls their sense of "common humanity." Institutional and cultural constraints require that the woman be weak and expressively compliant in relation to her husband, whose instrumentally mediated competitiveness in the economy earns for his family its level of economic security. Seeing her in the "weak wife" role, children learn to revere patriarchy and to devalue expressiveness as a relational stance against which instrumentality seems more powerful and valuable. This valuing of male instrumentality as more effective than female expressiveness is diffuse in the culture. But this valuational stance has no practical basis—except when framed by patriarchal ideology. One of Johnson's hopes is that the women's movement will produce the societal and cultural changes that lead to a systemwide reevaluation of expressiveness.

In the meantime, however, Johnson must deal with the question of how patriarchal structures are functional in the production of system equilibrium and social order. Johnson suggests (1993) that we ask, "functional for whom?" But with this question she moves beyond Parsonsian functionalism, which argues that functionality is to be understood in terms of the system per se. The question "functional for whom?" opens up issues of unequal power and conflicting interests, and points to a critical rather than a value-neutral stance for the theorist, a stance antithetical to functionalism. The question about women, the issue of gender, has, as it always does, made "the pot boil over."

Analytic Conflict Theory   The most influential theorist working on the issue of gender from the perspective of analytic conflict theory is Janet Chafetz (1984, 1988, 1990; see also Dunn, Almquist, and Chafetz, 1993), who, unlike Johnson, works in a network of similarly framed theoretical work (Rae Lesser Blumberg, 1978, 1979, 1984; Randall Collins, 1975; and anthropologist Peggy Sanday, 1974, 1981). Chafetz's approach is cross-cultural and trans-historical and seeks to theorize gender in all its particular societal patternings. More specifically, she focuses on gender inequality, or as she labels it, *sex stratification.* In starting with sex stratification, Chafetz is consistent with analytic conflict theory practices: she finds a recurrent form of social conflict and sets out to analyze, from a value-neutral stance, the structural conditions producing the conflict in greater or lesser degrees of intensity.

Chafetz then explores the social structures and conditions which affect the intensity of sex stratification—or the disadvantaging of women—in all societies and cultures. These include gender role differentiation, patriarchal ideology, family and work organization, and framing conditions such as fertility patterns, separation of household and work sites, economic surplus, technological sophistication, population density, and environmental harshness—all understood as variables. The interaction of these variables determines the degree of sex stratification, because they frame the key structures of household and economic production and the degree to which women move between the two areas. Chafetz's position is that women experience the least disadvantage when they can balance household responsibilities with a significant and independent role in marketplace production. The household/family is viewed not as an area outside of work, a zone of emotions and nurturance, but as an area in which work occurs—child care, housework, and sometimes also work (as on the family farm) for which there are extra-household material rewards. Women's access to those rewards either through household or marketplace production becomes the mitigation against social disadvantage, and the form of the household—resulting from the interplay of many other variables—is the key structure facilitating or obstructing this access.

Chafetz then goes on to focus on how gender equity may be purposively pursued, seeking to identify key structural points where change might improve women's condition. In her proactive stance toward gender equity Chafetz moves beyond the value neutrality which has been the hallmark of analytic conflict theory since Weber. The exploration of gender again leads the theorist—in this case a most disciplined practitioner—beyond the theory to issues of power and politics.

World-Systems Theory   World-systems theory takes global capitalism in all its historical phases as *the* system for sociological analysis. National societies and other distinct cultural groupings (for example, colonies and indigenous peoples) are significant structures in the world-system of global capitalism, as are the economic stratification of those societies and groupings (core, semiperipheral, and peripheral economies); the division of labor, capital, and power among and within them; and class relations within each societal unit. Since the defining process framing this theory's investigation is capitalism, individuals in all societal units typically are understood in terms of their role within capitalist arrangements for the creation of surplus value. This theory thus typically understands women's role in the social system only to the degree that their labor is part of capitalism—that is, when they are workers within capitalist production and markets. But a full and direct engagement with the issue of gender immediately throws this model of the social system into question.

Kathryn B. Ward (1984, 1985a, 1985b, 1988, 1990, 1993; Word and Pyle, 1995) argues that (1) the world-system cannot be understood until the labor of the household and the labor of the informal economy are properly factored in and (2) that because women compose much of this labor, women must be given special attention in world-systems theory and not simply subsumed under the title "worker." The household constitutes all the work done at home to maintain and reproduce the worker; the *in*formal economy is that organization of work in which there is *no* clear separation between labor and capital and *no* regulation of labor by law or capitalist organization. Ward argues that perhaps as much as 66 percent of the world's work is done in these two largely ignored, noncapitalist economies and that the proportion of the world's work done in these two economies is expanding *precisely as capitalism itself expands* globally. Answering the question "And what about the women?" in the world-system thus reveals a vast "subcontinent" of noncapitalist production coexisting, expanding, and interacting with global capitalism. In women's pattern of work globally—where the exigencies of household work are always present, and where women out of that base engage with informal and capitalist economies in an ever-shifting calculus—we find one point of entry for theorizing the structures of work within the world-system. Further, Ward argues that the particular contributions of women's unpaid labor to the world economy and male dominance over women must be understood and explained not simply as products of capitalism but as "distinctive phenomena properties with their own logic" (Ward, 1993:52).

Micro-Social Theories of Gender

Microsociological theorists have focused less on explaining women's social disadvantage than on explicating the phenomenon of gender as it enters into their understanding of society as human beings in interaction; they ask how gender is present in interactions and how interactions produce gender. The two main microsociological theories of gender are symbolic interactionism (Cahill, 1980; Deegan and Hill, 1987; Goffman, 1979) and ethnomethodology (Fenstermaker, Berk, 1985; Fenstermaker, West, and Zimmerman, 1991; West and Fenstermaker, 1993; West and Zimmerman, 1987).

Symbolic interactionism's theory of gender begins with a proposition central to any symbolic-interactionist analysis: "Gender identity, like other social identities, emerges out of social interaction and is incorporated into the individual's transsituational self [and] must be continually confirmed across varying interactional situations . . . because the self is subject to constant empirical tests" (Cahill, 1980:123). Symbolic interactionism reverses Freud's contention that identification with the same-sex parent is the key element *in developing* gender identity; it argues rather that in acquiring language the child learns that it is identified, and thus, to self-identify, as a "boy" or "girl" and thus, in turn, to identify with "mommy" or "daddy." Symbolic-interactionist accounts show individuals engaged in maintaining the gendered self in various situations; at the core of these accounts is a knowing individual who has a collection of ideas, of words in one's inner and outer conversations, about what it means to be a man or woman. The person brings a gendered self into situations and tries to act according to this internalized definition, which may be modified through interaction from situation to situation but is the repository of the gender component of people's transsituational behavior.

Ethnomethodology questions the stability of gender identity and looks at "how gender is done," that is, gender as an accomplishment by actors in various situations. Ethnomethodologists begin from Zimmerman's proposition (1978:11) that "properties of social life which seem objective, factual and transsituational, are actually managed accomplishments or achievements of local processes." Ethnomethodologists make the theoretically important distinction among *sex* (biological identification as male or female), *sex category* (social identification as male or female), and *gender* (behavior that meets social expectations for being male or female). Where the emphasis upon internalization of a fixed gender identity may reduce gender to as individual an attribute as sex—something that is inherently part of the individual—the ethnomethodological argument is that gender does not inhere in the person but is achieved in interaction in the situation. Because sex category is potentially an ever-present quality of an individual, the achievement of gender is potentially an ever-present quality in social situations. People's normative conceptions of appropriate male or female behavior are situationally activated. People in a situation know that they are "accountable" for gender performance to the degree that the situation permits a person to behave as a man or a woman within it and have other people so recognize her or his behavior. It is possible for people from different cultures—including class and race cultures—to find each other's behavior incomprehensible in terms of gender identity: what the other is doing is not recognized as being male- or female-appropriate behavior. On the other hand, ethnomethodological research has shown that divisions of household labor that appear vastly unequal from outside the household situation may be seen as fair and equal by both men and women in the situation because both parties accept and conform to normative expectations for doing gender within the household.

Both symbolic interactionism and ethnomethodology allow for and assume an institutional milieu of normative conceptions about gender. Goffman (1979) noted early, and symbolic interactionists, under the influence of postmodernism (Denzin, 1993), increasingly affirm that these conceptions are not accessed solely, or perhaps even primarily, through interaction with other people. Mediated messages—that is, media images in advertising, television, movies, books, magazines—tell both adults and children quite directly, without interactional intervention, how gender is enacted. These mediated messages offer what Goffman labels "displays" of gender: "simplified, exaggerated, stereotyped" information about the appropriate "alignments" for men and women in given interactions. This analysis produces a causal puzzle: is media imitating life or life, media? Here as in other instances, microsociological explorations of gender work successfully within their given paradigms without touching the essential male, privileged elite biases in those paradigms, challenges we raise in our discussion of feminist sociological theory later in this chapter.

VARIETIES OF CONTEMPORARY FEMINIST THEORY

The basis for any feminist sociological theory, including the one developed in the second half of this chapter, lies in contemporary feminist theory, that system of general ideas designed to describe and explain human social experiences from a woman-centered vantage point. In this section we present the themes that feminist theory offers for constructing feminist sociological theories. The "map" of feminist theory presented here is *one* construct, or ideal type, for patterning this complex body of intellectual work.[2]

[2]Several other classificatory systems already exist, for example, those developed by Chafetz (1988); Clough (1994); Glennon (1979); Jaggar (1983); Jaggar and Rothenberg (1984); Kirk and Okazawa-Rey (1998); Lengermann and Wallace (1985); Snitow, Stansell, and Thompson (1983); and Sokoloff (1980). Readers might turn to these for balance or amplification of the ideal type presented here. In combination, these efforts have generated a long list of types of feminist theory, including black feminism, conservatism, expressionism, instrumentalism, lesbian feminism, liberalism, Marxism, polarism, psychoanalytic feminism, radicalism, separatism, socialism, and synthesism. Our own typology attempts to include most of these theories, though not always as identified by these specific labels.

TABLE 9.1
OVERVIEW OF VARIETIES OF FEMINIST THEORY

Basic varieties of feminist theory—answers to the descriptive question, "What about the women?"	Distinctions within theories—answers to the explanatory question, "Why is women's situation as it is?"
Gender difference	
Women's location in, and experience of, most situations is *different* from that of men in the situation.	Cultural feminism Biological Institutional and socialization Social-psychological
Gender inequality	

Women's location in most situations is not only different but also less privileged than or *unequal* to that of men.	Liberal feminism
	Marxian
	    Marx and Engel's explanations
	    Contemporary Marxian explanations

Gender oppression	
Women are *oppressed,* not just different from or unequal to, but actively restrained, subordinated, molded, and used and abused by men.	Psychoanalytic feminism Radical feminism Socialist feminism
Structural oppression	
Women's experience of difference, inequality, and oppression varies by their social location within capitalism, patriarchy, and racism.	Socialist feminism Intersectionality theory
Feminism and postmodernism	

Our typology of feminist theory is organized around feminism's most basic question, *And what about the women?* The pattern of response to this question generates the main categories for our classification (see Table 9.1). Essentially we see four answers to the question "And what about the women?" The first is that women's location in, and experience of, most situations is *different* from that of the men in those situations. The second is that women's location in most situations is not only different from but also less privileged than or *unequal* to that of men. The third is that women's situation also has to be understood in terms of a direct power relationship between men and women. Women are *oppressed,* that is, restrained, subordinated, molded, and used and abused by men. The fourth is that women's experience of difference, inequality, and oppression varies according to their total locatedness within societies' arrangements *of structural oppression* or vectors of oppression and privilege—class, race, ethnicity, age, affectional preference, marital status, and global location. Each of the various types of feminist theory can be classified as a theory of *gender difference,* or of *gender inequality,* or of *gender oppression,* or of *structural oppression.* In our discussion we make distinctions within these basic categories in terms of their differing answers to the second or explanatory question, "Why then is all this as it is?" (The various types of answers are summarized in Table 9.1.) In addition, we note how all the answers are affected by feminism's qualifying question, "What about the differences among women?" We conclude this section with a discussion of the growing dialogue between feminism and postmodernism; but since postmodernist feminists do not conceptualize their work in terms of feminism's basic question, "What about the women?" its standing in this section is unique—as indicated by its placement in the chart.

This classification method gives one way to pattern the general body of contemporary feminist theory and the expanding literature on gender that has developed within sociology since the 1960s. As sociologists have turned their efforts to an exploration of feminist issues, they have typically used some portion of the existing body of sociological theory as a point of departure for what is called in the discipline the *sociology of gender.* Although the term *gender* is often used euphemistically in sociology for "women," the sociology of gender is, more precisely, the study of socially constructed male and female roles, relations, and identities (Acker, 1992)—and there is now a growing sociological literature on masculinity (for example, Arendell, 1995; Connell, 1990, 1995; Collinson and Hearn, 1996; Fine, Weis, Addelston, and Marusza, 1997; Hood, 1993; Kimmel, 1996; Messner, 1997; Pyke, 1996; Schwalbe, 1996). This focus on the relationship of men and women is not equivalent to a feminist theory which presents a critical woman-centered patterning of human experience. Nevertheless, some sociologists who begin from a sociology-of-gender standpoint have produced works of significance for feminist theory, and many sociologists are directly involved in producing feminist theory.

The remainder of this section explores the feminist theories of gender difference, of gender inequality, of gender oppression, and of structural oppression, describing in each case the general features of the approach, some key lines of variation within it, and its recommendations for change. Three notes of caution are, however, important. First, many theorists' work resists neat categorization. One must either talk about their main theoretical emphasis or distinguish among various of their theoretical statements. Second, one major trend in feminist work today is to weave together ideas drawn from various of the theories we describe, focusing on specific issues like the politics of the body or the nature of the state, in a practice one might name, using Kuhnian vocabulary, "normal theorizing." Third, this is a selective review. Given the volume of recent feminist and sociological writings on women's situation, comprehensiveness is beyond the scope of this chapter.

Gender Difference

At this point in the history of feminist thought, "difference" is an issue in five important debates. The first is whether the term "difference" itself is more appropriately used to describe differences between men and women, than is *gender differences,* the focus of discussion in this section, or to theorize on the issue of differences among women. Second is the possibility raised by postmodernists that gender is not an essential feature of human personhood but is instead a fluid and processual enactment within specific or contextualized interactions (Butler, 1990, 1993; Connell, 1992b; Flax, 1990; Frye, 1996; Nicholson, 1994; Thorne, 1993). The third debate is over the policy implications for feminists of a stand on the principle of gender difference—that is, of an argument about policies that address women's special needs, for example, for maternity leave or breast cancer research. Historically, this has been a significant argument used by feminists (Gordon, 1994; Skocpol, 1992), but many contemporary feminists are concerned about whether to move beyond "women-and-children-first" policies to policies which address inequities that affect all people, such as capitalism's organization of work or of health care (Bacchi, 1990; Barrett and Phillips, 1993; Fineman, 1995; Scott, 1990; Stacey, 1994; Vogel, 1993). The fourth is the debate on gender differences which has most resonance in popular engagements with feminism: the question over whether "male-specific" or "female-specific" traits are more appropriate "templates" for individual and social organization. Fifth is the issue of whether theories of gender difference are *ipso facto* "essentialist." "Essentialism" means that a thing or person possesses or lacks a particular quality as a part of the very terms or nature of its/her/his being. Most feminist theorists are uncomfortable with "essentialism" because they take as the purpose of their work the critical imperative "not to theorize the world but to change it," and essentialism denies the possibility of change. Feminist theoretical engagement with gender difference takes three main forms: cultural feminism, which argues for the worth of women's distinctive ways of being, explanatory theories which explore possible causes of gender difference, and phenomenological and existential theories which trace the implications of women's "Otherness."

Cultural Feminism   The argument of immutable gender difference was, of course, first used against women in male patriarchal discourse to claim that women were inferior and subservient to men. But that argument is reversed by some first-wave feminists who create a theory of *Cultural Feminism,* which extols the positive aspects of what was seen as "the female character" or "feminine personality." Theorists like Margaret Fuller, Frances Willard, Jane Addams, and Charlotte Perkins Gilman were proponents of a cultural feminism that argued that in the governing of the state society needed such women's virtues as cooperation, caring, pacifism, and nonviolence in the settlement of conflicts (Deegan and Hill, 1998; Donovan, 1985; Lengermann and Niebrugge-Brantley, 1998). This tradition has continued to the present day in arguments about women's distinctive standards for ethical judgment (Friedman, 1993; Gilligan, 1982; Held, 1993), about a mode of "caring attention" in women's consciousness (Fisher, 1995; Ruddick, 1980), about different achievement motivation patterns (Kaufman and Richardson, 1982), about a female style of communication (Bate and Taylor, 1988; Crawford, 1995; Tannen, 1990, 1993, 1994), about women's capacity for openness to emotional experience (Beutel and Marini, 1995; Lorde, 1984; Mirowsky and Ross, 1995), about women's fantasies of sexuality and intimacy (Hite, 1976; Radway, 1984; Snitow, Stansell, and Thompson, 1983), and about their lower levels of aggressive behavior and greater capacity for creating peaceful coexistence (A. Campbell, 1993; Ruddick, 1994; Wilson and Musick, 1997). Cultural feminism is typically though not exclusively more concerned with promoting the values of women's difference than with explaining its origins.

Explanatory Theories   Explanatory theories variously locate the causes of gender difference in biology, in institutional roles, in socialization, and in social interaction.

Sociologist and feminist Alice Rossi (1977, 1983) has linked the different biological functions of males and females to different patterns of hormonally determined development over the life cycle and this development, in turn, to sex-specific variation in such traits as sensitivity to light and sound and to differences in left and right brain connections. These differences, she argues, feed into different play patterns in childhood—which have been noted by Gilligan (1982), Lever (1978), and Best (1983)—the well-known female "math anxiety," and the apparent fact that women are more predisposed to care for infants in a nurturing way than are men. Rossi recommends that sociocultural arrangements be adjusted to compensate through social learning for each gender's biologically given disadvantages. Recent feminist biological research shows that many animal species do adjust sex-linked behaviors in response to environmental change (Fausto-Sterling, Gowaty, and Zuk, 1997).

Institutional explanations posit that gender differences result from the different roles that women and men come to play within various institutional settings. A major determinant of difference is seen to be the sexual division of labor that links women to the functions of wife, mother, and household worker, to the private sphere of home and family, and thus to a lifelong series of events and experiences very different from those of men. Women's roles as mothers and wives in producing and reproducing a female personality and culture have been analyzed by theorists as diverse as Berger and Berger (1983), J. Bernard (1981, 1982), Chodorow (1978), Risman and Ferree (1995), and M. Johnson (1989). Socialization theories look at the ways that children in particular (but also adults readying themselves, for instance, for marriage or motherhood) are prepared for playing these various life roles according to a gendered script (Best, 1983; Brown and Gilligan, 1992; Gilligan, 1982; Lever, 1978; Martin, 1998; Sidel, 1990). Some studies (e.g., Kirk, 1997) argue that women's experience of socialization and institutional role leads them to distinctive forms of political activism like environmental justice movements. But some sociologists see socialization and role theories as presenting too static and deterministic a model. They emphasize people's active work in reproducing gender in contextualized, ongoing interactional practices, where cultural typifications of gender are enacted, performed, experimented with, and even transformed. These theorists describe people as "doing gender" in all the various interactions of daily life—rather than carrying with them a gendered personality (Connell, Ashenden, Kessler, and Dowselt, 1982; Eder, Evans, and Parker, 1995; Passaro, 1996; Thorne, 1993; West and Fenstermaker, 1995; West and Zimmerman, 1987).

Existential and Phenomenological Analyses   Feminist thinkers offering existential and phenomenological analyses have developed one of the most enduring themes of feminist theory: the marginalization of women as Other in a male-created culture. This theme is given its classic formulation in Simone de Beauvoir's existential analysis in *The Second Sex* (1949/1957) but there have been myriad other important statements, including Bartsky (1992), Daly (1978), Griffin (1978, 1981), D. Smith (1987), and Tax (1970). In these explanations, the world people inhabit has been developed out of a culture created by men and assuming the male as subject, that is, as the consciousness from which the world is viewed and defined. That culture, at best, pushes women's experience and ways of knowing themselves to the very margins of conceptual framing and, at its most frightening, creates a construct of the woman as "the Other," an objectified being, who is assigned traits that represent the opposite of the agentic, subject male. (For de Beauvoir, following Hegel, Heidegger, and Sartre, it is a given that "Otherness is a fundamental category of human thought" [1949/1957:xiv], that binary opposition is one of the chief ways thought organizes culture, and that the individual experiences other people as a potential threat to the sovereignty of the subject's consciousness, restricting the capacity for ongoing self-actualization.) Women's difference from men results in part from this fact of cultural construction which excludes them and in part from their internalization of "Otherness." Crucial questions here are whether women can liberate themselves from the status of object/other and whether in that liberation they must become like men or can achieve a distinctive subjectivity. The tilt in this argument (a tilt developed radically by later French psychoanalytic feminists like Hélène Cixous [1976, 1994] and Luce Irigaray [1985a, b]) is that women will develop a consciousness and culture that is uniquely theirs.

In seeking to bring about change, theorists of difference demand that women's ways of being be recognized as viable alternatives to male modes and that public knowledge, academic scholarship, and the organization of social life be adjusted to take serious account of female ways of being. At its most militant, in cultural feminism, this theoretical approach makes the centuries-old feminist claim: that when a major infusion of women's ways becomes part of public life, the world will be a safer, more just place for us all.

Gender Inequality

Four themes characterize feminist theorizing of gender inequality. First, men and women are situated in society not only differently but also unequally. Specifically, women get less of the material resources, social status, power, and opportunities for self-actualization than do men who share their social location—be it a location based on class, race, occupation, ethnicity, religion, education, nationality, or any other socially significant factor. Second, this inequality results from the organization of society, not from any significant biological or personality differences between women and men. Third, although individual human beings may vary somewhat from each other in their profile of potentials and traits, no significant pattern of natural variation distinguishes the sexes. Instead, all human beings are characterized by a deep need for freedom to seek self-actualization and by a fundamental malleability that leads them to adapt to the constraints or opportunities of the situations in which they find themselves. To say that there is gender inequality, then, is to claim that women are situationally less empowered than men to realize the need they share with men for self-actualization. Fourth, all inequality theories assume that both women and men will respond fairly easily and naturally to more egalitarian social structures and situations. They affirm, in other words, that it is possible to change the situation. In this belief, theorists of gender inequality contrast with the theorists of gender difference, who present a picture of social life in which gender differences are, whatever their cause, more durable, more penetrative of personality, and less easily changed.

Liberal Feminism   The major expression of gender inequality theory is liberal feminism, which argues that women may claim equality with men on the basis of an essential human capacity for reasoned moral agency, that gender inequality is the result of a patriarchal and sexist patterning of the division of labor, and that gender equality can be produced by transforming the division of labor through the repatterning of key institutions—law, work, family, education, and media (Bem, 1993; Epstein, 1988; Friedan, 1963; Lorber, 1994; Rhode, 1997).

Historically the first element in the liberal feminist argument is the claim for gender equality. A key document for understanding the basis of this claim is the Declaration of Sentiments issued by the first women's rights convention at Seneca Falls, New York in 1848. Rewriting the Declaration of Independence, the signers declared that "We hold these truths to be self-evident: that all men and women ["and women" is added] are created equal; that they are endowed by their creator with certain inalienable rights; that among these are life, liberty, and the pursuit of happiness; that to secure these rights governments are instituted ["among men" is omitted], deriving their just powers from the consent of the governed"—and they continue in this vein to endorse the right of revolution when "any form of government becomes destructive of these ends." In this choice of a beginning, the women's movement laid claim to the intellectual discourses of the Enlightenment, the American and French Revolutions, and the Abolitionist Movement. They claimed for women the rights accorded to all human beings, under natural law, on the basis of the human capacity for reason and moral agency; asserted that laws which denied women their right to happiness were "contrary to the great precept of nature and of no . . . authority," and called for change in law and custom to allow women to assume their equal place in society. The denial of those rights by governments *instituted by men* violates natural law and is the tyrannical working out of patriarchal ideology and multiple practices of sexism. The radical nature of this foundational document is that it conceptualizes the woman not in the context of home and family but as an autonomous individual with rights in her own person (DuBois, 1973/1995).

Liberal feminism, thus, rests on the beliefs that (1) all human beings have certain essential features—capacities for reason, moral agency, and self-actualization; (2) the exercise of these capacities can be secured through legal recognition of universal rights; (3) the inequalities between men and women assigned by sex are social constructions having no basis in "nature," and (4) social change for equality can be produced by an organized appeal to a reasonable public and the use of the state. Contemporary feminist discourse has expanded these arguments with the introduction of the concept of *gender* as a way of understanding all the socially constructed features built around an idea of sex identity and used to produce inequality between persons considered male and persons considered female (e.g., Lorber, 1994; Ferree, Lorber, and Hess, 1999). It has also expanded to include a global feminism which confronts racism in North Atlantic societies and works for "the human rights of women" everywhere. And this discourse has continued to express many of its foundational statements in organizational documents like the National Organization for Women's Statement of Purpose and the Beijing Declaration; these organizational statements of purpose rely on an informing theory of human equality as a right which the state—local, national, international—must respect. These arguments are being freshly invoked in debates with the political right over reproductive freedom (Bordo, 1993; Pollitt, 1990; Solinger, 1998), in debates with post-modernists over the possibility and utility of formulating principles of rights (Green, 1995; Phillips, 1993; Williams, 1991), and in feminist considerations of the gendered character of liberal democratic theory and practice (Haney, 1996; Hirschmann and Di Stefano, 1996; Pateman, 1989; Phillips, 1993).

Contemporary liberal feminism's explanation of gender inequality turns on the interplay of four factors—the social construction of gender, the gendered division of labor, the doctrine and practice of public and private spheres, and patriarchal ideology. The sexual division of labor in modern societies divides production in terms both of gender and spheres denoted as "public" and "private"; women are given primary responsibility for the private sphere while men are given privileged access to the public sphere (which liberal feminists see as the locus of the true rewards of social life—money, power, status, freedom, opportunities for growth and self-worth). The fact that women have what access they do to the public sphere is, of course, one triumph of the women's movement—and of liberal feminism and of feminist sociology, as is the fact that women feel they can make some demands on men to assist in the work of the private sphere. The two spheres constantly interact in the lives of women (more than they do for men) and both spheres are still shaped by patriarchal ideology and sexism, which is also pervasive in contemporary mass media (Davis, 1997). On the one hand, women find their experience within the public sphere of education, work, politics, and public space still limited by practices of discrimination, marginalization and harassment (Benokraitis, 1997; Gardner, 1995; Hagan and Kay, 1995; Reskin and Padovic, 1994; Ridgeway, 1997). On the other hand, in the private sphere, they find themselves in a "time bind" as they return home from paid employment to "a second shift" of home and child care infused by an ideology of intensive mothering (Hays, 1996; Hochschild, 1989, 1997). These pressures on women work interactively in complex ways—and one feature of contemporary feminist theory is its attempts to understand these interactions. Women's ability to compete in career and profession is hindered by the demands of the private sphere (Waldfogel, 1997). The essentially patriarchal demands of the public sphere for "face time" and total commitment intensifies the stress of home commitments by shrinking women's resources of time and energy which in turn increase the demands on them for crisis management at home (Hochschild, 1997). The ideological link of women to the private sphere activities of caregiving, emotion management, the maintenance of routine and order translate into women's being expected to do this additional work in the public sphere and being frequently tracked into under-remunerated jobs in which these "womanly" skills are commodified and marketed (Adkins, 1995; Pierce, 1995). The patriarchal patterning of work and home puts the single mother, the woman trying to maintain home and children without the help of the male wage earner, at tremendous economic risk and is one factor in the increasing "feminization of poverty": the woman typically earns less than a man; the relationship of the single woman parent to any job is made both precarious and less negotiable because of the vagaries of her home responsibilities (Edin and Lein, 1997; Harris, 1996).

One theme in liberal feminist analysis of gender inequality is the problem of achieving equality in marriage. This theme is given its classic formulation in Jessie Bernard's study, *The Future of Marriage* (1972/1982). Bernard analyzes marriage as at one and

JESSIE BERNARD: A Biographical Sketch

Jessie Bernard's life and work were characterized by an extraordinary capacity for growth and outgrowth; she constantly moved beyond herself into new intellectual territory, a process she described in "My Four Revolutions: An Autobiographical Account of the American Sociological Association" (1973). Tracing Bernard's revolutions gives a history of women's participation in much of twentieth-century American sociology and of a thoughtful woman's journey to feminism.

Born Jessie Ravitch on June 8, 1903, in Minneapolis, she made her first outgrowth when she moved from her Jewish immigrant family to the University of Minnesota at the age of seventeen. At the university, she studied with Sorokin, who founded the Harvard sociology department, and with L. L. Bernard, who helped found the *American Sociological Review* and whom she married in 1925. Her study with Bernard gave her a grounding in positivistic sociology that showed in her later work in her ability to integrate quantitative research into increasingly qualitative and critical studies. She completed her Ph.D. at Washington University in St. Louis in 1935.

By the mid-1940s, the Bernards were at Pennsylvania State University, and Jessie was in the midst of outgrowing positivism. The Nazi holocaust destroyed her faith that science could know and produce a just world and she moved toward a sense of knowledge as contextualized rather than objective. She also began to establish an independent academic reputation. Her husband died in 1951, but she remained at Penn State until about 1960, teaching, writing, and raising her three children. In the sixties, she moved to Washington, D.C., to devote herself fully to writing and research.

The most dramatic outgrowth was in the last third of her life, from 1964 to her death in 1996. This period is significant for both Bernard's extraordinary output and what it says about career patterns in women's lives. During this period, Bernard established herself as a leading interpreter of the sociology of gender, authored twelve books and innumerable articles and presentations, and declined the ASA presidency to devote herself to research, writing, and the women's movement. In the light of Second Wave feminism, she rethought many of her writings on family and gender. Her major works include: *Marriage and Family among Negroes* (1956), *Academic Women* (1964), *The Sex Game: Communication between the Sexes* (1968), *Women and the Public Interest: An Essay on Policy and Protest* (1971), *The Future of Marriage* (1972), *The Future of Motherhood* (1974), *Women, Wives, Mothers: Values and Options* (1975), *The Female World* (1981), and *The Female World from a Global Perspective* (1987).

These works are characterized by four qualities: an ability to bring macro data to bear in analyzing micro interactions; an increasing recognition of the interplay between individual agency and social structures; an increasing emphasis on the contextuality of knowledge and the necessity for studying marginal groups in themselves, not in comparison to some dominant patriarchally determined type; and a transformation of her interest in women's lives from positivistic investigation to critical feminist analysis.

Bernard garnered many awards in her lifetime—the highest perhaps being the honor of having several awards named after her, awards designed, as Lipman-Blumen says, to mark "those who, like Jessie Bernard herself, have contributed intellectually, professionally, and humanely to the world of scholarship and feminism" (1979:55).

Sources: Bannister (1991), Bernard (1973), Howe and Cantor (1994), Lipman-Blumen (1979).

the same time a cultural system of beliefs and ideals, an institutional arrangement of roles and norms, and a complex of interactional experiences for individual women and men. Culturally, marriage is idealized as the destiny and source of fulfillment for women; a mixed blessing of domesticity, responsibility, and constraint for men; and for American society as a whole an essentially egalitarian association between husband and wife. Institutionally, marriage empowers the role of husband with authority and with the freedom, indeed, the obligation, to move beyond the domestic setting; it meshes the idea of male authority with sexual prowess and male power; and it mandates that wives be compliant, dependent, self-emptying, and essentially centered on the activities and demands of the isolated domestic household. Experientially then there are two marriages in any institutional marriage: the man's marriage, in which he holds to the belief of being constrained and burdened, while experiencing what the norms dictate—authority, independence, and a right to domestic, emotional, and sexual service by the wife; and the wife's marriage, in which she affirms the cultural belief of fulfillment, while experiencing normatively mandated powerlessness and dependence, an obligation to provide domestic, emotional, and sexual services, and a gradual "dwindling away" of the independent young person she was before marriage. The results of all this are to be found in the data that measure human stress: *married* women, whatever their claims to fulfillment, and *unmarried* men, whatever their claims to freedom, rank high on all stress indicators, including heart palpitations, dizziness, headaches, fainting, nightmares, insomnia, and fear of nervous breakdown; *unmarried* women, whatever their sense of social stigma, and *married* men rank low on all the stress indicators. Marriage then is good for men and bad for women and will cease to be so unequal in its impact only when couples feel free enough from the prevailing institutional constraints to negotiate the kind of marriage that best suits their individual needs and personalities. Recent studies have suggested that Bernard's analysis still holds for most marriages (Steil, 1997) but that some couples are achieving, through dedicated effort, the liberal feminist ideal of egalitarian marriage (Schwartz, 1994).

Liberal feminism's agenda for change is consistent with its analyses of the basis for claiming equality and the causes of inequality: they wish to eliminate gender as an organizing principle in the distribution of social "goods" and they are willing to invoke universal principles in their pursuit of equality. They pursue change through law—legislation, litigation, and regulation—and through appeal to the human capacity for reasoned moral judgments, that is, the capacity of the public to be moved by arguments for fairness. They argue for equal educational and economic opportunities; equal responsibility for the activities of family life; the elimination of sexist messages in family, education, and mass media; and individual challenges to sexism in daily life. Liberal feminists have shown remarkable creativity in redefining the strategies that will produce equality. In developing economic opportunities, they have worked through legislative change to ensure equality in education and to bar job discrimination; they have monitored regulatory agencies charged with enforcing this legislation; they have mobilized to have sexual harassment in the workplace legally defined as "job discrimination"; they have demanded both "pay equity" (equal pay for equal work) and "comparable worth" (equal pay for work of comparable value) (Acker, 1989; England, 1992; Kessler-Harris, 1990; Reskin, 1988; Rosenberg, 1992).

For liberal feminists, the ideal gender arrangement is one in which each individual acting as a free and responsible moral agent chooses the lifestyle most suitable to her or him and has that choice accepted and respected, be it for housewife or househusband, unmarried careerist or part of a dual-income family, childless or with children, heterosexual or homosexual. Liberal feminists see this ideal as one that enhances the practice of freedom and equality, central cultural ideals in America. Liberal feminism then is consistent with the dominant American ethos in its basic acceptance of democracy and capitalism, its reformist orientation, and its appeal to the values of individualism, choice, responsibility, and equality of opportunity.

Gender Oppression

Theories of gender oppression describe women's situation as the consequence of a direct power relationship between men and women in which men have fundamental and concrete interests in controlling, using, subjugating, and oppressing women—that is, in the practice of domination. By *domination,* oppression theorists mean any relationship in which one party (individual or collective), the *dominant,* succeeds in making the other party (individual or collective) the *subordinate,* an instrument of the dominant's will, and refuses to recognize the subordinate's independent subjectivity. Or conversely, from the subordinate's viewpoint, it is a relationship in which the subordinate's assigned significance is solely as an instrument of the will of the dominant (Lengermann and Niebrugge, 1995). Women's situation, then, for theorists of gender oppression, is centrally that of being used, controlled, subjugated, and oppressed by men. This pattern of gender oppression is incorporated in the deepest and most pervasive ways into society's organization, a basic structure of domination most commonly called *patriarchy.* Patriarchy is not the unintended and secondary consequence of some other set of factors—be it biology or socialization or sex roles or the class system. It is a primary power structure sustained by strong and deliberate intention. Indeed, to theorists of gender oppression, gender differences and gender inequality are by-products of patriarchy.

Whereas most earlier feminist theorists focused on issues of gender inequality, one hallmark of contemporary feminist theory is the breadth and intensity of its concern with oppression (Jaggar, 1983). A majority of contemporary feminist theorists in some measure subscribe to oppression theory, and many of the richest and most innovative theoretical developments within contemporary feminism have been the work of this cluster of theorists. We turn now to two major variants of gender oppression theory: psychoanalytic feminism and radical feminism.

Psychoanalytic Feminism   Contemporary psychoanalytical feminists attempt to explain patriarchy by reformulating the theories of Freud and his intellectual heirs (al-Hibri, 1981; Benjamin, 1985, 1988; Chodorow, 1978, 1990, 1994; Dinnerstein, 1976; Kittay, 1984).[3] These theories, broadly speaking, map and emphasize the emotional dynamics of personality, emotions often deeply buried in the subconscious or unconscious

---

[3]There is also a complex French feminist psychoanalytic tradition based in feminist translations of Jacques Lacan's reworkings of Freud; see Cixous, 1976, 1994; Irigaray, 1985a, b; Kurzweil, 1995.

areas of the psyche; they also highlight the importance of infancy and early childhood in the patterning of these emotions. In attempting to use Freud's theories, however, feminists have to undertake a fundamental reworking of his conclusions to follow through on directions implicit in Freud's theories while rejecting his gender-specific conclusions, which are notoriously sexist and patriarchal.

Psychoanalytical feminists operate with a particular model of patriarchy. Like all oppression theorists, they see patriarchy as a system in which men subjugate women, a universal system, pervasive in its social organization, durable over time and space, and triumphantly maintained in the face of occasional challenge. Distinctive to psychoanalytic feminism, however, is the view that this system is one that all men, in their individual daily actions, work continuously and energetically to create and sustain. Women resist only occasionally but are to be discovered far more often either acquiescing in or actively working for their own subordination. The puzzle that psychoanalytical feminists set out to solve is why men bring everywhere enormous, unremitting energy to the task of sustaining patriarchy and why there is an absence of countervailing energy on the part of women.

In searching for an explanation to this puzzle, these theorists give short shrift to the argument that a cognitive calculus of practical benefits is sufficient for male support for patriarchy. Cognitive mobilization does not seem a sufficient source for the intense energy that men invest in patriarchy, especially because, in light of the human capacity to debate and second-guess, men may not always and everywhere be certain that patriarchy is of unqualified value to them. Moreover, an argument anchored in the cognitive pursuit of self-interest would suggest that women would as energetically mobilize against patriarchy. Instead, these theorists look to those aspects of the psyche so effectively mapped by the Freudians: the zone of human emotions, of half-recognized or unrecognized desires and fears, and of neurosis and pathology. Here they find a clinically proven source of extraordinary energy and debilitation, one springing from psychic structures too deep to be recognized or monitored by individual consciousness. In searching for the energic underpinnings of patriarchy, psychoanalytical feminists have identified two possible explanations for male domination of women: the fear of death and the socio-emotional environment in which the personality of the young child takes form.

Fear of death, of the ceasing of one's individuality, is viewed in psychoanalytic theory as one of those existential issues that everyone, everywhere, must on occasion confront and as one that causes everyone, in that confrontation, to experience terror. Feminist theorists who develop this theme argue that women, because of their intimate and protracted involvement with bearing and rearing new life, are typically far less oppressed than men by the realization of their own mortality (al-Hibri, 1981; Dinnerstein, 1976). Men, however, respond with deep dread to the prospect of their individual extinction and adopt a series of defenses, all of which lead to their domination of women. Men are driven to produce things that will outlast them—art and architecture, wealth and weapons, science and religion. All these then become resources by which men can dominate women (and each other). Men also are driven—partly by envy of women's reproductive role, partly by their own passionate desire for immortality through offspring—to seek to control the reproductive process itself. They claim ownership of women, seek to control women's bodies, and lay claim through norms of legitimacy and paternity to the products of those bodies, children. Finally, driven by fear, men seek to separate themselves from everything that reminds them of their own mortal bodies: birth, nature, sexuality, their human bodies and natural functions, and women, whose association with so many of these makes them the symbol of them all. All of these aspects of existence must be denied, repressed, and controlled as men seek constantly to separate from, deny, and repress their own mortality. And women, who symbolize all these forbidden topics, also must be treated as Other: feared, avoided, controlled.

The second theme in psychoanalytic feminism centers on two facets of early child-hood development: (1) the assumption that human beings grow into mature people by learning to balance a never-resolved tension between the desire for freedom of action—*individuation*—and the desire for confirmation by another—*recognition;* and (2) the ob-servable fact that in all societies infants and children experience their earliest and most crucial development in a close, uninterrupted, intimate relationship with a woman, their mother or mother substitute (Benjamin, 1985, 1988; Chodorow, 1978, 1990, 1994; Din-nerstein, 1976; Doane and Hodges, 1992). As infants and young children, for consider-able periods lacking even language as a tool for understanding experience, individuals experience their earliest phases of personality development as an ongoing turbulence of primitive emotions: fear, love, hate, pleasure, rage, loss, desire. The emotional conse-quences of these early experiences stay with people always as potent but often uncon-scious "feeling memories." Central to that experiential residue is a cluster of deeply ambivalent feelings for the woman/mother/caregiver: need, dependence, love, posses-siveness, but also fear and rage over her ability to thwart one's will. Children's rela-tionship to the father/man is much more occasional, secondary, and emotionally uncluttered. From this beginning, the male child, growing up in a culture that positively values maleness and devalues femaleness and increasingly aware of his own male identity, attempts to achieve an awkwardly rapid separation of identity from the woman/mother. This culturally induced separation is not only partial but also destruc-tive in its consequences. In adulthood the emotional carryover from early childhood toward women—need, love, hate, possessiveness—energizes the man's quest for a woman of his own who meets his emotional needs and yet is dependent on and con-trolled by him—that is, he has an urge to dominate and finds mutual recognition diffi-cult. The female child, bearing the same feelings toward the woman/mother, discovers her own female identity in a culture that devalues women. She grows up with deeply mixed positive and negative feelings about herself and about the woman/mother and in that ambivalence dissipates much of her potential for mobilized resistance to her social subordination. She seeks to resolve her emotional carryover in adulthood by emphasiz-ing her capacities for according recognition—often submissively with males in acts of sexual attraction and mutually with females in acts of kinship maintenance and friend-ship. And rather than seeking mother substitutes, she re-creates the early infant-woman relationship by becoming a mother.

Psychoanalytical feminist theorists have extended their analyses beyond individual personality to Western culture. The emphases in Western science on a distinct separa-tion between "man" and "nature," on "man" as the "dominator" of "nature," and on a "scientific method" derived from these attitudes and promising "objective" truth have been challenged and reinterpreted as the projection by the overindividuated male ego of its own desire for domination and its own fear of intersubjective recognition (Jaggar and Bordo, 1989; Keller, 1985). Motifs in popular culture—such as the repeated positioning in both plot and image of the male as dominant over the female—are interpreted by psychoanalytical theorists as a sign of a breakdown in the requisite tensions between a need for individuation and a need for recognition (Benjamin, 1985, 1988; Brennan, 1994; Chancer, 1992). When this breakdown reaches, in a culture or personality, severe enough proportions, two pathologies result—the overindividuated dominator, who "recognizes" the other only through acts of control, and the underindividuated subordinate, who relinquishes independent action to find identity only as a mirror of the dominator.

Psychoanalytical feminists, then, explain women's oppression in terms of men's deep emotional need to control women, a drive arising from near-universal male neuroses centering on the fear of death and on ambivalence toward the mothers who reared them. Women either lack these neuroses or are subject to complementary neuroses, but in either case they are left psychically without an equivalent source of energy to resist domination. Much clinical psychiatric evidence supports the argument that these neuroses are in fact widespread in Western societies. But these theories, in drawing a straight line from universal human emotions to universal female oppression, fail to explore the intermediate social arrangements that link emotion to oppression and fail to suggest possible lines of variation in emotions, social arrangements, or oppression. Several theorists have discussed the unacknowledged ethnic, class, and nationality assumptions in these theories, their generalization from white, upper middle-class, North Atlantic family experience (Segura and Pierce, 1993; Spelman, 1988; Zhang, 1993). Moreover, and partly because of these omissions, psychoanalytic feminist theory suggests very few strategies for change, except perhaps that we restructure our childbearing practices and begin some massive psychocultural reworking of our orientation toward death. These theories thus give us some provocative insights into and deepen our understanding of the roots of gender oppression, but they require a great deal more elaboration of both sociological factors and change strategies.

Radical Feminism   Radical feminism is based on two emotionally charged central beliefs: (1) that women are of absolute positive value as women, a belief asserted against what they claim to be the universal devaluing of women; and (2) that women are everywhere oppressed—violently oppressed—by the system of patriarchy (T. Atkinson, 1974; Bunch, 1987; Chesler, 1994; Daly, 1993; C. Douglas, 1990; Dworkin, 1976, 1987, 1989; Echols, 1989; French, 1992; Frye, 1983; Griffin, 1978; Jeffreys, 1991; Millett, 1970; Rich, 1976, 1980, 1993; Richardson, 1996). In this passionate mixture of love and rage, radical feminists resemble the more militant mode of racial and ethnic groups, the "black is beautiful" claims of African Americans or the detailed "witnessing" of Jewish survivors of the Holocaust. Building on these core beliefs, radical feminists elaborate a theory of social organization, gender oppression, and strategies for change.

Radical feminists see in every institution and in society's most basic structures—heterosexuality, class, caste, race, ethnicity, age, and gender—systems of oppression in which some people dominate others. Of all these systems of domination and subordination, the most fundamental structure of oppression is gender, the system of patriarchy. Not only is patriarchy historically the first structure of domination and submission, but it continues as the most pervasive and enduring system of inequality, the basic societal model of domination (Lerner, 1986). Through participation in patriarchy, men learn how to hold other human beings in contempt, to see them as nonhuman, and to control them. Within patriarchy men see and women learn what subordination looks like. Patriarchy creates guilt and repression, sadism and masochism, manipulation and deception, all of which drive men and women to other forms of tyranny. Patriarchy, to radical feminists, is the least noticed and yet the most significant structure of social inequality.

Central to this analysis is the image of patriarchy as violence practiced by men and by male-dominated organizations against women. Violence may not always take the form of overt physical cruelty. It can be hidden in more complex practices of exploitation and control: in standards of fashion and beauty; in tyrannical ideals of motherhood, monogamy, chastity, and heterosexuality; in sexual harassment in the workplace; in the practices of gynecology, obstetrics, and psychotherapy; in unpaid household drudgery and underpaid wage work (MacKinnon, 1979, 1989; Rich, 1976, 1980; Thompson, 1994; Wolf, 1991). Violence exists whenever one group controls in its own interests the life chances, environments, actions, and perceptions of another group, as men do women.

But the theme of violence as overt physical cruelty lies at the heart of radical feminism's linking of patriarchy to violence: rape, sexual abuse, enforced prostitution, spouse abuse, incest, sexual molestation of children, hysterectomies and other excessive surgery, the sadism in pornography, the historic and cross-cultural practices of witch burning, the stoning to death of adulteresses, the persecution of lesbians, female infanticide, Chinese foot-binding, the abuse of widows, and the practice of clitorectomy (Barnett and LaViolette, 1993; Barry, 1979, 1997; Bart and Moran, 1993; Bergen, 1996; Buchwald, Fletcher, and Roth, 1993; MacKinnon, 1993; Owen, 1996; Russell, 1998; Sanday, 1996; Scully, 1990; Stiglmayer, 1994).

Patriarchy exists as a near-universal social form because men can muster the most basic power resource, physical force, to establish control. Once patriarchy is in place, the other power resources—economic, ideological, legal, and emotional—also can be marshaled to sustain it. But physical violence always remains its base, and in both interpersonal and intergroup relations, that violence is used to protect patriarchy from women's individual and collective resistance (Caputi, 1989; Faludi, 1991).

Men create and maintain patriarchy not only because they have the resources to do so but because they have real interests in making women serve as compliant tools. Women are a uniquely effective means of satisfying male sexual desire. Their bodies are essential to the production of children, who satisfy both practical and, as psychoanalysts have shown, neurotic needs for men. Women are a useful labor force. They can be ornamental signs of male status and power. As carefully controlled companions to both the child and the adult male, they are pleasant partners, sources of emotional support, and useful foils who reinforce the male's sense of central social significance. These useful functions mean that men everywhere seek to keep women compliant. But differing social circumstances give different rank orders to these functions and therefore lead to cross-cultural variations in the patterning of patriarchy. Radical feminists give us both an explanation of universal gender oppression *and* a model for understanding cross-cultural variations in this oppression.

How is patriarchy to be defeated? Radicals hold that this defeat must begin with a basic reworking of women's consciousness so that each woman recognizes her own value and strength; rejects patriarchal pressures to see herself as weak, dependent, and second-class; and works in unity with other women, regardless of differences among them, to establish a broad-based sisterhood of trust, support, appreciation, and mutual defense (McCaughey, 1997). With this sisterhood in place, two strategies suggest themselves: a critical confrontation with any facet of patriarchal domination whenever it is encountered; and a degree of separatism as women withdraw into women-run businesses, households, communities, centers of artistic creativity, and lesbian love relationships. Lesbian feminism, as a major strand in radical feminism, is the practice and belief that "erotic and/or emotional commitment to women is part of resistance to patriarchal domination" (Phelan, 1994; Taylor and Rupp, 1993:33).

How does one evaluate radical feminism? Emotionally each of us will respond to it in light of our own degree of personal radicalism, some seeing it as excessively critical and others as entirely convincing. But in attempting a theoretical evaluation, one should note that radical feminism incorporates arguments made by both socialist and psychoanalytical feminists about the reasons for women's subordination and yet moves beyond those theories. Radical feminists, moreover, have done significant research to support their thesis that patriarchy ultimately rests on the practice of violence against women. They have a reasonable though perhaps incomplete program for change. They have been faulted for their exclusive focus on patriarchy. This focus seems to simplify the realities of social organization and social inequality and thus to approach the issues of ameliorative change somewhat unrealistically.

Structural Oppression

Structural oppression theories, like gender oppression theories, recognize that oppression results from the fact that some groups of people derive direct benefits from controlling, using, subjugating, and oppressing other groups of people. These theories analyze how those interests in domination are enacted through mechanisms of social structure, that is, through recurring and routinized large-scale arrangements of social interaction. Structural oppression theorists see that these arrangements are always arrangements of power that have arisen out of history, that is, over time. They focus on the structures of patriarchy, capitalism, racism, and heterosexism, and they locate enactments of domination and experiences of oppression in the interplay of these structures, that is, in the way they mutually enforce each other. Structural oppression theorists do not absolve or deny the agency of individual dominants but they examine how that agency is the product of structural arrangements. In this section we look at two types of structural oppression theory, socialist feminism and intersectionality theory.

Socialist Feminism   The theoretical project of socialist feminism develops around three goals: (1) to achieve a critique of the distinctive yet interrelated oppressions of patriarchy and capitalism from a standpoint in women's experience; (2) to develop explicit and adequate methods for social analysis out of an expanded understanding of historical materialism; and (3) to incorporate an understanding of the significance of ideas into a materialist analysis of the determination of human affairs. Socialist feminists have set themselves the formal project of achieving both a synthesis of and a theoretical step beyond extant feminist theories. More specifically, socialist feminists seek to bring together what they perceive as the two broadest and most valuable feminist traditions: Marxian and radical feminist thought (Bartsky, 1992; Eisenstein, 1979; Fraser, 1989, 1997; Hansen and Philipson, 1990; Hartmann, 1979; Hartsock, 1983; Hennessey, 1992; Hennessey and Ingraham, 1997; Jaggar, 1983; MacKinnon, 1989; Rose, 1995; D. Smith, 1974, 1975, 1978, 1979, 1987, 1989, 1990a, 1990b, 1992, 1993; Vogel, 1995).

Radical feminism, as discussed above, is a critique of patriarchy. Marxian feminism, described here, has, traditionally, brought together Marxian class analysis and feminist social protest. But this amalgam—portrayed as an uneasy marriage (Hartmann, 1981; Shelton and Agger, 1993)—often produced not an intensified theory of gender oppression but a more muted statement of gender inequality as women's concerns were grafted onto, rather than made equal partners in, the critique of class oppression. While pure Marxian feminism is a relatively dormant theory in contemporary American feminism, it remains important as an influence on socialist feminism. Its foundation was laid by Marx and Engels (see Chapter 4). Their major concern was social class oppression, but they occasionally turned their attention to gender oppression, most famously in *The Origins of the Family, Private Property, and the State* (written by Engels in 1884 from extensive notes made by Marx in the year immediately preceding his death in 1883). We briefly summarize this book because it gives a good introduction to the classic Marxian theory of gender oppression and to the method of historical materialism.

The major argument of *The Origins* is that woman's subordination results not from her biology, which is presumably immutable, but from social relations that have a clear and traceable history and that can presumably be changed. In the context of nineteenth century thinking about gender, this was a radical, indeed, a feminist argument. The relational basis for women's subordination lies in the family, an institution aptly named from the Latin word for servant, because the family as it exists in complex societies is overwhelmingly a system in which men command women's services. Although the ideology of contemporary societies treats family as a fundamental and universal feature of social life, Engels and Marx produce archaeological and anthropological evidence to show that in the chronology of humanity's existence the family is a fairly recent relational invention, that for much of pre-history men and women lived in kin structures in which women enjoyed relative autonomy primarily because they had an independent economic base as gatherers, crafters, storers, and distributors of essential materials. The factor that destroyed this type of social system, producing what Engels calls "the world historic defeat of the female sex" (Engels, 1884/1970:87), was an economic one, specifically the replacement of hunting and gathering by herding and farming economies in which men's resources of strength, mobility, and a technology derived from their earlier hunting roles gave them a systematic advantage over women. This led to the invention of the concept of *property,* the idea and reality of a male class claiming as their own the communal resources for economic production. In these new economies, men as property owners needed both a compliant labor force—be it of slaves, captives, women-wives, or children—and heirs who would serve as a means of preserving and passing on property. Thus emerged the first *familia,* a master and his slave-servants, wife-servants, children-servants. Since then, the exploitation of labor has developed into increasingly complex structures of domination, most particularly class relations; the political order was created to safeguard these systems of domination; and the family itself has evolved along with the historical transformations of economic and property systems into an embedded and dependent institution, reflecting all the more massive injustices of the political economy and consistently enforcing the subordination of women. Engels and Marx conclude that only with the destruction of property rights through class revolution will women attain freedom of social, political, economic, and personal action.

Locating the origin of patriarchy in the emergence of property relations subsumes women's oppression under the general framework of Marxian class analysis. "Property"—understood not as personal possessions but as ownership of the resources necessary for social production (the means of production)—is the basis of class division because it creates a situation in which some groups are able to claim that they own the means of production while other groups work to do the producing. Marxian analysis focuses particularly upon how this class division works out under capitalism, the economic system of modern societies. The distinctive feature of capitalism is that the class that owns the means of production—the capitalists—operates on a logic of continuous capital accumulation; *capital* is wealth (money and other assets), which can be used to generate the material infrastructure of economic production. Unlike other forms of economic organization in which people may seek to exchange either goods or money for more goods, capitalists seek to exchange goods in order to amass wealth which in turn is invested in the material infrastructure of economic production to generate goods in order to generate more wealth. The mechanism by which capitalists turn goods into wealth is surplus value; surplus value is the difference between the compensation given to workers for their production and the value of the goods they produce; this surplus value (which we may understand as the difference between the cost of production and the price of the item—or profit) is appropriated by the capitalist who uses it to enhance his own lifestyle and power and, above all, to re-invest in the ongoing process of capital accumulation and expansion.

The compelling part of the Marxian analysis for feminist socialists is this analysis of class relations under capitalism—which they accept as a major source of oppression. The problematic part of the Marxian analysis is that it makes patriarchy a function of economic relations. Socialist feminists accept the radical argument and proof that patriarchy, while interacting with economic conditions, is an independent structure of oppression.

Socialist feminism sets out to bring together these dual knowledges—knowledge of oppression under capitalism and of oppression under patriarchy—into a unified explanation of all forms of social oppression. One term used to try to unify these two oppressions is *capitalist patriarchy* (Eisenstein, 1979; Hartmann, 1979; Kuhn and Wolpe, 1978). But the term perhaps more widely used is *domination,* defined above (under "Gender Oppression") as a relationship in which one party, *the dominant,* succeeds in making the other party, *the subordinate,* an instrument of the dominant's will and refuses to recognize the subordinate's independent subjectivity. Socialist feminism's explanations of oppression present domination as a large scale structural arrangement, a power relation between groups or categories of social actors. This structure of domination both patterns and is reproduced by the agency, the willful and intentional actions, of individual actors. Women are central to socialist feminism in two ways. First, as with all feminism, the oppression of women remains a primary topic for analysis. Second, women's location and experience of the world serve as the essential vantage point on domination in all its forms. Ultimately, though, these theorists are concerned with all experiences of oppression, either by women or by men. They also explore how some women, themselves oppressed, may yet actively participate in the oppression of other women, as, for example, privileged-class women in American society who oppress poor women. Indeed, one strategy of all socialist feminists is to confront the prejudices and oppressive practices *within* the community of women itself (Eisenstein, 1994; Lorde, 1984).

Both the focus on capitalist patriarchy and that on domination are linked to a commitment, either explicit or implicit, to historical materialism as an analytical strategy (Hennessey and Ingraham, 1997; Jaggar, 1983). *Historical materialism,* a basic principle in Marxian social theory, refers to the claim that the material conditions of human life, inclusive of the activities and relationships that produce those conditions, are the key factors that pattern human experience, personality, ideas, and social arrangements; that those conditions change over time because of dynamics imminent within them; and that history is a record of the changes in the material conditions of a group's life and of the correlative changes in experiences, personality, ideas, and social arrangements. Historical materialists hold that any effort at social analysis must trace in historically concrete detail the specifics of the group's material conditions and the links between those conditions and the experiences, personalities, events, ideas, and social arrangements characteristic of the group. In linking historical materialism to their focus on domination, socialist feminists attempt to realize their goal of a theory that probes the broadest of human social arrangements, domination, and yet remains firmly committed to precise, historically concrete analyses of the material and social arrangements that frame particular situations of domination.

The historical materialism that is a hallmark of socialist feminism shows clearly the school's indebtedness to Marxian thought. But in their use of this principle, socialist feminists move beyond the Marxians in three crucial ways: their redefinition of material conditions, their reevaluation of the significance of ideology, and their focus on domination. First, they broaden the meaning of the *material conditions* of human life. Marxians typically mean by this idea the economic dynamics of society, particularly the ways in which goods of a variety of types are created for and exchanged in the market. In these various exploitative arrangements, which make some wealthy and others poor, they locate the roots of class inequality and class conflict. Socialist feminist analysis includes economic dynamics and also, more broadly, other conditions that create and sustain human life: the human body, its sexuality and involvement in procreation and child rearing; home maintenance, with its unpaid, invisible round of domestic tasks; emotional sustenance; and the production of knowledge. In *all* these life-sustaining activities, exploitative arrangements profit some and impoverish others. Full comprehension of all these basic arrangements of life production and exploitation is the essential foundation for a theory of domination.

DOROTHY E. SMITH: A Biographical Sketch

Dorothy E. Smith explains that her sociological theory derives from her life experiences as a woman, particularly as a woman moving between two worlds—the male-dominated academic sphere and the essentially female-centered life of the single parent. Remembering herself at Berkeley in the early 1960s studying for a doctorate in sociology while single parenting, Smith reflects that her life seems to have been framed by what she sees as "not so much . . . a career as a series of contingencies, of accidents" (1979:151). This theme of contingency is one of many personal experiences that have led Smith to challenge sociological orthodoxy such as the image of the voluntary actor working through role conflicts.

Whether they occurred by accident or design, the following events appear to the outsider as significant stages in Smith's development. She was born in 1926 in Great Britain; she earned her bachelor's degree in sociology from the University of London in 1955 and her Ph.D. in sociology from the University of California at Berkeley in 1963. During this same period, she had "the experience of marriage, of immigration [to Canada] closely following marriage, of the arrival of children, of the departure of a husband rather early one morning, of the jobs that became available" (Smith, 1979:151). Of these events, Smith stresses, they "were moments in which I had in fact little choice and certainly little foreknowledge." The jobs that became available included research sociologist at Berkeley; lecturer in sociology at Berkeley; lecturer in sociology at the University of Essex, Colchester, England; associate professor and then professor in the department of sociology at the University of British Columbia; and since 1977, professor of sociology in education at the Ontario Institute for Studies in Education, Toronto.

Smith has written on a wide variety of topics, all connected by a concern with "bifurcation," sometimes as a central theme and sometimes as a motif. Smith sees the experience of bifurcation manifesting itself in the separation between social-scientific description and people's lived experience, between women's lived experience and the patriarchal ideal types they are given for describing that experience, between the micro-world and the macro-world

This redefinition of the concept of material conditions transforms the Marxian assumption that human beings are producers of goods into a theme of human beings as creators and sustainers of all human life. This shift brings us to the second point of difference between Marxian historical materialism and historical materialism as it is developed in socialist feminism, namely, the latter perspective's emphasis on what some Marxians might call, dismissively, *mental or ideational phenomena:* consciousness, motivation, ideas, social definitions of the situation, knowledge, texts, ideology, the will to act in one's interests or acquiesce to the interests of others.[4] To socialist feminists all these factors deeply affect human personality, human action, and the structures of domination that are realized through that action. Moreover, these aspects of human subjectivity are produced by social structures that are inextricably intertwined with, and as elaborate and powerful as, those

---

[4]Admittedly some neo-Marxians, notably the critical theorists, have also reevaluated the explanatory significance of ideology (see Chapter 4).

structures that dictate micro experience, and, especially, between the micro world of the oppressed and the micro world of the dominants whose actions create the macro structures of oppression. The concretization of these themes can be seen in a selective review of the titles of some of Smith's works: "The Statistics on Women and Mental Illness: How Not to Read Them" (1975), "What It Might Mean to Do a Canadian Sociology: The Everyday World as Problematic" (1976), "K is Mentally Ill: The Anatomy of a Factual Account" (1978), "Where There Is Oppression, There Is Resistance" (1979), "Women, Class and Family" (1981)—and, above all, "A Sociology for Women" (1979). In 1987 Smith produced her most extensive and integrated treatment of these themes in what has become a landmark in feminist sociology, *The Everyday World as Problematic.* She followed this with *The Conceptual Practices of Power* (1990) and *Texts, Facts and Femininity* (1990).

What Smith is producing for feminist sociologists, and indeed for all sociologists interested in the theoretical frontiers of the profession, is a sociology that integrates neo-Marxian concerns with the structures of domination and phenomenological insights into the variety of subjective and micro-interactional worlds. Smith sees these various everyday life-worlds as shaped by macro structures which are themselves shaped by the historical specifics of economic demand. What Smith wishes to avoid, in developing this line of reasoning, is a vision of the world in which the oppressors are consistently interpreted as individual actors making rational decisions on the basis of self-interest. What Smith sees is that self-interest itself is structurally situated, and what she calls for sociologists to focus on is always the ultimate structure producing the outcome at hand. But she believes that this structure can become known only by beginning with the outcome at hand, that is, by exploring the everyday worlds of situated individuals. Smith is concerned that much social science serves to obfuscate rather than clarify the structures that produce these worlds because much social science begins with an assumption that the structures are already known and can be known separately from the everyday life-worlds. Her recent work carries forward her project of a sociology for women through exploring macro structures as organizers of everyday/everynight worlds. She is particularly interested in developing her explorations of text-based organization and text-mediated social relations in people's everyday local practices. Here her work offers a sociological alternative to feminist postmodernism. The implications of Smith's work for sociological theory form the basis for much of this chapter.

that produce economic goods. Within all these structures, too, exploitative arrangements enrich and empower some while impoverishing and immobilizing others. Analysis of the processes that pattern human subjectivity is vital to a theory of domination, and that analysis also can be honed to precision by applying the principles of historical materialism.

The third difference between socialist feminists and Marxians is that the object of analysis for socialist feminists is not primarily class inequality but the complex intertwining of a wide range of social inequalities. Socialist feminism develops a portrait of social organization in which the public structures of economy, polity, and ideology interact with the intimate, private processes of human reproduction, domesticity, sexuality, and subjectivity to sustain a multifaceted system of domination, the workings of which are discernible both as enduring and impersonal social patterns and in the more varied subtleties of interpersonal relationships. To analyze this system, socialist feminists shuttle between a mapping of large-scale systems of domination and a situationally specific, detailed exploration of the mundane daily experiences of oppressed people. Their strategy for change rests in this process of discovery, in which they attempt to involve the oppressed groups that they study and through which they hope that both individuals and groups, in large and small ways, will learn to act in pursuit of their collective emancipation.

Within this general theoretical framing, socialist feminist analyses may be divided into three distinct emphases. First, *materialist feminism* emphasizes and situates gender relations within the structure of the contemporary capitalist class system, particularly as that system is now operating globally. The interest of materialist feminists is in the implications of global capitalism for women's lives and in the ways that women's labor contributes to the expanding wealth of capitalism. Within global capitalism, women as wage earners are more poorly paid than men because patriarchal ideology assigns them a lower social status. Because patriarchy assigns them the responsibility for the home, they are structurally more precariously positioned in wage-sector employment than men and thus more difficult to organize. These two factors make them an easy source of profit for the capitalist class. Further, capitalism depends on the unpaid production of women whose work as housewives, wives, and mothers subsidizes and disguises the real costs of reproducing and maintaining the work force. And women's work as consumers of goods and services for the household becomes a major source of capitalist profit-making (Hennessey and Ingraham, 1997; Vogel, 1995). A second emphasis in contemporary socialist feminism, given most form by Dorothy Smith and her students, is on the *relations of ruling*, the processes by which capitalist patriarchal domination are enacted through an interdependent system of control which includes not only the economy but the state and the privileged professions (including social science). The dynamics of this arrangement of control are explored through a focus on women's daily activities and experiences in the routine maintenance of material life. The relations of ruling are revealed as pervading and controlling women's daily production via "texts," extralocal, generalized requirements that seek to pattern and appropriate their labor— texts like health insurance forms, the school calendar, advertisements about the ideal home and the ideal female body (Campbell and Manicom, 1995; Currie, 1997). A third emphasis in socialist feminist discourse is represented by what materialist feminists, at least, describe as *cultural materialism* (Hennessey and Ingraham, 1997). Cultural materialists explore the many ways that state policies, social ideologies, and mass media messages interact with human subjectivity, both patterning and controlling thought and being repatterned by it. While cultural materialists explore the processes producing these messages, they do not necessarily locate the processes in a model of global capitalism and large-scale social class arrangements. Instead cultural materialists focus on the body, its depictions, meanings, and pleasures, and on politics as a struggle over how social groups and categories are represented (Clough, 1994; Davis, 1997; Walkerdine, 1997). "Cultural materialism rejects a systemic anticapitalist analysis linking the history of culture and meaning-making to capital's class system. . . . Instead, they focus almost exclusively on ideological, state, or cultural practices, anchor meaning in the body and its pleasures, or understand social change primarily in terms of the struggle over representation" (Hennessey and Ingraham, 1997:5).[5]

---

[5]Readers should note that there is disagreement among theorists as to the usage of these terms, especially *materialist feminism.* A good history of this controversy is Hennessey and Ingraham (1997).

Socialist feminists' program for change calls for a global solidarity among women to combat the abuses capitalism works in their lives, the lives of their communities, and the environment. They call on the feminist community to be ever vigilant about the dangers of their own co-optation into a privileged intelligentsia which serves capitalist interests. Their project is to mobilize people to use the state as a means for the effective redistribution of societal resources through the provision of an extensive safety net of public services like publicly supported education, health care, transportation, child care, housing; a progressive tax structure that reduces the wide disparities of income between rich and poor; and the guarantee of a living wage to all members of the community. They believe that this mobilization will be effective only if people become aware of and caring about the life conditions of others as well as their own. The feminist social scientist's duty is to make visible and experientially real the material inequalities that shape people's lives.

Intersectionality Theory   Theories of intersectionality begin with the understanding that women experience oppression in varying configurations and in varying degrees of intensity (C. Anderson, 1996; Anzaldúa, 1990; Aptheker, 1989; Caldwell, 1991; P. Collins, 1998; Crenshawe, 1989, 1991, 1997; E. Glenn, 1985; Lorde, 1984; Williams, 1991, 1995; Zinn and Dill, 1993). The explanation for that variation—and this explanation is the central subject of intersectionality theory—is that while all women potentially experience oppression on the basis of gender, women are, nevertheless, differentially oppressed by the varied intersections of other arrangements of social inequality. We may describe these arrangements of inequality as *vectors of oppression and privilege* (or in P. Collins's phrase, "the matrix of domination" [1990]), which include not only gender but also class, race, global location, sexual preference, and age. The variation of these intersections qualitatively alters the experience of being a woman—and this alteration, this diversity, must be taken into account in theorizing the experiences of "women." The argument in intersectionality theory is that the pattern of intersection itself produces a particular experience of oppression—not merely the salience of any one variable, the working out of one vector. Crenshawe (1989), for example, shows that black women frequently experience discrimination in employment because they are *black women,* but courts routinely refuse to recognize this discrimination—unless it can be shown to be a case of what is considered general discrimination, "sex discrimination" (read "white women") or "race discrimination" (read "black men"). In characterizing these as vectors of oppression *and* privilege we wish to suggest a fundamental insight of intersectionality theories—that the privilege exercised by some women and men turns on the oppression of other women and men. Theories of intersectionality at their core understand these arrangements of inequality as hierarchical structures based in unjust power relations. The theme of injustice signals the consistent critical focus of this analysis.

Intersectionality theory recognizes the fundamental link between ideology and power that allows dominants to control subordinates by creating a politics in which difference becomes a conceptual tool for justifying arrangements of oppression. In social practice, dominants use differences among people to justify oppressive practices by translating difference into models of inferiority/superiority; people are socialized to relate to difference not as a source of diversity, interest, and cultural wealth but evaluatively in terms of "better" or "worse." As Lorde (1984:115) argues, this "institutional rejection of difference is an absolute necessity in a profit economy which needs outsiders as surplus people." These ideologies operate in part by creating "a *mythical norm*" against which people evaluate others and themselves; in United States society this norm is "white, thin, male, young, heterosexual, christian, and financially secure" (Lorde, 1984:116). This norm not only allows dominants to control social production (both paid and unpaid); it also becomes part of individual subjectivity—an internalized rejection of difference that can operate to make people devalue themselves, reject people from different groups and create criteria within their own group for excluding, punishing, or marginalizing group members. Anzaldúa describes this last practice as "Othering," an act of definition done within a subordinated group to establish that a group member is unacceptable, an "other," by some criterion; this definitional activity, she points out, erodes the potential for coalition and resistance.

The intersection of vectors of oppression and privilege create variations both in the forms and the intensity of people's experience of oppression—"not all suffering is equal, there is a calculus of pain" (Arguelles, 1993). Much of the writing and research done out of an intersectionality perspective presents the concrete reality of people's lives as those lives are shaped by the intersections of these vectors. The most studied intersections by feminists are of gender and race (Amott and Mathhaei, 1991; Clark-Lewis, 1994; Dill, 1994; Jacobs, Thomas, and Lang, 1997); gender and class (Cohen, 1998; Foner, 1994; Gregson and Lowe, 1994; Seitz, 1995; Sugiman, 1994; Wrigley, 1995), and race, gender, class (Anderson and Collins, 1992; Edin and Lein, 1997; Rollins, 1985). Other analyses include gender and age (Findlen, 1995; Gibson, 1996; Lopata, 1996; Walker, 1995), gender and global location (Goodwin, 1994; Momsen, 1993; Rueschemeyer, 1994; Scheper-Hughes, 1992), and gender and sexual preference (Dunne, 1997).

In response to their material circumstances, women create interpretations and strategies for surviving and resisting the persistent exercise of unjust power. One part of the project of intersectionality theory is to give voice to the group knowledges worked out in specific life experiences created by historic intersections of inequality and to develop various feminist expressions of these knowledges—as for example, black feminist thought or chicana feminism (R. Brewer, 1989; P. Collins, 1990; Cordova et al., 1990; Alma Garcia, 1989; James and Ousia, 1993; Zandy, 1990).

Intersectionality theory develops a critique of work done in Second Wave (and First Wave) feminism where it sees that work reflecting the experience and concerns of white privileged-class feminists in North Atlantic societies. Some of this work of critique is paralleled by work done in postmodernism—but this parallelism should not be overstated. Intersectionality theory is one of the oldest traditions in feminism, at least in the United States, going back to, for example, Sojourner Truth's "Aint I a Woman" speech at the Akron Women's Rights Convention of 1852; the explosion of Black women's writings in the 1890s that led to statements like Anna Julia Cooper's (1892) *A Voice from the South by a Black Woman from the South,* or, later, Mary Church Terrell's *A Colored Woman in a White World* (1940). This critique has produced questions about what we mean by categories such as "woman," "gender," "race" and "sisterhood" (hooks, 1984; Kaminsky, 1994; Mohanty, 1991). It has focused on the diversity of experience in such seeming universals as "mothering" and "family" and has reinterpreted

PATRICIA HILL COLLINS: A Biographical Sketch

Patricia Hill Collins was born in 1948. By her own report, she grew up in a supportive and extended black working-class family located in a black community in Philadelphia; she moved from this secure base daily to attend an academically demanding public high school for girls, and then, more permanently, to earn her bachelor's degree at Brandeis University in 1969, and her M.A.T. at Harvard in 1970. During the 1970s she worked as a curriculum specialist in schools in Boston, Pittsburgh, Hartford, New York, and Washington, D.C. She returned to Brandeis to earn her Ph.D. in sociology in 1984. She has spent her career in higher education at the University of Cincinnati where she currently holds a dual appointment as Charles Phelps Taft Professor of Sociology and as Professor of African-American Studies.

Collins writes that her experiences of educational success were permeated by the counterexperience of being "the 'first,' or 'one of the few,' or the 'only' African-American and/or woman and/or working-class person in my schools, communities, and work settings" (1990:xi). In these situations, she found herself judged as being less than others who came from different backgrounds and learned that educational success seemed to demand that she distance herself from her black working-class background. This created in her a tension that produced "a loss of voice."

Her response to these tensions has been to formulate an alternative understanding of social theory and an alternative way of doing theory. This project led her to discover the theoretical voice of her community and to reclaim her own voice by situating it in that community. It culminated in *Black Feminist Thought* (1990) a landmark text in feminist and social theory that has been widely anthologized and for which Collins was honored with the Jessie Bernard Award and the C. Wright Mills Award. *Black Feminist Thought* presents social theory as the understandings of a specific group, black women; to this end, Collins draws on a wide range of voices, some famous, others obscure. What she presents is a community-based social theory that articulates that group's understanding of its oppression by intersections of race, gender, and class—and its historic struggle against that oppression. In this work, Collins uncovers the distinctive epistemology by which black women assess truth and validity; she also argues convincingly for a feminist standpoint epistemology. *Black Feminist Thought* suggests a direction for feminist social theory in particular and for social theory in general. In both practice and theory she has pursued her theory of intersectionality, helping to organize the ASA section, Race, Gender, Class; editing, with Margaret Anderson, the essay collection, *Race, Class and Gender* (1992); and authoring a multiplicity of articles in a wide range of journals.

Fighting Words: Black Women and The Search for Justice (1998) continues her struggle to redefine social theory not as the province and practice of an elite intellectual group but as the understandings variously situated groups have achieved about the social world. In this project, Collins repeats her emphatic call to sociologists to write and work as if social theory were part of the collective enterprise of social life and to make social theory meaningful and accessible to its publics.

theoretical works like the sociological-psychoanalytic studies of Chodorow and Benjamin (Dickerson, 1995; Glenn, Chang and Forcey, 1993; Mahoney and Yngvesson, 1992; Segura and Pierce, 1993; Zhang, 1993). This critique has prompted a repositioning of the understandings of "whiteness" by white feminists who seek to understand whiteness as a construction, the ways that whiteness results in privilege, what they can actively do to reduce racism, and how they can contribute to producing a more inclusive feminist analysis (Alcoff, 1998; A. Bailey, 1998; Breines, 1992; Chodorow, 1994; Frankenberg, 1993; Ward, 1994).

This process of theory-building, research, and critique, has brought intersectionality theory to one of its central themes and one of the central issues confronting feminism today: how to allow for the analytic principle and empirical fact of diversity among women while at the same time holding to the valuational and political position that specific groups of women share a distinctive standpoint. Explaining *standpoint,* Patricia Hill Collins (1998:224–225) proposes that it is the view of the world shared by a group characterized by a "heterogeneous commonality"; "shared," Collins argues, refers, as Marx suggests, to " 'circumstances directly encountered, given, and transmitted from the past.' " Thus, Collins concludes that a group's standpoint is constituted not out of some essentialism but out of a recognition that, as Black activist Fannie Lou Hamer says, " 'we're in this bag together.' " While vectors of oppression and privilege—race, class, gender, age, global location, sexual preference—intersect in all people's lives, these theorists argue that the way they intersect markedly affects the degree to which a common standpoint is affirmed. Among factors facilitating this affirmation are the group's existence over time, its sense of its own history as a group, its location in relatively segregated identifiable spaces, and its development of an intragroup system of social organizations and knowledges for coping with oppression. But a group standpoint is never monolithic or impermeable; the very fact that the group is constituted out of intersections of vectors means that group members can pivot between varying senses of self; group members frequently move from the home group into the larger society where their experience is that of "the outsider within" (P. Collins, 1990, 1998); moreover, the home group is subject to permeation by outside ideas and is not undifferentiated—it has its own internal dynamics of difference and may even be constituted by its existence at a cultural "borderland" (Anzaldúa, 1990). Intersectionality theorists warn that while it is easy to locate the experience of intersection and of standpoint in individuals, this reductionism is theoretically and politically dangerous, erasing the historic structures of unequal power that have produced the individual experience and obscuring the need for political change.

In developing an agenda for change, intersectionality theory turns to the knowledge of oppressed people and their long-held evaluative principles of faith and justice (Collins, 1990, 1998; hooks, 1984, 1990; Reagon, 1982/1995; Lorde, 1984). The theory argues for the need to bear witness, to protest, and to organize for change within the context of the oppressed community, for only within community can one keep faith in the eventual triumph of justice—a justice understood not in the narrow framing of legal rationality but as the working out within social institutions and social relations of the principles of fairness to and concern for others and oneself.

Feminism and Postmodernism

Postmodernist theory is described in Chapter 13. Here we offer an abbreviated description focusing on its relation to feminist theory.

Although feminist academic engagement with postmodernist ideas and vocabulary has gained ground in the 1990s (Clough, 1994; P. Collins, 1998; Hennessey and Ingraham, 1997; Mann and Kelley, 1997; Stacey and Thorne, 1996), postmodernism is used less as a theory of society than an epistemological approach by feminists—in the same way they might incorporate empiricism or phenomenology into their analyses. For postmodernism does not offer an answer to the fundamental question of feminist scholarship, "And what about the women?" Instead, postmodernism would respond with the counterquestion, "How are you constructing the category or concept of 'women'?" Thus, we argue, postmodernism is important to feminist theory primarily as "an oppositional epistemology," a strategy for questioning the claims to truth or knowledge advanced by a given theory (see also, P. Collins, 1998).

Postmodernist theory begins with the observation that we (that is, those of us living at the turn of the century) no longer live under conditions of modernity but of "postmodernity." This postmodern world is produced by the interplay of four major changes: an aggressively expansive stage in global capitalism; the weakening of centralized state power (with the collapse of the old imperial systems, the fragmentation of the communist bloc, and the rise of ethnic politics within nation states); the patterning of life by an increasingly powerful and penetrative technology that controls production and promotes consumerism; and the development of liberationist social movements based not in class but in other forms of identity—nationalism (the revolutions of formerly colonial states), race (the African American civil rights movement), gender (feminism as a global movement), sexual orientation (gay rights), and environmentalism. Liberationist movements may have been the most important of these developments producing the postmodern challenge to modernist epistemology and theory, as feminist philosopher Susan Bordo explains:

> [I]t was not . . . *any* professional intellectual voice who was ultimately responsible for uncovering the pretensions and illusions of the ideals of epistemological objectivity, foundations, and neutral judgment. That uncovering occurred first . . . in political practice. Its agents were the liberation movements of the sixties and seventies, emerging not only to make a claim to the legitimacy of marginalized cultures, unheard voices, suppressed narratives, but also to expose the perspectivity and partiality of the official accounts. . . . [The key questions now became] the historical, social questions: *Whose* truth? *Whose* nature? *Whose* version of reason? *Whose* history? *Whose* tradition?
> (Bordo, 1990:136–137)

The question "whose knowledge?" has proved to be radically transformative, opening debates not only about the relation of power to knowledge but about the basis of human claims to know. Postmodernists reject the basic principle of modernist epistemology, that humans can, by the exercise of pure reason, arrive at a complete and objective knowledge of the world, a knowledge which is a representation of reality, "a mirror of nature." They argue that this modernist principle gives rise to a number of epistemological errors—the *god-eye* view that locates the observer outside the world being observed; the *grand narrative* that holistically explains that world; *foundationalism* that identifies certain rules of analysis as always appropriate; *universalism* that asserts that there are discoverable principles that everywhere govern the world; *essentialism* that claims that people are constituted by core and unchanging qualities;

representation that presumes that one's statement about the world can accurately reflect the world. Postmodernism questions the existence both of "reason" as a universal, essential quality of the human mind and of the "reasoning subject" as a consistent, unified configuration of consciousness. Postmodernists portray the knowledge-making process as one of multiple representations of experience created by differently located discourse groups in which the establishment of any hegemonic knowledge-claim results from an effective exercise of power. They suggest alternative epistemological practices like *decentering,* which moves the understandings of nonprivileged groups to the center of discourse and knowledge; *deconstruction,* which shows how concepts, posed as accurate representations of the world, are historically constructed and contain contradictions; a focus on *difference,* which explores any knowledge construct not only for what it says but for what it erases or marginalizes, particularly through the application of modernist *binary logic* of "either/or."

Feminism and postmodernism both raise the question of *whose* knowledge or definitions are to count, and, to some degree, both engage in practices of decentering and deconstruction. If we look at popular slogans in feminist activism in the sixties and seventies, we see a dissolution of binary opposites—"The personal is political"; a challenging of traditional categories—"A woman without a man is like a fish without a bicycle"; an emphasis on decentering—"God is coming and, boy, is SHE pissed"; an understanding of language as contextual and relational—"If she says 'No,' it's rape"; and a sense of the world, no matter how material, as constructed out of power relations—"If men could menstruate, abortion would be a sacrament." Contemporary feminist theorists find in postmodernism a reinforcement and legitimation for their own insistence on the epistemological and political necessity for decentering and deconstruction. They have enriched their analyses by drawing on postmodernism's vocabulary: *discursive practices, discourse analysis, genealogy, code, intertextuality, representation, text, the Imaginary, difference, hyperreality, alterity.* Postmodernist epistemology, thus, provides some feminist scholars with an expanded possibility for naming their work and has become part of such accepted practices as the liberal feminist project of "deconstructing gender." This adoption of vocabulary is in the tradition of the achievement of Second Wave feminism, which developed a vocabulary to name women's oppression and empowerment. It has not involved an unthinking takeover but a sophisticated incorporation, sometimes keeping, sometimes blending, sometimes changing the original meanings. Many feminists—especially those working in text-based fields such as literature—also find the postmodernist understanding of the world as "representation," "text," and "discourse" useful for conceptualizing social life. Feminists in the social sciences sometimes adopt the image of social life as discourse and representation or use the direction it suggests to analyze what is present and what is obscured in the cultural and political representations affecting women's lives. Above all, the postmodernist "turn" pushes feminism to make reflexivity a permanent feature of theory-building, a way of ensuring that it will not become what it has set out to oppose—a hegemonic discourse that oppresses people through essentialist and universalist categories (Haraway, 1990; King, 1994; Nicholson, 1994; Sawicki, 1991). This directive has been particularly meaningful because it coincides with the questions raised by women of color, women from societies outside the North Atlantic, lesbians, and working-class women about Second Wave feminism's essentialist claims regarding "sisterhood," "woman," "Third World women," "sexuality," "family," "mothering," and "work." Jana Sawicki argues that feminists "have good reason to appeal to Foucault's negative freedom, that is, the freedom to disengage from our political identities, our presumptions about gender differences, and the categories and practices that define feminism. . . . Women are produced by patriarchal power at the same time they resist it. There are good reasons to be ambivalent about the liberatory possibilities of appealing to 'reason,' 'motherhood,' or the 'feminine' when they have also been the source of our oppression" (1991:102).

But the feminist relation to postmodernism is marked more strikingly by unease than embrace. Many feminists see postmodernism as exclusive in aspiration and therefore antithetical to the feminist project of inclusion. Evidence for this unease is postmodernism's arcane vocabulary, its location in the academy rather than in political struggle, and its nonreflexive grasp for hegemonic status in that academic discourse. Many feminists also question the "innocence" of the postmodernist challenge, wondering whether it is truly liberationist or is part of a politics of knowledge in which a privileged academic class responds to the challenges of marginalized persons with a technically complex argument to the effect that no location for speech can claim authority. Hartsock (1990:169) has made the classic statement of this concern: "Somehow it seems highly suspicious that it is at the precise moment when so many groups have been engaged in . . . redefinitions of the marginalized Others that suspicions emerge about the nature of the 'subject,' about the possibilities for a general theory which can describe the world, about historical 'progress.' " Another source of unease is that the postmodernist emphasis on an infinite regress of deconstruction and difference leads people away from collective, liberationist politics and toward a radical individualism that may conclude that " 'because every . . . one of us is different and special, it follows that every problem or crisis is exclusively our own, or, conversely, your problem—not mine' " (Jordan, 1992, in Collins, 1998:150). Above all, the postmodernist turn takes feminist scholars away from the materiality of inequality, injustice, and oppression and toward a neo-idealist posture that sees the world as "discourse," "representation," and "text." In severing the link to material inequality, postmodernism moves feminism away from its commitment to progressive change—the foundational project of any critical social theory.

A FEMINIST SOCIOLOGICAL THEORY

This section presents a synthesis of ideas implicit or explicit in the varieties of feminist theory described above in order to develop a statement of some fundamental principles for a feminist *sociological* theory. We identify five distinctive features of a feminist sociological theory: its sociology of knowledge, its model of society, its patterning of social interaction, its focus on a subjective level of social experience, and its integration of these levels of social life. Our synthesis draws on theorists writing out of a variety of disciplines, including sociology; the major influences are Benjamin, 1988; Bordo, 1993; Chodorow, 1978; P. Collins, 1990, 1998; Gilligan, 1982; Heilbrun, 1988; Hennessey and Ingraham, 1997; Lorde, 1984; MacKinnon, 1989; Rich, 1976, 1980; D. Smith, 1978, 1979, 1989, 1990a, 1990b, 1992, 1993; West and Fenstermaker, 1993; Williams, 1991, 1995.

A Feminist Sociology of Knowledge

A feminist sociology of knowledge sees everything that people label "knowledge of the world" as having four characteristics: (1) it is always created from the standpoint of embodied actors situated in groups that are differentially located in social structure; (2) it is, thus, always partial and interested, never total and objective; (3) it is produced in and varies among groups and, to some degree, among actors within groups; and (4) it is always affected by power relations—whether it is formulated from the standpoint of dominant or subordinate groups. This understanding of knowledge has been named "feminist standpoint epistemology" (Harding, 1986). A feminist sociological theory begins with a sociology of knowledge because feminists attempt to describe, analyze, and change the world from the standpoint of women; and because working from women's subordinated position in social relations, feminist sociological theorists see that knowledge is part of the system of power governing the production of knowledge, as it governs all production in society. Feminist sociological theory attempts to alter the balance of power within sociological discourse—and within social theory—by establishing the standpoint of women as one of the standpoints from which social knowledge is constructed.

In attempting to do sociology from the standpoint of women, feminist sociological theorists have to consider what constitutes a standpoint of women. A standpoint is the product of a social collectivity with a sufficient history and commonality of circumstance to develop a shared knowledge of social relations. Feminists, starting where Marx left off, have identified three crucial collectivities—owners, workers, *and women*—whose distinctive relationships to the processes of social production and reproduction constitute them as standpoint groups. Historically women under patriarchy whatever their class and race have been assigned to the tasks of social reproduction (childbearing, childrearing, housekeeping, food preparation, care of the ill and dependent, emotional and sexual service); patriarchy is a power relation in which women occupy a subordinate status as workers whose production is exploited and appropriated by men. Yet, any solidarity of women as a "class" in patriarchal production is fractured by other class configurations, including economic class and race class. While women's shared and historic relation to social reproduction in circumstances of subordination is the basis for the feminist claim of "the standpoint of women," in the daily workings of social power the intersection of gender inequality with race inequality, class inequality, geosocial inequality, and inequalities based on sexuality and age produces a complex system of unequally empowered standpoint groups relating through shifting arrangements of coalition and opposition. These intersectionalities are now an integral part of the feminist description and analysis of women's standpoint.

This understanding of knowledge as the product of different standpoint groups presents feminist sociological theory with the problem of how to produce a feminist sociological account that is both acceptable to sociologists and useful to feminism's emancipatory project, that is, how to avoid a collapse into relativism in which one account cancels out another. At least four strategies are used. One is asserting the validity of "webbed accounts," that is, of accounts woven together by reporting all the various actors' or standpoint groups' knowledges of an experience and describing the situations, including the dynamics of power, out of which the actors or groups came to create these versions (Haraway, 1988). A second strategy is that of privileging the accounts or standpoints of the less empowered actors or groups because a major factor in unequal power relations is that dominants' views are given both more credence and more circulation. The privileging of the standpoints of the disempowered is a part of the feminist emancipatory project but it also produces an important corrective to mainstream sociological theories by changing the angle of vision from which social processes are understood (Lorde, 1984). A third strategy is that the feminist theorist must be reflexive about and able to give an account of the stages through which she/he moves from knowledge of an individual's or group's standpoint to the generalizations of a sociological account, for that translation is an act of power (P. Collins, 1990, 1998; D. Smith, 1990a). A fourth strategy is for the social theorist to identify the particular location from which she or he speaks and thus to identify her or his partiality (in all meanings of that word) and its effect on the theory constructed. In keeping with this last strategy, we should declare the standpoint from which we create the theoretical synthesis presented here. We write from the relatively privileged class position of academic social scientists living in the contemporary United States, but also as women located within a particular intersection of vectors of oppression and privilege that makes us subject to experiences of racism, ageism, and heterosexism. We also write out of family heritages of membership in historically constituted standpoint groups shaped by poverty and by colonial status. This intermingling of current status and family history shapes both our interests and values. The synthesis we present here reflects oppression theories' concept of a just society as one that empowers all people to claim as a fundamental right (not a begrudged concession to need or a reward to the "deserving") a fair share of social goods—from the material essentials of food, clothing, shelter, health care, and education, to an absence of fear of violence, to a positive valuation of self in the particularities of one's group and individual identity.

The Macro-Social Order

In this and the sections that follow we operate within the established sociological conventions of vocabulary and conceptualization by organizing our presentation around such phrases as *macro-social, micro-social,* and *subjectivity.* Certainly one can extract much from feminist theory that relates to one or other of these established sociological concepts—although, as we shall see, much of what is extracted poses a fundamental critique of existing sociological assertions about these topics. But the critique goes deeper. Feminist theory is in the process of articulating a new conceptual vocabulary for sociology which moves outside and away from the bifurcation of macro-social versus micro-social/subjective, making that vision of social reality obsolete. We turn in the final part of this section to the newer concepts with which feminist sociologists are beginning to move beyond this older model of social reality.

Feminist sociology's view of the macro-social order emphasizes the impact of both social structure (or macro-objective productions) and ideology (or macro subjectivity) on actors' perceptions of social reality.

Feminist sociology begins by expanding the Marxian concept of economic production into a much more general concept of social production, that is, the production of all human social life. Along with the production of commodities for the market, social production for feminists also includes arrangements like the organization of housework, which produce the essential commodities and services of the household; of sexuality, which pattern and satisfy human desire; of intimacy, which pattern and satisfy human emotional needs for acceptance, approval, love, and self-esteem; of state and religion, which create the rules and laws of a community; and of politics, mass media, and academic discourse, which establish institutionalized, public definitions of the situation.

Thus framed and expanded, the Marxian model of intergroup relations remains visible in feminist theory's model of social organization. Each of these various types of social production is based on an arrangement by which some actors, controlling the resources crucial to that activity, act as dominants, or "masters," who dictate and profit from the circumstances of production. Within each productive sector, production rests on the work of subordinates, or "servants," whose energies create the world ordered into being by their masters and whose exploitation denies them the rewards and satisfactions produced by their work. Through feminist theory, we see, more vividly than through Marxian theory, the intimate association between masters and servants that may lie at the heart of production and the indispensability of the servant's work in creating and sustaining everything necessary to human social life. In intimate relations of exploitation, domination may be expressed not as coercion but as paternalism, "the combination of positive feelings toward the group with discriminatory intentions toward the group." Paternalism masks for both parties but does not transform a relationship of domination and subordination (Jackman, 1994:11). Social production occurs through a multidimensional structure of domination and exploitation that organizes class, gender, race, sex, power, and knowledge into overlapping hierarchies of intimately associated masters and workers.

The feminist model of stratification in social production offers a direct critique of the structural-functionalist vision of a society composed of a system of separate institutions and distinct though interrelated roles. Feminist theory claims that this image is not generalizable but that it depicts the experiences and vantage points of society's dominants—white, male, upper-class, and adult. Feminist research shows that women and other nondominants do not experience social life as a movement among compartmentalized roles. Instead, they are involved in a balancing of roles, a merging of role-associated interests and orientations, and, through this merging, in a weaving together of social institutions. Indeed, one indicator of the dominant group's control over the situations of production may be that its members can achieve this kind of purposive compartmentalization in *their* role behavior, a condition that serves to reproduce their control over situations. But feminist sociology stresses that this condition depends on the subordinate services of actors who cannot compartmentalize their lives and actions. Indeed, were these subordinate actors to compartmentalize similarly, the whole system of production in complex industrialized societies would collapse. In contrast to the structural-functional model, the feminist model emphasizes that the role-merging experience of women may be generalizable to the experience of many other subordinate "servant" groups whose work produces the fine-grained texture of daily life. The understandings that such subordinated groups have of the organization of social life may be very different from the understanding depicted in structural-functionalist theory; even their identification of key institutional spheres may differ. Yet their vantage point springs from situations necessary to society as it is presently organized and from work that makes possible the masters' secure sense of an institutionally compartmentalized world.

Further, feminism emphasizes the centrality of ideological domination to the structure of social domination. Ideology is an intricate web of beliefs about reality and social life that is institutionalized as public knowledge and disseminated throughout society so effectively that it becomes taken-for-granted knowledge for all social groups. Thus what feminists see as "public knowledge of social reality" is not an overarching culture, a consensually created social product, but a reflection of the interests and experiences of society's dominants and one crucial index of their power in society. What distinguishes this view from traditional Marxian analysis is that for feminists ideological control is a basic process in domination, and the hierarchical control of discourse and knowledge is a key element in societal domination.

Central to feminist concerns about the macro-social order is the macro-structural patterning of gender oppression. Feminist theorists argue that women's bodies constitute an essential resource in social production and reproduction and therefore become a site of exploitation and control. Gender oppression is reproduced by an ideological system of institutionalized knowledge that reflects the interests and experiences of men. Among other things, this gender ideology identifies men as the bearers of sociocultural authority and allocates to the male role the right to dominate and to the female role the obligation to serve in all dimensions of social production. Gender ideology constructs women as objects of male desire whose social value is determined by their fabrication of an appropriately molded body. Gender ideology also systematically flattens and distorts women's productive activities by (1) trivializing some of them, for example, housework; (2) idealizing to the point of unrecognizability other activities, for example, mothering; and (3) making invisible yet other crucial work, for example, women's multiple and vital contributions to the production of marketplace commodities. These ideological processes may be generalizable to the macro-structural production of all social subordination.

Capitalism and patriarchy, although analytically separate forms of domination, reinforce each other in numerous ways. For example, the organization of production into public and private spheres and the gendering of those spheres benefits both systems of domination. Capitalism benefits in that women's labor in the private sphere reproduces the worker at no cost to capital; further their responsibility for the private sphere makes women a marginal but always co-optable source of cheap labor, driving wages down generally. At the same time patriarchy benefits from this exploitation of the woman worker because it sustains her dependence on men. Women's difficult entry into the public sphere ensures that what "good" employment may be available there will go first to men. Women's experiences of sexual harassment on the job and of being hassled in public places are not incidental and insignificant micro events but examples of a power relation in which patriarchy helps police the borders for capital. This division is further complicated by the "race-ing" and "age-ing" as well as gendering of public and private.

The Micro-Social Order

At the micro-interactional level, feminist sociology (like some microsociological perspectives) focuses on how individuals take account of each other as they pursue objective projects or intersubjective meanings. Feminist sociological theory argues that the conventional models of interaction (social behaviorist and social definitionist—see Appendix) may depict how persons located as equals in macro-structural, power-conferring categories create meanings and negotiate relationships in the pursuit of joint projects; they may also depict how, from the vantage point of structural dominants, one experiences interaction with both equals and subordinates. But feminist theory suggests that when structural unequals interact there are many other qualities to their association than those suggested by the conventional models: that action is responsive rather than purposive, that there is a continuous enactment of power differentials, that the meaning of many activities is obscured or invisible, that access is not always open to those settings in which shared meanings are most likely to be created.

Most mainstream microsociology presents a model of purposive human beings setting their own goals and pursuing these in linear courses of action in which they (individually or collectively) strive to link means to ends. In contrast, feminist research shows, first, that women's lives have a quality of incidentalism, as women find themselves caught up in agendas that shift and change with the vagaries of marriage, husbands' courses of action, children's unpredictable impact on life plans, divorce, widowhood, and the precariousness of most women's wage-sector occupations. Second, in their daily activities, women find themselves not so much pursuing goals in linear sequences but responding continuously to the needs and demands of others. This theme has been developed from analysis of the emotional and relational symbiosis between mothers and daughters, through descriptions of intensely relational female play groups, to analyses of women in their typical occupations as teachers, nurses, secretaries, receptionists, and office helpers and accounts of women in their roles as wives, mothers, and community and kin coordinators. In calling women's activities "responsive," we are not describing them as passively reactive. Instead, we are drawing a picture of beings who are oriented not so much to their own goals as to the tasks of monitoring, coordinating, facilitating, and moderating the wishes, actions, and demands of others. In place of microsociology's conventional model of purposeful actors, then, feminist research presents a model of actors who are in their daily lives responsively located at the center of a web of others' actions and who in the long term find themselves located in one or another of these situations by forces that they can neither predict nor control.

Conventional micro-social theory assumes that the pressures in interactive situations toward collaboration and meaning construction are so great that actors, bracketing considerations of the macro structure, orient toward each other on an assumption of equality. Feminist research on interactions between women and men contradicts this idea, showing that these social interactions are pervasively patterned by influences from their macro-structural context. In their daily activities, women are affected by the fact that they are structurally subordinate to the men with whom they interact in casual associations, courtship, marriage, family, and wage work. Any interpersonal equality or dominance that women as individuals may achieve is effectively offset, within the interactive process itself, by these structural patterns—of which the most pervasive is the institution of gender. The macro-structural patterning of gender inequality is intricately woven through the interactions between women and men and affects not only its broad division of labor, in who sets and who implements projects, but also its processual details, which repeatedly show the enactment of authority and deference in seating and seating-standing arrangements, forms of address and conversation, eye contact, and the control of space and time. This assumption of inequality as a feature in interactive situations is intensified and complicated when factors of race and class are included in the feminist analytic frame.

Social definitionists assume that one of the major ongoing projects in social interaction is the construction of shared meanings. Actors, seeing each other in activity and interaction, form shared understandings through communication and achieve a common vantage point on their experiences. Feminists argue that this assumption must be qualified by the fact that micro interactions are embedded in and permeated by the macro structure. Women's everyday actions and relationships occur against an ideological backdrop of public or institutionalized understanding of everyday experience that flattens and distorts women's activity and experience. This ideology patterns the meanings assigned to activities in interaction. Men (dominants) in interaction with women are more likely to assign to women's activity meanings drawn from the macro structure of gender ideology than either to enter the situation with an attitude of open inquiry or to draw on any other macro-level typing for interpreting women's activity. Women, immersed in the same ideological interpretation of their experiences, stand at a point of dialectical tension, balancing this ideology against the actuality of their lives. A great diversity of meanings develops out of this tension. Social definitionists assume that actors, relating and communicating intimately and over long periods of time, create a common vantage point or system of shared understanding. Feminists' research on what may be the most intimate, long-term, male-female association, marriage, shows that, for all the reasons reported above, marriage partners remain strangers to each other and inhabit separate worlds of meaning. This "stranger-ness" may be greater for the dominant man, in the interests of effective control, than for the subordinate woman who must monitor the dominant's meanings (D. Smith, 1979).

A democratic ethos shapes both social-definitionist and social-behaviorist descriptions of interaction. Conventional models imply that people have considerable equality of opportunity and freedom of choice in moving in and out of interactional settings. Feminist research shows that the interactions in which women are most free to create with others meanings that depict their life experiences are those which occur when they are in relationship and communication with similarly situated women. Moreover, these associations can be deeply attractive to women because of the practical, emotional, and meaning-affirming support that they provide. Women, however, are not freely empowered to locate in these settings. Law, interactional domination, and ideology restrict and demean this associational choice so that, insidiously, even women become suspicious of its attractions. Under these circumstances, the association becomes not a free and open choice but a subterranean, circumscribed, and publicly invisible arena for relationship and meaning.

Finally, a feminist analysis of interactional practices may emphasize differences between men and women explainable in terms of deep psychic structures. Male training rewards individuation and the repudiation of the female so that the male understands at an early age that his claim to male privilege involves his distancing from female behaviors. Similarly, the female learns early that one of the duties of women—to men and to each other—is to recognize the subjectivity of the other through interactional gestures such as paying attention, commenting on actions done, using gestures to indicate approval and awareness. These behaviors permeate and explain not only interactions across gender but interactions within same-gender groups. Women are repeatedly shown as enacting more responsiveness to the other and engaging in more ongoing monitoring of the other's needs and desires. Men are more inclined to feel both the right and the duty to compartmentalize in order to attain individual projects and to feel that their responsiveness to the other is an act of generosity not a part of expected interactional behavior.

Subjectivity

Most sociological theories subsume the subjective level of social experience under micro-social action (micro subjectivity) or as "culture" or "ideology" at the macro level (macro subjectivity) (see Chapter 10; Appendix). Feminist sociology, however, insists that the actor's individual interpretation of goals and relationships must be looked at as a distinct level. This insistence, like so much of feminist sociology, grows out of the study of women's lives and seems applicable to the lives of subordinates in general. Women as subordinates are particularly aware of the distinctiveness of their subjective experience precisely because their own experience so often runs counter to prevailing cultural and micro-interactionally established definitions. When sociologists do look at the subjective level of experience, usually as part of the micro-social order, they focus on four major issues: (1) role taking and knowledge of the other; (2) the process of the internalization of community norms; (3) the nature of the self as social actor; and (4) the nature of the consciousness of everyday life. This section explores the feminist thesis on each of these issues.

The conventional sociological model of subjectivity (as presented to us in the theories of Mead [see Chapter 6] and Schutz) assumes that in the course of role taking, the social actor learns to see the self through the eyes of others deemed more or less the same as the actor. But feminist sociology shows that women are socialized to see themselves through the eyes of men. Even when significant others are women, they have been so socialized that they too take the male view of self and of other women. Women's experience of learning to role-take is shaped by the fact that they must, in a way men need not, learn to take the role of the genuine *other*, not just a social other who is taken to be much like oneself. The other for women is the male and is alien. The other for men is, first and foremost, men who are like them in a quality that the culture considers of transcendent importance: gender. Feminist theory emphasizes that this formula is complicated by the intersection of the vectors of oppression and privilege within individual lives.

Role taking usually is seen as culminating in the internalization of community norms via the social actor's learning to take the role of "the generalized other," a construct that the actor mentally creates out of the amalgam of macro- and micro-level experiences that form her or his social life. The use of the singular *other* indicates that microsociologists usually envision this imagined generalized other as a cohesive, coherent, singular expression of expectations. But feminists argue that in a male-dominated patriarchal culture, the generalized other represents a set of male-dominated community norms that force the woman to picture herself as "less than" or "unequal to" men. To the degree that a woman succeeds in formulating a sense of generalized other that accurately reflects the dominant perceptions of the community, she may have damaged her own possibilities for self-esteem and self-exploration. Feminist theory calls into question the existence of a unified generalized other for the majority of people. The subordinate has to pivot between a world governed by a dominant generalized other, or meaning system, and locations in "home groups" which offer alternative understandings and generalized others. The awareness of the possibility of multiple generalized others is essential to understanding the potential complexity of having or being a self.

Microsociologists describe the social actor as picturing the everyday world as something to be mastered according to one's particular interests. Feminist sociologists argue that women may find themselves so limited by their status as women that the idea of projecting their own plans onto the world becomes meaningless in all but theory. Further, women may not experience the life-world as something to be mastered according to their own particular interests. They may be socialized to experience that life-world as a place in which one balances a variety of actors' interests. Women may not have the same experience of control of particular spheres of space, free from outside interference. Similarly, their sense of time rarely can follow the simple pattern of first things first because they have as a life project the balancing of the interests and projects of others. Thus, women may experience planning and actions as acts of concern for a variety of interests, their own and others; may act in projects of cooperation rather than mastery; and may evaluate their ongoing experiences of role-balancing not as role conflicts but as a more appropriate response to social life than role compartmentalization.

Feminist sociologists have critically evaluated the thesis of a unified consciousness of everyday life that traditional microsociologists usually assume. Feminist sociologists stress that for women the most pervasive feature of the cognitive style of everyday life is that of a "bifurcated consciousness," developing along "a line of fault" between their own personal, lived, and reflected-on experience and the established types available in the social stock of knowledge to describe that experience (D. Smith, 1979, 1987). Everyday life itself thus divides into two realities for subordinates: the reality of actual, lived, reflected-on experience and the reality of social typifications. Often aware of the way that their own experience differs from that of the culturally dominant males with whom they interact, women may be less likely to assume a shared subjectivity. As biological and social beings whose activities are not perfectly regulated by patriarchal time, they are more aware of the demarcation between time as lived experience and time as a social mandate. A feminist sociology of subjectivity perhaps would begin here: How do people survive when their own experience does not fit the established social typifications of that experience? We know already that some do so by avoiding acts of sustained reflection; some by cultivating their own series of personal types to make sense of their experience; some by seeking community with others who share this bifurcated reality; some by denying the validity of their own experience.

What we have generalized here for women's subjectivity may be true for the subjectivity of all subordinates. (1) Their experience of role taking is complicated by their awareness that they must learn the expectations of an other who by virtue of differences in power is alien. (2) They must relate not to a generalized other but to many generalized others, in both the culture of the powerful and the various subcultures of the less empowered and the disempowered. (3) They do not experience themselves as purposive social actors who can chart their own course through life—although they may be constantly told that they can do so, especially within the American ethos. (4) Most pervasively, they live daily with a bifurcated consciousness, a sense of the line of fault between their own lived experiences and what the dominant culture tells them is the social reality.

Everything in this discussion has assumed a unified subject, that is, an individual woman or man with an ongoing, consistent consciousness and a sense of self. The unified subject is important to feminist theory because it is that subject who experiences pain and oppression, makes value judgments, and resists or accepts the world in place— the unified subject is the primary agent of social change. Yet, our discussion of subjectivity also raises questions about how unified this subject is; there are the problems of a subject whose generalized other is truly "other" or "alien," who experiences not *a* generalized other but many generalized others, whose consciousness is bifurcated, and whose self in its capacities for development and change may be viewed more as a process than a product. All these tendencies toward an understanding of the self as fragmented rather than as unified are inherent in feminist theorizing of the self—indeed, they are at the heart of feminist ideas about resistance and change. This sense of fragmentation is much intensified in postmodernist feminist critiques (discussed earlier in this chapter), a theoretical position which raises questions about the very possibility of "a unified subject or consciousness." If a self, any self, is subject to change from day to day or even moment to moment, if we can speak of "being not myself," then on what basis do we posit a self? Yet, feminist critics of postmodernism respond by beginning in the experience of women in daily life, who when they say "I was not myself" or "I have not been myself," assume a stable self from which they have departed and, further, by those very statements, some self that knows of the departure.

TOWARD AN INTEGRATIVE THEORY

The picture of social organization that emerges in feminist sociological theory is highly integrative. It combines economic activity with other forms of human social production (child rearing, emotional sustenance, knowledge, home maintenance, sexuality, and so on); it sees material production as elaborately linked with ideological production; it describes the interpenetration of apparently autonomous social institutions and apparently voluntary individual actions and relations; it connects structure to interaction and consciousness. In this vision of the world, feminist sociological theory addresses two classic dichotomies in sociological thinking, the debate over agency and structure and the division between macro and micro.

The debate among sociologists about agency and structure is a debate about how sociological explanations are to be constituted, about the explanatory significance of agency (human beings acting with relative autonomy to affect social life) or structure (the determinative effects on individual action of collective social arrangements) (see Chapter 11). Feminist sociological theory contributes to this debate by exploring the relationship between agency and structure in terms of feminism's position that social life is patterned by conflict between liberation and domination. On the one hand, feminist theory affirms the massive, enduring, and determinative social structures of patriarchy, capitalism, and racism. On the other hand, feminist theory centers in an oppositional politics and in a methodological focus on the embodied human subject, both of which are claims about the significance of human agency in history and in social analysis. Human agents are seen as living and acting within a complex field of power which they are determined by and which in their agency they both reproduce and contest. Social life may be understood as an ongoing series of enactments of oppression by agents who cannot be absolved from their responsibility for the reproduction of domination even when we can explain the social structures framing those enactments. Social life can also be understood as an ongoing series of individual and group responses to oppression, responses like coping, challenging, witnessing, subverting, rebelling, resisting—a politics of resistance in which individual and collective agency opposes structures and agents of domination. Significant to this oppositional politics is the existence and persistence of group standpoints; these group standpoints are ways of understanding society that develop out of social structural arrangements and that serve as motivations for individual and group reproduction of or resistance to domination (P. Collins, 1998). While the structural determinist may argue that standpoints are the product of social structures, feminist analysis points to the ongoing wonder and mystery of the human capacity to hope and act for better things even in circumstances of the most brutal oppression. Feminist analysis emphasizes the emotional responsiveness of embodied human subjects to structures, their capacity to respond in anger and to turn anger to constructive uses. The emotional response of anger—and the willingness to turn that anger into a stand against injustice or a demand for justice—cannot be accounted for by the structures of oppression which produce it (Lorde, 1984). In this affirmation, feminism bases its hope for a liberationist politics and offers a solution to the theoretical problematic of the structure versus agency debate.

Feminist theorists have also been developing a vocabulary for talking about the various and simultaneous realities of macro and micro relations. Dorothy Smith has introduced the concepts of "relations of ruling," "generalized, anonymous, impersonal texts," and "local actualities of lived experience" (Smith, 1987, 1990a, 1990b). *Relations of ruling* refers to the complex, nonmonolithic but intricately connected social activities that attempt to control human social production. Human social production must by its material nature occur at some moment in the *local actualities of lived experience* —that is, the places where some actual person sits while writing or reading a book (or plants food or produces clothing). The relations of ruling in late capitalist patriarchy manifest themselves through *texts* that are characterized by their essential *anonymity, generality, and authority*. These texts are designed to pattern and translate real-life, specific, individualized experience into a language form acceptable to the relations of ruling. This criterion of "acceptability" is met when the text imposes the dominants' definition on the situation. The texts may range from contracts to police reports to official boards-of-inquiry statements to school certificates to medical records. Everywhere they alter the material reality—reinterpreting what has occurred, determining what will be possible. Thus, in seeking to interact with the relations of ruling, even at a fairly local level, a given individual (such as a student applying for a summer job in a restaurant owned by a family friend) finds that she or he must fill out some texts (tax forms, for instance) which have been established not by the face-to-face employer but by part of the apparatus of ruling. These texts continuously create intersections between the relations of ruling and the local actualities of lived experience. It is important to observe that this intersection works both ways: at some series of moments in historic time, embodied actors, situated in absolutely individual locations, sit at desks or computer workstations or conference tables generating the forms that will become part of the apparatus of ruling.

All three aspects of social life—relations of ruling, local actualities of lived experience, and texts—are widespread, enduring, constant features of the organization of social life and of domination. All three features at the same time can and must be studied as the actions, relationships, and work of embodied human subjects. Each dimension has its distinctive internal dynamic—the drive for control in the relations of ruling, the drive for production and communication in the local actualities, the drive toward objectification and facticity in the generalized texts. This world is both gendered and coded by race. Thus, while no one can totally escape life in the local actuality—everyone has to be physically somewhere in time and space—women are much more deeply implicated in the never-ending maintaining of the local actualities and men are much freer to participate as dominants in the relations of ruling; and these same divisions are repeated for racial subordinates and dominants. The texts that strive for objectification and facticity are drawn in ways that make it impossible for all to share equally in the activity the text organizes and those inequalities are created along lines of race, gender, class, age, global location—that is, difference is an organizational principle of the texts of the relations of ruling. Through this lens the elements of structure and interaction are fused. Domination and production become the problematic, and their manifestations involve and thus absorb the age-old sociological distinctions of the macro-social, micro-social, and subjective aspects of social reality. In this, feminist theory is in accord with much of the work, discussed in Part Three of this book, on micro-macro and agency-structure integration.

SUMMARY

Feminist sociological theory grows out of feminist theory in general, that branch of the new scholarship on women that seeks to provide a system of ideas about human life that features woman as object and subject, doer and knower.

One effect of the contemporary feminist movement on sociology has been to expand the significance of the sociology of gender relations and of women's lives. Many sociological theories currently work to explore these issues. The macro-social theories of functionalism, analytic conflict theory, and neo-Marxian world-systems theory all explore the place of the household in social systems as a means of explaining women's social subordination. Symbolic interactionism and ethnomethodology, two micro-social theories, explore the ways in which gender is produced and reproduced in interpersonal relations.

Feminist scholarship is guided by four basic questions: *And what about the women? Why is women's situation as it is? How can we change and improve the social world?* and *What about differences among women?* Answers to these questions produce the varieties of feminist theory. This chapter patterns this variety to show four major groupings of feminist theory. Theories of gender difference see women's situation as different from men's, explaining this difference in terms of biosocial conditioning, institutional socialization, social interaction, and ontological constructions of woman as "other." Theories of gender inequality, notably by liberal feminists, emphasize women's claim to a fundamental right of equality and describe the unequal opportunity structures created by sexism. Gender oppression theories include feminist psychoanalytic theory and radical feminism; the former explains the oppression of women in terms of psychoanalytic descriptions of the male psychic drive to dominate; the latter, in terms of men's ability and willingness to use violence to subjugate women. Structural oppression theories include socialist feminism and intersectionality theory; socialist feminism describes oppression as arising from a patriarchal and a capitalist attempt to control social production and reproduction; intersectionality theories trace the consequences of class, race, gender, affectional preference, and global location for lived experience, group standpoints, and relations among women.

Feminist theory offers six key propositions as a basis for the revision of standard sociological theories. First, the practice of sociological theory must be based in a sociology of knowledge that recognizes the partiality of all knowledge, the knower as embodied and socially located, and the function of power in affecting what becomes knowledge. Second, macro social structures are based in processes controlled by dominants acting in their own interests and executed by subordinates whose work is made largely invisible and undervalued even to themselves by dominant ideology. Thus, dominants appropriate and control the productive work of society including not only economic production but also women's work of social reproduction. Third, micro-interactional processes in society are enactments of these dominant-subordinate power arrangements, enactments very differently interpreted by powerful and subordinate actors. Fourth, these conditions create in women's subjectivity a bifurcated consciousness along the line of fault caused by the juxtaposition of patriarchal ideology and women's experience of the actualities of their lives. Fifth, what has been said for women may be applicable to all subordinate peoples in some parallel, although not identical, form. Sixth, one must question the use of any categories developed by a traditionally male-dominated discipline and most particularly the divisions between micro- and macro-sociologies.

PART THREE

RECENT INTEGRATIVE DEVELOPMENTS IN SOCIOLOGICAL THEORY

10

MICRO-MACRO INTEGRATION

MICRO-MACRO EXTREMISM
THE MOVEMENT TOWARD MICRO-MACRO INTEGRATION
EXAMPLES OF MICRO-MACRO INTEGRATION
    Integrated Sociological Paradigm
    Multidimensional Sociology
    Subjective Levels of Analysis
    Micro-to-Macro Model
    The Micro Foundations of Macrosociology
BACK TO THE FUTURE: NORBERT ELIAS'S FIGURATIONAL
SOCIOLOGY
    The History of Manners
    Power and Civility

In this chapter, as well as the next, we deal with two important developments in recent sociological theory. Our concern in this chapter is with a dramatic development which occurred largely in the United States in the 1980s (although, as we will see, it had important precursors) and which continues to this day. That development is the growth in interest in the issue of the *micro-macro linkage*. In the following chapter we will deal with a parallel development that occurred largely in European sociological theory—the rise in interest in the *relationship between agency and structure*. As we will see, there are important similarities *and* crucial differences between the American micro-macro literature and the European work on agency and structure. The micro-macro and agency-structure literatures can, themselves, be seen as synthetic developments and thus as part of the broad movement toward theoretical synthesis discussed throughout Part Two of this book.

MICRO-MACRO EXTREMISM

Until recently, *one* of the major divisions in twentieth-century American sociological theory has been the conflict between extreme *microscopic* and *macroscopic*[1] theories (and theorists) and, perhaps more important, between those who have *interpreted* sociological theories in these ways (Archer, 1982). Such extreme theories and

---

[1]While the use of the terms *micro* and *macro* might suggest that we are dealing with a dichotomy, we are always aware of the fact that there is a *continuum* ranging from the micro to the macro end (see Appendix).

interpretations of theories have tended to heighten the image of a great chasm between micro and macro theories and, more generally, of conflict and disorder (Gouldner, 1970; Wardell and Turner, 1986a; Wiley, 1985) in sociological theory.

Although it is possible to interpret (and many have) the classic sociological theorists discussed in Part One of this book (Marx, Durkheim, Weber, Simmel) as either micro or macro extremists, the most defensible perspective, or at least the one that will orient this chapter, is that they were most generally concerned with the micro-macro linkage (Moscovici, 1993). Marx can be seen as being interested in the coercive and alienating effect of capitalist society on individual workers (and capitalists). Weber may be viewed as being focally concerned with the plight of the individual within the iron cage of a formally rational society. Simmel was interested primarily in the relationship between objective (macro) and subjective (or individual, micro) culture. Even Durkheim was concerned with the effect of macro-level social facts on individuals and individual behavior (for example, suicide). If we accept these characterizations of the classic sociological theorists, then it appears that much of the last century of American sociological theory has involved a loss of concern for this linkage and the dominance of micro and macro extremists—that is, the preeminence of theorists and theories that accord overwhelming power and significance to either the micro or the macro level. Thus, the theories discussed in Part Two of this book tended toward micro or macro extremism. On the macro-extreme side were structural functionalism, conflict theory, and some varieties of neo-Marxian theory (especially economic determinism). On the micro-extreme end were symbolic interactionism, ethnomethodology, exchange, and rational choice theory.

Among the most notable of the twentieth-century macro-extreme theories are Parsons's (1966) "cultural determinism";[2] Dahrendorf's (1959) conflict theory, with its focus on imperatively coordinated associations; and Peter Blau's macrostructuralism, epitomized by his proud announcement, "I am a structural determinist" (1977a:x). Macro-structural extremism comes from other sources as well (Rubinstein, 1986), including network theorists like White, Boorman, and Breiger (1976), ecologists like Duncan and Schnore (1959), and structuralists like Mayhew (1980). Few take a more extreme position than Mayhew, who says such things as, "In structural sociology the unit of analysis is always the social network, *never the individual*" (1980:349).

On the micro-extreme side we can point to a good portion of symbolic interactionism and the work of Blumer (1969a), who often seemed to have structural functionalism in mind as he positioned symbolic interactionism as a sociological theory seemingly single-mindedly concerned with micro-level phenomena (see Chapter 6 for a very different interpretation of Blumer's perspective). An even clearer case of micro extremism is exchange theory and George Homans (1974), who sought an alternative to structural functionalism and found it in the extreme micro orientation of Skinnerian behaviorism. Then there is ethnomethodology and its concern for the everyday practices of actors.

---

[2]Even as sympathetic an observer as Jeffrey Alexander (1987:296) admits Parsons's "own collectivist bias"; see also Coleman (1986:1310). However, while Parsons's greatest influence was in collectivistic theory, it is also possible to find within his work a strong micro-macro integrative theory.

Garfinkel (1967) was put off by the macro foci of structural functionalism and its tendency to turn actors into "judgmental dopes."

THE MOVEMENT TOWARD MICRO-MACRO INTEGRATION

While micro-macro extremism has characterized much of twentieth-century sociological theory, it has been possible, beginning mainly in the 1980s, to discern a movement, largely in American sociology, away from micro-macro extremism and toward a broad consensus that *the* focus, instead, should be on *the integration (or synthesis, linkage) of micro and macro theories and/or levels of social analysis.* This approach represents quite a change from that of the 1970s, when Kemeny argued: "So little attention is given to this distinction that the terms 'micro' and 'macro' are not commonly even indexed in sociological works" (1976:731). It could be argued that at least in this sense American sociological theorists have rediscovered the theoretical project of the early masters.

While developments in the 1980s and 1990s were particularly dramatic, isolated earlier works directly addressed the micro-macro linkage. For example, in the mid-1960s Helmut Wagner (1964) dealt with the relationship between small-scale and large-scale theories. At the end of the decade Walter Wallace (1969) examined the micro-macro continuum, but it occupied a secondary role in his analysis and was included as merely one of the "complications" of his basic taxonomy of sociological theory. In the mid-1970s Kemeny (1976) called for greater attention to the micro-macro distinction as well as to the ways in which micro and macro relate to one another.

However, it was in the 1980s that we witnessed a flowering of work on the micro-macro linkage issue. Collins argued that work on this topic "promises to be a significant area of theoretical advance for some time to come" (1986a:1350). In their introduction to a two-volume set of books, one devoted to macro theory (Eisenstadt and Helle, 1985a) and the other to micro theory (Helle and Eisenstadt, 1985), Eisenstadt and Helle concluded that "the confrontation between micro- and macro-theory belong[s] to the past" (1985b:3). Similarly, Münch and Smelser, in their conclusion to the anthology *The Micro-Macro Link* (Alexander et al., 1987), asserted: "Those who have argued polemically that one level is more fundamental than the other . . . must be regarded as in error. Virtually every contributor to this volume has correctly insisted on the mutual interrelations between micro and macro levels" (1987:385).

There are two major strands of work on micro-macro integration. Some theorists focus on integrating micro and macro *theories,* while others are concerned with developing a theory that deals with the linkage between micro and macro *levels* (Alford and Friedland, 1985; Edel, 1959) of social analysis. Above, for example, we quoted Eisenstadt and Helle (1985b:3), who concluded that the confrontation between micro and macro *theories* was behind us, while Münch and Smelser (1987:385) came to a similar conclusion about the need to choose between emphasizing either micro or macro *levels.* There are important differences between trying to integrate macro (for example, structural functionalism) and micro (for example, symbolic interactionism) theories and attempting to develop a theory that can deal with the relationship between macro (for example, social-structure) and micro (for example, personality) levels of social analysis.

Given this general introduction, we turn now to some examples of micro-macro integration. At a number of places throughout Part Two of this book, we dealt with efforts to integrate micro and macro *theories*. All the examples that follow focus on integrating micro and macro *levels of social analysis*.

EXAMPLES OF MICRO-MACRO INTEGRATION

Integrated Sociological Paradigm

This section begins with my own effort (Ritzer, 1979, 1981a) at micro-macro integration. The discussion here will be relatively brief, since the integrated sociological paradigm is also discussed in the Appendix. It is summarized there because it represents the metatheoretical schema that serves to orient and organize this book. In this section the focus is on what the integrated paradigm has to say about the micro-macro linkage issue.

It should be noted that my thinking on the integrated paradigm in general, and more specifically on micro-macro linkage, was shaped by the work of a number of predecessors, especially that of Abraham Edel (1959) and Georges Gurvitch (1964; see also Bosserman, 1968). Gurvitch operates with the belief that the social world can be studied in terms of "horizontal," or micro-macro, levels (Smelser [1997] identifies four), presented in ascending order from micro to macro: forms of sociality, groupings, social class, social structure, and global structures. To complement this hierarchy, Gurvitch also offers ten "vertical," or "depth," levels, beginning with the most objective social phenomena (for example, ecological factors, organizations) and ending with the most subjective social phenomena (collective ideas and values, the collective mind). Gurvitch crosscuts his horizontal and vertical dimensions in order to produce numerous levels of social analysis.

My work on the integrated sociological paradigm was motivated, in part, by the need to build upon Gurvitch's insights but to produce a more parsimonious model. It begins with the micro-macro continuum (Gurvitch's horizontal levels), ranging from individual thought and action to world-systems (see the Appendix, Figure A.1). To this continuum is added an objective-subjective continuum (Gurvitch's vertical levels), ranging from material phenomena like individual action and bureaucratic structures to nonmaterial phenomena like consciousness and norms and values (see the Appendix, Figure A.2). Like Gurvitch, I crosscut these two continua, but in this case the result is a far more manageable four, rather than many, levels of social analysis. Figure 10.1 depicts my major levels of social analysis.[3]

In terms of the micro-macro issue, my view is that it cannot be dealt with apart from the objective-subjective continuum. All micro and macro social phenomena are also either objective or subjective. Thus, the conclusion is that there are four major levels of social analysis *and* that sociologists must focus on the dialectical interrelationship

[3]I am reproducing this model here as well as in the Appendix (Figure A.3) because some instructors may not assign the Appendix to students.

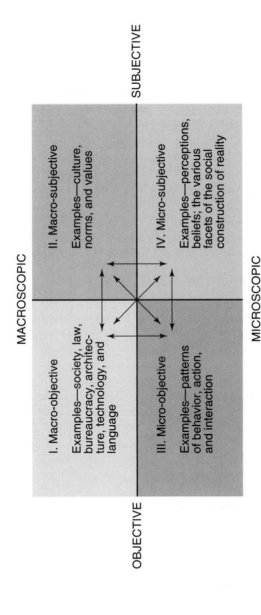

FIGURE 10.1

Ritzer's Major Levels of Social Analysis*

*Note that this is a "snapshot" in time. It is embedded in an ongoing historical process.

among these levels. The macro-objective level involves large-scale material realities like society, bureaucracy, and technology. The macro-subjective level encompasses large-scale nonmaterial phenomena like norms and values. At the micro levels, micro objectivity involves small-scale objective entities such as patterns of action and interaction, whereas micro subjectivity is concerned with the small-scale mental processes by which people construct social reality. Each of these four levels is important in itself, but of utmost importance is the dialectical relationship among and between them.

I have employed an integrative micro-macro approach in *Expressing America: A Critique of the Global Credit Card Society* (Ritzer, 1995). Specifically, I employ C. Wright Mills's (1959) ideas on the relationship between micro-level *personal troubles* and macro-level *public issues* to analyze the problems created by credit cards.

Personal troubles are those problems that affect an individual and those immediately around him or her. For example, a husband who batters his spouse is creating problems for his wife, other members of the family, and perhaps for himself (especially if the law is involved). However, the actions of a single husband who batters his wife are not going to create a public issue—those actions will not result in a public outcry to abandon marriage as a social institution. Public issues tend to be those that affect large numbers of people, perhaps society as a whole. The disintegration of marriage as an institution, in part as a result of widespread spouse battering, would be a public issue. There are various relationships between personal troubles and public issues. For example, widespread personal troubles can become a public issue, and a public issue can cause many personal troubles.

I examine a wide range of personal troubles and public issues associated with credit cards. I can illustrate my argument, and an integrated approach to the micro-macro linkage, by discussing the issue of consumer debt. At the macro level, aggregate consumer debt has become a public issue because a large and growing number of people are increasingly indebted to credit card companies. A by-product of this growing consumer debt is an increase in delinquencies and bankruptcies. Also at the macro level, and a public issue, is the role played by the government in encouraging consumer debt by its own tendency to accumulate debt. More important is the role played by the credit card firms in encouraging people to go into debt by doing everything they can to get as many credit cards into as many hands as possible. There is, for example, the increasing tendency for people to receive notices in the mail that they are eligible for preapproved credit cards. People can easily acquire a large number of credit cards with a huge collective credit limit. Perhaps the most reprehensible activities of the credit card firms involve their efforts to get cards into the hands of college and high school students. They are endeavoring to "hook" young people on a life of credit and indebtedness. Such activities are clearly a public issue that are causing personal troubles for untold numbers of people.

Turning to personal troubles, millions of people have gotten themselves into debt, sometimes irretrievably, as a result of the abuse of credit cards. People build up huge balances, sometimes surviving by taking cash advances on one card to make minimum payments on other cards. Overwhelmed, many people become delinquent and sometimes are forced to declare bankruptcy. As a result, some people spend years, in some cases the rest of their lives, trying to pay off old debts and restore their ability to get credit. Even if it does not go this far, many people are working long hours just to pay the interest on their credit card debt and are able to make little, if any, dent in their credit balance. Thus, one could say they are indentured for life to the credit card companies.

The kinds of personal troubles described here, when aggregated, create public issues for society. And, as we saw previously, public issues such as the policies and procedures of the credit card firms (for example, offering preapproved cards and recruiting students) help to create personal troubles. Thus, there is a dialectical relationship between personal troubles and public issues, each exacerbating the other. More generally, this example of credit cards illustrates the applicability of an integrated micro-macro approach to a pressing social problem.

Multidimensional Sociology

Jeffrey Alexander has offered what he calls a "new 'theoretical logic' for sociology" (1982:xv). That new logic affects "sociological thought at every level of the intellectual continuum" (Alexander, 1982:65). In this spirit, Alexander offers what he terms a *multidimensional sociology*. While *multidimensionality* has several meanings in his work, the most relevant here is Alexander's multidimensional sense of levels of social analysis.

We can begin with what Alexander (following Parsons) terms the *problem of order*. Alexander suggests that the micro-macro continuum ("an 'individual' or 'collective' level of analysis" [1982:93]) is involved in the way order is created in society. At the macro end of the continuum, order is externally created and is collectivist in nature; that is, order is produced by collective phenomena. At the micro end, order is derived from internalized forces and is individualistic in nature; that is, order stems from individual negotiation.

To the problem of order is added, in a classic Parsonsian position, the *problem of action*. Action involves a materialist-idealist continuum which parallels the objective-subjective continuum employed in my integrated sociological paradigm. At the material end, action is described as instrumental, rational, and conditional. At the nonmaterial pole, action is normative, nonrational, and affective. When we crosscut Alexander's order and action continua, we come up with four levels of social analysis that strongly resemble the four levels that I employ (see Figure 10.2).

Although the terminology is slightly different, there are few if any differences between the models offered by Alexander and me. The major difference lies in the way we relate the four levels. While I want to focus on the dialectical relationship among all four levels, Alexander seeks to grant priority to one of the levels.

Alexander believes that according privilege to the micro levels is "a theoretical mistake" (1987:295). He is highly critical of all theories, such as symbolic interactionism, that begin at the individual-normative level with nonrational voluntary agency and build toward the macro levels. From his point of view, the problem with these theories is that while maintaining notions of individual freedom and voluntarism, they are unable to deal with the unique (*sui generis*) character of collective phenomena. Alexander is also critical of theories such as exchange theory that start at the individual-instrumental level and move toward macro-level structures like the economy. Such theories are also unable to handle adequately macro-level phenomena. Thus, Alexander is critical of all

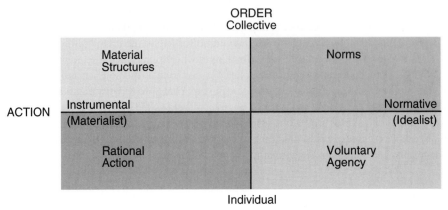

FIGURE 10.2
Alexander's Integrative Model

theories that have their origins at the micro levels and seek to explain macro-level phenomena from that base.

At the macro level, Alexander is critical of collective-instrumental theories (for example, economic and structural determinism) that emphasize coercive order and eliminate individual freedom. Basically, the problem is that such theories do not allow for individual agency.

While he expressed an interest in focusing on the relationships among all four of his levels, Alexander's sympathies (not surprisingly, given his Parsonsian and structural-functionalist roots) lay with the collective-normative level and theories that begin at that level. As he put it, "The hope for combining collective order and individual voluntarism lies with the normative, rather than the rationalist tradition" (Alexander, 1982:108). Central to this belief is his view that such an orientation is preferable because the sources of order are internalized (in the conscience) rather than externalized, as is the case with the collective-instrumental orientation. This focus on the internalization of norms allows for *both* order and voluntary agency.

Overall, Alexander argues that any individual, or micro, perspective is to be rejected because it ends with "randomness and complete unpredictability" rather than order (1985:27). Thus, "the general framework for social theory can be derived *only* from a collectivist perspective" (1985:28; italics added). And between the two collectivist perspectives, Alexander subscribes to the collective-normative position.

Thus, to Alexander social theorists must choose either a collectivist (macro) or individualist (micro) perspective. If they choose a collectivist position, they can incorporate only a "relatively small" element of individual negotiation. If, however, they choose an individualist theory, they are doomed to the "individualist dilemma" of trying to sneak into theory supraindividual phenomena to deal with the randomness inherent in their theory. This dilemma can be resolved only "if the formal adherence to individualism is abandoned" (Alexander, 1985:27).

Thus, while Alexander employs four levels of analysis that closely resemble those utilized by me, there is an important difference in the two models. Alexander accords priority to collective-normative theories and to a focus on norms in social life. I refuse to accord priority to any level and argue for the need to examine the dialectical relationship among and between all four levels. Alexander ends up giving inordinate significance to macro (subjective) phenomena, and as a result, his contribution to the development of a theory of micro-macro integration is highly limited. In a later work, Alexander said, "I believe theorists falsely generalize from a single variable to the immediate reconstruction of the whole" (1987:314). It can be argued that Alexander is one of these theorists, since he seeks to falsely generalize from the collective-normative level to the rest of the social world.

While not directly addressing Alexander's work, Giddens (1984) came to the similar conclusion that *all* work derived from the Parsonsian distinction between action and order inevitably ends up weak at the micro levels, especially on "the knowledgeability of social actors, as constitutive in part of social practices. I [Giddens] do not think that *any* standpoint which is heavily indebted to Parsons can cope satisfactorily with this issue at the very core of social theory" (1984:xxxvii).

However, it should be noted that Alexander has articulated a more truly integrative perspective, one that defines *micro* and *macro* in terms of one another. Here is the way he expresses this perspective: "The collective environments of action simultaneously inspire and confine it. If I have conceptualized action correctly, these environments will be seen as its products; if I can conceptualize the environments correctly, action will be seen as their end result" (Alexander, 1987:303). It appears that Alexander has a more complex, dialectical sense of the micro-macro nexus, one that is more similar to my integrated sociological paradigm than his earlier model.

Subjective Levels of Analysis

Norbert Wiley (1988) has offered a model of micro-macro relationships that closely resembles the models offered by Alexander and by me. What is distinctive about Wiley's approach is that it is purely subjective, whereas my approach and Alexander's involve both subjectivity *and* objectivity. Wiley makes clear his subjectivity by arguing that his starting point for the delineation of the levels is their relationship to the subject. The following are Wiley's four major levels of analysis, as well as the parallel level (in parentheses) within my work: self or individual (micro-subjective), interaction (micro-objective), social structure (macro-objective), culture (macro-subjective). While my (and Alexander's) four levels bear a striking resemblance to Wiley's levels, it is clear that objective reality is neglected by Wiley. In other words, in Wiley's work the levels of interaction and social structure, like the others, are defined subjectively.

Wiley's analysis begins with the micro-level self, or individual. Alexander, as we have seen, would clearly have trouble with such a point of origin. The view here is that it does not matter where one begins as long as one ultimately deals with the dialectical relationship among all levels of analysis. However, Wiley offers a highly limited conception of the micro-subjective level. Specifically, he gives undue importance to the self and therefore ignores a number of other important components of the micro-subjective level—mind, consciousness, the social construction of reality, and so on. To put it another way, the self, as social psychologists emphasize, far from exhausts the micro-subjective level.

Similarly, Wiley's concern with interaction, or the micro-objective level, is also limited. Much more goes on at this level than interaction. At the minimum, we must include action (including a conscious antecedent) and behavior (lacking such an antecedent) at this level. These clearly belong here because they are micro-level phenomena that cannot be included, at least totally, in Wiley's other, intrasubjective micro-level category. Furthermore, while interaction, action, and behavior may have a subjective component, they also have an objective existence; all three of them can come to be institutionalized in repetitive patterns. In my work, the subjective aspects of these processes are dealt with at the micro-subjective level, and the objective aspects come under the heading micro objectivity. In any case, we must deal with *both* their subjective and objective moments.

Wiley's conception of social structure and my sense of macro objectivity are closer than their micro analyses, even though Wiley continues his pattern by approaching this level from a subjective point of view. He writes of the "generic self" at this level, but he clearly implies the existence of macro-objective structures when he describes the generic self "as filler of roles and follower of rules" (Wiley, 1988:258). While Wiley emphasizes the subjective generic self here, I would place greatest importance on the objective structures (society, the world-system) that create the rules and the roles filled by the self.

There are few important differences between Wiley's cultural level and my macro subjectivity, because both are discussed in large-scale, subjective terms. The only quarrel here is that Wiley's thoughts on "pure meaning" at this level are too general and could profit from greater specificity and some discussion of such well-known sociological concepts as norms and values.

Wiley and I are similar not only in terms of our conceptualizations of the four major levels of social analysis but also in terms of our sense of the relationships among levels. Wiley talks of a continuing process of "emergence" that links lower to higher levels and of a process of "feedback" (also presumably continuous), which flows from higher to lower levels. Similarly, I am concerned with the dialectical (that is, the ongoing, multidirectional) relationship among all levels of social analysis. While my sense of the dialectical relationship among levels of social analysis may be seen as vaguer and more general than Wiley's emergence-feedback specification, there are many more kinds of relationships among and between levels of social analysis than Wiley suggests. A wide array of familiar sociological concepts (for example, externalization, objectification, socialization, internalization, social control) concern themselves with various aspects of the dialectical relationship between micro and macro levels.

While the micro-macro perspectives offered by Wiley and Alexander have both been summarized and critiqued from the point of view of my integrated paradigm, the overriding point is that all three perspectives offer virtually identical models of the major levels of social analysis. This commonality is particularly striking, since the three of us come at this issue from very different theoretical viewpoints—my dialectical approach; Alexander's multidimensional, neofunctionalist orientation; and Wiley's subjective viewpoint. We turn now to some very different approaches to the micro-macro linkage issue.

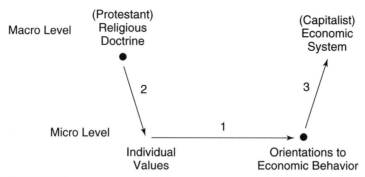

FIGURE 10.3
Coleman's Integrative Model

Micro-to-Macro Model

In his early thinking on this issue, James Coleman (1986, 1987) expressed an interest in the micro-macro relationship. (We dealt with Coleman's [1990] later and far more elaborate rational choice theory in Chapter 8.) However, Coleman focuses on the micro-to-macro problem and downplays the significance of the macro-to-micro issue. Thus, from the point of view of the more balanced micro-macro approaches offered by me, by Alexander, and by Wiley, Coleman's orientation to this issue is highly limited. A fully adequate approach to this problem must deal with *both* the micro-to-macro and the macro-to-micro problems.

Coleman begins by offering a partially adequate model of the micro-macro relationship. In doing so, he uses Weber's Protestant ethic thesis as an illustration. As shown in Figure 10.3, this model deals with *both* the macro-to-micro issue (arrow 2) and the micro-to-macro question (arrow 3); it also deals with the micro-to-micro relationship (arrow 1). While promising, this model is posed in causal terms, with arrows flowing in only one direction. A more adequate model would be dialectical, with all arrows pointing in both directions; that is, it would allow for feedback among all levels of analysis. However, the major weakness in Coleman's approach is that he wants to focus only on arrow 3, the micro-to-macro relationship. While this is important, it is no more important than the macro-to-micro relationship. An adequate micro-macro model must deal with *both* of these relationships.

Allen Liska (1990) sought to cope with the weaknesses in Coleman's approach by dealing with both the micro-to-macro and the macro-to-micro problems. Liska's model, like Coleman's, uses Weber's Protestant ethic thesis as an example (see Figure 10.4).

This model has two advantages over Coleman's approach. First, of course, is Liska's willingness to deal with the macro-to-micro linkage. Second is the detailing of a relationship (arrow *a*) between the two macro-level phenomena. However, Liska, like Coleman, utilizes one-way causal arrows, thereby losing sight of the dialectical relationship among all these factors.

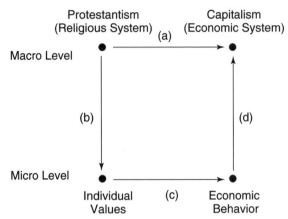

FIGURE 10.4
Liska's Macro-to-Micro and Micro-to-Macro Model

Liska employs a well-known scheme for dealing with macro phenomena as well as with the micro-macro linkage. That scheme involves three basic ways of describing macrophenomena. The first is *aggregation,* or the summation of individual properties in order to yield a group property. Thus, one could describe a group in terms of such things as its mean income or its suicide rate. The second is *structural,* and it involves relationships between individuals within a group; examples are relationships involving power or communication. Finally, there are *global* phenomena, which involve what are usually thought of as emergent properties, such as law and language.

In terms of the micro-macro linkage, Liska details the difficulties involved in using structural or global factors. These factors are qualitatively different from the characteristics of individual action, and it is difficult to know how they emerge out of the micro level. Sociologists use the idea of emergence to deal with global factors, but they know very little about how emergence actually works. Thus, Liska emphasizes the importance of aggregation as a micro-to-macro linkage. In this case, it is relatively clear how individual properties combine to yield group properties. Thus, for example, "Individual suicides can be aggregated, or 'combined,' over some social unit and expressed as a rate of that unit" (Liska, 1990:292). While aggregation may not be the most interesting way to move from the micro to the macro level, it has the advantage of being clear and less mystical than structural or global approaches.

Turning to the macro-to-micro issue, Liska argues for the importance of contextual variables as causes of micro-level phenomena. Here Liska includes aggregates, structural relations, and global properties as contexts of individual phenomena. He argues that sociologists have too frequently relied on micro-level factors when working on the individual level. By using macro-level, contextual factors, microsociologists would be moving in the direction of a greater understanding of the macro-to-micro linkage.

Liska's work comes down to a plea to sociologists who focus on either the macro or the micro level. Those who focus on the macro level have tended to ignore aggregation because it sounds too individualistic and does not have the emergent qualities of global or structural factors. Those who focus on the micro level have tended to use micro-level factors and to ignore contextual factors. Liska concludes that macro theorists should do more with aggregation and micro theorists more with contextual factors.

The Micro Foundations of Macrosociology

In an essay entitled "On the Microfoundations of Macrosociology," Randall Collins (1981a; see also 1981b) has offered a highly reductionistic orientation toward the micro-macro link question (for a critique, see Ritzer, 1985). In fact, despite the inherently integrative title of his essay, Collins labels his approach "radical microsociology." Collins's focus, the focus of radical microsociology, is what he calls "interaction ritual chains," or bundles of "individual chains of interactional experience, crisscrossing each other in space as they flow along in time" (1981a:998). In focusing on interaction ritual chains, Collins seeks to avoid what he considers to be even more reductionistic concerns with individual behavior and consciousness. Collins raises the level of analysis to interaction, chains of interaction, and the "marketplace" for such interaction. Collins thus rejects the extreme micro levels of thought and action (behavior) and is critical of the theories (such as phenomenology and exchange theory) that focus on these levels.

Collins also seeks to distance himself from macro theories and their concerns with macro-level phenomena. For example, he is critical of structural functionalists and their concern with macro-objective (structure) and macro-subjective (norms) phenomena. In fact, he goes so far as to say that "the terminology of norms ought to be dropped from sociological theory" (Collins, 1981a:991). He has a similarly negative attitude toward concepts associated with conflict theory, arguing, for example, that there are no "inherent objective" entities like property or authority; there are only "varying senses that people feel at particular places and times of how strong these enforcing coalitions are" (Collins, 1981a:997). His point is that only people do anything; structures, organizations, classes, and societies "never *do* anything. Any causal explanation must ultimately come down to the actions of real individuals" (Collins, 1975:12).

Collins seeks to show how "all macrophenomena" can be translated "into combinations of micro events" (1981a:985). Specifically, he argues that social structures may be translated empirically into "patterns of repetitive micro interaction" (Collins, 1981a:985).

Thus, in the end, Collins seeks *not* an integrated approach but the predominance of micro theory and micro-level phenomena (for a similar critique, see Giddens, 1984). As Collins puts it, "The effort coherently to reconstitute macro sociology upon radically empirical micro foundations is the crucial step toward a more successful sociological science" (1981b:82).

We can contrast Collins's orientation to that of Karin Knorr-Cetina (1981a). Although she, too, accords great importance to the interactional domain, Knorr-Cetina grants a greater role to both consciousness and macro-level phenomena in her work. Although Knorr-Cetina, like Collins, makes the case for a radical reconstruction of macro theory on a microsociological base, she is also willing to consider the much less radical course of simply integrating microsociological results into macro-social theory. In addition, she seems to take the position that the ultimate goal of

RANDALL COLLINS: An Autobiographical Sketch

I started becoming a sociologist at an early age. My father was working for military intelligence at the end of World War II and then joined the State Department as a foreign service officer. One of my earliest memories is of arriving in Berlin to join him in the summer of 1945. My sisters and I couldn't play in the park because there was live ammunition everywhere, and one day Russian soldiers came into our backyard to dig up a corpse. This gave me a sense that conflict is important and violence always possible.

My father's subsequent tours of duty took us to the Soviet Union, back to Germany (then under American military occupation), to Spain and South America. In between foreign assignments we would live in the States, so I went back and forth between being an ordinary American kid and being a privileged foreign visitor. I think this resulted in a certain amount of detachment in viewing social relationships. As I got older the diplomatic life looked less dramatic and more like an endless round of formal etiquette in which people never talked about the important politics going on; the split between backstage secrecy and front-stage ceremonial made me ready to appreciate Erving Goffman.

When I was too old to accompany my parents abroad, I was sent to a prep school in New England. This taught me another great sociological reality: the existence of stratification. Many of the other students came from families in the Social Register, and it began to dawn on me that my father was not in the same social class as the ambassadors and undersecretaries of state whose children I sometimes met.

I went on to Harvard, where I changed my major half a dozen times. I studied literature and tried being a playwright and novelist. I went from mathematics to philosophy; I read Freud and planned to become a psychiatrist. I finally majored in social relations, which covered sociology, social psychology, and anthropology. Taking courses from Talcott Parsons settled me onto a path. He covered virtually everything, from the micro to the macro and

microsociological research is a better understanding of the larger society, its structure, and institutions:

> I . . . believe in the seeming paradox that it is through micro-social approaches that we will learn most about the macro order, for it is these approaches which through their unashamed empiricism afford us a glimpse of the reality about which we speak. Certainly, we will not get a grasp of whatever is the whole of the matter by a microscopic recording of face-to-face interaction. However, it may be enough to begin with if we—for the first time—hear the macro order tick.
>
> (Knorr-Cetina, 1981a:41–42)

Thus, it seems clear that Knorr-Cetina takes a far more balanced position on the relationship between the macro and micro levels than does Collins.

An even more integrative position is taken by Aaron Cicourel (1981): "Neither micro nor macro structures are self-contained levels of analysis; they *interact* with each other at all times despite the convenience and sometimes the dubious luxury of across the range of world history. What I got from him was not so much his own theory but rather the ideal of what sociology could do. He also provided me with some important pieces of cultural capital: that Weber was less concerned with the Protestant Ethic than he was with comparing the dynamics of all the world religions and that Durkheim asked the key question when he tried to uncover the precontractual basis of social order.

I thought I wanted to become a psychologist and went to Stanford, but a year of implanting electrodes in rats' brains convinced me that sociology was a better place to study human beings. I switched universities and arrived in Berkeley in the summer of 1964, just in time to join the civil-rights movement. By the time the free-speech movement emerged on campus in the fall, we were veterans of sit-ins, and being arrested for another cause felt emotionally energizing when one could do it in solidarity with hundreds of others. I was analyzing the sociology of conflict at the same time that we were experiencing it. As the Vietnam War and the racial conflicts at home escalated, the opposition movement began to repudiate its nonviolent principles; many of us became disillusioned and turned to the cultural lifestyle of the hippie dropouts. If you didn't lose your sociological consciousness, it could be illuminating. I studied Erving Goffman along with Herbert Blumer (both of them Berkeley professors at the time) and began to see how all aspects of society—conflict, stratification, and all the rest—are constructed out of the interaction rituals of our everyday lives.

I never set out to be a professor, but by now I have taught in many universities. I tried to put everything together into one book, *Conflict Sociology* (1975), but it turned out I had to write another, *The Credential Society* (1979), to explain the inflationary status system in which we are all enmeshed. Taking my own analysis seriously, I quit the academic world and for a while made a living by writing a novel and textbooks. Eventually, attracted by some interesting colleagues, I got back into teaching. Our field is learning some tremendous things, from a new picture of world history down through the micro details of social emotions. One of the most important influences for me is my second wife, Judith McConnell. She organized women lawyers to break down discriminatory barriers in the legal profession, and now I am learning from her about the backstage politics of the higher judiciary. In sociology and in society, there is plenty yet to be done.

---

only examining one or the other level of analysis" (Cicourel, 1981:54). There is an implied criticism of Collins here, but Cicourel adopts another position that can be seen as a more direct critique of the kind of position adopted by Collins: "The issue is not simply one of dismissing one level of analysis or another, but showing how they must be integrated if we are not to be convinced about one level to the exclusion of the other by conveniently ignoring competing frameworks for research and theory" (1981:76). To his credit, Cicourel understands not only the importance of linking macro and micro levels but also the fact that that link needs to take place ontologically, theoretically, and methodologically.

Collins continued to subscribe to his micro-reductionistic position for some time. For example, in a later work Collins argued: "Macrostructure consists of nothing more than large numbers of microencounters, repeated (or sometimes changing over time and across space)" (1987b:195). He concluded, unashamedly: "This may sound as if I am giving a great deal of prominence to the micro. That is true" (Collins, 1987b:195).

However, it is worth noting that just one year later Collins (1988a) was willing to give the macro level greater significance. This approach led to a more balanced conception of the micro-macro relationship: "The micro-macro translation shows that everything macro is composed out of micro. Conversely, anything micro is part of the composition of macro; it exists in a macro context . . . it is possible to pursue the micro-macro connection fruitfully in either direction" (Collins, 1988a:244). The latter contention implies a more dialectical approach to the micro-macro relationship. Yet Collins (1988a:244), like Coleman, subscribes to the view that the "big challenge" in sociology is showing "how micro affects macro." Thus, while Collins has shown some growth in his micro-macro theory, it continues to be a highly limited approach.

BACK TO THE FUTURE: NORBERT ELIAS'S FIGURATIONAL SOCIOLOGY

Throughout this chapter we have dealt with some of the major recent American efforts at micro-macro integration. However, there is a European theorist, Norbert Elias, whose work is best discussed under this heading. (For a nice selection of his work, see Mennell and Goudsblom, 1998). Elias was involved in an effort to overcome the micro-macro distinction, and more generally to surmount the tendency of sociologists to distinguish between individuals and society (Dunning, 1986:5; Mennell, 1992). Elias's major work was done in the 1930s, but it has only recently begun to receive the recognition it deserves (Kilminster and Mennell, forthcoming; van Krieken, 1998). This is a good place to discuss his thinking on micro-macro integration and to introduce his basic theoretical ideas.

In order to help achieve his integrative goal, Elias proposed the concept of *figuration,* an idea which

> makes it possible to resist the socially conditioned pressure to split and polarize our conception of mankind, which has repeatedly prevented us from thinking of people as individuals *at the same time* as thinking of them as societies. . . . The concept of figuration therefore serves as a simple conceptual tool to loosen this social constraint to speak and think as if "the individual" and "society" were antagonistic as well as different.
>
> (Elias, 1978:129–130; italics added)

Figurations can be seen, above all, as processes. In fact, later in his life Elias came to prefer the term "process sociology" to describe his work (Mennell, 1992:252). Figurations are social processes involving the "interweaving" of people. They are *not* structures that are external to and coercive of relationships between people; they *are* those interrelationships. Individuals are seen as open and interdependent; figurations are made up of such individuals. Power is central to social figurations, which are, as a result, constantly in flux:

> At the core of changing figurations—indeed the very hub of the figuration process—is a fluctuating, tensile equilibrium, a balance of power moving to and fro, inclining first to one side and then to the other. This kind of fluctuating balance of power is a structural characteristic of the flow of every figuration.
>
> (Elias, 1978:131)

Figurations emerge and develop, but in largely unseen and unplanned ways.

Central to this discussion is the fact that the idea of a figuration applies at both the micro and macro levels, and to every social phenomenon between those two poles. The concept

> can be applied to relatively small groups just as well as to societies made up of thou-sands or millions of interdependent people. Teachers and pupils in a class, doctors and patients in a therapeutic group, regular customers at a pub, children at a nursery school—they all make up relatively comprehensible figurations with each other. But the inhabitants of a village, a city or a nation also form figurations, although in this in-stance the figurations cannot be perceived directly because the *chains of interdependence* which link people together are longer and more differentiated.
>
> (Elias, 1978:131; italics added)

Thus, Elias refuses to deal with the relationship between "individual" and "society," but focuses rather on "the relationship between people perceived as individuals and people perceived as societies" (Elias, 1986a:23). In other words, both individuals and societies (and every social phenomenon in between) involve people—human relationships. The idea of "chains of interdependence" underscored in the extract above is as good an image as any of what Elias means by figurations and what constitutes the focus of his sociology: "How and why people are bound together to form specific dynamic figura-tions is one of the central questions, perhaps even *the* central question, of sociology" (1969/1983:208).

Elias's notion of figuration is linked to the idea that individuals are open to, and in-terrelated with, other individuals. He argues that most sociologists operate with a sense of *homo clausus,* that is "an image of single human beings each of whom is ultimately absolutely independent of all others—an individual-in-himself" (Elias, 1969/1983:143). Such an image does not lend itself to a theory of figurations; an image of open, interde-pendent actors is needed for figurational sociology.

Given the concerns in this section of the book, we will focus on micro-macro inte-gration, but it should be pointed out that Elias's work is synthetic in a variety of other ways. For example, Elias was at least as upset over the theory-research split in sociol-ogy as he was over the micro-macro dichotomy. To him, theory is arid without data, and research is directionless without theory. The synthesis of theory and research, as well as the effort to interweave micro and macro, is clearest in the two volumes (*The History of Manners* [Elias, 1939/1978] and *Power and Civility* [Elias, 1939/1982]) that make up his best-known work, *The Civilizing Process* (Elias, 1939/1994). It is that work that will be the focus of this section.

Before we proceed, we must briefly explain why Elias is discussed here under the heading of micro-macro integration rather than in the next chapter, on agency-structure integration. After all, Elias was German in origin and the work on agency-structure is largely European, while it is Americans who dominate the work on micro-macro inte-gration. Although Elias's work could have been discussed in either chapter, it seems to fit best here because Elias is more interested in micro-level action and interaction than he is in the conscious, creative processes implied by a concern with agency. Indeed, a central aspect of Elias's theory is the unconscious and unplanned character of much of

NORBERT ELIAS: A Biographical Sketch

Norbert Elias had an interesting and instructive career. He produced his most important work in the 1930s, but it was largely ignored at the time and for many years thereafter. However, late in his life Elias and his work were "discovered," especially in England and the Netherlands. Today, Elias's reputation is growing, and his work is receiving increasing attention and recognition throughout the world. Elias lived until he was 93 (he died in 1990), long enough to bask belatedly in long-delayed recognition of the significance of his work.

Elias was born in Breslau, Germany, in 1897 (Mennell, 1992). His father was a small manufacturer and the family lived a comfortable existence. The home was apparently a loving one and it imbued Elias with a self-confidence that was to stand him in good stead later when his work was not recognized:

I put that down to the great feeling of security I had as a child . . . I have a basic feeling of great security, a feeling that in the end things will turn out for the best, and I attribute that to an enormous emotional security which my parents gave me as an only child.

I knew very early on what I wanted to do; I wanted to go to university, and I wanted to do research. I knew that from when I was young, and I have done it, even though sometimes it seemed impossible . . . I had great confidence that in the end my work would be recognized as a valuable contribution to knowledge about humanity.

(Elias, cited in Mennell, 1992:6–7)

Elias served in the German army in World War I and returned after the war to study philosophy and medicine at the University of Breslau. Although he progressed quite far in his medical studies, he eventually dropped them in favor of the study of philosophy. His work in medicine gave him a sense of the interconnections among the various parts of the human body, and that view shaped his orientation to human interconnections—his concern for figurations. Elias received his Ph.D. in January 1924; only then did he go to Heidelberg to learn sociology.

Elias received no pay at Heidelberg, but he did become actively involved in sociology circles at the university. Max Weber had died in 1920, but a salon headed by his wife, Marianne, was active, and Elias became involved in it. He also associated with Max Weber's brother, Alfred, who held a chair in sociology at the university, as well as with Karl Mannheim (described by Elias [1994:34] as "unquestionably brilliant"), who was slightly ahead of Elias in terms of career progress. In fact, Elias became Mannheim's friend and unpaid, unofficial assistant. When Mannheim was offered a position at the University of Frankfurt in 1930,

---

what transpires in the social world. In addition, as we will see, the first volume of *The Civilizing Process, The History of Manners,* focuses more on micro issues, and the second, *Power and Civility*, is oriented more to macro issues.

The History of Manners

If Weber can be seen as being concerned with the rationalization of the West, Elias's focal interest is on the *civilization* of the Occident (Bogner, Baker, and Kilminster, 1992; for an application of his ideas to another part of the world—Singapore—see Stauth,

Elias went with him as his paid and official assistant (on the relationship between the two men and their work, see Kilminster, 1993).

Adolph Hitler came to power in February 1933, and soon after, Elias, like many other Jewish scholars (including Mannheim), went into exile, at first in Paris and later in London (it is believed that Elias's mother died in a concentration camp in 1941). It was in London that he did most of the work on *The Civilizing Process,* which was published in German in 1939. There was no market in Germany then for books written by a Jew, and Elias never received a penny of royalties from that edition. In addition, the book received scant recognition in other parts of the world.

Both during the war and for almost a decade after, Elias bounced around with no secure employment and remained marginal to British academic circles. However, in 1954 Elias was offered two academic positions, and he accepted the one at Leicester. Thus, Elias *began* his formal academic career at the age of 57! Elias's career blossomed at Leicester, and a number of important publications followed. However, Elias was disappointed with his tenure at Leicester because he failed in his effort to institutionalize a developmental approach that could stand as an alternative to the kind of static approaches (of Talcott Parsons and others) that were then preeminent in sociology. He was also disappointed that few students adopted his approach; he continued to be a voice in the wilderness, even at Leicester, where the students tended to regard him as an eccentric "voice from the past" (Mennell, 1992:22). Reflective of this feeling of being on the outside is a recurrent dream reported by Elias during those years in which a voice on the telephone repeats, "'Can you speak louder? I can't hear you'" (Mennell, 1992:23). It is interesting to note that throughout his years at Leicester *none* of his books was translated into English and few English sociologists of the day were fluent in German.

However, on the Continent, especially in the Netherlands and Germany, Elias's work began to be rediscovered in the 1950s and 1960s. In the 1970s Elias began to receive not only academic, but public, recognition in Europe. Throughout the rest of his life Elias received a number of significant awards, an honorary doctorate, a *Festschrift* in his honor, and a special double issue of *Theory, Culture and Society* devoted to his work.

Interestingly, while Elias has now received wide recognition in sociology (including inclusion in this text), his work has received that recognition during a period in which sociology is growing *less* receptive to his kind of work. That is, the rise of postmodern thinking has led sociologists to question any grand narrative, and Elias's major work, *The Civilizing Process,* is, if nothing else, a grand narrative in the old style. That is, it is concerned with the long-term historical development (admittedly with ebbs and flows) of civilization in the West. The growth of postmodern thinking threatens to limit interest in Elias's work just as it is beginning to receive wide attention.

1997). By the way, Elias is not arguing that there is something inherently good, or better, about civilization as it occurs in the West, or anywhere else for that matter. Nor is he arguing that civilization is inherently bad, although he does recognize that various difficulties have arisen in Western civilization. More generally, Elias (1968/1994:188) is not arguing that to be more civilized is to be better, or conversely that to be less civilized is worse. In saying that people have become more civilized, we are not necessarily saying that they have become better (or worse); we are simply stating a sociological fact. Thus, Elias is concerned with the sociological study of what he calls the "sociogenesis" of civilization in the West (as we will see shortly).

Specifically, Elias is interested in the gradual changes (Elias, 1997) that took place in the behavior and psychological makeup of people in the West. It is an analysis of these changes that is his concern in *The History of Manners*. In the second volume of *The Civilizing Process, Power and Civility,* Elias turns to the societal changes that accompany, and are closely related to, these behavioral and psychological changes. Overall, Elias is concerned with "the connections between changes in the structure of society and changes in the structure of behavior and psychical makeup" (1939/1994:xv).

In his study of the history of manners, Elias is interested in the gradual, historical transformation of a variety of very mundane behaviors in the direction of what we would now call civilized behavior (although there are also periods of "decivilization"; see Elias, 1995). Although he begins with the Middle Ages, Elias makes it clear that there is not, and cannot be, such a thing as a starting (or ending) point for the development of civilization: "Nothing is more fruitless, when dealing with long-term social processes, than to attempt to locate an absolute beginning" (Elias, 1969/1983:232). That is, civilizing processes can be traced back to ancient times, continue to this day, and will continue into the future. Civilization is an ongoing developmental process that Elias is picking up, for convenience, in the Middle Ages. He is interested in tracing such things as changes in what embarrasses us, our increasing sensitivity, how we've grown increasingly observant of others, and our sharpened understanding of others. However, the best way of gaining an understanding of what Elias is doing is not through abstractions, but through a discussion of some of his concrete examples.

Behavior at the Table   Elias examines what books (and other sources) on manners written between the thirteenth and nineteenth centuries had to say about how to comport oneself at the dinner table (as well as on the issues discussed in the next several sections). Elias's most basic point is that the threshold of embarrassment has gradually advanced. What people did at the table with little or no embarrassment in the thirteenth century would cause much mortification in the nineteenth century. What is regarded as distasteful is over time increasingly likely to be *"removed behind the scenes of social life"* (Elias, 1939/1994:99).

For example, a thirteenth-century poem warned, "A number of people gnaw on a bone and then put it back in the dish—this is a serious offense" (Elias, 1939/1994:68). Another thirteenth-century volume warns, "It is not decent to poke your fingers into your ears or eyes, as some people do, or to pick your nose while eating" (Elias, 1939/1994:71). Clearly, the implication of these warnings is that many people at that time engaged in such behaviors and that it generally caused them, or those around them, no embarrassment. There was a perceived need for such admonitions because people did not know that such behavior was "uncivilized." As time goes by there is less and less need to warn people about such things as picking one's nose while eating. Thus, a late sixteenth-century document says, "Nothing is more improper than to lick your fingers, to touch the meats and put them into your mouth with your hand, to stir sauce with your fingers, or to dip bread into it with your fork and then suck it" (Elias, 1939/1994:79). Of course, there *are* things, picking one's nose for example, more improper than licking one's fingers, but by this time civilization has already progressed to the point that it is widely recognized that such behaviors are uncivilized. With nose picking safely behind the scenes, society found other, less egregious behaviors that it defined as uncivilized.

One of Elias's points in this context, and in others, is that these changes are not made rationally. He sees their sources more in emotions than in rational considerations. (For example, in his discussion of the increasing restrictions on spitting, Elias contends that the motivation for them came from social consideration and not from medical concerns; such restrictions existed long before there was any scientific evidence about the potentially unhealthy effects of spittle.) And, as was already pointed out, these changes are not brought about consciously, but rather emerge unconsciously. As Elias puts it, "Obviously, individual people did not at some past time intend this change, this 'civilization,' and gradually realize it by conscious, 'rational,' purposive measures" (1939/1982). Another central point is that these changes generally emanate from a single source (especially, as we will see, the court in French society) and then disperse throughout society. Here is the way Elias summarizes these points:

> Certain forms of behavior are placed under prohibition, not because they are unhealthy [a rational reason] but because they lead to an offensive sight and disagreeable associations; shame at offering such a spectacle, originally absent, and fear of arousing such associations are gradually spread from the standard setting circles to larger circles by numerous authorities and institutions. However, once such feelings are aroused and firmly established in society by means of certain rituals . . . they are constantly reproduced so long as the structure of human relations is not fundamentally altered.
>
> (Elias, 1939/1994:104)

Natural Functions A similar trend is found in the performance of natural functions. A fourteenth-century book used by schoolchildren, among others, found it necessary to offer advice on the expelling of wind:

> To contract an illness: Listen to the old maxim about the sound of wind. If it can be purged without a noise that is best. But it is better that it be emitted with a noise than it be held back. . . .
>
> . . . The sound of farting, especially of those who stand on elevated ground, is horrible. One should make sacrifices with the buttocks pressed firmly together . . .
>
> . . . let a cough hide the explosive sound . . . Follow the law of Chiliades: Replace farts with coughs.
>
> (Elias, 1939/1994:106)

Here we see things being openly discussed that by the nineteenth century (and certainly today) it was no longer necessary to mention because it had come to be well known that the behaviors in question were uncivilized. Further, we are likely to be startled by such a discussion, which offends our contemporary sense of propriety. But all this reflects the process of civilization and the movement of the "frontier of embarrassment" (Elias, 1939/1994:107). Things that could be discussed openly have over time progressively moved beyond that frontier. The fact that we are startled by reading advice on farting reflects the fact that the frontier today is very different from what it was in the fourteenth century.

Elias relates this change in the notion of the appropriate way to expel wind to changes in social figurations, especially in the French court. More people were living in closer proximity and in more permanent interdependence. Therefore, there was a greater need to regulate people's impulses and to get them to practice greater restraint. The control over impulses that began in the higher echelons of the court were eventually transmitted to those of lower social status. The need to extend these restraints was made necessary by further figurational changes, especially people of different statuses moving closer together, becoming more interdependent, and by the decreasing rigidity of the stratification system, which made it easier for those of lower status to interact with those of higher status. As a result, to put it baldly, there was increasingly just as much need for the lower classes to control their wind (and many other behaviors) as there was for the upper classes. At the same time, those from the upper classes needed to control their wind in the presence not only of peers, but of social inferiors as well.

Elias sums up his discussion of such natural functions:

> Society is gradually beginning to suppress the positive pleasure component in certain functions more and more strongly by the arousal of anxiety; or, more exactly, it is rendering this pleasure 'private' and 'secret' (i.e. suppressing it within the individual), while fostering the negatively charged affects—displeasure, revulsion, distaste—as the only feelings customary in society.
>
> (Elias, 1939/1994:117)

Blowing One's Nose   A similar process is seen in the restraints on blowing one's nose. For example, a fifteenth-century document warned, "Do not blow your nose with the same hand that you use to hold the meat" (Elias, 1939/1994:118). Or, in the sixteenth century, the reader is informed, "Nor is it seemly, after wiping your nose, to spread out your handkerchief and peer into it as if pearls and rubies might have fallen out of your head" (Elias, 1939/1994:119). However, by the late eighteenth century these kinds of details are avoided in sources of advice: "Every voluntary movement of the nose . . . is impolite and puerile. To put your fingers into your nose is a revolting impropriety. . . . You should observe, in blowing your nose, all the rules of propriety and cleanliness" (Elias, 1939/1994:121). As Elias says, "The 'conspiracy of silence' is spreading" (1939/1994:121). That is, things that could be discussed openly a century or two before are now discussed more discreetly, or not at all. The "shame frontier" as it relates to blowing one's nose, and many other things, has progressed. Shame has come to be attached to things (for example, blowing one's nose, farting) that in the past were not considered shameful. More and more walls are being erected between people so that things that could formerly be done in the presence of others are now hidden from view.

Sexual Relations   Elias describes the same general trend in sexual relations. In the Middle Ages it was common for many people, including men and women, to spend the night together in the same room. And, it was not uncommon for them to sleep naked. However, over time, it came to be viewed as increasingly shameful to show oneself naked in the presence of the opposite sex. As an example of "uncivilized" sexual behavior, Elias describes the following wedding customs beginning in the Middle Ages:

> The procession into the bridal chamber was led by the best man. The bride was undressed by the bridesmaids; she had to take off all finery. The bridal bed had to be mounted in the presence of witnesses if the marriage was to be valid. They were "laid together." "Once

in bed you are rightly wed," the saying went. In the later Middle Ages this custom gradually changed to the extent that the couple was allowed to lie on the bed in their clothes.
. . . Even in the absolutist society of France, bride and bridegroom were taken to bed by
the guests, undressed, and given their nightdress.

(Elias, 1939/1994:145–146)

Clearly, this changed further over time with the advance of civilization. Today, everything that occurs in the wedding bed is concealed, taking place behind the scenes and
out of the sight of all observers. More generally, sexual life has been taken out of the
larger society and enclosed within the nuclear family.

One key point here, which applies more generally, is that civilization involves a
change in the way human drives are controlled. That is, there is movement from either
a relative absence of control, or largely external control, to the more contemporary situation in which the emphasis is on self-control.

In the area of sexuality, as in all others, the civilizing process does *not* occur in a
straight line; rather there are many forward, backward, and even sideways movements
over time. However, there is still a discernible trend in sexuality and elsewhere that can
be described as the civilizing process:

> The process of civilization of the sex drive, seen on a large scale, runs parallel to those of
> other drives, no matter what sociogenetic differences of detail may always be present . . .
> control grows ever stricter. The instinct is slowly but progressively suppressed from the
> public life of society. . . . And this restraint, like all others, is enforced less and less by
> direct physical force. It is cultivated in the individual from an early age as habitual self-
> restraint by the structure of social life, by the pressure of social institutions in general, and
> by certain executive organs of society (above all, the family) in particular. Thereby the
> social commands and prohibitions become increasingly part of the self.
>
> (Elias, 1939/1994:154)

Overall, in the *History of Manners* Elias is concerned with changes in the way individuals think, act, and interact. He sometimes speaks of this, in general, as a change in
"personality structure," but Elias seems to be describing more than changes in personality; he is also describing changes in the way people act and interact. Taken together,
it could be argued that the *History of Manners* focuses largely on micro-level concerns.
However, two factors militate against such an interpretation. First, Elias often deals in
The History of Manners with concomitant macro-level changes (in the court, for example) and he argues that "the structures of personality and of society evolve in indissolu-
ble interrelationship" (1968/1994:188). Second, *The History of Manners* is written with
the awareness that the second volume, *Power and Civility,* dealing focally with these
more macro-level changes, is to accompany it. Nonetheless, even though Elias wishes
to avoid the micro-macro dichotomy, *The Civilizing Process* consists of two separate
volumes, one focally concerned with micro issues and the second interested mainly in
macro questions.

Power and Civility

If self-constraint is the key to the civilizing process, then what Elias is concerned with
in *Power and Civility* are the changes in social constraint that are associated with this
rise in self-restraint. It is useful to begin this discussion of *Power and Civility* with
Elias's summary of *The History of Manners:*

It has been shown in detail above how constraints through others from a variety of angles are converted into self-restraints, how the more animalic human activities are progressively thrust behind the scenes of men's communal social life and invested with feelings of shame, how the regulation of the whole instinctual and affective life by steady self-control becomes more and more stable, more even and more all-embracing.

(Elias, 1939/1982:230)

However, Elias, despite his later overt rejection of the micro-macro distinction, seems to announce that in *Power and Civility* he is dealing with another, more "macroscopic" level of analysis:

This basic tissue resulting from the many single plans and actions of men can give rise to changes and patterns that no individual person has planned or created. From this interdependence of people arises an order sui generis, an order more compelling and stronger than the will and reason of the individual people composing it. It is this order of interweaving human impulses and strivings, this social order, which determines the course of historical change; it underlies the civilizing process.

(Elias, 1939/1982:230)

These are strong, almost Durkheimian words, depicting a unique *(sui generis)* and compelling reality that "determines the course of historical change." In spite of Elias's later rhetoric about the need to overcome the micro-macro distinction, such a position is not, in the main, supported by *Power and Civility,* which tends at times to deal with the effect, sometimes the determining effect, of macro structures on micro-level phenomena. (However, I hasten to add that Elias often says that he is merely interested in the covariation of macro and micro phenomena, or the connection between "specific changes in the structure of human relations and the corresponding changes in the structure of the personality" [1939/1982:231].)

Reflective of his difficulties in dealing with micro and macro in an integrated way is the fact that Elias distinguishes between *psychogenetic* and *sociogenetic* investigations. In a psychogenetic investigation, one focuses on individual psychology, while sociogenetic investigations have a larger radius and a longer-range perspective focusing on "the overall structure, not only of a single state society but of the social field formed by a specific group of interdependent societies, and of the sequential order of its evolution" (Elias, 1939/1982:287–288).

Lengthening Interdependency Chains　What is this macro-structural change that is of such great importance to the process of civilization? It can be described as the lengthening of "interdependency chains":

From the earliest period of the history of the Occident to the present, social functions have become more and more differentiated under the pressure of competition. The more differentiated they become, the larger grows the number of functions and thus of people on whom the individual constantly depends in all his actions, from the simplest and most commonplace to the more complex and uncommon. As more and more people must attune their conduct to that of others, the web of actions must be organized more and more strictly and accurately, if each individual action is to fulfil its social function. The individual is compelled to regulate his conduct in an increasingly differentiated, more even and stable manner . . . the more complex and stable control of conduct is increasingly instilled in the individual from his earliest years as an automatism, a self-compulsion that he cannot resist even if he consciously wishes to.

(Elias, 1939/1982:232–233)

The result of all this is "the lengthening of the chains of social action and interdependence," which is what contributes to the corresponding need for individuals to moderate their emotions by developing the "habit of connecting events in terms of chains of cause and effect" (Elias, 1939/1982:236).

Thus, to Elias, the increasing differentiation of social functions plays a key role in the civilization process. In addition to, and in conjunction with, this differentiation is the importance of what Elias calls "a total reorganization of the social fabric" (1939/1982:234). Here he is describing the historical process which witnessed the emergence of increasingly stable central organs of society that monopolize the means of physical force and of taxation. Crucial to this development is the emergence of a king with absolute status, as well as of the court society (especially in France and during the reign of Louis XIV, although the courts of Europe came to be closely linked). What Elias calls a "royal mechanism" is operating here—kings are able to emerge in a specific figuration where competing functional groups are ambivalent (they were characterized by both mutual dependency and hostility) and power is evenly distributed between them, thus prohibiting a decisive conflict or a decisive compromise. As Elias puts it, "Not by chance, not whenever a strong ruling personality is born, but when a specific social structure provides the opportunity, does the central organ attain that optimal power which usually finds expression in strong autocracy" (1939/1982:174). In other words, a king emerges when the appropriate figuration is in place.

The king's court took on special importance for Elias because it was here that changes took place that eventually affected the whole of society. In contrast to the warrior, whose short chains of dependence made it relatively easy for him to engage in violent behavior, the court noble, with much longer chains of dependence on many other nobles, found it necessary to be increasingly sensitive to others. The noble also found it increasingly difficult to give free play to his emotions through violence or any other action. The noble was further limited by the fact that the king was gaining increasing control over the means of violence. "The monopolization of physical violence, the concentration of arms and armed men under one authority . . . forces unarmed men in the pacified social spaces to restrain their own violence through foresight or reflection; in other words it imposes on people a greater or lesser degree of self-control" (Elias, 1939/1982:239). The monopoly of violence is intimately related to the ability of the king to monopolize taxation, since taxes are what allow the king to pay for control over the means of violence (Elias, 1939/1982:208). In fact, Elias describes a situation that involves the interplay of these two monopolies: "The financial means thus flowing into this central authority maintains its monopoly of military force, while this in turn maintains the monopoly of taxation" (1939/1982:104). In addition, the increase in the king's income is accompanied by a reduction of the nobility's, and this disparity serves to further enhance the power of the king (Elias, 1969/1983:155).

The nobles play a key role in the civilization process because changes that take place among this elite group are gradually disseminated throughout society:

It is in this courtly society that the basic stock of models of conduct is formed which then, fused with others and modified in accordance with the position of the groups carrying them, spread, with the compulsion to exercise foresight, to ever-wider circles of functions. Their special situation makes the people of courtly society, more than any other Western group affected by this movement, specialists in the elaboration and moulding of social conduct.

(Elias, 1939/1982:258)

Furthermore, these changes that started in the West began to spread through many other parts of the world.

The rise of the king and the court and the transition from warrior to courtier (or the "courtization" of the warrior) represent for Elias a key "spurt" in the civilizing process. This idea of "spurts" is central to Elias's theory of social change; he does not view change as a smooth, unilinear process, but rather one with much stopping and starting— much to-and-fro movement.

While Elias gives great importance to the rise of the court,[4] the ultimate cause of the decisive changes that ensued is the change in the entire social figuration of the time. That is, the key was the changes in various relationships among groups (for example, between warriors and nobles), as well as changes in the relationships among individuals in those groups. Furthermore, this figuration was constraining on nobles and king alike: "Princes and aristocratic groups are apt to appear as people leading a free and unconstrained life. Here . . . it emerged very clearly to what constraints upper classes, and not least their most powerful member, the absolute monarch, are subjected" (Elias, 1969/1983:266).

From the dominance of the king and his nobles there is gradual movement toward a state. In other words, once a private monopoly (by the king) of arms and taxes is in place, the ground is set for the public monopoly of those resources—that is, the emergence of the state. There is a direct link between the growth of the king and later the state as controlling agencies in society and the development of a parallel controlling agency within the individual. Together, they begin to wield unprecedented power over the individual's ability to act on his or her emotions. It is not that before this time people totally lacked self-control, but self-control grew more continuous and stable, affecting more and more aspects of people's lives. Elias's argument is very close to Durkheim's when he contends that with the longer chains of interdependence, "the individual learns to control himself more steadily; he is now less a prisoner of his passions" (1939/1982:241).

An interesting aspect of Elias's argument is that he recognizes that this control over passions is not an unmitigated good. Life has grown less dangerous, but it has also become less pleasurable. Unable to express their emotions directly, people need to find other outlets, such as in their dreams or through books. In addition, what were external struggles may come to be internalized as, in Freudian terms, battles between the id and superego. (Elias's thinking on the individual was heavily influenced by Freudian theory.) Thus, while the greater control over passions brings a welcome reduction in violence, it also brings with it increasing boredom and restlessness.

[4]For an interesting study of the court, the bourgeoisie, and their impact on Mozart, see Elias, 1993.

The longer dependency chains are associated not only with greater affective control, but with increasing sensitivity to others and to the self. Furthermore, people's judgments become more finely shaded and nuanced, making them better able to judge and control both themselves and others. Before the rise of the court society, people had to protect themselves from violence and death. Afterward, as this danger receded, people could afford to grow more sensitive to far more subtle threats and actions. This greater sensitivity is a key aspect of the civilizing process and a key contributor to its further development.

Of great importance in the civilizing process is the socializing of the young so that they develop self-restraint. However, as is true more generally, the increase in self-restraint has its problems: "The civilizing of the human young, is never a process entirely without pain; it always leaves scars" (Elias, 1939/1982:244).

SUMMARY

The focus in this chapter is micro-macro integration. This development represents a return to the concerns of the early giants of sociological theory and a move away from the theoretical extremism, either micro or macro, that characterized much of twentieth-century American sociological theory. While little attention was given to the micro-macro issue prior to the 1980s, during that decade and through the 1990s interest in the topic exploded. The works came from both the micro and the macro extremes as well as various points between them. Some of this work focused on integrating micro and macro theories, while the rest was concerned with the linkage between micro and macro levels of social analysis. In addition to this basic difference, there are important differences among those working on integrating theories and levels.

The heart of the chapter is a discussion of several major examples of work integrating micro and macro levels of social analysis. Three works, those by Ritzer, Alexander, and Wiley, develop very similar micro-macro models of the social world. While there are important differences among these works, their similar images of the social world reflect considerable consensus among those seeking to link micro and macro levels of social analysis.

A much more limited example is offered by Coleman, who focuses on the micro-to-macro linkage. This work is criticized for its failure to deal also with the macro-to-micro linkage, as well as for its lack of a dialectical image of the social world. Liska's work is discussed in this context because of its effort to overcome the limitations of Coleman's micro-to-macro focus and to deal, as well, with the macro-to-micro issue. Liska emphasizes the importance of aggregation and contextual factors in dealing with the micro-macro linkage. Collins's effort at micro-macro integration is discussed and criticized for its micro reductionism—its tendency to reduce macro phenomena to micro phenomena.

The chapter closes with a detailed examination of the work of one of the European precursors of American work on micro-macro integration—Norbert Elias. Of particular relevance are his thoughts on figurational sociology, as well as his historical-comparative study of the relationship between micro-level manners and macro-level changes in the court and the state.

11

AGENCY-STRUCTURE
INTEGRATION

INTRODUCTION

MAJOR EXAMPLES OF AGENCY-STRUCTURE INTEGRATION
  Structuration Theory
  Culture and Agency
  Habitus and Field
  Colonization of the Life-World

MAJOR DIFFERENCES IN THE AGENCY-STRUCTURE
LITERATURE

AGENCY-STRUCTURE AND MICRO-MACRO LINKAGES
  Basic Similarities
  Fundamental Differences

INTRODUCTION

As was pointed out in the previous chapter, paralleling the growth in interest in American sociological theory in the micro-macro issue has been an increase in interest among European theorists in the relationship between agency and structure. In fact, this interest is so intense that Fuller (1998) has called it a "craze." For example, Margaret Archer has contended that "the problem of structure and agency has rightly come to be seen as the basic issue in modern social theory" (1988:ix). In fact, she argues that dealing with this linkage (as well as a series of other linkages implied by it) has become the "acid test" of a general social theory and the "central problem" in theory (Archer, 1988:x). Earlier, Dawe went even further than Archer: *"Here, then, is the problematic around which the entire history of sociological analysis could be written: the problematic of human agency"* (1978:379). Implied in Dawe's concern with agency is also an interest in social structure as well as the constant tension between them.[1]

At a superficial level the micro-macro and agency-structure issues sound similar, and they are often treated as if they resemble one another greatly. However, there are other ways to think of both agency-structure and micro-macro issues that make the significant differences between these two conceptualizations quite clear.

---

[1]In fact, agency is often used in such a way as to include a concern for structure (Abrams, 1982:xiii).

While *agency* generally refers to micro-level, individual human actors,[2] it can also refer to (macro) collectivities that act. For example, Burns sees human agents as including "individuals as well as organized groups, organizations and nations" (1986:9). Touraine (1977) focuses on social classes as actors. If we accept such collectivities as agents, then we cannot equate agency and micro-level phenomena. In addition, while *structure* usually refers to large-scale social structures, it can also refer to micro structures such as those involved in human interaction. Giddens's definition of *systems* (which is closer to the usual meaning of structure than his own concept of structure) implies both types of structures, since it involves "reproduced relations between actors or collectivities" (1979:66). Thus both agency and structure can refer to either micro-level or macro-level phenomena or to both.

Turning to the micro-macro distinction, *micro* often refers to the kind of conscious, creative actor of concern to many agency theorists, but it can also refer to a more mindless "behaver" of interest to behaviorists, exchange theorists, and rational choice theorists. Similarly, the term *macro* can refer not only to large-scale social structures but also to the cultures of collectivities. Thus micro may or may not refer to "agents" and macro may or may not refer to "structures."

When we look closely at the micro-macro and agency-structure schemas, we find that there are substantial differences between them.

MAJOR EXAMPLES OF AGENCY-STRUCTURE INTEGRATION

Structuration Theory

One of the best-known and most articulated efforts to integrate agency and structure is Anthony Giddens's structuration theory (Bryant and Jary, forthcoming; Cohen, 1989; Craib, 1992; Held and Thompson, 1989). Giddens goes so far as to say, "Every research investigation in the social sciences or history is involved in relating action [often used synonymously with *agency*] to structure . . . there is no sense in which structure 'determines' action or vice versa" (1984:219).

While he is not a Marxist, there is a powerful Marxian influence in Giddens's work, and he even sees *The Constitution of Society* as an extended reflection on Marx's inherently integrative dictum: "Men make history, but they do not make it just as they please; they do not make it under circumstances chosen by themselves, but under circumstances directly encountered, given, and transmitted from the past" (1869/1963:15).[3]

Marx's theory is but one of many theoretical inputs into structuration theory. At one time or another, Giddens has analyzed and critiqued most major theoretical orientations and derived a range of useful ideas from many of them. Structuration theory is

---

[2]A variety of contemporary theorists, especially those associated with poststructuralism and postmodernism, have questioned and even rejected the idea of human agency. See, for example, M. Jones (1996).

[3]I agree with according Marx such a central place in structuration theory and, more generally, in theories that integrate agency and structure. As I concluded in my own metatheoretical work, Marx's work is the best "exemplar for an integrated sociological paradigm" (Ritzer, 1981a:232).

extraordinarily eclectic; in fact, Craib (1992:20–31) outlines nine major inputs into Giddens's thinking.

Giddens surveys a wide range of theories that begin with either the individual/agent (for example, symbolic interactionism) or the society/structure (for example, structural functionalism) and rejects both of these polar alternatives. Rather, Giddens argues that we must begin with "recurrent social practices" (1989:252). Giving slightly more detail, he argues: "The basic domain of the study of the social sciences, according to the theory of structuration, is neither the experience of the individual actor, nor the existence of any form of social totality, but social practices ordered across time and space" (Giddens, 1984:2).

At its core Giddens's structuration theory, with its focus on social practices, is a theory of the relationship between agency and structure. According to Bernstein, "the very heart of the theory of structuration" is "intended to illuminate the duality and dialectical interplay of agency and structure" (1989:23). Thus, agency and structure cannot be conceived of apart from one another; they are two sides of the same coin. In Giddens's terms, they are a duality (in the next section we will discuss Archer's critique of this orientation). All social action involves structure, and all structure involves social action. Agency and structure are inextricably interwoven in ongoing human activity or practice.

As pointed out earlier, Giddens's analytical starting point is human practices, but he insists that they be seen as recursive. That is, activities are "not brought into being by social actors but are continually recreated by them via the very means whereby they express themselves as actors. In and through their activities agents produce the conditions that make these activities possible" (Giddens, 1984:2). Thus, activities are not produced by consciousness, by the social construction of reality, nor are they produced by social structure. Rather, in expressing themselves as actors, people are engaging in practice, and it is through that practice that both consciousness and structure are produced. Focusing on the recursive character of structure, Held and Thompson argue that "structure is reproduced in and through the succession of situated practices which are organized by it" (1989:7). The same thing can be said about consciousness. Giddens is concerned with consciousness, or reflexivity. However, in being reflexive, the human actor is not merely self-conscious but is also engaged in the monitoring of the ongoing flow of activities and structural conditions. Bernstein argues that "agency itself is reflexively and recursively implicated in social structures" (1989:23). Most generally, it can be argued that Giddens is concerned with the dialectical process in which practice, structure, and consciousness are produced. Thus, Giddens deals with the agency-structure issue in a historical, processual, and dynamic way.

Not only are social actors reflexive, but so are the social researchers who are studying them. This idea leads Giddens to his well-known ideas on the "double hermeneutic." Both social actors and sociologists use language. Actors use language to account for what they do, and sociologists, in turn, use language to account for the actions of social actors. Thus, we need to be concerned with the relationship between lay and scientific language. We particularly need to be aware of the fact that the social scientist's understanding of the social world may have an impact on the understandings of the actors being studied. In that way, social researchers can alter the world they are studying and thus lead to distorted findings and conclusions.

Elements of Structuration Theory   Let us discuss some of the major components of Giddens's structuration theory, starting with his thoughts on agents, who, as we have seen, continuously monitor their own thoughts and activities as well as their physical and social contexts. In their search for a sense of security, actors rationalize their world. By rationalization Giddens means the development of routines that not only give actors a sense of security, but enable them to deal efficiently with their social lives. Actors also have motivations to act, and these motivations involve the wants and desires that prompt action. Thus, while rationalization and reflexivity are continuously involved in action, motivations are more appropriately thought of as potentials for action. Motivations provide overall plans for action, but most of our action, in Giddens's view, is not directly motivated. Although such action is not motivated and our motivations are generally unconscious, motivations play a significant role in human conduct.

Also within the realm of consciousness, Giddens makes a (permeable) distinction between discursive and practical consciousness. *Discursive consciousness* entails the ability to describe our actions in words. *Practical consciousness* involves actions that the actors take for granted, without being able to express in words what they are doing. It is the latter type of consciousness that is particularly important to structuration theory, reflecting a primary interest in what is done rather than what is said.

Given this focus on practical consciousness, we make a smooth transition from agents to agency, the things that agents actually *do.* "Agency concerns events of which an individual is a perpetrator. . . . Whatever happened would not have happened if that individual had not intervened" (Giddens, 1984:9). Thus, Giddens gives great (his critics say too much) weight to the importance of agency (Baber, 1991). Giddens takes great pains to separate agency from intentions because he wants to make the point that actions often end up being different from what was intended; in other words, intentional acts often have unintended consequences. The idea of unintended consequences plays a great role in Giddens's theory and is especially important in getting us from agency to the social-system level.

Consistent with his emphasis on agency, Giddens accords the agent great power. In other words, Giddens's agents have the ability to make a difference in the social world. Even more strongly, agents make no sense without power; that is, an actor ceases to be an agent if he or she loses the capacity to make a difference. Giddens certainly recognizes that there are constraints on actors, but this does not mean that actors have no choices and make no difference. To Giddens, power is logically prior to subjectivity because action involves power, or the ability to transform the situation. Thus, Giddens's structuration theory accords power to the actor and action and is in opposition to theories that are disinclined to such an orientation and instead grant great importance either to the intent of the actor (phenomenology) or to the external structure (structural functionalism).

The conceptual core of structuration theory lies in the ideas of structure, system, and duality of structure. *Structure* is defined as "the structuring properties [*rules and resources*] . . . the properties which make it possible for discernibly similar social practices to exist across varying spans of time and space and which lend them systemic form" (Giddens, 1984:17). Structure is made possible by the existence of rules and resources. Structures themselves do not exist in time and space. Rather, social phenomena have the capacity to become structured. Giddens contends that "structure only exists in and through the activities of human agents" (1989:256). Thus, Giddens offers a very unusual definition of *structure* that does not follow the Durkheimian pattern of viewing structures as external to and coercive of actors. He takes pains to avoid the impression that structure is "outside" or "external" to human action. "In my usage, structure is what gives form and shape to social life, but it is not *itself* that form and shape" (Giddens, 1989:256). As Held and Thompson put it, structure to Giddens is not a framework "like the girders of a building or the skeleton of a body" (1989:4).

Giddens does not deny the fact that structure can be constraining on action, but he feels that sociologists have exaggerated the importance of this constraint. Furthermore, they have failed to emphasize the fact that structure "is *always* both constraining and enabling" (Giddens, 1984:25, 163; italics added). Structures often allow agents to do things they would not otherwise be able to do. While Giddens deemphasizes structural constraint, he does recognize that actors can lose control over the "structured properties of social systems" as they stretch away in time and space. However, he is careful to avoid Weberian iron-cage imagery and notes that such a loss of control is *not* inevitable.

The conventional sociological sense of structure is closer to Giddens's concept of social system (Thompson, 1989:60). Giddens defines *social systems* as reproduced social practices, or "reproduced relations between actors or collectivities organized as regular social practices" (1984:17, 25). Thus, the idea of social system is derived from Giddens's focal concern with practice. Social systems do *not* have structures, but they do exhibit structural properties. Structures do not themselves exist in time and space, but they do become manifested in social systems in the form of reproduced practices. While some social systems may be the product of intentional action, Giddens places greater emphasis on the fact that such systems are often the unanticipated consequences of human action. These unanticipated consequences may become unrecognized conditions of action and feed back into it. These conditions may elude efforts to bring them under control, but nevertheless actors continue in their efforts to exert such control.

Thus structures are "instantiated" in social systems. In addition, they are also manifest in "memory traces orienting the conduct of knowledgeable human agents" (Giddens, 1984:17). As a result, rules and resources manifest themselves at both the macro level of social systems and the micro level of human consciousness.

We are now ready for the concept of *structuration,* which is premised on the idea that "[t]he constitution of agents and structures are not two independently given sets of phenomena, a dualism, but represent a duality . . . the structural properties of social systems are both medium and outcome of the practices they recursively organize," or "the moment of the production of action is also one of reproduction in the contexts of the day-to-day enactment of social life" (Giddens, 1984:25, 26). It is clear that structuration involves the dialectical relationship between structure and agency (Rachlin, 1991). Structure and agency are a duality; neither can exist without the other.

As has already been indicated, *time* and *space* are crucial variables in Giddens's theory. Both depend on whether other people are present temporally or spatially. The primordial condition is face-to-face interaction, in which others are present at the same time and in the same space. However, social systems extend in time and space, so others may no longer be present. Such distancing in terms of time and space is made increasingly possible in the modern world by new forms of communication and transportation. Gregory (1989) argues that Giddens devotes more attention to time than to space. Underscoring the importance of space, Saunders contends that "any sociological analysis of *why* and *how* things happen will need to take account of *where* (and when) they happen" (1989:218). The central sociological issue of social order depends on how well social systems are integrated over time and across space. One of Giddens's most widely recognized achievements in social theory is his effort to bring the issues of time and space to the fore.

We end this section by bringing Giddens's very abstract structuration theory closer to reality by discussing the research program that can be derived from it. First, instead of focusing on human societies, structuration theory would concentrate on "the orderings of institutions across time and space" (Giddens, 1989:300). (Institutions are viewed by Giddens as clusters of practices, and he identifies four of them—symbolic orders, political institutions, economic institutions, and law.) Second, there would be a focal concern for changes in institutions over time and space. Third, researchers would need to be sensitive to the ways in which the leaders of various institutions intrude on and alter social patterns. Fourth, structurationists would need to monitor, and be sensitive to, the impact of their findings on the social world. Most generally, Giddens is deeply concerned with the "shattering impact of modernity" (1989:301), and the structurationist should be concerned with the study of this pressing social problem.

There is much more to structuration theory than can be presented here; Giddens goes into great detail about the elements of the theory already outlined and discusses many others as well. Along the way he analyzes, integrates, and/or critiques a wide range of theoretical ideas. More recently, he is devoting increasing attention to utilizing his theory for critical analysis of the modern world (Giddens, 1990, 1991, 1992; see Chapter 12). Unlike many others, Giddens has gone beyond a program statement for agency-structure integration; he has given a detailed analysis of its various elements and, more important, has focused on the nature of the interrelationship. What is most satisfying about Giddens's approach is the fact that his key concern, structuration, is defined in inherently integrative terms. The constitutions of agents and structures are not independent of one another; the properties of social systems are seen as both medium and outcome of the practices of actors, and those system properties recursively organize the practices of actors.

Layder, Ashton, and Sung (1991) have sought empirical evidence of Giddens's structuration theory in a study of the transition from school to work. Although they generally support his theoretical approach, their most important conclusion is that structure and agency are not as intertwined as Giddens suggests: "Thus we conclude that empirically structure and action are interdependent (and thus, deeply implicated in each other), *but partly autonomous and separable domains*" (Layder, Ashton, and Sung, 1991:461; italics added). As we will see in the following section, this conclusion is consistent with the position taken by Margaret Archer.

Criticisms   Ian Craib (1992) has offered the most systematic criticism of Giddens's structuration theory (for a more general critique, see Mestrovic, 1998). First, Craib argues that because Giddens focuses on social practices, his work lacks "ontological depth." That is, Giddens fails to get at the social structures that underlie the social world. Second, his effort at theoretical synthesis does not mesh well with the complexity of the social world. To deal with this complexity, rather than a single synthetic theory, "we require a range of theories that might be quite incompatible" (Craib, 1992:178). The social world is also, in Craib's view, quite messy, and that messiness cannot be dealt with adequately by a single, conceptually neat approach like structuration theory. Giddens's approach also serves to limit the potential contributions that could be derived by employing the full range of sociological theories. In rejecting metatheories like positivism and theories like structural functionalism, Giddens is unable to derive useful ideas from them. Even when he does draw upon other theories, Giddens uses only some aspects of those theories, and as a result, he does not get all he can out of them. Third, since Giddens offers no base point from which he can operate, he lacks an adequate basis for critical analysis of modern society (see Chapter 12). As a result, his criticisms tend to have an ad hoc quality rather than emanating systematically from a coherent theoretical core. Fourth, Giddens's theory, in the end, seems quite fragmented. His eclecticism leads him to accumulate various theoretical bits and pieces that do not necessarily hold together well. Finally, it is difficult, if not impossible, to know exactly what Giddens is talking about (Mestrovic, 1998:207). Many times throughout his analysis, Craib indicates that he is unsure about, is guessing at, Giddens's meaning.

Given the number and severity of the criticisms, Craib asks, Why, then, deal with structuration theory at all? He offers two basic reasons. First, many of Giddens's ideas (for example, structures as both constraining and enabling) have become integral parts of contemporary sociology. Second, anyone working in social theory today will need to take into account, and respond to, Giddens's work. Craib closes with the faintest of praise for Giddens's work: "I find it difficult to conceive of any social theory that would not find *something* in his work on which to build. *For the time being,* at any rate, structuration theory will be the food at the centre of the plate" (1992:196; italics added).

Culture and Agency

Margaret Archer (1988) has moved the agency-structure literature in another direction by focusing on the linkage between agency and culture. In fact, this approach is derived from an earlier work by Archer (1982) in which she critiqued Giddens's structuration theory and sought to articulate a systems-theory alternative to it. We begin with this earlier work because it provides a backdrop for her later theory of culture and agency.

Archer's focus is on *morphogenesis;* stemming from systems theory (see Chapter 9), this is the process by which complex interchanges lead not only to changes in the structure of the system but also to an end product—structural elaboration. (While morphogenesis implies change, *morphostasis* is the opposite, an absence of change.) Morphogenesis implies that there are emergent properties that are separable from the actions and interactions that produced them. Once structures have emerged, they react upon and alter action and interaction. The morphogenetic perspective looks at this process over time, seeing endless sequences and cycles of structural change, alterations in action and interaction, and structural elaboration.

Criticisms of Giddens   One key difference between Giddens and Archer is Giddens's case for dualities as opposed to Archer's critique of Giddens's devotion to dualities and her case for the utility of using (analytic) dualisms for analyzing the social world (Archer, 1996; Willmott, 1997). In her view, structure (and culture) and agency are analytically distinct, although they are intertwined in social life. Archer clearly has Giddens in mind when she argues that "too many have concluded too quickly that the task is therefore how to look at both faces of the same medallion at once. . . . [This] foregoes the possibility of examining the interplay between them over time. . . . Any form of conceptualization which prevents examination of this interplay should therefore be resisted" (Archer, 1988:xii). Archer's main fear is that thinking in terms of dualities of "parts" and "people" will mean that "their influences upon one another cannot be unravelled" (1988:xiv).

In our view, both dualities and dualisms have a role to play in analyzing the social world. In some cases it may be useful to separate structure and action, or micro and macro, in order to look at the way in which they relate to one another. In other cases, it may help to look at structure and action and micro and macro as dualities that are inseparable. In fact, it may well be that the degree to which the social world is characterized by dualities or dualisms is an empirical question. That is, in one case the social setting might better be analyzed using dualities, while in another case it might be better to use dualisms. Similar points could also be made about different moments in time. We should be able to study and measure the degree of dualities and dualisms in any social setting at any given time.

A second major criticism of Giddens is that his structuration theory does not seem to have any end result. There is just an endless cycle of agency and structure without any direction. In contrast, Archer's morphogenetic approach leads in the direction of structural elaboration. There are many other critiques of Giddens from the perspective of Archer's morphogenetic approach, but the key point for us here is that morphogenesis is the background for, and plays a key role in, culture-agency theory.

Morphogenesis, Culture, Agency   Archer begins with the premise that the problem of structure and agency has "overshadowed" the issue of culture and agency. She sees, as do most sociologists, a distinction between the two. However, the distinction is a conceptual one, since structure and culture are obviously intertwined in the real world (Hays, 1994). While structure is the realm of material phenomena and interests, culture involves nonmaterial phenomena and ideas. Not only are structure and culture substantively different, but they are also relatively autonomous.[4] Thus, in Archer's view, structure and culture must be dealt with as relatively autonomous, not "clamped together in a conceptual vice" (1988:ix). However, in spite of the revival of "cultural sociology" (Lamont and Wuthnow, 1990), cultural analysis lags far behind structural analysis. (Archer describes "cultural analysis as a poor relation" [1988:xii]; she says that, as a result, there has been little discussion of the relationship between culture and agency.)

---

[4]For an argument against these views of culture and for the idea that culture should be seen as social structure, see Hays (1994). Social structure, for Hays, is composed of "systems of social relations and systems of meaning" (1994:65).

Within morphogenetic theory, the focus in the realm of structure is on how structural conditioning affects social interaction and on how this interaction, in turn, leads to structural elaboration. The parallel concern within the cultural domain is on how cultural conditioning affects sociocultural interaction and, again, on how this interaction leads to cultural elaboration. In both cases, time is accorded a central place in morphogenetic theory. Cultural conditioning refers to the parts, or components, of the cultural system. Sociocultural interaction deals with the relationships between cultural agents. The relationship between cultural conditioning and sociocultural interaction is, then, a variant of the (cultural) structure-agency issue.

Archer begins with the cultural system "because any Socio-Cultural action, wherever it is situated historically, takes place in the context of innumerable interrelated theories, beliefs and ideas which had developed prior to it, and, as will be seen, exert a conditional influence on it" (1988:xix). The sociocultural system logically predates sociocultural action and interaction and affects, and is affected by, such action. Finally, cultural elaboration comes after sociocultural action and interaction and the changes induced in them by alterations in the sociocultural system. Archer is interested in explaining not only cultural elaboration in general but also its specific manifestations. Here is the way Archer summarizes her temporal, dialectical approach to the relationship among the three "stages": "Thus Cultural Elaboration is the future which is forged in the present, hammered out of past inheritance by current innovation" (1988:xxiv).

There is also a conflict-and-order dimension to Archer's theorizing. The parts of the cultural system may be either contradictory or complementary. This helps determine whether agents will engage in orderly or conflictual relationships with one another. These relationships, in turn, will aid in determining whether cultural relationships are stable or changing.

In terms of agency, Archer is concerned with specifying the ways in which the cultural system impinges on sociocultural action. In addition, she is interested in the effect of social relationships on agents. Then there is the issue of the ways in which agents respond to, and react upon, the cultural system. Archer expresses her focal concern with the culture-agency nexus in the following manner: "Our prime interest in the Cultural System lies precisely in its two-fold relationship with human agency; that is with its effects upon us . . . and our effects on it" (1988:143). Agents have the ability either to reinforce or to resist the influence of the cultural system.

Archer sees culture as being on a par with the social system and as being analyzable using a similar, systems-theory perspective. She distinguishes her approach to culture from three other general orientations. The first is downward conflation, or the idea that culture is a macro phenomenon that acts on actors behind their backs. The second is upward conflation, or the view that one group imposes its world view on others. Finally, there is central conflation, which Archer associates with Giddens's approach. Part of her criticism of Giddens's thinking is that he refuses to analyze separately the cultural system and the sociocultural level. As Archer puts her preferred position, "Culture is the product of human agency but at the same time any form of social interaction is embedded in it" (1988:77–78).

Four general positions lie at the base of Archer's theory. First, the cultural system is made up of components that have a logical relationship to one another. Second, the cultural system has a causal impact on the sociocultural system. Third, there is a causal relationship among the individuals and groups that exist at the sociocultural level. Finally, changes at the sociocultural level lead to elaboration of the cultural system.

While Archer is making the case for the study of the relationship between culture and agency under the broad heading "morphogenesis" (Archer, 1995), her objective in later work is the unified analysis of the relationship between structure, culture, and agency. Here, she gets at the reciprocal impact of structure and culture as well as the relative impact of both on agency.

Habitus and Field

Pierre Bourdieu's (1984a:483) theory is animated by the desire to overcome what he considers to be the false opposition between objectivism and subjectivism, or in his words, the "absurd opposition between individual and society" (Bourdieu, 1990:31). As Bourdieu puts it, "the most steadfast (and, in my eyes, the most important) intention guiding my work has been to overcome" the opposition between objectivism and subjectivism (1989:15).

He places Durkheim and his study of social facts (see Chapter 1) and the structuralism of Saussure, Lévi-Strauss, and the structural Marxists (see Chapter 13) within the objectivist camp. These perspectives are criticized for focusing on objective structures and ignoring the process of social construction by which actors perceive, think about, and construct these structures and then proceed to act on that basis. Objectivists ignore agency and the agent, whereas Bourdieu favors a position that is structuralist without losing sight of the agent. "My intention was to bring real-life actors back in who had vanished at the hands of Lévi-Strauss and other structuralists, especially Althusser" (Bourdieu, cited in Jenkins, 1992:18).

This goal moves Bourdieu (1980/1990:42) in the direction of a subjectivist position, one that during his days as a student was dominated by Sartre's existentialism. In addition, Schutz's phenomenology, Blumer's symbolic interactionism, and Garfinkel's ethnomethodology are thought of as examples of subjectivism, focusing on the way agents think about, account for, or represent the social world while ignoring the objective structures in which those processes exist. Bourdieu sees these theories as concentrating on agency and ignoring structure.

Instead, Bourdieu focuses on the dialectical relationship between objective structures and subjective phenomena:

> On the one hand, the objective structures . . . form the basis for . . . representations and constitute the structural constraints that bear upon interactions: but, on the other hand, these representations must also be taken into consideration particularly if one wants to account for the daily struggles, individual and collective, which purport to transform or to preserve these structures.
>
> (Bourdieu, 1989:15)

To sidestep the objectivist-subjectivist dilemma, Bourdieu (1977:3) focuses on *practice,* which he sees as the outcome of the dialectical relationship between structure and agency. Practices are not objectively determined, nor are they the product of free will.

(Another reason for Bourdieu's focus on practice is that such a concern avoids the often irrelevant intellectualism that he associates with objectivism and subjectivism.)

Reflecting his interest in the dialectic between structure and the way people construct social reality, Bourdieu labels his own orientation "constructivist structuralism," "structuralist constructivism," or "genetic structuralism." Here is the way Bourdieu defines genetic structuralism:

> The analysis of objective structures—those of different fields—is inseparable from the analysis of the genesis, within biological individuals, of the mental structures which are to some extent the product of the incorporation of social structures; inseparable, too, from the analysis of the genesis of these social structures themselves: the social space, and of the groups that occupy it, are the products of historical struggles (in which agents participate in accordance with their position in the social space and with the mental structures through which they apprehend this space).
>
> (Bourdieu, 1990:14)

He subscribes, at least in part, to a structuralist perspective, but it is one that is different from the structuralism of Saussure and Lévi-Strauss (as well as the structural Marxists). While they, in turn, focused on structures in language and culture, Bourdieu argues that structures also exist in the social world itself. Bourdieu sees "objective structures [as] independent of the consciousness and will of agents, which are capable of guiding and constraining their practices or their representations" (1989:14). He simultaneously adopts a constructivist position which allows him to deal with the genesis of schemes of perception, thought, and action as well as of social structures.

While Bourdieu seeks to bridge structuralism and constructivism, and he succeeds to some degree, there is a bias in his work in the direction of structuralism. It is for this reason that he (along with Foucault and others—see Chapter 13) is thought of as a poststructuralist. There is more continuity in his work with structuralism than there is with constructivism. Unlike the approach of most others (for example, phenomenologists, symbolic interactionists), Bourdieu's constructivism ignores subjectivity and intentionality. He does think it important to include within his sociology the way people, on the basis of their position in social space, perceive and construct the social world. However, the perception and construction that takes place in the social world is both animated and constrained by structures. This is well reflected in one of his own definitions of his theoretical perspective: "The analysis of objective structures . . . is inseparable from the analysis of the genesis, within biological individuals, of the mental structures which are to some extent the product of the incorporation of social structures; inseparable, too, from the analysis of the genesis of these social structures themselves" (Bourdieu, 1990:14). We can describe what he is interested in as the relationship "between social structures and mental structures" (Bourdieu, 1984a:471).

Thus, some microsociologists would be uncomfortable with Bourdieu's perspective and would see it as little more than a more fully adequate structuralism. According to Wacquant, "Although the two moments of analysis are equally necessary, they are not equal: epistemological priority is granted objectivist rupture over subjectivist understanding" (1992:11). As Jenkins puts it, "In his sociological heart of hearts he [Bourdieu] is as committed to an objectivist view of the world as the majority of those whose

PIERRE BOURDIEU: A Biographical Sketch

As of this writing, Pierre Bourdieu holds the prestigious chair in sociology at College de France (Jenkins, 1992). Born in a small rural town in southeast France in 1930, Bourdieu grew up in a lower-middle-class household (his father was a civil servant). In the early 1950s he attended, and received a degree from, a prestigious teaching college in Paris, Ecole Normale Superieure. However, he refused to write a thesis, in part because he objected to the mediocre quality of his education and to the authoritarian structure of the school. He was put off by, and was active in the opposition against, the strong communist, especially Stalinist, orientation of the school.

Bourdieu taught briefly in a provincial school, but was drafted in 1956 and spent two years in Algeria with the French Army. He wrote a book about his experiences and remained in Algeria for two years after his army tenure was over. He returned to France in 1960 and worked for a year as an assistant at the University of Paris. He attended the lectures of the anthropologist Lévi-Strauss at College de France and worked as an assistant to the sociologist Raymond Aron. Bourdieu moved to the University of Lille for three years and then returned to the powerful position of Director of Studies at L'Ecole Practique des Hautes Etudes in 1964.

In the succeeding years Bourdieu became a major figure in Parisian, French, and ultimately world intellectual circles. His work has had an impact on a number of different fields, including education, anthropology, and sociology. He gathered a group of disciples around him in the 1960s, and since then his followers have collaborated with him and made intellectual contributions of their own. In 1968 the Centre de Sociologie Européenne was founded and Bourdieu has been its director since that time. Associated with the center was a unique publishing venture, *Actes de la Recherche en Sciences Sociales,* that has been an important outlet for the work of Bourdieu and his supporters.

When Raymond Aron retired in 1981, the chair at College de France became open, and most of the leading French sociologists (for example, Raymond Boudon and Alain Touraine) were in competition for it. However, the chair was awarded to Bourdieu. Since that time Bourdieu has, if anything, been a more prolific author than he was before, and his reputation has continued to grow (for more on Bourdieu, see Swartz, 1997:15–51).

An interesting aspect of Bourdieu's work is the way in which his ideas have been shaped in ongoing, sometimes explicit, sometimes implicit, dialogue with others. For example, many of his early ideas were formed in a dialogue with two of the leading scholars of the day during his years of training—Jean-Paul Sartre and Claude Lévi-Strauss. From the existentialism of Sartre, Bourdieu got a strong sense of actors as creators of their social worlds.

work he so sternly dismisses" (1992:91). Or conversely, "At the end of the day, perhaps the most crucial weakness in Bourdieu's work is his inability to cope with subjectivity" (Jenkins, 1992:97). Yet there is a dynamic actor in Bourdieu's theory, an actor capable of *"intentionless invention* of regulated improvisation" (1977:79). The heart of Bourdieu's work, and of his effort to bridge subjectivism and objectivism, lies in his concepts of habitus and field (Aldridge, 1998), as well as their dialectical relationship to one another (Swartz, 1997). While habitus exist in the minds of actors, fields exist outside their minds. We will examine these two concepts in some detail over the next few pages.

However, Bourdieu felt that Sartre had gone too far and accorded the actors too much power and in the process ignored the structural constraints on them. Pulled in the direction of structure, Bourdieu naturally turned to the work of the preeminent structuralist, Lévi-Strauss. At first Bourdieu was strongly drawn to this orientation; in fact, he described himself for a time as a "'blissful structuralist'" (cited in Jenkins, 1992:17). However, some of his early research led him to the conclusion that structuralism was as limiting, albeit in a different direction, as existentialism. He objected to the fact that the structuralists saw themselves as privileged observers of people who are presumed to be controlled by structures of which they are unconscious. Bourdieu came to have little regard for a field that focused solely on such structural constraints, saying that sociology

> would perhaps not be worth an hour's trouble if it solely had as its end the intention of exposing the wires which activate the individuals it observes—if it forgot that it has to do with men, even those who, like puppets, play a game of which they do not know the rules—if, in short, it did not give itself the task of restoring to men the meaning of their actions.
>
> (Bourdieu, cited in Robbins, 1991:37)

Bourdieu defined one of his basic objectives in reaction to the excesses of structuralism: "'My intention was to bring real-life actors back in who had vanished at the hands of Lévi-Strauss and other structuralists . . . through being considered as epiphenomena of structures'" (cited in Jenkins, 1992:17–18). In other words, Bourdieu wanted to integrate at least a part of Sartre's existentialism with Lévi-Strauss's structuralism.

Bourdieu's thinking was also profoundly shaped by Marxian theory and the Marxists. As we have seen, as a student Bourdieu objected to some of the excesses of the Marxists and he later rejected the ideas of structural Marxism. While Bourdieu cannot be thought of as a Marxist, there are certainly ideas derived from Marxian theory that run through his work. Most notable is his emphasis on practice (praxis) and his desire to integrate theory and (research) practice in his sociology. (It could be said that instead of existentialism or structuralism, Bourdieu is doing "praxeology.") There is also a liberationist strand in his work in which he can be seen as being interested in freeing people from political and class domination. But, as was the case with Sartre and Lévi-Strauss, Bourdieu can best be seen as creating his ideas by using Marx and the Marxists as a point of departure.

There are traces of the influence of other theorists in his work, especially that of Weber and of the leading French sociological theorist, Emile Durkheim. However, Bourdieu resists being labeled as a Marxian, Weberian, Durkheimian, or anything else. He regards such labels as limiting, oversimplifying, and doing violence to his work. In a sense, Bourdieu has developed his ideas in a critical dialogue that started while he was a student and continues to this day: "Everything that I have done in sociology and anthropology I have done as much against what I was taught as thanks to it" (Bourdieu, in Bourdieu and Wacquant, 1992:204).

Habitus We begin with the concept for which Bourdieu is most famous—habitus.[5] *Habitus* are the "mental, or cognitive structures" through which people deal with the social world. People are endowed with a series of internalized schemes through which they perceive, understand, appreciate, and evaluate the social world. It is through such schemes that people both produce their practices and perceive and evaluate them.

---

[5]This idea was not created by Bourdieu but is, rather, a traditional philosophical idea that he resuscitated (Wacquant, 1989).

Dialectically, habitus are "the product of the internalization of the structures" of the social world (Bourdieu, 1989:18). In fact, we can think of habitus as "internalized, 'embodied' social structures" (Bourdieu, 1984a:468). They reflect objective divisions in the class structure, such as age groups, genders, and social classes. A habitus is acquired as a result of long-term occupation of a position within the social world. Thus, habitus varies depending on the nature of one's position in that world; not everyone has the same habitus. However, those who occupy the same position within the social world tend to have similar habitus. (To be fair to Bourdieu, we must report that he makes statements such as that his work has been guided "by the desire to reintroduce the agent's practice, his or her capacity for invention and improvisation" [Bourdieu, 1990:13].)

In this sense, habitus can also be a collective phenomenon. The habitus allows people to make sense out of the social world, but the existence of a multitude of habitus means that the social world and its structures do not impose themselves uniformly on all actors.

The habitus available at any given time have been created over the course of collective history: "The habitus, the product of history, produces individual and collective practices, and hence history, in accordance with the schemes engendered by history" (Bourdieu, 1977:82). The habitus manifested in any given individual is acquired over the course of individual history and is a function of the particular point in social history in which it occurs. Habitus is both durable and transposable—that is, transferable from one field to another. However, it is possible for people to have an inappropriate habitus, to suffer from what Bourdieu calls *hysteresis*. A good example is someone who is uprooted from an agrarian existence in a contemporary precapitalist society and put to work on Wall Street. The habitus acquired in a precapitalist society would not allow one to cope very well with life on Wall Street.

The habitus both produces and is produced by the social world. On the one hand, habitus is a "structuring structure"; that is, it is a structure that structures the social world. On the other hand, it is a "structured structure"; that is, it is a structure which is structured by the social world. In other terms, Bourdieu describes habitus as the *"dialectic of the internalization of externality and the externalization of internality"* (1977:72). Thus, habitus allows Bourdieu to escape from having to choose between subjectivism and objectivism, to "escape from under the philosophy of the subject without doing away with the agent . . . as well as from under the philosophy of the structure but without forgetting to take into account the effects it wields upon and through the agent" (Bourdieu and Wacquant, 1992:121–122).

It is practice that mediates between habitus and the social world. On the one hand, it is through practice that the habitus is created; on the other, it is as a result of practice that the social world is created. Bourdieu expresses the mediating function of practice when he defines the habitus as "the system of structured and structuring dispositions which is constituted by practice and constantly aimed at practical . . . functions" (cited in Wacquant, 1989:42; see also Bourdieu, 1977:72). While practice tends to shape habitus, habitus, in turn, serves to both unify and generate practice.

Although habitus is an internalized structure that constrains thought and choice of action, it does *not* determine them. This lack of determinism is one of the main things that distinguishes Bourdieu's position from that of mainstream structuralists. The habitus merely "suggests" what people should think and what they should choose to do. People engage in a conscious deliberation of options, although this decision-making process reflects the operation of the habitus. The habitus provides the principles by which people make choices and choose the strategies that they will employ in the social world. As Bourdieu and Wacquant picturesquely put it, "people are not fools." However, people are not fully rational either (Bourdieu has disdain for rational choice theory); they act in a "reasonable" manner—they have practical sense. There is a logic to what people do; it is the "logic of practice" (Bourdieu, 1980/1990).

Robbins underscores the point that practical logic is "'polythetic'—that is to say that practical logic is capable of sustaining simultaneously a multiplicity of confused and logically (in terms of formal logic) contradictory meanings or theses because the overriding context of its operation is practical" (1991:112). This statement is important not only because it underscores the difference between practical logic and rationality (formal logic), but also because it reminds us of Bourdieu's "relationism." The latter is important in this context because it leads us to recognize that habitus is *not* an unchanging, fixed structure, but rather is adapted by individuals who are constantly changing in the face of the contradictory situations in which they find themselves.

The habitus functions "below the level of consciousness and language, beyond the reach of introspective scrutiny and control by the will" (Bourdieu, 1984a:466). While we are not conscious of habitus and its operation, it manifests itself in our most practical activities, such as the way we eat, walk, talk, and even blow our noses. The habitus operates as a structure, but people do not simply respond mechanically to it or to external structures that are operating on them. Thus, in Bourdieu's approach we avoid the extremes of unpredictable novelty and total determinism.

Field   We turn now to the "field," which Bourdieu thinks of relationally rather than structurally. The *field* is a network of relations among the objective positions within it (Bourdieu and Wacquant, 1992:97). These relations exist apart from individual consciousness and will. They are *not* interactions or intersubjective ties among individuals. The occupants of positions may be either agents or institutions, and they are constrained by the structure of the field. There are a number of semi-autonomous fields in the social world (for example, artistic [Bourdieu and Darbel, 1969/1990; Fowler, 1997], religious, higher education), all with their own specific logics and all generating among actors a belief about the things that are at stake in a field.

Bourdieu sees the field, by definition, as an arena of battle: "The field is also a field of struggles" (Bourdieu and Wacquant, 1992:101). It is the structure of the field that both "undergirds and guides the strategies whereby the occupants of these positions seek, individually or collectively, to safeguard or improve their position, and to impose the principle of hierarchization most favorable to their own products" (Bourdieu, cited in Wacquant, 1989:40). The field is a type of competitive marketplace in which various kinds of capital (economic, cultural, social, symbolic) are employed and deployed. However, it is the field of power (of politics) that is of the utmost importance; the hierarchy of power relationships within the political field serve to structure all the other fields.

Bourdieu lays out a three-step process for the analysis of a field. The first step, reflecting the primacy of the field of power, is to trace out the relationship of any specific field to the political field. The second step is to map out the objective structure of the relations among positions within the field. Finally, the analyst should seek to determine the nature of the habitus of the agents who occupy the various types of positions within the field.

The positions of various agents in the field are determined by the amount and relative weight of the capital they possess (Anheier, Gerhards, and Romo, 1995). Bourdieu even uses military imagery to describe the field, calling it an arena of "strategic emplacements, fortresses to be defended and captured in a field of struggles" (1984a:244). It is capital that allows one to control one's own fate as well as the fate of others (on the negative aspects of capital, see Portes and Landolt, 1996). Bourdieu usually discusses four types of capital (for a discussion of a slightly different formulation of types of capital applied to the genesis of the state, see Bourdieu, 1994). The idea is, of course, drawn from the economic sphere and the meaning of *economic capital* is obvious. *Cultural capital* involves various kinds of legitimate knowledge; *social capital* consists of valued social relations between people; *symbolic capital* stems from one's honor and prestige.

Occupants of positions within the field employ a variety of *strategies*. This idea shows, once again, that Bourdieu's actors have at least some freedom: "The habitus does not negate the possibility of *strategic* calculation on the part of agents" (Bourdieu, 1993:5; italics added). However, strategies do not refer "to the purposive and preplanned pursuit of calculated goals . . . but to the active deployment of objectively oriented 'lines of action' that obey regularities and form coherent and socially intelligible patterns, even though they do not follow conscious rules or aim at the premeditated goals posited by a strategist" (Wacquant, 1992:25). It is via strategies that "the occupants of these positions seek, individually or collectively, to safeguard or improve their position and to impose the principle of hierarchization most favorable to their own products. The strategies of agents depend on their positions in the field" (Bourdieu and Wacquant, 1992:101).

Bourdieu sees the state as the site of the struggle over the monopoly of what he calls *symbolic violence.* This is a "soft" form of violence—"violence which is exercised upon a social agent with his or her complicity" (Bourdieu and Wacquant, 1992:167). Symbolic violence is practiced indirectly, largely through cultural mechanisms, and stands in contrast to the more direct forms of social control that sociologists often focus on. The educational system is the major institution through which symbolic violence is practiced on people (Bourdieu and Passeron, 1970/1990; for an application of the idea of symbolic violence to the status of women, see Krais, 1993). The language, the meanings, the symbolic system of those in power is imposed on the rest of the population. This serves to buttress the position of those in power by, among other things, obscuring what they are doing from the rest of society and getting "the dominated [to] accept as legitimate their own condition of domination" (Swartz, 1997:89). More generally, Bourdieu (1996) sees the educational system as deeply implicated in reproducing existing power and class relations. It is in his ideas on symbolic violence that the political aspect of Bourdieu's work is clearest. That is, Bourdieu is interested in the emancipation of people from this violence and, more generally, from class and political domination (Postone, LiPuma, and Calhoun, 1993:6). Yet Bourdieu is no naive utopian; a better description of his position might be "reasoned utopianism" (Bourdieu and Wacquant, 1992:197).

In underscoring the importance of *both* habitus and field, Bourdieu is rejecting the split between methodological individualists and methodological holists and adopting a position that has recently been termed "methodological relationism" (Ritzer and Gindoff, 1992). That is, Bourdieu is focally concerned with the *relationship* between habitus and field. He sees this as operating in two main ways. On the one hand, the field *conditions* the habitus; on the other, the habitus *constitutes* the field as something that is meaningful, that has sense and value, and that is worth the investment of energy.

Applying Habitus and Field   Bourdieu does not simply seek to develop an abstract theoretical system; he also relates it to a series of empirical concerns and thereby avoids the trap of pure intellectualism. We will illustrate the application of his theoretical approach in his empirical study *Distinction,* which examines the aesthetic preferences of different groups throughout society.

Distinction   In this work, Bourdieu is attempting, among other things, to demonstrate that culture can be a legitimate object of scientific study. He is attempting to reintegrate culture in the sense of "high culture" (for example, preferences for classical music) with the anthropological sense of culture, which looks at all its forms, both high and low. More specifically, in this work Bourdieu is linking taste for refined objects with taste for the most basic food flavors.

Because of structural invariants, especially field and habitus, the cultural preferences of the various groups within society (especially classes and fractions of classes) constitute coherent systems. Bourdieu is focally concerned with variations in aesthetic "taste," the acquired disposition to differentiate among the various cultural objects of aesthetic enjoyment and to appreciate them differentially. Taste is also practice that serves, among other things, to give an individual, as well as others, a sense of his or her place in the social order. Taste serves to unify those with similar preferences *and* to differentiate them from those with different tastes. That is, through the practical applications and implications of taste, people classify objects and thereby, in the process, classify themselves. We are able to categorize people by the tastes they manifest, for example, by their preferences for different types of music or movies. These practices, like all others, need to be seen in the context of all mutual relationships, that is, within the totality. Thus, seemingly isolated tastes for art or movies are related to preferences in food, sports, or hairstyles.

Two interrelated fields are involved in Bourdieu's study of taste—class relationships (especially within fractions of the dominant class) and cultural relationships (for a critique of this distinction, see Erickson, 1996). He sees these fields as a series of positions in which a variety of "games" are undertaken. The actions taken by the agents (individual or collective) who occupy specific positions are governed by the structure of the field, the nature of the positions, and the interests associated with them. However, it is also a game that involves self-positioning and use of a wide range of strategies to allow one to excel at the game. Taste is an opportunity both to experience and to assert one's position within the field. But the field of social class has a profound effect on one's ability to play this game; those in the higher classes are far better able to have their tastes accepted and to oppose the tastes of those in the lower classes. Thus, the world of cultural works is related to the hierarchical world of social class and is itself both hierarchical and hierarchizing.

Needless to say, Bourdieu also links taste to his other major concept, habitus. Tastes are shaped far more by these deep-rooted and long-standing dispositions than they are by surface opinions and verbalizations. Peoples' preferences for even such mundane aspects of culture as clothing, furniture, or cooking are shaped by the habitus. And it is these dispositions "that forge the unconscious unity of a class" (Bourdieu, 1984a:77). Bourdieu puts this more colorfully later: "Taste is a matchmaker . . . through which a habitus confirms its affinity with other habitus" (1984a:243). Dialectically, of course, it is the structure of the class that shapes the habitus.

While both field and habitus are important to Bourdieu, it is their dialectical relationship that is of utmost importance and significance; field and habitus mutually define one another:

> The dispositions constituting the cultivated *habitus* are only formed, only function and are only valid in a *field,* in the relationship with a field . . . which is itself a 'field of possible forces,' a 'dynamic' situation in which forces are only manifested in their relationship with certain dispositions. This is why the same practices may receive opposite meanings and values in different fields, in different configurations, or in opposing sectors of the same field.
>
> (Bourdieu, 1984a:94; italics added)

Or, as Bourdieu puts it, in more general terms: "There is a strong correlation between social positions and the dispositions of the agents who occupy them" (1984a:110). It is out of the relationship between habitus and field that practices, cultural practices in particular, are established.

Bourdieu sees culture as a kind of economy, or marketplace. In this marketplace people utilize cultural rather than economic capital. This capital is largely a result of people's social class origin and their educational experience. In the marketplace, people accrue more or less capital and either expend it to improve their position or lose it, thereby causing their position within the economy to deteriorate.

People pursue distinction in a range of cultural fields—the beverages they drink (Perrier or cola), the automobiles they drive (Mercedes Benz or Ford Escort), the newspapers they read (*The New York Times* or *USA Today*), or the resorts they visit (The French Riviera or Disney World). Relationships of distinction are objectively inscribed in these products and reactivated each time they are appropriated. In Bourdieu's view, "The total field of these fields offers well-nighly inexhaustible possibilities for the pursuit of distinction" (1984a:227). The appropriation of certain cultural goods (for example, a Mercedes Benz) yields "profit," while that of others (an Escort) yields no gain, or even a "loss."

Bourdieu (1998:9) takes pains to make it clear that he is not simply arguing, following Thorstein Veblen's (1899/1994) famous theory of conspicuous consumption, that the "driving force of all human behavior was the search for distinction." Rather, he contends that his main point "is that to exist within a social space, to occupy a point or to be an individual within a social space, is to differ, to be different . . . being inscribed in the space in question, he or she . . . is endowed with categories of perception, with classificatory schemata, with a certain *taste,* which permits her to make differences, to discern, to distinguish" (Bourdieu, 1994/1998:9). Thus, for example, one who chooses to own a grand piano is different from one who opts for an accordion. That one choice (the piano) is worthy of distinction while another (the accordion) is considered vulgar is a result of the dominance of one point of view and the symbolic violence practiced against those who adopt another viewpoint.

There is a dialectic between the nature of the cultural products and tastes. Changes in cultural goods lead to alterations in taste, but changes in taste are also likely to result in transformations in cultural products. The structure of the field not only conditions the desires of the consumers of cultural goods but also structures what the producers create in order to satisfy those demands.

Changes in taste (and Bourdieu sees all fields temporally) result from the struggle between opposing forces in both the cultural (the supporters of old versus new fashions, for example) and the class (the dominant versus the dominated fractions within the dominant class) arenas. However, the heart of the struggle lies within the class system, and the cultural struggle between, for example, artists and intellectuals is a reflection of the interminable struggle between the different fractions of the dominant class to define culture, indeed the entire social world. It is oppositions within the class structure that condition oppositions in taste and in habitus. While Bourdieu gives great importance to social class, he refuses to reduce it to merely economic matters or to the relations of production but sees class as defined by habitus as well.

Bourdieu offers a distinctive theory of the relationship between agency and structure within the context of a concern for the dialectical relationship between habitus and field. His theory is also distinguished by its focus on practice (in the preceding case, aesthetic practices) and its refusal to engage in arid intellectualism. In that sense it represents a return to the Marxian concern for the relationship between theory and practice.

Homo Academicus In *Homo Academicus,* Bourdieu (1984b) has a variety of objectives, including applying his theoretical arsenal to an analysis of French academia (see Krais, 1996, for an application to German academia). In describing the field of concern in this work, Bourdieu provides us with a number of now-familiar ideas:

> The university field is, like any other field, the locus of a struggle to determine the conditions and the criteria of legitimate membership and legitimate hierarchy, that is, to determine which properties are pertinent, effective and liable to function as capital so as to generate the specific profits guaranteed by the field.
>
> (Bourdieu, 1984b:11)

More specifically, Bourdieu's concern is the relationship between the objective positions of different academic fields, their corresponding habitus, and the struggle between them. In addition, Bourdieu wants to link the academic field and what takes place in it to the larger field of power. As Bourdieu puts the latter relationship in this case, the structure of higher education "reproduces in specifically academic logic the structure of the field of power to which it gives access" (1984b:38). And, dialectically, the structure of the academic field through selection and indoctrination contributes to the reproduction of the field of power.

Bourdieu finds that French academia is divided between the dominant fields of law and medicine and the subordinate fields of science and, to a lesser extent, arts. This division parallels that of the field of power, in which those with social competence are temporally dominant and those with scientific competence are socially subordinate. However, the matter is greatly complicated by the fact that academia is both a social hierarchy (reflecting the field of power as well as the social stratification system, and in which political and economic power reign) and a cultural hierarchy ruled by cultural capital derived from scientific authority or intellectual renown. In the cultural domain, the hierarchy of the academic disciplines is reversed: science is on top, with law and medicine ranking lower. Thus, most generally, the opposition between the economic-political and the cultural fields is being fought out in the French university system.

This struggle is being waged not only between the faculties, but also *within* the arts faculty, which is caught between the social and the scientific. Thus, the arts faculty is "a privileged vantage-point for observing the struggle between the two kinds of university power" (Bourdieu, 1984b:73). Some members of the arts faculty have social (or academic) power derived from their role within the university as a place for the transmission of legitimate knowledge. Their capital is acquired within the university through their control of the educational process and of the production of the next generation of academicians. Others in the arts faculty have scientific power derived from their intellectual renown within their particular field. These two types of academicians struggle for power within the arts faculties of the field of the French university system.

Whatever type of capital an academician has, it takes time to acquire it. The process of acquiring capital leads to an interesting dynamic between established professors and the graduate students and junior faculty members who aspire to their positions. Those in power control the aspirants, who must be docile and submissive. However, the aspirants have complicity in this process. As Bourdieu puts it, "one is only hooked if one is in the pool" (1984b:89). Master professors must hold neophytes back from becoming independent too soon, but they must not frustrate them so much that they defect and go to work for rival professors. The number and prestige of subordinates serves to enhance the prestige of an established professor. Further, large numbers of students draw other students into the fold. In this way, and others, "capital breeds capital" (Bourdieu, 1984b:91). Ambitious students are drawn to ambitious professors with the result that their affinities are much more social than intellectual.

Bourdieu uses this example to attack the intellectual mediocrity of the university system. To succeed, one must conform rather than be innovative. More practically, time spent on accruing academic power (such as through participation on committees) is time taken away from intellectual pursuits. It takes a lot of time to accumulate and maintain academic power—time that cannot be devoted to more intellectual pursuits. All of this, to Bourdieu, is not the product of conscious choice on the part of academics, but rather results from the dynamics of the interaction of positions in the academic field.

Bourdieu also uses this relationship between senior and junior academicians to analyze the academic revolution that took place in France in 1968. Reared in the cozy academic system described above, older professors were unprepared for the coming disturbances. Some of the new entrants, for their part, refused to wait as patiently, or as long, as had their predecessors. Thus, for both young and senior professors, there was a clash between extant habitus and the changing nature of the field. Older professors continued to work "without any conscious orchestration to defend the social constants of the professorial body" (Bourdieu, 1984b:137). They were alarmed by the number of new entrants who were able to gain entry without paying the expected dues; these new-comers were seen as gaining entrance at a "cut price." It was these new faculty members who, even though they occupied subordinated academic positions, aligned themselves with students to create the revolution.

However, in Bourdieu's view, the conflict took place not between the old and young faculty members, but rather between two groups of younger faculty members. On the one hand, there were the younger faculty members who internalized the habitus of the older generation and who had the possibility of ascending the academic hierarchy. Arrayed against them was a second group of younger faculty with a different habitus, stemming from the fact that they had few, if any, career prospects. (Those who see their chances of upward mobility blocked are likely to be the ones who protest.)

Bourdieu also argues that different faculties reacted differently to the crisis. The faculties most likely to be involved were those that served "as a refuge for students who, in the previous state of the system, would have been excluded or would have dropped out" (Bourdieu, 1984b:165). Sociology and psychology were two such fields: "These ill-defined academic positions, which give access to social positions which in their turn are ill-defined, are well designed to allow their occupants to surround themselves and their future with an aura of indeterminacy and vagueness" (Bourdieu, 1984b:165). Those with maladjusted or vague expectations were more likely to participate in the crisis. Sociology played a key role in triggering the crisis not only for the reasons already cited, but also because it attracted "students from the dominant class with a low level of academic attainment" (Bourdieu, 1984b:170). It was in sociology that such students came into contact with teachers with few career prospects, and it was the resulting interaction that played a key role in fueling the rebellion. As Bourdieu puts it, there was a "structural affinity between the students and subordinate teachers" (1984b:171). They came together not consciously, but because of similarities in their habitus and their positions within the respective fields (student and faculty).

Concluding Thoughts   Bourdieu is one of those thinkers (another is Garfinkel) who is considered a theorist but who rejects that label. He says that he is not "producing a general discourse on the social world" (Bourdieu and Wacquant, 1992:159). Bourdieu rejects pure theory that lacks an empirical base, but he also disdains pure empiricism performed in a theoretical vacuum. Rather, he sees himself engaged in research which is "inseparably empirical and theoretical . . . *research without theory is blind, and theory without research is empty*" (Bourdieu and Wacquant, 1992:160, 162).

Overall, I find myself in accord with Jenkins when he argues that "Bourdieu's intellectual project is longstanding, relatively coherent and cumulative. It amounts to nothing less than an attempt to construct a theory of social practice and society" (1992:67). Calhoun sees Bourdieu as a critical theorist, which in this context is defined more broadly than simply those associated with the Frankfurt school. Calhoun defines critical theory as "the project of social theory that undertakes simultaneously critique of received categories, critique of theoretical practice, and critical substantive analysis of social life in terms of the possible, not just the actual" (1993:63).

Although Bourdieu is offering a theory, his theory does not have universal validity. For example, he says that there are "no transhistoric laws of the relations between fields" (Bourdieu and Wacquant, 1992:109). The nature of the actual relations between fields is always an empirical question. Similarly, the nature of habitus changes with altered historical circumstances: "Habitus . . . is a transcendental but a *historical transcendental* bound up with the structure and history of a field" (Bourdieu and Wacquant, 1992:189).

Colonization of the Life-World

We discussed Habermas's earlier ideas in Chapter 4, on neo-Marxian theory, under the heading "Critical Theory." While, as we will see, Habermas's perspective can still be thought of, at least in part, as being a neo-Marxian orientation, it has broadened considerably and is increasingly difficult to contain within that, or any other, theoretical category. Habermas's theory has grown and become more diverse as he has addressed, and incorporated, the ideas of a wide number of sociological theorists, most recently and most notably those of George Herbert Mead, Talcott Parsons, Alfred Schutz, and Emile Durkheim. In spite of the difficulties involved in categorizing Habermas's innovative theoretical perspective, we will discuss his most recent ideas, which can be broadly thought of as the "colonization of the life-world," under the heading "agency-structure issue." Habermas (1991:251) makes it clear that he is engaging in "paradigm combination"; that is, he is creating his agency-structure perspective by integrating ideas drawn from action and systems theory. It is, at least in part, in his thoughts on the life-world that Habermas deals with agency. Structure is dealt with primarily in Habermas's ideas on the social system, which, as we will see, is the force that is colonizing the life-world. What does Habermas mean by life-world, system, and colonization? We address these phenomena and their interrelationship, as well as other key ideas in Habermas's most recent theorizing, in this section.

Before we get to these concepts, it should be made clear that Habermas's major focus continues to be on communicative action. Free and open communication remains both his theoretical baseline and his political objective. It also has the methodological function, much like Weber's ideal types, of allowing him to analyze variations from the model: "The construction of an unlimited and undistorted discourse can serve at most as a foil for setting off more glaringly the rather ambiguous developmental tendencies in modern society" (Habermas, 1987a:107). Indeed, his focal interest in the colonization of the life-world is the ways in which that process is adversely affecting free communication.

Habermas also retains an interest in the Weberian process of rationalization, specifically the issue of the differential rationalization of life-world and system and the impact of this difference on the colonization of the former by the latter (for a somewhat counter view, see Bartos, 1996). In Weberian terms, the *system* is the domain of formal rationality, while the *life-world* is the site of substantive rationality. The *colonization of the life-world,* therefore, involves a restatement of the Weberian thesis that in the modern world, formal rationality is triumphing over substantive rationality and coming to dominate areas that were formerly defined by substantive rationality. Thus, while Habermas's theory has taken some interesting new turns, it retains its theoretical roots, especially in its Marxian and Weberian orientations.

The Life-World   This concept is derived from phenomenological sociology in general and, more specifically, the theories of Alfred Schutz (Bowring, 1996). But Habermas interprets the ideas of George Herbert Mead as also contributing to insights about the life-world. To Habermas, the life-world represents an internal perspective (while, as we will see, the system represents an external viewpoint): "Society is conceived from the perspective of the acting subject" (1987a:117). Thus, there is only one society; life-world and system are simply different ways of looking at it.

Habermas views the life-world and communicative action as "complementary" concepts. More specifically, communicative action can be seen as occurring within the life-world:

> The lifeworld is, so to speak, the transcendental site where speaker and hearer meet, where they reciprocally raise claims that their utterances fit the world . . . and where they can criticize and confirm those validity claims, settle their disagreements, and arrive at agreements.
>
> (Habermas, 1987a:126)

The life-world is a "context-forming background of processes of reaching understanding" through communicative action (Habermas, 1987a:204). It involves a wide range of unspoken presuppositions about mutual understanding that must exist and be mutually understood for communication to take place.

Habermas is concerned with the rationalization of the life-world, which involves, for one thing, increasingly rational communication in the life-world. He believes that the more rational the life-world becomes, the more likely it is that interaction will be controlled by "rationally motivated mutual understanding." Such understanding, or a rational method of achieving consensus, is based ultimately on the authority of the better argument.

Habermas sees the rationalization of the life-world as involving the progressive differentiation of its various elements. The life-world is composed of culture, society, and personality (note the influence of Parsons and his action systems). Each of these refers to interpretive patterns, or background assumptions, about culture and its effect on action, appropriate patterns of social relations (society), and what people are like (personality) and how they are supposed to behave. Engaging in communicative action and achieving understanding in terms of each of these themes leads to the reproduction of the life-world through the reinforcement of culture, the integration of society, and the formation of personality. While these components are closely intertwined in archaic societies, the rationalization of the life-world involves the "growing differentiation between culture, society and personality" (Habermas, 1987a:288).

System   While the life-world represents the viewpoint of acting subjects on society, system involves an external perspective that views society "from the observer's perspective of someone not involved" (Habermas, 1987a:117). In analyzing systems, we are attuned to the interconnection of actions, as well as the functional significance of actions and their contributions to the maintenance of the system. Each of the major components of the life-world (culture, society, personality) has corresponding elements in the system. Cultural reproduction, social integration, and personality formation take place at the system level.

The system has its roots in the life-world, but ultimately it comes to develop its own structural characteristics. Examples of such structures include the family, the judiciary, the state, and the economy. As these structures evolve, they grow more and more distant from the life-world. As in the life-world, rationalization at the system level involves progressive differentiation and greater complexity. These structures also grow more self-sufficient. As they grow in power, they exercise more and more steering capacity over the life-world. They come to have less and less to do with the process of achieving consensus and, in fact, limit the occurrence of that process in the life-world. In other words, these rational structures, instead of enhancing the capacity to communicate and reach understanding, threaten those processes through the exertion of external control over them.

Social Integration and System Integration   Given the preceding discussion of life-world and system, Habermas concludes: *"The fundamental problem of social theory* is how to connect in a satisfactory way the two conceptual strategies indicated by the notions of 'system' and 'lifeworld'"* (1987a:151; italics added). Habermas labels those two conceptual strategies "social integration" and "system integration."

The perspective of *social integration* focuses on the life-world and the ways in which the action system is integrated through either normatively guaranteed or communicatively achieved consensus. Theorists who believe that society is integrated through social integration begin with communicative action and see society *as* the life-world. They adopt the internal perspective of the group members, and they employ a hermeneutic approach in order to be able to relate their understanding to that of the members of the life-world. The ongoing reproduction of society is seen as a result of the actions undertaken by members of the life-world to maintain its symbolic structures. It is also seen only from their perspective. Thus, what is lost in this hermeneutic approach is the outsider's viewpoint as well as a sense of the reproductive processes that are occurring at the system level.

The perspective of *system integration* is focally concerned with the system and the way in which it is integrated through external control over individual decisions that are not subjectively coordinated. Those who adopt this perspective see society as a self-regulating system. They adopt the external perspective of the observer, but this perspective prohibits them from really getting at the structural patterns that can be understood only hermeneutically from the internal perspective of members of the life-world.

Thus, Habermas concludes that while each of these two broad perspectives has something to offer, both have serious limitations. On the basis of his critique of social and system integration, Habermas offers his alternative, which seeks to integrate these two theoretical orientations: he sees society as a system that has to fulfill conditions for the maintenance of sociocultural life-worlds. The formula-societies are *systematically stabilized* complexes of action of *socially integrated* groups. . . . [I] stand for the heuristic proposal that we view society as an entity that, in the course of social evolution, gets differentiated *both* as a *system* and a *lifeworld.*

(Habermas, 1987a:151–152; italics added)

Having argued that he is interested in *both* system and life-world, Habermas makes it clear at the end of the above quotation that he is also concerned with the evolution of the two. While both evolve in the direction of increasing rationalization, that rationalization takes different forms in life-world and system, and that differentiation is the basis of the colonization of the life-world.

Colonization   Crucial to the understanding of the idea of colonization is the fact that Habermas sees society as being composed of *both* life-world and system. Furthermore, while both concepts were closely intertwined in earlier history, today there is an increasing divergence between them; they have become "decoupled." While both have undergone the process of rationalization, that process has taken different forms in the two settings. Although Habermas sees a dialectical relationship between system and life-world (they both limit and open up new possibilities for one another), his main concern is with the way in which system in the modern world has come to control the life-world. In other words, he is interested in the breakdown of the dialectic between system and life-world and the growing power of the former over the latter.[6]

Habermas contrasts the increasing rationality of system and life-world. The rationalization of the life-world involves growth in the rationality of communicative action. Furthermore, action that is oriented toward achieving mutual understanding is increasingly freed from normative constraint and relies more and more on everyday language. In other words, social integration is achieved more and more through the processes of consensus formation in language.

But the result of this is the fact that the demands on language grow and come to overwhelm its capacities. Delinguistified media (especially money in the economic system and power in the political system and its administrative apparatus)—having become differentiated in, and emanating from, the system—come to fill the void and replace, to at least some degree, everyday language. Instead of language coordinating action, it is money and power that perform that function. Life becomes monetarized and bureaucratized.

More generally, the increasingly complex system "unleashes system imperatives that burst the capacity of the lifeworld they instrumentalize" (Habermas, 1987a:155). Thus, Habermas writes of the "violence" exercised over the life-world by the system through the ways in which it restricts communication. This violence, in turn, produces "pathologies" within the life-world. Habermas embeds this development within a view of the history of the world:

---

[6]However, Habermas also sees problems (domination, self-deception) *within* the life-world (Outhwaite, 1994:116).

The far-reaching uncoupling of system and lifeworld was a necessary condition for the transition from the stratified class societies of European feudalism to the economic class societies of the early modern period; but the capitalist pattern of modernization is marked by a *deformation,* a reification of the symbolic structures of the lifeworld under the imperatives of subsystems differentiated out via money and power and rendered self-sufficient.

(Habermas, 1987a:283; italics added)

It might be noted that by linking the deformities to capitalism, Habermas continues, at least in this sense, to operate within a neo-Marxian framework. However, when he looks at the modern world, Habermas is forced to abandon a Marxian approach (Sitton, 1996), since he concludes that the deformation of the life-world is "no longer localizable in any class-specific ways" (1987a:333). Given this limitation, and in line with his roots in critical theory, Habermas demonstrates that his work is also strongly influenced by Weberian theory. In fact, he argues that the distinction between life-world and system, and the ultimate colonization of the life-world, allows us to see in a new light the Weberian thesis "of a modernity at variance with itself" (Habermas, 1987a:299). In Weber, this conflict exists primarily between substantive and formal rationality and the triumph in the West of the latter over the former. To Habermas, the rationalization of the system comes to triumph over the rationalization of the life-world, with the result that the life-world comes to be colonized by the system.

Habermas adds specificity to his thoughts on colonization by arguing that the main forces in the process are "formally organized domains of action" at the system level, such as the economy and the state. In traditional Marxian terms, Habermas sees modern society as subject to recurrent systemic crises. In seeking to deal with these crises, institutions like the state and the economy undertake actions that adversely affect the life-world, leading to pathologies and crises within it. Basically, the life-world comes to be denuded by these systems, and communicative action comes to be less and less directed to the achievement of consensus. Communication becomes increasingly rigidified, impoverished, and fragmented, and the life-world itself seems poised on the brink of dissolution. This assault on the life-world worries Habermas greatly, given his concern for the communicative action that takes place within it. However, no matter how extensive the colonization by the system, the life-world is "never completely husked away" (Habermas, 1987a:311).

If the essential problem in the modern world is the uncoupling of system and life-world and the domination of the life-world by the system, then the solutions are clearcut. On the one hand, life-world and system need to be recoupled. On the other, the dialectic between system and life-world needs to be reinstated so that, instead of the latter being deformed by the former, the two become mutually enriching and enhancing. While the two were intertwined in primitive society, the rationalization process that has occurred in both system and life-world makes it possible that the future recoupling will produce a level of system, life-world, and their interrelationship unprecedented in human history.

Thus, once again, Habermas is back to his Marxian roots. Marx, of course, did not look back in history for the ideal state but saw it in the future in the form of communism and the full flowering of species-being. Habermas, too, does not look back to archaic societies where nonrationalized system and life-world were more unified but looks to a future state involving the far more satisfactory unification of rationalized system and life-world.

Habermas also reinterprets the Marxian theory of basic struggles within society. Marx, of course, emphasized the conflict between proletariat and capitalist and traced it to the exploitative character of the capitalist system. Habermas focuses not on exploitation but on colonization and sees many of the struggles of recent decades in this light. That is, he sees social movements such as those oriented to greater equality, increased self-realization, the preservation of the environment, and peace "as reactions to system assaults on the lifeworld. Despite the diversity of interests and political projects of these heterogeneous groups, they have resisted the colonization of the life-world" (Seidman, 1989:25). The hope for the future clearly lies in resistance to the encroachments on the life-world and in the creation of a world in which system and life-world are in harmony and serve to mutually enrich one another to a historically unprecedented degree.

MAJOR DIFFERENCES IN THE AGENCY-STRUCTURE LITERATURE

As is the case with work on micro-macro integration in the United States, there are significant differences among Europeans working on the agency-structure issue. For example, there is considerable disagreement in the literature on the nature of the agent. Most of those working within this realm (for example, Giddens, Bourdieu) tend to treat the agent as an individual actor, but Touraine's "actionalist sociology" treats collectivities such as social classes as agents. In fact, Touraine defines *agency* as "an organization directly implementing one or more elements of the system of historical action and therefore intervening directly in the relations of social domination" (1977:459). A third, middle-ground position on this issue is taken by Burns and Flam (see also Crozier and Friedberg, 1980), who regard either individuals or collectivities as agents. This lack of agreement on the nature of the agent is a source of substantial differences in the agency-structure literature.

There is considerable disagreement even among those who focus on the individual actor as agent. For example, Bourdieu's agent, dominated by habitus, seems far more mechanical than Giddens's (or Habermas's) agent. Bourdieu's habitus involves "systems of durable, transposable *dispositions,* structuring structures, that is, as principles of the generation and structuring of practices and representations" (1977:72). The habitus is a source of strategies "without being the product of a genuine strategic intention" (Bourdieu, 1977:73). It is neither subjectivistic nor objectivistic but combines elements of both. It clearly rejects the idea of an actor with "the free and willful power to constitute" (Bourdieu, 1977:73). Giddens's agents may not have intentionality and free will either, but they have much more willful power than do Bourdieu's. Where Bourdieu's agents seem to be dominated by their habitus, by internal ("structuring") structures, the agents in Giddens's work are the perpetrators of action. They have at least some choice, at least the possibility of acting differently than they do. They have power, and they make a difference in their worlds (see also Lukes, 1977). Most important, they constitute (and are constituted by) structures. In contrast, in Bourdieu's work a sometimes seemingly disembodied habitus is involved in a dialectic with the external world.[7]

Similarly, there are marked disagreements among agency-structure theorists on precisely what they mean by structure.[8] Some adopt a specific structure as central, such as the organization in the work of Crozier and Friedberg and Touraine's relations of social domination as found in political institutions and organizations; others (for example, Burns, 1986:13) focus on an array of social structures, such as bureaucracy, the polity, the economy, and religion. Giddens offers a very idiosyncratic definition of *structure* ("recursively organized sets of rules and resources" [1984:25]) that is at odds with virtually every other definition of *structure* in the literature (Layder, 1985). However, his definition of *systems* as reproduced social practices is very close to what many sociologists mean by structure. In addition to the differences among those working with structure, differences exist between these theorists and others. Archer, as we have seen, excoriates Giddens (and implicitly all the others) for focusing on structure to the exclusion of culture.

The attempts at agency-structure linkage flow from a variety of very different theoretical directions. For example, within social theory Giddens seems to be animated by functionalism and structuralism versus phenomenology, existentialism, and ethnomethodology and, more generally, by new linguistic structuralism, semiotics, and hermeneutics (Archer, 1982), while Archer is influenced mainly by systems theory, especially that of Walter Buckley. One result is that Giddens's agents tend to be active and creative people ("corporeal beings" with selves) involved in a continual flow of conduct, while Archer's are often reduced to systems, particularly the sociocultural system. Bourdieu seeks to find a satisfactory alternative to subjectivism and objectivism within anthropological theory. Habermas seeks to synthesize ideas derived from Marx, Weber, critical theorists, Durkheim, Mead, Schutz, and Parsons.

There is a strain toward either the agency or the structural direction in Europe. Certainly Bourdieu is pulling strongly in the direction of structure, while Giddens has a more powerful sense of agency than do most other theorists of this genre (Layder, 1985:131). In spite of the existence of pulls in the directions of agency and structure, what is distinctive about the European work on agency and structure, as compared to American micro-macro work, is a much stronger sense of the need to refuse to separate the two and to deal with them dialectically (for example, Giddens, Bourdieu, Habermas). In the American micro-macro literature, one parallel to the European efforts to deal with agency and structure dialectically is my attempt to deal dialectically with the integration of the micro-macro and objective-subjective continua.

Dietz and Burns (1992) have made an effort to offer a view of agency and structure that reflects the strengths and weaknesses of earlier work. Four criteria must be met in

---

[7]Although I am emphasizing the differences between Giddens and Bourdieu on agency, Giddens (1979:217) sees at least some similarities between the two perspectives.

[8]I am focusing here mainly on Europeans who deal with social structure and not those who see structure as hidden, underlying elements of culture.

order for agency to be attributed to a social actor.[9] First, the actor must have power; the actor must be able to make a difference. Second, the actions undertaken by an agent must be intentional. Third, the actor must have some choice, some free play. The result is that observers can make only probabilistic statements about what actors may do. Finally, agents must be reflexive, monitoring the effects of their actions and using that knowledge to modify the bases of action. Overall, agency is viewed as a continuum; all actors have agency to some degree and no actor has full, unconstrained agency.

The other, structural side of the equation, from Dietz and Burns' point of view, are the constraints on agency. First, even if an agent can imagine certain actions, they simply may not be possible, given technological and physical realities. Second, structure (especially rules) makes certain actions seem necessary while others appear impossible. Finally, agency is limited by other agents who have sanctioning power, both positive and negative.

AGENCY-STRUCTURE AND MICRO-MACRO LINKAGES

Basic Similarities

The most general similarity between the work in the United States and that in Europe is the desire for integration and synthesis. Beyond this shared interest, there has been a tendency for both Americans and Europeans to be animated in their thinking by their aversion to the excesses of extant dominant theories. Both Americans and Europeans have attacked the macro determinism of structural functionalism. There is a similar aversion to the excesses of structuralism, although the feeling is stronger in Europe, where structuralism made far greater inroads than it did in the United States. In Europe structural functionalism and structuralism are seen as emphasizing structure and giving agency little or no importance (see, for example, Giddens, 1979:50). In America they are seen as focusing on the macro level and giving little attention to micro-level phenomena.

Similarly, theorists on both sides of the ocean have been wary of the excesses of micro/agency theories such as symbolic interactionism, ethnomethodology, and existentialism and phenomenology. The shared concern here is that these theories have little to say about the macro/structural level, with the result that actors are accorded far too much voluntarism. For example, Giddens argues: "Symbolic interactionism has placed most emphasis upon regarding social life as an active accomplishment of purposive, knowledgeable actors . . . the subsequent evolution of this tradition . . . has not successfully developed modes of institutional analysis" (1979:50). Similarly, as we saw in Chapter 10, Alexander believes that according privilege to the micro level is "a theoretical mistake" (1987:295).

Fundamental Differences

The most general differences between the American micro-macro literature (Elias is an exception) and the European work on agency and structure has been discussed in terms

---

[9]Like most other agency-structure theorists, Dietz and Burns downplay or ignore the agent's body (see Shilling and Mellor, 1996; Shilling, 1997b).

of the major terminological differences between agency-structure and micro-macro work. These, however, do not exhaust the differences between the two literatures.

Of great interest in this section is Giddens's (1984:139; see also, Archer, 1995) case "against" the micro-macro dualism. Giddens (1984:141) seems to be opposed to setting micro and macro off in opposition to one another, to fostering "the micro/macro distinction." He is opposed to the "phoney war" between microsociology and macrosociology, as well as the "unhappy division of labour [that] tends to come into being between them" (Giddens, 1984:139). More specifically, Giddens criticizes Collins for his overemphasis on the micro level and the corresponding weakness of his approach at the macro level (a view which is shared by some American theorists [for example, Porpora, 1989; Ritzer, 1985]). However, Giddens's opposition is to the micro-macro dualism; it appears that he would be less opposed to those who treat the relationship as a duality.

One of the central differences between American and European theorists is their images of the actor. What is distinctive about American theory is the much greater influence of behaviorism as well as of exchange theory, derived, in part, from a behavioristic perspective. Thus, American theorists share the interest of (some) Europeans in conscious, creative action, but it is limited by a recognition of the importance of mindless behavior. This tendency to see the actor as behaving mindlessly is being enhanced now by the growing interest in rational choice theory in American sociology. The image here is of an actor more or less automatically choosing the most efficient means to ends.[10] The influence of rational choice theory in the United States promises to drive an even greater wedge between European and American conceptions of action and agency.

At the macro/structure level, Europeans have been inclined to focus on social structure. In cases where there has not been a single-minded focus on it, social structure has not been adequately differentiated from culture. (Indeed, this is the motivation behind Archer's [1988] recent work.) On the other hand, there has been a much greater tendency in the United States to deal with *both* structure and culture in efforts aimed at micro-macro integration. For example, in my own work (see Chapter 10), I differentiated macro objectivity (mainly social structure) and macro subjectivity (mainly culture) and sought to deal with their dialectical interrelationship with micro objectivity and micro subjectivity.

Another difference in the macro/structure issue stems from differences in theoretical influence in the United States and Europe. In the United States, the main influence on thinking on the macro/structure issue has been structural functionalism. The nature of that theory has led American theorists to focus on both large-scale social structures *and* culture. In Europe, the main influence has been structuralism, which has a much more wide-ranging sense of structures, extending all the way from micro structures of the mind to macro structures of society. Culture has been of far less importance to structuralists than to structural functionalists.

Another key difference between the two literatures is the fact that the micro-macro issue is subsumable under the broader issue of levels of analysis (Edel, 1959; Jaffee, 1998; Ritzer, 1981a, 1989b; Wiley, 1988), while the concern for agency and structure is

---

[10]DeVille (1989) sees such an actor as robotlike.

not. We can clearly think of the micro-macro linkage in terms of some sort of vertical hierarchy, with micro-level phenomena on the bottom, macro-level phenomena at the top, and meso-level entities in between. The agency-structure linkage seems to have no clear connection to the levels-of-analysis issue, since both agency and structure can be found at any level of social analysis.

The agency-structure issue is much more firmly embedded in a historical, dynamic framework than is the micro-macro issue (Sztompka, 1991; again Elias is a clear exception, but of course he is European). This characteristic is clearest in the work of Giddens, Habermas, and Archer, but it is manifest throughout the literature on agency and structure. In contrast, theorists who deal with micro-macro issues are more likely to depict them in static, hierarchical, ahistorical terms. Nevertheless, at least some of those who choose to depict the micro-macro relationship rather statically make it clear that they understand the dynamic character of the relationship: "The study of levels of social reality and their interrelationship is inherently a *dynamic* rather than a static approach to the social world. . . . A dynamic and historical orientation to the study of levels of the social world can be seen as integral parts of a more general *dialectical* approach" (Ritzer, 1981a:208; see also Wiley, 1988:260).

Finally, we must mention that morality is a central issue to agency-structure theorists but is largely ignored in the micro-macro literature. This difference may be traced, in part, to differences in theoretical roots and reference groups. Agency-structure theory has much more powerful roots in, and a stronger orientation to, philosophy, including its great concern with moral issues. In contrast, micro-macro theory is largely indigenous to sociology and oriented to the hard sciences as a reference group—areas where moral issues are of far less concern than they are in philosophy. The result is that a sense of moral concern, even moral outrage, is far more palpable in the agency-structure than the micro-macro literature.

SUMMARY

This chapter deals with the largely European literature on the agency-structure linkage. This literature has a number of similarities to the American work on micro-macro integration, but there are also a number of substantial differences between the literatures.

While a large number of contemporary European theorists are dealing with the agency-structure relationship, the bulk of this chapter is devoted to the work of four major examples of this type of theorizing. The first is Giddens's structuration theory. The core of Giddens's theory is his refusal to treat agents and structures apart from one another; they are seen as being mutually constitutive. Next is Archer's theory of the culture-agency relationship. Archer is critical of Giddens's refusal to separate agent and structure for analytic purposes. More generally, she is critical of agency-structure theorists for ignoring culture, and she seeks to rectify this problem by dealing with the agency-culture relationship. We then turn to Bourdieu's theory, which focuses primarily on the relationship between habitus and field. Finally, we analyze Habermas's recent ideas on life-world and system and the colonization of the life-world by the system.

Following a discussion of these specific agency-structure works, we return to a more general discussion of this literature. We begin with a discussion of major differences in this literature, including differing views on the nature of the agent and structure. Another source of difference is the varying theoretical traditions on which these works are based. Some of these works strain in the direction of agency, while others pull in the direction of structure.

The next issue is the similarities between the agency-structure and micro-macro literatures. Both literatures share an interest in integration and are wary of the excesses of micro/agency and macro/structural theories. There are, however, far more differences than similarities between these literatures. There are differences in their images of the actor, the ways in which structure is conceived, the theories from which their ideas are derived, the degree to which they may be subsumed under the idea of levels of analysis, the extent to which they are embedded in a historical, dynamic framework, and the degree to which they are concerned with moral issues.

PART FOUR

FROM MODERN TO POSTMODERN SOCIAL THEORY (AND BEYOND)

12

CONTEMPORARY
THEORIES OF MODERNITY

CLASSICAL THEORISTS ON MODERNITY

THE JUGGERNAUT OF MODERNITY
   Modernity and Its Consequences
   Modernity and Identity
   Modernity and Intimacy

THE RISK SOCIETY
   Creating the Risks
   Coping with the Risks

McDONALDIZATION, GLOBALIZATION/AMERICANIZATION, AND
THE NEW MEANS OF CONSUMPTION
   McDonaldization
   Globalization or Americanization?
   The New Means of Consumption
   Risky or Not?

MODERNITY AND THE HOLOCAUST
   A Product of Modernity
   The Role of Bureaucracy
   The Holocaust and McDonaldization

MODERNITY'S UNFINISHED PROJECT
   Habermas versus Postmodernists

INFORMATIONALISM AND THE NETWORK SOCIETY

There is a debate raging in sociology today between those who continue to see contemporary society as a modern world and those who argue that a substantial change has taken place in recent years and that we have moved into a new, postmodern world. The final two chapters of this book are devoted to these two theoretical positions. In this chapter we discuss the work of contemporary representatives of those who continue to see the world in modern terms, while in the next (and concluding) chapter, we will offer an overview of the ideas of some of the most important postmodern theorists.

CLASSICAL THEORISTS ON MODERNITY

Before discussing the work of contemporary thinkers on modernity, we remind the reader that most of the classical sociologists were engaged in an analysis and critique of modern society. Such analysis is clear, for example, in the work of the four major classical sociological theorists: Marx, Weber, Durkheim, and Simmel. All were working at the point of the emergence and ascendancy of modernity. While all four were well aware of the advantages of modernity, what animated their work most was a critique of the problems posed by the modern world.

For Marx, of course, modernity was defined by the capitalist economy. Marx recognized the advances brought about by the transition from earlier societies to capitalism. However, in his work he restricted himself largely to a critique of that economic system and its deformities (alienation, exploitation, and so on).

To Weber, the most defining problem of the modern world was the expansion of formal rationality at the expense of the other types of rationality and the resulting emergence of the iron cage of rationality. People were being increasingly imprisoned in this iron cage and, as a result, were progressively unable to express some of their most human characteristics. Of course, Weber recognized the advantages of the advance of rationalization—for example, the strengths of the bureaucracy over earlier organizational forms—but he was most concerned with the problems posed by rationalization.

In Durkheim's view, modernity was defined by its organic solidarity and the weakening of the collective conscience. While organic solidarity brought with it greater freedom and more productivity, it also posed a series of unique problems. For example, with such a weakening of the common morality, people tended to find themselves adrift meaninglessly in the modern world. In other words, they found themselves to be suffering from anomie.

The fourth of the classical theorists, Georg Simmel, will receive a bit more detailed treatment here, in large part because he has recently been described as *both* a modernist (Frisby, 1992) and as a postmodernist (Weinstein and Weinstein, 1993; Jaworski, 1997). Since he fits to some degree in both categories, Simmel represents an important bridge between this chapter and the next. We will deal with the case for Simmel as a modernist here; in the next chapter we will discuss the contention that he is a postmodernist.

Frisby accepts the point of view that "Simmel is the first sociologist of modernity" (1992:59). Simmel is seen as investigating modernity primarily in two major interrelated sites—the city and the money economy. The city is where modernity is concentrated or intensified, whereas the money economy involves the diffusion of modernity, its extension (Frisby, 1992:69).

Poggi (1993) picks up the theme of modernity as it relates to money, especially in Simmel's *Philosophy of Money*. As Poggi sees it, three views of modernity are expressed in that work. The first is that modernization brings with it a series of advantages to human beings, especially the fact that they are able to express various potentialities that are unexpressed, concealed, and repressed in premodern society. In this sense, Simmel sees modernity "as an 'epiphany,' that is, as the express manifestation of powers intrinsic to the human species, but previously unrevealed" (Poggi, 1993:165). Second, Simmel deals with the powerful effect of money on modern society. Finally, there is Simmel's concentration on the adverse consequences of money for modernity, especially alienation. The issue of alienation brings us back to the central issue in Simmel's sociological theory in general, as well as in his sociology of modernity: the "tragedy of culture," the growing gap between objective and subjective culture, or as Simmel put it,

" 'the atrophy of individual culture and the hypertrophy of objective culture' " (cited in Frisby, 1992:69).

In Frisby's view, Simmel concentrates on the "experience" of modernity. The key elements of that experience—time, space, and contingent causality—are central aspects of at least some of the contemporary theories of modernity to be discussed in this chapter:

> The experience of modernity is viewed by Simmel as discontinuous of *time* as transitory, in which both the fleeting moment and the sense of presentness converge; *space* as the dialectic of distance and proximity . . . and *causality* as contingent, arbitrary and fortuitous.
>
> (Frisby, 1992:163–164)

While it is certainly possible to view Simmel as a postmodernist, and as we will see in the next chapter, he does seem to have more in common with postmodernists than do the other classical social theorists, the fact remains that it is at least equally appropriate to see him as a modernist. Almost certainly, the foci of much of his attention—especially the city and the money economy—are at the heart of modernity. Thus, even in the case of Simmel, and certainly in the cases of Marx, Weber, and Durkheim, it is best to think of these theorists as doing sociologies of modernity.

By 1920 all four of these classical sociological theorists were dead. As we move into the twenty-first century, it is obvious that the world is a very different place than it was in 1920. While there is great disagreement over when the postmodern age began (assuming for the moment that it did), no one puts that date before 1920. The issue is whether the changes in the world since that time are modest and continuous with those associated with modernity, or are so dramatic and discontinuous that the contemporary world is better described by a new term—postmodern. That issue informs the discussion in this chapter and the next.

In this chapter we will examine the thoughts of several contemporary theorists (there are many others [for example, Lefebvre, 1962/1995; Touraine, 1995; P. Wagner, 1994; Wood, 1997] whose work we will not have space to deal with) who in various ways and to varying degrees see the contemporary world as still best described as modern.

THE JUGGERNAUT OF MODERNITY

In an effort not only to be consistent with his structuration theory (see Chapter 11), but also to create an image to rival those of classical thinkers like Weber and his iron cage, Anthony Giddens (1990; see Mestrovic, 1998, for a bitter critique of Giddens's theory of modernity) has described the modern world (with its origins in seventeenth-century Europe) as a "juggernaut." More specifically, he is using this term to describe an advanced stage of modernity—radical, high, or late modernity. In so doing, Giddens is arguing against those who have contended that we have entered a postmodern age, although he holds out the possibility of some type of postmodernism in the future. However, while we still live in a modern age, in Giddens's view today's world is very different from the world of the classical sociological theorists.

Here is the way Giddens describes the juggernaut of modernity:

> a runaway engine of enormous power which, collectively as human beings, we can drive to some extent but which also threatens to rush out of our control and which could rend

itself asunder. The juggernaut crushes those who resist it, and while it sometimes seems to have a steady path, there are times when it veers away erratically in directions we cannot foresee. The ride is by no means wholly unpleasant or unrewarding; it can often be exhilarating and charged with hopeful anticipation. But, so long as the institutions of modernity endure, we shall never be able to control completely either the path or the pace of the journey. In turn, we shall never be able to feel entirely secure, because the terrain across which it runs is fraught with risks of high consequence.

(Giddens, 1990:139)

Modernity in the form of a juggernaut is extremely dynamic, it is a " 'runaway world' " with great increases in the pace, scope, and profoundness of change over prior systems (Giddens, 1991:16). Giddens is quick to add that this juggernaut does not follow a single path. Furthermore, it is not of one piece, but rather is made up of a number of conflicting and contradictory parts. Thus, Giddens is telling us that he is not offering us an old-fashioned grand theory, or at least not a simple, unidirectional grand narrative.

The idea of a juggernaut fits nicely with structuration theory, especially with the importance in that theory of time and space. The image of a juggernaut is of something that is moving along *through time* and *over physical space.* However, this image does *not* fit well with Giddens's emphasis on the power of the agent; the image of a juggernaut seems to accord this modern mechanism far more power than the agents who steer it (Mestrovic, 1998:155). This problem is consistent with the more general criticism that there is a disjunction between the emphasis on agency in Giddens's purely theoretical work and the substantive historical analyses which "point to the dominance of system tendencies against our ability to change the world" (Craib, 1992:149).

Modernity and Its Consequences

Giddens defines modernity in terms of four basic institutions. The first is *capitalism,* characterized, familiarly, by commodity production, private ownership of capital, propertyless wage labor, and a class system derived from these characteristics. The second is *industrialism,* which involves the use of inanimate power sources and machinery to produce goods. Industrialism is not restricted to the workplace, and it affects an array of other settings, such as "transportation, communication and domestic life" (Giddens, 1990:56). While Giddens's first two characteristics of modernity are hardly novel, the third—*surveillance capacities*—is, although it owes a deep debt to the work of Michel Foucault (see Chapter 13). As Giddens defines it, "Surveillance refers to the supervision of the activities of subject populations [mainly, but not exclusively] in the political sphere" (1990:58). The final institutional dimension of modernity is military power, or the *control of the means of violence,* including the industrialization of war. In addition, it should be noted that in his analysis of modernity, at least at the macro level, Giddens focuses on the *nation-state* (rather than the more conventional sociological focus on society), which he sees as radically different from the type of community characteristic of premodern society.

Modernity is given dynamism by three essential aspects of Giddens's structuration theory: distanciation, disembedding, and reflexivity. The first is *time and space separation, or distanciation* (although this process of increasing separation, like all aspects of Giddens's work, is not unilinear; it is dialectical). In premodern societies, time was always linked with space, and the measurement of time was imprecise. With modernization, time was standardized and the close linkage between time and space was broken. In this sense, both time and space were "emptied" of content; no particular time or space was privileged; they became pure forms. In premodern societies, space was defined largely by physical presence and therefore by localized spaces. With the coming of modernity, space is progressively torn from place. Relationships with those who are physically absent and increasingly distant become more and more likely. To Giddens, place becomes increasingly "phantasmagoric"; that is, "locales are thoroughly penetrated by and shaped in terms of social influences quite distant from them . . . the 'visible form' of the locale conceals the distanciated relations which determine its nature" (Giddens, 1990:19).

Time and space distanciation is important to modernity for several reasons. First, it makes possible the growth of rationalized organizations like bureaucracies and the nation-state, with their inherent dynamism (in comparison to premodern forms) and their ability to link local and global domains. Second, the modern world is positioned within a radical sense of world history, and it is able to draw upon that history to shape the present. Third, such distanciation is a major prerequisite for Giddens's second source of dynamism in modernity—disembedding.

As Giddens defines it, *disembedding* involves "the 'lifting out' of social relations from local contexts of interaction and their restructuring across indefinite spans of time-space" (1990:21). There are two types of disembedding mechanisms that play a key role in modern societies; both of them can be included under the heading of abstract systems. The first is symbolic tokens, the best known of which is money. Money allows for time-space distanciation—we are able to engage in transactions with others who are widely separated from us by time and/or space. The second is expert systems, defined as "systems of technical accomplishment or professional expertise that organise large areas of the material and social environments in which we live today" (Giddens, 1990:27). The most obvious expert systems involve professionals like lawyers and physicians, but everyday phenomena like our cars and homes are created and affected by expert systems. Expert systems provide guarantees (but not without risks) of performance across time and space.

Trust is very important in modern societies dominated by abstract systems and with great time-space distanciation. The need for trust is related to this distanciation: "We have no need to trust someone who is constantly in view and whose activities can be directly monitored" (Giddens, 1991:19). Trust becomes necessary when, as a result of increasing distanciation in terms of either time or place, we no longer have full information about social phenomena (Craib, 1992:99). Trust is defined "as confidence in the reliability of a person or systems, regarding a given set of outcomes or events, where that confidence expresses a faith in the probity or love of another, or in the correctness of abstract principles (technical knowledge)" (Giddens, 1990:34). Trust is of great importance not only in modern society in general, but also to the symbolic tokens and expert systems that serve to disembed life in the modern world. For example, in order for the money economy and the legal system to work, people must have trust in them.

The third dynamic characteristic of modernity is its *reflexivity*. While reflexivity is a fundamental feature of Giddens's structuration theory (as well as of human existence, in his view), it takes on special meaning in modernity, where "social practices are constantly examined and reformed in the light of incoming information about those very practices, thus constitutively altering their character" (Giddens, 1990:38). Everything is open to reflection in the modern world, including reflection itself, leaving us with a pervasive sense of uncertainty. Furthermore, the problem of the double hermeneutic (see Chapter 11) recurs here because the reflection of experts on the social world tends to alter that world.

The disembedded character of modern life raises a number of distinctive issues. One is the need for trust in abstract systems in general, and expert systems in particular. In one of his more questionable metaphors, Giddens sees children as being "inoculated" with a "dosage" of trust during childhood socialization. This aspect of socialization serves to provide people with a "protective cocoon," which, as they mature into adulthood, helps to give them a measure of ontological security and trust. This trust tends to be buttressed by the series of routines that we encounter on a day-to-day basis. However, there are new and dangerous risks associated with modernity that always threaten our trust and threaten to lead to pervasive ontological *in*security. As Giddens sees it, while the disembedding mechanisms have provided us with security in various areas, they have also created a distinctive "risk profile." Risk is global in intensity (nuclear war can kill us all) and in the expansion of contingent events that affect large numbers of people around the world (for example, changes in the worldwide division of labor). Then there are risks traceable to our efforts to manage our material environment. Risks also stem from the creation of institutional risk environments such as global investment markets. People are increasingly aware of risks and religion and customs are increasingly less important as ways of believing that those risks can be transformed into certainties. A wide range of publics are now likely to know of the risks we face. Finally, there is a painful awareness that expert systems are limited in their ability to deal with these risks. It is these risks that give modernity the feeling of a runaway juggernaut and fill us with ontological insecurity.

What has happened? Why are we suffering the negative consequences of being aboard the juggernaut of modernity? Giddens suggests several reasons. The first is *design faults* in the modern world; those who designed elements of the modern world made mistakes. The second is *operator failure;* the problem is traceable not to the designers, but to those who run the modern world. Giddens, however, gives prime importance to two other factors—*unintended consequences* and *reflexivity of social knowledge*. That is, the consequences of actions for a system can never be forecast fully, and new knowledge is continually sending systems off in new directions. For all these reasons, we cannot completely control the juggernaut, the modern world.

However, rather than giving up, Giddens suggests the seemingly paradoxical course of *utopian realism*. That is, he seeks a balance between utopian ideals and the realities of life in the modern world. He also accords importance to the role that social movements can play in dealing with some of the risks of the modern world and pointing us toward a society in which those risks are ameliorated.

Giddens's (1994) effort to find a compromise political position is manifest in the title of one of his later books, *Beyond Left and Right: The Future of Radical Politics.* With extant political positions moribund, Giddens proposes a reconstituted "radical politics" which is based on utopian realism and oriented toward addressing the problems of poverty, environmental degradation, arbitrary power and force, and violence in social life. Giddens's political position involves an acceptance of at least some aspects of capitalism (e.g. markets) and rejection of many aspects of socialism (e.g. a revolutionary subject). Thus, Giddens has chosen to walk a very narrow and difficult political tightrope.

Given his views on modernity, where does Giddens stand on postmodernity? For one thing, he rejects most, if not all, of the tenets we usually associate with postmodernism. For example, of the idea that systematic knowledge is impossible, Giddens says that such a view would lead us "to repudiate intellectual activity altogether" (1990:47). However, while he sees us as living in an era of high modernity, Giddens believes it is possible now to gain a glimpse of postmodernity. Such a world would, in his view, be characterized by a postscarcity system, increasingly multilayered democratization, demilitarization, and the humanization of technology. However, there are clearly no guarantees that the world will move in the direction of some, to say nothing of all, of these postmodern characteristics. Yet, reflexively, Giddens believes that in writing about such eventualities he (and others) can play a role in helping them come to pass.

Modernity and Identity

While *The Consequences of Modernity* is a largely macro-oriented work, *Modernity and Self-Identity* (Giddens, 1991) focuses more on the micro aspects of late modernity, especially the self. Although Giddens certainly sees the self as dialectically related to the institutions of modern society, most of his attention here is devoted to the micro end of the continuum. We, too, will focus on the micro issues, but we should not lose sight of the larger dialectic:

> Transformations in self-identity and globalisation . . . are the two poles of the dialectic of the local and the global in conditions of high modernity. Changes in intimate aspects of personal life . . . are directly tied to the establishment of social connections of very wide scope . . . for the first time in human history, 'self' and 'society' are interrelated in a global milieu.
>
> (Giddens, 1991:32)

As we have seen, Giddens defines the modern world as reflexive, and he argues that the "reflexivity of modernity extends into the core of the self . . . the self becomes a *reflexive project*" (1991:32). That is, the self comes to be something to be reflected upon, altered, even molded. Not only does the individual become responsible for the creation and maintenance of the self, but this responsibility is continuous and all-pervasive. The self is a product both of self-exploration and of the development of intimate social relationships. In the modern world, even the body gets "drawn into the reflexive organisation of social life" (Giddens, 1991:98). We are responsible for the design not only of our selves, but also (and relatedly) of our bodies. Central to the reflexive creation and maintenance of the self is the appearance of the body and its appropriate demeanor in a variety of settings and locales. The body is also subject to a variety of "regimes" (for example, diet and exercise books) that not only help individuals mold their bodies, but also contribute to self-reflexivity as well as to the reflexivity of modernity in general. The result, overall, is an obsession with our bodies and our selves within the modern world.

The modern world brings with it the *"sequestration of experience,"* or the "connected processes of concealment which set apart the routines of ordinary life from the following phenomena: madness; criminality; sickness and death; sexuality; and nature" (Giddens, 1991:149, 156). Sequestration occurs as a result of the growing role of abstract systems in everyday life. This sequestration brings us greater ontological security, but it is at the cost of the "exclusion of social life from fundamental existential issues which raise central moral dilemmas for human beings" (Giddens, 1991:156).

While modernity is a double-edged sword, bringing both positive and negative developments, Giddens perceives an underlying "looming threat of *personal meaninglessness"* (1991:201). All sorts of meaningful things have been sequestered from daily life; they have been repressed. However, dialectically, increasing self-reflexivity leads to the increasing likelihood of the return of that which has been repressed. Giddens sees us moving into a world in which "on a collective level and in day-to-day life moral/ existential questions thrust themselves back to centre-stage" (1991:208). The world beyond modernity, for Giddens, is a world characterized by "remoralization." Those key moral and existential issues that have been sequestered will come to occupy center stage in a society that Giddens sees as being foreshadowed, and anticipated, in the self-reflexivity of the late modern age.

Modernity and Intimacy

Giddens picks up many of these themes in *The Transformation of Intimacy* (1992). In this work Giddens focuses on ongoing transformations of intimacy that show movement toward another important concept in Giddens's thinking about the modern world—the *pure relationship,* or "a situation where a social relation is entered into for its own sake, for what can be derived by each person from a sustained association with another; and which is continued only so far as it is thought by both parties to deliver enough satisfactions for each individual to stay within it" (Giddens, 1992:58). In the case of intimacy, a pure relationship is characterized by emotional communication with self and other in a context of sexual and emotional equality. The democratization of intimate relationships can lead to the democratization not only of interpersonal relations in general, but of the macro-institutional order as well. The changing nature of intimate relations, in which women ("the emotional revolutionaries of modernity" [Giddens, 1992:130]) have taken the lead and men have been "laggards," has revolutionary implications for society as a whole.

In the modern world intimacy and sexuality (and, as we have seen, much else) have been sequestered. However, while this sequestration was liberating in various senses from intimacy in traditional societies, it is also a form of repression. The reflexive effort to create purer intimate relationships must be carried out in a context separated from larger moral and ethical issues. However, this modern arrangement comes under pressure as people, especially women, attempt reflexive construction of themselves and others. Thus, Giddens is arguing not for sexual liberation or pluralism, but rather for a larger ethical and moral change, a change that he sees already well under way in intimate relationships:

> We have no need to wait around for a sociopolitical revolution to further programmes of emancipation, nor would such a revolution help very much. Revolutionary processes are already well under way in the infrastructure of personal life. The transformation of intimacy presses for psychic as well as social change and such change, going 'from the bottom up,' could potentially ramify through other, more public, institutions.
>
> Sexual emancipation, I think, can be the medium of a wide-ranging emotional reorganisation of social life.
>
> (Giddens, 1992:181–182)

THE RISK SOCIETY

We have already touched on the issue of risk in Giddens's work on modernity. As Giddens says,

> Modernity is a risk culture. I do not mean by this that social life is inherently more risky than it used to be; for most people that is not the case. Rather, the concept of risk becomes fundamental to the way both lay actors and technical specialists organise the social world. Modernity reduces the overall riskiness of certain areas and modes of life, yet at the same time introduces new risk parameters largely or completely unknown to previous eras.
>
> (Giddens, 1991:3–4)

Thus, Giddens (1991:28) describes as "quite accurate" the thesis of the work to be discussed in this section, Ulrich Beck's *Risk Society: Toward a New Modernity* (1992; Bronner, 1995).

In terms of this discussion, the subtitle of Beck's work is of great importance, since it indicates that he, like Giddens, rejects the notion that we have moved into a postmodern age. Rather, in Beck's view we continue to exist in the modern world, albeit in a new form of modernity. The prior, "classical" stage of modernity was associated with industrial society, while the emerging new modernity and its technologies are associated with the risk society (Clark, 1997). While we do not yet live in a risk society, we no longer live only in an industrial society; that is, the contemporary world has elements of both. In fact, the risk society can be seen as a type of industrial society, since many of those risks are traceable to industry. Beck offers the following overview of his perspective:

> *Just as modernization dissolved the structure of feudal society in the nineteenth century and produced the industrial society, modernization today is dissolving industrial society and another modernity is coming into being. . . . The thesis of this book is: we are witnessing not the end but the* beginning *of modernity—that is, of a modernity* beyond *its classical industrial design.*
>
> (Beck, 1992:10)

What, then, is this new modernity? And what is the risk society that accompanies it?

Beck labels the new, or better yet newly emerging, form *reflexive modernity*. A process of individualization has taken place in the West. That is, agents are becoming

ANTHONY GIDDENS: A Biographical Sketch

Anthony Giddens is Great Britain's most important contemporary social theorist and one of a handful of the world's most influential theorists. Giddens was born on January 18, 1938 (Clark, Modgil, and Modgil, 1990). He studied at the University of Hull, the London School of Economics, and the University of London. Giddens was appointed Lecturer at the University of Leicester in 1961. His early work was empirical and focused on the issue of suicide. By 1969 he had moved to the position of Lecturer in Sociology at the prestigious Cambridge University, as well as Fellow of King's College. He engaged in cross-cultural work that led to the first of his books to achieve international fame, *The Class Structure of Advanced Societies* (1975). Over the next decade, or so, Giddens published a number of important theoretical works. In those works he began a step-by-step process of building his own theoretical perspective, which has come to be known as structuration theory. The years of work culminated in 1984 with the appearance of a book, *The Constitution of Society: Outline of the Theory of Structuration,* which constitutes the most important single statement on Giddens's theoretical perspective. In 1985 Giddens was appointed Professor of Sociology at the University of Cambridge.

Giddens has been a force in sociological theory for well over two decades. In addition, he has played a profound role in shaping contemporary British sociology. For one thing, he has served as a consulting editor for two publishing companies—Macmillan and Hutchinson. A large number of books have been produced under his editorship. More important, he was a cofounder of Polity Press, a publisher that has been both extremely active and influential, especially in sociological theory. Giddens has also published an American-style textbook, *Sociology* (1987), that has been a worldwide success.

As a theorist, Giddens has been highly influential in the United States, as well as many other parts of the world. Interestingly, his work has often been less well received in his home country of Great Britain than in many other parts of the world. This lack of acceptance at home may be attributable, in part, to the fact that Giddens has succeeded in winning the worldwide theoretical following that many other British social theorists sought and failed to achieve. As Craib says, "Giddens has perhaps realized the fantasies of many of us who committed ourselves to sociology during the period of intense and exciting debate out of which structuration theory developed" (1992:12).

Giddens's career took a series of interesting turns in the 1990s (Bryant and Jary, still forthcoming). Several years of therapy led to a greater interest in personal life and books such as *Modernity and Self-Identity* (1991) and *The Transformation of Intimacy* (1992). Therapy also gave him the confidence to take on a more public role and to become an advisor to British Prime Minister Tony Blair. In 1997 he became Director of the highly prestigious London School of Economics (LSE). He has moved to strengthen the scholarly reputation of LSE as well as to increase its voice in public discourse in Great Britain and around the world. There is some feeling that all this has had an adverse effect on Giddens's scholarly work (his books of the 1990s lacked the depth and sophistication of his earlier works), but for the moment he is clearly focused on being a force in public life.

increasingly free of structural constraints and are, as a result, better able to reflexively create not only themselves, but also the societies in which they live. For example, instead of being determined by their class situations, people operate more or less on their own. Left to their own devices, people have been forced to be more reflexive. Beck makes the case about the importance of reflexivity in the example of social relationships in such a world: "The newly formed social relationships and social networks now have to be individually chosen; social ties, too, are becoming *reflexive,* so that they have to be established, maintained, and constantly renewed by individuals" (1992:97).

Beck sees a break within modernity and a transition from classical industrial society to the risk society, which, while different from its predecessor, continues to have many of the characteristics of industrial society. The central issue in classical modernity was wealth and how it could be distributed more evenly. In advanced modernity the central issue is risk and how it can be prevented, minimized, or channeled. In classical modernity the ideal was equality, while in advanced modernity it is safety. In classical modernity people achieved solidarity in the search for the positive goal of equality, but in advanced modernity the attempt to achieve that solidarity is found in the search for the largely negative and defensive goal of being spared from dangers.

Creating the Risks

The risks are, to a large degree, being produced by the sources of wealth in modern society. Specifically, industry and its side effects are producing a wide range of hazardous, even deadly, consequences for society and, as a result of globalization (Featherstone, 1990; Robertson, 1992), the world as a whole. Using the concepts of time and space, Beck makes the point that these modern risks are not restricted to place (a nuclear accident in one geographic locale could affect many other nations) or time (a nuclear accident could have genetic effects that might affect future generations).

While social class is central in industrial society and risk is fundamental to the risk society, risk and class are not unrelated. Says Beck,

> The history of risk distribution shows that, like wealth, risks adhere to the class pattern, only inversely: wealth accumulates at the top, risks at the bottom. To that extent, risks seem to *strengthen,* not to abolish, class society. Poverty attracts an unfortunate abundance of risks. By contrast, the wealthy (in income, power, or education) can *purchase* safety and freedom from risk.
>
> (Beck, 1992:35)

What is true for social classes is also true for nations. That is, to the degree that it is possible, risks are centered in poor nations, while the rich nations are able to push many risks as far away as possible. Further, the rich nations profit from the risks they produce by, for example, producing and selling technologies that help prevent risks from occurring or deal with their adverse effects once they do occur.

However, neither wealthy individuals, nor the nations that produce risks, are safe from risks. In this context, Beck discusses what he calls the "boomerang effect," whereby the side effects of risk "strike back even at the centers of their production. The agents of modernization themselves are emphatically caught in the maelstrom of hazards that they unleash and profit from" (1992:37).

Coping with the Risks

While advanced modernization produces the risks, it also produces the reflexivity that allows it to question itself and the risks it produces. In fact, it is often the people themselves, the victims of the risks, who begin to reflect on those risks. They begin to observe and to collect data on the risks and their consequences for people. They become experts who come to question advanced modernity and its dangers. They do this, in part, because they can no longer rely on scientists to do this for them. Indeed, Beck is very hard on scientists for their role in the creation and maintenance of the risk society: "Science has *become the protector of a global contamination of people and nature.* In that respect, it is no exaggeration to say that in the way they deal with risks in many areas, the sciences *have squandered until further notice their historic reputation for rationality"* (1992:70).

While in classical industrial society nature and society were separated, in advanced industrial society nature and society are deeply intertwined. That is, changes in society often affect the natural environment, and those changes, in turn, affect society. Thus, according to Beck, today "nature *is* society and society is also *'nature'"* (1992:80). Thus nature has been politicized, with the result that natural scientists, like social scientists, have had their work politicized.

The traditional domain of politics, the government, is losing power because the major risks are emanating from what Beck calls "sub politics," for example, large companies, scientific laboratories, and the like. It is in the subpolitical system that "the structures of a new society are being implemented with regard to the ultimate goals of progress in knowledge, outside the parliamentary system, not in opposition to it, but simply ignoring it" (Beck, 1992:223). This is part of what he calls the "unbinding of politics," where politics is no longer left to the central government, but is increasingly becoming the province of various subgroups, as well as of individuals. These subgroups and individuals can be more reflexive and self-critical than a central government can, and they have the capability to reflect upon, to better deal with, the array of risks associated with advanced modernity. Thus, dialectically, advanced modernity has generated both unprecedented risks and unprecedented efforts to deal with those risks (Beck, 1996).

McDONALDIZATION, GLOBALIZATION/AMERICANIZATION, AND THE NEW MEANS OF CONSUMPTION

In my own work, I have addressed the issue of modernity in three ways—the McDonaldization of society, the relationship between McDonaldization and globalization/Americanization, and the development of the new means of consumption.

McDonaldization

The theoretical impetus for *The McDonaldization of Society* (Ritzer, 1993, 1996, 1998)[1] is Weber's work on rationality. With McDonaldization the focus is on the fact that

---

[1]For some of the debate surrounding the McDonaldization thesis, see Alfino, Caputo, and Wynyard, 1998; Smart, 1999.

the fast-food restaurant represents a contemporary paradigm of formal rationality. Thus, one could argue that in Weber's day the model of a formally rational system was a bureaucracy, while today the fast-food restaurant represents an even better paradigm of this type of rationality. The bureaucracy is still with us, but the fast-food restaurant better exemplifies this type of rationality. This implies that not only is formal rationality still with us, but so is the modern world of which this type of rationality is a key component.

There are four dimensions of formal rationality—efficiency, predictability, an emphasis on quantity rather than quality, and control through the substitution of nonhuman for human technologies—and this form of rationality tends to bring with it the irrationality of rationality. Efficiency means the search for the best means to the end; in the fast-food restaurant, the drive-through window is a good example of heightening the efficiency of obtaining a meal. Predictability means a world of no surprises; the Big Mac in Los Angeles is indistinguishable from the one in New York; similarly, the one we consume tomorrow or next year will be just like the one we eat today. Rational systems tend to emphasize quantity, usually large quantities, rather than quality. The Big Mac is a good example of this emphasis on quantity rather than quality. Instead of the human qualities of a chef, fast-food restaurants rely on nonhuman technologies like unskilled cooks following detailed directions and assembly-line methods applied to the cooking and serving of food. Finally, such a formally rational system brings with it various irrationalities, most notably the demystification and dehumanization of the dining experience.

Thus, the fast-food restaurant brings new heights to formal rationality in general, as well as to each of its specific dimensions. Furthermore, innumerable other businesses and other sectors of the social world are emulating some or all of the innovations put in place by the fast-food restaurant. If we equate formal rationality with modernity, then the success and spread of the fast-food restaurant, as well as the degree to which it is serving as a model for much of the rest of society, indicate that we continue to live in a modern world. Buttressing this argument is the fact that the fast-food restaurant is Fordist in various ways, most notably in the degree to which it utilizes assembly-line principles and technologies. Similarly, it is built on industrial principles, thereby standing in contradiction to the view that we have moved into a postindustrial society (Hage and Powers, 1992). While there may be other changes in the economy which support the idea of a postindustrial society, the fast-food restaurant and the many other elements of the economy that are modeled after it do not. I have also examined credit cards from the point of view of the rationalization thesis (Ritzer, 1995). What credit cards have done is to McDonaldize the receipt and expenditure of credit. Instead of fast food, what the modern bank is doing is dispensing fast money.

Each of the dimensions of McDonaldization apply to the credit card. The whole process of obtaining a loan has been made more efficient. Instead of a long and cumbersome application process, there are just a few simple questions to answer. And if that is not efficient enough, many people are frequently offered preapproved cards. Predictability is best exemplified by the fact that the credit card serves to make consumption more predictable; one can even consume without any cash on hand. The emphasis for most people is the number of credit cards they can acquire and the collective credit limits of those cards, with little regard to the adverse effect a large amount of debt has on the quality of their lives. Decisions about whether or not to issue a new card or to raise a credit limit are increasingly left to ever more sophisticated computer programs with little or no input from humans on a case-by-case basis. Ultimately, the highly rationalized credit card business has a series of irrationalities, including the dehumanization associated with dealing with nonhuman technologies and robotlike bank employees who engage in tightly scripted interaction with customers.

Thus, the credit card, like the fast-food restaurant, can be seen as part of our McDonaldized, formally rationalized, and therefore ultimately modern society. The two examples discussed here—the fast-food restaurant, and the credit card—indicate advancement in rationality, and therefore modernization, over their predecessors—the local diner and a personal loan. Is such advancement still in the realm of modernity, or do we need a new concept, like postmodernism, to describe it?

What we can say, with some confidence, is that the two cases discussed here indicate that rationality and therefore modernity are alive and well in the contemporary world. Even if everything else falls under the heading of postmodernism (which is highly doubtful), the continuation of at least some modern elements minimally calls into question the most extreme claims of the postmodernists. More extremely, if many other aspects of today's world are also found to be better described as modern, then the claims that we have entered a postmodern world may be either premature or in error.

Globalization or Americanization?

One of the issues raised by McDonaldization is whether it is better described as a process of globalization or Americanization (Ritzer, 1998:71–94).

Americanization The issue of Americanization is not commonly thought of as part of social theory, but even a classical theorist like Georg Simmel (1991:27) was concerned with the growing "Americanism" of his day. Among other things, for Simmel this stood for the "enormous desire for happiness of modern man" and, more negatively, for "modern 'covetousness.'" Over the years a number of works, generally outside of social theory, have addressed the issue of Americanization (Duhamel, 1931; Duignan and Gann, 1992; Emmison, 1997; Kuisel, 1993; McCreary, 1964; Servan-Schreiber, 1968; Williams, 1962). More generally, modernization theory (Archer, 1990), which was a popular social theory for a time, was related to the idea of Americanization. Modernization theorists tended to laud Western, especially American, developments and to urge the rest of the world to move in that direction.

At the most general level, Americanization is simply a term to describe the impact of America and its norms, values, structures, and institutions on the rest of the world. However, most of the literature on Americanization has been produced by non-Americans with the result that it has usually had a critical orientation. Thus, McCreary (1964:1) describes Americanization as "a catchall for anything of which the speaker morally and emotionally disapproves."

McDonald's and most of its McDonaldized derivatives are products of American society that have been aggressively exported to the rest of the world. For example, today McDonald's opens new outlets overseas at a far greater rate than it does in the United

States and already about half of its profits come from outside the United States. As an American export, McDonald's is radically altering what and how the rest of the world eats. Furthermore, while it is being embraced by people around the world, it is simultaneously condemned by intellectuals and other public leaders. Thus, as an American export, as well as one that is often condemned, McDonald's (and other McDonaldized systems) clearly reflect the process of Americanization.

Globalization   While Americanization has been of little direct concern to social theorists, one of the hot topics in contemporary social theory is globalization. In the forefront on this issue has been Roland Robertson (1992:61, 64) who has argued that social theorists should adopt "a specifically global point of view" and "treat the global condition as such." More specific, and telling, is Robertson's (1992:60; see also, Featherstone, 1990:1) argument that "there is a general autonomy and 'logic' to the globalization process, which operates in *relative* independence of strictly societal and other conventionally studied sociocultural processes."

It is the focus on largely autonomous global processes that distinguishes globalization theory. Appadurai (1990), for example, has identified a number of "third cultures" that are at least partially autonomous, transcend national boundaries, and exist globally. For example, the *finanscape* involves the "movement of megamonies through national turnstiles at blinding speed" (Appadurai, 1990:298). International trade in stocks, bonds, and currencies is part of the finanscape. Then there is the *ethnoscape* involving the movement of large numbers of people through tourism. International chains of hotels and Disney with its theme parks not only in the United States but in Japan and France would be involved in the ethnoscape. One other example is the *technoscape* employing technologies that girdle the world. The Internet is a perfect example of an element of the technoscape.

The point is that all these "third cultures" transcend any specific nation state, including the United States. As a result, globalization theory stands in opposition to any theory that focuses on a specific nation, especially Americanization theory and its focus on the United States.

Is McDonaldization better thought of as an example of Americanization or of globalization? McDonald's itself was created in the United States and virtually all the major players in not only the fast-food industry but other McDonaldized sectors have their roots in the United States. McDonald's and many other McDonaldized businesses have become international in reach, but they still retain their American base and their American roots. Some day all these may lose their American base and become largely autonomous like the third cultures described above, but at the moment they are still far better described by Americanization than globalization. However, even though it does not relate well to McDonaldization, globalization theory represents a powerful perspective that is likely to attract increasing attention in social theory.

The New Means of Consumption

I have most recently addressed the rise of the "new means of consumption" in the United States in the more than half century since the end of World War II (Ritzer, 1999). McDonald's (and more generally the fast-food industry) is one of the new means of consumption, but there are many others, such as shopping malls, megamalls (e.g., Mall of America), cybermalls, superstores (e.g., Toys "R" Us), discounters (Wal-Mart), cruise lines, Las Vegas casino-hotels, Disney-type theme parks, and so on.

The concept of the new means of consumption is derived from the work of Karl Marx. However, like most other modern theorists, Marx focused mainly on production; that is, he had a productivist bias. Given the realities that he was dealing with—the early days of the industrial revolution and capitalism—a focus on production in general, and the means of production in particular, was sensible. However, in recent years, to the degree that production and consumption can be clearly separated, production has grown increasingly less important (for example, fewer workers are involved in goods production), especially in the United States, while consumption has grown in importance (more people work in consumption-related service jobs and many more spend a large portion of their leisure time consuming). In such a society, it makes sense to shift our focus from the means of production to the means of consumption.

Strikingly, Marx had a great deal to say about consumption, especially in his well-known work on commodities. Much less well known and visible is the fact that Marx (following Adam Smith, as he often did) employed the concept "means of consumption" that is one of the centerpieces of my recent book.

Marx defined the *means of production* as "commodities that possess a form in which they . . . enter productive consumption" (1884/1991:471). The *means of consumption* he defined as "commodities that possess a form in which they enter individual consumption of the capitalist and working class" (1884/1991:471). Under this heading, Marx differentiates between subsistence and luxury consumption (Smith made a similar distinction). On the one hand are the "necessary means of consumption," or those "that enter the consumption of the working class" (Marx, 1884/1991:479). On the other are the "luxury means of consumption, which enter the consumption only of the capitalist class, i.e., can be exchanged only for the expenditure of surplus-value, which does not accrue to the workers" (Marx, 1884/1991:479). Thus, basic foodstuffs would be subsistence means of consumption while elegant automobiles (say, a Rolls Royce) would be luxury means of consumption.

While Marx is to be lauded for his early interest in commodities, consumption, and the means of consumption, there is a logical problem in the way he uses the last concept, especially in comparison to the paired notion of means of production. The means of production occupy an intermediate position between workers and products; they are the means that make possible both the production of commodities and the control and exploitation of the workers. In contrast, in the way Marx uses the idea, the means of consumption are not means but rather the end products in his model of consumption; they are those things (either subsistence or luxury) that are consumed. In other words, there is *no* distinction in Marx's work between consumer goods and what we term here the means of consumption (for example, shopping malls and cruise ships). To put it another way, in his work there is no parallel in the realm of consumption to the mediating and expediting role played by the means of production.

Thus, while Marx used the term *means of consumption*, he used it in a logically inappropriate way and in a way that is different from the way it is employed here. For one thing, the means of consumption play the same mediating role in consumption that the means of production play in Marx's theory of production. That is, just as the means of production are those entities that make it possible for the proletariat to produce commodities and to be controlled and exploited as workers, the means of consumption are defined as those things that make it possible for people to acquire goods and services and for the same people to be controlled and exploited as consumers.

The concept of the means of consumption appears, at least in passing, in various other places (Simmel, 1907/1978:477; Zukin, 1991), but most notably in one of Jean Baudrillard's early works, *The Consumer Society* (1970/1998). At this point in his career Baudrillard was still heavily influenced by Marxian theory, although he was to break with that approach in a few years en route to becoming today's preeminent postmodern social theorist. Characteristically, Baudrillard does not define the concept, but the way he uses it makes it clear that (unlike Marx) he is not conflating the means of consumption with the commodities to be consumed, but is following the definition we are using. Baudrillard's paradigm of the means of consumption is the Parisian "drugstore." Here is a description of one such drugstore:

> Any resemblance to an American pharmacy is tucked into one small corner. The rest of this amazing establishment is more like a mini-department store with everything from books to cameras, toys, French and foreign newspapers and magazines, clothing, and a booming takeout business in carved-on-the-spot sandwiches, salads, and soft drinks as well as caviar, pate de foie gras, and elaborate picnic hampers. Le Drugstore's outdoor cafe offers what it claims is an "authentic" American menu.
>
> (Rothenberg and Rothenberg, 1993:38)

The Parisian "drugstore" is clearly a means of consumption in that it is a means, a social and economic structure, that enables consumers to acquire an array of commodities.

But this is merely Baudrillard's starting point. He goes on to talk about an entire community as the "drugstore writ large." In this context he describes a community, Parly 2, with its shopping center, swimming pool, clubhouse, and housing developments. The shopping center is an example of the new means of consumption. Other examples discussed by Baudrillard are holiday resorts (ski resorts, Club Med) and airport terminals.

Baudrillard was quite prescient in writing about the significance of these new means of consumption in the late 1960s. However, he did little with the idea and related phenomena. Furthermore, he erred in focusing on the Parisian drugstore because of its limited impact on the rest of the world. In fact, today that drugstore has been swamped by the importation of the kinds of means of consumption that occupy our attention here— fast-food restaurants, chains of all sorts, Euro Disney, and so on. Nonetheless, Baudrillard's sense of the means of consumption is the closest in the literature to the way the concept is employed in this discussion.

All of the new means of consumption are modern in the sense that they are largely new innovations that have come into existence and boomed in the last half century. Like McDonald's, they are largely American innovations that have not only transformed consumption in the United States, but have been aggressively exported to much of the rest of the world where they are having an even more profound effect on consumption. Within the United States they are so successful that they are serving as models for such diverse settings as universities, hospitals, museums, airports, sports stadia, even churches. The latter, which can be seen as serving consumers, are coming to look more and more like the new means of consumption.

The new means of consumption are modern in a more important sense; they are highly rationalized or McDonaldized:

Efficiency. The mall, for example, can be described as a highly efficient selling machine. This, in turn, makes it a highly efficient "buying machine" from the customer's perspective. Consumption is obviously made far more efficient for the consumer by having virtually all shops in one location that also has a large adjacent parking lot. Similar efficiencies are provided by superstores for customers in search of a specific type of product.

Calculability. Las Vegas hotels compete to see which one can offer the most hotel rooms, the largest casino, the "loosest slots," the biggest entertainment attraction. A similar competition takes place among the largest cruise lines, which boast about how many people their ships can carry, how long and wide the ships are, how many tons they weigh, how many different kinds of attractions they offer, and so on. In discount department stores, including Wal-Mart, customers are led to believe they can rely on three quantifiable things—low prices, a large number and a wide variety of goods. The same belief prevails about discount malls, although it often turns out to be illusory. The set prices for a daily or weekly pass at Disney World, as well as the abundant signs indicating how long a wait one can expect at a given attraction, illustrate similar calculability in the means of consuming tourism.

Predictability. The predictability one finds in McDonald's is evident in more upscale chains such as Hard Rock Cafe. For example, the menu, the taste of the food, even the guitars on the wall are the same whether one is in Osaka, Berlin, or San Francisco. Chain stores such as Pottery Barn, Crate and Barrel, the Gap, and J. Crew can be seen as having raised standardization to a new high. These chains have brought high design to the mass market, but at the cost of identical products being sold in identical stores. Ironically, while these chains offer uniformity and predictability, they tout themselves as offering individuality.

Control through Nonhuman rather than Human Technology. The shopping mall can be seen as highly controlled technologically throughout all aspects of its operation. Tight control is exercised over temperature, lighting, events, and merchandise. The aim is to control customers. Time and space are controlled by making the malls windowless; there are few doors to beckon one outside; the uniformity of malls means they could be anywhere; in many cases there are no clocks; the maintenance and periodic remodeling make it seem as if the malls do not age; there is overall an unreal perfection about the malls. Consumers float for hours in malls without an awareness of the passing of time. By inducing this state, malls make it likely that consumers will encounter many shops and see more goods and services and purchase more of them. Malls control what we purchase not only by deciding what is included and excluded, but also by employing the principle of "adjacent attraction," through which mundane objects are made to seem more desirable by surrounding them with diverse, more exotic objects. Malls manage the emotions of consumers by offering bright, cheery and upbeat environments. Children are singled out for special attention and on this count can be described as growing up in a controlled environment. Even greater control is exerted over employees, who can be seen as mall prisoners.

Thus, we can view the new means of consumption as highly rational and therefore largely modern phenomena. We will return to the new means of consumption in Chapter 13 where we will discuss the application of several postmodern ideas to these modern phenomena.

Risky or Not?

One of the seeming contradictions in this discussion is the emphasis in the work of Giddens and especially of Beck on risk in the modern world as opposed to the predictability that I see as characteristic of McDonaldized societies. A predictable world is one without surprises, including the surprises produced by risky undertakings. Can these two views be reconciled?

Giddens and Beck are operating at one level of analysis, while I am working at quite another level. Giddens and Beck are interested mainly in extraordinary events and circumstances, such as accidents associated with nuclear power plants and weapons. Clearly there are great risks here, risks that can have adverse effects over great expanses of time and space. In contrast, I am focally concerned with the more mundane aspects of our lives, such as the hamburger or tacos we eat at lunchtime or the credit cards we use to pay for them. Just as clearly, there are few, if any, risks here—we will get the burger or taco we expected and the fast-food restaurant will be paid by the credit card company.

But there is a deeper issue here: Can the risky events and circumstances described by Giddens and Beck be McDonaldized? I think that the answer is not only that they can be McDonaldized, but they have been rationalized to a very high degree. A nuclear power plant certainly operates efficiently, works predictably, relies on quantitative measures, and employs a wide range of nonhuman technologies, but like all other McDonaldized systems, it produces irrationalities of rationality, including the rare but devastating accident.

Furthermore, the Weberian theory of rationality, especially its sense of the irrationality of rationality, accounts very well for most of the risks described by Giddens and Beck. Most risky settings have been rationalized to a high degree, but irrationalities are an ever-present possibility. In fact, Beck makes this point, but in the context of a misguided rejection of the Weberian thesis: "Max Weber's concept of 'rationalization' no longer grasps this late modern reality, produced by successful rationalization. *Along with the growing capacity of technical options (Zweckrationalität) grows the incalculability of their consequences*" (1992:22). The problem is that the irrationalities associated with risky enterprises are far more consequential than those associated with a fast-food restaurant. A nuclear accident is far more grave than a burned burger or a rejected credit card.

When Beck ventures into the realm covered by McDonaldization he comes very close to echoing that thesis:

Individualization means market dependency in all dimensions of living. The forms of existence that arise are the isolated *mass market,* not conscious of itself, and *mass consumption* of generically designed housing, furnishings, articles of daily use, as well as opinions, habits, attitudes and lifestyles launched and adopted through the mass media. In other words, individualization delivers people over to an *external control and standardization* that was unknown in the enclaves of familial and feudal subcultures.

(Beck, 1992:132)

Similarly, in his reflexive world of many options, Giddens sees something like McDonaldization in the same domain I have explored: "Of course, there are standardising influences too—most notably, in the form of commodification" (1991:5). More generally, Giddens says, "The abstract systems of modernity create large areas of relative security for the continuance of day-to-day life" (1991:133).

Yet another difference is the fact that Giddens (England) and Beck (Germany) are writing from a European vantage point, whereas I am writing from an American point of view. Europe of the 1970s and 1980s, the years when all three theorists were forming their ideas, were the years of East-West confrontation and the danger of nuclear war. That danger was felt more strongly in Europe than in the United States, in part because of Europe's proximity to the former Soviet Union and in part because of its direct experience with the ravages of war. This sentiment leads Giddens to say, for example, "The world in which we live today is a fraught and dangerous one" (1990:10). While far from being immune to the danger, as a rule Americans have tended to see the world as not nearly so dangerous.

MODERNITY AND THE HOLOCAUST

While to me the modern paradigm of formal rationality is the fast-food restaurant, to Zygmunt Bauman (1989, 1991) it is the Holocaust, the systematic destruction of the Jews by the Nazis. As Bauman puts it, "Considered as a complex purposeful operation, the Holocaust may serve as a paradigm of modern bureaucratic rationality" (1989:149). To many it will seem obscene to discuss fast-food restaurants and the Holocaust in the same context. Yet, there is a clear line in sociological thinking about modern rationality from the bureaucracy to the Holocaust and then to the fast-food restaurant. Weber's principles of rationality can be applied usefully and meaningfully to each. The perpetrators of the Holocaust employed the bureaucracy as one of their major tools. The conditions that made the Holocaust possible, especially the formally rational system, continue to exist today. Indeed, what the process of McDonaldization indicates is not only that formally rational systems persist, but that they are expanding dramatically. Thus, in Bauman's view, under the right set of circumstances the modern world would be ripe for an even greater abomination (if such a thing is possible) than the Holocaust.

A Product of Modernity

Rather than viewing the Holocaust, as most do, as an abnormal event, Bauman sees it as in many ways a "normal" aspect of the modern, rational world:

The truth is that every "ingredient" of the Holocaust—all of those many things that rendered it possible—was normal; "normal" not in the sense of the familiar . . . but in the sense of being fully in keeping with everything we know about our civilization, its guiding spirit, its priorities, its immanent vision of the world.

(Bauman, 1989:8)

Thus, the Holocaust, to Bauman, was a product of modernity and *not,* as most people view it, a result of the breakdown of modernity or a special route taken within it (Joas, 1998; Varcoe, 1998). In Weberian terms, there was an "elective affinity" between the Holocaust and modernity.

For example, the Holocaust involved the application of the basic principles of industrialization in general, and the factory system in particular, to the destruction of human beings:

[Auschwitz] was also a mundane extension of the modern factory system. Rather than producing goods, the raw material was human beings and the end-product was death, so many units per day marked carefully on the manager's production charts. The chimneys, the very symbol of the modern factory system, poured forth acrid smoke produced by burning human flesh. The brilliantly organized railroad grid of modern Europe carried a new kind of raw material to the factories. It did so in the same manner as with other cargo. . . . Engineers designed the crematoria; managers designed the system of bureaucracy that worked with a zest and efficiency. . . . What we witnessed was nothing less than a massive scheme of social engineering.

(Feingold, cited in Bauman, 1989:8)

What the Nazis succeeded in doing was bringing together the rational achievements of industry and the rational bureaucracy, and then bringing both to bear on the objective of destroying people. Modernity, as embodied in these rational systems, was not a sufficient condition for the Holocaust, but it was clearly a necessary condition. Without modernity and rationality, "the Holocaust would be unthinkable" (Bauman, 1989:13).

The Role of Bureaucracy

The German bureaucracy did more than carry out the Holocaust, in a very real sense it created the Holocaust. The task of "getting rid of the Jews," as Hitler defined it, was picked up by the German bureaucrats, and as they resolved a series of day-to-day problems, extermination emerged as the best means to the end as it was defined by Hitler and his henchmen. Thus, Bauman argues that the Holocaust was not the result of irrationality, or premodern barbarity, but rather it was the product of the modern, rational bureaucracy. It was not crazed lunatics who created and managed the Holocaust, but highly rational and otherwise quite normal bureaucrats.

In fact, previous efforts, such as emotional and irrational pogroms, could not have accomplished the mass extermination that characterized the Holocaust. Such a mass extermination required a highly rationalized and bureaucratized operation. An irrational outburst like a pogrom might kill some people, but it could never successfully carry on a mass extermination of the scale undertaken in the Holocaust. As Bauman puts it, "Rage and fury are pitiably primitive and inefficient tools of mass annihilation. They normally peter out before the job is done" (1989:90). In contrast, modern genocide as it was perpetrated by the Nazis had a seemingly rational purpose, the creation of a "better" society (unfortunately, to the Nazis, a better society was one that was free of "evil" Jews). And, the Nazis and their bureaucrats went about achieving that goal in a cold and methodical manner.

Unlike most observers, Bauman does not see the bureaucracy as simply a neutral tool that can be propelled in any direction. Bauman sees the bureaucracy as "more like . . . loaded dice" (1989:104). While it can be used for either cruel or humane purposes, it is more likely to favor inhuman processes. "It is programmed to measure the optimum in such terms as would not distinguish between one human object and another, or between human and inhuman objects" (Bauman, 1989:104). And given its basic characteristics, the bureaucracy would see the inhuman task through to the end, and beyond. In addition to their normal operations, bureaucracies have a number of well-known incapacities, and they too fostered the Holocaust. For example, means often become ends in bureaucracies, and in this case the means, killing, often came to be the end.

Of course, the bureaucracy and its officials could not and did not create the Holocaust on their own; other factors were required. For one thing, there was the unquestioned control of the state apparatus with its monopoly of the means of violence over the rest of society. In other words, there were few if any countervailing power bases in Nazi Germany. And the state, of course, was controlled by Adolph Hitler, who had the ability to get the state to do his bidding. For another thing, there was a distinctly modern and rational form of anti-Semitism in which Jews were systematically set apart from the rest of society and portrayed as if they were preventing Germany from becoming a "perfect" society. In order to accomplish this goal, the Germans had to exterminate those who stood in the way of achieving a perfect society. German science (itself highly rationalized) was employed to help define the Jews as defective. Once they were defined as defective, and as a barrier to the perfect society, then it followed that the only solution was their elimination. And once it was determined that they should be eliminated, then the only important issue facing the bureaucrat was finding the most efficient way of bringing about this end.

Another factor here is that there is no place for moral considerations in modern structures like bureaucracies. Whether it was right or wrong to exterminate the Jews was a nonissue. The absence of such moral concerns is another reason that the Holocaust is such a modern phenomenon.

The Holocaust and McDonaldization

The Holocaust had all the characteristics of "McDonaldization." There was certainly an emphasis on efficiency. For example, gas was determined to be a far more efficient method of killing large numbers of people than were bullets. The Holocaust had the predictability of an assembly line, with the long lines of trains snaking into the death camps, the long rows of people winding into the "showers," and the "production" of large stacks of bodies to be disposed of at the end of the process. It was calculable in the sense that the emphasis was on quantitative factors such as how many people could be killed and in how short a time.

> For railway managers, the only meaningful articulation of their object is in terms of tonnes per kilometre. They do not deal with humans, sheep, or barbed wire; they only deal with cargo, and this means an entity consisting entirely of measurements and devoid

of quality. For most bureaucrats, even such a category as cargo would mean too strict a quality-bound restriction. They deal only with the financial effects of their actions. Their object is money.

(Bauman, 1989:103)

There was certainly little attention paid to the quality of the life, or even of the death, of the Jews as they marched inexorably to the gas chambers. In another, quantitative sense, the Holocaust was the most extreme of mass exterminations:

> Like everything else done in the modern—rational, planned, scientifically informed, expert, efficiently managed, co-ordinated—way, the Holocaust left behind and put to shame all its alleged pre-modern equivalents, exposing them as primitive, wasteful and ineffective by comparison. Like everything else in our modern society, the Holocaust was an accomplishment in every respect superior. . . . It towers high above the past genocidal episodes."

(Bauman, 1989:89)

Finally, the Holocaust used nonhuman technologies, such as the rules and regulations of the camps and the assembly-line operation of the ovens, to control both inmates and guards.

Of course, the characteristic of McDonaldization that best fits the Holocaust is the irrationality of rationality, especially dehumanization. Here Bauman makes use of the idea of distanciation to make the point that the victims can be dehumanized because the bureaucrats making decisions about them have no personal contact with them. Furthermore, the victims are objects to be moved about and disposed of, numbers on a ledger, they are not human beings. In sum, "German bureaucratic machinery was put in the service of a goal incomprehensible in its irrationality" (Bauman, 1989:136).

One of Bauman's most interesting points is that the rational system put in place by the Nazis came to encompass the victims, the Jews. The ghetto was transformed into "an extension of the murdering machine" (Bauman, 1989:23). Thus,

> the leaders of the doomed communities performed most of the preliminary bureaucratic work the operation required (supplying the Nazis with the records and keeping the files on their prospective victims), supervised the productive and distributive activities needed to keep the victims alive until the time when the gas chambers were ready to receive them, policed the captive population so that law-and-order tasks did not stretch the ingenuity or resources of the captors, secured the smooth flow of the annihilation process by appointing the objects of its successive stages, delivered the selected objects to the sites from which they could be collected with minimum of fuss, and mobilized the financial resources needed to pay for the last journey.

(Bauman, 1989:118)

(This is similar to the idea that in a McDonaldized world, the customers become unpaid workers in the system, making their own salads, cleaning up after themselves, and so on.) In "ordinary genocide," the murderers and the murdered are separated from one another. The murderers are planning to do something terrible to their victims, with the result that the resistance of potential victims is likely. However, such resistance is far less likely when the victims are an integral part of a "system" created by the perpetrators.

In their actions, the Jews who cooperated with the Nazis were behaving rationally. They were doing what was necessary to, for example, keep themselves alive for another day or be selected as people deserving of special, more favorable treatment. They were even using rational tools, such as calculating that the sacrifice of a few would save the many, or that if they didn't cooperate many more would die. However, in the end, such actions were irrational in that they helped expedite the process of genocide and they reduced the likelihood of resistance to it.

Modernity has prided itself on being civilized, on having safeguards in place so that something like the Holocaust could never occur. But it did occur; the safeguards were not sufficient to prevent it. Today, the forces of rationalization remain in place and are, if anything, stronger. And there is little to suggest that the safeguards needed to prevent rationalization from running amok are any stronger today than they were in the 1940s. As Bauman says, "None of the societal conditions that made Auschwitz possible has truly disappeared, and no effective measures have been undertaken to prevent . . . Auschwitz-like catastrophes" (1989:11). Necessary to prevent another Holocaust are a strong morality and pluralistic political forces. But there are likely to be times when a single power comes to predominate and there is little to lead us to believe that a strong enough moral system is in place to prevent another confluence of a powerful leader and an eager and willing bureaucracy.

MODERNITY'S UNFINISHED PROJECT

Jurgen Habermas is arguably not only today's leading social theorist, but also the leading defender of modernity and rationality in the face of the assault on those ideas by postmodernists (and others). According to Seidman:

> In contrast to many contemporary intellectuals who have opted for an anti- or postmodernist position, Habermas sees in the institutional orders of modernity structures of rationality. Whereas many intellectuals have become cynical about the emancipatory potential of modernity . . . Habermas continues to insist on the utopian potential of modernity. In a social context in which faith in the Enlightenment project of a good society promoted by reason sees a fading hope and spurned idol, Habermas remains one of its strongest defenders.
>
> (Seidman, 1989:2)

Habermas (1987b) sees modernity as an "unfinished project," implying that there is far more to be done in the modern world before we can begin thinking about the possibility of a postmodern world (Scambler, 1996).

In Chapter 11 we covered a good portion of Habermas's thinking on modernity in our discussion of his ideas on system, life-world, and the colonization of the life-world by the system. Habermas (1986:96) can be seen as doing a "theory of the pathology of modernity" since he regards modernity as being at variance with itself. By this he means that the rationality (largely formal rationality) that has come to characterize social systems is different from, and in conflict with, the rationality that characterizes the life-world. Social systems have grown increasingly complex, differentiated, integrated, and characterized by instrumental reason. The life-world, too, has witnessed increasing differentiation and condensation (but of the knowledge bases and value spheres of truth, goodness, and beauty), secularization, and institutionalization of norms of reflexivity and criticism (Seidman, 1989:24). A rational society would be one in which *both* system and life-world were permitted to rationalize in their own way, following their own logics. The rationalization of system and life-world would lead to a society with material abundance and control over its environments as a result of rational systems *and* one of truth, goodness, and beauty stemming from a rational life-world. However, in the modern world, the system has come to dominate and to colonize the life-world. The result is that while we may be enjoying the fruits of system rationalization, we are being deprived of the enrichment of life that would come from a life-world that was allowed to flourish. Many of the social movements that have arisen at the "borders" between life-world and system in the last few decades are traceable to a resistance against the colonization and impoverishment of the life-world.

In analyzing the way in which the system colonizes the life-world, Habermas sees himself in alignment with much of the history of social thought:

> The main strand of social theory—from Marx via Spencer and Durkheim to Simmel, Weber and Lukács—has to be understood as the answer to the entry of system-environment boundaries into society itself [Habermas's life-world], to the genesis of the "internal foreign country" . . . which has been understood as the *hallmark of modernity.*
> (Habermas, 1991:255–256; italics added)

In other words, the "hallmark of modernity" to Habermas, as well as to most of classical theory, has been, in Habermas's terms, the colonization of the life-world by the system.

What, then, for Habermas would constitute the completion of modernity's project? It seems clear that the final product would be a fully rational society in which both system and life-world rationality were allowed to express themselves fully without one destroying the other. We currently suffer from an impoverished life-world, and that problem must be overcome. However, the answer does not lie in the destruction of systems (especially the economic and administrative systems), since it is they that provide the material prerequisites needed to allow the life-world to rationalize.

One of the issues Habermas (1987b) deals with is the increasing problems confronted by the modern, bureaucratic, social welfare state. Many of those associated with such a state recognize the problems, but their solution is to deal with them at the system level by, for example, simply adding a new subsystem to deal with the problems. However, Habermas does not think the problems can be solved in this way. Rather, they must be solved in the relationship between system and life-world. First, "restraining barriers" must be put in place to reduce the impact of system on life-world. Second, "sensors" must be built in order to enhance the impact of life-world on system. Habermas concludes that contemporary problems cannot be solved "by systems learning to function better. Rather, impulses from the lifeworld must be able to enter into the self-steering of functional systems" (1987b:364). These would constitute important steps toward the creation of mutually enriching life-world and system. It is here that social movements enter the picture, because they represent the hope of a recoupling of system and life-world so that the two can rationalize to the highest possible degree.

JURGEN HABERMAS: A Biographical Sketch

Jurgen Habermas is arguably the most important social thinker in the world today. Born in Düsseldorf, Germany, on June 18, 1929, his family was middle-class and rather traditional. Habermas's father was director of the Chamber of Commerce. In his early teens, during World War II, Habermas was profoundly affected by the war. The end of the war brought new hope and opportunities for many Germans, including Habermas. The fall of Nazism brought optimism about the future of Germany, but Habermas was disappointed in the lack of dramatic progress in the years immediately after the war. With the end of Nazism, all sorts of intellectual opportunities arose, and once-banned books became available to the young Habermas. These included Western and German literature, as well as tracts written by Marx and Engels. Between 1949 and 1954 Habermas studied a wide range of topics (for example, philosophy, psychology, German literature) in Göttingen, Zurich, and Bonn. However, none of the teachers at the schools at which Habermas studied were illustrious, and most were compromised by the fact that they either supported the Nazis overtly or simply continued to carry out their academic responsibilities under the Nazi regime. Habermas received his doctorate from the University of Bonn in 1954 and worked for two years as a journalist.

In 1956 Habermas arrived at the Institute for Social Research in Frankfurt and became associated with the Frankfurt school. Indeed, he became research assistant to one of the most illustrious members of that school, Theodor Adorno, as well as an associate of the institute (Wiggershaus, 1994). While the Frankfurt school is often thought of as highly coherent, that was not Habermas's view:

> For me there was never a consistent theory. Adorno wrote essays on the critique of culture and also gave seminars on Hegel. He presented a certain Marxist background—and that was it.
>
> (Habermas, cited in Wiggershaus, 1994:2)

While he was associated with the Institute for Social Research, Habermas demonstrated from the beginning an independent intellectual orientation. A 1957 article by Habermas got him into trouble with the leader of the institute, Max Horkheimer. Habermas urged critical thought and practical action, but Horkheimer was afraid that such a position would jeopardize the publicly funded Institute. Horkheimer strongly recommended that Habermas be dismissed from the Institute. Horkheimer said of Habermas, " 'He probably has a good, or even

Habermas sees little hope in the United States, which seems intent on buttressing system rationality at the cost of a continuing impoverishment of the life-world. However, Habermas does see hope in Europe, which has the possibility of putting "an end to the confused idea that the normative content of modernity that is stored in rationalized lifeworlds could be set free only by means of ever more complex systems" (1987b:366). Thus, Europe has the possibility of assimilating "in a decisive way the legacy of Occidental rationalism" (Habermas, 1987b:366). That legacy translates today into restraints on system rationality in order to allow life-world rationality to flourish to the extent that the two types of rationalities can coexist as equals within the brilliant, career as a writer in front of him, but he would only cause the Institute immense damage'" (cited in Wiggershaus, 1994:555). The article was eventually published, but not under the auspices of the institute and with virtually no reference to it. Eventually, Horkheimer enforced impossible conditions on Habermas's work and the latter resigned.

In 1961 Habermas became a privatdocent and completed his "Habilitation" (a second dissertation required by German universities) at the University of Marburg. Having already published a number of notable works, Habermas was recommended for a professorship of philosophy at the University of Heidelberg even before he had completed his Habilitation. He remained at Heidelberg until 1964, when he moved on to the University of Frankfurt as professor of philosophy and sociology. From 1971 to 1981 he was the director of the Max Planck Institute. He returned to the University of Frankfurt as professor of philosophy, and in 1994 he became an emeritus professor at that institution. He has won a number of prestigious academic prizes and has been awarded honorary professorships at a number of universities.

For many years, Habermas was the world's leading neo-Marxist. However, over the years his work has broadened to involve many different theoretical inputs. Habermas continues to hold out hope for the future of the modern world. It is in this sense that Habermas writes of modernity's unfinished project. While Marx focused on work, Habermas is concerned mainly with communication, which he considers to be a more general process than is work. While Marx focused on the distorting effect of the structure of capitalist society on work, Habermas is concerned with the way the structure of modern society distorts communication. While Marx sought a future world involving full and creative labor, Habermas seeks a future society characterized by free and open communication. Thus, there are startling similarities between the theories of Marx and Habermas. Most generally, both are modernists who believed or believe that in their time modernity's project (creative and fulfilling work for Marx, open communication for Habermas) has not yet been completed. Yet, both have faith that in the future that project will be completed.

It is this commitment to modernism, and his faith in the future, that sets Habermas apart from many leading contemporary thinkers, such as Jean Baudrillard and other postmodernists. While the latter are often driven to nihilism, Habermas continues to believe in his lifelong (and modernity's) project. Similarly, while other postmodernists (for example, Lyotard) reject the possibility of creating grand narratives, Habermas continues to work on and support what is perhaps the most notable grand theory in modern social theory. Much is at stake for Habermas in his battle with the postmodernists. If they win out, Habermas may come to be seen as the last great modernist thinker. If Habermas (and his supporters) emerge victorious, he may be viewed as the savior of the modernist project and of grand theory in the social sciences.

modern world. Such a full partnership between system and life-world rationality would constitute the completion of modernity's project. Since we remain a long way from that goal, we are far from the end of modernity, let alone on the verge, or in the midst, of postmodernity.

Habermas versus Postmodernists

Habermas makes a case not only for modernity, but also against the postmodernists. Habermas offered some early criticisms in an essay, "Modernity versus Postmodernity"

(1981), which has achieved wide recognition.[2] In that essay, Habermas raises the issue of whether, in light of the failures of the twentieth century, we "should try to hold on to the *intentions of the Enlightenment,* feeble as they may be, or should we declare the entire project of modernity a lost cause?" (1981:9). Habermas, of course, is not in favor of giving up on the Enlightenment project or, in other words, modernity. Rather, he chooses to focus on the "mistakes" of those who do reject modernity. One of the latter's most important mistakes is their willingness to give up on science, especially a science of the life-world. The separation of science from the life-world, and the leaving of it to experts, would, if done in conjunction with the creation of other autonomous spheres, involve the surrender of "the project of modernity altogether" (Habermas, 1981:14). Habermas refuses to give up on the possibility of a rational, "scientific" understanding of the life-world as well as on the possibility of the rationalization of that world.

Holub (1991) has offered an overview of Habermas's most important criticisms of the postmodernists. First, the postmodernists are equivocal about whether they are producing serious theory or literature. If we treat them as producing serious theory, then their work becomes incomprehensible because of "their refusal to engage in the institutionally established vocabularies" (Holub, 1991:158). On the other hand, if we treat the work of the postmodernists as literature, "then their arguments forfeit all logical force" (Holub, 1991:158). In either case, it becomes almost impossible to critically analyze the work of the postmodernists seriously, because they can always claim that we do not understand their words or their literary endeavors.

Second, Habermas feels that the postmodernists are animated by normative sentiments, but what those sentiments are is concealed from the reader. Thus, the reader is unable to understand what postmodernists are really up to, why they are critiquing society, from their stated objectives. Furthermore, while they have hidden normative sentiments, the postmodernists overtly repudiate such sentiments. The lack of such overt sentiments prevents postmodernists from developing a self-conscious praxis aimed at overcoming the problems they find in the world. In contrast, the fact that Habermas's normative sentiments (free and open communication) are overt and clearly stated makes the source of his critiques of society clear, and it provides the base for political praxis.

Third, Habermas accuses postmodernism of being a totalizing perspective that fails "to differentiate phenomena and practices that occur within modern society" (Holub, 1991:159). For example, the view of the world as dominated by power and surveillance is not fine-grained enough to allow for meaningful analysis of the real sources of oppression in the modern world.

Finally, the postmodernists are accused of ignoring that which Habermas finds absolutely central—everyday life and its practices. This oversight constitutes a double loss for postmodernists. On the one hand, they are closed off from an important source for the development of normative standards. After all, the rational potential that exists in everyday life is an important source of Habermas's ideas on communicative rationality (Cooke, 1994). On the other hand, the everyday world also constitutes the

---

[2]There is a sense that in his later work Habermas has offered a softer and more fine-grained critique of the postmodernists (Peters, 1994).

ultimate goal for work in the social sciences, since it is there that theoretical ideas can have an impact on praxis.

Habermas (1994:107) offers a good summary of his views on modernity-postmodernity and a useful transition to the next chapter of this text in which we will deal with postmodern social theory: "The concept of modernity no longer comes with a promise of happiness. But despite all the talk of postmodernity, there are no visible rational alternatives to this form of life. What else is left for us, then, but at least to search out practical improvements *within* this form of life?"

INFORMATIONALISM AND THE NETWORK SOCIETY

One of the most recent contributions to modern social theory is a trilogy authored by Manuel Castells (1996, 1997, 1998) with the overarching title, *The Information Age: Economy, Society and Culture*. Castells (1996:4) articulates a position opposed to postmodern social theory, which he sees as indulging in "celebrating the end of history, and, to some extent, the end of Reason, giving up on our capacity to understand and make sense":

> The project informing this book swims against streams of destruction, and takes excep-
> tion to various forms of intellectual nihilism, social skepticism, and political cynicism. I
> believe in rationality, and the possibility of calling upon reason . . . I believe in the
> chances of meaningful social action . . . And, yes, I believe in spite of a long tradition of
> sometimes tragic intellectual errors, that observing, analyzing, and theorizing is a way of
> helping to build a different, better world.
>
> (Castells, 1996:4)

Castells examines the emergence of a new society, culture, and economy in light of the revolution, begun in the United States in the 1970s, in informational technology (television, computers, and so on). This revolution led, in turn, to a fundamental restructuring of the capitalist system beginning in the 1980s and to the emergence of what Castells calls "informational capitalism." Also emerging were "informational societies" (although there are important cultural and institutional differences among these societies). Both are based on "informationalism" ("a mode of development in which the main source of productivity is the qualitative capacity to optimize the combination and use of factors of production on the basis of knowledge and information" [Castells, 1998:7]). The spread of informationalism, especially informational capitalism, leads to the emergence of oppositional social movements based on self and identity ("the process by which a social actor recognizes itself and constructs meaning primarily on the basis of a given cultural attribute or set of attributes, to the exclusion of a broader reference to other social structures" [Castells, 1996:22]). Such movements bring about the contemporary equivalent of what Marxists call "class struggle." The hope against the spread of informational capitalism and the problems it causes (exploitation, exclusion, threats to self and identity) is not the working class, but a diverse set of social movements (e.g., ecological, feminist) based primarily on identity.

At the heart of Castells's analysis is what he calls the information technology paradigm with five basic characteristics. First, these are technologies that act on information. Second, since information is part of all human activity, these technologies have a pervasive effect. Third, all systems using information technologies are defined by a "networking logic" allowing them to affect a wide variety of processes and organizations. Fourth, the new technologies are highly flexible, allowing them to adapt and change constantly. Finally, the specific technologies associated with information are merging into a highly integrated system.

In the 1980s there emerged a new, increasingly profitable global informational economy. "It is *informational* because the productivity and competitiveness of units or agents in this economy (be it firms, regions, or nations) fundamentally depend upon their capacity to generate, process, and apply efficiently knowledge-based information" (Castells, 1996:66). It is global because it has the *"capacity to work as a unit in real time on a planetary scale"* (Castells, 1996:92). This was made possible, for the first time, by the new information and communication technologies. And it is "informational, not just information-based, because the cultural-institutional attributes of the whole social system must be included in the diffusion and implementation of the new technological paradigm" (Castells, 1996:91). While it is global, there are differences, and Castells distinguishes among regions that lie at the heart of the new global economy (North America, the European Union, and the Asian Pacific). Thus, we are talking about a regionalized, global economy. In addition, there is considerable diversity within each region and of crucial importance is the fact that while some areas of the globe are included, others are excluded and they suffer grave negative consequences. Whole areas of the world (e.g., sub-Saharan Africa) are excluded, as are parts of the privileged regions such as the inner cities in the United States.

Accompanying the rise of the new global informational economy is the emergence of a new organizational form, the network enterprise. Among other things, the network enterprise is characterized by flexible (rather than mass) production, new management systems (frequently adapted from Japanese models), organizations based on a horizontal rather than a vertical model, and the intertwining of large corporations in strategic alliances. However, most importantly, the fundamental component of organizations is a series of networks. It is this that leads Castells (1996:171) to argue that "a new organizational form has emerged as characteristic of the informational/global economy: the *network enterprise*" defined as *"that specific form of enterprise whose system of means is constituted by the intersection of segments of autonomous systems of goals."* The network enterprise is the materialization of the culture of the global informational economy, and it makes possible the transformation of signals into commodities through the processing of knowledge. As a result, the nature of work is being transformed (e.g., the individualization of work through such things as flex-time), although the precise nature of this transformation varies from one nation to another.

Castells (1996:373) also discusses the emergence (accompanying the development of multimedia out of the fusion of the mass media and computers) of the culture of *real virtuality, "a system in which reality itself (that is, people's material/symbolic existence) is entirely captured, fully immersed in a virtual image setting, in the world of make-believe, in which appearances are not just on the screen through which experience is communicated, but they become the experience."* In contrast to the past dominated by "the space of places" (e.g., cities like New York or London), a new spatial logic, the "space of flows," has emerged. We have become a world dominated by processes rather than physical locations (although the latter obviously continue to exist). Similarly, we have entered an era of "timeless time" in which, for example, information is instantly available anywhere on the globe.

Going beyond the network enterprise, Castells (1996:469, 470; italics added) argues that the "dominant functions and processes in the information age are increasingly organized around *networks*" defined as sets of "interconnected nodes." Networks are open, capable of unlimited expansion, dynamic, and able to innovate without disrupting the system. However, the fact that our age is defined by networks does not mean the end of capitalism. In fact, at least at the moment, networks allow capitalism to become, for the first time, truly global and organized on the basis of global financial flows, exemplified by the much-discussed global "financial casino" that is a wonderful example of not only a network, but also an informational system. Money won and lost here is now far more important than that earned through the production process. Money has come to be separated from production; we are in a capitalist age defined by the endless search for money.

However, as we saw above, Castells does not see the development of networks, the culture of real virtuality, informationalism, and especially their use in informational capitalism as going unchallenged. These are opposed by individuals and collectivities with identities of their own which they seek to defend. Thus, "God, nation, family, and community will provide unbreakable, eternal codes around which a counter-offensive will be mounted" (Castells, 1997:66). However, it is important to recognize that these countermovements must rely on information and networks in order to succeed. Thus, they are deeply implicated in the new order. In this context, Castells describes a wide range of social movements including the Zapatistas in Chiapas, Mexico, the American militia, the Japanese cult *Aum Shinrikyo,* environmentalism, feminism, and the gay movement.

What of the state? In Castells's view, it is increasingly powerless in this new world of the globalization of the economy and its dependence on global capital markets. Thus, for example, states have become unable to protect their welfare programs because imbalances around the globe will lead capital to gravitate toward those states with low welfare costs. Also eroding the power of the state are global communications which flow freely in and out of any country. Then there is the globalization of crime and the creation of global networks that are beyond the control of any single state. Also weakening the state is the growth of multilateralism, the emergence of super nation-states such as the European Union, and internal divisions. While they will continue to exist, Castells (1997:304) sees states becoming *"nodes of a broader network of power."* The dilemma facing the state is that if it represents its national constituencies, it will be less effective in the global system, but if it focuses on the latter, it will fail to adequately represent its constituencies.

An example of the failure of the state is the Soviet Union. It simply was incapable of adapting to the new informationalism and world of networks. For example, the Soviet state monopolized information, but this was incompatible with a world in which success is associated with the free flow of information. As it fell apart, the old Soviet Union proved easy prey for global criminal elements. Ironically, while Russia today is excluded from the global information society, it is deeply implicated in global criminality.

Given his critical orientation, especially to informational capitalism and its threats to self, identity, welfare, as well as its exclusion of vast portions of the world, Castells (1998: 359) concludes that as they are currently constituted, our "economy, society and culture . . . limit collective creativity, confiscate the harvest of information technology, and deviate our energy into self-destructive confrontation." However, it need not be this way since there "is nothing that cannot be changed by conscious, purposive social action" (Castells, 1998:360).

Castells offers the first sustained sociological analysis of our new computerized world and there are many insights to be derived from his work. Two major weaknesses stand out. First, this is primarily an empirical study (relying on secondary data) and Castells takes pains to avoid using a series of theoretical resources that might have enhanced his work. Second, he remains locked in a productivist perspective and fails to deal with the implications of his analysis for consumption. Nonetheless, Castells has clearly offered us an important beginning in our effort to gain a better understanding of the emerging world he describes.

SUMMARY

In this chapter we have surveyed a number of theoretical perspectives that continue to see the contemporary world in modern terms. Anthony Giddens sees modernity as a juggernaut that offers a number of advantages but also poses a series of dangers. Among the dangers underscored by Giddens are the risks associated with the modern juggernaut. These dangers are the key issue in Beck's work on the risk society. The modern world is seen as being characterized by risk and the need on the part of people to prevent risk and to protect themselves from it. I see rationality as the key characteristic of contemporary society, although it is amplified by McDonaldization. While I view the fast-food restaurant as the paradigm of rationality and modernity, Bauman sees the Holocaust as occupying that position. An emphasis on the fast-food restaurant, and much more extremely, on the Holocaust, indicates the irrationalities, and more generally the dangers, associated with modernity and increasing rationalization. Next, we discussed Habermas's work on modernity as an unfinished project. Habermas, too, focuses on rationality, but his concern is with the dominance of system rationality and impoverishment of the rationality of the life-world. Habermas sees the completion of modernity in the mutually enriching rationalization of system and life-world.

The final section is devoted to a discussion of the recent work of Manuel Castells. Castells is concerned with the growth of informationalism and the development of the network society. It is mainly the computer and the information flows it permits that have transformed the world and in the process created a series of problems such as the exclusion of great parts of the world, and even some pockets in the United States, from this system and its rewards.

Given these views on modernity, we turn in the next and final chapter of this book to a discussion of a variety of ideas associated with postmodernity.

13

STRUCTURALISM, POSTSTRUCTURALISM, AND THE EMERGENCE OF POSTMODERN SOCIAL THEORY

STRUCTURALISM
  Roots in Linguistics
  Anthropological Structuralism: Claude Lévi-Strauss
  Structural Marxism
POSTSTRUCTURALISM
  The Ideas of Michel Foucault
POSTMODERN SOCIAL THEORY
  Moderate Postmodern Social Theory: Fredric Jameson
  Extreme Postmodern Social Theory: Jean Baudrillard
  Postmodern Social Theory and Sociological Theory
  Applying Postmodern Social Theory
CRITICISMS AND POST-POSTMODERN SOCIAL THEORY

This book has been largely about *modern* social theory. However, the use of the term "modern" implies that there are developments that follow modern sociological theory. This idea seems strange, since we are accustomed to thinking of things that are modern as the latest, most up-to-date developments. However, in the last several decades, and in many different fields (art, architecture, literature, and so on), there has been a range of developments that scholars have come to think of as *post*modern. The implication is not only that these things come after the modern, but that there were problems with the modern that the postmodernists are pointing out and endeavoring to deal with.

In sociological theory, the modern (as well as the classical) theories discussed throughout the preceding pages continue to be important—in fact, preeminent—within the discipline. Yet, postmodern social theory is having an increasingly important impact on sociological theory, and it is now possible to identify postmodern developments, theoretical perspectives, and theorists. Furthermore, one would expect sociological theorists, as those closest to the humanities, to be most open to postmodernism. As at least some sociological theorists grow more postmodern in their orientation, we can expect that other, more empirically inclined sociologists will come to be influenced by at least some aspects of postmodern social theory.

In discussing postmodern social theory it is necessary to shift our focus from *socio-logical* theories to *social* theories. While the distinction between the two is not clear-cut, sociological theories tend to reflect developments that have occurred largely within sociology and that are of interest mainly to sociologists. Social theories tend to be multidisciplinary. In fact, at least some of the theories discussed earlier in this book, especially the neo-Marxian and agency-structure theories, might be better described as social theories. In any case, it is clear that postmodern theories are best viewed as social theories.

In this chapter, we deal with the emergence of what, in fact, does come after modern social theory by tracing the line of development from structuralism to poststructuralism and ultimately to what now has come to be known as postmodern social theory.

Following Lash (1991:ix), we take "the structuralism which swept through French so-cial thought in the 1960s" as the starting point for the emergence of poststructuralism and postmodernism. Structuralism itself was a reaction against French humanism, especially the existentialism of Jean-Paul Sartre. In his early work Sartre focused on the individual, especially individual freedom. At that point he adhered to the view that what people do is determined by them and not by social laws or larger social structures. However, later in his career, Sartre was more drawn to Marxian theory and while he continued to focus on the "free individual," that individual was now "situated in a massive and oppressive social structure which limits and alienates his activities" (Craib, 1976:9).

In her analysis of Sartre's work, Gila Hayim (1980) sees continuity between his early and his late work. In *Being and Nothingness,* published in 1943, Sartre focuses more on the free individual and takes the view that "existence is defined by and through one's acts. . . . *One is what one does*" (Hayim, 1980:3). At the same time, Sartre attacks the structuralist view of "objective structures as completely determinis-tic of behavior" (Hayim, 1980:5). For Sartre and existentialists in general, actors have the capacity to go beyond the present, to move toward the future. For Sartre, then, peo-ple are free; they are responsible for everything that they do; they have no excuses. In some senses, these "staggering responsibilities of freedom" (Hayim, 1980:17) are a tremendous source of anguish to people. In other senses, this responsibility is a source of optimism to people—their fates are in their hands. In the *Critique of Dialectical Reason,* published in 1963, Sartre devotes more attention to social structures, but even here he emphasizes the "human prerogative for transcendence—the surpassing of the given" (Hayim, 1980:16). Sartre is critical of various Marxists (structural Marxists) who overemphasize the role and place of social structure. "Dogmatic Marxists have, by Sartre's view, eliminated the humanistic component of Marx's original idea" (Hayim, 1980:72). As an existentialist, Sartre *always* retained this humanism. It is against the backdrop of the humanism of existentialism that one must see the rise of structuralism, poststructuralism, and postmodernism.

STRUCTURALISM

Structuralism obviously involves a focus on structures, but they are not in the main the same structures that concern the structural functionalists (see Chapter 3). While the lat-ter, indeed most, sociologists, are concerned with *social* structures, of primary concern to structuralists are *linguistic* structures. This shift from social to linguistic structures is what has come to be known as the *linguistic turn* which dramatically altered the nature of the social sciences (Lash, 1991:ix). The focus of a good many social scientists shifted from social structure to language (see, for example, the earlier discussions of Habermas's work on communication, or the conversational analyses of some ethnomethodologists) or more generally to signs of various sorts.

Roots in Linguistics

Structuralism emerged from diverse developments in various fields. The source of modern structuralism and its strongest bastion to this day is linguistics. The work of the Swiss linguist Ferdinand de Saussure (1857–1913) stands out in the development of structural linguistics and, ultimately, structuralism in various other fields (Culler, 1976). Of particular interest to us is Saussure's differentiation between *langue* and *parole,* which was to have enormous significance. *Langue* is the formal, grammatical system of language. It is a system of phonic elements whose relationships are governed, Saussure and his followers believed, by determinate laws. Much of linguistics since Saussure's time has been oriented to the discovery of those laws. The existence of *langue* makes *parole* possible. *Parole* is actual speech, the way that speakers use language to express themselves. Although Saussure recognized the significance of people's use of language in subjective and often idiosyncratic ways, he believed that the individual's use of language cannot be the concern of the scientifically oriented linguist. Such a linguist must look at *langue,* the formal system of language, not at the subjective ways in which it is used by actors.

Langue, then, can be viewed as a system of signs—a structure—and the meaning of each sign is produced by the relationship among signs within the system. Especially important here are relations of difference, including binary oppositions. Thus, for example, the meaning of the word "hot" comes not from some intrinsic properties of the word, but from the word's relationship with, its binary opposition to, the word "cold." Meanings, the mind, and ultimately the social world are shaped by the structure of language. Thus, instead of an existential world of people shaping their surroundings, we have here a world in which people, as well as other aspects of the social world, are being shaped by the structure of language.

The concern for structure has been extended beyond language to the study of all sign systems. This focus on the structure of sign systems has been labeled "semiotics" and has attracted many followers (Gottdiener, 1994; Hawkes, 1977). *Semiotics* is broader than structural linguistics, because it encompasses not only language but also other sign and symbol systems, such as facial expressions, body language, literary texts, indeed all forms of communication.

Roland Barthes is often seen as the true founder of semiotics. Barthes extended Saussure's ideas to all areas of social life. Not only language but also social behaviors are representations, or signs: "Not just language, but wrestling matches are also signifying practices, as are TV shows, fashions, cooking and just about everything else in everyday life" (Lash, 1991:xi). The "linguistic turn" came to encompass all social phenomena which, in turn, came to be reinterpreted as signs.

Anthropological Structuralism: Claude Lévi-Strauss

A central figure in French structuralism—indeed Kurzweil (1980:13) calls him "the father of structuralism"—is the French anthropologist Claude Lévi-Strauss. While structure takes various forms in Lévi-Strauss's work, what is important for our purposes is that he can be seen as extending Saussure's work on language to anthropological issues—for example, to myths in primitive societies. However, Lévi-Strauss also applied structuralism more broadly to all forms of communication. His major innovation was to reconceptualize a wide array of social phenomena (for instance, kinship systems) as systems of communication, thereby making them amenable to structural analyses. The exchange of spouses, for example, can be analyzed in the same way as the exchange of words; both are social exchanges that can be studied through the use of structural anthropology.

We can illustrate Lévi-Strauss's (1967) thinking with the example of the similarities between linguistic systems and kinship systems. First, terms used to describe kinship, like phonemes in language, are basic units of analysis to the structural anthropologist. Second, neither the kinship terms nor the phonemes have meaning in themselves. Instead, both acquire meaning only when they are integral parts of a larger system. Lévi-Strauss even used a system of binary oppositions in his anthropology (for example, the raw and the cooked) much like those employed by Saussure in linguistics. Third, Lévi-Strauss admitted that there is empirical variation from setting to setting in both phonemic and kinship systems, but even these variations can be traced to the operation of general, although implicit, laws.

All of this is very much in line with the linguistic turn, but Lévi-Strauss ultimately went off in a number of directions that are at odds with that turn. Most importantly, he argued that both phonemic systems and kinship systems are the products of the structures of the mind. However, they are not the products of a conscious process. Instead, they are the products of the unconscious, logical structure of the mind. These systems, as well as the logical structure of the mind from which they are derived, operate on the basis of general laws. Most of those who have followed the linguistic turn have not followed Lévi-Strauss in the direction of defining the underlying structure of the mind as the most fundamental structure.

Structural Marxism

Another variant of structuralism that enjoyed considerable success in France (and many other parts of the world) was structural Marxism, especially the work of Louis Althusser, Nicos Poulantzas, and Maurice Godelier.

Although we have presented the case that modern structuralism began with Saussure's work in linguistics, there are those who argue that it started with the work of Karl Marx: "When Marx assumes that structure is not to be confused with visible relations and explains their hidden logic, he inaugurates the modern structuralist tradition" (Godelier, 1972b:336). Although structural Marxism and structuralism in general are both interested in "structures," each field conceptualizes structure differently.

At least some structural Marxists share with structuralists an interest in the study of structure as a prerequisite to the study of history. As Maurice Godelier said, "The study of the internal functioning of a structure must precede and illuminate the study of its genesis and evolution" (1972b:343). In another work, Godelier said, "The inner *logic* of these systems must be analyzed *before* their *origin* is analyzed" (1972a:xxi). Another view shared by structuralists and structural Marxists is that structuralism should be concerned with the structures, or systems, that are formed out of the interplay of social relations. Both schools see structures as real (albeit invisible), although they differ markedly on the nature of the structure that they consider real. For Lévi-Strauss the focus is on the structure of the mind, whereas for structural Marxists it is on the underlying structure of society.

Perhaps most important, both structuralism and structural Marxism reject empiricism and accept a concern for underlying invisible structures. Godelier argued: "What both structuralists and Marxists reject are the empiricist definitions of what constitutes a social structure" (1972a:xviii). Godelier also made this statement:

> For Marx as for Lévi-Strauss a structure is *not* a reality that is *directly* visible, and so directly observable, but a *level of reality* that exists *beyond* the visible relations between men, and the functioning of which constitutes the underlying logic of the system, the subjacent order by which the apparent order is to be explained.
>
> (Godelier, 1972a:xix)

Godelier went even further and argued that such a pursuit defines all science: "What is visible is a *reality* concealing *another,* deeper reality, which is hidden and the discovery of which is the very purpose of scientific cognition" (1972a:xxiv).

In spite of these similarities, structural Marxism did not in the main participate in the linguistic turn then taking place in the social sciences. For example, the focal concern continued to be social and economic, not linguistic, structures. Moreover, structural Marxism continued to be associated with Marxian theory, and many French social thinkers were becoming at least as impatient with Marxian theory as they were with existentialism.

POSTSTRUCTURALISM

While it is impossible to pinpoint such a transition with any precision, Charles Lemert (1990) traces the beginning of poststructuralism to a 1966 speech by Jacques Derrida, one of the acknowledged leaders of this approach, in which he proclaimed the dawning of a new poststructuralist age. In contrast to the structuralists, especially those who followed the linguistic turn and who saw people constrained by the structure of language, Derrida reduced language to "writing" which does not constrain its subjects. Furthermore, Derrida also saw social institutions as nothing but writing and therefore unable to constrain people. In contemporary terms, Derrida deconstructed language and social institutions (Trifonas, 1996), and when he had finished, all he found there was writing. While there is still a focus here on language, writing is *not* a structure that constrains people. Furthermore, while the structuralists saw order and stability in the language system, Derrida sees language as disorderly and unstable. Different contexts give words different meanings. As a result, the language system cannot have the constraining power over people that the structuralists think it does. Furthermore, it is impossible for scientists to search for the underlying laws of language. Thus, Derrida offers what is ultimately a subversive, deconstructive perspective. As we will see, subversion and deconstruction become even more important with the emergence of postmodernism, and it is poststructuralism that laid the groundwork for postmodernism.

The object of Derrida's hostility is the logocentrism (the search for a universal system of thought that reveals what is true, right, beautiful, and so on) that has dominated Western social thought. This approach has contributed to what Derrida describes as the "historical repression and suppression of writing since Plato" (1978:196). Logocentrism has led to the closure not only of philosophy, but also of the human sciences. Derrida is interested in deconstructing, or "dismantling," the sources of this closure—this repression—thereby freeing writing from the things that enslave it. An apt phrase to describe Derrida's focus is "the deconstruction of logocentrism" (1978:230). More generally, *deconstruction* involves the decomposition of unities in order to uncover hidden differences (Smith, 1996:208).

A good concrete example of Derrida's thinking is his discussion of what he calls the "theatre of cruelty." He contrasts this concept against the traditional theater, which he sees as dominated by a system of thought that he calls representational logic (a similar logic has dominated social theory). That is, what takes place on the stage "represents" what takes place in "real life," as well as the expectations of writers, directors, and so on. This "representationalism" is the theater's god, and it renders the traditional theater theological. A theological theater is a controlled, enslaved theater:

> The stage is theological for as long as its structure, following the entirety of tradition, comports the following elements: an author-creator who, absent and from afar, is armed with a text and keeps watch over, assembles, regulates the time or the meaning of representation. . . . He lets representation represent him through representatives, directors or actors, *enslaved* interpreters . . . who . . . more or less directly represent the thought of the "creator." *Interpretive slaves* who faithfully execute the providential designs of the "master." . . . Finally, the theological stage comports a *passive,* seated public, a public of spectators, of consumers, of enjoyers.
>
> (Derrida, 1978:235; italics added)

Derrida envisions an alternative stage (an alternative society?) in which "speech will cease to govern the stage" (1978:239). That is, the stage will no longer be governed by, for example, authors and texts. The actors will no longer take dictation; the writers will no longer be the dictators of what transpires on the stage. However, this does not mean that the stage will become anarchic. While Derrida is not crystal clear on his alternative stage, we get a hint when he discusses the "construction of a stage whose clamor has not yet been pacified into words" (1978:240). Or, "the theatre of cruelty would be the art of difference and of expenditure without economy, without reserve, without return, without history" (Derrida, 1978:247).

It is clear that Derrida is calling for a radical deconstruction of the traditional theater. More generally, he is implying a critique of society in general, which is in the thrall of logocentrism. Just as he wants to free the theater from the dictatorship of the writer, he wants to see society free of the ideas of all the intellectual authorities who have created the dominant discourse. In other words, Derrida wants to see us all be free to be writers.

Implied here is another well-known concern of the poststructuralists (and postmodernists): *decentering.* In a sense, Derrida wants the theater to move away from its traditional "center," its focus on writers (the authorities) and their expectations, and to give the actors more free play. This point, too, can be generalized to society as a whole. Derrida associates the center with *the* answer and therefore ultimately with death. The center is linked with the absence of that which is essential to Derrida: "play and difference" (1978:297). Theater or society without play and difference—that is, static theater or society—can be seen as being dead. In contrast, a theater or a world without a center would be one which is infinitely open, ongoing, and self-reflexive. Derrida concludes that the future "is neither to be awaited nor to be refound" (1978:300). His point is that we are not going to find the future in the past, nor should we passively await our fate. Rather, the future is to be found, is being made, is being written, in what we are doing.

Having debunked Western logocentrism and intellectual authority, in the end Derrida leaves us without an answer; in fact, there is *no* single answer (Cadieux, 1995). The search for the answer, the search for Logos, has been destructive and enslaving. All we are left with is the process of writing, of acting, with play and with difference.

The Ideas of Michel Foucault

Although Derrida is an extremely important poststructuralist, the most important thinker associated with this approach is Michel Foucault (Smart, forthcoming). Foucault's work illustrates yet another difference between poststructuralism and structuralism. While structuralism was overwhelmingly influenced by linguistics, Foucault's approach, and poststructuralism more generally, shows a variety of theoretical inputs (Smart, 1985). This variety makes Foucault's work provocative and difficult to handle. Furthermore, the ideas are not simply adopted from other thinkers but are transformed as they are integrated into Foucault's unusual theoretical orientation. Thus, Weber's theory of rationalization has an impact, but to Foucault it is found only in certain "key sites," and it is not an "iron cage"; there is always resistance. Marxian ideas (Smart, 1983) are found in Foucault's work, but Foucault does not restrict himself to the economy; he focuses on a range of institutions. He is more interested in the "micro-politics of power" than in the traditional Marxian concern with power at the societal level. He practices hermeneutics in order to better understand the social phenomena of concern to him. Moreover, Foucault has no sense of some deep, ultimate truth; there are simply ever more layers to be peeled away. There is a phenomenological influence, but Foucault rejects the idea of an autonomous, meaning-giving subject. There is a strong element of structuralism but no formal rule-governed model of behavior. Finally, and perhaps most importantly, Foucault adopts Nietzsche's interest in the relationship between power and knowledge, but that link is analyzed much more sociologically by Foucault. This multitude of theoretical inputs is one of the reasons that Foucault is thought of as a poststructuralist.

There is yet another sense in which Foucault's work is clearly poststructuralist. That is, in his early work Foucault was heavily influenced by structuralism, but as his work progressed that influence declined and other inputs moved his theory in a variety of other directions. Let us look at the evolution of Foucault's work.

Two ideas are at the core of Foucault's methodology—"archaeology of knowledge" (Foucault, 1966) and "genealogy of power" (Foucault, 1969). While there is a sense in his work that the latter succeeds the former, Mitchell Dean (1994) has made a convincing case that the two coexist and mutually support one another in his substantive work.

Alan Sheridan (1980:48) contends that Foucault's archaeology of knowledge involves a search for "a set of rules that determine the conditions of possibility for all that can be said within the particular discourse at any given time." To put it another way, archaeology is the search for the "general system of the formation and transformation of statements [into discursive formations]" (Dean, 1994:16). The search for such a "general system," or such "rules," as well as the focus on *discourse*—spoken and written "documents"—reflects the early influence of structuralism on Foucault's work. In analyzing these documents, Foucault does not seek to "understand" them as would a hermeneuticist. Rather, Foucault's archaeology "organises the document, divides it up, distributes it, orders, arranges it in levels, establishes series, distinguishes between what is relevant and what is not, discovers elements, defines unities, describes relations" (Dean, 1994:15). Discourse and the documents it produces are to be analyzed, described, and organized; they are irreducible and not subject to interpretation seeking some "deeper" level of understanding. Also ruled out by Foucault is the search for origins; it is the documents themselves that are important and not their point of origination.

Foucault is particularly interested in those discourses "that seek to rationalise or systematise themselves in relation to particular ways of 'saying the true'" (Dean, 1994:32). As we will see, this concern leads him in the direction of the study of discourses that relate to the formation of human sciences such as psychology. Archaeology is able to distance and detach itself from "the norms and criteria of validity of established sciences and disciplines in favour of the internal intelligibility of the ensembles so located, their conditions of emergence, existence, and transformation" (Dean, 1994:36).

The concern for "saying the truth" relates directly to Foucault's genealogy of power since, as Foucault comes to see it, knowledge and power are inextricably intertwined (Foucault is here heavily indebted to the philosophy of Nietzsche). Genealogy is a very distinctive type of intellectual history, "a way of linking historical contents into organised and ordered *trajectories* that are neither the simple unfolding of their origins nor the necessary realisation of their ends. It is a way of analysing multiple, open-ended, heterogeneous trajectories of discourses, practices, and events, and of establishing their patterned relationships, without recourse to regimes of truth that claim pseudonaturalistic laws or global necessities" (Dean, 1994:35–36; italics added). Thus, genealogy is at odds with other types of historical studies that accord centrality to such laws or necessities. Everything is contingent from a genealogical perspective. Genealogy is inherently critical, involving a "tireless interrogation of what is held to be given, necessary, natural or neutral" (Dean, 1994:20).

More specifically, genealogy is concerned with the relationship between knowledge and power within the human sciences and their "practices concerned with the regulation of bodies, the government of conduct, and the formation of self" (Dean, 1994:154). Foucault is interested in the "conditions which hold at any one moment for the 'saying the true'" within the human sciences (Dean, 1994:24). Thus, "where archaeology had earlier addressed the rules of formation of discourse, the new critical and genealogical description addresses both the rarity of statements and the power of the affirmative" (Dean, 1994:33). In terms of the relationship between Foucault's two methods, archaeology performs tasks that are necessary in order to do genealogy. Specifically, archaeology involves empirical analyses of historical discourses, while genealogy undertakes a serial and critical analysis of these historical discourses and their relationship to issues of concern in the contemporary world.

Thus, genealogy is to be a "history of the present." However, this is not to be confused with "presentism," which involves the "unwitting projection of a structure of interpretation that arises from the historian's own experience or context onto aspects of the past under study" (Dean, 1994:28). Instead, Foucault seeks to illuminate the present using "historical resources to reflect upon the contingency, singularity, interconnections, and potentialities of diverse trajectories of those elements which compose present social arrangements as experience" (Dean, 1994:21). There is no determinism here; the present is not a necessary outcome of past developments. Foucault is oriented to the critical use of history to make present possibilities intelligible.

In his genealogy of power, Foucault is concerned with how people govern themselves and others through the production of knowledge. Among other things, he sees knowledge generating power by constituting people as subjects and then governing the subjects with the knowledge. He is critical of the hierarchization of knowledge. Because the highest-ranking forms of knowledge (the sciences) have the greatest power, they are singled out for the most severe critique. Foucault is interested in techniques, the technologies that are derived from knowledge (especially scientific knowledge), and how they are used by various institutions to exert power over people. Although he sees links between knowledge and power, Foucault does not see a conspiracy by elite members of society. Such a conspiracy would imply conscious actors, whereas Foucault is more inclined to see structural relationships, especially between knowledge and power. Looking over the sweep of history, Foucault does not see progress from primitive brutishness to more modern humaneness based on more sophisticated knowledge systems. Instead, Foucault sees history lurching from one system of domination (based on knowledge) to another. Although this is a generally bleak image, on the positive side Foucault believes that knowledge-power is always contested; there is always ongoing resistance to it. Foucault looks at historical examples, but he is interested primarily in the modern world. As he puts it, he is "writing the history of the present" (Foucault, 1979:31).

With this background, let us look at some of Foucault's specific, substantive works. In *Madness and Civilization* (1965; Foucault, 1995), Foucault is doing an archaeology of knowledge, specifically of psychiatry. He begins with the Renaissance, when madness and reason were not separated. However, between 1650 and 1800 (the classical period), distance between them is established, and ultimately reason comes to subjugate madness. In other words Foucault is describing "a broken dialogue" between reason and madness (1965:x). He describes the end result:

> Here reason reigned in the pure state, in a triumph arranged for it in advance over a frenzied unreason. Madness was thus torn from that imaginary freedom which still allowed it to flourish on the Renaissance horizon. Not so long ago, it had floundered about in broad daylight: in *King Lear,* in *Don Quixote.* But in less than a half-century, it had been sequestered and, in the fortress of confinement, bound to Reason, to the rules of morality and to their monotonous nights.

(Foucault, 1965:64)

There is a clear Weberian, iron-cage imagery here—the "monotonous nights" to be spent by the "mad" (the irrational) in the iron cage constructed by those with reason (rationality).

The scientific psychology of the nineteenth century eventually arose out of the separation of the mad from the sane in the eighteenth century (psychiatry is labeled a "monologue of reason about madness" [Foucault, 1965:xi]). At first, medicine was in charge of the physical and moral treatment of the mad, but later scientific psychological medicine took over the moral treatment. "A purely psychological medicine was made possible only when madness was alienated in guilt" (Foucault, 1965:182–183). Later, Foucault says, "What we call psychiatric practice is a certain moral tactic contemporary with the end of the eighteenth century, preserved in the rights of asylum life, and overlaid by the myths of positivism" (1965:276). Thus for Foucault, psychology (and psychiatry) is a moral enterprise, not a scientific endeavor, aimed against the mad, who are progressively unable to protect themselves from this "help." He sees the mad as being sentenced by so-called scientific advancement to a "gigantic moral imprisonment."

Needless to say, Foucault here rejects the idea that over the years we have seen scientific, medical, and humanitarian advances in the treatment of the mad. What he sees, instead, are increases in the ability of the sane and their agents (physicians, psychologists, psychiatrists) to oppress and repress the mad, who, we should not forget, had been on equal footing with the sane in the seventeenth century. The most recent development is that now the mad are less judged by these external agents; "madness is ceaselessly called upon to judge itself" (Foucault, 1965:265). In many senses such internalized control is the most repressive form of control. Clearly, Foucault's archaeology of knowledge leads him to very different conclusions from those of traditional historians about the history and current status of the mad and their relationship to the sane (and their agents). In addition, he is looking at the roots of the human sciences (especially psychology and psychiatry) in the distinction between the mad and the sane and the exertion of moral control over the mad. This is part of his more general thesis about the role of the human sciences in the moral control of people.

As for Foucault's structuralism in this early work, he argues that madness occurs at two "levels," and at "a deeper level madness is a form of discourse" (1965:96). Specifically, madness, at least in the classical age, is not mental or physical changes; instead, "delirious language is the ultimate truth of madness" (Foucault, 1965:97). But there is an even broader structuralism operating in this early work: "Let classical culture formulate, *in its general structure,* the experience it had of madness, an experience which crops up with the same meanings, in the identical order of its inner logic, in both the order of speculation and in the order of institutions, in *both discourse and decree,* in both word and watchword—wherever, in fact, a signifying element can assume for us the value of a language" (Foucault, 1965:116; italics added).

Foucault continues to use a structuralist method in *The Birth of the Clinic,* in which he focuses on medical discourse and its underlying structure: "What counts in the things said by men is not so much what they may have thought or the extent to which these things represent their thoughts, as *that which systematizes them from the outset,* thus making them thereafter endlessly accessible to new discourses and open to the task of transforming them" (1975:xiv; italics added).

In *Madness and Civilization,* medicine was an important precursor of the human sciences, and that is an even more central theme in *The Birth of the Clinic.* (As Foucault said, "The science of man . . . was medically . . . based" [1975:36].) Prior to the nineteenth century, medicine was a classificatory science, and the focus was on a clearly ordered system of diseases. But in the nineteenth century, medicine came to focus on diseases as they existed in individuals and the larger society (epidemics). Medicine came to be extended to healthy people (preventive care), and it adopted a normative posture distinguishing between healthy and unhealthy and, later, normal and pathological states. Medicine had become, again, a forerunner of the human sciences that were to adopt this normal-pathological stance toward people.

As yet, however, there was no clinical structure in medicine. The key was the development of the clinic where patients were observed in bed. Here Foucault uses a key term, the *gaze,* in this case a "gaze that was at the same time knowledge" (1975:81). In other words, knowledge was derived from what physicians could see in contrast to what they read in books. As a structuralist, Foucault saw the gaze as a kind of language, "a language without words" (1975:68), and he was interested in the deep structure of that "language." The ability to see and touch (especially in autopsies) sick (or dead) people was a crucial change and an important source of knowledge. Foucault says of the autopsy, "The living night is dissipated in the brightness of death" (1975:146). Foucault sees the anatomo-clinical gaze as the "great break" in Western medicine. Thus, there was not an evolution of knowledge, but an epistemic change. Doctors were no longer playing the same game; it was a different game with different rules. *The* game was that people (patients) had become the object of scientific knowledge and practice (instead of the disease as an entity). In terms of his structuralist orientation, what had changed was the nature of discourse—names of diseases, groupings, field of objects, and so forth (Foucault, 1975:54).

Once again, medicine takes on for Foucault the role of forerunner to the human sciences. "It is understandable, then, that medicine should have had such importance in the constitution of the sciences of man—an importance that is not only methodological, but ontological, in that it concerns man's becoming an object of positive knowledge" (Foucault, 1975:197). Specifically on the medical autopsy, Foucault says, "Death left its old tragic heaven and became the lyrical core of man: his invisible truth, his visible secret" (1975:172). In fact, for Foucault the broader change is the individual as subject and object of his own knowledge, and the change in medicine is but one "of the more visible witnesses to these changes in the fundamental structures of experience" (1975:199).

Many of the same themes appear in *Discipline and Punish* (Foucault, 1979), but now we see more of the genealogy of power and much less on structuralism, discourse, and the like. Here "power and knowledge directly imply one another" (Foucault, 1979:27). In this work Foucault is concerned with the period between 1757 and the 1830s, a period during which the torture of prisoners was replaced by control over them by prison rules. (Characteristically, Foucault sees this change developing in an irregular way; it does not evolve rationally.) The general view is that this shift from torture to rules represented a humanization of the treatment of criminals; it had grown more kind, less painful, and less cruel. The reality, from Foucault's point of view, was that punishment had grown more rationalized ("the executioner [in the guillotine] need be no more than a meticulous watchman" [1979:13]) and in many ways impinged more on prisoners. The early torture of prisoners may have made for good public displays, but it was "a bad economy of power" because it tended to incite unrest among the viewers of the spectacle (Foucault, 1979:79). The link between knowledge and power was clear in the case of torture; with the development of rules, that link became far less clear. The new system of rules was "more regular, more effective, more constant, and more detailed in its effects; in short, which increase its effects while diminishing its economic cost" (Foucault, 1979:80–81). The new system was not designed to be more humane, but "to punish better . . . to insert the power to punish more deeply into the social body" (Foucault, 1979:82). In contrast to torture, this new technology of the power to punish occurred earlier in the deviance process, was more numerous, more bureaucratized, more efficient, more impersonal, more invariable, more sober, and involved the surveillance not just of criminals but of the entire society.

This new technology, a technology of disciplinary power, was based on the military model. It involved not a single overarching power system, but rather a system of micro powers. Foucault describes a "micro-physics of power" with "innumerable points of confrontation" (1979:26–27) and resistance (Brenner, 1994). He identifies three instruments of disciplinary power. First is *hierarchical observation,* or the ability of officials to oversee all they control with a single *gaze.* Second is the ability to make *normalizing judgments* and to punish those who violate the norms. Thus, one might be negatively judged and punished on the dimensions of time (for being late), activity (for being inattentive), and behavior (for being impolite). Third is the use of *examination* to observe subjects and to make normalizing judgments about people. The third instrument of disciplinary power involves the other two.

Foucault does not simply take a negative view toward the growth of the disciplinary society; he sees that it has positive consequences as well. For example, he sees discipline as functioning well within the military and industrial factories. However, Foucault communicates a genuine fear of the spread of discipline, especially as it moves into the state-police network for which the entire society becomes a field of perception and an object of discipline.

Foucault does not see discipline sweeping uniformly through society. Instead, he sees it "swarming" through society and affecting bits and pieces of society as it goes. Eventually, however, most major institutions are affected. Foucault asks rhetorically, "Is it surprising that prisons resemble factories, schools, barracks, hospitals, which all resemble prisons?" (1979:228). In the end, Foucault sees the development of a carceral system in which discipline is transported "from the penal institution to the entire social body" (1979:298). Although there is an iron-cage image here, as usual Foucault sees the operation of forces in opposition to the carceral system; there is an ongoing structural dialectic in Foucault's work.

Although Foucault's greater emphasis on power in *Discipline and Punish* is evident in the discussion to this point, he is also concerned in this work with his usual theme of the emergence of the human sciences. The transition from torture to prison rules constituted a switch from punishment of the body to punishment of the soul or the will. This change, in turn, brought with it considerations of normality and morality. Prison officials and the police came to judge the normality and morality of the prisoner. Eventually, this ability to judge was extended to other "small-scale judges," such as psychiatrists and educators. From all this adjudication emerged new bodies of scientific penal knowledge, and these served as the base of the modern "scientifico-legal complex." The new mode of subjugation was that people were defined as the object of knowledge, of scientific discourse. The key point is that the modern human sciences have their roots here. Foucault bitterly depicts the roots of the human sciences in the disciplines: "These sciences, which have so delighted our 'humanity' for over a century, have their technical matrix in the petty, malicious minutiae of the disciplines and their investigations" (1979:226).

One other point about *Discipline and Punish* is worth mentioning. Foucault is interested in the way that knowledge gives birth to technologies that exert power. In this context, he deals with the Panopticon. A *Panopticon* is a structure that allows officials the possibility of complete observation of criminals. In fact, officials need not always be present; the mere existence of the structure (and the possibility that officials might be there) constrains criminals. The Panopticon might take the form of a tower in the center of a circular prison from which guards could see into all cells. The Panopticon is a tremendous source of power for prison officials because it gives them the possibility of total surveillance. More important, its power is enhanced because the prisoners come to control themselves; they stop themselves from doing various things because they fear that they *might* be seen by the guards. There is a clear link here among knowledge, technology, and power. Furthermore, Foucault returns to his concern for the human sciences, for he sees the Panopticon as a kind of laboratory for the gathering of information about people. It was the forerunner of the social-scientific laboratory and other social-science techniques for gathering information about people. At still another level, Foucault sees the Panopticon as the base of "a whole type of society" (1979:216), the disciplinary society.[1]

Finally, we can look at the first volume of *The History of Sexuality* (Foucault, 1980). Again, the emphasis is on the genealogy of power. To Foucault, sexuality is "an especially dense transfer point for relations of power" (1980:103). He sees his goal as being to "define the regime of power-knowledge-pleasure that *sustains* the discourse on human sexuality in our part of the world" (Foucault, 1980:11). He examines the way that sex is put into discourse and the way that power permeates that discourse.

Foucault takes issue with the conventional view that Victorianism had led to the repression of sexuality in general and of sexual discourse in particular. In fact, he argues the exact opposite position—that Victorianism led to an explosion in discourses on sexuality. As a result of Victorianism, there was more analysis, stocktaking, classification, specification, and quantitative/causal study of sexuality. Said Foucault, "People will ask themselves why we were so bent on ending the rule of silence regarding what was the noisiest of our preoccupations" (1980:158). This was especially the case in schools, where instead of repression of sexuality, "the question of sex was a constant preoccupation" (1980:27). Here is the way that Foucault sums up the Victorian hypothesis and his alternative view:

---

[1]For an interesting use of this idea, see Zuboff (1988), who views the computer as a modern Panopticon that gives superiors virtually unlimited surveillance over subordinates.

MICHEL FOUCAULT: A Biographical Sketch

When he died of AIDS in 1984 at 57 years of age, "Michel Foucault was perhaps the single most famous intellectual in the world" (J. Miller, 1993:13). That fame was derived from a fascinating body of work that has influenced thinkers in a number of different fields, including sociology. Foucault also led an extremely interesting life, and the themes that characterized his life tended to define his work as well. In fact, it could be argued that through his work Foucault was seeking to better understand himself and the forces that led him to lead the life that he did.

Among Foucault's last works was a trilogy devoted to sex—*The History of Sexuality* (1976), *The Care of the Self* (1984), and *The Use of Pleasure* (1984). These works reflected Foucault's lifelong obsession with sex. A good deal of Foucault's life seems to have been defined by this obsession, in particular his homosexuality and his sadomasochism. During a trip to San Francisco in 1975, Foucault visited and was deeply attracted to the city's flourishing gay community. Foucault appears to have been drawn to the impersonal sex that flourished in the infamous bathhouses of that time and place. His interest and participation in these settings and activities were part of a lifelong interest in "'the overwhelming, the unspeakable, the creepy, the stupefying, the ecstatic'" (cited in J. Miller, 1993:27). In other words, in his life (and his work) Foucault was deeply interested in "limit experiences" (where people [including himself] purposely push their minds and bodies to the breaking point) like the impersonal sadomasochistic activities that took place in and around those bathhouses. It was Foucault's belief that it was during such limit experiences that great personal and intellectual breakthroughs and revelations became possible.

Thus, sex was related to limit experiences, and both, in turn, were related in his view to death: "'I think the kind of pleasure I would consider as *the* real pleasure would be so deep,

We must therefore abandon the hypothesis that modern industrial societies ushered in an age of increased sexual repression. We have not only witnessed a visible explosion of unorthodox sexualities . . . never have there existed more centers of power; never more attention manifested and verbalized . . . never more sites where the intensity of pleasures and the persistency of power catch hold, only to spread elsewhere.

(Foucault, 1980:49)

Once again, Foucault accords a special place to medicine and its discourses on sexuality. Whereas to most, medicine is oriented to the scientific analysis of sexuality, Foucault sees more morality than science in the concerns of medicine. (In fact, Foucault is characteristically hard on medicine, seeing the aim of its discourse "not to state the truth, but to prevent its very emergence" [1980:55].) Also involved in the morality of sexuality is religion, especially Western Christianity, the confession, and the need for the subject to tell the truth about sexuality. All this is related to the human sciences and their interest in gaining knowledge of the subject. Just as people confessed to their priests, they also confessed to their doctors, their psychiatrists, and their sociologists. The confession, especially the sexual confession, came to be cloaked in scientific terms.

so intense, so overwhelming that I couldn't survive it. . . . Complete total pleasure . . . for me, it's related to death'" (Foucault, cited in J. Miller, 1993:27). Even in the fall of 1983, when he was well aware of AIDS and the fact that homosexuals were disproportionately likely to contract the disease, he plunged back into the impersonal sex of the bathhouses of San Francisco: *"He took AIDS very seriously. . . . When he went to San Francisco for the last time, he took it as a 'limit-experience'"* (cited in J. Miller, 1993:380).

Foucault also had a limit experience with LSD at Zabriskie Point in Death Valley in the spring of 1975. There Foucault tried LSD for the first time, and the drug pushed his mind to the limit: "'The sky has exploded . . . and the stars are raining down upon me. I know this is not true, but it is the Truth'" (cited in J. Miller, 1993:250). With tears streaming down his face, Foucault said, "'I am very happy. . . . Tonight I have achieved a fresh perspective on myself. . . . I now understand my sexuality. . . . We must go home again'" (cited in J. Miller, 1993:251).

Prior to his experience with LSD, Foucault had been hard at work doing the research for his history of sexuality. He planned to approach that work much as he had approached his previous work on madness and other issues. But after his limit experience with LSD, he totally rethought the project. Among other things, that project came to focus more on the self. It is perhaps that new focus that Foucault anticipated when, during his LSD trip, he spoke of going home (to the self) again.

Foucault pushed himself to the limit not only in his personal life, but also in his work. Indeed, it could be argued that the extreme natures of both tended to feed off one another. Whatever else one may say about Foucault's work, it clearly was enormously creative; it pushed up against and perhaps even went beyond the limits of creativity. His work was a limit experience for him, and the study of it can be a "limit experience" for the reader.

Because he was operating at the limit, Foucault's life and work defy simple definition. This incapacity would be just fine with Foucault, given the fact that he once wrote, "'Do not ask who I am and do not ask me to remain the same. . . . More than one person, doubtless like me, writes in order to have no face'" (Foucault, cited in J. Miller, 1993:19).

In the West, "the project of the science of the subject has gravitated, in ever-narrowing circles, around the question of sex" (Foucault, 1980:70). Questions aimed at ascertaining who we are increasingly have come to be directed to sex. Foucault sums this all up: "Sex, the explanation of everything" (1980:78).

Instead of focusing on the repression of sexuality, Foucault argues that the scientific study of sex should focus on the relationship between sex and power. Again, that power does not reside in one central source; it exists in a variety of micro settings. Furthermore, as is always the case with Foucault, there is resistance to the imposition of power over sex. Power and the resistance to power are everywhere.

Prior to the eighteenth century, society sought control over death, but beginning in that century the focus shifted to control over life, especially sex. Power over life (and sex) took two forms. First, there was the "anatomo-politics of the human body," in which the goal was to discipline the human body (and its sexuality).[2] Second, there was the "bio-politics of population," in which the object was to control and regulate population

---

[2]Foucault's work played a key role in the development of the sociology of the body and of a new journal, *Body and Society* (Featherstone and Turner, 1995).

growth, health, life expectancy, and so forth. In both cases, society came to see "life as a political object" (Foucault, 1980:145). Sex was central in both cases: "Sex was a means of access both to the life of the body and the life of the species" (Foucault, 1980:146). In the modern West, sex has become more important than the soul (and we know how important that is in Foucault's work) and almost as important as life itself. Through knowledge of sexuality, society is coming to exercise more power over life itself. Yet despite this increase in control, Foucault holds out the hope of emancipation:

> It is the agency of sex that we must break away from, if we aim—through a tactical reversal of the various mechanisms of sexuality—to counter the grips of power with the claims of bodies, pleasures, and knowledges, in their multiplicity and their possibility of resistance. The rallying point for the counterattack against the deployment of sexuality ought not to be sex-desire, but bodies and pleasures.
>
> (Foucault, 1980:157)

Dean (1994) argues that from the late 1970s until his death in 1984, Foucault's work shifted from the micro politics of power in the direction of a concern for *governmentalities,* or the "heterogeneous, non-subjective processes in which practices and techniques of governance have come to depend on discursive representations of their fields of intervention and operation" (Dean, 1994:78). In contrast to other theorists, Foucault's focus is not specifically on the state, but "the practices and rationalities that compose the means of rule and government" (Dean, 1994:153). Thus, in terms of the will to knowledge in the human sciences, Foucault is concerned with the way bodies are regulated, the way conduct is governed, and the ways in which the self is formed. More generally, he was concerned with self-government, the government of others, and the government of the state. In most general terms, government to Foucault is concerned with "the conduct of conduct" (Dean, 1994:176).

Foucault has now been dead for nearly two decades, and while some of the early French poststructuralists (for example, Derrida) continue to be active, poststructuralism has been overtaken and passed by postmodern theory. It has always been difficult to draw a clear line between poststructuralism and postmodern theory; indeed there is no such line. Postmodern thinking can be seen as an extension and an exaggeration of poststructuralism. Whether or not one can clearly differentiate between the two, it is abundantly clear that postmodernism has become the most important development not only in sociological theory, but in a wide range of academic and nonacademic fields.

POSTMODERN SOCIAL THEORY

Sociology today faces a situation that a number of fields, mainly in the liberal arts, confronted a decade ago:

> The postmodern moment had arrived and perplexed intellectuals, artists, and cultural entrepreneurs wondered whether they should get on the bandwagon and join the carnival, or sit on the sidelines until the new fad disappeared into the whirl of cultural fashion.
>
> (Kellner, 1989b:1–2)

While many sociologists, and some sociological theorists, still consider postmodern social theory to be a fad (and it continues to look to some more like a carnival than a serious scholarly endeavor), the simple fact is that postmodern social theory can no longer be ignored by sociological theorists. In contemporary social theory, it has been "the hottest game in town" (Kellner, 1989b:2). It has been so hot, in fact, that at least one theorist has urged that we stop using the term because it has been "worn frail by overexertion" (Lemert, 1994b:142). That is, it has been abused by both supporters and detractors, as well as in the course of the overheated debate between them.

Given the importance of postmodern social theory and the heat that it has generated, the objective here is to offer at least a brief introduction to postmodern thinking (Antonio, 1998; Ritzer, 1997). However, this is no easy matter. For one thing, there is great diversity among the generally highly idiosyncratic postmodern thinkers, so it is difficult to offer generalizations on which the majority would agree. Smart (1993), for example, has differentiated among three postmodernist positions.[3] The first, or extreme, postmodernist position is that there has been a radical rupture and modern society has been replaced by a postmodern society. Exponents of this point of view include Jean Baudrillard, Gilles Deleuze and Felix Guattari (1972/1983; Bogard, 1998; *Theory, Culture and Society,* 1997). The second position is that while a change has taken place, postmodernism grows out of, and is continuous with, modernism. This orientation is adhered to by Marxian thinkers like Fredric Jameson, Ernesto Laclau, and Chantal Mouffe and by postmodern feminists such as Nancy Fraser and Linda Nicholson. Finally, there is the position, adopted by Smart himself, that rather than viewing modernism and postmodernism as epochs, we can see them as engaged in a long-running and ongoing set of relationships, with postmodernism continually pointing out the limitations of modernism. While useful, Smart's typology would likely be dismissed by postmodernists as greatly simplifying the great diversity of their ideas and distorting them in the process.

While no term has greater resonance today among scholars in a wide range of disciplines than does "postmodern," there is enormous ambiguity and controversy over exactly what the term means. For clarity it is useful to distinguish among the terms "postmodernity," "postmodernism," and "postmodern social theory."[4] *Postmodernity* refers to a historical epoch that is generally seen as following the modern era; *postmodernism* to cultural products (in art, movies, architecture, and so on) that differ from modern cultural products; and *postmodern social theory* to a way of thinking that is distinct from modern social theory. Thus, the postmodern encompasses *a new historical epoch, new cultural products,* and *a new type of theorizing about the social world.* All these, of course, share the perspective that something new and different has happened in recent years that can no longer be described by the term "modern," and that those new developments are replacing modern realities.

To address the first of these concepts, there is a widespread belief that the modern era is ending, or has ended, and we have entered a new historical epoch of *postmodernity.* Lemert argues that the birth of postmodernism can be traced, at least symbolically, to

> the death of modernist architecture at 3:32 P.M., July 15, 1972—the moment at which the Pruitt-Igoe housing project in St. Louis was destroyed. . . . This massive housing project in St. Louis represented modernist architecture's arrogant belief that by building the

---

[3]Rosenau (1992) distinguishes between skeptical and affirmative postmodern thinkers.
[4]Here I follow the distinction made by Best and Kellner (1991:5).

biggest and best public housing planners and architects could eradicate poverty and human misery. To have recognized, and destroyed the symbol of that idea was to admit the failure of modernist architecture, and by implication modernity itself.

(Lemert, 1990:233; following Jencks, 1977)

The destruction of Pruitt-Igoe is a reflection of differences between modernists and postmodernists over whether it is possible to find rational solutions to society's problems. To take another example, Lyndon Johnson's war on poverty in the 1960s was typical of the way modern society believed it could discover and implement rational solutions to its problems. It could be argued that in the 1980s the Reagan administration and its general unwillingness to develop massive programs to deal with such problems was representative of a postmodern society and the belief that there is no single rational answer to various problems. Thus, we might conclude that somewhere between the presidential administrations of Kennedy and Johnson and Reagan, the United States moved from being a modern to a postmodern society. In fact, the destruction of Pruitt-Igoe occurred within that time frame.

The second concept, *postmodernism,* relates to the cultural realm in which it is argued that postmodern products have tended to supplant modern products. In art, as we will see shortly, Jameson (1984) contrasts Andy Warhol's postmodern, almost photographic and unemotional painting of Marilyn Monroe to Edvard Munch's modern and highly painful *The Scream.* In the realm of television, the show *Twin Peaks* is generally taken to be a good example of postmodernism, while *Father Knows Best* is a good example of a modern television program. In the movies, *Blade Runner* may be seen as a postmodern work, while the *Ten Commandments* would certainly qualify as a modern movie.

Third, and of much more direct relevance to us here, is the emergence of *postmodern social theory* and its differences from modern theory. Modern social theory sought a universal, ahistorical, rational foundation for its analysis and critique of society. For Marx, that foundation was species-being, while for Habermas it was communicative reason. Postmodern thinking rejects this "foundationalism" and tends to be relativistic, irrational, and nihilistic. Following Nietzsche and Foucault, among others, postmodernists have come to question such foundations, believing that they tend to privilege some groups and downgrade the significance of others, give some groups power and render other groups powerless.

Similarly, postmodernists reject the ideas of a grand narrative or a metanarrative. It is in the rejection of these ideas that we encounter one of the most important postmodernists, Jean-François Lyotard. Lyotard (1984:xxiii) begins by identifying modern (scientific) knowledge with the kind of single grand synthesis (or "metadiscourse") that we have associated with the work of theorists like Marx and Parsons. The kinds of grand narratives he associates with modern science include "the dialectics of Spirit, the hermeneutics of meaning, the emancipation of the rational or working subject, or the creation of wealth" (Lyotard, 1984:xxiii).

If modern knowledge is identified in Lyotard's view with metanarratives, then postmodern knowledge involves a rejection of such grand narratives. As Lyotard puts it: "Simplifying to the extreme, I define *postmodern* as incredulity to metanarratives" (1984:xxiv). More strongly, he argues: "Let us wage war on totality . . . let us activate the differences" (Lyotard, 1984:82). In fact, postmodern social theory becomes a celebration of a range of different theoretical perspectives: "Postmodern knowledge is not simply a tool of authorities; it refines our sensitivity to differences and reinforces our ability to tolerate the incommensurable" (Lyotard, 1984:xxv). In these terms, sociology has moved beyond the modern period, into the postmodern period, in its search for a range of more specific syntheses. In the view of Fraser and Nicholson, Lyotard prefers "smallish, localized narrative[s]" to the metanarratives, or the grand narratives, of modernity (1988:89). The new syntheses discussed throughout this book may be seen as examples of such "smallish," "localized" sociological narratives.

While Lyotard rejects the grand narrative in general, Baudrillard rejects the idea of a grand narrative in sociology. For one thing, Baudrillard rejects the whole idea of the social. For another, rejecting the social leads to a rejection of the metanarrative of sociology that is associated with modernity:

> . . . the great organizing principle, the grand narrative of the Social which found its support and justification in ideas on the rational contract, civil society, progress, power, production—that all this may have pointed to something that once existed, but exists no longer. The age of the perspective of the social (coinciding rightly with that ill-defined period known as modernity) . . . is over.
>
> (Bogard, 1990:10)

Thus, postmodern social theory stands for the rejection of metanarratives in general and of grand narratives within sociology in particular.

Postmodern social theory has, to a large degree, been the product of nonsociologists (Lyotard, Derrida, Jameson, and others). In recent years, a number of sociologists have begun to operate within a postmodern perspective, and postmodern social theory can be seen, at least to some degree, as *part* of the classical sociological tradition. Take, for example, the recent reinterpretation of the work of Georg Simmel entitled *Postmodern(ized) Simmel* (Weinstein and Weinstein, 1993; 1998). Weinstein and Weinstein recognize that there is a strong case to be made for Simmel as a liberal modernist who offers a grand narrative of the historical trend toward the dominance of objective culture—the "tragedy of culture." However, they also argue that an equally strong case can be made for Simmel as a postmodern theorist. Thus, they acknowledge that both alternatives have validity and, in fact, that one is no more true than the other. Weinstein and Weinstein argue: "To our minds 'modernism' and 'postmodernism' are not exclusive alternatives but discursive domains bordering each other" (1993:21). They note they could be doing a modernist interpretation of Simmel, but feel that a postmodernist explication is more useful. Thus, they express the very postmodern view: "There is no essential Simmel, only different Simmels read through the various positions in contemporary discourse formations" (Weinstein and Weinstein, 1993:55).

What sort of arguments do Weinstein and Weinstein make in defense of a postmodernized Simmel? For one thing, Simmel is seen as being generally opposed to totalizations; indeed he is inclined to detotalize modernity. In spite of, and aside from, the theory of the "tragedy of culture," Simmel was primarily an essayist and a storyteller, and he dealt mainly with a range of specific issues rather than with the totality of the social world.

Simmel is also described by Weinstein and Weinstein, as he is by others, as a *flaneur,* or someone who is something of an idler. More specifically, Simmel is described as a so-ciologist who idled away his time analyzing a wide range of social phenomena. He was interested in all of them for their aesthetic qualities; they all existed "to titillate, astonish, please or delight him" (Weinstein and Weinstein, 1993:60). Simmel is described as spending his intellectual life wandering through a wide range of social phenomena de-scribing one or another as the mood moved him. This approach led Simmel away from a totalized view of the world and toward a concern for a number of discrete, but impor-tant, elements of that world.

Bricoleur is another term used to describe Simmel. A *bricoleur* is a kind of intellec-tual handyman who makes do with whatever happens to be available to him. Available to Simmel are a wide range of fragments of the social world, or "shards of objective cul-ture," as Weinstein and Weinstein (1993:70) describe them in Simmelian terms. As a *bricoleur* Simmel cobbles together whatever ideas he can find in order to shed light on the social world.

There is no need to go too deeply into the details of Weinstein and Weinstein's inter-pretation of a postmodernized Simmel. The illustrative points already made make it clear that such an interpretation is as reasonable as the modernized vision. It would be far harder to come up with similar postmodern views of the other major classical theorists, although one could certainly find aspects of their work that are consistent with postmod-ern social theory. Thus, as Seidman (1991) makes clear, most of sociological theory *is* modernist, but as the case of Simmel illustrates, there are postmodern intimations in even that most modernist of traditions.

Another place to look for intimations of postmodern social theory is among the critics of modern theory *within* sociological theory. As several observers (Antonio, 1991; Best and Kellner, 1991; Smart, 1993) have pointed out, a key position is occupied by C. Wright Mills (1959). First, Mills actually used the term "postmodern" to describe the post-Enlightenment era which we were entering: "We are at the ending of what is called The Modern Age. . . . The Modern Age is being succeeded by a post-modern period" (Mills, 1959:165–166). Second, he was a severe critic of modern grand theory in sociol-ogy, especially as it was practiced by Talcott Parsons. Third, Mills favored a socially and morally engaged sociology. In his terms, he wanted a sociology that linked broad public issues to specific private troubles.

While there are intimations of postmodern social theory in the work of Simmel and Mills (and many others), it is not there that we find postmodern theory itself. For example, Best and Kellner contend that Mills "is very much a modernist, given to sweeping socio-logical generalization, totalizing surveys of sociology and history, and a belief in the power of the sociological imagination to illuminate social reality and to change society" (1991:8).

Given this general background, let us turn to a more concrete discussion of postmod-ern social theory. We will focus on a few of the ideas associated with two of the most im-portant postmodern social theorists: Fredric Jameson and Jean Baudrillard.

Moderate Postmodern Social Theory: Fredric Jameson

The dominant position on the issue of postmodernity is clearly that there is a radical dis-juncture between modernity and postmodernity. However, there are some postmodern theorists who argue that while postmodernity has important differences from modernity, there are also continuities between them. The best-known of these arguments is made by Fredric Jameson (1984) in an essay entitled "Postmodernism, or The Cultural Logic of Late Capitalism," as well as later in a book of essays with the same title (Jameson, 1991). That title is clearly indicative of Jameson's Marxian position that capitalism, now in its "late" phase, continues to be the dominant feature in today's world, but it has spawned a new cultural logic—postmodernism. In other words, while the cultural logic may have changed, the underlying economic structure is continuous with earlier forms of capitalism. Furthermore, capitalism continues to be up to its same old tricks of spawning a cultural logic in order to help it maintain itself.

In writing in this vein, Jameson is clearly rejecting the claim made by many postmodernists (for example, Lyotard, Baudrillard) that Marxian theory is perhaps the grand narrative par excellence and therefore has no place in, or relevance to, postmodernity. Jameson is not only rescuing Marxian theory, but endeavoring to show that it offers the best theoretical explanation of postmodernity. Interestingly, while Jameson is generally praised for his insights into the culture of postmodernism, he is often criticized, especially by Marxists, for offering an inadequate analysis of the economic base of this new cultural world.

Also consistent with the work of Marx, and unlike most theorists of postmodernism, Jameson (1984:86) sees both positive and negative characteristics, "catastrophe and progress all together," associated with postmodern society. Marx, of course, saw capitalism in this way: productive of liberation and very valuable advancements and *at the same time* the height of exploitation and alienation.

Jameson begins by recognizing that postmodernism is usually associated with a radical break, but then after discussing a number of things usually associated with postmodernism, he asks, "Does it imply any more fundamental change or break than the periodic style—and fashion—changes determined by an older high modernist imperative of stylistic innovation?" (1984:54). He responds that while there certainly have been aesthetic changes, those changes continue to be a function of underlying economic dynamics:

> What has happened is that aesthetic production today has become integrated into commodity production generally: the frantic economic urgency of producing fresh waves of ever more novel-seeming goods (from clothing to airplanes), at ever greater rates of turnover, now assigns an increasingly essential structural function and position to aesthetic innovation and experimentation. Such economic necessities then find recognition in the institutional support of all kinds available for the newer art, from foundations and grants to museums and other forms of patronage.
>
> (Jameson, 1984:56)

The continuity with the past is even clearer and more dramatic in the following:

> This whole global, yet American, postmodern culture is the internal and superstructural expression of a whole new wave of American military and economic domination throughout the world: in this sense, as throughout class history, the underside of culture is blood, torture, death and horror.
>
> (Jameson, 1984:57)

Jameson (following Ernest Mandel) sees three stages in the history of capitalism. The first stage, analyzed by Marx, is market capitalism, or the emergence of unified national markets. The second stage, analyzed by Lenin, is the imperialist stage with the emergence of a global capitalist network. The third stage, labeled by Mandel (1975) and Jameson as "late capitalism," involves "a prodigious expansion of capital into hitherto uncommodified areas" (Jameson, 1984:78). This expansion, "far from being inconsistent with Marx's great 19th-century analysis, constitutes on the contrary the purest form of capital yet to have emerged" (Jameson, 1984:78). Said Jameson, "The Marxist framework is still indispensable for understanding the new historical content, which demands not modification of the Marxist framework, but an expansion of it" (cited in Stephanson, 1989:54). For Jameson, the key to modern capitalism is its multinational character and the fact that it has greatly increased the range of commodification.

These changes in the economic structure have been reflected in cultural changes. Thus, Jameson associates realist culture with market capitalism, modernist culture with monopoly capitalism, and postmodern culture with multinational capitalism. This view seems to be an updated version of Marx's base-superstructure argument, and many have criticized Jameson for adopting such a simplistic perspective. However, Jameson has tried hard to avoid such a "vulgar" position and has described a more complex relationship between the economy and culture. Nonetheless, even a sympathetic critic like Featherstone concludes, "It is clear that his view of culture largely works within the confines of a base-superstructure model" (1989:119).

Capitalism has gone from a stage in monopoly capitalism in which culture was at least to some degree autonomous to an explosion of culture in multinational capitalism:

> A prodigious expansion of culture throughout the social realm, to the point at which everything in our social life—from economic value and state power to practices and to the very structure of the psyche itself—can be said to have become "cultural" in some original and as yet untheorized sense. This perhaps startling proposition is, however, substantively quite consistent with the previous diagnosis of a society of the image or the simulacrum [this term will be defined shortly], and a transformation of the "real" into so many pseudo-events.
>
> (Jameson, 1984:87)

Jameson describes this new form as a "cultural dominant." As a cultural dominant, postmodernism is described as a "force field in which very different kinds of cultural impulses . . . must make their way" (Jameson, 1984:57). Thus, while postmodernism is "a new systematic cultural norm," it is made up of a range of quite heterogeneous elements (Jameson, 1984:57). By using the term "cultural dominant," Jameson also clearly means that while postmodern culture is controlling, there are various other forces that exist within today's culture.

Fredric Jameson offers a comparatively clear image of a postmodern society composed of four basic elements (a fifth, its late capitalistic character, has already been discussed). First, postmodern society is characterized by superficiality and lack of depth. Its cultural products are satisfied with surface images and do not delve deeply into the underlying meanings. A good example is Andy Warhol's famous painting of Campbell soup cans which appear to be nothing more than perfect representations of those cans. To use a key term associated with postmodern theory, the picture is a *simulacrum* in which one cannot distinguish between the original and the copy. A simulacrum is also a copy of a copy; Warhol was reputed to have painted his soup cans not from the cans themselves, but from a photograph of the cans. Jameson describes a simulacrum as "the identical copy for which no original ever existed" (1984:66). A simulacrum is, by definition, superficial, lacking in depth.

Second, postmodernism is characterized by a waning of emotion or affect. As his example, Jameson contrasts another of Warhol's paintings—another near-photographic representation, this time of Marilyn Monroe—to a classic modernist piece of art—Edvard Munch's *The Scream*. *The Scream* is a surreal painting of a person expressing the depth of despair, or in sociological terms, anomie or alienation. Warhol's painting of Marilyn Monroe is superficial and expresses no genuine emotion. This reflects the fact that to the postmodernists, the alienation and anomie that caused the kind of reaction depicted by Munch is part of the now-past modern world. In the postmodern world alienation has been replaced by fragmentation. Since the world and the people in it have become fragmented, the affect that remains is "free-floating and impersonal" (Jameson, 1984:64). There is a peculiar kind of euphoria associated with these postmodern feelings, or what Jameson prefers to call "intensities." He gives as an example, a photorealist cityscape "where even automobile wrecks gleam with some new hallucinatory splendour" (Jameson, 1984:76). Euphoria based on automobile disasters in the midst of urban squalor is, indeed, a peculiar kind of emotion. Postmodern intensity also occurs when "the body is plugged into the new electronic media" (Donougho, 1989:85).

Third, there is a loss of historicity. We cannot know the past. All we have access to are texts about the past, and all we can do is produce yet other texts about that topic. This loss of historicity has led to the "random cannibalization of all styles of the past" (Jameson, 1984:65–66). The result leads us to another key term in postmodern thinking—*pastiche*. Since it is impossible for historians to find the truth about the past, or even to put together a coherent story about it, they are satisfied with creating pastiches, or hodgepodges of ideas, sometimes contradictory and confused, about the past. Further, there is no clear sense of historical development, of time passing. Past and present are inextricably intertwined. For example, in historical novels such as E. L. Doctorow's *Ragtime,* we see the "disappearance of the historical referent. This historical novel can no longer set out to represent historical past; it can only 'represent' our ideas and stereotypes about that past" (Jameson, 1984:71). Another example is the movie *Body Heat,* which while clearly about the present, creates an atmosphere reminiscent of the 1930s. In order to do this,

> the object world of the present-day—artifacts and appliances, even automobiles, whose styling would serve to date the image—is elaborately edited out. Everything in the film, therefore, conspires to blur its official contemporaneity and to make it possible for you to receive the narrative as though it were set in some eternal Thirties, beyond historical time.
>
> (Jameson, 1984:68)

A movie like *Body Heat* or a novel like *Ragtime* is "an elaborated symptom of the waning of our historicity" (Jameson, 1984:68). This loss of temporality, this inability to distinguish between past, present, and future, is manifested at the individual level in a kind of schizophrenia. For the postmodern individual, events are fragmented and discontinuous.

Fourth, there is a new technology associated with postmodern society. Instead of productive technologies like the automobile assembly line, we have the dominance of *re*productive technologies, especially electronic media like the television set and the computer. Rather than the "exciting" technology of the industrial revolution, we have technologies like television, "which articulates nothing but rather implodes, carrying its flattened image surface within itself" (Jameson, 1984:79). The implosive, flattening technologies of the postmodern era give birth to very different cultural products than the explosive, expanding technologies of the modern era did.

In sum, Jameson presents us with an image of postmodernity in which people are adrift and unable to comprehend the multinational capitalist system or the explosively growing culture in which they live. As a paradigm of this world, and of one's place in it, Jameson offers the example of Los Angeles's Hotel Bonaventure, designed by a famous postmodern architect, John Portman. One of the points that Jameson makes about the hotel is that one is unable to get one's bearings in the lobby. The lobby is an example of what Jameson means by *hyperspace,* an area where modern conceptions of space are useless in helping us to orient ourselves. In this case, the lobby is surrounded by four absolutely symmetrical towers which contain the rooms. In fact, the hotel had to add color coding and directional signals to help people find their way. But the key point is that, as designed, people had great difficulty getting their bearings in the hotel lobby.

This situation in the lobby of the Hotel Bonaventure is a metaphor for our inability to get our bearings in the multinational economy and cultural explosion of late capitalism. Unlike many postmodernists, Jameson as a Marxist is unwilling to leave it at that and comes up with at least a partial solution to the problem of living in a postmodern society. What we need, he says, are cognitive maps in order to find our way around (Jagtenberg and Mekie, 1997). Yet, these are not, cannot be, the maps of old. Thus, Jameson awaits a

> breakthrough to some as yet unimaginable new mode of representing . . . [late capitalism], in which we may again begin to grasp our positioning as individual and collective subjects and regain a capacity to act and struggle which is at present neutralized by our spatial as well as our social confusion. The political form of postmodernism, if there ever is any, will have as its vocation the invention and projection of a global cognitive mapping, on a social as well as a spatial scale.
>
> (Jameson, 1984:92)

These cognitive maps can come from various sources—social theorists (including Jameson himself, who can be seen as providing such a map in his work), novelists, and people on an everyday basis who can map their own spaces. Of course, the maps are not ends in themselves to a Marxist like Jameson, but are to be used as the basis for radical political action in postmodern society.

The need for maps is linked to Jameson's view that we have moved from a world that is defined temporally to one that is defined spatially. Indeed, the idea of hyperspace, and the example of the lobby of the Hotel Bonaventure, reflect the dominance of space in the postmodern world. Thus, for Jameson, the central problem today is "the loss of our ability to *position ourselves within this space and to cognitively map it*" (Jameson, in Stephanson, 1989:48).

Interestingly, Jameson links the idea of cognitive maps to Marxian theory, specifically the idea of class consciousness: "'Cognitive mapping' was in reality nothing but a code word for 'class consciousness' . . . only it proposed the need for class consciousness of a new and hitherto undreamed of kind, while it also inflected the account in the direction of that new spatiality implicit in the postmodern" (1989:387).

The great strength of Jameson's work is his effort to synthesize Marxian theory and postmodernism. While he should be praised for this effort, the fact is that his work often displeases *both* Marxists and postmodernists. According to Best and Kellner, "His work is an example of the potential hazards of an eclectic, multiperspectival theory which attempts to incorporate a myriad of positions, some of them in tension or contradiction with each other, as when he produces the uneasy alliance between classical Marxism and extreme postmodernism" (1991:192). More specifically, for example, some Marxists object to the degree to which Jameson has accepted postmodernism as a cultural dominant, and some postmodernists criticize his acceptance of a totalizing theory of the world.

Extreme Postmodern Social Theory: Jean Baudrillard

If Jameson is among the more moderate of postmodern social theorists, then Jean Baudrillard is one of the most radical and outrageous of this genre. Unlike Jameson, Baudrillard was trained as a sociologist, but his work has long since left the confines of that discipline; indeed, it cannot be contained by any discipline, and Baudrillard would in any case reject the whole idea of disciplinary boundaries.

Following Kellner (1989d; forthcoming), we offer a brief overview of the twists and turns in Baudrillard's work. His earliest work, going back to the 1960s, was both modernist (Baudrillard did not use the term "postmodernism" until the 1980s) and Marxian in its orientation. His early works involved a Marxian critique of the consumer society. However, this work was already heavily influenced by linguistics and semiotics, with the result that Kellner contends that it is best to see this early work as "a semiological supplement to Marx's theory of political economy." However, it was not long before Baudrillard began to criticize the Marxian approach (as well as structuralism) and ultimately to leave it behind.

In *The Mirror of Production,* Baudrillard (1973/1975) came to view the Marxian perspective as the mirror image of conservative political economy. In other words, Marx (and the Marxists) bought into the same world view as the conservative supporters of capitalism. In Baudrillard's view, Marx was infected by the "virus of bourgeois thought" (1973/1975:39). Specifically, Marx's approach was infused with conservative ideas like "work" and "value." What was needed was a new, more radical orientation.

Baudrillard articulated the idea of symbolic exchange as an alternative to—the radical negation of—economic exchange (D. Cook, 1994). Symbolic exchange involved an uninterrupted cycle of "taking and returning, giving and receiving," a "*cycle* of gifts and countergifts" (Baudrillard, 1973/1975:83). Here was an idea that did not fall into the trap that ensnared Marx; symbolic exchange was clearly outside of, and opposed to, the logic of capitalism. The idea of symbolic exchange implied a political program aimed at creating a society characterized by such exchange. For example, Baudrillard is critical of the working class and seems more positive to the new left, or hippies. However, Baudrillard soon gave up on *all* political objectives.

Instead, Baudrillard turned his attention to the analysis of contemporary society, which, as he sees it, is dominated no longer by production, but rather by the "media, cybernetic models and steering systems, computers, information processing, entertainment and knowledge industries and so forth" (Kellner, 1989d:61). Emanating from these systems is a veritable explosion of signs (Harris, 1996). It could be said that we have moved from a society dominated by the mode of production to one controlled by the code of production. The objective has shifted from exploitation and profit to domination by the signs and the systems that produce them. Furthermore, while there was a time when the signs stood for something real, now they refer to little more than themselves and other signs; signs have become self-referential. We can no longer tell what is real; the distinction between signs and reality has *imploded.* More generally, the postmodern world (for now Baudrillard is operating squarely within that world) is a world characterized by such implosion as distinguished from the explosions (of productive systems, of commodities, of technologies, and so on) that characterized modern society. Thus, just as the modern world underwent a process of differentiation, the postmodern world can be seen as undergoing *dedifferentiation.*

Another way that Baudrillard, like Jameson, describes the postmodern world is that it is characterized by *simulations;* we live in "the age of simulation" (Baudrillard, 1983:4; Der Derian, 1994). The process of simulation leads to the creation of *simulacra,* or "reproductions of objects or events" (Kellner, 1989d:78). With the distinction between signs and reality imploding, it is increasingly difficult to tell the real from those things that simulate the real. For example, Baudrillard talks of "the dissolution of TV into life, the dissolution of life into TV" (1983:55). Eventually, it is the representations of the real, the simulations, that come to be predominant. We are in the thrall of these simulations, which "form a spiralling, circular system with no beginning or end" (Kellner, 1989d:83).

Baudrillard (1983) describes this world as *hyperreality.* For example, the media cease to be a mirror of reality, but become that reality, or even more real than that reality. The tabloid news shows that are so popular on TV these days (for example, *Inside Edition*) are good examples (another is "infomercials") because the falsehoods and distortions they peddle to viewers are more than reality—they are hyperreality. The result is that what is real comes to be subordinated and ultimately dissolved altogether. It becomes impossible to distinguish the real from the spectacle. In fact, "real" events increasingly take on the character of the hyperreal. For example, the trial of former football great O. J. Simpson for the murders of Nicole Simpson and Ronald Goldman seemed hyperreal and perfect fodder for the hyperreal TV shows like *Inside Edition.* In the end, there is no more reality, only hyperreality.

In all this, Baudrillard is focusing on culture, which he sees as undergoing a massive and "catastrophic" revolution. That revolution involves the masses becoming increasingly passive, rather than increasingly rebellious, as they were to the Marxists. Thus, the mass is seen as a "'black hole' [that] absorbs all meaning, information, communication, messages and so on, thereby rendering them meaningless . . . masses go sullenly on their ways, ignoring attempts to manipulate them" (Kellner, 1989d:85). Indifference, apathy, and inertia are all good terms to describe the masses saturated with media signs, simulacra, and hyperreality. The masses are not seen as manipulated by the media, but the media are being forced to supply their escalating demands for objects and spectacles. In a sense, society itself is imploding into the black hole that is the masses. Summing up much of this theory, Kellner concludes,

> Acceleration of inertia, the implosion of meaning in the media, the implosion of the so-
> cial in the mass, the implosion of the mass in a dark hole of nihilism and meaningless-
> ness; such is the Baudrillardian postmodern vision.
>
> (Kellner, 1989d:118)

As extraordinary as this analysis may seem, Baudrillard was even more bizarre, scan-dalous, irreverent, promiscuous, playful, or as Kellner says, "carnivalesque," in *Symbolic Exchange and Death* (1976/1993). Baudrillard sees contemporary society as a death culture, with death being the "paradigm of all social exclusion and discrimination" (Kellner, 1989d:104). The emphasis on death also reflects the binary opposition of life and death. In contrast, societies characterized by symbolic exchange end binary oppo-sitions in general and more specifically the opposition between life and death (and, in the process, the exclusion and discrimination that accompanies a death culture). It is the anxiety about death and exclusion that leads people to plunge themselves even more deeply into the consumer culture.

Holding up symbolic exchange as the preferred alternative to contemporary society began to seem too primitive to Baudrillard (1979/1990), and he came to regard *seduction* as the preferred alternative, perhaps because it fit better with his emerging sense of postmodernism. Seduction "involves the charms of pure and mere games, superficial rituals" (Kellner, 1989d:149). Baudrillard is extolling the power and virtues of seduc-tion, with its meaninglessness, playfulness, depthlessness, "non-sense," and irrational-ity, over a world characterized by production.

In the end, Baudrillard is offering a fatal theory. Thus, in one of his later works, *America,* Baudrillard says that in his visit to that country, he "sought the finished form of the future catastrophe" (1986/1989:5). There is no revolutionary hope as there is in Marx's work. Nor is there even the possibility of reforming society as Durkheim hoped. Rather, we seem doomed to a life of simulations, hyperreality, and implosion of every-thing into an incomprehensible black hole. While vague alternatives like symbolic ex-change and seduction can be found in Baudrillard's work, he generally shies away from extolling their virtues or articulating a political program aimed at their realization.

Postmodern Social Theory and Sociological Theory

There are those who believe that postmodern social theory, especially in its more radi-cal forms, represents an incommensurable alternative to sociological theory. In one sense, it is seen as not being theory, at least in the sense that we conventionally use the term. At the beginning of this book, sociological theory was defined as "the 'big ideas' in sociology that have stood the test of time (or promise to), idea systems that deal with major social issues and are far-reaching in scope." It seems to me that the radical ideas of a postmodernist like Baudrillard fit this definition quite well. Baudrillard certainly offers a number of "big ideas" (simulations, hyperreality, symbolic exchange, seduction). They are ideas that show every promise of standing the test of time. And Baudrillard certainly deals with major social issues (for example, the control of the media); his ideas have implications for a substantial part, if not all, of the social world. Thus, I would say that Baudrillard is offering a sociological theory, and if that can be said of Baudrillard, it can certainly be said of Jameson and most other postmodernists.

The real threat of postmodern social theory is more in its form than in its substance. In rejecting grand narratives, postmodernists are rejecting most of what we usually think of as sociological theory. Baudrillard (and other postmodernists) do not offer grand narratives, but rather bits and pieces of ideas that often seem to contradict one another. If the postmodernists win the day, the sociological theory of the future will look very different from today's theory. But even if the form is nearly unrecognizable, the content will still involve important, wide-ranging ideas about social issues.

Whatever the future may hold, at the moment postmodern social theorists are producing an unusually large number of important and exciting ideas. Those ideas cannot be ignored and may, as they are internalized in sociology, push sociological theory in some new and unforeseen directions.

Applying Postmodern Social Theory

In Chapter 12 we encountered my work on the new means of consumption (Ritzer, 1999). They were described as modern phenomena both because they are recent innovations and because they are highly rationalized. However, their high degree of rationalization not only enables them in various ways, but also creates problems for them. It is in the responses to these problems that we can see the utility of postmodern social theory, especially the ideas of Jean Baudrillard.

Just as Max Weber alerts us to the rationalization process, he also sensitizes us to the problems associated with rationalization, especially disenchantment. One of Max Weber's most general theses is that as a result of rationalization the Western world has grown increasingly disenchanted (Schneider, 1993:ix). Disenchantment involves the displacement of "magical elements of thought" (Gerth and Mills, 1958:51). As Schneider (1993:ix) puts it, "Max Weber saw history as having departed a deeply enchanted past en route to a disenchanted future—a journey that would gradually strip the natural world both of its magical properties and of its capacity for meaning." Or, "In the face of the seemingly relentless advance of science and bureaucratic social organization, he believed, enchantment would be hounded further and further from the institutional centers of our culture. Carried to an extreme, this process would turn life into a tale which, whether told by an idiot or not, would certainly signify nothing, having been evacuated of meaning" (Schneider, 1993:xiii).

Disenchantment poses a major problem for the new means of consumption. Disenchanted settings are simply not very attractive to consumers who are unlikely to return to such sites over and over. As a result, the new means of consumption need to find a way of re-enchanting themselves and it is this notion of re-enchantment that leads us to postmodern social theory because postmodernists accord great centrality to this process of re-enchantment:

> Postmodernity . . . brings "re-enchantment" of the world after the protracted and earnest, though in the end inconclusive, modern struggle to dis-enchant it (or, more exactly, the resistance to dis-enchantment, hardly ever put to sleep, was all along the "postmodern thorn" in the body of modernity). The mistrust of human spontaneity, of drives, impulses and inclinations resistant to prediction and rational justification, has been all but replaced by the mistrust of unemotional, calculating reason. Dignity has been returned to emotions; legitimacy to the "inexplicable," nay *irrational* . . . The postmodern world is one in which *mystery* is no more a barely tolerated alien awaiting a deportation order . . . We learn to live with events and acts that are not only not-yet-explained, but (for all we know about what we will ever know) inexplicable. We learn again to respect ambiguity, to feel regard for human emotions, to appreciate actions without purpose and calculable rewards.
>
> (Bauman, 1993:33)

For example, Baudrillard (1983/1990:51) argues that the previously discussed "seduction" offers the possibility of re-enchanting our lives. Rather than the complete clarity and visibility associated with modernity, seduction offers "the play and power of illusion." Re-enchantment constitutes the way out of the dilemma posed by the disenchantment of the world in general and of the means of consumption in particular. In order to continue to attract, control, and exploit consumers, the cathedrals of consumption undergo a continual process of re-enchantment.

Spectacle is the key to the re-enchantment of the new means of consumption (DeBord, 1967/1994). We will define a spectacle as a dramatic public display. In this case, these displays are oriented toward re-enchanting the new means of consumption. Spectacles may be created intentionally, or they may be partially or wholly unintentional. We will concern ourselves here with the latter, especially through the previously discussed postmodern processes of simulation and implosion.

Simulations   Perhaps the most important reason for creating simulations, or transforming "real" phenomena into simulations, is that they can be made more spectacular than their authentic counterparts and, therefore, a greater lure to consumers. Take Las Vegas, which has become the ultimate in simulated spectacle because it has created so many artificial settings in one location. Where else can you find New York City, Monte Carlo, Bellagio, Venice, and Paris within a few minutes walk of one another? Even if you went to one of those "real" cities, you would be able to experience only it and not the others. In any case, the tourist areas of those cities have themselves become simulations.

Las Vegas hotel-casinos have a field day with the line between reality and unreality. The Bellagio is a simulation of the Italian region of the same name, but it also houses $260 million in original fine art by such masters as Renoir, Cezanne, and Picasso. At about the same time that Bellagio openend, the Rio hotel-casino hosted a six-month exhibit of treasures from Russia's Romanov Dynasty. It included Peter the Great's throne and a Faberge pen used by Czar Nicholas to abdicate in 1917. These "real" artifacts were housed in a replica of the Russian royal galleries including "a reproduction neogothic ceiling from high density foam." King Tut's tomb in the Luxor hotel is called a "museum" even though everything in it is a reproduction. However, its gift shop sells "genuine ancient coins, 18th century Egyptian engravings, oil lamps and other artifacts." Said an art critic, "The museum had all fakes, and the gift shop had the real thing. It just summed up Las Vegas for me" (Binkley, 1998:B10).

Huxtable, following Umberto Eco (and Baudrillard), argues that the "unreal has become the reality . . . The real now imitates the imitation" (cited in Huxtable, 1997a:64, 65). For example, the clearly simulated and unreal Disney World has become the model not only for Disney's town of Celebration, but many other communities throughout the United States. Seaside, Florida, and Kentlands, Maryland, are two examples of popular communities that have tried to emulate the ersatz small-town America that is championed by Disney World. Specifically, Huxtable emphasizes the growing importance of fake, synthetic, artificial, simulated architecture: "Real architecture has little place in the unreal America" (Huxtable, 1997a:3).

Our environment has come to be dominated by entertainment and to emulate the theme park. Huxtable's (1997b:1) architectural model of this is the casino, New York, New York, and more generally Las Vegas: "the real fake reaches its apogee in places like Las Vegas . . . The outrageously fake fake has developed its own indigenous style and life style to become a real place . . . this is the real, real fake at the highest, loudest and most authentically inauthentic level of illusion and invention." Huxtable (1997b:40) argues that visitors seem to find things such as the artificial rainforests, volcanos, and rock formations in Las Vegas far more impressive than the real thing. In fact, a spokesperson for the industry goes so far as to make the case *against* reality: "'You get a very artificial appearance with real rock.'"

Implosion Imploded worlds represent a kind of spectacle that draws consumers into them and leads them to consume. It is simply amazing to find interpenetrated settings and activities that, not too long ago, were clearly distinguished from one another. Only a few decades ago people had to trek from one locale to another for various goods and services; now they can find that variety in a single mall. Similarly, it wasn't that many years ago that if one wanted to gamble, one went to Las Vegas, but if one wanted to visit a theme park, one went to Orlando (or Anaheim). Now, one can go to the MGM Grand or Circus Circus in Las Vegas, for example, and find both a casino and a theme park on the hotel's grounds. Your local Wal-Mart, or corner service station, might well encompass a satellite fast-food restaurant. REI in Seattle not only offers you mountain climbing shoes, but even a mountain to practice on. Thus, another spectacular and enchanting aspect of many of the new means of consumption is that so many different things have imploded into them and they, in turn, have imploded into so many other settings.

The changes in Las Vegas are related to a more general implosion of the boundaries between touring and consuming. Of course, touring always involved the consumption of tourist activities and sites. Along the way, tourists generally were interested in purchasing everything from trinkets to trophies. Now, however, we are seeing more and more instances in which the main objective of touring *is* the consumption of goods. For one thing, mega-malls have become tourist destinations. The lure of a mega-mall vacation is that mega-malls have something for everyone—water parks, roller coasters and amusement parks for the children; shops, restaurants, and bars for the adults. This combination is spectacular and a powerful lure to the traveler. Airlines offer day trips to Mall of America; bus lines offer package trips that might involve visits of several days to the mall. Mall of America attracted 12 million tourists in 1995, more than the combined number of visitors to Walt Disney World, the Grand Canyon, and Graceland. In Canada, the largest tourist attraction is *not* Niagara Falls, but rather the Edmonton Mall.

Potomac Mills outside Washington had 4.5 million visitors in 1995. By comparison, 4 million visited Arlington National Cemetery, 2.5 million journeyed to Colonial Williamsburg, and only 1 million visited Mount Vernon. Franklin Mills, outside Philadelphia, drew 6 million visitors in 1995, four times as many as visited the Liberty Bell. NikeTown is Chicago's largest tourist attraction. Many tourist destinations are surrounded by outlet or discount malls that are the fastest-growing segment of not only the mall business, but also the travel industry. People are almost as apt to journey to such locales for the malls as they are for the sea or the air. Indeed, it often seems as if almost as many people are at the malls as are on the beach.

Also worth noting in this context are the cruise ships that, incredibly, have malls on board and that turn the islands on their itinerary into little more than indigenous malls. There are even cruises devoted to shopping with the focus on the onboard shops, catalogues, and shopping forays in selected ports.

In spite of such efforts at re-enchantment, an inherent dilemma confronts the new means of consumption. In whatever way they have accomplished it, they have managed to become re-enchanted and, as a result, have grown far more attractive to consumers and effective in luring them into consumption. The problem is that these efforts at re-enchantment may be rationalized (or McDonaldized) from their inception. Even if they are not, the new means of consumption are often so enormous and/or encompass so many settings that they are forced to rationalize that which re-enchants consumers. In rationalizing these forms of re-enchantment they are, by definition, disenchanting them. Can rationalized forms of re-enchantment remain enchanting and attractive to consumers? Can the cathedrals of consumption continually generate new, nonrationalized forms of re-enchantment? Time will tell, but it is clear that there is an inherent contradiction at the heart of the new means of consumption that could ultimately prove to be their undoing.

CRITICISMS AND POST-POSTMODERN SOCIAL THEORY

Debates about poststructural and postmodern social theory ordinarily generate an enormous amount of heat. Supporters are often gushing in their praise, while detractors are frequently driven into what can only be described as a blind rage. For example, John O'Neill (1995) writes of the "the insanity of postmodernism" (p. 16); describes it as offering "a great black sky of nonsense" (p. 191) and as "an already dead moment of the mind" (p. 199). Leaving aside the extreme rhetoric, what are some of the major criticisms of postmodern social theory (bearing in mind that given the diversity of postmodern social theories, general criticisms of those theories are of questionable validity and utility)?

(1) Postmodern theory is criticized for its failure to live up to modern scientific standards, standards that postmodernists eschew. To the scientifically oriented modernist, it is impossible to know whether or not the contentions of postmodernists are true. To put it in more formal terms, virtually everything that the postmodernists have to say is viewed by modernists as not being falsifiable, that is, their ideas cannot be disproved, especially by empirical research (Frow, 1991; Kumar, 1995). Of course, this criticism assumes the existence of a scientific model, of reality, and of a search for and existence of truth. All of these assumptions would, naturally, be rejected by postmodernists.

(2) Since the knowledge produced by postmodernists cannot be seen as constituting a body of scientific ideas, it might be better to look at postmodern social theory as ideology (Kumar, 1995). Once we do that, it is no longer a matter of whether or not the ideas are true, but simply whether or not we believe in them. Those who believe in one set of ideas have no grounds to argue that their ideas are any better or worse than any other set of ideas.

(3) Because they are unconstrained by the norms of science, postmodernists are free to do as they please; to "play" with a wide range of ideas. Broad generalizations are offered, often without qualification. Furthermore, in expressing their positions, postmodern social theorists are not restricted to the dispassionate rhetoric of the modern scientist. The excessive nature of much of postmodern discourse makes it difficult for most of those outside the perspective to accept its basic tenets.

(4) Postmodern ideas are often so vague and abstract that it is difficult, if not impossible, to connect them to the social world (Calhoun, 1993). Relatedly, meanings of concepts tend to change over the course of a postmodernist's work, but the reader, unaware of the original meanings, is unclear about any changes.

(5) Despite their propensity to criticize the grand narratives of modern theorists, postmodern social theorists often offer their own varieties of such narratives. For example, Jameson is often accused of employing Marxian grand narratives and totalizations.

(6) In their analyses, postmodern social theorists often offer critiques of modern society, but those critiques are of questionable validity since they generally lack a normative basis with which to make such judgments.

(7) Given their rejection of an interest in the subject and subjectivity, postmodernists often lack a theory of agency.

(8) Postmodern social theorists are best at critiquing society, but they lack any vision of what society ought to be.

(9) Postmodern social theory leads to profound pessimism.

(10) While postmodern social theorists grapple with what they consider to be major social issues, they often end up ignoring what many consider the key problems of our time.

(11) While one can find adherents among them, as we saw in Chapter 9 the feminists have been particularly strong critics of postmodern social theory. Feminists have tended to be critical of the postmodern rejection of the subject, of its opposition to universal, cross-cultural categories (like gender and gender oppression), of its excessive concern with difference, of its rejection of truth, and of its inability to develop a critical political agenda.

We could obviously enumerate many other criticisms of postmodern social theory in general, to say nothing of many specific criticisms of each postmodern theorist. However, the above gives the reader a good sense of the range of those criticisms. Whatever the merits of these critiques, the central issue is whether or not postmodern theory has produced a set of interesting, insightful and important ideas that are apt to affect social theory long into the future. It should be clear from this chapter that such ideas exist in profusion within postmodern social theory.

While postmodern social theory is only beginning to have a powerful impact on American sociology, in many areas it is long past its prime and in decline. Interestingly, it is in French social theory, the source of the best in poststructuralism and postmodernism, that we find the most determined efforts to move beyond postmodern theory.

Given their rejection of the human subject, the postmodernists are accused of anti-humanism (Ferry and Renaut, 1985/1990:30) Thus, the post-postmodernists are seeking to rescue humanism (and subjectivity) from the postmodern critique that had presumably left such an idea for dead. For example, Lilla (1984b:20) argues that what is being sought is "a new defense of universal, rational norms in morals and politics, and especially a defense of human rights."

Another strand of "post-postmodern social theory" involves an effort to reinstate the importance of liberalism in the face of the postmodern assault on the liberal grand narrative (Lilla, 1994a). The works of the poststructuralists/postmodernists (e.g. Foucault's *Discipline and Punish*), even when they were couched in highly abstract theoretical terms, were read by the French as attacks on structures in general, especially the structure of liberal bourgeois society and its "governmentalities." Not only did postmodern theorists question such a society, but this also led to the view that there was no way of escaping the reach of that society's power structure. Issues thought dead during the heyday of postmodern theory—"human rights, constitutional government, representation, class, individualism" (Lilla, 1994b:16)—have attracted renewed attention. The nihilism of postmodernism has been replaced by a variety of sympathetic orientations to liberal society. One could say that this revival of interest in liberalism (as well as humanism) indicates a restoration of interest in, and sympathy for, modern society.

Other aspects of post-postmodern social theory are made clear in Gilles Lipovetsky's (1987/1994), *The Empire of Fashion: Dressing Modern Democracy*. Lipovetsky takes on, quite explicitly, the poststructuralists and postmodernists. Here is the way he articulates the position taken by them and to which he is opposed, at least to some degree:

> In our societies, fashion is in the driver's seat. In less than half a century, attractiveness and evanescence have become the organizing principles of modern collective life. We live in societies where the trivial predominates . . . Should we be dismayed by this? Does it announce the slow but inexorable decline of the West? Must we take it as a sign of the decadence of the democratic ideal? Nothing is more commonplace or widespread than the tendency to stigmatize—not without cause, moreover—the consumerist bent of democracies; they are represented as devoid of any great mobilizing collective projects, lulled into a stupor by the private orgies of consumerism, infantilized by 'instant' culture, by advertising, by politics-as-theater.
>
> (Lipovetsky, 1987/1994:6)

In contrast, while he recognizes the problems associated with it, Lipovetsky (1987/1994:6) argues that fashion is "the primary agent of the spiraling movement toward individualism and the consolidation of liberal societies." Thus, Lipovetsky does not share the gloomy view of the postmodernists; he sees not only the negative, but also the positive, side of fashion and has a generally optimistic view of the future of society.

While Lipovetsky has much that is positive to say about fashion, consumerism, individualism, democracy and modern society, he also recognizes the problems associated with each. He concludes that we live in "neither the best of worlds nor the worst . . . Fashion is neither angel nor devil . . . Such is the greatness of fashion, which always refers us, as individuals, back to ourselves; such is the misery of fashion, which renders us increasingly problematic to ourselves and others" (Lipovetsky, 1987/1994:240–241). Intellectuals are warned not to dismiss fashion (and the rest) just because it offends their intellectual sympathies. It is for being dismissive of such important phenomena as fashion (and liberalism, democracy, and so on) that Lipovetsky attacks the poststruc-turalists/postmodernists and others (e.g. critical theorists). In any case, the assault on fashion (and other aspects of modern society) has led us to lose sight of the fact that "the age of fashion remains the major factor in the process that has drawn men and women collectively away from obscurantism and fanaticism, has instituted an open public space and shaped a more lawful, more mature, more skeptical humanity" (Lipovetsky, 1987/1994:12).

While his paradigm is clothing, Lipovetsky argues that fashion is a form of social change that is a distinctive product of the Occident. In contrast to the postmodernists who were resistant to the idea of origins, Lipovetsky traces the origins of fashion to the upper classes in the West in the late Middle Ages. Fashion is a form of change charac-terized by a brief time span, largely fanciful shifts, and the ability to affect a wide vari-ety of sectors of the social world. A number of factors came together in the West to give birth to the fashion form, especially its consecration of both individuality and novelty.

Fashion has been a force in the rise of individuality by allowing people to express themselves and their individuality in their clothing even while they might also be at-tending to collective changes in fashion. Similarly, it has been a factor in greater equal-ity by allowing those lower in the stratification system to at least dress like those who ranked above them. Fashion also permitted frivolous self-expression. Most generally, it is linked to increasing individualism and the democratization of society as a whole.

The discussion in this section should not be taken to mean that post- or anti-postmodern social theory exhausts contemporary French theory, but it is clearly one of the dominant themes in that theory. Postmodern social theory is not dead in contempo-rary France. Jean Baudrillard continues to write and there are others whose work we have not had time to discuss. There are, for example, the contributions of the French urbanist and architect, Paul Virilio. In a fascinating series of books, Virilio (1983, 1986, 1991a, 1991b, 1995) has focused on the study of speed (dromology) in the postmodern world. For example, in *Lost Dimension*, Virilio (1991a) discusses how physical dis-tances and barriers have disappeared in the face of the growing importance of speed; space has been replaced by time; the material has been replaced by the immaterial. Thus, in the case of the city, its physical boundaries have been breached forever by, among other things, high-speed communication. The modern world defined by space has given way to a postmodern world defined by time.

More importantly for our purposes, postmodern social theory is not only alive and well, but on the ascendancy, in the United States. However, we need to look beyond in-tellectual fashion in the United States (or France) and realize that whether or not post-modern/poststructural ideas are in or out of fashion in any given place at any given moment, they will be of continuing significance to social theory in general for some time to come. We will eventually move beyond postmodern social theory, but social theory in general will never quite be the same again.

SUMMARY

This chapter covers a wide range of important and interrelated developments in the re-cent history of sociological theory. The source of many of these developments is the revolution that took place in linguistics and led to a search for the underlying structures of language. Structuralism, as this revolution came to be called, affected a number of fields, including anthropology (especially the work of Lévi-Strauss) and Marxian theory (structural Marxism, in particular).

While structuralism continues to affect the thinking of social theorists, it gave birth to a movement known as poststructuralism. As the name suggests, poststructuralism built on the ideas of structuralism but went well beyond them to create a distinctive mode of thought. The most important of the poststructuralists is Michel Foucault. In a series of important books, Foucault created a number of theoretical ideas that are likely to be influential for many decades to come.

Emerging, in part, out of poststructuralism is an enormously influential development known as postmodern theory. Many fields have been influenced by postmodern thinking—art, architecture, philosophy, and sociology. There are a wide variety of postmodern social theories, and we have examined a moderate version offered by Fredric Jameson and a radical alternative offered by Jean Baudrillard. At the minimum, postmodern social theory represents a challenge to sociological theory. At the maximum, it stands as a rejection of much, if not all, sociological theory. The chapter closes with some of the major criticisms of postmodern social theory and a discussion of the significance of post-postmodern social theory.

SOCIOLOGICAL METATHEORIZING AND A METATHEORETICAL SCHEMA FOR ANALYZING SOCIOLOGICAL THEORY

METATHEORIZING IN SOCIOLOGY
  Pierre Bourdieu's Reflexive Sociology
THE IDEAS OF THOMAS KUHN
SOCIOLOGY: A MULTIPLE-PARADIGM SCIENCE
TOWARD A MORE INTEGRATED SOCIOLOGICAL PARADIGM
  Levels of Social Analysis: An Overview
  Levels of Social Analysis: A Model

One of the most recent developments in sociological theory is the growth in interest in sociological metatheorizing. While theorists take the social world as their subject matter, metatheorists engage in *the systematic study of the underlying structure of sociological theory* (Ritzer, 1991b; Zhao, forthcoming). Among our goals in this Appendix is a look at the increase in interest in metatheorizing in sociology and the basic parameters of this approach. Furthermore, the entire structure of this book rests on a specific set of metatheoretical perspectives developed by the author (Ritzer, 1975a, 1981a). Thus, another objective of this Appendix is to present the metatheoretical ideas that inform the text, but before we can do that, we need to present an overview of metatheorizing in sociology.

METATHEORIZING IN SOCIOLOGY

Sociologists are not the only ones to do meta-analysis, that is, to reflexively study their own discipline. Others who do such work include philosophers (Radnitzky, 1973), psychologists (Gergen, 1973, 1986; Schmidt et al., 1984), political scientists (Connolly, 1973), a number of other social scientists (various essays in Fiske and Shweder, 1986), and historians (White, 1973).

Beyond the fact that meta-analysis is found in other fields, various kinds of sociologists, not just metatheorists, do such analysis (Zhao, 1991). We can group the types of meta-analysis in sociology under the heading "metasociology," which we can define as *the reflexive study of the underlying structure of sociology in general, as well as of its various components*—substantive areas (for example, R. Hall's [1983] overview of occupational sociology), concepts (Rubinstein's [1986] analysis of the concept of "structure"), methods (*metamethods;* for example, Brewer and Hunter's [1989] and Noblit and Hare's [1988] efforts to synthesize sociological methods), data (*meta-data-analysis;*[1] for example, Fendrich, 1984; Hunter, Schmidt, and Jackson, 1982; Polit and Falbo, 1987; Wolf, 1986), and theories. It is the latter, *metatheorizing,* that will concern us in this Appendix.

What distinguishes work in this area is not so much the process of metatheorizing (or systematically studying theories, which all metatheorists share) but rather the nature of the end products. There are three varieties of metatheorizing, largely defined by differences in end products (Ritzer, 1991a, 1991b, 1991c, 1992b, 1992c). The first type, *metatheorizing as a means of attaining a deeper understanding of theory* (M_U), involves the study of theory in order to produce a better, more profound understanding of extant theory (Ritzer, 1988). M_U is concerned, more specifically, with the study of theories, theorists, and communities of theorists, as well as the larger intellectual and social contexts of theories and theorists. The second type, *metatheorizing as a prelude to theory development* (M_P), entails the study of extant theory in order to produce new sociological theory. There is also a third type, *metatheorizing as a source of perspectives that overarch sociological theory* (M_O), in which the study of theory is oriented toward the goal of producing a perspective, one could say *a* metatheory, that overarches some part or all of sociological theory. (As we will see, it is this type of metatheorizing that provided the framework used in constructing this book.) Given these definitions, let us examine each type of metatheorizing in greater detail.

The first type of metatheorizing, M_U, is composed of four basic subtypes, all of which involve the formal or informal study of sociological theory to attain a deeper understanding of it. The first subtype (internal-intellectual) focuses on intellectual or cognitive issues that are internal to sociology. Included here are attempts to identify major cognitive paradigms (Ritzer, 1975a, 1975b; see also the discussion below) and "schools of thought" (Sorokin, 1928), more dynamic views of the underlying structure of sociological theory (Harvey, 1982, 1987; Wiley, 1979; Nash and Wardell, 1993; Holmwood and Stewart, 1994), and the development of general metatheoretical tools with which to analyze existing sociological theories and to develop new theories (Alexander et al., 1987; Edel, 1959; Gouldner, 1970; Ritzer, 1989b, 1990a; Wiley, 1988). The second subtype (internal-social) also looks within sociology, but it focuses on social rather than cognitive factors. The main approach here emphasizes the communal aspects of various sociological theories and includes efforts to identify the major "schools" in the history of sociology (Bulmer, 1984, 1985; Cortese, 1995; Tiryakian, 1979, 1986), the more formal, network approach to the study of the ties among groups of sociologists (Mullins, 1973, 1983), as well as studies of theorists themselves that examine their institutional affiliations, their career patterns, their positions within the field of sociology, and so on (Gouldner, 1970; Camic, 1992). The third variant (external-intellectual) turns to other academic disciplines for ideas, tools, concepts, and theories that can be used in the analysis of sociological theory (for example, Brown, 1987, 1990a). Baker (1993) has looked at the implications of chaos theory, with its roots in physics, for sociological theory. Bailey has argued that while explicit attention to metatheorizing may be relatively new in sociology, "general systems theory has long been marked by widespread metatheorizing" (1994:27). Such metatheorizing was made necessary by the multidisciplinary character of systems theory and the need to study and bring together ideas from different fields. He later continues, arguing that social-systems theory "embraces metatheorizing" (Bailey, 1994:82).

---

[1]I have labeled this (somewhat awkwardly) "meta-data-analysis" in order to differentiate it from the more generic meta-analysis. In meta-data-analysis the goal is to seek ways of cumulating research results across research studies. In his introduction to Wolf's *Meta-Analysis,* Niemi defines *meta-analysis* as "the application of statistical procedures to collections of empirical findings from individual studies for the purpose of integrating, synthesizing, and making sense of them" (Wolf, 1986:5).

In fact, Bailey uses a metatheoretical approach to analyze developments in systems theory (see Chapter 5) and their relationship to developments in sociological theory.

Finally, the external-social approach shifts to a more macro level to look at the larger society (national setting, sociocultural setting, etc.) and the nature of its impact on sociological theorizing (for example, Vidich and Lyman, 1985).

Of course, specific metatheoretical efforts can combine two or more types of M_U. For example, Jaworski has shown how Lewis Coser's 1956 book, *Functions of Social Conflict* (see Chapter 3), "was a deeply personal book and a historically situated statement" (1991:116). Thus, Jaworski touches on the impact of his family (internal-social) and of the rise of Hitler in Germany (external-social) on Coser's life and work. Jaworski also deals with the effect of external-intellectual (American radical political thought) and internal-intellectual (industrial sociology) factors on Coser's thinking. Thus, Jaworski combines all four subtypes of M_U in his analysis of Coser's work on social conflict.

Most metatheorizing in sociology is not M_U; rather, it is the second type, metatheorizing as a prelude to the development of sociological theory (M_P). Most important classical and contemporary theorists developed their theories, at least in part, on the basis of a careful study of, and reaction to, the work of other theorists. Among the most important examples are Marx's theory of capitalism (see Chapter 1), developed out of a systematic engagement with Hegelian philosophy as well as other ideas, such as political economy and utopian socialism; Parsons's action theory (see Chapter 3), developed out of a systematic study of the work of Durkheim, Weber, Pareto, and Marshall; Alexander's (1982–83) multidimensional, neofunctional theory, based on a detailed study of the work of Marx, Weber, Durkheim, and Parsons; and Habermas's (1987a) communication theory, based on his examination of the work of various critical theorists, as well as that of Marx, Weber, Parsons, Mead, and Durkheim. Let us look in more detail at M_P as it was practiced by Karl Marx.

In *Economic and Philosophic Manuscripts of 1844,* Marx (1932/1964) develops his theoretical perspective on the basis of a detailed and careful analysis and critique of the works of political economists like Adam Smith, Jean-Baptiste Say, David Ricardo, and James Mill; philosophers like G. W. F. Hegel, the Young Hegelians (for example, Bruno Bauer), and Ludwig Feuerbach; utopian socialists like Etienne Cabet, Robert Owen, Charles Fourier, and Pierre Proudhon; and a variety of other major and minor intellectual schools and figures. It seems safe to say that in almost its entirety the *Manuscripts of 1844* is a metatheoretical treatise in which Marx develops his own ideas out of an engagement with a variety of idea systems.

What of Marx's other works? Are they more empirical? Less metatheoretical? In his preface to *The German Ideology* (Marx and Engels, 1845–46/1970), C. J. Arthur describes that work as composed mainly of "detailed line by line polemics against the writings of some of their [Marx and Engels's] contemporaries" (1970:1). In fact, Marx himself describes *The German Ideology* as an effort "to set forth together our conception as opposed to the ideological one of German philosophy, in fact to settle accounts with our former philosophical conscience. The intention was carried out in the form of a critique of post-Hegelian philosophy" (1859/1970:22). *The Holy Family* (Marx and Engels, 1845/1956) is, above all, an extended critique of Bruno Bauer, the Young Hegelians, and their propensity toward speculative "critical criticism."[2] In their foreword, Marx and Engels make it clear that this kind of metatheoretical work is a prelude to their coming theorizing: "We therefore give this polemic as a preliminary to the independent works in which we . . . shall present our positive

---

[2]In fact, the book is subtitled *Against Bruno Bauer and Co.*

view" (1845/1956:16). In the *Grundrisse* Marx (1857–58/1974) chooses as his metatheoretical antagonists the political economist David Ricardo and the French socialist Pierre Proudhon (Nicolaus, 1974). Throughout the *Grundrisse* Marx is struggling to solve an array of theoretical problems, in part through a critique of the theories and theorists mentioned here and in part through an application of ideas derived from Hegel. In describing the introduction to the *Grundrisse,* Nicolaus says that it "reflects in its every line the struggle of Marx against Hegel, Ricardo and Proudhon. From it, Marx carried off the most important objective of all, namely the basic principles of writing history dialectically" (1974:42). *A Contribution to the Critique of Political Economy* (Marx, 1859/1970) is, as the title suggests, an effort to build a distinctive economic approach on the basis of a critique of the works of the political economists.

Even *Capital* (1867/1967)—which is admittedly one of Marx's most empirical works, since he deals more directly with the reality of the capitalist work world through the use of government statistics and reports—is informed by Marx's earlier metatheoretical work and contains some metatheorizing of its own. In fact, the subtitle, *A Critique of Political Economy,* makes the metatheoretical roots absolutely clear. However, Marx is freer in *Capital* to be much more "positive," that is, to construct his own distinctive theoretical orientation. This freedom is traceable, in part, to his having done much of the metatheoretical groundwork in earlier works. Furthermore, most of the new metatheoretical work is relegated to the so-called fourth volume of *Capital,* published under the title *Theories of Surplus Value* (Marx, 1862–63/1963, 1862–63/1968). *Theories* is composed of many extracts from the work of the major political economists (for example, Smith, Ricardo) as well as critical analysis of them by Marx. In sum, it is safe to say that Marx was, largely, a metatheorist, perhaps the *most* metatheoretical of all classical sociological theorists.

While we have singled out Marx for detailed discussion, virtually all classical and contemporary theorists were metatheorists, and, more specifically, they practiced M_P.

There are a number of examples of the third type of metatheorizing, M_O. They include Wallace's (1988) "disciplinary matrix," Ritzer's (1979, 1981a) "integrated sociological paradigm" (discussed later in this Appendix), Furfey's (1953/1965) positivistic metasociology, Gross's (1961) "neodialectical" metasociology, Alexander's (1982) "general theoretical logic for sociology," and Alexander's (1995) later effort to develop a postpositivist approach to universalism and rationality. A number of theorists (Bourdieu and Wacquant, 1992; Emirbayer, 1997; Ritzer and Gindoff, 1992, 1994) have been engaged in an effort to create what Ritzer and Gindoff have called "methodological relationism"[3] to complement the extant overarching perspectives of "methodological individualism" (Bhargava, 1992) and "methodological holism." Methodological relationism is derived from a study of works on micro-macro and agency-structure integration, as well as a variety of works in social psychology.

The three varieties of metatheory are ideal types. In actual cases there is often considerable overlap in the objectives of metatheoretical works. Nevertheless, those who do one type of metatheorizing tend to be less interested in achieving the objectives of the other two types. Of course, there are sociologists who at one time or another have done all three types of metatheorizing. For example, Alexander (1982–83) creates overarching perspectives (M_O) in the first volume of *Theoretical Logic in Sociology,* uses them in the next three volumes to achieve a better understanding (M_U) of the classic theorists, and later sought to help create neofunctionalism (M_P) as a theoretical successor to structural functionalism (Alexander and Colomy, 1990a).

[3]Swartz (1997) does a particularly good job of delineating this metatheory as well as the other metatheories that inform Bourdieu's theorizing.

Pierre Bourdieu's Reflexive Sociology

An important contemporary metatheorist (although he would resist that label, indeed any label) is Pierre Bourdieu. Bourdieu calls for a reflexive sociology: "For me, sociology ought to be meta but *always vis-à-vis itself*. It must use its own instruments to find out what it is and what it is doing, to try to know better where it stands" (Bourdieu and Wacquant, 1992:191; see also, Meisenhelder, 1997). Or, using an older and less well defined label ("sociology of sociology") for metasociology, Bourdieu says, "The sociology of sociology is a fundamental dimension of sociological epistemology" (Bourdieu and Wacquant, 1992:68). Sociologists, who spend their careers "objectivizing" the social world, ought to spend some time objectivizing their own practices. Thus, sociology "continually turns back onto itself the scientific weapons it produces" (Bourdieu and Wacquant, 1992:214). Bourdieu even rejects certain kinds of metatheorizing (for example, the internal-social and internal-intellectual forms of M_U) as "a complacent and intimist return upon the private *person* of the sociologist or with a search for the intellectual *Zeitgeist* that animates his or her work" (Bourdieu and Wacquant, 1992:72; for a discussion of Bourdieu's more positive view of even these kinds of metatheorizing, see Wacquant, 1992:38). However, a rejection of certain kinds of metatheorizing does not represent a rejection of the undertaking in its entirety. Clearly, following the logic of *Homo Academicus,* (1984b; see Chapter 11), Bourdieu would favor examining the habitus and practices of sociologists within the fields of sociology as a discipline and the academic world, as well as the relationship between those fields and the fields of stratification and politics. His work *Distinction* (1984a) would lead Bourdieu to concern himself with the strategies of individual sociologists, as well as of the discipline itself, to achieve distinction. For example, individual sociologists might use jargon to achieve high status in the field, and sociology might wrap itself in a cloak of science so that it could achieve distinction vis-à-vis the world of practice. In fact, Bourdieu has claimed that the scientific claims of sociology and other social sciences "are really euphemized assertions of power" (Robbins, 1991:139). Of course, this position has uncomfortable implications for Bourdieu's own work:

> Bourdieu's main problem during the 1980s has been to sustain his symbolic power whilst simultaneously undermining the scientificity on which it was originally founded. Some would say that he has tied the noose around his own neck and kicked away the stool from beneath his feet.
>
> (Robbins, 1991:150)

Given his commitment to theoretically informed empirical research, Bourdieu would also have little patience with most, if not all, forms of M_O which he has described as "universal metadiscourse on knowledge of the world" (Bourdieu and Wacquant, 1992:159). More generally, Bourdieu would reject metatheorizing as an autonomous practice, setting metatheorizing apart from theorizing about and empirically studying the social world (see Wacquant, 1992:31).

Bourdieu makes an interesting case for metatheorizing when he argues that sociologists need to *"avoid being the toy of social forces in [their] practice of sociology"* (Bourdieu and Wacquant, 1992:183). The only way to avoid such a fate is to understand the nature of the forces acting upon the sociologist at a given point in history. Such forces can be understood only via metatheoretical analysis, or what Bourdieu calls "socioanalysis" (Bourdieu and Wacquant, 1992:210). Once sociologists understand the nature of the forces (especially external-social and external-intellectual) operating on them, they will be in a better position to control the impact of those forces on their work. As Bourdieu puts it, in personal terms, "I continually use sociology to try to cleanse my work of . . . social determinants" (Bourdieu and Wacquant, 1992:211). Thus, the goal of metatheorizing from Bourdieu's point of view is not to undermine sociology, but to free it from those forces which determine it. Of course, what Bourdieu says of his own efforts is equally true of metatheoretical endeavors in general. While he strives to limit the effect of external factors on his work, Bourdieu is aware of the limitations of such efforts: "I do not for one minute believe or claim that I am fully liberated from them [social determinants]" (Bourdieu and Wacquant 1992:211).

Similarly, Bourdieu wishes to free sociologists from the symbolic violence committed against them by other, more powerful sociologists. This objective invites internal-intellectual and internal-social analyses of sociology in order to uncover the sources and nature of that symbolic violence. Once the latter are understood, sociologists are in a better position to free themselves of, or at least limit, their effects. More generally, sociologists are well positioned to practice "epistemological vigilance" in order to protect themselves from these distorting pressures (Bourdieu, 1984b:15).

What is most distinctive about Bourdieu's metatheoretical approach is his refusal to separate metatheorizing from the other facets of sociology.[4] That is, he believes that sociologists should be continually reflexive as they are doing their sociological analyses. They should reflect on what they are doing, and especially on how it might be distorting what they are examining, during their analyses. This reflection would limit the amount of "symbolic violence" against the subjects of study.

Although Bourdieu is doing a distinctive kind of metatheoretical work, it is clear that his work is, at least in part, metatheoretical. Given his growing significance in social theory, the association of Bourdieu's work with metatheorizing is likely to contribute further to the growth of interest in metatheorizing in sociology.

With this overview, we now turn to the specific metatheoretical approach that undergirds this book. As will become clear, it involves a combination of M_U and M_O. We begin with a brief review of the work of Thomas Kuhn, and then we examine my (M_U) analysis of sociology's multiple paradigms. Finally, we review the metatheoretical tool—the integrated sociological paradigm (M_O)—that is the source of the levels of analysis used to analyze sociological theories throughout this book.

THE IDEAS OF THOMAS KUHN

In 1962 the philosopher of science Thomas Kuhn published a rather slim volume entitled *The Structure of Scientific Revolutions* (Hoyningen-Huene, 1993). Because this work grew out of philosophy, it appeared fated to a marginal status within sociology, especially because it focused on the hard sciences (physics, for example) and had little directly to say about the social sciences. However, the theses of the book proved extremely interesting to people in a wide range of fields (for example, Hollinger, 1980, in history; Searle, 1972, in linguistics; Stanfield, 1974, in economics), and to none was it more important than to sociologists. In 1970 Robert Friedrichs published the first important work from a Kuhnian perspective, *A Sociology of Sociology*. Since then there has been a steady stream of work from this perspective (Eckberg and Hill, 1979; Effrat, 1972; Eisenstadt and Curelaru, 1976; Falk and Zhao, 1990a, 1990b; Friedrichs, 1972a; Greisman, 1986; Guba and Lincoln, 1994; Lodahl and Gordon, 1972; Phillips, 1973, 1975; Quadagno, 1979; Ritzer, 1975a, 1975b, 1981b;

---

[4]This leads Swartz (1997:11) to argue that "Bourdieu does not share Ritzer's (1988) vision of establishing sociological metatheory as a legitimate subfield within the discipline of sociology."

Rosenberg, 1989; Snizek, 1976; Snizek, Fuhrman, and Miller, 1979). There is little doubt that Kuhnian theory is an important variety of M_U, but what exactly is Kuhn's approach?

One of Kuhn's goals in *The Structure of Scientific Revolutions* was to challenge commonly held assumptions about the way in which science changes. In the view of most laypeople and many scientists, science advances in a cumulative manner, with each advance building inexorably on all that preceded it. Science has achieved its present state through slow and steady increments of knowledge. It will advance to even greater heights in the future. This conception of science was enunciated by the physicist Sir Isaac Newton, who said, "If I have seen further, it is because I stood on the shoulders of giants." But Kuhn regarded this conception of cumulative scientific development as a myth and sought to debunk it.

Kuhn acknowledged that accumulation plays some role in the advance of science, but the truly major changes come about as a result of revolutions. Kuhn offered a theory of how major changes in science occur. He saw a science at any given time as dominated by a specific *paradigm* (defined for the moment as a fundamental image of the science's subject matter). *Normal science* is a period of accumulation of knowledge in which scientists work to expand the reigning paradigm. Such scientific work inevitably spawns *anomalies,* or findings that cannot be explained by the reigning paradigm. A *crisis* stage occurs if these anomalies mount, and this crisis may ultimately end in a scientific revolution. The reigning paradigm is overthrown as a new one takes its place at the center of the science. A new dominant paradigm is born, and the stage is set for the cycle to repeat itself. Kuhn's theory can be depicted diagrammatically:

Paradigm I   →   Normal Science   →   Anomalies   →
Crisis   →   Revolution   →   Paradigm II

It is during periods of revolution that the truly great changes in science take place. This view places Kuhn clearly at odds with most conceptions of scientific development.

The key concept in Kuhn's approach, as well as in this section, is the paradigm. Unfortunately, Kuhn is vague on what he means by a paradigm (Alcala-Campos, 1997). According to Margaret Masterman (1970), he used it in at least twenty-one different ways. We will employ a definition of *paradigm* that we feel is true to the sense and spirit of Kuhn's early work.

A paradigm serves to differentiate one scientific community from another. It can be used to differentiate physics from chemistry or sociology from psychology. These fields have different paradigms. It can also be used to differentiate between different historical stages in the development of a science (Mann, Grimes, and Kemp, 1997). The paradigm that dominated physics in the nineteenth century is different from the one that dominated it in the early twentieth century. There is a third usage of the paradigm concept, and it is the one that is most useful to us here. Paradigms can differentiate among cognitive groupings *within* the same science. Contemporary psychoanalysis, for example, is differentiated into Freudian, Jungian, and Horneyian paradigms (among others)—that is, there are *multiple paradigms* in psychoanalysis—and the same is true of sociology and of most other fields.

I can now offer a definition of *paradigm* that I feel is true to the sense of Kuhn's original work:

A paradigm is a fundamental image of the subject matter within a science. It serves to define what should be studied, what questions should be asked, how they should be asked, and what rules should be followed in interpreting the answers obtained. The paradigm is the broadest unit of consensus within a science and serves to differentiate one scientific

GEORGE RITZER: Autobiography as a Metatheoretical Tool

Biographical and autobiographical work is useful in helping us understand the work of sociological theorists, and of sociologists generally. The historian of science, Thomas Hankin, explains it this way:

[A] fully integrated biography of a scientist which includes not only his personality, but also his scientific work and the intellectual and social context of his times, [is] . . . still the best way to get at many of the problems that beset the writing of history of science . . . science is created by individuals, and however much it may be driven by forces outside, these forces work through the scientist himself. Biography is the literary lens through which we can best view this process.

(Hankin, 1979:14)

What Hankin asserts about scientists generally informs my orientation to the biographies of sociological theorists, including myself. This autobiographical snippet is designed to suggest at least a few ways in which biography can be a useful tool for metatheoretical analysis.

While I have taught in sociology departments for more than thirty years, have written extensively about sociology, and have lectured all over the world on the topic, none of my degrees are in sociology. This lack of a formal background in the field has led to lifelong study of sociology in general and sociological theory in particular. It has also, at least in one sense, aided my attempt to understand sociological theory. Because I had not been trained in a particular "school," I came to sociological theory with few prior conceptions and biases. Rather, I was a student of all "schools of thought"; they were all equally grist for my theoretical mill.

My first metatheoretical work, *Sociology: A Multiple Paradigm Science* (1975a), sought not only to lay out sociology's separable, and often conflicting, paradigms but also to make the case for paradigm linking, leaping, bridging, and integrating. Uncomfortable with paradigmatic conflict, I wanted to see more harmony and integration in sociology. That desire led to the publication of *Toward an Integrated Sociological Paradigm* (1981a), in which I more fully developed my sense of an integrated paradigm. The interest in resolving theoretical conflict led to a focus on micro-macro (1990a) and agency-structure (Ritzer and Gindoff, 1994) integration as well as the larger issue of theoretical syntheses (1990b).

---

community (*or subcommunity*) from another. It subsumes, defines, and interrelates the exemplars, *theories* [italics added], and methods and instruments that exist within it.

(Ritzer, 1975a:7)

With this definition we can begin to see the relationship between paradigms and theories. *Theories are only part of larger paradigms.* To put it another way, a paradigm may encompass two or more *theories,* as well as different *images* of the subject matter, *methods* (and instruments), and *exemplars* (specific pieces of scientific work that stand as a model for all those who follow).

SOCIOLOGY: A MULTIPLE-PARADIGM SCIENCE

My work on the paradigmatic status of sociology (Ritzer, 1975a, 1975b, 1980) provides the basis for the metatheoretical perspective that has guided the analysis of sociological theory

My interest in metatheoretical work is explained by my desire to understand theory better and to resolve unnecessary conflict within sociological theory. In *Metatheorizing in Sociology* (1991b) and in an edited volume, *Metatheorizing* (1992b), I made a case for the need for the systematic study of sociological theory. I believe that we need to do more of this in order to understand theory better, produce new theory, and produce new overarching theoretical perspectives (or metatheories). Metatheoretical study is also oriented to clarifying contentious issues, resolving disputes, and allowing for greater integration and synthesis.

Having spent many years seeking to clarify the nature of sociological theory, in the early 1990s I grew weary of the abstractions of metatheoretical work. I sought to apply the various theories that I had learned to very concrete aspects of the social world. I had done a little with this in the 1980s, applying Weber's theory of rationalization to fast-food restaurants (1983) and the medical profession (Ritzer and Walczak, 1988). I revisited the 1983 essay and the result was a book, *The McDonaldization of Society* (1993, 1996), which argued that while in Weber's day the model of the rationalization process was the bureaucracy, today the fast-food restaurant has become a better model of that process (additional essays on this topic are to be found in *The McDonaldization Thesis* [1998]). In *Expressing America: A Critique of the Global Credit Card Society,* I turned my attention to another everyday economic phenomenon, which I analyzed not only from the perspective of rationalization theory, but from other perspectives including Georg Simmel's theoretical ideas on money.

This work on fast-food restaurants and credit cards led to the realization that what I was really interested in was the sociology of consumption, a field little developed in the United States, at least in comparison to Great Britain and other European nations. That led to *Enchanting a Disenchanted World: Revolutionizing the Means of Consumption* (1999), in which I used Weberian, Marxian, and postmodern theory to analyze the revolutionary impact of a range of new means of consumption (superstores, megamalls, cybermalls, home shopping television, casinos, theme parks, cruise ships, as well as fast-food restaurants and other franchises) on the way Americans and the rest of the world consume goods and services.

While I cannot rule out a return to more metatheoretical issues, my current plans are to continue to apply social theory to the realm of consumption. I also envision exploring the relationship between various social theories of rationalization and the McDonaldization thesis.

Source: Adapted (and updated) from George Ritzer, "I Never Metatheory I Didn't Like," *Mid-American Review of Sociology,* 15:21–32, 1991.

throughout this book. In my view, there are *three* paradigms that dominate sociology, with several others having the potential to achieve paradigmatic status. I label the three paradigms the *social-facts, social-definition,* and *social-behavior* paradigms. Each paradigm is analyzed in terms of the four components of a paradigm.

The Social-Facts Paradigm

1 *Exemplar:* The model for social factists is the work of Emile Durkheim, particularly *The Rules of Sociological Method* and *Suicide.*

2 *Image of the subject matter:* Social factists focus on what Durkheim termed social facts, or large-scale social structures and institutions. Those who subscribe to the social-facts paradigm focus not only on these phenomena but on their effect on individual thought and action.

3 *Methods:* Social factists are more likely than those who subscribe to the other paradigms to use the interview-questionnaire[5] and historical-comparative methods.

4 *Theories:* The social-facts paradigm encompasses a number of theoretical perspectives. *Structural-functional* theorists tend to see social facts as neatly interrelated and order as maintained by general consensus. *Conflict* theorists tend to emphasize disorder among social facts as well as the notion that order is maintained by coercive forces in society. Although structural functionalism and conflict theory are the dominant theories in this paradigm, there are others, including *systems* theory.

The Social-Definition Paradigm

1 *Exemplar:* To social definitionists, the unifying model is Max Weber's work on social action.

2 *Image of the subject matter:* Weber's work helped lead to an interest among social definitionists in the way actors define their social situations and the effect of these definitions on ensuing action and interaction.

3 *Methods:* Social definitionists, although they are most likely to use the interview-questionnaire method, are more likely to use the observation method than those in any other paradigm (Prus, 1996). In other words, observation is the distinctive methodology of social definitionists.

4 *Theories:* There are a wide number of theories that can be included within social definitionism: *action theory, symbolic interactionism, phenomenology, ethnomethodology,* and *existentialism.*

The Social-Behavior Paradigm

1 *Exemplar:* The model for social behaviorists is the work of the psychologist B. F. Skinner.

2 *Image of the subject matter:* The subject matter of sociology to social behaviorists is the unthinking *behavior* of individuals. Of particular interest are the rewards that elicit desirable behaviors and the punishments that inhibit undesirable behaviors.

3 *Methods:* The distinctive method of social behaviorism is the experiment.

4 *Theories:* Two theoretical approaches in sociology can be included under the heading "social behaviorism." The first is *behavioral sociology,* which is very close to pure psychological behaviorism. The second, which is much more important, is *exchange theory.*[6]

TOWARD A MORE INTEGRATED SOCIOLOGICAL PARADIGM

In addition to detailing the nature of sociology's multiple paradigms, I sought to make the case for more paradigmatic integration in sociology. Although there is reason for extant par-

---

[5]William Snizek (1976) has shown that the interview-questionnaire is dominant in *all* paradigms.

[6]Analyses of this paradigm schema include Eckberg and Hill (1979); Friedheim (1979); Harper, Sylvester, and Walczak (1980); Snizek (1976); and Staats (1976).

adigms to continue to exist, there is also a need for a more integrated paradigm.[7] Contrary to a claim by Nash and Wardell (1993), I am *not* arguing for a new hegemonic position in sociology; I am *not* arguing that "the current diversity represents an undesirable condition needing elimination" (Nash and Wardell, 1993:278). On the contrary, I am arguing for *more* diversity through the development of an integrated paradigm to supplement extant paradigms. Like Nash and Wardell, I *favor* theoretical diversity.

Extant paradigms tend to be one-sided, focusing on specific levels of social analysis while paying little or no attention to the others. This characteristic is reflected in the social factists' concern with macro structures; the social definitionists' concern with action, interaction, and the social construction of reality; and the social behaviorists' concern with behavior. It is this kind of one-sidedness that has led to a growing interest in a more integrated approach among a wide range of sociologists (Ritzer, 1991d). (This is but part of a growing interest in integration within and even among many social sciences; see especially Mitroff and Kilmann, 1978.) For example, Robert Merton, representing social factism, saw it and social definitionism as mutually enriching, as "opposed to one another in about the same sense as ham is opposed to eggs: they are perceptively different but mutually enriching" (1975:30).

The key to an integrated paradigm is the notion of *levels* of social analysis (Ritzer, 1979, 1981a). As the reader is well aware, *the social world is not really divided into levels.* In fact, social reality is best viewed as an enormous variety of social phenomena that are involved in continuing interaction and change. Individuals, groups, families, bureaucracies, the polity, and numerous other highly diverse social phenomena represent the bewildering array of phenomena that make up the social world. It is extremely difficult to get a handle on such a large number of wide-ranging and mutually interpenetrating social phenomena. Some sort of conceptual schema is clearly needed, and sociologists have developed a number of such schemas in an effort to deal with the social world. The idea of levels of social analysis employed here should be seen as but one of a large number of such schemas that can be, and have been, used for dealing with the complexities of the social world.

Levels of Social Analysis: An Overview

Although the idea of levels is implicit in much of sociology, it has received relatively little explicit attention. (However, there does seem to be some explicit interest in this issue, as reflected, for example, in the work of Hage [1994a], Whitmeyer [1994], and especially Jaffee [1998] and Smelser [1997].) In concentrating on levels here, we are making explicit what has been implicit in sociology.

The close of this Appendix will offer a conceptualization of the major levels of social analysis. An adequate understanding of that conceptualization requires some preliminary differentiations. As you will see, two continua of social reality are useful in developing the major levels of the social world. The first is the *microscopic-macroscopic* continuum. Thinking of the social world as being made up of a series of entities ranging from those large in scale to those small in scale is relatively easy, because it is so familiar. Most people in their day-to-day lives conceive of the social world in these terms. As we saw in Chapter 10, a number of thinkers have worked with a micro-macro continuum. For laypeople and academics alike, the continuum is based on the simple idea that social phenomena vary greatly

---

[7]There are other possibilities, including a postmodern paradigm (Milovanovic, 1995) and a more interparadigmatic dialogue (Chriss, 1996).

in size. At the macro end of the continuum are such large-scale social phenomena as groups of societies (for example, the capitalist world-system), societies, and cultures. At the micro end are individual actors and their thoughts and actions. In between are a wide range of meso-level phenomena—groups, collectivities, social classes, and organizations. We have little difficulty recognizing these distinctions and thinking of the world in micro-macro terms. There are no clear dividing lines between the micro social units and the macro units. Instead, there is a continuum ranging from the micro to the macro ends.

The second continuum is the *objective-subjective* dimension of social analysis. At each end of the micro-macro continuum (and everywhere in between) we can differentiate between objective and subjective components. At the micro, or individual, level, there are the subjective mental processes of an actor and the objective patterns of action and interaction in which he or she engages. *Subjective* here refers to something that occurs solely in the realm of ideas; *objective* relates to real, material events. This same differentiation is found at the macro end of the continuum. A society is made up of objective structures, such as governments, bureaucracies, and laws, and subjective phenomena, such as norms and values.

Now let us turn to the work of several sociologists on the objective-subjective continuum. As we saw in Chapter 1, an important influence on Karl Marx was German idealism, particularly the work of G. W. F. Hegel. The Hegelian dialectic was a subjective process taking place within the realm of ideas. Although affected by this view, Marx and, before him, the Young Hegelians, were dissatisfied with the dialectic because it was not rooted in the objective, material world. Marx, building on the work of Ludwig Feuerbach and others, sought to extend the dialectic to the material world. On the one hand, he was concerned with real, sentient actors rather than idea systems. On the other hand, he came to focus on the objective structures of capitalist society, primarily the economic structure. Marx became increasingly interested in the real material structures of capitalism and the contradictions that exist among and within them. This is not to say that Marx lost sight of subjective ideas; in fact, notions of false and class consciousness play a key role in his work. It is the materialism-idealism split, as manifest in the work of Marx and others, that is one of the major philosophical roots of the objective-subjective continuum in modern sociology.

We can also find this continuum, although in a different form, in the work of Emile Durkheim (see Chapter 1). In his classic work on methodology, Durkheim differentiated between material (objective) and nonmaterial (subjective) social facts. In *Suicide,* Durkheim said, "The social fact is sometimes materialized as to become an element of the external world" (1897/1951:313). He discussed architecture and law as two examples of material (objective) social facts. However, most of Durkheim's work emphasizes nonmaterial (subjective) social facts:

> Of course it is true that not all social consciousness achieves such externalization and materialization. Not all aesthetic spirit of a nation is embodied in the works it inspires; not all morality is formulated in clear precepts. The greater part is diffused. There is a large collective life which is at liberty; all sorts of currents come, go, circulate everywhere, cross and mingle in a thousand different ways, and just because they are constantly mobile are never crystallized in an objective form. Today a breath of sadness and discouragement descends on society: tomorrow, one of joyous confidence will uplift all hearts.
>
> (Durkheim, 1897/1951:315)

These social currents do not have material existence; they can exist only within the consciousness of individuals and between them. In *Suicide,* Durkheim concentrated on examples of this kind of social fact. He related differences in suicide rates to differences in social currents. For example, where there are strong currents of anomie (normlessness), we find high rates of anomic suicide. Social currents such as anomie, egoism, and altruism clearly do not have a material existence, although they may have a material effect by causing differences in suicide rates. Instead, they are intersubjective phenomena that can exist only in the consciousness of people.

Peter Blau (1960) differentiated between institutions (subjective entities) and social structures (objective entities). He defined *subjective institutions* as "the common values and norms embodied in a culture or subculture" (Blau, 1960:178). Conversely, there are *social structures* that are "the networks of social relations in which processes of social interaction become organized and through which social positions of individuals and subgroups become differentiated" (Blau, 1960:178).

It can be argued that the objective-subjective continuum plays a crucial role in the thought of people like Marx, Durkheim, Blau, and many others. But there is a rather interesting problem in their use of the continuum: they employ it almost exclusively at the macroscopic level. However, it also can be applied at the microscopic level. Before giving an example, we need to underscore the point that we must deal not only with the microscopic-macroscopic and objective-subjective continua *but also with the interaction between them.*

One example of the use of the objective-subjective continuum at the microscopic level is an empirical study by Mary and Robert Jackman (1973) of what they called "objective and subjective social status." Their micro-subjective concern was "the individual's perception of his own position in the status hierarchy" (Jackman and Jackman, 1973:569). Micro subjectivity in this study involved the feelings, perceptions, and mental aspects of the actors' positions in the stratification system. These are related to various components of the micro-objective realm that include the actor's socioeconomic status, social contacts, amount of capital owned, ethnic group membership, or status as a breadwinner or a union member. Instead of dealing with actors' feelings, these dimensions involve the more objective characteristics of the individuals—the patterns of action and interaction in which they actually engage.

Interest in the microscopic aspect of the objective-subjective continuum is manifest in both the social-definition and social-behavior paradigms. Both tend to focus on micro-objective patterns of action and interaction, but they part company on the micro-subjective dimension. All the theoretical components of the social-definition paradigm (for example, symbolic interactionism, ethnomethodology, and phenomenology) share an interest in micro subjectivity—the feelings and thoughts of actors. However, the social behaviorists reject the idea that it is necessary to study the micro-subjective components of social life. This rejection is exemplified by B. F. Skinner's (1971) attack on what he called the idea of "autonomous man." To Skinner, we imply that people are autonomous when we attribute to them such ideas as feeling, minding, freedom, and dignity. To Skinner, the idea that people have such an inner, autonomous core is a mystical, metaphysical position of the kind that must be eliminated from the social sciences: "Autonomous man serves to explain only the things we are not yet able to explain in other ways. His existence depends on our ignorance, and he naturally loses status as we come to know more about behavior" (1971:12). Although we need to reject this kind of political diatribe, the key point is this: the microscopic level has *both* a subjective and an objective dimension.

Levels of Social Analysis: A Model

The most important thinker on the issue of levels of social reality was the French sociologist Georges Gurvitch. Although he did not use the same terms, Gurvitch (1964) had a sense of *both* micro-macro and objective-subjective continua. Even more important, he had a

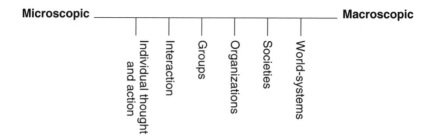

Microscopic _____ **Macroscopic**

Individual thought and action | Interaction | Groups | Organizations | Societies | World-systems

FIGURE A.1
The Microscopic-Macroscopic Continuum, with Identification of Some Key Points on the
Continuum

profound sense of how these two continua are related. To his credit, he also steadfastly refused to treat the two continua and their interrelationships as static tools but used them to underscore the dynamic quality of social life. But Gurvitch has one major difficulty: his
analytical schema is extremely complex and cumbersome.

The social world is very complicated, and in order to get a handle on it, we need relatively
simple models. The simple model we are seeking is formed out of the intersection of the
two continua of levels of social reality discussed in the last several pages. The first, the
microscopic-macroscopic continuum, can be depicted as in Figure A.1.

The objective-subjective continuum presents greater problems, yet it is no less important
than the micro-macro continuum. In general, an objective social phenomenon has a real, material existence. We can think of the following, among others, as objective social phenomena:
actors, action, interaction, bureaucratic structures, law, and the state apparatus. It is possible
to see, touch, or chart all these objective phenomena. However, there are social phenomena
that exist *solely* in the realm of ideas; they have no material existence. These are sociological
phenomena such as mental processes, the social construction of reality (Berger and Luckmann, 1967), norms, values, and many elements of culture. The problem with the objective-
subjective continuum is that there are many phenomena in the middle that have *both* objective
and subjective elements. The family, for example, has a real material existence as well as
a series of subjective mutual understandings, norms, and values. Similarly, the polity is
composed of objective laws and bureaucratic structures as well as subjective political norms
and values. In fact, it is probably true that the vast majority of social phenomena are mixed
types representing some combination of objective and subjective elements. Thus it is best to
think of the objective-subjective continuum as two polar types with a series of variously
mixed types in the middle. Figure A.2 shows the objective-subjective continuum.

Although these continua are interesting in themselves, the interrelationship of the two
continua is what concerns us here. Figure A.3 is a schematic representation of the intersection of these two continua and the four major levels of social analysis derived from it.

The contention here is that an integrated sociological paradigm must deal with the four
basic levels of social analysis identified in the figure and their interrelationships (for similar
models, see Alexander, 1985a; Wiley, 1988). It must deal with macro-objective entities like
bureaucracy, macro-subjective realities like values, micro-objective phenomena like patterns
of interaction, and micro-subjective facts like the process of reality construction. We must
remember that in the real world, all these gradually blend into the others as part of the larger
social continuum, but we have made some artificial and rather arbitrary differentiations in
order to be able to deal with social reality. These four levels of social analysis are posited for
heuristic purposes and are not meant to be accurate depictions of the social world.

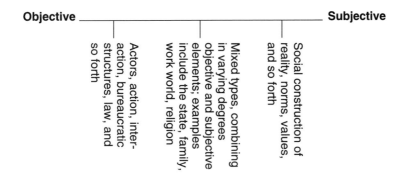

FIGURE A.2
The Objective-Subjective Continuum, with Identification of Some Mixed Types

While there is much to be gained from the development of an integrated sociological paradigm, one can expect resistance from many quarters. Lewis has argued that opposition to an integrated paradigm comes from those theorists, "paradigm warriors" (Aldrich, 1988), who are intent on defending their theoretical turf, come what may:

> Much of the objection to an integrated paradigm is not on theoretical, but on political grounds; an integrated paradigm threatens the purity and independence—and perhaps even the existence—of theoretical approaches which derive their inspiration from *opposition* to existing theory. . . . An integrated paradigm, such as Ritzer proposes, allows and even encourages a broader perspective than some find comfortable. Adopting an integrated paradigm means relinquishing belief in the ultimate truth of one's favorite theory. . . . Acceptance of an integrated paradigm requires an understanding, and indeed an appreciation, of a broad range of theoretical perspectives—an intellectually challenging task. . . . Although Ritzer does not discuss the issue, this author maintains that overcoming massive *intellectual agoraphobia* presents the greatest challenge to acceptance of an integrated paradigm.
>
> (Lewis, 1991:228–229)

An obvious question is how the four levels of the integrated paradigm relate to the three paradigms discussed earlier, as well as to the integrated paradigm. Figure A.4 relates the four levels to the three paradigms.

The social-facts paradigm focuses primarily on the macro-objective and macro-subjective levels. The social-definition paradigm is concerned largely with the micro-subjective world and that part of the micro-objective world that depends on mental processes (action). The social-behavior paradigm deals with that part of the micro-objective world that does not involve the minding process (behavior). Whereas the three extant paradigms cut across the levels of social reality horizontally, an integrated paradigm cuts across vertically. This depiction makes it clear why the integrated paradigm does not supersede the others. Although each of the three existing paradigms deals with a given level or levels in great detail, the integrated paradigm deals with all levels but does not examine any given level in anything like the degree of intensity of the other paradigms. Thus the choice of a paradigm depends on the kind of question being asked. Not all sociological issues require an integrated approach, but at least some do.

What has been outlined in the preceding pages is a model for the image of the subject matter of an integrated sociological paradigm. This sketch needs to be detailed more sharply,

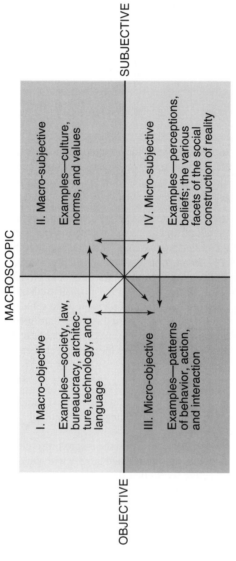

FIGURE A.3

Ritzer's Major Levels of Social Analysis*

*Note that this is a "snapshot" in time. It is embedded in an ongoing historical process.

LEVELS OF SOCIAL REALITY

SOCIOLOGICAL PARADIGMS

Macro-subjective
Macro-objective

Micro-subjective
Micro-objective

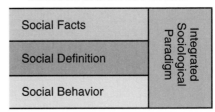

FIGURE A.4
Levels of Social Analysis and the Major Sociological Paradigms

but that is a task for another time (see Ritzer, 1981a). The goal of this discussion is not the development of a new sociological paradigm but the delineation of an overarching metatheoretical schema (M_O) that allows us to analyze sociological theory in a coherent fashion. The model developed in Figure A.3 forms the basis for this book.

Sociological theory is analyzed using the four levels of social analysis depicted in Figure A.3. This figure provides us with a metatheoretical tool that can be used in the comparative analysis of sociological theories. It enables us to analyze the concerns of a theory and how they relate to the concerns of all other sociological theories.

To be avoided at all costs is the simple identification of a theory or a theorist with specific levels of social analysis. Although it is true, given the preceding description of the current paradigmatic status of sociology, that sociological theorists who adhere to a given paradigm tend to focus on a given level or levels of social analysis, it often does them an injustice simply to equate the breadth of their work with one or more levels. For example, Karl Marx is often thought of as focusing on macro-objective structures—in particular, on the economic structures of capitalism. But the use of the schema in which there are multiple levels of social analysis allows us to see that Marx had rich insights regarding *all* levels of social reality and their interrelationships. Similarly, symbolic interactionism is generally considered a perspective that deals with micro subjectivity and micro objectivity, but it is not devoid of insights into the macroscopic levels of social analysis (Maines, 1977).

It is also important to remember that the use of levels of social analysis to analyze a theory tends to break up the wholeness, the integrity, and the internal consistency of the theory. Although the levels are useful for understanding a theory and comparing it to others, one must take pains to deal with the interrelationship among levels and with the totality of a theory.

In sum, the metatheoretical schema outlined in Figure A.3, the development of which was traced in this Appendix, provides the basis for the analysis of the sociological theories discussed in this book.

REFERENCES

Abbott, Carroll, Brown, Charles R., and Crosbie, Paul V.
1973   "Exchange as Symbolic Interaction: For What?" *American Sociological Review* 38:504–506.

Abel, Emily
1991   *Who Cares for the Elderly? Public Policy and the Experience of Adult Daughters.* Philadelphia: Temple University Press.

Aboulafia, Mitchell
1986   *The Mediating Self: Mead, Sartre, and Self-Determination.* New Haven: Yale University Press.

Abrahamsen, Rita
1997   "The Victory of Popular Forces or Passive Revolution? A Neo-Gramscian Perspective on Democratisation." *Journal of Modern African Studies* 35:129–152.

Abrahamson, Mark
1978   *Functionalism.* Englewood Cliffs, N.J.: Prentice-Hall.

Abrahamsson, Bengt
1970   "Homans on Exchange." *American Journal of Sociology* 76:273–285.

Abrams, Philip
1968   *The Origins of British Sociology: 1834–1914.* Chicago: University of Chicago Press.
1982   *Historical Sociology.* Ithaca, N.Y.: Cornell University Press.

Abrams, Philip, Deem, Rosemary, Finch, Janet, and Rock, Paul
1981   *Practice and Progress: British Sociology 1950–1980.* London: Allen and Unwin.

Acker, Joan
1989   *Doing Comparable Worth.* Philadelphia: Temple University Press.
1990   "Hierarchies, Jobs, Bodies." *Gender & Society* 4:139–158.
1992   "Gendered Institutions: From Sex Roles to Gendered Institutions." *Contemporary Sociology* 21:565–568.

Adkins, Lisa
1995   *Gendered Work: Sexuality, Family, and the Labour Market.* Bristol, Penn.: Open University Press.

Adler, Freda, and Laufer, William S. (eds.)
1995   *The Legacy of Anomie Theory.* New Brunswick, N.J.: Transaction Publishers.

Agger, Ben
1998   *Critical Social Theories: An Introduction.* Boulder, Colo.: Westview.

Agger, Ben (ed.)
1978   *Western Marxism: An Introduction.* Santa Monica, Calif.: Goodyear.

Alcala-Campos, Raul
1997   "Thomas S. Kuhn: Between Modernity and Postmodernity." *Acta
            Sociologica* 19:59–77.
Alcoff, Linda Martin
1998   "What Should White People Do?" *Hypatia* 13:6–26.
Aldrich, Howard
1988   "Paradigm Warriors: Donaldson versus the Critics of Organization Theory."
            Organization Studies 9:19–25.
Aldridge, Alan
1998   "Habitus and Cultural Capital in the Field of Personal Finance." *Sociological
            Review* 46:1–23.
Alexander, Jeffrey C.
1981   "Revolution, Reaction, and Reform: The Change Theory of Parsons's Middle
            Period." *Sociological Inquiry* 51:267–280.
1982   *Theoretical Logic in Sociology.* Vol. 1, *Positivism, Presuppositions, and
            Current Controversies.* Berkeley: University of California Press.
1982–1983   *Theoretical Logic in Sociology.* 4 vols. Berkeley: University of California
            Press.
1983   *Theoretical Logic in Sociology.* Vol. 4, *The Modern Reconstruction of
            Classical Thought: Talcott Parsons.* Berkeley: University of California
            Press.
1984   "The Parsons Revival in German Sociology." In R. Collins (ed.),
            Sociological Theory—1984. San Francisco: Jossey-Bass: 394–412.
1985a   "The 'Individualist Dilemma' in Phenomenology and Interactionism." In
            S. N. Eisenstadt and H. J. Helle (eds.), *Macro-Sociological Theory,* Vol. 1.
            London: Sage: 25–51.
1987a   "Action and Its Environments." In J. C. Alexander et al. (eds.), *The Micro-
            Macro Link.* Berkeley: University of California Press: 289–318.
1987b   *Twenty Lectures: Sociological Theory Since World War II.* New York:
            Columbia University Press.
1988b   "Culture and Political Crisis: 'Watergate' and Durkheimian Sociology." In
            J. C. Alexander (ed.), *Durkheimian Sociology: Cultural Studies.* Cambridge:
            Cambridge University Press: 187–224.
1988c   "Introduction: Durkheimian Sociology and Cultural Studies Today." In J. C.
            Alexander (ed.), *Durkheimian Sociology: Cultural Studies.* Cambridge:
            Cambridge University Press: 1–21.
1992   "Shaky Foundations: The Presuppositions and Internal Contradictions of
            James Coleman's *Foundations of Social Theory.*" *Theory and Society*
            21:203–217.
1993   "The Return of Civil Society." *Contemporary Sociology* 22:797–803.
1995   *Fin de Siecle Social Theory: Relativism, Reduction, and the Problem of
            Reason.* London: Verso.
1998a   *Neofunctionalism and After.* London: Blackwell.
1998b   *Real Civil Societies: Dilemmas of Institutionalization.* London: Sage.
Alexander, Jeffrey C. (ed.)
1985a   *Neofunctionalism.* Beverly Hills, Calif.: Sage.
1988   *Durkheimian Sociology: Cultural Studies.* Cambridge: Cambridge
            University Press.

Alexander, Jeffrey C., and Colomy, Paul
1985 "Toward Neo-Functionalism." *Sociological Theory* 3:11–23.
1990a "Neofunctionalism: Reconstructing a Theoretical Tradition." In G. Ritzer (ed.), *Frontiers of Social Theory: The New Syntheses*. New York: Columbia University Press: 33–67.
1992 "Traditions and Competition: Preface to a Postpositivist Approach to Knowledge Cumulation." In G. Ritzer (ed.), *Metatheorizing*. Newbury Park, Calif.: Sage: 27–52.
Alexander, Jeffrey C., and Colomy, Paul (eds.)
1990b *Differentiation Theory and Social Change: Comparative and Historical Perspectives*. New York: New York University Press.
Alexander, Jeffrey C., and Giesen, Bernhard
1987 "From Reduction to Linkage: The Long View of the Micro-Macro Link." In J. C. Alexander et al. (eds.), *The Micro-Macro Link*. Berkeley: University of California Press: 1–42.
Alexander, Jeffrey C., Giesen, Bernhard, Münch, Richard, and Smelser, Neil J. (eds.)
1987 *The Micro-Macro Link*. Berkeley: University of California Press.
Alexander, Jeffrey C., Smith, Philip, and Sherwood, Steven Jay
1993 "Risking Enchantment: Theory and Method in Cultural Studies." *Newsletter of the Sociology of Culture Section of the American Sociological Association* 8:10–14.
Alfino, Mark, Caputo, John S., and Wynyard, Robin (eds.)
1998 *McDonaldization Revisited: Critical Essays on Consumer Culture*. Westport, Conn.: Praeger.
Alford, Robert R., and Friedland, Roger
1985 *Powers of Theory: Capitalism, the State, and Democracy*. Cambridge: Cambridge University Press.
Alger, Janet M., and Alger, Steven F.
1997 "Beyond Mead: Symbolic Interaction between Humans and Felines." *Society and Animals* 5:65–81.
al-Hibri, Azizah
1981 "Reproduction, Mothering and the Origins of Patriarchy." In J. Trebilcot (ed.), *Mothering: Essays in Feminist Theory*. Totowa, N.J.: Rowman and Allanheld: 81–93.
Allen, Paula Gunn
1991 *Grandmothers of the Light: A Medicine Woman's Sourcebook*. Boston: Beacon Press.
Allen, Paula Gunn (ed.)
1989 *Spider Woman's Granddaughters: Traditional Tales and Contemporary Writing by Native American Women*. Boston: Beacon Press.
Alt, John
1985–1986 "Reclaiming C. Wright Mills." *Telos* 66:6–43.
Althusser, Louis
1969 *For Marx*. Harmondsworth, Eng.: Penguin.
Alway, Joan
1995a *Critical Theory and Political Possibilities*. Westport, Conn.: Greenwood Press.
1995b "The Trouble with Gender: Tales of the Still Missing Feminist Revolution in Sociological Theory." *Sociological Theory* 13:209–226.

Amin, Ash (ed.)
1994   *Post-Fordism: A Reader.* Oxford: Blackwell.

Amin, Samir
1977   *Unequal Development: An Essay on the Social Formations of Peripheral Capitalism.* New York: Monthly Review Press.

Amott, Teresa L., and Matthaei, Julie A.
1991   *Race, Gender, and Work: A Multicultural Economic History of Women in the United States.* Boston: South End Press.

Amsterdamska, Olga
1985   "Institutions and Schools of Thought." *American Journal of Sociology* 91:332–358.

Andersen, Margaret, and Collins, Patricia Hill
1992   *Race, Class and Gender.* Belmont, Calif.: Wadsworth.

Anderson, Brom
1987–1988   "The Gospel According to Jameson." *Telos* 74:116–125.

Anderson, Cynthia D.
1996   "Understanding the Inequality Problematic: From Scholarly Rhetoric to Theoretical Reconstruction." *Gender & Society* 10:729–746.

Anderson, Leon, Snow, David A., and Cress, Daniel
1994   "Negotiating the Public Realm: Stigma Management and Collective Action among the Homeless." *Research in Community Sociology* 4, supplement: 121–143.

Anderson, Perry
1984   *In the Tracks of Historical Materialism.* Chicago: University of Chicago Press.
1990a   "A Culture in Contraflow—I." *New Left Review* 180:41–78.
1990b   "A Culture in Contraflow—II." *New Left Review* 182:85–137.

Anderson, R. J., Hughes, J. A., and Sharrock, W. W.
1987   "Executive Problem Finding: Some Material and Initial Observations." *Social Psychology Quarterly* 50:143–159.

Anheier, Helmut K., Gerhards, Jurgen, and Romo, Frank P.
1995   "Forms of Capital and Social Structure in Cultural Fields: Examining Bourdieu's Social Topography." *American Journal of Sociology* 100:859–903.

Antonio, Robert J.
1979   "Domination and Production in Bureaucracy." *American Sociological Review* 44:895–912.
1981   "Immanent Critique as the Core of Critical Theory: Its Origins and Development in Hegel, Marx and Contemporary Thought." *British Journal of Sociology* 32:330–345.
1985   "Values, History and Science: The Metatheoretic Foundations of the Weber-Marx Dialogues." In R. J. Antonio and R. M. Glassman (eds.), *A Weber-Marx Dialogue.* Lawrence: University Press of Kansas: 20–43.
1990   "The Decline of the Grand Narrative of Emancipatory Modernity: Crisis or Renewal in Neo-Marxian Theory?" In G. Ritzer (ed.), *Frontiers of Social Theory: The New Syntheses.* New York: Columbia University Press: 88–116.
1991   "Postmodern Storytelling versus Pragmatic Truth-Seeking: The Discursive Bases of Social Theory." *Sociological Theory* 9:154–163.

1998   "Mapping Postmodern Social Theory." In Alan Sica (ed.), *What Is Social Theory? The Philosophical Debates.* Oxford: Blackwell: 22–75.

Antonio, Robert J., and Glassman, Ronald M. (eds.)
1985   *A Weber-Marx Dialogue.* Lawrence: University Press of Kansas.

Antonio, Robert J., and Kellner, Douglas
1992   "Metatheorizing Historical Rupture: Classical Theory and Modernity." In G. Ritzer (ed.), *Metatheorizing.* Beverly Hills, Calif.: Sage: 88–106.
1994   "The Future of Social Theory and the Limits of Postmodern Critique." In D. R. Dickens and A. Fontana (eds.), *Postmodernism and Social Inquiry.* New York: Guilford Press: 127–152.
forthcoming *Theorizing Modernity.* London: Sage.

Anzaldúa, Gloria (ed.)
1990   *Making Face, Making Soul/Hacienda Caras: Creative and Critical Perspectives by Women of Color.* San Francisco: Aunt Lute Foundation Books.

Appadurai, Arjun
1990   "Disjunction and Difference in the Global Cultural Economy." In Mike Featherstone (ed.), *Global Culture: Nationalism, Globalization and Modernity.* London: Sage: 295–310.

Aptheker, Bettina
1989   *Tapestries of Life: Women's Work, Women's Consciousness and the Meaning of Daily Experience.* Amherst: University of Massachusetts Press.

Archer, Margaret S.
1982   "Morphogenesis versus Structuration: On Combining Structure and Action." *British Journal of Sociology* 33:455–483.
1985   "Structuration versus Morphogenesis." In S. N. Eisenstadt and H. J. Helle (eds.), *Macro-Sociological Theory.* London: Sage: 58–88.
1988   *Culture and Agency: The Place of Culture in Social Theory.* Cambridge: Cambridge University Press.
1990   "Theory, Culture and Post-Industrial Society." In Mike Featherstone (ed.), *Global Culture: Nationalism, Globalization and Modernity.* London: Sage: 97–120.
1995   *Realist Social Theory: The Morphogenetic Approach.* Cambridge: Cambridge University Press.
1996   "Social Integration and System Integration: Developing the Distinction." *Sociology* 30: 679–699.

Arguelles, Lourdes
1993   Plenary Address: "Intellectual Foundations of Women's Studies: Beyond Political Correctness." National Women's Studies Association, Washington, D.C., June.

Arendell, Terry
1995   *Fathers and Divorce.* Thousand Oaks, Calif.: Sage.

Aron, Raymond
1965   *Main Currents in Sociological Thought,* Vol. 1. New York: Basic Books.

Aronson, Ronald
1995   *After Marxism.* New York: Guilford Press.

Arthur, C. J.
1970   "Editor's Introduction." In K. Marx and F. Engels, *The German Ideology,* Part 1. New York: International Publishers: 4–34.

Asante, Molefi Kete
1996   "The Afrocentric Metatheory and Disciplinary Implications." In Mary F.
            Rogers (ed.), *Multicultural Experiences, Multicultural Theories*. New York:
            McGraw-Hill: 61–73.
Ascher, Carol, de Salvo, Louise, and Ruddick, Sara
1984   *Between Women*. Boston: Beacon Press.
Athens, Lonnie
1995   "Mead's Vision of the Self: A Pair of 'Flawed Diamonds.' " *Studies in
            Symbolic Interaction* 18:245–261.
Atkinson, J. Maxwell
1984a   *Our Masters' Voices: The Language and Body Language of Politics*. New
            York: Methuen.
1984b   "Public Speaking and Audience Responses: Some Techniques for Inviting
            Applause." In J. M. Atkinson and J. Heritage (eds.), *Structures of Social
            Action*. Cambridge: Cambridge University Press: 370–409.
Atkinson, Paul
1988   "Ethnomethodology: A Critical Review." *Annual Review of Sociology*
            14:441–465.
Atkinson, Ti-Grace
1974   *Amazon Odyssey*. New York: Link Books.
Baber, Zaheer
1991   "Beyond the Structure/Agency Dualism: An Evaluation of Giddens' Theory
            of Structuration." *Sociological Inquiry* 61:219–230.
Bacchi, Carol Lee
1990   *Same Difference: Feminism and Sexual Difference*. Sydney: Allen and
            Unwin.
Bailey, Alison
1998   "Locating Traitorous Identities: Toward a View of Privilege Cognizant White
            Character." *Hypatia* 13:27–42.
Bailey, Cathryn
1997   "Making Waves and Drawing Lines: The Politics of Defining the
            Vicissitudes of Feminism." *Hypatia* 12:16–28.
Bailey, Kenneth D.
1987   "Globals, Mutables and Immutables: An Alternative Approach to
            Micro/Macro Analysis." Paper presented at the meetings of the American
            Sociological Association, Chicago, Illinois.
1990   *Social Entropy Theory*. Albany: State University of New York Press.
1994   *Sociology and the New Systems Theory: Toward a Theoretical Synthesis*.
            Albany: State University of New York Press.
1997   "System and Conflict: Toward a Symbiotic Reconciliation." *Quality and
            Quantity* 31:425–442.
1998   "Structure, Structuration, and Autopoesis: The Emerging Significance of
            Recursive Theory." In Jennifer M. Lehmann (ed.), *Current Perspectives in
            Social Theory*, Vol. 18. Greenwich, Conn.: JAI Press: 131–154.
Baker, Patrick L.
1993   "Chaos, Order, and Sociological Theory." *Sociological Inquiry* 63: 123–149.
Baker, Wayne E.
1990   "Market Networks and Corporate Behavior." *American Journal of Sociology*
            96:589–625.

Baldwin, Alfred
1961   "The Parsonian Theory of Personality." In M. Black (ed.), *The Social Theories of Talcott Parsons.* Englewood Cliffs, N.J.: Prentice-Hall: 153–190.
Baldwin, John C.
1986   *George Herbert Mead: A Unifying Theory for Sociology.* Newbury Park, Calif.: Sage.
1988a   "Mead and Skinner: Agency and Determinism." *Behaviorism* 16:109–127.
1988b   "Mead's Solution to the Problem of Agency." *Sociological Inquiry* 58:139–162.
Baldwin, John D., and Baldwin, Janice I.
1986   *Behavior Principles in Everyday Life.* 2nd ed. Englewood Cliffs, N.J.: Prentice-Hall.
Ball, Richard A.
1978   "Sociology and General Systems Theory." *American Sociologist* 13:65–72.
Ball, Terence
1991   "History: Critique and Irony." In T. Carver (ed.), *The Cambridge Companion to Marx.* Cambridge: Cambridge University Press: 124–142.
Banks, Alan, Billings, Dwight, and Tice, Karen
1996   "Appalachian Studies and Postmodernism." In Mary F. Rogers (ed.), *Multicultural Experiences, Multicultural Theories.* New York: McGraw-Hill: 81–90.
Banner, Lois
1984   *Women in Modern America: A Brief History.* New York: Harcourt Brace Jovanovich.
Bannister, Robert
1991   *Jessie Bernard: The Making of a Feminist.* New Brunswick, N.J.: Rutgers University Press.
Baran, Paul, and Sweezy, Paul M.
1966   *Monopoly Capital: An Essay on the American Economic and Social Order.* New York: Monthly Review Press.
Barber, Bernard
1993   *Constructing the Social System.* New Brunswick, N.J.: Transaction.
1994   "Talcott Parsons on the Social System: An Essay in Clarification and Elaboration." *Sociological Theory* 12:101–105.
Barnett, Ola W., and LaViolette, Alyce D.
1993   *It Could Happen to Anyone: Why Battered Women Stay.* Newbury, Calif.: Sage.
Barrett, Michele
1985   "Introduction." In F. Engels, *Origins of the Family, Private Property and the State.* New York: Penguin.
1989   *Women's Oppression Today.* Rev. ed. New York: Verso.
Barrett, Michele, and Phillips, Ann (eds.)
1993   *Destabilizing Theory: Contemporary Feminist Debates.* Stanford, Calif.: Stanford University Press.
Barry, Kathleen
1979   *Female Sexual Slavery.* Englewood Cliffs, N.J.: Prentice-Hall.
1993   *The Prostitution of Sexuality: The Global Exploitation of Women.* New York: New York University Press.

Bart, Pauline, and Moran, Eileen Geil (eds.)
1993   *Violence against Women: The Bloody Footprints.* Newbury Park, Calif.:
            Sage.
Bartos, Ottomar J.
1996   "Postmodernism, Postindustrialism, and the Future." *Sociological Quarterly*
            37:307–325.
Bartsky, Sandra Lee
1992   *Feminism and Domination: Studies in the Phenomenology of Oppression.*
            New York: Routledge.
Bate, Barbara, and Taylor, Anita (eds.)
1988   *Women Communicating: Studies of Women's Talk.* Norwood, N.J.: Ablex.
Baudrillard, Jean
1970/1998   *The Consumer Society.* London: Sage.
1972/1981   *For a Critique of the Political Economy of the Sign.* St. Louis: Telos Press.
1973/1975   *The Mirror of Production.* St. Louis: Telos Press.
1976/1993   *Symbolic Exchange and Death.* London: Sage.
1979/1990   *Seduction.* New York: St. Martin's.
1980–1985/ *Cool Memories.* London: Verso.
1990
1983   *Simulations.* New York: Semiotext(e).
1983/1990   *Fatal Strategies.* New York: Semiotext(e).
1986/1989   *America.* London: Verso.
1990/1993   *The Transparency of Evil: Essays on Extreme Phenomena.* London: Verso.
Baum, Rainer C., and Lechner, Frank J.
1981   "National Socialism: Toward an Action-Theoretical Perspective."
            Sociological Inquiry 51:281–308.
Bauman, Zygmunt
1976   *Towards a Critical Sociology: An Essay on Commonsense and
            Emancipation.* London: Routledge and Kegan Paul.
1989   *Modernity and the Holocaust.* Ithaca, N.Y.: Cornell University Press.
1990   "From Pillars to Post." *Marxism Today,* February:20–25.
1991   *Modernity and Ambivalence.* Ithaca, N.Y.: Cornell University Press.
1992   *Intimations of Postmodernity.* London: Routledge.
1993   *Postmodern Ethics.* Oxford: Basil Blackwell.
Beck, Ulrich
1992   *Risk Society: Towards a New Modernity.* London: Sage.
1996   "World Risk Society as Cosmopolitan Society?" *Theory, Culture and Society*
            13:1–32.
Becker, Howard S., and McCall, Michal M. (eds.)
1990   *Symbolic Interaction and Cultural Studies.* Chicago: University of Chicago
            Press.
Becker, Uwe
1988   "From Social Scientific Functionalism to Open Functional Logic." *Theory
            and Society* 17:865–883.
Bell, Daniel
1992   "George C. Homans (11 August 1910–29 May 1989)." *Proceedings of the
            American Philosophical Society* 136:587–593.
Bem, Sandra Lipsitz
1993   *The Lenses of Gender: Transforming Debates on Sexual Inequality.* New
            Haven: Yale University Press.

Benford, Robert D., and Hunt, Scott A.
1992   "Dramaturgy and Social Movements: The Social Construction and Communication of Power." *Sociological Inquiry* 62:36–55.
Beniger, James R., and Savory, Laina
1981   "Social Exchange: Diffusion of a Paradigm." *American Sociologist* 16:240–250.
Benjamin, Jessica
1985   "The Bonds of Love: Rational Violence and Erotic Domination." In H. Eisenstein and A. Jardine (eds.), *The Future of Difference.* New Brunswick, N.J.: Rutgers University Press: 41–70.
1988   *The Bonds of Love: Psychoanalysis, Feminism, and the Problem of Domination.* New York: Pantheon.
Benokraitis, Nijole
1997   *Subtle Sexism: Current Practice and Prospects for Change.* Thousand Oaks, Calif.: Sage.
Benston, Margaret
1970   *The Political Economy of Women's Liberation.* New York: Monthly Review Press. Reprint.
Bergen, Raquel Kennedy
1996   *Wife Rape: Understanding the Response of Survivors and Service Providers.* Thousand Oaks, Calif.: Sage.
Berger, Brigette, and Berger, Peter
1983   *The War over the Family: Capturing the Middle Ground.* Garden City, N.Y.: Anchor.
Berger, Joseph, Eyre, Dana P., and Zelditch, Morris, Jr.
1989   "Theoretical Structures and the Micro/Macro Problem." In J. Berger, M. Zelditch, Jr., and B. Anderson (eds.), *Sociological Theories in Progress: New Formulations.* Newbury Park, Calif.: Sage: 11–32.
Berger, Joseph, Wagner, David G., and Zelditch, Morris, Jr.
1989   "Theory Growth, Social Processes and Metatheory." In J. Turner (ed.), *Theory Building in Sociology: Assessing Theoretical Cumulation.* Newbury Park, Calif.: Sage 19–42.
Berger, Peter
1963   *Invitation to Sociology.* New York: Doubleday.
Berger, Peter and Kellner, Hansfried
1964   "Marriage and the Social Construction of Reality." In P. Dreitzel (ed.), *Recent Sociology.* No. 2, *Patterns of Communicative Behavior.* New York: Macmillan.
Berger, Peter, and Luckmann, Thomas
1967   *The Social Construction of Reality.* Garden City, N.Y.: Anchor.
Bergeson, Albert
1984   "The Critique of World-System Theory: Class Relations or Division of Labor?" In R. Collins (ed.), *Sociological Theory—1984.* San Francisco: Jossey-Bass: 365–372.
Bernard, Jessie
1971   *Women and the Public Interest.* Chicago: Aldine.
1973   "My Four Revolutions: An Autobiographical Account of the American Sociological Association." *American Journal of Sociology* 78:773–792.
1981   *The Female World.* New York: Free Press.
1972/1982   *The Future of Marriage.* 2nd ed. New Haven: Yale University Press.

1987   *The Female World from a Global Perspective.* Bloomington: Indiana
                University Press.

Bernard, Thomas
1983   *The Consensus-Conflict Debate: Form and Content in Sociological
                Theories.* New York: Columbia University Press.

Bernikow, Louise (ed.)
1974   *The World Split Open: Four Centuries of Women Poets in England and
                America, 1552–1950.* New York: Vintage.

1980   *Among Women.* New York: Harper.

Bernstein, J. M.
1995   *Recovering Ethical Life: Jurgen Habermas and the Future of Critical
                Theory.* London: Routledge.

Bernstein, Richard J.
1971   *Praxis and Action: Contemporary Philosophies of Human Activity.*
                Philadelphia: University of Pennsylvania Press.

1989   "Social Theory as Critique." In D. Held and J. B. Thompson (eds.), *Social
                Theory of Modern Societies: Anthony Giddens and His Critics.* Cambridge:
                Cambridge University Press: 19–33.

Besnard, Philippe
1983a   "The 'Année Sociologique' Team." In P. Besnard (ed.), *The Sociological
                Domain.* Cambridge: Cambridge University Press: 11–39.

Besnard, Philippe (ed.)
1983b   *The Sociological Domain.* Cambridge: Cambridge University Press.

Best, Raphaela
1983   *We've All Got Scars: What Boys and Girls Learn in Elementary School.*
                Bloomington: University of Indiana Press.

Best, Steven, and Kellner, Douglas
1991   *Postmodern Theory: Critical Interrogations.* New York: Guilford Press.

Beutel, Ann M., and Marini, Margaret Mooney
1995   "Gender and Values." *American Sociological Review* 60:436–448.

Bhargava, Rajeev
1992   *Individualism in Social Science: Forms and Limits of a Methodology.*
                Oxford: Clarendon Press.

Bian, Yanjie
1997   "Bringing Strong Ties Back In: Indirect Ties, Network Bridges, and Job
                Searches in China." *American Sociological Review* 62:366–385.

Binkley, Christina
1998   "Gambling on Culture: Casinos Invest in Fine Art." *The Wall Street Journal,*
                April 15:10.

Bird, Caroline
1979   *The Two Paycheck Family.* New York: Rawson, Wade.

Birnbaum, Pierre, and Todd, Jane Marie
1995   "French Jewish Sociologists between Reason and Faith: The Impact of the
                Dreyfus Affair." *Jewish Social Studies* 2:1–35.

Bittner, Egon
1973   "Objectivity and Realism in Sociology." In G. Psathas (ed.),
                Phenomenological Sociology: Issues and Applications. New York: Wiley:
                109–125.

Blalock, Hubert, and Wilken, Paul
1979   *Intergroup Processes: A Micro-Macro Perspective.* New York: Free Press.

Blau, Peter
1960   "Structural Effects." *American Sociological Review* 25:178–193.
1964   *Exchange and Power in Social Life.* New York: Wiley.
1975a   Introduction, "Parallels and Contrasts in Structural Inquiries." In P. Blau
            (ed.), *Approaches to the Study of Social Structure.* New York: Free Press:
            1–20.
1975b   "Parameters of Social Structure." In P. Blau (ed.), *Approaches to the Study of
            Social Structure.* New York: Free Press: 220–253.
1977a   *Inequality and Heterogeneity: A Primitive Theory of Social Structure.* New
            York: Free Press.
1977b   "A Macrosociological Theory of Social Structure." *American Sociological
            Review* 83:26–54.
1980   "A Fable about Social Structure." *Social Forces* 58:777–788.
1987a   "Contrasting Theoretical Perspectives." In J. C. Alexander et al. (eds.), *The
            Micro-Macro Link.* Berkeley: University of California Press: 71–85.
1987b   "Microprocess and Macrostructure." In K. Cook (ed.), *Social Exchange
            Theory.* Beverly Hills, Calif.: Sage: 83–100.
1994   *Structural Contexts of Opportunities.* Chicago: University of Chicago Press.
1997   "On Limitations of Rational Choice Theory for Sociology." *American
            Sociologist* 28:16–21.
Blau, Peter, and Merton, Robert K. (eds).
1981   *Continuities in Structural Inquiry.* Beverly Hills, Calif: Sage
Blau, Peter, and Schwartz, Joseph E.
1997   *Crosscutting Social Circles: Testing a Macrostructural Theory of Intergroup
            Relations.* New Brunswick, NJ: Transaction Pubs..
Bleich, Harold
1977   *The Philosophy of Herbert Marcuse.* Washington, D.C.: University Press of
            America.
Bleicher, Josef
1980   *Contemporary Hermeneutics: Hermeneutics as Method, Philosophy and
            Critique.* London: Routledge and Kegan Paul.
Blum, Linda M.
1991   *Between Feminism and Labor: The Significance of the Comparable Worth
            Movement.* Berkeley: University of California Press.
Blum, Nancy S.
1991   "The Management of Stigma by Alzheimer Family Caregivers." *Journal of
            Contemporary Ethnography* 20:263–284.
Blumberg, Rae Lesser
1978   *Stratification: Socio-Economic and Sexual Inequality.* Dubuque, Iowa:
            William C. Brown.
1979   "A Paradigm for Predicting the Position of Women: Policy Implications and
            Problems." In J. Lipman-Blumen and J. Bernard (eds.), *Sex Roles and Social
            Policy.* Beverly Hills, Calif.: Sage: 113–142.
1984   "A General Theory of Gender Stratification." In R. Collins (ed.), *Sociological
            Theory.* San Francisco: Jossey-Bass.
Blumer, Herbert
1954/1969   "What Is Wrong with Social Theory?" In H. Blumer, *Symbolic Interaction.*
            Englewood Cliffs, N.J.: Prentice-Hall: 140–152.
1955/1969   "Attitudes and the Social Act." In H. Blumer, *Symbolic Interaction.*
            Englewood Cliffs, N.J.: Prentice-Hall: 90–100.

1956/1969	"Sociological Analysis and the 'Variable.' " In H. Blumer, *Symbolic Interaction*. Englewood Cliffs, N.J.: Prentice-Hall: 127–139.
1962/1969	"Society as Symbolic Interaction." In H. Blumer, *Symbolic Interaction*. Englewood Cliffs, N.J.: Prentice-Hall: 78–89.
1969a	*Symbolic Interaction: Perspective and Method.* Englewood Cliffs, N.J.: Prentice-Hall.
1969b	"The Methodological Position of Symbolic Interactionism." In H. Blumer, *Symbolic Interaction*. Englewood Cliffs, N.J.: Prentice-Hall: 1–60.
1974	"Comments on 'Parsons as a Symbolic Interactionist.' " *Sociological Inquiry* 45:59–62.
1980	Comment: "Mead and Blumer: The Convergent Methodological Perspectives of Social Behaviorism and Symbolic Interactionism." *American Sociological Review* 45:409–419.
1990	*Industrialization as an Agent of Social Change: A Critical Analysis.* New York: Aldine de Gruyter.

Boden, Deirdre
1990a	"The World as It Happens: Ethnomethodology and Conversation Analysis." In G. Ritzer (ed.), *Frontiers of Social Theory: The New Syntheses*. New York: Columbia University Press: 185–213.
1990b	"People Are Talking: Conversation Analysis and Symbolic Interaction." In H. S. Becker and M. McCall (eds.), *Symbolic Interactionism and Cultural Studies*. Chicago: University of Chicago Press: 244–273.

Bogard, William
1990	"Closing Down the Social: Baudrillard's Challenge to Contemporary Sociology." *Sociological Theory* 8:1–15.
1998	"Sense and Segmentarity: Some Markers of a Deleuzian-Guattarian Sociology." *Sociological Theory* 16:52–74.

Bogner, Arthur, Baker, Adelheid, and Kilminster, Richard
1992	"The Theory of the Civilizing Process—An Idiographic Theory of Modernization." *Theory, Culture, and Society* 9:23–52.

Bolt, Christine
1993	*The Women's Movements in the United States and Britain from the 1740's to the 1920's.* Amherst: University of Massachusetts Press.

Bookman, Ann, and Morgen, Sandra (eds.)
1988	*Women and the Politics of Empowerment.* Philadelphia: Temple University Press.

Bordo, Susan
1990	"Feminism, Postmodernism, and Gender-Scepticism." In L. Nicholson (ed.), *Feminism/Postmodernism*. New York: Routledge: 133–156.
1993	*Unbearable Weight: Feminism, Western Culture and the Body.* Berkeley: University of California Press.

Borges, Jorges
1964	*Labrynths.* New York: Modern Library.

Bosserman, Phillip
1968	*Dialectical Sociology: An Analysis of the Sociology of Georges Gurvitch.* Boston: Porter Sargent.

Bottomore, Tom
1984	*The Frankfurt School.* Chichester, Eng.: Ellis Horwood.

Bourdieu, Pierre
1977   *Outline of a Theory of Practice.* London: Cambridge University Press.
1980/1990   *The Logic of Practice.* Stanford, Calif.: Stanford University Press.
1984b   *Homo Academicus.* Stanford, Calif.: Stanford University Press.
1989   "Social Space and Symbolic Power." *Sociological Theory* 7:14–25.
1990   *In Other Words: Essays Toward a Reflexive Sociology.* Cambridge: Polity Press.
1993   *The Field of Cultural Production: Essays on Art and Leisure.* New York:
            Columbia University Press.
1994   "Rethinking the State: Genesis and Structure of the Bureaucratic Field."
            Sociological Theory 12:1–18.
1996   *The State Nobility.* Stanford, Calif.: Stanford University Press.
1998   *Practical Reason.* Stanford, Calif.: Stanford University Press.
Bourdieu, Pierre, and Darbel, Alain
1969/1990   *The Love of Art: European Art Museums and their Public.* Stanford, Calif.:
            Stanford University Press.
Bourdieu, Pierre, and Passeron, Jean-Claude
1970/1990   *Reproduction in Education, Society and Culture.* London: Sage.
Bourdieu, Pierre, and Wacquant, Loïc J. D.
1992   "The Purpose of Reflexive Sociology (The Chicago Workshop)." In P.
            Bourdieu and L. J. D. Wacquant (eds.), *An Invitation to Reflexive Sociology.*
            Chicago: University of Chicago Press: 61–215.
Bourricaud, François
1981   *The Sociology of Talcott Parsons.* Chicago: University of Chicago Press.
Bowles, Samuel, and Gintis, Herbert
1987   *Democracy and Capitalism: Property, Community, and the Contradictions of
            Modern Social Thought.* New York: Basic Books.
Bowring, Finn
1996   "A Lifeworld without a Subject: Habermas and Pathologies of Modernity."
            Telos 106:77–104.
Bramson, Leon
1961   *The Political Context of Sociology.* Princeton, N.J.: Princeton University Press.
Braverman, Harry
1974   *Labor and Monopoly Capital: The Degradation of Work in the Twentieth
            Century.* New York: Monthly Review Press.
Breines, Wini
1992   *Young, White and Miserable: Growing Up Female in the Fifties.* Boston:
            Beacon Press.
Brennan, Teresa
1994   *History after Lacan.* New York: Routledge.
1997   "The Two Forms of Consciousness." *Theory, Culture and Society* 14:89–96.
Brenner, Neil
1994   "Foucault's New Functionalism." *Theory and Society* 23:679–709.
Brewer, John, and Hunter, Albert
1989   *Multimethod Research: A Synthesis of Styles.* Newbury Park, Calif.: Sage.
Brewer, Rose M.
1989   "Black Women and Feminist Sociology: The Emerging Perspective."
            American Sociologist 20:57–71.
Brinton, Mary C.
1992   *Women and the Economic Miracle: Gender and Work in Postwar Japan.*
            Berkeley: University of California Press.

Brinton, Mary C. (ed.)
1993   "Gender and Work." *Rationality and Society* 5:5–116.
Bronner, Stephen Eric
1995   "Ecology, Politics, and Risk: The Social Theory of Ulrich Beck." *Capital, Nature and Socialism* 6:67–86.
Brown, Lyn Mikel, and Gilligan, Carol
1992   *Meeting at the Crossroads: Women's Psychological and Personal Development.* Cambridge, Mass.: Harvard University Press.
Brown, Richard
1987   *Society as Text: Essays on Rhetoric, Reason and Reality.* Chicago: University of Chicago Press.
1990a   "Social Science and the Poetics of Public Truth." *Sociological Forum* 5:55–74.
1990b   "Rhetoric, Textuality, and the Postmodern Turn in Sociological Theory." *Sociological Theory* 8:188–197.
Brubaker, Rogers
1984   *The Limits of Rationality: An Essay on the Social and Moral Thought of Max Weber.* London: Allen and Unwin.
Bruder, Kurt A.
1998   "Monastic Blessings: Deconstructing and Reconstructing the Self." *Symbolic Interaction* 21:87–116.
Brugger, Bill
1995   "Marxism, Asia, and the 1990s." *Positions* 3:630–641.
Brustein, William, and Falter, Jurgen W.
1994   "The Sociology of Nazism: An Interest-Based Account." *Rationality and Society* 6:369–399.
Bryant, Christopher G. A.
1985   *Positivism in Social Theory and Research.* New York: St. Martin's.
Bryant, Christopher G. A., and Jary, David
forthcoming "Anthony Giddens." In George Ritzer (ed.), *The Blackwell Companion to Major Social Theorists.* Oxford, England, and Cambridge, Mass.: Blackwell.
Buchwald, Emilie, Fletcher, Pamela R., and Roth, Martha (eds.)
1993   *Transforming a Rape Culture.* Minneapolis: Milkweed.
Buckley, Kerry W.
1989   *Mechanical Man: John Broadus Watson and the Beginnings of Behaviorism.* New York: Guilford Press.
Buckley, Walter
1967   *Sociology and Modern Systems Theory.* Englewood Cliffs, N.J.: Prentice-Hall.
Buffalohead, W. Roger
1996   "Reflections on Native American Cultural Rights and Resources." In Mary F. Rogers (ed.), *Multicultural Experiences, Multicultural Theories.* New York: McGraw-Hill: 154–156.
Bulmer, Martin
1984   *The Chicago School of Sociology: Institutionalization, Diversity, and the Rise of Sociological Research.* Chicago: University of Chicago Press.
1985   "The Chicago School of Sociology: What Made It a 'School'?" *History of Sociology: An International Review* 5:62–77.

1996   "The Sociological Contributions to Social Policy Research." In Jon Clark (ed.), *James Coleman.* London: Falmer Press: 103–118.

Bunch, Charlotte
1987   *Passionate Politics: Feminist Theory in Action.* New York: St. Martin's.

Burawoy, Michael
1979   *Manufacturing Consent: Changes in the Labor Process under Monopoly Capitalism.* Chicago: University of Chicago Press.
1990   "Marxism as Science: Historical Challenges and Theoretical Growth." *American Sociological Review* 55:775–793.

Burger, Thomas
1976   *Max Weber's Theory of Concept Formation: History, Laws and Ideal Types.* Durham, N.C.: Duke University Press.

Burke, Peter
1986   "Strengths and Weaknesses of the History of Mentalities." *History of European Ideas* 7:439–451.

Burns, Tom R.
1986   "Actors, Transactions, and Social Structure: An Introduction to Social Rule System Theory." In U. Himmelstrand (ed.), *Sociology: The Aftermath of Crisis.* London: Sage: 8–37.

Burns, Tom R., and Flam, Helena
1986   *The Shaping of Social Organization: Social Rule System Theory with Applications.* Beverly Hills, Calif.: Sage.

Burris, Val
1979   "Introduction." In "The Structuralist Influence in Marxist Theory and Research." *Insurgent Sociologist* 9:4–17.

Burt, Ronald
1982   *Toward a Structural Theory of Action: Network Models of Social Structure, Perception, and Action.* New York: Academic Press.
1992   *Structural Holes: The Social Structure of Competition.* Cambridge, Mass.: Harvard University Press.

Bushell, Don, and Burgess, Robert
1969   "Some Basic Principles of Behavior." In R. Burgess and D. Bushell (eds.), *Behavioral Sociology.* New York: Columbia University Press: 27–48.

Butler, Judith
1990   *Gender Trouble: Feminism and the Subversion of Identity.* New York: Routledge.
1993   *Bodies That Matter: On the Discursive Limits of "Sex."* New York: Routledge.

Buttel, Frederick H. (ed.)
1990   "Symposium: Evolution and Social Change." *Sociological Forum* 5:153–212.

Button, Graham
1987   "Answers as Interactional Products: Two Sequential Practices Used in Interviews." *Social Psychology Quarterly* 50:160–171.
1991   "Introduction: Ethnomethodology and the Foundational Respecification of the Human Sciences." In G. Button (ed.), *Ethnomethodology and the Human Sciences.* Cambridge: Cambridge University Press: 1–19.

Buxton, William
1985   *Talcott Parsons and the Capitalist Nation-State: Political Sociology as a Strategic Vocation.* Toronto: University of Toronto Press.

Cadieux, R. D.
1995   "Dialectics and the Economy of Difference." *Dialectical Anthropology*
            20:319–340.
Caldwell, Paulette
1991   "A Hair Piece: Perspectives on the Intersection of Race and Gender." *Duke
            Law Journal* 36:365–96.
Calhoun, Craig
1993   "Habitus, Field, and Capital: The Question of Historical Specificity." In C.
            Calhoun, E. LiPuma and M. Postone (eds.), *Bourdieu: Critical Perspectives.*
            Chicago: University of Chicago Press: 61–88.
Callari, Antonio, Cullenberg, Stephen, and Biewener, Carole (eds.)
1995   *Marxism in the Postmodern Age: Confronting the New World Order.* New
            York: Guilford Press.
Callinicos, Alex
1989   "Introduction: Analytical Marxism." In Alex Callinicos (ed.), *Marxist
            Theory.* Oxford: Oxford University Press, 1989: 1–16.
1990   *Against Postmodernism: A Marxist Critique.* New York: St. Martin's.
Camic, Charles
1989   "*Structure* after 50 Years: The Anatomy of a Charter." *American Journal of
            Sociology* 95:38–107.
1990   "An Historical Prologue." *American Sociological Review* 55:313–319.
1992   "Reputation and Predecessor Selection: Parsons and the Institutionalists."
            American Sociological Review 57:421–445.
Camic, Charles (ed.)
1997   *Reclaiming the Sociological Classics: The State of Scholarship.* Oxford:
            Blackwell.
Campbell, Anne
1993   *Men, Women and Aggression.* New York: Basic Books.
Campbell, Colin
1982   "A Dubious Distinction? An Inquiry into the Value and Use of Merton's
            Concepts of Manifest and Latent Function." *American Sociological Review*
            47:29–44.
Campbell, Marie, and Manicom, Ann
1995   *Knowledge, Experience, and Ruling Relations: Studies in the Social
            Organization of Knowledge.* Toronto: University of Toronto Press.
Caplan, Paula
1993   *Lifting a Ton of Feathers: A Woman's Guide to Surviving in the Academic
            World.* Toronto: University of Toronto Press.
Caputi, Jane
1989   "The Sexual Politics of Murder." *Gender & Society* 3:437–456.
Caraway, Nancie
1991   *Segregated Sisterhood: Racism and the Politics of American Feminism.*
            Knoxville: University of Tennessee Press.
Carden, Maren Lockwood
1974   *The New Feminist Movement.* New York: Russell Sage Foundation.
Carleheden, Mikael, and Gabriels, Rene
1996   "An Interview with Jurgen Habermas." *Theory, Culture and Society* 13:1–17.
Carver, Terrell
1983   *Marx and Engels: The Intellectual Relationship.* Bloomington: Indiana
            University Press.

Carveth, Donald
1982   "Sociology and Psychoanalysis: The Hobbesian Problem Revisited."
    Canadian Journal of Sociology 7:201–229.
Castells, Manuel
1996a "The Net and the Self: Working Notes for a Critical Theory of the
    Informational Society." *Critique of Anthropology* 16:9–38.
1996b *The Rise of the Network Society.* Malden, Mass.: Blackwell.
1997   *The Power of Identity.* Malden, Mass.: Blackwell.
1998   *End of Millennium.* Malden, Mass.: Blackwell.
Cerullo, John J.
1994   "The Epistemic Turn: Critical Sociology and the 'Generation of 68.' "
    International Journal of Politics, Culture and Society. 8:169–181.
Chafetz, Janet Saltzman
1984   *Sex and Advantage.* Totowa, N.J.: Rowman and Allanheld.
1988   *Feminist Sociology: An Overview of Contemporary Theories.* Itasca, Ill.:
    Peacock.
1990   *Gender Equity: An Integrated Theory of Stability and Change.* Newbury
    Park, Calif.: Sage.
1997   "Feminist Theory and Sociology: Underutilized Contributions for
    Mainstream Theory." *Annual Review of Sociology* 23:97–190.
Chafetz, Janet Saltzman, and Dworkin, Anthony Gary
1986   *Female Revolt: Women's Movements in World and Historical Perspectives.*
    Totowa, N.J.: Rowman and Allanheld.
Chamberlain, Marian K. (ed.)
1988   *Women in Academe: Progress and Prospects.* New York: Russell Sage.
Chancer, Lynn S.
1992   *Sadomasochism in Everyday Life: The Dynamics of Power and
    Powerlessness.* New Brunswick, N.J.: Rutgers University Press.
Chapin, Mark
1994   "Functional Conflict Theory: The Alcohol Beverage Industry, and the Alco-
    holism Treatment Industry." *Journal of Applied Social Sciences* 18:169–182.
Chapoulie, Jean-Michel
1996   "Everett Hughes and the Chicago Tradition." *Sociological Theory* 14:3–29.
Charmaz, Kathy
1991   *Good Days, Bad Days: The Self in Chronic Illness and Time.* New
    Brunswick, N.J.: Rutgers University Press.
Charon, Joel M.
1998   *Symbolic Interactionism: An Introduction, an Interpretation, an Integration.*
    6th ed. Englewood Cliffs, N.J.: Prentice-Hall.
Chase-Dunn, Christopher, and Hall, Thomas D.
1994   "The Historical Evolution of World-Systems." *Sociological Inquiry*
    64:257–280.
Chaves, Mark, and Cann, David E.
1992   "Regulation, Pluralism, and Religious Market Structure: Explaining
    Religion's Vitality." *Rationality and Society* 4:272–290.
Chayko, Mary
1993   "What Is Real in the Age of Virtual Reality? 'Reframing' Frame Analysis for
    a Technological World." *Symbolic Interaction* 16:171–181.
Chesler, Phyllis
1994   *Patriarchy: Notes of an Expert Witness.* Boston: Common Courage Press.

Chinchilla, Norma Stoltz
1990   "Revolutionary Popular Feminism in Nicaragua: Articulating Class, Gender and National Sovereignty." *Gender & Society* 4:370–397.
1991   "Marxism, Feminism and the Struggle for Democracy in Latin America." *Gender & Society* 5:291–310.
Chitnis, Anand C.
1976   *The Scottish Enlightenment: A Social History.* Totowa, N.J.: Rowman and Littlefield.
Chodorow, Nancy
1978   *The Reproduction of Mothering: Psychoanalysis and the Sociology of Gender.* Berkeley: University of California Press.
1990   *Feminism and Psychoanalytic Theory.* New Haven: Yale University Press.
1994   *Femininities, Masculinity, Sexualities: Freud and Beyond.* Lexington: University of Kentucky Press.
Chriss, James J.
1993a   "Durkheim's Cult of the Individual as Civil Religion: Its Appropriation by Erving Goffman." *Sociological Spectrum* 13:251–275.
1993b   "Looking Back on Goffman: The Excavation Continues." *Human Studies* 16:469–483.
1995   "Testing Gouldner's Coming Crisis Thesis: On the Waxing and Waning of Intellectual Influence." *Current Perspectives in Social Theory* 15:33–61.
1996   "Toward an Interparadigmatic Dialogue on Goffman." *Sociological Perspectives* 39:333–339.
Cicourel, Aaron
1974   *Cognitive Sociology: Language and Meaning in Social Interaction.* New York: Free Press.
1981   "Notes on the Integration of Micro- and Macro-Levels of Analysis." In K. Knorr-Cetina and A. Cicourel (eds.), *Advances in Social Theory and Methodology.* New York: Methuen: 51–79.
Cixous, Hélène
1976   "The Laugh of the Medusa." Keith Cohen and Paula Cohen (trans.). *Signs* 1:875–893.
1994   *The Hélène Cixous Reader.* Susan Sellers (ed.). New York: Routledge.
Cixous, Hélène, and Clement, Catherine (eds.)
1986   *The Newly Born Woman.* Minneapolis: University of Minnesota Press.
Clark, Jon (ed.)
1996   *James S. Coleman.* London: Falmer Press.
Clark, Jon, Modgil, Celia, and Modgil, Sohan (eds.)
1990   *Anthony Giddens: Consensus and Controversy.* London: Falmer Press.
Clark, Nigel
1997   "Panic Ecology: Nature in the Age of Superconductivity." *Theory, Culture and Society* 14:77–96.
Clark, Priscilla P., and Clark, Terry Nichols
1982   "The Structural Sources of French Structuralism." In I. Rossi (ed.), *Structural Sociology.* New York: Columbia University Press: 22–46.
Clarke, Simon
1990   "The Crisis of Fordism or the Crisis of Social Democracy?" *Telos* 83:71–98.
Clark-Lewis, Elizabeth
1994   *Living In, Living Out: African American Domestics in Washington, D.C. 1910–1940.* Washington, D.C.: Smithsonian Institution Press.

Clawson, Dan
1980   *Bureaucracy and the Labor Process: The Transformation of U.S. Industry,*
            1860–1920. New York: Monthly Review Press.
Clawson, Dan, Neustadtl, Alan, and Bearden, James
1986   "The Logic of Business Unity: Corporate Contributions to the 1980
            Congressional Elections." *American Sociological Review* 51:797–811.
Clayman, Steven E.
1988   "Displaying Neutrality in Television News Interviews." *Social Problems*
            35:474–492.
1993   "Booing: The Anatomy of a Disaffiliative Response." *American Sociological*
            Review 58:110–130.
Clough, Patricia Ticineto
1994   *Feminist Thought: Desire, Power and Academic Discourse.* Cambridge,
            Mass: Blackwell.
Cobble, Dorothy Sue (ed.)
1993   *Women and Unions: Forging a Partnership.* Ithaca, N.Y.: ILR Press.
Cockburn, Cynthia
1991   *In the Way of Women: Men's Resistance to Sex Equality in Organizations.*
            Ithaca, N.Y.: ILR Press.
Cohen, G. A.
1978   *Karl Marx's Theory of History: A Defence.* Princeton, N.J.: Princeton
            University Press.
1978/1986   "Marxism and Functional Explanation." In J. Roemer (ed.), *Analytical*
            Marxism. Cambridge: Cambridge University Press: 221–234.
Cohen, Ira
1989   *Structuration Theory.* London: Macmillan.
Cohen, Jean L., and Arato, Andrew
1992   *Civil Society and Political Theory.* Cambridge, Mass.: MIT Press.
Cohen, Percy
1968   *Modern Social Theory.* New York: Basic Books.
Cohen, Philip N.
1998   "Replacing Housework in the Service Economy: Gender, Class, and Race-
            Ethnicity in Service Spending." *Gender & Society* 12:219–231.
Coleman, James S.
1968   Review of Harold Garfinkel, *Studies in Ethnomethodology. American*
            Sociological Review 33:126–130.
1971   "Community Disorganization and Conflict." In R. Merton and R. Nisbet
            (eds.), *Contemporary Social Problems.* 3rd ed. New York: Harcourt Brace
            Jovanovich: 657–708.
1986   "Social Theory, Social Research, and a Theory of Action." *American Journal*
            of Sociology 91:1309–1335.
1987   "Microfoundations and Macrosocial Behavior." In J. C. Alexander et al.
            (eds.), *The Micro-Macro Link.* Berkeley: University of California Press:
            153–173.
1989   "Rationality and Society." *Rationality and Society* 1:5–9.
1990   *Foundations of Social Theory.* Cambridge: Belknap Press of Harvard
            University Press.
1990a   "Columbia in the 1950s." In B. Berger (ed.), *Authors of Their Own Lives:*
            Intellectual Autobiographies by Twenty American Sociologists. Berkeley:
            University of California Press: 75–103.

1993a	"The Design of Organizations and the Right to Act." *Sociological Forum* 8:527–546.
1993b	"The Rational Reconstruction of Society." *American Sociological Review* 58:1–15.
1994	"A Vision for Sociology." *Society* 32:29–34.

Colfax, J. David, and Roach, Jack L.

1971	*Radical Sociology.* New York: Basic Books.

Collins, Patricia Hill

1990	*Black Feminist Thought: Knowledge, Consciousness and Empowerment.* Boston: Unwin Hyman.
1996	"Sociological Visions and Revisions." *Contemporary Sociology* 25:329–331.
1998	*Fighting Words: Black Women and the Search for Justice.* Minneapolis: University of Minnesota Press.

Collins, Randall

1975	*Conflict Sociology: Toward an Explanatory Science.* New York: Academic Press.
1979	*The Credential Society.* New York: Academic Press.
1980	"Weber's Last Theory of Capitalism: A Systematization." *American Sociological Review* 45:925–942.
1981a	"On the Microfoundations of Macrosociology." *American Journal of Sociology* 86:984–1014.
1981b	"Micro-Translation as Theory-Building Strategy." In K. Knorr-Cetina and A. Cicourel (eds.), *Advances in Social Theory and Methodology.* New York: Methuen: 81–108.
1981c	"Introduction." In R. Collins (ed.), *Sociology since Midcentury: Essays in Theory Cumulation.* New York: Academic Press: 1–9.
1985	*Weberian Sociological Theory.* Cambridge: Cambridge University Press.
1986a	"Is 1980s Sociology in the Doldrums?" *American Journal of Sociology* 91:1336–1355.
1986b	"The Passing of Intellectual Generations: Reflections on the Death of Erving Goffman." *Sociological Theory* 4:106–113.
1987a	"Interaction Ritual Chains, Power and Property: The Micro-Macro Connection as an Empirically Based Theoretical Problem." In J. C. Alexander et al. (eds.), *The Micro-Macro Link.* Berkeley: University of California: 193–206.
1987b	"A Micro-Macro Theory of Intellectual Creativity: The Case of German Idealistic Philosophy." *Sociological Theory* 5:47–69.
1988a	"The Micro Contribution to Macro Sociology." *Sociological Theory* 6:242–253.
1988b	"The Durkheimian Tradition in Conflict Sociology." In J. C. Alexander (ed.), *Durkheimian Sociology: Cultural Studies.* Cambridge: Cambridge University Press: 107–128.
1989a	"Sociology: Proscience or Antiscience?" *American Sociological Review* 54:124–139.
1989b	"Toward a Neo-Meadian Sociology of Mind." *Symbolic Interaction* 12:1–32.
1990	"Conflict Theory and the Advance of Macro-Historical Sociology." In G. Ritzer (ed.), *Frontiers of Social Theory: The New Syntheses.* New York: Columbia University Press: 68–87.

1993 "What Does Conflict Theory Predict about America's Future?" *Sociological Perspectives* 22:861–870.

1997a "An Asian Route to Capitalism: Religious Economy and the Origins of Self-Transforming Growth in Japan." *American Sociological Review* 62:843–865.

1997b "A Sociological Guilt Trip: Comment on Connell." *American Journal of Sociology* 102:1558–1564.

Collinson, David L., and Hearn, Jeff (eds.)

1996 *Men as Managers, Managers as Men: Critical Perspectives on Men, Masculinities and Managements.* Thousand Oaks, Calif.: Sage.

Colomy, Paul

1986 "Recent Developments in the Functionalist Approach to Change." *Sociological Focus* 19:139–158.

1990a "Introduction: The Functionalist Tradition." In P. Colomy (ed.), *Functionalist Sociology.* Brookfield, Vt.: Elgar Publishing: xiii–lxii.

1990b "Introduction: The Neofunctionalist Movement." In P. Colomy (ed.), *Neofunctionalist Sociology.* Brookfield, Vt.: Elgar Publishing: xi–xii.

1990c "Uneven Differentiation and Incomplete Institutionalization: Political Change and Continuity in the Early American Nation." In J. C. Alexander and P. Colomy (eds.), *Differentiation Theory and Social Change: Comparative and Historical Perspectives.* New York: Columbia University Press: 119–162.

1990d "Strategic Groups and Political Differentiation in the Antebellum United States." In J. C. Alexander and P. Colomy (eds.), *Differentiation Theory and Social Change: Comparative and Historical Perspectives.* New York: Columbia University Press: 222–264.

Colomy, Paul, and Rhoades, Gary

1994 "Toward a Micro Corrective of Structural Differentiation Theory." *Sociological Perspectives* 37:547–583.

Comte, Auguste

1830–1842/ 1974 *The Positive Philosophy.* New York: AMS Press.

1851–1854/ 1976 *System of Positive Philosophy.* 4 vols. New York: Burt Franklin.

Connell, R. W.

1990 "A Whole New World: Remaking Masculinity in the Context of the Environmental Movement." *Gender & Society* 4:452–478.

1992a "A Sober Anarchism." *Sociological Theory* 10:88–98.

1992b "A Very Straight Gay: Masculinity, Homosexual Experience and the Dynamics of Gender." *American Sociological Review* 57:735–751.

1995 *Masculinities.* Berkeley: University of California Press.

1996 "Men and the Women's Movement." In Mary F. Rogers (ed.), *Multicultural Experiences, Multicultural Theories.* New York: McGraw-Hill: 409–415.

1997 "How Is Classical Theory Classical?" *American Journal of Sociology* 102:1511–1557.

Connell, R. W., Ashenden, Dean J., Kessler, Sandra, and Dowselt, Gary W.

1982 *Making the Difference: Schools, Families and Social Division.* Boston: Allen and Unwin.

Connerton, Paul (ed.)
1976   *Critical Sociology.* Harmondsworth, Eng.: Penguin.
Connolly, William E.
1973   "Theoretical Self-Consciousness." *Polity* 6:5–35.
Cook, Deborah
1994   "Symbolic Exchange in Hyperreality." In D. Kellner (ed.), *Baudrillard: A Critical Reader.* Oxford: Blackwell: 150–167.
1996   *The Culture Industry Revisited: Theodor W. Adorno on Mass Culture.* Lanham, Md.: Rowman and Littlefield.
Cook, Gary
1993   *George Herbert Mead: The Making of a Social Pragmatist.* Urbana: University of Illinois Press.
Cook, Judith, and Fonow, Mary Margaret
1986   "Knowledge and Women's Interests: Issues of Epistemology and Methodology in Feminist Sociological Research." *Sociological Inquiry* 56:2–29.
Cook, Karen S.
1987b   "Emerson's Contributions to Social Exchange Theory." In K. S. Cook (ed.), *Social Exchange Theory.* Beverly Hills, Calif.: Sage: 209–222.
Cook, Karen S. (ed.)
1987a   *Social Exchange Theory.* Beverly Hills, Calif.: Sage.
Cook, Karen S., and Emerson, Richard M.
1978   "Power, Equity, Commitment in Exchange Networks." *American Sociological Review* 43:721–739.
Cook, Karen S., Emerson, Richard M., Gillmore, Mary B., and Yamagishi, Toshio
1983   "The Distribution of Power in Exchange Networks: Theory and Experimental Results." *American Journal of Sociology* 89:275–305.
Cook, Karen S., and Gillmore, Mary R.
1984   "Power, Dependence, and Coalitions." *Advances in Group Processes* 1:27–58.
Cook, Karen S., O'Brien, Jodi, and Kollock, Peter
1990   "Exchange Theory: A Blueprint for Structure and Process." In G. Ritzer (ed.), *Frontiers of Social Theory: The New Syntheses.* New York: Columbia University Press: 158–181.
Cook, Karen S., and Whitmeyer, J. M.
1992   "Two Approaches to Social Structure: Exchange Theory and Network Analysis." *Annual Review of Sociology* 18:109–127.
forthcoming "Richard Emerson." In George Ritzer (ed.) *The Blackwell Companion to Major Social Theorists.* Oxford, England, and Cambridge, Mass.: Blackwell.
Cooke, Maeve
1994   *Language and Reason: A Study of Habermas's Pragmatics.* Cambridge, Mass. MIT Press.
Cooley, Charles H.
1902/1964   *Human Nature and the Social Order.* New York: Scribner's.
Cordova, Teresa, Cantu, Norma, Cardena, Gilbert, Garcia, Juan, Sierra, Christine M. (eds.)
1990   *Chicana Voices: Intersections of Class, Race, and Gender.* Austin, Tex.: National Association for Chicano Studies.

Cormack, Patricia
1996   "The Paradox of Durkheim's Manifesto: Reconsidering *The Rules of Sociological Method.*" *Theory and Society* 25:85–104.
Cornell, Bradford
1995   "A Hypothesis Regarding the Origins of Ethnic Discrimination." *Rationality and Society* 7:4–30.
Cortese, Anthony
1995   "The Rise, Hegemony, and Decline of the Chicago School of Sociology, 1892–1945." *Social Science Journal* 32:235–254.
Coser, Lewis
1956   *The Functions of Social Conflict.* New York: Free Press.
1967   *Continuities in the Study of Social Conflict.* New York: Free Press.
1975a   Presidential Address: "Two Methods in Search of a Substance." *American Sociological Review* 40:691–700.
1975b   "Structure and Conflict." In P. Blau (ed.), *Approaches to the Study of Social Structure.* New York: Free Press: 210–219.
1977   *Masters of Sociological Thought.* 2nd ed. New York: Harcourt Brace Jovanovich.
Cott, Nancy F.
1977   *The Bonds of Womanhood: Women's Sphere in New England, 1780–1835.* New Haven: Yale University Press.
Cottrell, Leonard S., Jr.
1980   "George Herbert Mead: The Legacy of Social Behaviorism." In R. K. Merton and M. W. Riley (eds.), *Sociological Traditions from Generation to Generation: Glimpses of the American Experience.* Norwood, N.J.: Ablex.
Couch, C. J., Saxton, S. L., and Katovich, M. A.
1986a   *Studies in Symbolic Interaction: The Iowa School,* Part A. Greenwich, Conn.: JAI Press.
1986b   *Studies in Symbolic Interaction: The Iowa School,* Part B. Greenwich, Conn.: JAI Press.
Coulter, Jeff
1983   *Rethinking Cognitive Theory.* New York: St. Martin's.
1989   *Mind in Action.* Atlantic Highlands, N.J.: Humanities Press.
Craib, Ian
1976   *Existentialism and Sociology: A Study of Jean-Paul Sartre.* Cambridge: Cambridge University Press.
1993   *Anthony Giddens.* London: Routledge.
Crawford, Mary
1995   *Talking Difference: On Gender and Language.* Newbury Park, Calif.: Sage.
Crenshawe, Kimberle
1989   "Demarginalizing the Intersection of Race and Sex: A Black Feminist Critique of Antidiscrimination Doctrine, Feminist Theory, and Antiracist Politics." *University of Chicago Legal Forum:*139–167.
1991   "Mapping the Margins: Intersectionality, Identity Politics, and Violence against Women of Color." *Stanford Law Review* 43:6.
1997   "Intersectionality and Identity Politics: Learning from Violence against Women of Color." In M. Shanley and U. Narayan (eds.), *Reconstructing Political Theory: Feminist Perspectives.* University Park, Penn.: Pennsylvania State University Press.

Crippen, Timothy
1994   "Toward a Neo-Darwinian Sociology: Its Nomological Principles and Some Illustrative Applications." *Sociological Perspectives* 37:309–335.

Crombie, A. C.
1986   "What Is the History of Science?" *History of European Ideas* 7:21–31.

Cronk, George
1987   *The Philosophical Anthropology of George Herbert Mead.* New York: Peter Lang.

Crook, Stephen
1995   *Adorno: The Stars Down to Earth and Other Essays on the Irrational in Culture.* London: Routledge.

Crozier, Michel, and Friedberg, Erhard
1980   *Actors and Systems: The Politics of Collective Action.* Chicago: University of Chicago Press.

Culler, Jonathan
1976   *Ferdinand de Saussure.* Harmondsworth, Eng.: Penguin.

Currie, Dawn H.
1997   "Decoding Femininity: Advertisements and Their Teenage Readers." *Gender & Society* 11:453–477.

Curtis, Bruce
1981   *William Graham Sumner.* Boston: Twayne.

Dahms, Harry
1997   "Theory in Weberian Marxism: Patterns of Critical Social Theory in Lukács and Habermas." *Sociological Theory* 15:181–214.

1998   "Beyond the Carousel of Reification: Critical Social Theory after Lukács, Adorno, and Habermas." *Current Perspectives in Social Theory* 18:3–62.

Dahrendorf, Ralf
1958   "Out of Utopia: Toward a Reorientation of Sociological Analysis." *American Journal of Sociology* 64:115–127.

1959   *Class and Class Conflict in Industrial Society.* Stanford, Calif.: Stanford University Press.

1968   *Essays in the Theory of Society.* Stanford, Calif.: Stanford University Press.

Daly, Mary
1978   *Gyn/Ecology: The MetaEthics of Radical Feminism.* Boston: Beacon.

1993   *Outercourse: The Be-dazzling Voyage.* San Francisco: Harper.

Dandaneau, Steven P.
1992   "Immanent Critique of Post-Marxism." *Current Perspectives in Social Theory* 12:155–177.

Daniels, Arlene Kaplan
1988   *Invisible Careers: Women Civic Leaders from the Volunteer World.* Chicago: University of Chicago Press.

Davis, Kingsley
1959   "The Myth of Functional Analysis as a Special Method in Sociology and Anthropology." *American Sociological Review* 24:757–772.

Davis, Kingsley, and Moore, Wilbert
1945   "Some Principles of Stratification." *American Sociological Review* 10:242–249.

Davis, Laurel R.
1997   *The Swimsuit Issue and Sport: Hegemonic Masculinity in* Sports Illustrated. Albany: State University of New York Press.

Dawe, Alan
1978   "Theories of Social Action." In T. Bottomore and R. Nisbet (eds.), *A History of Sociological Analysis.* New York: Basic Books: 362–417.
Dean, Mitchell
1994   *Critical and Effective Histories: Foucault's Methods and Historical Sociology.* London: Routledge.
de Beauvoir, Simone
1949/1957   *The Second Sex.* New York: Vintage.
Debord, Guy
1967/1994   *The Society of the Spectacle.* New York: Zone Books.
Deckard, Barbara Sinclair
1979   *The Women's Movement: Political, Socioeconomic and Psychological Issues.* New York: Harper & Row.
Deegan, Mary Jo
1988   *Jane Addams and the Men of the Chicago School, 1892–1918.* New Brunswick, N.J.: Transaction Books.
1991   *Women in Sociology: A Bio-Bibliographical Sourcebook.* Westport, Conn.: Greenwood Press.
Deegan, Mary Jo, and Hill, Michael R. (eds.)
1998   *With Her in Ourland: Sequel to Herland.* By Charlotte Perkins Gilman. Westport, Conn.: Praeger.
Delanty, Gerard
1997   "Habermas and Occidental Rationalism: The Politics of Identity, Social Learning, and the Cultural Limits of Moral Universalism." *Sociological Theory* 15:30–59.
Deleuze, Gilles, and Guattari, Felix
1972/1983   *Anti-Oedipus: Capitalism and Schizophrenia.* Minneapolis: University of Minnesota Press.
Demerath, Nicholas, and Peterson, Richard (eds.)
1967   *System, Change and Conflict.* New York: Free Press.
Densimore, Dana
1973   "Independence from the Sexual Revolution." In A. Koedt et al. (eds.), *Radical Feminism.* New York: Quadrangle: 107–118.
Denzin, Norman
1990a   "Harold and Agnes: A Feminist Narrative Undoing." *Sociological Theory* 9:198–216.
1990b   "Reading Rational Choice Theory." *Rationality and Society* 2:172–189.
1991   "Back to Harold and Agnes." *Sociological Theory* 9:280–285.
1992   *Symbolic Interactionism and Cultural Studies: The Politics of Interpretation.* Oxford: Blackwell.
1993   "Sexuality and Gender: An Interactionist/Poststructuralist Reading." In P. England (ed.), *Theory on Gender/Feminism on Theory.* New York: Aldine de Gruyter: 199–223.
Der Derian, James
1994   "Simulation: The Highest Stage of Capitalism?" In D. Kellner (ed.), *Baudrillard: A Critical Reader.* Oxford: Blackwell: 189–208.
Derrida, Jacques
1978   *Writing and Difference.* Chicago: University of Chicago Press.

DeVault, Marjorie L.
1991   *Feeding the Family: The Social Organization of Caring as Gendered Work.*
            Chicago: University of Chicago Press.
DeVille, Phillippe
1989   "Human Agency and Social Structure in Economic Theory: The General
            Equilibrium Theory and Beyond." Paper presented at the conference on
            "Social Theory and Human Agency," Swedish Collegium for Advanced
            Study in the Social Sciences, Uppsala, Sweden, Sept. 29–Oct. 1.
Diamond, Timothy
1992   *Making Grey Gold: Narratives of Nursing Home Care.* Chicago: University
            of Chicago Press.
Dickerson, Bette J. (ed.)
1995   *African American Single Mothers: Understanding Their Lives and Families.*
            Newbury Park, Calif.: Sage.
Dietz, Thomas, and Burns, Tom R.
1992   "Human Agency and the Evolutionary Dynamics of Culture." *Acta
            Sociologica* 35:187–200.
Dill, Bonnie Thornton
1994   *Across the Boundaries of Race and Class: An Exploration of Work and
            Family among Black Female Domestic Servants.* New York: Garland.
Dinnerstein, Dorothy
1976   *The Mermaid and the Minotaur.* New York: Harper & Row.
Di Stefano, Christine
1991   *Configurations of Masculinity: A Feminist Perspective on Modern Political
            Theory.* Ithaca, N.Y.: Cornell University Press.
Ditton, Jason (ed.)
1980   *The View from Goffman.* New York: St. Martin's.
Doane, Janice, and Hodges, Devon
1992   *From Klein to Kristeva: Psychoanalytic Feminism and the Search for the
            "Good Enough" Mother.* Ann Arbor: University of Michigan Press.
Dobb, Maurice
1964   *Studies in the Development of Capitalism.* Rev. ed. New York: International
            Publishers.
Donougho, Martin
1989   "Postmodern Jameson." In D. Kellner (ed.), *Postmodernism, Jameson,
            Critique.* Washington, D.C.: Maisonneuve Press: 75–95.
Donovan, Josephine
1985   *Feminist Theory: The Intellectual Traditions of American Feminism.* New
            York: Ungar.
Douglas, Carol Ann
1990   *Love and Politics: Radical Feminist and Lesbian Theories.* San Francisco:
            Ism Press.
Douglas, Jack
1980   "Introduction to the Sociologies of Everyday Life." In J. Douglas et al.
            (eds.), *Introduction to the Sociologies of Everyday Life.* Boston: Allyn and
            Bacon: 1–19.

Dowd, James J.
1996   "An Act Made Perfect in Habit: The Self in the Postmodern Age." *Current Perspectives in Social Theory* 16:237–263.
DuBois, Ellen Carol
1973/1995   "The Radicalism of the Women's Suffrage Movement." In Claire Goldberg Moses and Heidi Hartmann (eds.), *U.S. Women in Struggle.* Chicago: University of Illinois Press: 42–51.
Duhamel, Georges
1931   *America the Menace: Scenes from the Life of the Future.* Boston: Houghton Mifflin.
Duignan, Peter, and Gann, Lewis
1992   *The Rebirth of the West: The Americanization of the Democratic World.* Oxford: Basil Blackwell.
Duncan, O. D., and Schnore, L. F.
1959   "Cultural, Behavioral and Ecological Perspectives in the Study of Social Organization." *American Journal of Sociology* 65:132–146.
Dunn, Robert G.
1997   "Self, Identity, and Difference: Mead and the Poststructuralists." *Sociological Quarterly* 38:687–705.
Dunning, Eric
1986   "Preface." In N. Elias and E. Dunning, *Quest for Excitement: Sport and Leisure in the Civilizing Process.* Oxford: Blackwell: 1–18.
Durkheim, Emile
1887/1993   *Ethics and the Sociology of Morals.* Buffalo: Prometheus Books.
1892/1997   *Montesquieu: Quid Secundatus Politicae Scientiae Instituendae Contulerit.* Oxford: Durkheim Press.
1893/1960   *Montesquieu and Rousseau: Forerunners of Sociology.* Ann Arbor: University of Michigan Press.
1893/1964   *The Division of Labor in Society.* New York: Free Press.
1895/1964   *The Rules of Sociological Method.* New York: Free Press.
1897/1951   *Suicide.* New York: Free Press.
1912/1965   *The Elementary Forms of Religious Life.* New York: Free Press.
1928/1962   *Socialism.* New York: Collier Books.
Dworkin, Andrea
1976   *Our Blood: Prophecies and Discourses on Sexual Politics.* New York: Perigee Books.
1987   *Intercourse.* New York: Free Press.
1989   *Letters from the War Zone: Writings 1976–1987.* New York: Dutton.
Echols, Alice
1989   *Daring to Be Bad: Radical Feminism in America, 1967–1975.* Minneapolis: University of Minnesota Press.
Eckberg, Douglas Lee, and Hill, Lester
1979   "The Paradigm Concept and Sociology: A Critical Review." *American Sociological Review* 44:925–937.
Edel, Abraham
1959   "The Concept of Levels in Social Theory." In L. Gross (ed.), *Symposium on Sociological Theory.* Evanston, Ill.: Row Peterson: 167–195.

Eder, Donna, with Evans, Catherine Colleen and Parker, Stephen
1995   *School Talk: Gender and Adolescent Culture.* New Brunswick, N.J.: Rutgers
            University Press.
Eder, Klaus
1990   "The Rise of Counter-Culture Movements against Modernity: Nature as a
            New Field of Class Struggle." *Theory, Culture and Society* 7:21–47.
Edin, Kathryn, and Lein, Laura
1997   *Making Ends Meet: How Single Mothers Survive Welfare and Low-Wage
            Work.* New York: Russell Sage Foundation.
Edwards, Richard
1979   *Contested Terrain: The Transformation of the Workplace in the Twentieth
            Century.* New York: Basic Books.
Effrat, Andrew
1972   "Power to the Paradigms: An Editorial Introduction." *Sociological Inquiry*
            42:3–33.
Ehrmann, Jacques
1970   "Introduction." In J. Ehrmann (ed.), *Structuralism.* Garden City, N.Y.:
            Anchor: vii–xi.
Eisen, Arnold
1978   "The Meanings and Confusions of Weberian 'Rationality.' " *British Journal
            of Sociology* 29:57–70.
Eisenstadt, S. N.
1973   *Tradition, Change and Modernity.* New York: Wiley.
Eisenstadt, S. N., with Curelaru, M.
1976   *The Form of Sociology: Paradigms and Crises.* New York: Wiley.
Eisenstadt, S. N., and Helle, H. J. (eds.)
1985a   *Macro-Sociological Theory: Perspectives on Sociological Theory,* Vol. 1.
            London: Sage.
1985b   "General Introduction to Perspectives on Sociological Theory." In S. N.
            Eisenstadt and H. J. Helle (eds.), *Macro-Sociological Theory.* London:
            Sage: 1–3.
Eisenstein, Zillah
1979   *Capitalist Patriarchy and the Case for Socialist Feminism.* New York:
            Monthly Review Press.
1994   *The Color of Gender: Reimaging Democracy.* Berkeley: University of
            California Press.
Ekeh, Peter P.
1974   *Social Exchange Theory: The Two Traditions.* Cambridge, Mass.: Harvard
            University Press.
Elias, Norbert
1939/1978   *The Civilizing Process.* Part 1, *The History of Manners.* New York:
            Pantheon.
1939/1982   *The Civilizing Process.* Part 2, *Power and Civility.* New York: Pantheon.
1939/1994   *The Civilizing Process.* Oxford: Blackwell.
1968/1994   "Introduction to the 1968 Edition." In N. Elias, *The Civilizing Process.*
            Oxford: Blackwell: 181–215.
1969/1983   *The Court Society.* New York: Pantheon.
1978   *What Is Sociology?* New York: Columbia University Press.
1986a   "Introduction." In N. Elias and E. Dunning, *Quest for Excitement: Sport and
            Leisure in the Civilizing Process.* Oxford: Blackwell: 19–62.

1986b	"An Essay on Sport and Violence." In N. Elias and E. Dunning, *Quest for Excitement: Sport and Leisure in the Civilizing Process*. Oxford: Blackwell: 150–174.
1987/1992	*Time: An Essay*. Oxford: Blackwell.
1993	*Mozart: Portrait of a Genius*. Berkeley: University of California Press.
1994	*Reflections on a Life*. Cambridge: Polity Press.
1995	"Technicization and Civilization." *Theory, Culture and Society* 12:7–42.
1997	"Towards a Theory of Social Processes." *British Journal of Sociology* 48:355–383.

Elias, Norbert, and Dunning, Eric
1986   *Quest for Excitement: Sport and Leisure in the Civilizing Process*. Oxford: Blackwell.

Elster, Jon
1982   "Marxism, Functionalism and Game Theory: The Case for Methodological Individualism." *Theory and Society* 11:453–482.
1985   *Making Sense of Marx*. Cambridge: Cambridge University Press.
1986   "Further Thoughts on Marxism, Functionalism, and Game Theory." In J. Roemer (ed.), *Analytical Marxism*. Cambridge: Cambridge University Press: 202–220.

Emerson, Richard M.
1962   "Power-Dependence Relations." *American Sociological Review* 27:31–40.
1972a   "Exchange Theory, Part I: A Psychological Basis for Social Exchange." In J. Berger, M. Zelditch, Jr., and B. Anderson (eds.), *Sociological Theories in Progress*, Vol. 2. Boston: Houghton Mifflin: 38–57.
1972b   "Exchange Theory, Part II: Exchange Relations and Networks." In J. Berger, M. Zelditch, Jr., and B. Anderson (eds.), *Sociological Theories in Progress*, Vol. 2. Boston: Houghton Mifflin: 58–87.
1976   "Social Exchange Theory." In A. Inkeles, J. Coleman, and N. Smelser (eds.), *Annual Review of Sociology*, Vol. 2. Palo Alto, Calif.: Annual Reviews: 335–362.
1981   "Social Exchange Theory." In M. Rosenberg and R. H. Turner (eds.), *Social Psychology: Sociological Perspectives*. New York: Basic Books: 30–65.

Emirbayer, Mustafa
1996   "Useful Durkheim." *Sociological Theory* 14:109–130.
1997   "Manifesto for a Relational Sociology." *American Journal of Sociology* 103:281–317.

Emmison, Michael
1997   "Transformations of Taste: Americanisation, Generational Change and Australian Cultural Consumption." *Australian and New Zealand Journal of Sociology* 33:322–343.

Engels, Friedrich
1884/1970   *The Origins of the Family, Private Property and the State*. New York: International Publishers.
1890/1972   "Letter to Joseph Bloch." In R. C. Tucker (ed.), *The Marx-Engels Reader*. New York: Norton: 640–642.

England, Paula
1992   *Comparable Worth: Theories and Evidence*. New York: Aldine de Gruyter.
1993   *Theory on Gender/Feminism on Theory*. New York: Aldine de Gruyter.

England, Paula, and Kilbourne, Barbara Stanek
1990   "Feminist Critiques of the Separative Model of the Self." *Rationality and Society* 2:156–171.

Epstein, Cynthia Fuchs
1988   *Deceptive Distinctions: Sex, Gender, and the Social Order.* New Haven: Yale
            University Press.
Erickson, Bonnie H.
1996   "Culture, Class, and Connections." *American Journal of Sociology*
            102:217–251.
Eriksson, Bjorn
1993   "The First Formulation of Sociology: A Discursive Innovation of the 18th
            Century." *Archives of European Sociology* 34:251–276.
Esposito, Elena
1996   "From Self-Reference to Autology: How to Operationalize a Circular
            Approach." *Social Science Information* 35:269–281.
Esser, Hartmut
1993   "The Rationality of Everyday Behavior: A Rational Choice Reconstruction
            of the Theory of Action by Alfred Schutz." *Rationality and Society* 5:7–31.
Etzioni, Amitai
1988   *The Moral Dimension: Toward a New Economics.* New York: Free Press.
Evans, Sara
1980   *Personal Politics: The Roots of the Women's Liberation Movement in the
            Civil Rights Movement and the New Left.* New York: Vintage.
Faghirzadeh, Saleh
1982   *Sociology of Sociology: In Search of . . . Ibn-Khaldun's Sociology Then and
            Now.* Teheran: Soroush Press.
Faia, Michael A.
1986   *Dynamic Functionalism: Strategy and Tactics.* Cambridge: Cambridge
            University Press.
Falk, William, and Zhao, Shanyang
1990a   "Paradigms, Theories and Methods in Contemporary Rural Sociology: A
            Partial Replication." *Rural Sociology* 54:587–600.
1990b   "Paradigms, Theories and Methods Revisited: We Respond to Our Critics."
            Rural Sociology 55:112–122.
Faludi, Susan
1991   *Backlash: The Undeclared War against American Women.* New York:
            Crown.
Fararo, Thomas J.
1989   "The Spirit of Unification in Sociological Theory." *Sociological Theory*
            7:175–190.
1993   "General Social Equilibrium: Toward Theoretical Synthesis." *Sociological
            Theory* 11:291–313.
1996   "Foundational Problems in Theoretical Sociology." In Jon Clark (ed.), *James
            S. Coleman.* London: Falmer Press: 263–284.
Fararo, Thomas J., and Skvoretz, John
1986   "E-State Structuralism: A Theoretical Method." *American Sociological
            Review* 51:591–602.
Farberman, Harvey A.
1991   "Symbolic Interaction and Postmodernism: Close Encounter of a Dubious
            Kind." *Symbolic Interaction* 14:471–488.
Farganis, James
1975   "A Preface to Critical Theory." *Theory and Society* 2:483–508.

Faris, R. E. L.
1970   *Chicago Sociology: 1920–1932.* Chicago: University of Chicago Press.
Farnham, C. (ed.)
1987   *The Impact of Feminist Research on the Academy.* Bloomington: Indiana
            University Press.
Farrell, Chad R.
1997   "Durkheim, Moral Individualism and the Dreyfus Affair." *Current
            Perspectives in Social Theory* 17:313–330.
Faught, Jim
1980   "Presuppositions of the Chicago School in the Work of Everett Hughes."
            American Sociologist 15:72–82.
Fausto-Sterling, Anne, and Gowaty, Patricia Adair, and Zuk, Marlene
1997   "Evolutionary Psychology and Darwinian Feminism." *Feminist Studies*
            23:403–417.
Featherstone, Mike
1989   "Postmodernism, Cultural Change, and Social Practice." In D. Kellner (ed.),
            Postmodernism, Jameson, Critique. Washington, D.C.: Maisonneuve Press:
            117–138.
Featherstone, Mike (ed.)
1990   *Global Culture: Nationalism, Globalization and Modernity.* London: Sage.
Featherstone, Mike, and Turner, Bryan
1995   "Body and Society: An Introduction." *Body and Society* 1:1–12.
Feenberg, Andrew
1996   "Marcuse or Habermas: Two Critiques of Technology." *Inquiry* 39:45–70.
Femia, Joseph
1995   "Pareto's Concept of Demagogic Plutocracy." *Government and Opposition*
            30:370–392.
Fendrich, Michael
1984   "Wives' Employment and Husbands' Distress: A Meta-Analysis and a
            Replication." *Journal of Marriage and the Family* 46:871–879.
Fenstermaker, Sarah, West, Candace, and Zimmerman, Don
1991   "Gender Inequality: New Conceptual Terrain." In R. L. Blumberg (ed.),
            Gender, Family and Economy: The Triple Overlap. Newbury Park, Calif.:
            Sage: 293–307.
Fenstermaker Berk, Sarah
1985   *The Gender Factory: The Appointment of Work in American Households.*
            New York: Plenum.
Ferguson, Ann
1987   "Sex and Work: Women as a New Revolutionary Class in the United States."
            In R. S. Gottlieb (ed.), *An Anthology of Western Marxism.* New York: Oxford
            University Press.
Ferree, Myra Marx, and Hall, Elaine
1996   "Rethinking Stratification from a Feminist Perspective: Gender, Race, and
            Class in Mainstream Textbooks." *American Sociological Review*
            61:929–950.
Ferree, Myra Marx, and Martin, Patricia Yancy (eds.)
1995   *Feminist Organizations: Harvest of the New Women's Movement.*
            Philadelphia: Temple University Press.

Ferree, Myra Marx, Lorber, Judith, and Hess, Beth (eds.)
1999   *Revisioning Gender.* Thousand Oaks, Calif.: Sage.
Ferry, Luc, and Renaut, Alain
1985/1990   *French Philosophy of the Sixties: An Essay on Antihumanism.* Amherst:
              University of Massachusetts Press.
Findlen, Barbara (ed.)
1995   *Listen Up: Voices from the Next Feminist Generation.* Seattle, Wash.: Seal
              Press.
Fine, Gary Alan
1988   "On the Macrofoundations of Microsociology: Meaning, Order, and
              Comparative Context." Paper presented at the meetings of the American
              Sociological Association, Atlanta, Georgia.
1990   "Symbolic Interactionism in the Post-Blumerian Age." In G. Ritzer (ed.),
              Frontiers of Social Theory: The New Syntheses. New York: Columbia
              University Press: 117–157.
1992   "Agency, Structure, and Comparative Contexts: Toward a Synthetic
              Interactionism." *Symbolic Interaction* 15:87–107.
1993   "The Sad Demise, Mysterious Disappearance, and Glorious Triumph of
              Symbolic Interactionism." *Annual Review of Sociology* 19:61–87.
1995   "A Second Chicago School? The Development of a Postwar American
              Sociology." In Gary Alan Fine (ed.), *A Second Chicago School? The
              Development of a Postwar American Sociology.* Chicago: University of
              Chicago Press: 1–16.
1996   *Kitchens: The Culture of Restaurant Work.* Berkeley: University of
              California Press.
Fine, Gary Alan, and Kleinman, Sherryl
1983   "Network and Meaning: An Interactionist Approach to Social Structure."
              Symbolic Interaction 6:97–110.
1986   "Interpreting the Sociological Classics: Can There Be a 'True' Meaning of
              Mead?" *Symbolic Interaction* 9:129–146.
Fine, Gary Alan, and Manning, Philip
forthcoming   "Erving Goffman." In George Ritzer (ed.), *The Blackwell Companion to
              Major Social Theorists.* Oxford, England, and Cambridge, Mass.: Blackwell.
Fine, Michelle, Weis, Lois, Addelston, Judi, and Marusza, Julia
1997   "(In) Secure Times: Constructing White Working-Class Masculinities in the
              Late 20th Century." *Gender & Society* 11:52–68.
Fine, William F.
1979   *Progressive Evolutionism and American Sociology, 1890–1920.* UMI
              Research Press (n.p.).
Fineman, Martha Albertson
1995   *The Neutered Mother, the Sexual Family and Other Twentieth Century
              Tragedies.* New York: Routledge.
Fischer, Norman
1984   "Hegelian Marxism and Ethics." *Canadian Journal of Political and Social
              Theory* 8:112–138.
Fisher, Berenice, and Strauss, Anselm
1979   "George Herbert Mead and the Chicago Tradition of Sociology—Parts 1 and
              2." *Symbolic Interaction* 2:9–25; 2:9–19.

Fisher, Sue
1995   *Nursing Wounds: Nurse Practitioners, Doctors, Women Patients and the Negotiation of Meaning.* New Brunswick, N. J.: Rutgers University Press.

Fiske, Donald W., and Shweder, Richard A. (eds.)
1986   *Metatheory in Social Science: Pluralisms and Subjectivities.* Chicago: University of Chicago Press.

Fitzpatrick, Ellen
1990   *Endless Crusade: Women Social Scientists and Progressive Reform.* New York: Oxford University Press.

Flax, Jane
1990   *Thinking Fragments: Psychoanalysis, Feminism and Postmodernism in the Contemporary West.* Berkeley: University of California Press.

Folbre, Nancy
1993   "Macro, Micro, Choice and Structure." In P. England (ed.), *Theory on Gender/Feminism on Theory.* New York: Aldine de Gruyter.

Foner, Nancy
1994   *The Caregiving Dilemma: Work in an American Nursing Home.* Berkeley: University of California Press.

Foster, John Bellamy
1994   "*Labor and Monopoly Capital* Twenty Years After: An Introduction." *Monthly Review* 46:1–13.

Foucalt, Michel
1965   *Madness and Civilization: A History of Insanity in the Age of Reason.* New York: Vintage.
1966   *The Order of Things: An Archaeology of the Human Sciences.* New York: Vintage.
1969   *The Archaeology of Knowledge and the Discourse on Language.* New York: Harper Colophon.
1975   *The Birth of the Clinic: An Archaeology of Medical Perception.* New York: Vintage.
1979   *Discipline and Punish: The Birth of the Prison.* New York: Vintage.
1980   *The History of Sexuality.* Vol. 1, *An Introduction.* New York: Vintage.
1985   *The Use of Pleasure. The History of Sexuality.* Vol. 2. New York: Pantheon.
1995   "Madness, the Absence of Work." *Critical Inquiry* 21:290–298.

Fowler, Bridget
1997   *Pierre Bourdieu and Cultural Theory: Critical Investigations.* London: Sage.

Fox, Renee C.
1997   "Talcott Parsons, My Teacher." *American Scholar* 66:395–410.

Frank, André Gunder
1966/1974   "Functionalism and Dialectics." In R. S. Denisoff, O. Callahan, and M. H. Levine (eds.), *Theories and Paradigms in Contemporary Sociology.* Itasca, Ill.: Peacock: 342–352.

Frankenberg, Ruth
1993   *White Women, Race Matters: The Social Construction of Whiteness.* Minneapolis: University of Minnesota Press.

Frankfurt Institute for Social Research
1973   *Aspects of Sociology.* London: Heinemann.

Franklin, Adrian
1996   "On Fox-Hunting and Angling: Norbert Elias and the 'Sportisation' Process." *Journal of Historical Sociology* 9:432–456.

Franks, David D., and Gecas, Viktor
1992   "Autonomy and Conformity in Cooley's Self-Theory: The Looking-Glass Self and Beyond." *Symbolic Interaction* 15:49–68.
Fraser, Nancy
1989   *Unruly Practices: Power, Discourse and Gender in Contemporary Social Theory.* Minneapolis: University of Minnesota Press.
1997   *Justice Interruptus: Critical Reflections on the "Postsocialist" Condition.* New York: Routledge.
Fraser, Nancy, and Bartsky, Sandra Lee (eds.)
1991   *Revaluing French Feminism: Critical Essays on Difference, Agency and Culture.* Bloomington: Indiana University Press.
Fraser, Nancy, and Nicholson, Linda
1988   "Social Criticism without Philosophy: An Encounter between Feminism and Postmodernism." In A. Ross (ed.), *Universal Abandon: The Politics of Postmodernism.* Minneapolis: University of Minnesota Press: 83–104.
Freese, Lee
1994   "The Song of Sociobiology." *Sociological Perspectives* 37:337–373.
French, Marilyn
1992   *The War against Women.* New York: Summit.
Friedan, Betty
1963   *The Feminine Mystique.* New York: Dell.
1981   *The Second Stage.* New York: Summit.
Friedheim, Elizabeth
1979   "An Empirical Comparison of Ritzer's Paradigms and Similar Metatheories: A Research Note." *Social Forces* 58:59–66.
Friedman, Debra, and Hechter, Michael
1988   "The Contribution of Rational Choice Theory to Macrosociological Research." *Sociological Theory* 6:201–218.
1990   "The Comparative Advantages of Rational Choice Theory." In G. Ritzer (ed.), *Frontiers of Social Theory: The New Syntheses.* New York: Columbia University Press: 214–229.
Friedman, George
1981   *The Political Philosophy of the Frankfurt School.* Ithaca, N.Y.: Cornell University Press.
Friedman, Marilyn
1993   *What Are Friends For? Feminist Perspectives on Personal Relationships and Moral Theory.* Ithaca, N.Y.: Cornell University Press.
Friedrichs, Robert
1970   *A Sociology of Sociology.* New York: Free Press.
1972a   "Dialectical Sociology: Toward a Resolution of Current 'Crises' in Western Sociology." *British Journal of Sociology* 13:263–274.
1972b   "Dialectical Sociology: An Exemplar for the 1970's." *Social Forces* 50:447–455.
Frisby, David
1981   *Sociological Impressionism: A Reassessment of Georg Simmel's Social Theory.* London: Heinemann.
1984   *Georg Simmel.* Chichester, Eng.: Ellis Horwood.
1992   *Simmel and Since: Essays on Georg Simmel's Social Theory.* London: Routledge.

Frye, Marilyn
1983   *The Politics of Reality: Essays in Feminist Theory.* Trumansburg, N.Y.:
              Crossings Press.
1996   "The Necessity of Differences: Constructing a Positive Category of
              Women." *Signs* 21:991–1010.
Fuchs, Stephan, and Ward, Steven
1994a   "What Is Deconstruction, and Where and When Does It Take Place? Making
              Facts in Science, Building Cases in Law." *American Sociological Review*
              59:481–500.
1994b   "The Sociology and Paradoxes of Deconstruction: A Reply to Agger."
              American Sociological Review 59:506–510.
Fudge, Judith, and McDermott, Patricia (eds.)
1991   *Just Wages: A Feminist Assessment of Pay Equity.* Toronto: University of
              Toronto Press.
Fuhrman, Ellsworth R.
1980   *The Sociology of Knowledge in America: 1883–1915.* Charlottesville:
              University of Virginia Press.
Fuhrman, Ellsworth R., and Snizek, William
1990   "Neither Proscience nor Antiscience: Metasociology as Dialogue."
              Sociological Forum 5:17–31.
Fullbrook, Mary
1978   "Max Weber's 'Interpretive Sociology.' " *British Journal of Sociology*
              29:71–82.
Fuller, Steve
1998   "From Content to Context: A Social Epistemology of the Structure-Agency
              Craze." In Alan Sica (ed.), *What Is Social Theory? The Philosophical
              Debates.* Oxford: Blackwell: 92–117.
Furfey, Paul
1953/1965   *The Scope and Method of Sociology: A Metasociological Treatise.* New
              York: Cooper Square Publishers.
Gabaccia, Donna (ed.)
1992   *Seeking Common Ground: Multidisciplinary Studies of Immigrant Women in
              the United States.* Westport, Conn.: Greenwood Press.
Gabin, Nancy F.
1990   *Feminism in the Labor Movement: Women and United Auto Workers
              1935–1975.* Ithaca, N.Y.: Cornell University Press.
Gans, Herbert J.
1972   "The Positive Functions of Poverty." *American Journal of Sociology*
              78:275–289.
1994   "Positive Functions of the Undeserving Poor: Uses of the Underclass in
              America." *Politics and Society* 22:269–283.
Gans, Herbert J., and Marx, Gary T.
1992   "Sociological Amnesia: The Noncumulation of Normal Social Science."
              Sociological Forum 7:701–710.
Garcia, Alma M.
1989   "The Development of Chicana Feminist Discourse 1970–1980." *Gender &
              Society* 3:217–238.

Garcia, Angela
1991   "Dispute Resolution without Disputing: How the Interactional Organization
            of Mediation Hearings Minimizes Argument." *American Sociological
            Review* 56:818–835.
Gardiner, Jean
1979   "Women's Domestic Labor." In Z. Eisenstein (ed.), *Capitalist Patriarchy
            and the Case for Socialist Feminism.* New York and London: Monthly
            Review Press.
Gardiner, Judith Kegan
1993   "Towards a Feminist Theory of Self: Repressive Dereification and the
            Subject in Process." *NWSA Journal* 5:303–323.
Gardner, Carol Brooks
1991   "Stigma and the Public Self: Notes on Communication, Self, and Others."
            Journal of Contemporary Ethnography 20:251–262.
1995   *Passing By: Gender and Public Harassment.* Los Angeles: University of
            California Press.
Garfinkel, Harold
1963   "A Conception of, and Experiments with, 'Trust' as a Condition of Stable
            and Concerted Actions." In O. J. Harvey (ed.), *Motivation in Social
            Interaction.* New York: Ronald: 187–238.
1967   *Studies in Ethnomethodology.* Englewood Cliffs, N.J.: Prentice-Hall.
1974   "The Origins of the Term 'Ethnomethodology.'" In R. Turner (ed.),
            Ethnomethodology. Harmondsworth, Eng.: Penguin: 15–18.
1988   "Evidence for Locally Produced, Naturally Accountable Phenomena of
            Order, Logic, Reason, Meaning, Method, etc. in and as of the Essential
            Quiddity of Immortal Ordinary Society (I of IV): An Announcement of
            Studies." *Sociological Theory* 6:103–109.
1991   "Respecification: Evidence for Locally Produced, Naturally Accountable
            Phenomena of Order, Logic, Reason, Meaning, Method, etc. in and as of the
            Essential Haecceity of Immortal Ordinary Society (I): An Announcement of
            Studies." In G. Button (ed.), *Ethnomethodology and the Human Sciences.*
            Cambridge: Cambridge University Press: 10–19.
Garland, Anne Witte
1988   *Women Activists: Challenging the Abuse of Power.* New York: Feminist
            Press.
Gartman, David
1998   "Postmodernism; or, the Cultural Logic of Post-Fordism?" *Sociological
            Quarterly* 39:119–137.
Gaziano, Emanuel
1996   "Ecological Metaphors as Scientific Boundary Work: Innovation and
            Authority in Interwar Sociology and Biology." *American Journal of
            Sociology* 101:874–907.
Gelb, Joyce, and Paley, Marian Lief
1982   *Women and Public Policies.* Princeton, N.J.: Princeton University Press.
Geras, Norman
1987   "Post-Marxism?" *New Left Review* 163:40–82.
Gergen, Kenneth J.
1973   "Social Psychology as History." *Journal of Personality and Social
            Psychology* 26:309–320.

1986 "Correspondence versus Autonomy in the Language of Understanding Human Action." In D. W. Fiske and R. A. Shweder (eds.), *Metatheory in Social Science: Pluralisms and Subjectivities.* Chicago: University of Chicago Press: 136–162.

Gerstein, Dean
1987 "To Unpack Micro and Macro: Link Small with Large and Part with Whole." In J. C. Alexander et al. (eds.), *The Micro-Macro Link.* Berkeley: University of California Press: 86–111.

Gerth, Hans, and Mills, C. Wright
1958 *From Max Weber.* New York: Oxford University Press.

Gerth, Hans, and Mills, C. Wright (eds.)
1953 *Character and Social Structure.* New York: Harcourt, Brace and World.

Gerth, Nobuko
1993 "Hans H. Gerth and C. Wright Mills: Partnership and Partisanship." *International Journal of Politics, Culture and Society* 7:133–154.

Gibson, Diane
1996 "Broken Down by Age and Gender: 'The Problem of Old Women' Redefined." *Gender & Society* 10:433–448.

Giddens, Anthony
1972 "Introduction: Durkheim's Writings in Sociology and Social Philosophy." In A. Giddens (ed.), *Emile Durkheim: Selected Writings.* Cambridge: Cambridge University Press: 1–50.

1975 *The Class Structure of Advanced Societies.* New York: Harper & Row.

1976 *New Rules of Sociological Method: A Positive Critique of Interpretive Sociologies.* New York: Basic Books.

1979 *Central Problems in Social Theory: Action, Structure and Contradiction in Social Analysis.* Berkeley: University of California Press.

1981 *The Contemporary Critique of Historical Materialism.* Berkeley: University of California Press.

1982 *Profiles and Critiques in Social Theory.* Berkeley: University of California Press.

1984 *The Constitution of Society: Outline of the Theory of Structuration.* Berkeley: University of California Press.

1987 "Structuralism, Post-Structuralism and the Production of Culture." In A. Giddens and J. H. Turner (eds.), *Social Theory Today.* Stanford, Calif.: Stanford University Press: 195–223.

1989 "A Reply to My Critics." In D. Held and J. B. Thompson (eds.), *Social Theory of Modern Societies: Anthony Giddens and His Critics.* Cambridge: Cambridge University Press: 249–301.

1990 *The Consequences of Modernity.* Stanford, Calif.: Stanford University Press.

1991 *Modernity and Self-Identity: Self and Society in the Late Modern Age.* Stanford, Calif.: Stanford University Press.

1992 *The Transformation of Intimacy: Sexuality, Love and Eroticism in Modern Societies.* Stanford, Calif.: Stanford University Press.

1994 *Beyond Left and Right: The Future of Radical Politics.* Stanford, Calif.: Stanford University Press.

1995 *Politics, Sociology and Social Theory: Encounters with Classical and Contemporary Social Thought.* Stanford, Calif.: Stanford University Press.

Giddings, Paula
1984   *When and Where I Enter: The Impact of Black Women on Race and Sex in America.* New York: William Morrow.
Gilbert, Sandra M., and Gubar, Susan
1979   *The Madwoman in the Attic: The Woman Writer and the Nineteenth-Century Literary Imagination.* New Haven: Yale University Press.
Gilligan, Carol
1982   *In a Different Voice: Psychological Theory and Women's Development.* Cambridge, Mass.: Harvard University Press.
Giminez, Martha E.
1990   "The Dialectics of Waged and Unwaged Work." In J. Collins and M. Giminez (eds.), *Work without Wages.* Albany: State University of New York Press.
1991   "The Mode of Reproduction in Transition: A Marxist-Feminist Analysis of the Effects of Reproductive Technologies." *Gender & Society* 5:334–359.
Glatzer, Wolfgang
1998   "The German Sociological Association: Origins and Developments." Paper presented at the meetings of the International Sociological Association, Montreal, Canada.
Glazer, Nona
1993   *Women's Paid and Unpaid Labor: The Work Transfer in Health Care and Retailing.* Philadelphia: Temple University Press.
Glenn, Evelyn Nakano
1985   "Racial Ethnic Women's Labor: The Intersection of Race, Gender, and Class Oppression." *Review of Radical Political Economics* 17:86–108.
Glenn, Evelyn Nakano, Chang, Grace, and Forcey, Linda Rennie (eds.)
1993   *Mothering.* New York: Routledge.
Glenn, Phillip J.
1989   "Initiating Shared Laughter in Multi-Party Conversations." *Western Journal of Speech Communications* 53:127–149.
Glennon, Lynda M.
1979   *Women and Dualism.* New York: Longman.
Gluckman, Max
1959   *Custom and Conflict in Africa.* Glencoe, Ill.: Free Press.
Godelier, Maurice
1972a   *Rationality and Irrationality in Economics.* London: NLB.
1972b   "Structure and Contradiction in *Capital.*" In R. Blackburn (ed.), *Readings in Critical Social Theory.* London: Fontana: 334–368.
Goffman, Erving
1959   *Presentation of Self in Everyday Life.* Garden City, N.Y.: Anchor.
1961   *Encounters: Two Studies in the Sociology of Interaction.* Indianapolis: Bobbs-Merrill.
1963a   *Behavior in Public Places: Notes on the Social Organization of Gatherings.* Glencoe, Ill.: Free Press.
1963b   *Stigma: Notes on the Management of Spoiled Identity.* Englewood Cliffs., N.J.: Prentice-Hall.
1967   *Interaction Ritual: Essays on Face-to-Face Behavior.* Garden City, N.Y.: Anchor.

1971   *Relations in Public: Microstudies of the Public Order.* New York: Basic
            Books.
1972   *Strategic Interaction.* New York: Ballantine.
1974   *Frame Analysis: An Essay on the Organization of Experience.* New York:
            Harper Colophon.
1977   "The Arrangement between the Sexes." *Theory and Society* 40:301–331.
1979   *Gender Advertisements.* New York: Harper and Row.
Golden, Martha
1994   *Wild Women Don't Wear No Blues.* New York: Anchor.
Golden, Stephanie
1992   *The Women Outside: Meanings and Myths of Homelessness.* Berkeley:
            University of California Press.
Goldfield, Michael, and Gilbert, Alan
1997   "The Limits of Rational Choice Theory." *National Political Science Review*
            6:205–228.
Goldscheider, Frances K., and Waite, Linda J.
1991   *New Families, No Families? The Transformation of the American Home.*
            Berkeley: University of California Press.
Goldstone, Jack A., and Opp, Karl-Dieter (eds.)
1994   "Rationality, Revolution, and 1989 in Eastern Europe." *Rationality and
            Society* 6:3–179.
Gonos, George
1977   " 'Situation' versus 'Frame': The 'Interactionist' and the 'Structuralist'
            Analyses of Everyday Life." *American Sociological Review* 42:854–867.
1980   "The Class Position of Goffman's Sociology: Social Origins of an American
            Structuralism." In J. Ditton (ed.), *The View from Goffman.* New York: St.
            Martin's: 134–169.
Goode, William J.
1960   "A Theory of Role Strain." *American Sociological Review* 25:483–496.
Goodwin, Charles
1979   "The Interactive Construction of a Sentence in Natural Conversation." In G.
            Psathas (ed.), *Everyday Language: Studies in Ethnomethodology.* New York:
            Irvington: 97–121.
1984   "Notes on Story Structure and the Organization of Participation." In J. M.
            Atkinson and J. Heritage (eds.), *Structures of Social Action.* Cambridge:
            Cambridge University Press: 225–246.
Goodwin, Jan
1994   *Price of Honor: Muslim Women Lift the Veil of Silence on the Islamic World.*
            New York: Little, Brown.
Gordon, Linda
1994   *Pitied but Not Entitled: Single Mothers and the History of Welfare.* New
            York: Free Press.
Gottdiener, Mark
1993   "Ideology, Foundationalism, and Sociological Theory." *Sociological
            Quarterly* 34:653–671.
1994   "Semiotics and Postmodernism." In D. R. Dickens and A. Fontana (eds.),
            Postmodernism and Social Inquiry. New York: Guilford Press: 155–181.
Gouldner, Alvin
1958   "Introduction." In E. Durkheim, *Socialism and Saint-Simon.* Yellow Springs,
            Ohio: Antioch Press.

1959/1967   "Reciprocity and Autonomy in Functional Theory." In N. Demerath and R. Peterson (eds.), *System, Change and Conflict.* New York: Free Press: 141–169.

1960   "The Norm of Reciprocity." *American Sociological Review* 25:161–178.

1970   *The Coming Crisis of Western Sociology.* New York: Basic Books.

Gramsci, Antonio

1917/1977   "The Revolution against 'Capital.' " In Q. Hoare (ed.), *Antonio Gramsci: Selections from Political Writings (1910–1920).* New York: International Publishers: 34–37.

1932/1975   *Letters from Prison: Antonio Gramsci.* Lynne Lawner (ed.). New York: Harper Colophon.

1971   *Selections from the Prison Notebooks.* New York: International Publishers.

Granovetter, Mark

1973   "The Strength of Weak Ties." *American Journal of Sociology* 78:1360–1380.

1983   "The Strength of Weak Ties: A Network Theory Revisited." In R. Collins (ed.), *Sociological Theory—1983.* San Francisco: Jossey-Bass: 201–233.

1985   "Economic Action and Social Structure: The Problem of Embeddedness." *American Journal of Sociology* 91:481–510.

Greatbatch, David, and Dingwall, Robert

1997   "Argumentative Talk in Divorce Mediation Sessions." *American Sociological Review* 62:151–170.

Green, Donald, and Shapiro, Ian

1994   *Pathologies of Rational Choice Theory: A Critique of Applications in Political Science.* New Haven, Conn.: Yale University Press.

Green, Karen

1995   *The Woman of Reason: Feminism, Humanism, and Political Thought.* New York: Continuum.

Gregory, Derek

1989   "Presences and Absences: Time-Space Relations and Structuration Theory." In D. Held and J. B. Thompson (eds.), *Social Theory of Modern Societies: Anthony Giddens and His Critics.* Cambridge: Cambridge University Press: 185–214.

Gregson, Nicki, and Lowe, Michelle

1994   *Servicing the Middle Class: Class, Gender and Waged Domestic Labor.* New York: Routledge.

Greisman, Harvey C.

1986   "The Paradigm That Failed." In R. C. Monk (ed.), *Structures of Knowing.* Lanham, Md.: University Press of America: 273–291.

Greisman, Harvey C., and Ritzer, George

1981   "Max Weber, Critical Theory and the Administered World." *Qualitative Sociology* 4:34–55.

Grewal, Idepal, and Kaplan, Caren (eds.)

1994   *Scattered Hegemonies: Postmodernity and Transnational Feminist Culture.* Minneapolis: University of Minnesota Press.

Griffin, Susan

1978   *Women and Nature: The Roaring within Her.* New York: Harper & Row.

1979   *Rape, the Power of Consciousness.* New York: Harper & Row.

1981   *Pornography as Silence: Culture's Revenge against Nature.* New York: Harper & Row.

Gross, Llewellyn
1961   "Preface to a Metatheoretical Framework for Sociology." *American Journal of Sociology* 67:125–136.
Grossberg, Lawrence, and Nelson, Cary
1988   "Introduction: The Territory of Marxism." In C. Nelson and L. Grossberg (eds.), *Marxism and the Interpretation of Culture.* Urbana: University of Illinois Press: 1–13.
Guba, Egon G., and Lincoln, Yvonna S.
1994   "Competing Paradigms in Qualitative Research." in Norman K. Denzin and Yvonna S. Lincoln (eds.), *Handbook of Qualitative Research.* Thousand Oaks, Calif.: Sage: 105–117.
Gubbay, Jon
1997   "A Marxist Critique of Weberian Class Analyses." *Sociology* 31:73–89.
Gurney, Patrick J.
1981   "Historical Origins of Ideological Denial: The Case of Marx in American Sociology." *American Sociologist* 16:196–201.
Gurvitch, Georges
1964   *The Spectrum of Social Time.* Dordrecht, Neth.: D. Reidel.
Habermas, Jurgen
1970   *Toward a Rational Society.* Boston: Beacon Press.
1971   *Knowledge and Human Interests.* Boston: Beacon Press.
1973   *Theory and Practice.* Boston: Beacon Press.
1975   *Legitimation Crisis.* Boston: Beacon Press.
1979   *Communication and the Evolution of Society.* Boston: Beacon Press.
1981   "Modernity versus Postmodernity." *New German Critique* 22:3–14.
1984   *The Theory of Communicative Action.* Vol. 1, *Reason and the Rationalization of Society.* Boston: Beacon Press.
1986   *Autonomy and Solidarity: Interviews.* Peter Dews (ed.). London: Verso.
1987a   *The Theory of Communicative Action.* Vol. 2, *Lifeworld and System: A Critique of Functionalist Reason.* Boston: Beacon Press.
1987b   *The Philosophical Discourse of Modernity: Twelve Lectures.* Cambridge, Mass.: MIT Press.
1991   "A Reply." In A. Honneth and H. Joas (eds.), *Communicative Action: Essays on Jurgen Habermas's* The Theory of Communicative Action. Cambridge: Cambridge University Press: 215–264.
1994   *The Past as Future.* Interviewed by Michael Haller. Lincoln: University of Nebraska Press.
Hagan, John, and Kay, Fiona
1995   *Gender in Practice: A Study of Lawyers' Lives.* New York: Oxford University Press.
Hage, Jerald
1980   *Theories of Organization.* New York: Wiley.
1994a   "Constructing Bridges between Sociological Paradigms and Levels: Trying to Make Sociological Theory More Complex, Less Fragmented, and Politicized." In J. Hage (ed.), *Formal Theory in Sociology: Opportunity or Pitfall?* Albany: State University Press of New York: 152–168.
Hage, Jerald (ed.)
1994b   *Formal Theory in Sociology: Opportunity or Pitfall?* Albany: State University Press of New York.

Hage, Jerald, and Powers, Charles H.
1992   *Post-Industrial Lives: Roles and Relationships in the 21st Century.* Newbury Park, Calif.: Sage.

Haines, Valerie
1988   "Is Spencer's Theory an Evolutionary Theory? *American Journal of Sociology* 93:1200–1223.
1992   "Spencer's Philosophy of Science." *British Journal of Sociology* 43:155–172.

Halfpenny, Peter
1982   *Positivism and Sociology: Explaining Social Life.* London: Allen and Unwin.

Hall, John R.
1992   "Where History and Sociology Meet: Forms of Discourse and Sociohistorical Inquiry." *Sociological Theory* 10:164–193.

Hall, Richard
1983   "Theoretical Trends in the Sociology of Occupations." *Sociological Quarterly* 24:5–23.

Hall, Stuart
1988   "Brave New World." *Marxism Today* October:24–29.

Hall, Stuart, and Jameson, Fredric
1990   "Clinging to the Wreckage: A Conversation." *Marxism Today* September:28–31.

Halliday, Fred
1990   "The Ends of the Cold War." *New Left Review* 180:5–23.

Halls, W. D.
1996   "The Cultural and Educational Influences of Durkheim, 1900–1945." *Durkheimian Studies* 2:122–132.

Handel, Warren
1982   *Ethnomethodology: How People Make Sense.* Englewood Cliffs, N.J.: Prentice-Hall.

Haney, Lynne
1996   "Homeboys, Babies, Men in Suits: The State and the Reproduction of Male Dominance." *American Sociological Review* 61:759–778.

Hankin, Thomas L.
1979   "In Defense of Biography: The Use of Biography in the History of Science." *History of Science* 17:1–16.

Hansen, Karen V., and Philipson, Ilene (eds.)
1990   *Women, Class and the Feminist Imagination: A Socialist-Feminist Reader.* Philadelphia: Temple University Press.

Haraway, Donna
1988   "Situated Knowledge: The Science Question in Feminism and the Privilege of Partial Perspective." *Feminist Studies* 14:575–600.
1989   *Primate Visions: Gender, Race and Nature in the World of Modern Science.* New York: Routledge.
1990   "A Manifesto for Cyborgs: Science, Technology, and Socialist Feminism in the 1980s." In L. Nicholson (ed.), *Feminism/Postmodernism.* New York: Routledge: 190–233.

Harding, Sandra
1986   *The Science Question in Sociology.* Ithaca, N.Y.: Cornell University Press.
1991   *Whose Science? Whose Knowledge? Thinking from Women's Lives.* Ithaca, N.Y.: Cornell University Press.

Harding, Sandra (ed.)
1987   *Feminism and Methodology.* Bloomington: Indiana University Press.
Harding, Sandra, and Hintikka, Merrill B. (eds.)
1983   *Discovering Reality: Feminist Perspectives on Epistemology, Metaphysics,
            Methodology and Philosophy of Science.* Boston: Reidel.
Hardy-Fanta, Carol
1993   *Latina Politics/Latino Politics.* Philadelphia: Temple University Press.
Harper, Diane Blake, Sylvester, Joan, and Walczak, David
1980   "An Empirical Comparison of Ritzer's Paradigms and Similar Metatheories:
            Comment on Friedheim." *Social Forces* 59:513–517.

Harris, David
1996   *A Society of Signs?* London: Routledge.

Harris, Kathleen Mullan
1996   "Life after Welfare: Women, Work, and Repeat Dependency." *American
            Sociological Review* 61:407–426.

Harris, Maxine
1991   *Sisters of the Shadow.* Norman: University of Oklahoma Press.

Hartmann, Heidi
1979   "Capitalism, Patriarchy and Job Segregation by Sex." In Z. Eisenstein (ed.),
            Capitalist Patriarchy and the Case for Socialist Feminism. New York:
            Monthly Review Press: 206–247.
1981   "The Unhappy Marriage of Marxism and Feminism: Towards a More
            Progressive Union." In Lydia Sargent (ed.) *Women and Revolution.* Boston:
            South End Press.

Hartsock, Nancy
1983   *Money, Sex and Power: Towards a Feminist Historical Materialism.* New
            York: Longman.
1990   "Foucault on Power: A Theory for Women?" In L. Nicholson (ed.),
            Feminism/Postmodernism. New York: Routledge: 157–175.

Harvey, David
1989   *The Condition of Postmodernity: An Enquiry into the Origins of Cultural
            Change.* Oxford: Blackwell.

Harvey, Lee
1982   "The Use and Abuse of Kuhnian Paradigms in the Sociology of Knowledge."
            British Journal of Sociology 16:85–101.
1987   "The Nature of 'Schools' in the Sociology of Knowledge: The Case of the
            'Chicago School.' " *Sociological Review* 35:245–278.

Hawkes, Terence
1977   *Structuralism and Semiotics.* London: Methuen.
Hawthorn, Geoffrey
1976   *Enlightenment and Despair.* Cambridge: Cambridge University Press.
Hayim, Gila
1980   *The Existential Sociology of Jean-Paul Sartre.* Amherst: University of
            Massachusetts Press.
Hays, Sharon
1994   "Structure and Agency and the Sticky Problem of Culture." *Sociological
            Theory* 12:57–72.
1996   *The Cultural Contradictions of Motherhood.* New Haven, Conn.: Yale
            University Press.

Hazelrigg, Lawrence
1972   "Class, Property and Authority: Dahrendorf's Critique of Marx's Theory of
            Class." *Social Forces* 50:473–487.
Hearn, Frank
1997   *Moral Order and Social Disorder: The American Search for Civil Society.*
            New York: Aldine de Gruyter.
Heath, Anthony
1976   *Rational Choice and Social Exchange: A Critique of Exchange Theory.*
            Cambridge: Cambridge University Press.
Hechter, Michael
1983a   "Introduction." In M. Hechter (ed.), *The Microfoundations of
            Macrosociology.* Philadelphia: Temple University Press: 3–15.
1983b   "A Theory of Group Solidarity." In Michael Hechter (ed.), *The
            Microfoundations of Macrosociology.* Philadelphia: Temple University
            Press: 16–57.
1987   *Principles of Group Solidarity.* Berkeley: University of California Press.
Hechter, Michael, and Kanazawa, Satoshi
1997   "Sociological Rational Choice Theory." In John Hagan and Karen S. Cook
            (eds.), *Annual Review of Sociology,* Vol. 23. Palo Alto, Calif.: Annual
            Reviews: 191–214.
Heckathorn, Douglas D.
1997   "Overview: The Paradoxical Relationship between Sociology and Rational
            Choice." *The American Sociologist* 28:6–15.
Heckathorn, Douglas D., and Broadhead, Robert S.
1996   "Rational Choice, Public Policy and AIDS." *Rationality and Society*
            8:235–260.
Hedstrom, Peter, and Swedberg, Richard
1996   "Rational Choice, Empirical Research, and the Sociological Tradition."
            European Sociological Review 12:127–146.
Hegel, G. W. F.
1807/1967   *The Phenomenology of Mind.* New York: Harper Colophon.
1821/1967   *The Philosophy of Right.* Oxford: Clarendon Press.
Hegtvedt, Karen A., Thompson, Elaine A., and Cook, Karen S.
1993   "Power and Equity: What Counts in Attributions for Exchange Outcomes?"
            Social Psychology Quarterly 56:100–119.
Heilbron, Johan
1995   *The Rise of Social Theory.* London: Polity Press.
Heilbrun, Carolyn
1988   *Writing a Woman's Life.* New York: Norton.
Heins, Volker
1993   "Weber's Ethic and the Spirit of Anti-Capitalism." *Political Studies*
            41:269–283.
Hekman, Susan
1980   *Weber, the Ideal Type, and Contemporary Social Theory.* Notre Dame, Ind.:
            University of Notre Dame Press.
Held, David
1980   *Introduction to Critical Theory: Horkheimer to Habermas.* Berkeley:
            University of California Press.

Held, David, and Thompson, John B.
1989   "Editors' Introduction." In D. Held and J. B. Thompson (eds.), *Social Theory of Modern Societies: Anthony Giddens and His Critics.* Cambridge: Cambridge University Press: 1–18.

Held, Virginia
1993   *Feminist Morality: Transforming Culture, Society and Politics.* Chicago: University of Chicago Press.

Helle, H. J., and Eisenstadt, S. N. (eds.)
1985   *Micro-Sociological Theory: Perspectives on Sociological Theory,* Vol. 2. London: Sage.

Hennessey, Rosemary
1992   *Materialist Feminism and the Politics of Discourse.* New York: Routledge.

Hennessey, Rosemary, and Ingraham, Chrys
1997   "Introduction: Reclaiming Anticapitalist Feminism." In R. Hennessey and C. Ingraham (eds.), *Materialist Feminism.* New York and London: Routledge: 1–14.

Heritage, John
1984   *Garfinkel and Ethnomethodology.* Cambridge: Polity Press.

Heritage, John, and Atkinson, J. Maxwell
1984   "Introduction." In J. M. Atkinson and J. Heritage (eds.), *Structures of Social Action.* Cambridge: Cambridge University Press: 1–15.

Heritage, John, and Greatbatch, David
1986   "Generating Applause: A Study of Rhetoric and Response in Party Political Conferences." *American Journal of Sociology* 92:110–157.

Heritage, John, and Watson, D. R.
1979   "Formulations as Conversational Objects." In G. Psathas (ed.), *Everyday Language: Studies in Ethnomethodology.* New York: Irvington: 187–201.

Herrnstein, Richard J., and Murray, Charles
1994   *The Bell Curve: Intelligence and Class Structure in American Life.* New York: Free Press.

Hesse, Mary
1995   "Habermas and the Force of Dialectical Argument." *History of European Ideas* 21:367–378.

Hewitt, John P.
1984   *Self and Society: A Symbolic Interactionist Social Psychology.* 3rd ed. Boston: Allyn and Bacon.

Hewitt, Nancy
1992   "Compounding Differences." *Feminist Studies* 18:313–326.

Heyl, John D., and Heyl, Barbara S.
1976   "The Sumner-Porter Controversy at Yale: Pre-Paradigmatic Sociology and Institutional Crisis." *Sociological Inquiry* 46:41–49.

Hilbert, Richard A.
1990   "Ethnomethodology and the Micro-Macro Order." *American Sociological Review* 55:794–808.
1991   "Norman and Sigmund: Comment on Denzin's 'Harold and Agnes.' " *Sociological Theory* 9:264–268.
1992   *The Classical Roots of Ethnomethodology: Durkheim, Weber and Garfinkel.* Chapel Hill: University of North Carolina Press.

Hill, Greg
1997   "History, Necessity, and Rational Choice Theory." *Rationality and Society*
            9:189–213.
Himes, Joseph
1966   "The Functions of Racial Conflict." *Social Forces* 45:1–10.
Hindess, Barry
1986   "Actors and Social Relations." In M. L. Wardell and S. Turner (eds.),
            Sociological Theory in Transition. Boston: Allen and Unwin: 113–126.
1988   *Choice, Rationality, and Social Theory*. London: Unwin Hyman.
Hinkle, Roscoe
1980   *Founding Theory of American Sociology: 1881–1915*. London: Routledge
            and Kegan Paul.
1994   *Developments in American Sociological Theory: 1915–1950*. Albany: State
            University of New York Press.
Hinkle, Roscoe, and Hinkle, Gisela
1954   *The Development of American Sociology*. New York: Random House.
Hirsch, Paul, Michaels, Stuart, and Friedman, Ray
1987   " 'Dirty Hands' versus 'Clean Models': Is Sociology in Danger of Being
            Seduced by Economics?" *Theory and Society* 16:317–336.
Hirschmann, Nancy J., and Di Stefano, Christine (eds.)
1996   *Revisioning the Political: Feminist Reconstructions of Traditional Concepts
            in Western Political Theory*. Boulder, Colo.: Westview.
Hite, Shere
1976   *The Hite Report: A Nationwide Study of Female Sexuality*. New York: Dell.
Hobsbawm, Eric J.
1965   *Primitive Rebels*. New York: Norton.
Hochschild, Arlie
1983   *The Managed Heart: Commercialization of Human Feeling*. Berkeley:
            University of California Press.
1997   *The Time Bind: When Work Becomes Home and Home Becomes Work*. New
            York: Metropolitan Books.
Hochschild, Arlie, with Machung, Anne
1989   *The Second Shift*. New York: Avon Books.
Hoecker-Drysdale, Susan
1994   *Harriet Martineau: First Woman Sociologist*. New York: Berg.
Hofstadter, Richard
1959   *Social Darwinism in American Thought*. New York: Braziller.
Hollinger, David
1980   "T. S. Kuhn's Theory of Science and Its Implications for History." In G.
            Gutting (ed.), *Paradigms and Revolutions*. Notre Dame, Ind.: Notre Dame
            University Press: 195–222.
Holmwood, John
1996   *Founding Sociology: Talcott Parsons and the Idea of General Theory*. Essex:
            Longman.
Holmwood, John, and Stewart, Alexander
1994   "Synthesis and Fragmentation in Social Theory: A Progressive Solution."
            Sociological Theory 12:83–100.
Holton, Robert J., and Turner, Bryan S.
1986   *Talcott Parsons on Economy and Society*. London: Routledge and
            Kegan Paul.

Holub, Robert C.
1991   *Jurgen Habermas: Critic in the Public Sphere.* London: Routledge.
Homans, George C.
1958   "Social Behavior as Exchange." *American Journal of Sociology* 63:597–606.
1961   *Social Behavior: Its Elementary Forms.* New York: Harcourt, Brace and
            World.
1962   *Sentiments and Activities.* New York: Free Press.
1967   *The Nature of Social Science.* New York: Harcourt, Brace and World.
1969   "The Sociological Relevance of Behaviorism." In R. Burgess and D. Bushell
            (eds.), *Behavioral Sociology.* New York: Columbia University Press: 1–24.
1971   "Commentary." In H. Turk and R. Simpson (eds.), *Institutions and Social
            Exchange.* Indianapolis: Bobbs-Merrill: 363–374.
1974   *Social Behavior: Its Elementary Forms.* Rev. ed. New York: Harcourt Brace
            Jovanovich.
1984   *Coming to My Senses: The Autobiography of a Sociologist.* New Brunswick,
            N.J.: Transaction Books.
Homans, George C., and Schneider, David M.
1955   *Marriage, Authority and Final Causes: A Study of Unilateral Cross-Cousin
            Marriage.* New York: Free Press.
Hood, Jane C. (ed.)
1993   *Men, Work and Family.* Newbury Park, Calif.: Sage.
Hook, Sidney
1965   "Pareto's Sociological System." In J. H. Meisel (ed.), *Pareto and Mosca.*
            Englewood Cliffs, N.J.: Prentice-Hall: 57–61.
Hooks, Bell
1984   *Feminist Theory: From Margin to Center.* Boston: South End Press.
1989   *Talking Back: Thinking Feminist, Thinking Black.* Boston: South End Press.
1990   *Yearning: Race, Gender, and Cultural Politics.* Boston: South End Press.
Horowitz, Irving L.
1962/1967   "Consensus, Conflict, and Cooperation." In N. Demerath and R. Peterson
            (eds.), *System, Change and Conflict.* New York: Free Press: 265–279.
1983   *C. Wright Mills: An American Utopian.* New York: Free Press.
Howe, Harriet and Muriel Cantor
1994   "Jessie Bernard: The Unfolding of the Female World." *Sociological Inquiry*
            64:10–22.
Hoyningen-Huene, Paul
1993   *Reconstructing Scientific Revolutions: Thomas S. Kuhn's Philosophy of
            Science.* Chicago: University of Chicago Press.
Huaco, George
1966   "The Functionalist Theory of Stratification: Two Decades of Controversy."
            Inquiry 9:215–240.
1986   "Ideology and General Theory: The Case of Sociological Functionalism."
            Comparative Studies in Society and History 28:34–54.
Huber, Joan
1976   "Sociology." *Signs: Journal of Women in Culture and Society* 1, part
            1:685–697.
1991   *Macro-Micro Linkages in Sociology.* Newbury Park, Calif.: Sage.
Hughes, John A., Martin, Peter J., and Sharrock, W. W.
1995   *Understanding Classical Sociology: Marx, Weber and Durkheim.*
            London: Sage.

Humphery, Kim
1998   *Shelf Life: Supermarkets and the Changing Cultures of Consumption.*
            Cambridge: Cambridge University Press.
Hunter, Allen
1988   "Post-Marxism and the New Social Movements." *Theory and Society*
            17:885–900.
Hunter, J. E., and Schmidt, F. L.
1989   *Methods of Meta-Analysis: Correcting Error and Bias in Research Findings.*
            Newbury Park, Calif.: Sage.
Hunter, J. E., Schmidt, F. L., and Jackson, G. B.
1982   *Meta-Analysis: Cumulating Research Findings across Studies.* Beverly Hills,
            Calif.: Sage.
Huxtable, Ada Louise
1997a   *The Unreal America: Architecture and Illusion.* New York:
            The New Press, 1997.
1997b   "Living with the Fake and Liking It." *New York Times,* sec. 2, March 30: 1.
Imber, Jonathan B. (ed.)
1997   "The Place of Rational Choice in Sociology." *American Sociologist* 28:3–87.
Inbar, Michael
1996   "The Violation of Normative Rules and the Issue of Rationality in Individual
            Judgments." In Jon Clark (ed.), *James S. Coleman.* London: Falmer Press:
            227–262.
Irigaray, Luce
1985a   *Speculum of the Other Woman.* Gillian Gill (trans.). Ithaca, N.Y.: Cornell
            University Press.
1985b   *This Sex Which Is Not Our Own.* Catherine Porter (trans.). Ithaca, N.Y.:
            Cornell University Press.
Irving, Katrina
1989   "(Still) Hesitating on the Threshold: Feminist Theory and the Question of the
            Subject." *NWSA Journal* 1:630–645.
Iwao, Sumko
1993   *The Japanese Woman: Traditional Image and Changing Reality.* New York:
            Free Press.
Jackman, Mary R.
1994   *The Velvet Glove: Paternalism and Conflict in Gender, Class, and Race
            Relations.* Berkeley: University of California Press.
Jackman, Mary R., and Jackman, Robert W.
1973   "An Interpretation of the Relation between Objective and Subjective Social
            Status." *American Sociological Review* 38:569–582.
Jacobs, Bruce A.
1992   "Drugs and Deception: Undercover Infiltration and Dramaturgical Theory."
            Human Relations 45:1293–1310.
Jacobs, Sue-Ellen, Thomas, Wesley, and Lang, Sabine (eds.)
1997   *Two-Spirit People: Native American Gender Identity, Sexuality, and
            Spirituality.* Urbana: University of Illinois Press.
Jaffee, David
1998   *Levels of Socio-Economic Development Theory.* Westport, Conn.: Praeger.
Jaggar, Alison M.
1983   *Feminist Politics and Human Nature.* Totowa, N.J.: Rowman and Allanheld.

Jaggar, Alison M. (ed.)
1994   *Living with Contradictions: Controversies in Feminist-Social Ethics.*
            Boulder, Colo.: Westview Press.
Jaggar, Alison M., and Bordo, Susan (eds.)
1989   *Gender/Body/Knowledge: Feminist Reconstructions of Being and Knowing.*
            New Brunswick, N.J.: Rutgers University Press.
Jaggar, Alison M., and Rothenberg, Paula (eds.)
1984   *Feminist Frameworks.* 2nd ed. New York: McGraw-Hill.
Jagtenberg, Tom, and McKie, David
1997   *Eco-Impacts and the Greening of Postmodernity: New Maps for*
            Communication Studies, Cultural Studies and Sociology. Thousand Oaks,
            Calif.: Sage.
James, Selma, and Costa, Mariarosa Dallacosa
1973   *The Power of Women and the Subversion of Community.* Bristol, Eng.:
            Falling Wall Press.
James, Stanlie M., and Busia, Abema P. A. (eds.)
1993   *Theorizing Black Feminisms.* New York: Routledge.
Jameson, Fredric
1984   "Postmodernism, or the Cultural Logic of Late Capitalism." *New Left Review*
            146:53–92.
1989   "Afterword—Marxism and Postmodernism." In D. Kellner (ed.),
            Postmodernism, Jameson, Critique. Washington, D.C.: Maisonneuve Press:
            369–387.
1991   *Postmodernism, or, The Cultural Logic of Late Capitalism.* Durham, N.C.:
            Duke University Press.
Janeway, Elizabeth
1981   *Powers of the Weak.* New York: Morrow Quill.
Jaworski, Gary Dean
1991   "The Historical and Contemporary Importance of Coser's *Functions.*"
            Sociological Theory 9:116–123.
1995   "Simmel in Early American Sociology: Translation as Social Action."
            International Journal of Politics, Culture and Society 8:389–417.
1997   *Georg Simmel and the American Prospect.* Albany: State University of New
            York Press.
Jay, Martin
1973   *The Dialectical Imagination.* Boston: Little, Brown.
1984   *Marxism and Totality: The Adventures of a Concept from Lukács to*
            Habermas. Berkeley: University of California Press.
1986   *Permanent Exiles: Essays on the Intellectual Migration from Germany to*
            America. New York: Columbia University Press.
1988   *Fin-de-Siecle Socialism and Other Essays.* New York: Routledge.
Jefferson, Gail
1979   "A Technique for Inviting Laughter and Its Subsequent Acceptance
            Declination." In G. Psathas (ed.), *Everyday Language: Studies in*
            Ethnomethodology. New York: Irvington: 79–96.
1984   "On the Organization of Laughter in Talk about Troubles." In J. M. Atkinson
            and J. Heritage (eds.), *Structures of Social Action.* Cambridge: Cambridge
            University Press: 346–369.
Jeffreys, Sheila
1991   *Anticlimax: A Feminist Perspective on the Sexual Revolution,* New York:
            New York University Press.

Jencks, Charles
1977   *The Language of Post-Modern Architecture.* New York: Rizzoli.
Jenkins, Richard
1992   *Pierre Bourdieu.* London: Routledge.
Joas, Hans
1981   "George Herbert Mead and the 'Division of Labor': Macrosociological
            Implications of Mead's Social Psychology." *Symbolic Interaction*
            4:177–190.
1985   *G. H. Mead: A Contemporary Re-examination of His Thought.* Cambridge,
            Mass.: MIT Press.
1993   *Pragmatism and Social Theory.* Chicago: University of Chicago Press.
1996   *The Creativity of Action.* Chicago: University of Chicago Press.
1998   "Bauman in Germany: Modern Violence and the Problems of German Self-
            Understanding." *Theory, Culture and Society* 15:47–55.
Johnson, Allan G.
1997   *The Gender Knot: Unraveling Our Patriarchal Legacy.* Philadelphia: Temple
            University Press.
Johnson, Chalmers
1966   *Revolutionary Change.* Boston: Little, Brown.
Johnson, Doyle Paul
1981   *Sociological Theory: Classical Founders and Contemporary Perspectives.*
            New York: Wiley.
Johnson, Miriam
1988   *Strong Women, Weak Wives: The Search for Gender Equality.* Berkeley:
            University of California Press.
1989   "Feminism and the Theories of Talcott Parsons." In R. A. Wallace (ed.),
            Feminism and Sociological Theory. Newbury Park, Calif.: Sage: 101–118.
Johnson-Odum, Cheryl, and Strobel, Margaret
1992   *Expanding the Boundaries of Women's History: Essays on Women in the
            Third World.* Bloomington: Indiana University Press.
Johnston, Barry V.
1995   *Pitirim Sorokin: An Intellectual Biography.* Lawrence, Kan.: University of
            Kansas Press.
Jones, Greta
1980   *Social Darwinism and English Thought: The Interaction between Biological
            and Social Theory.* Atlantic Highlands, N.J.: Humanities Press.
Jones, Mark Peter
1996   "Posthuman Agency: Between Theoretical Traditions." *Sociological Theory*
            14:290–309.
Jones, Robert Alun
1983   "The New History of Sociology." *Annual Review of Sociology* 9:447–469.
1994   "The Positive Science of Ethics in France: German Influences in *De la
            Division du Travail Social.*" *Sociological Forum* 9:37–57.
forthcoming "Emile Durkheim." In George Ritzer (ed.), *The Blackwell Companion to
            Major Social Theorists.* Oxford, England, and Cambridge, Mass.: Blackwell.
Jordan, June
1992   *Technical Difficulties: African-American Notes on the State of the Union.*
            New York: Pantheon.

Kalberg, Stephen
1980   "Max Weber's Types of Rationality: Cornerstones for the Analysis of
            Rationalization Processes in History." *American Journal of Sociology*
            85:1145–1179.
1985   "The Role of Ideal Interests in Max Weber's Comparative Historical
            Sociology." In R. J. Antonio and R. M. Glassman (eds.), *A Weber-Marx
            Dialogue*. Lawrence: University Press of Kansas: 46–67.
1990   "The Rationalization of Action in Max Weber's Sociology of Religion."
            Sociological Theory 8:58–84.
1994   *Max Weber's Comparative-Historical Sociology*. Chicago: University of
            Chicago Press.
Kaldor, Mary
1990   "After the Cold War." *New Left Review* 180:25–40.
Kaminsky, Amy
1994   "Gender, Race, *Raza*." *Feminist Studies* 20:7–31.
Kandal, Terry R.
1988   *The Woman Question in Classical Sociological Theory*. Miami: International
            Universities Press.
Kanigel, Robert
1997   *The One Best Way: Frederick Winslow Taylor and the Enigma of Efficiency*.
            New York: Viking.
Kanter, Rosabeth Moss
1977   *Men and Women of the Corporation*. New York: Basic Books.
Karady, Victor
1983   "The Durkheimians in Academe: A Reconsideration." P. Besnard (ed.), *The
            Sociological Domain*. Cambridge: Cambridge University Press.
Kasler, Dirk
1985   "Jewishness as a Central Formation-Milieu of Early German Sociology."
            History of Sociology: An International Review 6:69–86.
Kasper, Anne
1986   "Consciousness Re-Evaluated: Interpretive Theory and Feminist
            Scholarship." *Sociological Inquiry* 56:30–49.
Kaufman, Debra R., and Richardson, Barbara L.
1982   *Achievement and Women: Challenging the Assumptions*. New York: Free Press.
Kaye, Howard L.
1991   "A False Convergence: Freud and the Hobbesian Problem of Order."
            Sociological Theory 9:87–105.
Keller, Evelyn Fox
1985   *Reflections on Gender and Science*. New Haven, Conn.: Yale University Press.
Kellner, Douglas
1988   "Postmodernism as Social Theory: Some Challenges and Problems." *Theory,
            Culture and Society* 5:239–269.
1989b   "Introduction: Jameson, Marxism, and Postmodernism." In D. Kellner (ed.),
            Postmodernism, Jameson, Critique. Washington, D.C.: Maisonneuve
            Press: 1–42.
1989c   *Critical Theory, Marxism, and Modernity*. Baltimore: Johns Hopkins
            University Press.
1990a   "The Postmodern Turn: Positions, Problems, and Prospects." In G. Ritzer
            (ed.), *Frontiers of Social Theory: The New Syntheses*. New York: Columbia
            University Press: 255–286.

1990c   *Television and the Crisis of Democracy.* Boulder, Colo.: Westview Press.
1993   "Critical Theory Today: Revisiting the Classics." *Theory, Culture and Society* 10:43–60.
1995   "Marxism, the Information Superhighway, and the Struggle for the Future." *Humanity and Society* 19:41–56.
forthcoming "Jean Baudrillard." In George Ritzer (ed.), *The Blackwell Companion to Major Social Theorists.* Oxford, England, and Cambridge, Mass.: Blackwell.

Kellner, Douglas (ed.)
1989a   *Postmodernism, Jameson, Critique.* Washington, D.C.: Maisonneuve Press.
1989d   *Jean Baudrillard: From Marxism to Postmodernism and Beyond.* Cambridge: Polity Press.
1994   *Baudrillard: A Critical Reader.* Oxford: Blackwell.

Kelly-Godol, Joan
1983   "The Social Relation of the Sexes: Methodological Implications of Women's History." In E. Abel and E. K. Abel (eds.), *The Signs Reader: Women, Gender and Scholarship.* Chicago: University of Chicago Press.

Kemeny, Jim
1976   "Perspectives on the Micro-Macro Distinction." *Sociological Review* 24:731–752.

Kent, Raymond A.
1981   *A History of British Empirical Sociology.* Aldershot, Hants, Eng.: Gower.

Kessler, Suzanne J., and McKenna, Wendy
1978   *Gender: An Ethnomethodological Approach.* Chicago: University of Chicago Press.

Kessler-Harris, Alice
1990   *A Woman's Wage: Symbolic Meanings and Social Consequences.* Lexington: University of Kentucky Press.

Kettler, David, and Meja, Volker
1995   *Karl Mannheim and the Crisis of Liberalism.* New Brunswick, N.J.: Transaction Publishers.

Kiely, Ray
1998   "Globalization, Post-Fordism and the Contemporary Context of Development." *International Sociology* 13:95–115.

Kilminster, Richard
1993   "Norbert Elias and Karl Mannheim: Closeness and Distance." *Theory, Culture and Society* 10:81–114.

Kilminster, Richard, and Mennell, Stephen
forthcoming "Norbert Elias." In George Ritzer (ed.), *The Blackwell Companion to Major Social Theorists.* Oxford, England, and Cambridge, Mass.: Blackwell.

Kimmel, Michael
1996   *Manhood in America: A Cultural History.* New York: Free Press.

Kimmel, Michael S., and Messner, Michael A. (eds.)
1992   *Men's Lives.* New York: Macmillan.

Kimmerling, Baruch
1992   "Sociology, Ideology, and Nation-Building: The Palestinians and Their Meaning in Israeli Sociology." *American Sociological Review* 57:446–460.

King, Katie
1994   *Theory in Its Feminist Travels: Conversation in U.S. Women's Movements.* Bloomington: Indiana University Press.

Kirk, Gwyn
1997   "Standing on Solid Ground: A Materialist Ecological Feminism." In
            R. Hennessey and C. Ingraham (eds.) *Materialist Feminism*. New York:
            Routledge: 345–363.
Kirk, Gwyn, and Okazawa-Rey, Margo (eds.)
1998   *Women's Lives: Multicultural Perspectives*. Mt. View, Calif.: Mayfield.
Kirkpatrick, Graeme
1994   "Philosophical Foundations of Analytical Marxism." *Science and Society*
            58:34–52.
Kittay, Eva Feder
1984   "Womb Envy: An Explanatory Concept." In Joyce Trebilcot (ed.),
            Mothering: Essays in Feminist Theory. Totowa, N.J.: Rowman and
            Allanheld: 94–128.
Klein, Hilary Manette
1989   "Marxism, Psychoanalysis and Mother Nature." *Feminist Studies* 15:255–278.
Kleinman, Sherryl
1996   *Opposing Ambitions: Gender and Identity in an Alternative Organization*.
            Chicago: University of Chicago Press.
Knorr-Cetina, Karin D.
1981a   "Introduction: The Micro-Sociological Challenge of Macro-Sociology:
            Towards a Reconstruction of Social Theory and Methodology." In K. Knorr-
            Cetina and A. Cicourel (eds.), *Advances in Social Theory and Methodology*.
            New York: Methuen: 1–47.
1981b   *The Manufacture of Knowledge: An Essay on the Constructivist and
            Contextual Nature of Science*. Oxford: Pergamon Press.
Knox, John
1963   "The Concept of Exchange in Sociological Theory: 1884 and 1961." *Social
            Forces* 41:341–346.
Kohn, Melvin L.
1976   "Occupational Structure and Alienation." *American Journal of Sociology*
            82:111–127.
Kolb, William L.
1944   "A Critical Evaluation of Mead's 'I' and 'Me' Concepts." *Social Forces*
            22:291–296.
Korenbaum, Myrtle
1964   Translator's preface to Georges Gurvitch, *The Spectrum of Social Time*.
            Dordrecht, Neth.: D. Reidel: ix–xxvi.
Krais, Beate
1993   "Gender and Symbolic Violence: Female Oppression in the Light of Pierre
            Bourdieu's Theory of Social Practice." In C. Calhoun, E. LiPuma, and M.
            Postone (eds.), *Bourdieu: Critical Perspectives*. Chicago: University of
            Chicago Press: 156–177.
1996   "The Academic Disciplines: Social Field and Culture." *Comparative Social
            Research* 2:93–111.
Kramarae, Cheris, and Spender, Dale (eds.)
1991   *The Knowledge Explosion: Generations of Feminist Scholarship*. New York:
            Macmillan.
Kristeva, Julia
1986   *The Kristeva Reader*. Tori Moi (trans. and ed.). New York: Columbia
            University Press.

Kuhn, Annette, and Wolpe, Ann Marie (eds.)
1978   *Feminism and Materialism: Women and Modes of Production.* London:
            Routledge.
Kuhn, Manford
1964   "Major Trends in Symbolic Interaction Theory in the Past Twenty-Five
            Years." *Sociological Quarterly* 5:61–84.
Kuhn, Thomas
1962   *The Structure of Scientific Revolutions.* Chicago: University of Chicago
            Press.
1970   *The Structure of Scientific Revolutions.* 2nd ed. Chicago: University of
            Chicago Press.
Kuisel, Richard
1993   *Seducing the French: The Dilemma of Americanization.* Berkeley, Calif.:
            University of California Press.
Kurzweil, Edith
1980   *The Age of Structuralism: Lévi-Strauss to Foucault.* New York: Columbia
            University Press.
1987   "Psychoanalysis as the Macro-Micro Link." In J. C. Alexander et al. (eds.),
            The Micro-Macro Link. Berkeley: University of California Press: 237–254.
1995   *Freudians and Feminists.* Boulder, Colo.: Westview Press.
Laclau, Ernesto
1990   "Coming Up for Air." *Marxism Today,* March:25, 27.
Laclau, Ernesto, and Mouffe, Chantal
1985   *Hegemony and Socialist Strategy: Towards a Radical Democratic Politics.*
            London: Verso.
1987   "Post-Marxism without Apologies." *New Left Review* 166:79–106.
Lamont, Michele, and Wuthnow, Robert
1990   "Betwixt and Between: Recent Cultural Sociology in Europe and the United
            States." In G. Ritzer (ed.), *Frontiers of Social Theory: The New Syntheses.*
            New York: Columbia University Press: 287–315.
Lamphere, Louise
1987   *From Working Girls to Working Mothers: Immigrant Women in a New
            England Industrial Community.* Ithaca, N.Y.: Cornell University Press.
Landry, Donna, and MacLean, Gerald
1993   *Materialist Feminisms.* Cambridge, Mass.: Blackwell.
Langsdorf, Lenore
1995   "Treating Method and Form as Phenomena: An Appreciation of Garfinkel's
            Phenomenology of Social Action." *Human Studies* 18:177–188.
Lash, Scott
1988   "Discourse or Figure? Postmodernism as a 'Regime of Signification.' "
            Theory, Culture & Society 5:311–336.
1991   "Introduction." In *Post-Structuralist and Post-Modernist Sociology.*
            Aldershot, Eng.: Edward Elgar: ix–xv.
Lash, Scott, and Urry, John
1987   *The End of Organized Capitalism.* Cambridge: Polity.
Laslett, Barbara, and Thorne, Barrie
1992   "Considering Dorothy Smith's Sociology." *Sociological Theory* 10:60–63.
Laslett, Barbara, and Thorne, Barrie (eds.)
1997   *Feminist Sociology: Life Histories of a Movement.* New York: Routledge.

Laws, Judith Long, and Schwartz, Pepper
1977   *Sexual Scripts: The Social Construction of Female Sexuality.* Hinsdale, Ill.:
            Dryden.
Layder, Derek
1985   "Power, Structure and Agency." *Journal for the Theory of Social Behaviour*
            15:131–149.
Layder, Derek, Ashton, David, and Sung, Johnny
1991   "The Empirical Correlates of Action and Structure: The Transition from
            School to Work." *Sociology* 25:447–464.
Leach, Edmund
1974   *Claude Lévi-Strauss.* New York: Penguin.
Lefebvre, Henri
1962/1995   *Introduction to Modernity.* London: Verso.
1968   *The Sociology of Marx.* New York: Vintage.
Lehman, Edward W.
1988   "The Theory of the State versus the State of Theory." *American Sociological
            Review* 53:807–823.
Leidner, Robin
1991   "Stretching the Boundaries of Liberalism: Democratic Innovation in a
            Feminist Organization." *Signs* 16:263–289.
Lemert, Charles
1979   *Sociology and the Twilight of Man: Homocentrism and Discourse in
            Sociological Theory.* Carbondale: Southern Illinois University Press.
1990   "The Uses of French Structuralisms in Sociology." In G. Ritzer (ed.),
            Frontiers of Social Theory: The New Syntheses. New York: Columbia
            University Press: 230–254.
1992a   "Sociological Metatheory and Its Cultured Despisers." In G. Ritzer (ed.),
            Metatheorizing. Newbury Park, Calif.: Sage: 124–134.
1992b   "Subjectivity's Limit: The Unsolved Riddle of the Standpoint." *Sociological
            Theory* 10:63–72.
1994a   "The Canonical Limits of Durkheim's First Classic." *Sociological Forum*
            9:87–92.
1994b   "Social Theory at the Early End of a Short Century." *Sociological Theory*
            12:140–152.
Lemert, Charles (ed.)
1981   *French Sociology: Rupture and Renewal since 1968.* New York: Columbia
            University Press.
1993   *Social Theory: The Multicultural and Classical Readings.* Boulder, Colo.:
            Westview Press.
LeMoyne, Terri, Falk, William, and Neustadtl, Alan
1994   "Hyperrationality: Historical Antecedents and Contemporary Outcomes
            within Japanese Manufacturing." *Sociological Spectrum* 14:221–240.
Lengermann, Patricia Madoo
1979   "The Founding of the *American Sociological Review.*" *American
            Sociological Review* 44:185–198.
Lengermann, Patricia Madoo, and Niebrugge-Brantley, Jill
1990   "Feminist Sociological Theory: The Near-Future Prospects." In G. Ritzer
            (ed.), *Frontiers of Social Theory: The New Syntheses.* New York: Columbia
            University Press: 316–344.

1995   "Intersubjectivity and Domination: A Feminist Analysis of the Sociology of
                Alfred Schutz." *Sociological Theory* 13:25–36.
1998   *The Women Founders: Sociology and Social Theory, 1830–1930.* New York:
                McGraw-Hill.
forthcoming   "Early Women Sociologists." In George Ritzer, *Classical Sociology.* New
                York: McGraw-Hill: 294–328.
Lengermann, Patricia Madoo, and Wallace, Ruth A.
1985   *Gender in America: Social Control and Social Change.* Englewood Cliffs,
                N.J.: Prentice-Hall.
Lennon, Kathleen, and Whitford, Margaret (eds.)
1994   *Knowing the Difference.* New York: Routledge.
Lenzer, Gertrud (ed.)
1975   *Auguste Comte and Positivism: The Essential Writings.* Magnolia, Mass.:
                Peter Smith.
Leonard, Diana, and Allen, Sheila (eds.)
1991   *Sexual Divisions Revisited.* New York: St. Martin's.
Lepenies, Wolf
1988   *Between Literature and Science: The Rise of Sociology.* Cambridge:
                Cambridge University Press.
Lerner, Gerda
1986   *The Creation of Patriarchy.* New York: Oxford.
1993   *The Creation of Feminist Consciousness.* New York: Oxford.
Lerner, Gerda (ed.)
1972   *Black Women in White America: A Documentary History.* New York: Vintage.
Lester, David (ed.)
1972   *Emile Durkheim: Le Suicide One Hundred Years Later.* Philadelphia: Charles
                Press.
Lever, Janet
1978   "Sex Differences in the Complexity of Children's Play and Games."
                American Sociological Review 43:471–483.
Levi, Margaret, Cook, Karen S., O'Brien, Jodi A., and Faye, Howard
1990   "The Limits of Rationality." In K. S. Cook and M. Levi (eds.), *The Limits of
                Rationality.* Chicago: University of Chicago Press.
Levidow, Les
1990   "Foreclosing the Future." *Science as Culture* 8:59–90.
Levine, Andrew, Sober, Elliot, and Wright, Erik Olin
1987   "Marxism and Methodological Individualism." *New Left Review* 162:67–84.
Levine, Donald
1981   "Rationality and Freedom: Weber and Beyond." *Sociological Inquiry*
                51:5–25.
1989   "Simmel as a Resource for Sociological Metatheory." *Sociological Theory*
                7:161–174.
1991a   "Simmel and Parsons Reconsidered." *American Journal of Sociology*
                96:1097–1116.
1991b   "Simmel as Educator: On Individuality and Modern Culture." *Theory,
                Culture and Society* 8:99–118.
1995   *Visions of the Sociological Tradition.* Chicago: University of Chicago Press.
Levine, Donald, Carter, Ellwood B., and Gorman, Eleanor Miller
1976a   "Simmel's Influence on American Sociology—I." *American Journal of
                Sociology* 81:813–845.

1976b   "Simmel's Influence on American Sociology—II." *American Journal of Sociology* 81:1112–1132.

Lévi-Strauss, Claude
1949   *Les Structures Elementaires de la Parente.* Paris: Presses Universitaires de France.
1963   *Totemism.* Boston: Beacon Press.
1967   *Structural Anthropology.* Garden City, N.Y.: Anchor.

Lewis, J. David, and Smith, Richard L.
1980   *American Sociology and Pragmatism: Mead, Chicago Sociology, and Symbolic Interaction.* Chicago: University of Chicago Press.

Lewis, Reba Rowe
1991   "Forging New Syntheses: Theories and Theorists." *American Sociologist,* Fall/Winter:221–230.

Lilla, Mark
1994   "The Legitimacy of the Liberal Age." In M. Lilla (ed.), *New French Thought: Political Philosophy.* Princeton, N.J.: Princeton University Press: 3–34.

Lindner, Rolf
1996   *The Reportage of Urban Culture: Robert Park and the Chicago School.* Cambridge: Cambridge University Press.

Lipman-Blumen, Jean
1979   "Jessie Bernard." In *International Encyclopedia of the Social Sciences,* Vol. 18. New York: Free Press: 49–56.
1984   *Gender Roles and Power.* Englewood Cliffs, N.J.: Prentice-Hall.

Lipovetsky, Gilles
1987/1994   *The Empire of Fashion: Dressing Modern Democracy.* Princeton, N.J.: Princeton University Press.

Liska, Allen E.
1990   "The Significance of Aggregate Dependent Variables and Contextual Independent Variables for Linking Macro and Micro Theories." *Social Psychology Quarterly* 53:292–301.

Liska, Allen E., and Warner, Barbara
1991   "Functions of Crime: A Paradoxical Process." *American Journal of Sociology* 96:1441–1463.

Lockwood, David
1956   "Some Remarks on *The Social System.*" *British Journal of Sociology* 7:134–146.

Lodahl, Janice B., and Gordon, Gerald
1972   "The Structure of Scientific Fields and the Functioning of University Graduate Departments." *American Sociological Review* 37:57–72.

Lodge, Peter
1986   "Connections: W. I. Thomas, European Social Thought and American Sociology." In R. C. Monk (ed.), *Structures of Knowing.* Lanham, Md.: University Press of America: 135–160.

Longino, Helen E.
1993   "Feminist Standpoint Theory and the Problems of Knowledge." *Signs* 19:201–212.

Lopata, Helena Znaniecka
1996   *Current Widowhood: Myths and Realities.* Thousand Oaks, Calif.: Sage.

Lorber, Judith
1994   *Paradoxes of Gender.* New Haven, Conn.: Yale University Press.
Lorde, Audre
1984   *Sister Outsider: Essays and Speeches.* Trumansburg, N.Y.: Crossings Press.
Lougee, Carolyn C.
1976   *Le Paradis des Femmes: Women, Salons and Social Stratification in Seventeenth-Century France.* Princeton, N.J.: Princeton University Press.
Lovejoy, Arthur
1948   *Essays in the History of Ideas.* Baltimore: Johns Hopkins University Press.
Lovell, David W.
1992   "Socialism, Utopianism and the 'Utopian Socialists.' " *History of European Ideas* 14:185–201.
Lowy, Michael
1996   "Figures of Weberian Marxism." *Theory and Society* 25:431–446.
Luhmann, Niklas
1980/1981/ *Gesellschaftsstruktur und Semantik. Studien zur Wissenssoziologie der*
1989/1995   *modernen Gesellschaft.* 4 vols. Frankfurt am Main: Suhrkamp.
1982a   "The World Society as a Social System." *International Journal of General Systems* 8:131–138.
1982b   *The Differentiation of Society.* New York: Columbia University Press.
1982/1986   *Liebe als Passion/Love as Passion.* Frankfurt am Main: Suhrkamp/Cambridge: Polity Press.
1984/1995   *Soziale Systeme. Grundreiner allgemeinen Theorie/Social Systems: Outline of a General Theory.* Frankfurt am Main: Suhrkamp/Stanford, Calif.: Stanford University Press.
1985   "Complexity and Meaning." In S. Aida et al. (eds.), *The Science and Praxis of Complexity.* Tokyo: United Nations University: 99–104.
1986   "The Autopoiesis of Social Systems." In R. F. Geyer and J. van der Zouwen (eds.), *Sociocybernetic Paradoxes: Observation, Control and Evolution of Self-Steering Systems.* London: Sage: 172–192.
1986/1989   *Okologische Kommunikation. Kann die moderne Gesellschaft sich auf okologische Gefahrdungen einstellen?/Ecological Communication.* Opladen: Westdeutscher Verlag/Cambridge: Polity Press.
1987   "Modern Systems Theory and the Theory of Society." In V. Meja, D. Misgeld, and N. Stehr (eds.), *Modern German Sociology.* New York: Columbia University Press: 173–186.
1988   *Die Wirtschaft der Gesellschaft.* Frankfurt am Main: Suhrkamp.
1990a   *Die Wissenschaft der Gesellschaft.* Frankfurt am Main: Suhrkamp.
1990b   "The Paradox of System Differentiation and the Evolution of Society." In J. C. Alexander and P. Colomy (eds.), *Differentiation Theory and Social Change: Comparative and Historical Perspectives.* New York: Columbia University Press: 409–440.
1991   *Soziologie des Risikos.* Berlin; New York: de Gruyter.
1993   *Das Recht der Gesellschaft.* Frankfurt am Main: Suhrkamp.
1995   *Die Kunst der Gesellschaft.* Frankfurt am Main: Suhrkamp.
1997   *Die Gesellschaft der Gesellschaft.* 2 vols. Frankfurt am Main: Suhrkamp.
Lukács, Georg
1922/1968   *History and Class Consciousness.* Cambridge, Mass.: MIT Press.
1991   "Georg Simmel." *Theory, Culture and Society* 8:145–150.

Lukes, Steven
1972   *Emile Durkheim: His Life and Work.* New York: Harper & Row.
1977   "Power and Structure." In S. Lukes, *Essays in Social Theory.* London:
            Macmillan: 3–29.
Luscher, Kurt
1990   "The Social Reality of Perspectives: On G. H. Mead's Potential Relevance
            for the Analysis of Contemporary Societies." *Symbolic Interaction* 13:1–18.
Luttrell, Wendy
1992   " 'The Teachers, They All Had Their Pets': Concepts of Gender, Knowledge
            and Power." *Signs* 18:505–546.
Luxemburg, Rosa
1971   "Women's Suffrage and Class Struggle." In D. Howard (ed.), *Selected
            Political Writings.* New York: Monthly Review Press: 219–220.
Luxenberg, Stan
1985   *Roadside Empires: How the Chains Franchised America.* New York: Viking.
Lyman, Stanford, and Scott, Marvin
1970   *A Sociology of the Absurd.* New York: Appleton-Century-Crofts.
Lynch, Michael
1985   *Art and Artifact in Laboratory Science: A Study of Shop Work and Shop Talk
            in a Research Laboratory.* London: Routledge and Kegan Paul.
1991   "Pictures of Nothing? Visual Construals in Social Theory." *Sociological
            Theory* 9:1–21.
1993   *Scientific Practice and Ordinary Action: Ethnomethodology and Social
            Studies of Science.* Cambridge: Cambridge University Press.
Lynch, Michael, and Bogen, David
1991   "In Defense of Dada-Driven Analysis." *Sociological Theory* 9:269–276.
Lyotard, Jean-François
1984   *The Postmodern Condition.* Minneapolis: University of Minnesota Press.
Mackay, Robert W.
1974   "Words, Utterances and Activities." In R. Turner (ed.), *Ethnomethodology:
            Selected Readings.* Harmondsworth, Eng.: Penguin: 197–215.
MacKinnon, Catherine
1979   *Sexual Harassment of Working Women.* New Haven, Conn.: Yale University
            Press.
1982   "Feminism, Marxism, Method and the State: An Agenda for Theory." In
            N. O. Keohane et al. (eds.), *Feminist Theory: A Critique of Ideology.*
            Chicago: University of Chicago Press: 1–30.
1989   *Towards a Feminist Theory of the State.* Cambridge, Mass.: Harvard
            University Press.
1993   *Only Words.* Cambridge, Mass.: Harvard University Press.
Mahoney, Maureen A., and Yngvesson, Barbara
1992   "The Construction of Subjectivity and the Paradox of Resistance:
            Reintegrating Feminist Anthropology and Psychology." *Signs* 18:44–73.
Maines, David R.
1977   "Social Organization and Social Structure in Symbolic Interactionist
            Thought." In A. Inkeles, J. Coleman, and N. Smelser (eds.), *Annual Review
            of Sociology.* Vol. 3. Palo Alto, Calif.: Annual Reviews: 259–285.
1988   "Myth, Text, and Interactionist Complicity in the Neglect of Blumer's
            Macrosociology." *Symbolic Interaction* 11:43–57.

1989a   "Repackaging Blumer: The Myth of Herbert Blumer's Astructural Bias." *Symbolic Interaction* 10:383–413.

1989b   "Herbert Blumer on the Possibility of Science in the Practice of Sociology: Further Thoughts." *Journal of Contemporary Ethnography* 18:160–177.

1996   "On Postmodernism, Pragmatism, and Plasterers: Some Interactionist Thoughts and Queries." *Symbolic Interaction* 19:323–340.

Maines, David, Bridger, Jeffrey C., and Ulmer, Jeffery T.

1996   "Mythic Facts and Park's Pragmatism: On Predecessor-Selection and Theorizing in Human Ecology." *Sociological Quarterly* 37:521–549.

Maines, David R., and Morrione, Thomas J.

1990   "On the Breadth and Relevance of Blumer's Perspective: Introduction to His Analysis of Industrialization." In H. Blumer, *Industrialization as an Agent of Social Change: A Critical Analysis.* New York: Aldine de Gruyter.

Mandel, Ernest

1975   *Late Capitalism.* London: New Left Books.

Mandelbaum, Jenny

1989   "Interpersonal Activities in Conversational Storytelling." *Western Journal of Speech Communications* 53:114–126.

Manent, Pierre

1994/1998   *The City of Man.* Princeton, N.J.: Princeton University Press.

Manis, Jerome, and Meltzer, Bernard (eds.)

1978   *Symbolic Interaction: A Reader in Social Psychology.* 3rd ed. Boston: Allyn and Bacon.

Mann, Michael

1986   *The Sources of Social Power,* Vol. 1. New York: Cambridge University Press.

Mann, Susan A., Grimes, Michael D., and Kemp, Alice Abel

1997   "Paradigm Shifts in Family Sociology? Evidence from Three Decades of Family Textbooks." *Journal of Family Issues* 18:315–349.

Mann, Susan A., and Kelley, Lori R.

1997   "Standing at the Crossroads of Modernist Thought—Collins, Smith, and the New Feminist Epistemologies." *Gender & Society* 11:391–408.

Mannheim, Karl

1931/1936   "The Sociology of Knowledge." In K. Mannheim, *Ideology and Utopia.* New York: Harcourt, Brace and World: 264–311.

Manning, Philip

1991   "Drama as Life: The Significance of Goffman's Changing Use of the Theatrical Metaphor." *Sociological Theory* 9:70–86.

1992   *Erving Goffman and Modern Sociology.* Stanford, Calif.: Stanford University Press.

Manning, Philip, and Ray, George

1993   "Shyness, Self-Confidence, and Social Interaction." *Social Psychology Quarterly* 56:178–192.

Manuel, Frank

1962   *The Prophets of Paris.* Cambridge, Mass.: Harvard University Press.

Marcuse, Herbert

1958   *Soviet Marxism: A Critical Analysis.* New York: Columbia University Press.

1964   *One-Dimensional Man.* Boston: Beacon Press.

1969   *An Essay on Liberation.* Boston: Beacon Press.

Marini, Margaret M.
1988   "Sociology of Gender." In E. F. Borgatta and K. S. Cook (eds.), *The Future of Sociology.* Beverly Hills, Calif.: Sage: 374–393.
Markovsky, Barry
1987   "Toward Multilevel Sociological Theories: Simulations of Actor and Network Effects." *Sociological Theory* 5:101–117.
Marks, Elaine, and de Courtivron, Isabelle (eds.)
1980   *New French Feminisms.* Amherst: University of Massachusetts Press.
Marlaire, Courtney L., and Maynard, Douglas W.
1990   "Standardized Testing as an Interactional Phenomenon." *Sociology of Education* 63:83–101.
Martin, Karin
1998   "Becoming a Gendered Body: Practices of Preschools." *American Sociological Review* 63:494–511.
Martin, Wendy
1972   *The American Sisterhood: Writings of the Feminist Movement from Colonial Times to Present.* New York: Harper & Row.
Marx, Karl
1842/1977   "Communism and the *Augsburger Allegemeine Zeitung.*" In D. McLellan (ed.), *Karl Marx: Selected Writings.* New York: Oxford University Press: 20.
1847/1963   *The Poverty of Philosophy.* New York: International Publishers.
1852/1970   "The Eighteenth Brumaire of Louis Bonaparte." In R. C. Tucker (ed.), *The Marx-Engels Reader.* New York: Norton: 436–525.
1857–1858/ *Pre-Capitalist Economic Formations,* Eric J. Hobsbawm (ed.). New York:
1964   International Publishers.
1857–1858/ *The Grundrisse: Foundations of the Critique of Political Economy.* New
1974   York: Random House.
1859/1970   *A Contribution to the Critique of Political Economy.* New York: International Publishers.
1862–1863/ *Theories of Surplus Value,* Part I. Moscow: Progress Publishers.
1963
1862–1863/ *Theories of Surplus Value,* Part II. Moscow: Progress Publishers.
1968
1867/1967   *Capital: A Critique of Political Economy,* Vol. 1. New York: International Publishers.
1869/1963   *The 18th Brumaire of Louis Bonaparte.* New York: International Publishers.
1884/1991   *Capital,* Vol. 2. New York: Vintage Books.
1932/1964   *The Economic and Philosophic Manuscripts of 1844,* Dirk J. Struik (ed.). New York: International Publishers.
Marx, Karl, and Engels, Friedrich
1845/1956   *The Holy Family.* Moscow: Foreign Language Publishing House.
1845–1846/ *The German Ideology,* Part 1. C. J. Arthur (ed.). New York: International
1970   Publishers.
1848/1948   *Manifesto of the Communist Party.* New York: International Publishers.
Maryanski, Alexandra
1994   "The Pursuit of Human Nature in Sociobiology and Evolutionary Sociology." *Sociological Perspectives* 37:375–389.

Maryanski, Alexandra, and Turner, Jonathan H.
1991 "The Offspring of Functionalism: French and British Structuralism." *Sociological Theory* 9:106–115.
1992 *The Social Cage: Human Nature and the Evolution of Society.* Stanford, Calif.: Stanford University Press.

Masterman, Margaret
1970 "The Nature of a Paradigm." In I. Lakatos and A. Musgrove (eds.), *Criticism and the Growth of Knowledge.* Cambridge: Cambridge University Press: 59–89.

Masters, William, and Johnson, Virginia
1966 *Human Sexual Response.* Boston: Little, Brown.

Matthews, Fred H.
1977 *Quest for an American Sociology: Robert E. Park and the Chicago School.* Montreal: McGill University Press.

Matthews, Glenna
1992 *Women's Power and Women's Place in the United States 1630–1970.* New York: Oxford University Press.

Maturana, Humberto R., and Varela, F. G.
1980 *Autopoiesis and Cognition: The Realization of the Living.* Dordrecht, Neth.: Reidel.

Mauss, Marcel
1954 *The Gift.* Ian Cunnison (trans.). London: Cohen and West.

Mayer, Tom
1994 *Analytical Marxism.* Thousand Oaks, Calif.: Sage.

Mayhew, Bruce
1980 "Structuralism versus Individualism: Part I, Shadowboxing in the Dark." *Social Forces* 59:335–375.
1981 "Structuralism versus Individualism: Part II, Ideological and Other Obfuscations." *Social Forces* 59:627–648.

Maynard, Douglas W.
1991a "Interaction and Asymmetry in Clinical Discourse." *American Journal of Sociology* 97:448–495.
1991b "Goffman, Garfinkel and Games." *Sociological Theory* 9:277–279.

Maynard, Douglas W., and Clayman, Steven E.
1991 "The Diversity of Ethnomethodology." *Annual Review of Sociology* 17:385–418.

McCarthy, Thomas
1982 *The Critical Theory of Jurgen Habermas.* Cambridge, Mass.: MIT Press.
1984 "Translator's Introduction." In J. Habermas, *The Theory of Communicative Action.* Boston: Beacon Press.

McCaughey, Martha
1997 *Real Knockouts: The Physical Feminism of Women's Self-Defense.* New York: New York University Press.

McCreary, Edward A.
1964 *The Americanization of Europe: The Impact of Americans and American Business on the Uncommon Market.* Garden City, N.Y.: Doubleday.

McDermott, Patrice
1994 *Politics and Scholarship: Feminist Academic Journals and the Production of Knowledge.* Champaign: University of Illinois Press.

McGuire, Gail M., and Reskin, Barbara F.
1993 "Authority Hierarchies of Race and Sex." *Gender & Society* 7:487–506.

McKinney, John C.
1966 *Constructive Typology and Social Theory.* New York: Appleton-Century-Crofts.
McLean, Paul D.
1998 "A Frame Analysis of Favor Seeking in the Renaissance: Agency, Networks, and Political Culture." *American Journal of Sociology* 104:51–91.
McLellan, David
1973 *Karl Marx: His Life and Thought.* New York: Harper Colophon.
McLellan, David (ed.)
1971 *The Thought of Karl Marx.* New York: Harper Torchbooks.
McMahon, A. M.
1984 "The Two Social Psychologies: Postcrises Directions." In R. H. Turner and J. F. Short (eds.), *Annual Review of Sociology,* Vol. 10. Palo Alto, Calif.: Annual Reviews: 121–140.
McMahon, Martha
1995 *Engendering Motherhood: Identity and Self-Transformation in Women's Lives.* New York: Guilford Press.
McPhail, Clark, and Rexroat, Cynthia
1979 "Mead vs. Blumer." *American Sociological Review* 44:449–467.
1980 Rejoinder: "*Ex Cathedra* Blumer or *Ex Libris* Mead?" *American Sociological Review* 45:420–430.
Mead, George Herbert
1934/1962 *Mind, Self and Society: From the Standpoint of a Social Behaviorist.* Chicago: University of Chicago Press.
1936 *Movements of Thought in the Nineteenth Century.* Chicago: University of Chicago Press.
1938/1972 *The Philosophy of the Act.* Chicago: University of Chicago Press.
1959 *The Philosophy of the Present.* LaSalle, Ill.: Open Court Publishing.
1982 *The Individual and the Social Self: Unpublished Work of George Herbert Mead.* Chicago: University of Chicago Press.
Mehan, Hugh, and Wood, Houston
1975 *The Reality of Ethnomethodology.* New York: Wiley.
Meiksins, Peter
1994 "Labor and Monopoly Capital for the 1990s: A Review and Critique of the Labor Process Debate." *Monthly Review* 46:45–59.
Meisenhelder, Tom
1997 "Pierre Bourdieu and the Call for a Reflexive Sociology." *Current Perspectives in Social Theory* 17:159–183.
Meltzer, Bernard
1964/1978 "Mead's Social Psychology." In J. Manis and B. Meltzer (eds.), *Symbolic Interaction: A Reader in Social Psychology.* 3rd ed. Boston: Allyn and Bacon: 15–27.
Meltzer, Bernard, Petras, James, and Reynolds, Larry
1975 *Symbolic Interactionism: Genesis, Varieties and Criticisms.* London: Routledge and Kegan Paul.
Menard, Scott
1995 "A Developmental Test of Mertonian Anomie Theory." *Journal of Research in Crime and Delinquency* 32:136–174.
Mennell, Stephen
1992 *Norbert Elias: An Introduction.* Oxford: Blackwell.

Mennell, Stephen, and Goudsblom, Johan (eds.)
1998   *Norbert Elias: On Civilization, Power, and Knowledge.* Chicago: University
            of Chicago Press.
Merton, Robert K.
1949/1968   "Manifest and Latent Functions." In R. K. Merton, *Social Theory and Social
            Structure.* New York: Free Press: 73–138.
1968   *Social Theory and Social Structure.* New York: Free Press.
1975   "Structural Analysis in Sociology." In P. Blau (ed.), *Approaches to the Study
            of Social Structure.* New York: Free Press: 21–52.
1976   *Sociological Ambivalence.* New York: Free Press.
1980   "Remembering the Young Talcott Parsons." *American Sociologist* 15:68–71.
1986   "Comments." In S. Lindenberg, J. S. Coleman, and S. Nowak (eds.),
            Approaches to Social Theory. New York: Russell Sage Foundation: 61–62.
1989   "The Sorokin–Merton Correspondence on 'Puritanism, Pietism and Science,'
            1933–34." *Science in Context* 3:291–298.
1995   "Opportunity Structure: The Emergence, Diffusion, and Differentiation of a
            Sociological Concept, 1930s–1950s." In F. Adler and W. S. Laufer (eds.),
            The Legacy of Anomie Theory. New Brunswick, N.J.: Transaction Publishers.
Messner, Michael A.
1997   *Politics of Masculinities: Men in Movements.* Thousand Oaks, Calif.: Sage.
Mestrovic, Stjepan G.
1988   *Emile Durkheim and the Reformation of Sociology.* Totowa, N.J.: Rowman
            and Littlefield.
1992   *Durkheim and Postmodern Culture.* New York: Aldine de Gruyter.
1998   *Anthony Giddens: The Last Modernist.* London: Routledge.
Mészáros, István
1995   *Beyond Capital.* New York: Monthly Review Press.
Meyrowitz, Joshua
1995   "New Sense of Politics: How Television Changes the Political Drama."
            Research in Political Sociology 7:117–138.
Miller, David
1973   *George Herbert Mead: Self, Language and the World.* Austin: University of
            Texas Press.
1981   "The Meaning of Role-Taking." *Symbolic Interaction* 4:167–175.
1982a   "Introduction." In G. H. Mead, *The Individual and the Social Self:
            Unpublished Work of George Herbert Mead.* Chicago: University of Chicago
            Press: 1–26.
1982b   Review of J. David Lewis and Richard L. Smith, *American Sociology and
            Pragmatism. Journal of the History of Sociology* 4:108–114.
1985   "Concerning J. David Lewis' Response to My Review of *American
            Sociology and Pragmatism.*" *Journal of the History of Sociology* 5:131–133.
Miller, James
1993   *The Passion of Michel Foucault.* New York: Anchor Books.
Miller, Jean Baker
1976   *Toward a New Psychology of Women.* Boston: Beacon Press.
Miller, W. Watts
1993   "Durkheim's Montesquieu." *British Journal of Sociology* 44:693–712.
Millett, Kate
1970   *Sexual Politics.* Garden City, N.Y.: Doubleday.

Millman, Marcia
1991   *Warm Hearts and Cold Cash: The Intimate Dynamics of Families and Money*. New York: Free Press.
Mills, C. Wright
1951   *White Collar*. New York: Oxford University Press.
1956   *The Power Elite*. New York: Oxford University Press.
1959   *The Sociological Imagination*. New York: Oxford University Press.
1960   *Listen Yankee: The Revolution in Cuba*. New York: McGraw-Hill.
1962   *The Marxists*. New York: Dell.
Milovanovic, Dragan
1995   "Dueling Paradigms: Modernist versus Postmodernist Thought." *Humanity and Society* 19:19–44.
Mirowsky, John, and Ross, Catherine E.
1995   "Sex Differences in Distress: Real or Artifact?" *American Sociological Review* 60:449–468.
Mitchell, Jack N.
1978   *Social Exchange, Dramaturgy and Ethnomethodology: Toward a Paradigmatic Synthesis*. New York: Elsevier.
Mitchell, Juliet
1975   *Psychoanalysis and Feminism*. New York: Vintage.
Mitroff, Ian
1974   "Norms and Counter-Norms in a Select Group of the Apollo Moon Scientists: A Case Study of the Ambivalence of Scientists." *American Sociological Review* 39:579–595.
Mitroff, Ian, and Kilmann, Ralph
1978   *Methodological Approaches to Social Science*. San Francisco: Jossey-Bass.
Mitzman, Arthur
1969   *The Iron Cage: An Historical Interpretation of Max Weber*. New York: Grosset and Dunlap.
Mizruchi, Mark
1990   "Cohesion, Structural Equivalence, and Similarity of Behavior: An Approach to the Study of Corporate Political Power." *Sociological Theory* 8:16–32.
1994   "Social Network Analysis: Recent Achievements and Current Controversies." *Acta Sociologica* 37:329–343.
Mizruchi, Mark S., and Koenig, Thomas
1986   "Economic Sources of Corporate Political Consensus: An Examination of Interindustry Relations." *American Sociological Review* 51:482–491.
Mohanty, Chandra Talpade
1991   "Under Western Eyes: Feminist Scholarship and Colonial Discourses." In C. Mohanty, A. Russo, L. Torres (eds.), *Third World Women and the Politics of Feminism*. Bloomington: Indiana University Press:
Moi, Toril (ed.)
1986   *The Kristeva Reader*. New York: Columbia University Press.
Molm, Linda D.
1988   "The Structure and Use of Power: A Comparison of Reward and Punishment Power." *Social Psychology Quarterly* 51:108–122.
1989   "Punishment Power: A Balancing Process in Power-Dependence Relations." *American Journal of Sociology* 94:1392–1418.

1991   "Affect and Social Exchange: Satisfaction in Power-Dependence Relations."
            American Sociological Review 56:475–493.
1994   "Is Punishment Effective? Coercive Strategies in Social Exchange." *Social
            Psychology Quarterly* 57:75–94.
1997   *Coercive Power in Exchange.* Cambridge: Cambridge University Press.
Molm, Linda D., and Cook, Karen S.
1995   "Social Exchange and Exchange Networks." In K. S. Cook, G. A. Fine, and
            J. S. House (eds.), *Sociological Perspectives on Social Psychology.* Boston:
            Allyn and Bacon: 209–235.
Molm, Linda D., Quist, Theron M., and Wisely, Phillip A.
1994   "Imbalanced Structures, Unfair Strategies: Power and Justice in Social
            Exchange." *American Sociological Review* 59:98–121.
Mommsen, Wolfgang J.
1974   *The Age of Bureaucracy.* New York: Harper & Row.
Momsen, Janet (ed.)
1993   *Women and Change in the Caribbean.* Bloomington: Indiana University
            Press.
Moore, Wilbert E.
1978   "Functionalism." In T. Bottomore and R. Nisbet (eds.), *A History of
            Sociological Analysis.* New York: Basic Books: 321–361.
Moraga, Cherrie, and Anzaldua, Gloria
1981   *This Bridge Called My Back: Writings by Radical Women of Color.*
            Watertown, Mass.: Persephone Press.
Morgan, Leslie A.
1991   *After Marriage Ends: Economic Consequences for Midlife Women.* Newbury
            Park, Calif.: Sage.
Morgan, Robin
1970   *Sisterhood Is Powerful: An Anthology of Writings from the Women's
            Liberation Movement.* New York: Vintage.
Morrione, Thomas J.
1988   "Herbert G. Blumer (1900–1987): A Legacy of Concepts, Criticisms, and
            Contributions." *Symbolic Interaction* 11:1–12.
Morrow, Raymond A.
1994   "Critical Theory, Poststructuralism, and Critical Theory." *Current
            Perspectives in Social Theory* 14:27–51.
Morrow, Raymond A., and Brown, David D.
1994   *Critical Theory and Methodology.* Thousand Oaks, Calif.: Sage.
Morse, Chandler
1961   "The Functional Imperatives." In M. Black (ed.), *The Social Theories of
            Talcott Parsons.* Englewood Cliffs, N.J.: Prentice-Hall: 100–152.
Morton, Donald
1996   "The Politics of Queer Theory in the (Post)Modern Moment." In Mary F.
            Rogers (ed.), *Multicultural Experiences, Multicultural Theories.* New York:
            McGraw-Hill: 90–98.
Moscovici, Serge
1993   *The Invention of Society.* Cambridge, Mass.: Polity, 1993.
Moses, Claire Goldberg, and Rabine, Leslie Wahl
1993   *Feminism, Socialism and French Romanticism.* Bloomington: Indiana
            University Press.

Mouffe, Chantal
1988   "Radical Democracy: Modern or Postmodern?" In A. Ross (ed.), *Universal Abandon? The Politics of Postmodernism.* Minneapolis: University of Minnesota Press: 31–45.
Mouzelis, Nicos
1997   "In Defence of the Sociological Canon: A Reply to David Parker." *Sociological Review* 97:244–253.
Mueller-Vollmer, Kurt
1985   "Language, Mind and Artifact: An Outline of Hermeneutic Theory since the Enlightenment." In K. Mueller-Vollmer (ed.), *The Hermeneutics Reader.* New York: Continuum: 1–53.
Mullins, Nicholas
1973   *Theories and Theory Groups in Contemporary American Sociology.* New York: Harper & Row.
1983   "Theories and Theory Groups Revisited." In R. Collins (ed.), *Sociological Theory—1983.* San Francisco: Jossey-Bass: 319–337.
Münch, Richard
1987   "The Interpenetration of Microinteraction and Macrostructures in a Complex and Contingent Institutional Order." In J. C. Alexander, et al. (eds.), *The Micro-Macro Link.* Berkeley: University of California Press: 319–336.
1991   "American and European Social Theory: Cultural Identities and Social Forms of Theory Production." *Sociological Perspectives* 34:313–336.
Münch, Richard, and Smelser, Neil J.
1987   "Relating the Micro and Macro." In J. C. Alexander, et al. (eds.), *The Micro-Macro Link.* Berkeley: University of California Press. 356–387.
Musolf, Gil Richard
1994   "William James and Symbolic Interactionism." *Sociological Focus* 27:303–314.
Nash, Bradley, Jr., and Wardell, Mark
1993   "The Control of Sociological Theory: In Praise of the Interregnum." *Sociological Inquiry* 63:276–292.
Natanson, Maurice
1973a   "Introduction." In A. Schutz, *Collected Papers I: The Problem of Social Reality.* The Hague: Martinus Nijhoff: xxv–xlvii.
1973b   *The Social Dynamics of George H. Mead.* The Hague: Martinus Nijhoff.
Nedelmann, Birgitta, and Sztompka, Piotr
1993   "Introduction." In B. Nedelmann and P. Sztompka (eds.), *Sociology in Europe: In Search of Identity.* Berlin: Walter de Gruyter: 1–23.
Newman, Katherine S.
1993   *Declining Fortunes: The Withering of the American Dream.* New York: Basic Books.
Nicholson, Linda
1994   "Interpreting Gender." *Signs* 20:79–105.
Nicolaus, Martin
1974   "Foreword." In K. Marx, *The Grundrisse.* New York: Random House: 7–63.
Nisbet, Robert
1959   "Comment." *American Sociological Review* 24:479–481.
1967   *The Sociological Tradition.* New York: Basic Books.

Noblit, George W., and Hare, R. Dwight
1988   *Meta-Ethnography: Synthesizing Qualitative Studies.* Newbury Park, Calif.:
            Sage.
Olson, Richard
1993   *The Emergence of the Social Sciences. 1642–1792.* New York: Twayne.
O'Neill, William L.
1971   *A History of Feminism in America.* Chicago: Quadrangle Books.
Orbell, John
1993   "*Hamlet* and the Psychology of Rational Choice under Uncertainty."
            Rationality and Society 5:127–140.
Orbuch, Terri L.
1997   "People's Accounts Count: The Sociology of Accounts." In John Hagan and
            Karen S. Cook (eds.), *Annual Review of Sociology,* Vol. 23. Palo Alto, Calif.:
            Annual Reviews: 455–478.
Orr, Catherine M.
1997   "Charting the Currents of the Third Wave." *Hypatia* 12:29–43.
Osterberg, Dag
1988   *Metasociology: An Inquiry into the Origins and Validity of Social Thought.*
            Oslo: Norwegian University Press.
Outhwaite, William
1994   *Habermas: A Critical Introduction.* Stanford, Calif.: Stanford University
            Press.
Owen, David (ed.)
1997   *Sociology after Postmodernism.* London: Sage.
Pareto, Vilfredo
1935   *A Treatise on General Sociology.* 4 vols. New York: Dover.
Park, Robert E.
1927/1973   "Life History." *American Journal of Sociology* 79:251–260.
Parker, David
1997   "Why Bother with Durkheim?" *Sociological Review* 45:122–146.
Parker, Mike, and Slaughter, Jane
1990   "Management-by-Stress: The Team Concept in the US Auto Industry."
            Science as Culture 8:27–58.
Parsons, Talcott
1934–1935   "The Place of Ultimate Values in Sociological Theory." *International
            Journal of Ethics* 45:282–316.
1937   *The Structure of Social Action.* New York: McGraw-Hill.
1942   "Some Sociological Aspects of the Fascist Movements." *Social Forces*
            21:138–147.
1947   "Certain Primary Sources and Patterns of Aggression in the Social Structure
            of the Western World." *Psychiatry* 10:167–181.
1949   *The Structure of Social Action.* 2nd ed. New York: McGraw-Hill.
1951   *The Social System.* Glencoe, Ill.: Free Press.
1954a   "The Prospects of Sociological Theory." In T. Parsons (ed.), *Essays in
            Sociological Theory.* New York: Free Press: 348–369.
1954b   "The Present Position and Prospects of Systematic Theory in Sociology." In
            T. Parsons. (ed.), *Essays in Sociological Theory.* New York: Free Press:
            212–237.

1954c	"Age and Sex in the Social Structure of the United States." In T. Parsons (ed.), *Essays in Sociological Theory.* New York: Free Press.
1960	"A Sociological Approach to the Theory of Organizations." In T. Parsons (ed.), *Structure and Process in Modern Societies.* New York: Free Press: 16–58.
1961	"Some Considerations on the Theory of Social Change." *Rural Sociology* 26:219–239.
1964	"Levels of Organization and the Mediation of Social Interaction." *Sociological Inquiry* 34:207–220.
1966	*Societies.* Englewood Cliffs, N.J.: Prentice-Hall.
1970a	*Social Structure and Personality.* New York: Free Press.
1970b	"On Building Social System Theory: A Personal History." *Daedalus* 99:826–881.
1971	*The System of Modern Societies.* Englewood Cliffs, N.J.: Prentice-Hall.
1974	"Comment on Turner, 'Parsons as a Symbolic Interactionist.' " *Sociological Inquiry* 45:62–65.
1975	"Social Structure and the Symbolic Media of Interchange." In P. Blau (ed.), *Approaches to the Study of Social Structure.* New York: Free Press: 94–100.
1977a	"General Introduction." In T. Parsons (ed.), *Social Systems and the Evolution of Action Theory.* New York: Free Press: 1–13.
1977b	"On Building Social System Theory: A Personal History." In T. Parsons (ed.), *Social Systems and the Evolution of Action Theory.* New York: Free Press: 22–76.
1990	"Prolegomena to a Theory of Social Institutions." *American Sociological Review* 55:319–333.

Parsons, Talcott, and Platt, Gerald
1973   *The American University.* Cambridge, Mass.: Harvard University Press.
Parsons, Talcott, and Shils, Edward A. (eds.)
1951   *Toward a General Theory of Action.* Cambridge, Mass.: Harvard University Press.
Passaro, Joanne
1996   *The Unequal Homeless: Men in the Streets, Women in Their Place.* New York: Routledge.
Pateman, Carol
1989   *The Disorder of Women: Democracy, Feminism, and Political Theory.* Stanford, Calif.: Stanford University Press.
Paulsen, Micheal B., and Feldman, Kenneth A.
1995   "Toward a Reconceptualization of Scholarship: A Human Action System with Functional Imperatives." *Journal of Higher Education* 66:615–640.
Peel, J. D. Y.
1971   *Herbert Spencer: The Evolution of a Sociologist.* New York: Basic Books.
Pelaez, Eloina, and Holloway, John
1990   "Learning to Bow: Post-Fordism and Technological Determinism." *Science as Culture* 8:15–26.
Pemberton, Gayle
1992   *The Hottest Water in Chicago: Family, Race, Time and American Culture.* Boston: Faber and Faber.
Perinbanayagam, Robert S.
1985   *Signifying Acts: Structure and Meaning in Everyday Life.* Carbondale: Southern Illinois University Press.

Perrin, Robert
1976   "Herbert Spencer's Four Theories of Social Evolution." *American Journal of Sociology* 81:1339–1359.
Perry, Wilhelmia E., Abbott, James R., and Hutter, Mark
1997   "The Symbolic Interactionist Paradigm and Urban Sociology." *Research in Urban Sociology* 4:59–92.
Peters, Michael
1994   "Habermas, Post-Structuralism and the Question of Postmodernity: The Defiant Periphery." *Social Analysis* 36:3–20.
Peterson, V. Spike, and Runyan, Anne Sisson
1993   *Global Gender Issues.* Boulder, Colo.: Westview Press.
Phelan, Sandra
1989   *Identity Politics: Lesbian Feminism and the Limits of Community.* Philadelphia: Temple University Press.
Phelan, Shane
1994   *Getting Specific: Postmodern Lesbian Politics.* Minneapolis: University of Minnesota Press.
Phillips, Anne
1993   *Democracy and Difference.* University Park: Pennsylvania State University Press.
Phillips, Derek
1973   "Paradigms, Falsifications and Sociology." *Acta Sociologica* 16:13–31.
1975   "Paradigms and Incommensurability." *Theory and Society* 2:37–62.
Piccone, Paul
1990   "Paradoxes of *Perestroika.*" *Telos* 84:3–32.
Pickering, Mary
1993   *Auguste Comte: An Intellectual Biography.* Vol. 1. Cambridge: Cambridge University Press.
1997   "A New Look at Auguste Comte." In Charles Camic (ed.), *Reclaiming the Sociological Classics: The State of Scholarship.* Oxford: Blackwell: 11–44.
forthcoming "Auguste Comte." In George Ritzer (ed.), *The Blackwell Companion to Major Social Theorists.* Oxford, England, and Cambridge, Mass.: Blackwell.
Pierce, Jennifer
1995   *Gender Trials: Emotional Lives in Contemporary Law Firms.* Berkeley: University of California Press.
Poggi, Gianfranco
1993   *Money and the Modern Mind: Georg Simmel's Philosophy of Money.* Berkeley: University of California Press.
Polit, Denise F., and Falbo, Toni
1987   "Only Children and Personality Development: A Quantitative Review." *Journal of Marriage and the Family* 49:309–325.
Pollitt, Katha
1990   " 'Fetal Rights': A New Assault on Feminism." *Nation* March 26:17–23.
Pollner, Melvin
1987   *Mundane Reason: Reality in Everyday and Sociological Discourse.* Cambridge: Cambridge University Press.
1991   "Left of Ethnomethodology: The Rise and Decline of Radical Reflexivity." *American Sociological Review* 56:370–380.

Porpora, Douglas
1989   "Four Concepts of Social Structure." *Journal for the Theory of Social
            Behaviour* 19:195–211.
Portes, Alejandro, and Landolt, Patricia
1996   "The Downside of Social Capital." *American Prospect* 26:18–21.
Postone, Moishe, LiPuma, Edward, and Calhoun, Craig
1993   "Introduction: Bourdieu and Social Theory." In C. Calhoun, E. LiPuma, and
            M. Postone (eds.), *Bourdieu: Critical Perspectives.* Chicago: University of
            Chicago Press: 1–13.
Powers, Charles H.
1986   *Vilfredo Pareto.* Newbury Park, Calif.: Sage.
Prus, Robert
1996   *Symbolic Interaction and Ethnographic Research: Intersubjectivity and the
            Study of Human Lived Experience.* Albany: State University of
            New York Press.
Przeworski, Adam
1985   *Capitalism and Social Democracy.* Cambridge: Cambridge University Press.
Puner, Helen Walker
1947   *Freud: His Life and His Mind.* New York: Dell.
Pyke, Karen D.
1996   "Class-Based Masculinities: The Interdependence of Gender, Class, and
            Interpersonal Power." *Gender & Society* 10:527–549.
Quadagno, Jill
1979   "Paradigms in Evolutionary Theory: The Sociobiological Model of Natural
            Selection." *American Sociological Review* 44:100–109.
1990   "Race, Class and Gender in the United States Welfare State: Nixon's Failed
            Family Assistance Plan." *American Sociological Review* 55:11–28.
Rachlin, Allan
1991   "Rehumanizing Dialectic: Toward an Understanding of the Interpenetration
            of Structure and Subjectivity." *Current Perspectives in Social Theory*
            11:255–269.
Radnitzky, Gerard
1973   *Contemporary Schools of Metascience.* Chicago: Regnery.
Radway, Janice
1984   *Reading the Romance: Women, Patriarchy and Popular Literature.* Chapel
            Hill: University of North Carolina Press.
Rambo, Eric
1995   "Conceiving Best Outcomes within a Theory of Utility Maximization: A
            Culture-Level Critique." *Sociological Theory* 13:145–162.
Rammstedt, Otthein
1991   "On Simmel's Aesthetics: Argumentation in the Journal *Jugend,*
            1897–1906." *Theory, Culture and Society* 8:125–144.
Rawls, Anne Warfield
forthcoming "Harold Garfinkel." In George Ritzer (ed.), *The Blackwell Companion to
            Major Social Theorists.* Oxford, England, and Cambridge, Mass.: Blackwell.
Reagon, Bernice Johnson
1982/1995   "My Black Mothers and Sisters; or, On Beginning a Cultural
            Autobiography." In C. Goldberg and H. Hartmann (eds.), *U.S. Women in
            Struggle.* Chicago: University of Illinois Press: 296–310.

Reed, Evelyn
1970   *Women's Liberation.* New York: Pathfinder Press.
Reedy, W. Jay
1994   "The Historical Imaginary of Social Science in Post-Revolutionary France: Bonald, Saint-Simon, Comte." *History of the Human Sciences* 7:1–26.
Reinharz, Shulamit
1993   *A Contextualized Chronology of Women's Sociological Work.* Waltham, Mass.: Brandeis University Press.
Reitzes, Donald C., and Reitzes, Dietrich C.
1993   "The Social Psychology of Robert E. Park: Human Nature, Self, Personality and Social Structure." *Symbolic Interaction* 16:39–63.
Reskin, Barbara
1988   "Bringing the Men Back In: Sex Differences and the Devaluation of Women's Work." *Gender & Society* 2:58–81.
Reskin, Barbara, and Padavic, Irene
1994   *Women and Men at Work.* Thousand Oaks, Calif.: Pine Forge Press.
Rhoades, Lawrence J.
1981   *A History of the American Sociological Association.* Washington, D.C.: American Sociological Association.
Rhode, Deborah L.
1997   *Speaking of Sex: The Denial of Gender Inequality.* Cambridge, Mass.: Harvard University Press.
Rich, Adrienne
1976   *Of Woman Born: Motherhood as Experience and Institution.* New York: Bantam.
1979   *On Lies, Secrets and Silences: Selected Prose 1966–1978.* New York: Norton.
1980   "Compulsory Heterosexual and Lesbian Experience." In C. R. Stimson and E. S. Person (eds.), *Women, Sex, and Sexuality.* Chicago: University of Chicago Press: 62–91.
1993   *What Is Found There: Notebooks on Poetry and Politics.* New York: Norton.
Richardson, Diane (ed.)
1996   *Theorising Heterosexuality.* Buckingham, U.K., and Bristol, Penn.: Open University Press.
Ridgeway, Cecelia
1997   "Interaction and the Conservation of Gender Inequality: Considering Employment." *American Sociological Review* 62:218–235.
Risman, Barbara, and Ferree, Myra Marx
1995   "Making Gender Visible." *American Sociological Review* 60:5:775–782.
Risman, Barbara, and Schwarz, Pepper (eds.)
1989   *Gender in Intimate Relationships: A Microstructural Approach.* Belmont, Calif.: Wadsworth.
Ritzer, George
1975   *Sociology: A Multiple Paradigm Science.* Boston: Allyn and Bacon.
1975c   "Professionalization, Bureaucratization and Rationalization: The Views of Max Weber." *Social Forces* 53:627–634.

1979   "Toward an Integrated Sociological Paradigm." In W. Snizek et al. (eds.), *Contemporary Issues in Theory and Research.* Westport, Conn.: Greenwood Press: 25–46.

1980   *Sociology: A Multiple Paradigm Science.* Rev. ed. Boston: Allyn and Bacon.

1981a   *Toward an Integrated Sociological Paradigm: The Search for an Exemplar and an Image of the Subject Matter.* Boston: Allyn and Bacon.

1981b   "Paradigm Analysis in Sociology: Clarifying the Issues." *American Sociological Review* 46:245–248.

1983   "The McDonaldization of Society." *Journal of American Culture* 6:100–107.

1985   "The Rise of Micro-Sociological Theory." *Sociological Theory* 3:88–98.

1987   "The Current State of Metatheory." *Sociological Perspectives: The Theory Section Newsletter* 10:1–6.

1988   "Sociological Metatheory: Defending a Subfield by Delineating Its Parameters." *Sociological Theory* 6:187–200.

1989a   "Metatheorizing as a Prelude to Theory Development." Paper presented at the meetings of the American Sociological Association, San Francisco.

1989b   "Of Levels and 'Intellectual Amnesia.' " *Sociological Theory* 7:226–229.

1990a   "Micro-Macro Linkage in Sociological Theory: Applying a Metatheoretical Tool." In G. Ritzer (ed.), *Frontiers of Social Theory: The New Syntheses.* New York: Columbia University Press: 347–370.

1990b   "The Current Status of Sociological Theory: The New Syntheses." In G. Ritzer (ed.), *Frontiers of Social Theory: The New Syntheses.* New York: Columbia University Press: 1–30.

1990c   Special mini-issue on metatheory. *Sociological Forum* 5:1–74.

1991a   "Metatheorizing in Sociology." *Sociological Forum* 5:3–15.

1991b   *Metatheorizing in Sociology.* Lexington, Mass.: Lexington Books.

1991c   "Recent Explorations in Sociological Metatheorizing." *Sociological Perspectives* 34:237–390.

1991d   "The Recent History and the Emerging Reality of American Sociological Theory: A Metatheoretical Interpretation." *Sociological Forum* 6:269–287.

1991e   "Hyperrationality: An Extension of Weberian and Neo-Weberian Theory." In G. Ritzer, *Metatheorizing in Sociology.* Lexington, Mass.: Lexington Books: 93–115.

1992a   *Classical Sociological Theory.* New York: McGraw-Hill.

1992c   "Metatheorizing in Sociology: Explaining the Coming of Age." In G. Ritzer (ed.), *Metatheorizing.* Newbury Park, Calif.: Sage: 7–26.

1993   *The McDonaldization of Society.* Thousand Oaks, Calif.: Pine Forge Press.

1995   *Expressing America: A Critique of the Global Credit Card Society.* Thousand Oaks, Calif.: Pine Forge Press.

1996   *The McDonaldization of Society,* revised ed. Thousand Oaks, Calif.: Pine Forge Press.

1997   *Postmodern Social Theory.* New York: McGraw-Hill.

1998   *The McDonaldization Thesis.* London: Sage.

1999   *Enchanting a Disenchanted World: Revolutionizing the Means of Consumption.* Thousand Oaks, Calif.: Pine Forge Press.

Ritzer, George (ed.)

1990d   *Frontiers of Social Theory: The New Syntheses.* New York: Columbia University Press.

1992b   *Metatheorizing.* Newbury Park, Calif.: Sage.

Ritzer, George, and Bell, Richard
1981   "Emile Durkheim: Exemplar for an Integrated Sociological Paradigm?"
            Social Forces 59:966–995.
Ritzer, George, and Gindoff, Pamela
1992   "Methodological Relationism: Lessons for and from Social Psychology."
            Social Psychology Quarterly 55:128–140.
1994   "Agency-Structure, Micro-Macro, Individualism-Holism-Relationism: A
            Metatheoretical Explanation of Theoretical Convergence between the United
            States and Europe." In P. Sztompka (ed.), *Agency and Structure: Reorienting
            Social Theory.* Amsterdam: Gordon and Breach: 3–23.
Ritzer, George, and LeMoyne, Terri
1991   "Hyperrationality: An Extension of Weberian and Neo-Weberian Theory." In
            G. Ritzer, *Metatheorizing in Sociology.* Lexington, Mass.: Lexington Books:
            93–115.
Ritzer, George, and Trice, Harrison
1969   *An Occupation in Conflict: A Study of the Personnel Manager.* Ithaca, N.Y.:
            ILR Press.
Ritzer, George, and Walczak, David
1988   "Rationalization and the Deprofessionalization of Physicians." *Social Forces*
            67:1–22.
Robbins, Derek
1991   *The Work of Pierre Bourdieu.* Boulder, Colo.: Westview Press.
Robertson, Roland
1992   *Globalization: Social Theory and Global Culture.* London: Sage.
Rocher, Guy
1975   *Talcott Parsons and American Sociology.* New York: Barnes and Noble.
Rock, Paul
1979   *The Making of Symbolic Interactionism.* Totowa, N.J.: Rowman and
            Littlefield.
Roemer, John
1982   *A General Theory of Exploitation and Class.* Cambridge, Mass.: Harvard
            University Press.
1986a   "Introduction." In J. Roemer (ed.), *Analytical Marxism.* Cambridge:
            Cambridge University Press: 1–7.
1986b   " 'Rational Choice' Marxism: Some Issues of Method and Substance." In J.
            Roemer (ed.), *Analytical Marxism.* Cambridge: Cambridge University Press:
            191–201.
Roemer, John (ed.)
1986c   *Analytical Marxism.* Cambridge: Cambridge University Press.
Rogers, Mary
1983   *Sociology, Ethnomethodology, and Experience: A Phenomenological
            Critique.* New York: Cambridge University Press.
1996b   "Theory—What? Why? How?" In Mary F. Rogers (ed.), *Multicultural
            Experiences, Multicultural Theories.* New York: McGraw-Hill: 11–16.
forthcoming "Alfred Schutz." In George Ritzer (ed.), *The Blackwell Companion to Major
            Social Theorists.* Oxford, England, and Cambridge, Mass.: Blackwell.
Rogers, Mary F. (ed.)
1996a   *Multicultural Experiences, Multicultural Theories.* New York: McGraw-Hill.

Rollins, Judith
1985   *Between Women: Domestics and Their Employers.* Philadelphia: Temple
            University Press.
Rose, Arnold
1962   "A Systematic Summary of Symbolic Interaction Theory." In A. Rose (ed.),
            Human Behavior and Social Processes. Boston: Houghton Mifflin.
Rose, Gillian
1984   *Dialectic of Nihilism: Post-Structuralism and Law.* New York: Blackwell.
Rose, Nancy E.
1995   *Workfare or Fair Work: Women, Welfare, and Government Work Programs.*
            New Brunswick, N.J.: Rutgers University Press.
Rosenau, Pauline Marie
1992   *Post-Modernism and the Social Sciences: Insights, Inroads, and Intrusions.*
            Princeton, N.J.: Princeton University Press.
Rosenberg, Alexander
1988   *Philosophy of Social Science.* Boulder, Colo.: Westview Press.
Rosenberg, Morris
1989   "Self-Concept Research: A Historical Review." *Social Forces* 68:34–44.
Rosenberg, Rosalind
1982   *Beyond Separate Spheres: Intellectual Roots of Modern Feminism.* New
            Haven, Conn.: Yale University Press.
Rosenthal, Naomi, Fingrutd, Meryl, Ethier, Michele, and Karant, Roberta
1985   "Social Movements and Network Analysis: A Case Study of Nineteenth-
            Century Women's Reform in New York State." *American Journal of
            Sociology* 90:1022–1054.
Ross, Dorothy
1991   *The Origins of American Social Science.* Cambridge: Cambridge
            University Press.
Rossi, Alice
1974   *The Feminist Papers: From Adams to de Beauvoir.* New York: Bantam.
1977   "A Biosocial Perspective on Parenting." *Daedalus* 106:9–31.
1983   "Gender and Parenthood." *American Sociological Review* 49:1–19.
Rothenberg, Sheila, and Rothenberg, Robert S.
1993   "The Pleasures of Paris." *USA Today* (Magazine), March:38ff.
Rowbotham, Sheila
1973   *Women's Consciousness, Man's World.* Middlesex, Eng.: Pelican.
1989   *Hidden from History: 300 Years of Women's Oppression and the Fight
            against It.* Winchester, Mass.: Unwin Hyman.
Rubin, Gayle
1975   "The Traffic in Women: Notes on the Political Economy of Sex." In R.
            Reiter (ed.), *Towards an Anthropology of Women.* New York: Monthly
            Review Press.
Rubin, Lillian
1976   *Worlds of Pain: Life in the Working Class Family.* New York:
            Basic Books.
1979   *Intimate Strangers: Men and Women Together.* New York: Harper & Row.
1985   *Just Friends: The Role of Friendship in Our Lives.* New York: Harper & Row.
Rubenstein, David
1986   "The Concept of Structure in Sociology." In M. L. Wardell and S. P. Turner
            (eds.), *Sociological Theory in Transition.* Boston: Allen and Unwin: 80–94.

Ruddick, Sara
1980   "Maternal Thinking." *Feminist Studies* 6:342–367.
1994   "Notes towards a Feminist Maternal Peace Politics." In A. Jaggar (ed.),
            Living with Contradictions: Controversies in Feminist Social Ethics.
            Boulder, Colo.: Westview Press.
Rueschemeyer, Marilyn (ed.)
1994   *Women in the Politics of Postcommunist Eastern Europe.* Armonk and
            London: M. E. Sharpe.
Russell, Diana E.
1998   *Dangerous Relationships: Pornography, Misogyny, and Rape.* Thousand
            Oaks, Calif.: Sage.
Ryan, Barbara
1992   *Feminism and the Women's Movement: Dynamics of Change in Social
            Movement Ideology.* New York: Routledge.
Ryan, Mary
1990   *Women in Public: From Barriers to Ballots, 1825–1880.* Baltimore: Johns
            Hopkins University Press.
Ryan, William
1971   *Blaming the Victim.* New York: Pantheon.
Sacks, Karen
1988   *Caring by the Hour: Women, Work, and Organizing at Duke Medical Center.*
            Urbana: University of Illinois Press.
Safa, Helen Icken
1990   "Women's Social Movements in Latin America." *Gender & Society*
            4:354–369.
Salamini, Leonardo
1981   *The Sociology of Political Praxis: An Introduction to Gramsci's Theory.*
            London: Routledge and Kegan Paul.
Salomon, A.
1945   "German Sociology." In G. Gurvitch and W. F. Moore (eds.), *Twentieth
            Century Sociology.* New York: Philosophical Library: 586–614.
1963/1997   "Georg Simmel Reconsidered." In Gary D. Jaworski, *Georg Simmel and the
            American Prospect.* Albany: State University of New York Press: 91–108.
Sanday, Peggy Reeves
1974   "Female Status in the Public Domain." In M. Rosaldo and L. Lamphere
            (eds.), *Women, Culture and Society: A Theoretical Overview.* Stanford,
            Calif.: Stanford University Press: 189–206.
1981   *Female Power and Male Dominance.* Cambridge: Cambridge
            University Press.
1990   *Fraternity Gang Rape: Sex, Brotherhood and Privilege on Campus.* New
            York: New York University Press.
1996   *A Woman Scorned: Acquaintance Rape on Trial.* New York: Doubleday.
Sargent, Lydia (ed.)
1981   *Women and Revolution: A Discussion of the Unhappy Marriage of Marxism
            and Feminism.* Boston: South End Press.
Satoshi, Kamata
1982   *Japan in the Passing Lane.* New York: Pantheon.
Saunders, Peter
1989   "Space, Urbanism and the Created Environment." In D. Held and J. B.
            Thompson (eds.), *Social Theory of Modern Societies: Anthony Giddens and
            His Critics.* Cambridge: Cambridge University Press: 215–234.

Savage, Mike, and Witz, Anne (eds.)
1992   *Gender and Bureaucracy.* Oxford: Blackwell.
Sawicki, Jana
1991   *Disciplining Foucault: Feminism, Power and the Body.* New York:
            Routledge.
Scaff, Lawrence
1989   *Fleeing the Iron Cage: Culture, Politics, and Modernity in the Thought of
            Max Weber.* Berkeley: University of California Press.
1993   "Life contra Ratio: Music and Social Theory." *Sociological Theory*
            11:234–240.
Scambler, Graham
1996   "The 'Project of Modernity' and the Parameters for a Critical Sociology: An
            Argument with Illustrations from Medical Sociology." *Sociology* 30:567–581.
Schegloff, Emanuel
1979   "Identification and Recognition in Telephone Conversation Openings." In G.
            Psathas (ed.), *Everyday Language: Studies in Ethnomethodology.* New York:
            Irvington: 23–78.
1987   "Between Macro and Micro: Contexts and Other Connections." In J. C.
            Alexander et al. (eds.), *The Micro-Macro Link.* Berkeley: University of
            California Press: 207–234.
1992   "Repair after Next Turn: The Last Structurally Provided Defense of
            Intersubjectivity in Conversation." *American Journal of Sociology*
            97:1295–1345.
Scheper-Hughes, Nancy
1992   *Death without Weeping: The Violence of Everyday Life in Brazil.* Berkeley:
            University of California Press.
Schimank, Uwe
1996   *Theorien Gesellschaftlicher Differenzierung.* Opladen: Leske and Budrich.
Schmidt, Neal, Gooding, Richard Z., Noe, Raymond A., and Kirsch, Michael
1984   "Meta-Analyses of Validity Studies Published between 1964 and 1982 and
            the Investigation of Study Characteristics." *Personnel Psychology*
            37:407–422.
Schmitt, Raymond L., and Schmitt, Tiffani Mari
1996   "Community Fear of AIDS as Enacted Emotion: A Comparative
            Investigation of Mead's Concept of the Social Act." *Studies in Symbolic
            Interaction* 20:91–119.
Schmutz, Corinne
1996   "The Service Industry and Marx's Fetishism of Commodities." *Humanity
            and Society* 20:102–105.
Schneider, Louis
1967   *The Scottish Moralists: On Human Nature and Society.* Chicago: University
            of Chicago Press.
1971   "Dialectic in Sociology." *American Sociological Review* 36:667–678.
Schneider, Mark A.
1993   *Culture and Disenchantment.* Chicago: University of Chicago Press.
Schroeter, Gerd
1985   "Dialogue, Debate, or Dissent? The Difficulties of Assessing Max Weber's
            Relation to Marx." In R. J. Antonio and R. M. Glassman (eds.), *A Weber-
            Marx Dialogue.* Lawrence: University of Kansas Press: 2–13.

Schroyer, Trent
1970   "Toward a Critical Theory of Advanced Industrial Society." In H. P. Dreitzel
            (ed.), *Recent Sociology: No. 2.* New York: Macmillan: 210–234.
1973   *The Critique of Domination.* Boston: Beacon Press.

Schulin, Ernst
1981   "German 'Geistesgeschichte,' American 'Intellectual History,' and French
            'Histoire des Mentalities' since 1900: A Comparison." *History of European
            Ideas* 1:195–214.

Schultz, Ruth W.
1995   "The Improbable Adventures of an American Scholar: Robert K. Merton."
            American Sociologist 26:68–77.

Schutz, Alfred
1932/1967   *The Phenomenology of the Social World.* Evanston, Ill.: Northwestern
            University Press.

Schwalbe, Michael L.
1993   "Goffman against Postmodernism: Emotion and the Reality of the Self."
            Symbolic Interaction 16:333–350.
1996   *Unlocking the Iron Cage: The Men's Movement, Gender Politics and
            American Culture.* New York: Oxford University Press.

Schwanenberg, Enno
1971   "The Two Problems of Order in Parsons' Theory: An Analysis from Within."
            Social Forces 49:569–581.

Schwartz, Justin
1995   "In Defence of Exploitation." *Economics and Philosophy* 11:275–307.

Schwartz, Pepper
1994   *Peer Marriage: How Love between Equals Really Works.* New York:
            Free Press.

Schweber, Silvan S.
1991   "Auguste Comte and the Nebular Hypothesis." In R. T. Bienvenu and M.
            Feingold (eds.), *In the Presence of the Past: Essays in Honor of Frank
            Manuel.* Dordrecht, Neth.: Kluwer: 131–191.

Schwendinger, Julia, and Schwendinger, Herman
1974   *Sociologists of the Chair.* New York: Basic Books.

Schwinn, Thomas
1998   "False Connections: Systems and Action Theories in Neofunctionalism and
            in Jurgen Habermas." *Sociological Theory* 16:75–95.

Scimecca, Joseph
1977   *The Sociological Theory of C. Wright Mills.* Port Washington, N.Y.:
            Kennikat Press.

Sciulli, David
1986   "Voluntaristic Action as a Distinct Concept: Theoretical Foundations of
            Societal Constitutionalism." *American Sociological Review* 51:743–766.

Sciulli, David, and Gerstein, Dean
1985   "Social Theory and Talcott Parsons in the 1980s." *Annual Review of
            Sociology* 11:369–387.

Scott, Joan
1990   "Deconstructing Equality-versus-Difference." In M. Hirsch and E. F. Keller
            (eds.), *Conflicts in Feminism.* New York: Routledge.

Scully, Diana
1980   *Men Who Control Health: The Miseducation of Obstetrician-Gynecologists.* Boston: Houghton Mifflin.
1990   *Understanding Sexual Violence: A Study of Convicted Rapists.* Boston: Unwin Hyman.

Searle, John
1972   "Chomsky's Revolution in Linguistics." *New York Review of Books* 18:16–24.

Segura, Denise A., and Pierce, Jennifer
1993   "Chicana/o Family Structure and Gender Personality: Chodorow, Familism, and Psychoanalytic Sociology Revisited." *Signs* 19:62–91.

Seidman, Steven
1983   *Liberalism and the Origins of European Social Theory.* Berkeley: University of California Press.
1989   "Introduction." In S. Seidman (ed.), *Jurgen Habermas on Society and Politics: A Reader.* Boston: Beacon Press: 1–25.
1991   "The End of Sociological Theory: The Postmodern Hope." *Sociological Theory* 9:131–146.
1994a   *Contested Knowledge: Social Theory in the Postmodern Age.* Oxford: Blackwell.
1994b   "Symposium: Queer Theory/Sociology: A Dialogue." *Sociological Theory* 12:166–177.

Seitz, Virginia Rinaldo
1995   *Women, Development, and Communities for Empowerment in Appalachia.* Albany: State University of New York Press.

Seligman, Adam B.
1993a   "The Representation of Society and the Privatization of Charisma." *Praxis International* 13:68–84.
1993b   *The Idea of Civil Society.* New York: Free Press.

Servan-Schreiber, J.-J.
1968   *The American Challenge.* New York: Atheneum.

Sewart, John J.
1978   "Critical Theory and the Critique of Conservative Method." *American Sociologist* 13:15–22.

Shalin, Dmitri
1986   "Pragmatism and Social Interactionism." *American Sociological Review* 51:9–29.
1993   "Modernity, Postmodernism, and Pragmatist Inquiry: An Introduction." *Symbolic Interaction* 16:303–332.

Sharrock, Wes, and Anderson, Bob
1986   *The Ethnomethodologists.* Chichester, Eng.: Ellis Horwood.

Shaw, Linda L.
1991   "Stigma and the Moral Careers of Ex-Mental Patients Living in Board and Care." *Journal of Contemporary Ethnography* 20:285–305.

Shelton, Beth Anne
1992   *Women, Men and Time: Gender Differences in Paid Work, Housework and Leisure.* New York: Greenwood Press.

Shelton, Beth Anne, and Agger, Ben
1993 "Shotgun Wedding, Unhappy Marriage, No-Fault Divorce? Rethinking the Feminism-Marxism Relationship." In P. England (ed.), *Theory on Gender/Gender on Theory*. New York: Aldine de Gruyter.

Sheridan, Alan
1980 *Michel Foucault: The Will to Truth*. London: Tavistock.

Sherlock, Steve
1997 "The Future of Commodity Fetishism." *Sociological Focus* 30:61–78.

Sherman, Suzanne
1992 *Lesbian and Gay Marriage: Private Commitments, Public Ceremonies*. Philadelphia: Temple University Press.

Shibutani, Thomas
1988 "Herbert Blumer's Contribution to Twentieth-Century Sociology." *Symbolic Interaction* 11:23–31.

Shilling, Chris
1997 "The Undersocialised Conception of the Embodied Agent in Modern Sociology." *Sociology* 31:737–754.

Shilling, Chris, and Mellor, Philip A.
1996 "Embodiment, Structuration Theory and Modernity: Mind/Body Dualism and the Repression of Sensuality." *Body and Society* 2:1–15.

Shils, Edward
1996 "The Sociology of Robert E. Park." *American Sociologist* 27:88–106.

Shirazi-Mahajan, Faegheh
1995 "A Dramaturgical Approach to Hijab in Post-Revolutionary Iran." *Critique* 7:35–51.

Showalter, Elaine
1971 *Women's Liberation and Literature*. New York: Harcourt Brace Jovanovich.

Shreve, Anita
1989 *Women Together, Women Alone: The Legacy of the Consciousness Raising Movement*. New York: Viking.

Sidel, Ruth
1990 *On Her Own: Growing Up in the Shadow of the American Dream*. New York: Viking.
1994 *Battling Bias: The Struggle for Identity and Community on College Campuses*. New York: Viking.

Sijuwade, Philip O.
1995 "Counterfeit Intimacy: A Dramaturgical Analysis of Erotic Performance." *Social Behavior and Personality* 23:369–376.

Silber, Ilana Friedrich
1993 "Monasticism and the 'Protestant Ethic': Asceticism, Rationality and Wealth in the Medieval West." *British Journal of Sociology* 44:103–123.

Simmel, Georg
1907/1978 *The Philosophy of Money*, Tom Bottomore and David Frisby (eds. and trans.), London: Routledge and Kegan Paul.
1991 "Money in Modern Culture." *Theory, Culture and Society* 8:17–31.

Simon, Herbert
1957 *Administrative Behavior*. New York: Free Press.

Sitton, John F.
1996   "Disembodied Capitalism: Habermas's Conception of the Economy."
            Sociological Forum 13:61–83.
Sjoberg, Gideon, Gill, Elizabeth, Littrell, Boyd, and Williams, Norma
1997   "The Reemergence of John Dewey and American Pragmatism." In Norman
            K. Denzin (ed.), *Studies in Symbolic Interaction*, Vol. 21. Greenwich, Conn.:
            JAI Press: 73–92.
Skinner, B. F.
1971   *Beyond Freedom and Dignity.* New York: Knopf.
Skocpol, Theda
1979   *States and Social Revolutions.* Cambridge: Cambridge University Press.
1986   "The Dead End of Metatheory." *Contemporary Sociology* 16:10–12.
1992   *Protecting Soldiers and Mothers: The Political Origins of Social Policy in
            the United States.* Cambridge, Mass.: Harvard University Press.
Slater, Don
1997   *Consumer Culture and Modernity.* Cambridge: Polity Press.
Slater, Phil
1977   *Origin and Significance of the Frankfurt School: A Marxist Perspective.*
            London: Routledge and Kegan Paul.
Smart, Barry
1983   *Foucault, Marxism and Critique.* London: Routledge and Kegan Paul.
1985   *Michel Foucault.* Chichester, Eng.: Ellis Horwood.
1993   *Postmodernity.* London: Routledge.
forthcoming "Michel Foucault." In George Ritzer (ed.), *The Blackwell Companion to
            Major Social Theorists.* Oxford, England, and Cambridge, Mass.: Blackwell.
Smart, Barry (ed.)
1999   *Resisting McDonaldization.* London: Sage.
Smelser, Neil
1959   *Social Change in the Industrial Revolution.* Chicago: University of
            Chicago Press.
1962   *Theory of Collective Behavior.* New York: Free Press.
1987   "Depth Psychology and the Social Order." In J. C. Alexander et al. (eds.),
            The Micro-Macro Link. Berkeley: University of California Press: 267–286.
1988   "Sociological Theory: Looking Forward." *Perspectives: The Theory Section
            Newsletter* 11:1–3.
1992   "The Rational Choice Perspective: A Theoretical Assessment." *Rationality
            and Society* 4:381–410.
1997   *Problematics of Sociology: The Georg Simmel Lectures, 1995.* Berkeley:
            University of California Press.
Smith, Cyril
1997   "Friedrich Engels and Marx's Critique of Political Economy." *Capital and
            Class* 62:123–142.
Smith, David Norman
1996   "The Social Construction of Enemies: Jews and the Representation of Evil."
            Sociological Theory 14:203–240.
Smith, Dorothy
1974   "Women's Perspective as a Radical Critique of Sociology." *Sociological
            Inquiry* 44:7–13.

1975   "An Analysis of Ideological Structures and How Women Are Excluded: Consideration for Academic Women." *Canadian Review of Sociology and Anthropology* 12:353–369.

1978   "A Peculiar Eclipsing: Women's Exclusion from Man's Culture." *Women's Studies International Quarterly* 1:281–295.

1979   "A Sociology for Women." In J. A. Sherman and E. T. Beck (eds.), *The Prism of Sex: Essays in the Sociology of Knowledge.* Madison: University of Wisconsin Press.

1987   *The Everyday World as Problematic: A Feminist Sociology.* Boston: Northeastern University Press.

1989   "Sociological Theory: Methods of Writing Patriarchy." In R. A. Wallace (ed.), *Feminism and Sociological Theory.* Newbury Park, Calif.: Sage: 34–64.

1990a   *The Conceptual Practices of Power: A Feminist Sociology of Knowledge.* Boston: Northeastern University Press.

1990b   *Texts, Facts and Femininity: Exploring the Relations of Ruling.* London: Routledge and Kegan Paul.

1992   "Sociology from Women's Experience: A Reaffirmation." *Sociological Theory* 10:88–98.

1993   "High Noon in Textland: A Critique of Clough." *Sociological Quarterly* 34:183–192.

Smith, Dorothy, and Griffith, Alison
1985   "Coordinating the Uncoordinated: How Mothers Manage the School Day." Paper presented at the annual meeting of the American Sociological Association, Washington, D.C.

Smith, Norman Erik
1979   "William Graham Sumner as an Anti-Social Darwinist." *Pacific Sociological Review* 22:332–347.

Smith, T. V.
1931   "The Social Philosophy of George Herbert Mead." *American Journal of Sociology* 37:368–385.

Snitow, Ann Barr
1979   "Mass Market Romance: Pornography for Women Is Different." *Radical History Review* 20:141–163.

Snitow, Ann Barr, Stansell, Christine, and Thompson, Sharon
1983   *Powers of Desire: The Politics of Sexuality.* New York: Monthly Review Press.

Snizek, William E.
1976   "An Empirical Assessment of 'Sociology: A Multiple Paradigm Science.' " *American Sociologist* 11:217–219.

Snizek, William E., Fuhrman, Ellsworth, R., and Miller, Michael K. (eds.)
1979   *Contemporary Issues in Theory and Research.* Westport, Conn.: Greenwood Press.

Snow, David
1986   "Frame Alignment Processes, Micromobilization, and Movement Participation." *American Sociological Review* 51:464–481.

Sokoloff, Natalie
1980   *Between Money and Love: The Dialectics of Women's Home and Market Work.* New York: Praeger.

1992   *Black Women and White Women in the Professions: Occupational Segregation by Race and Gender 1960–1980.* New York: Routledge.

Solinger, Rickie (ed.)
1998   *Abortion Wars: A Half Century of Struggle, 1950–2000.* Berkeley:
            University of California Press.
Sorokin, Pitirim
1928   *Contemporary Sociological Theories.* New York: Harper.
1937–1941   *Social and Cultural Dynamics.* 4 vols. New York: American Book.
1956   *Fads and Foibles in Modern Sociology and Related Sciences.* Chicago:
            Regnery.
1963   *A Long Journey: The Autobiography of Pitirim Sorokin.* New Haven, Conn.
            College and University Press.
Speier, Matthew
1970   "The Everyday World of the Child." In J. Douglas (ed.), *Understanding
            Everyday Life.* Chicago: Aldine: 188–217.
Spelman, Elizabeth
1988   *Inessential Woman: The Problem of Exclusion in Feminist Thought.* Boston:
            Beacon Press.
Spender, Dale
1980   *Man Made Language.* London: Routledge and Kegan Paul.
1982   *Women of Ideas (And What Men Have Done to Them).* London: Routledge
            and Kegan Paul.
1989   *The Writing or the Sex? Or Why You Don't Have to Read Women's Writing to
            Know It's No Good.* New York: Pergamon Press.
Spender, Dale (ed.)
1983   *Feminist Theorists: Three Centuries of Key Women Thinkers.* New York:
            Random House.
Staats, Arthur W.
1976   "Skinnerian Behaviorism: Social Behaviorism or Radical Behaviorism?"
            American Sociologist 11:59–60.
Stacey, Judith
1994   "The Future of Feminist Difference." *Contemporary Sociology* 23:
            482–486.
1996   *In the Name of the Family: Rethinking Family Values in the Postmodern Age.*
            Boston: Beacon Press.
Stacey, Judith, and Thorne, Barrie
1985   "The Missing Feminist Revolution in Sociology." *Social Problems*
            32:301–316.
1996   "Is Sociology Still Missing Its Feminist Revolution?" *Perspectives: The ASA
            Theory Section Newsletter* 18:1–3.
Stanfield, Ron
1974   "Kuhnian Scientific Revolutions and the Keynesian Revolution." *Journal of
            Economic Issues* 8:97–109.
Stanley, Liz (ed.)
1990   *Feminist Praxis: Research Theory and Epistemology in Feminist Sociology.*
            London: Routledge.
Stanton, Donna
1985   "Language and Revolution: The Franco-American Dis-Connection." In H.
            Eisenstein and A. Hardine (eds.), *The Future of Difference.* New Brunswick,
            N.J.: Rutgers University Press: 73–87.

Stauth, Georg
1997 " 'Elias in Singapore': Civilizing Processes in a Tropical City." *Thesis-Eleven* 50:51–70.
Steil, Janice M.
1997 *Marital Equality: Its Relationship to the Well-Being of Husbands and Wives.* Thousand Oaks, Calif.: Sage.
Stephanson, Anders
1989 "Regarding Postmodernism: A Conversation with Fredric Jameson." In D. Kellner (ed.), *Postmodernism, Jameson, Critique.* Washington, D.C.: Maisonneuve Press: 43–74.
Stetson, Dorothy McBride, and Mazur, Amy G. (eds.)
1995 *Comparative State Feminism.* Thousand Oaks, Calif.: Sage.
Stiglmayer, Alexandra (ed.)
1994 *Mass Rape: The War Against Women in Bosnia-Herzogovina.* Translations by Marion Faber. Lincoln: University of Nebraska Press.
Stockard, Jean, and Johnson, Miriam
1980 *Sex Roles: Sex Inequality and Sex Role Development.* Englewood Cliffs, N.J.: Prentice-Hall.
Stolte, John F.
1987 "Legitimacy, Justice, and Productive Exchange." In K. S. Cook (ed.), *Social Exchange Theory.* Beverly Hills, Calif.: Sage: 190–208.
Stones, Rob
1991 "Strategic Context Analysis: A New Research Strategy for Structuration Theory." *Sociology* 25:673–695.
Strauss, Anselm
1996 "Everett Hughes: Sociology's Mission." *Symbolic Interaction* 19:271–283.
Strenski, Ivan
1997 *Durkheim and the Jews of France.* Chicago: University of Chicago Press.
Strom, Sharon Hartman
1992 *Beyond the Typewriter: Gender, Class and the Origins of Modern American Office Work.* Urbana: University of Illinois Press.
Stryker, Sean
1998 "Communicative Action in New Social Movements: The Experience of the Students for a Democratic Society." *Current Perspectives in Social Theory* 18:79–98.
Stryker, Sheldon
1980 *Symbolic Interactionism: A Social Structural Version.* Menlo Park, Calif.: Benjamin/Cummings.
Sugiman, Pamela
1994 *Labour's Dilemma: The Gender Politics of Auto Workers in Canada, 1937–1979.* Toronto: University of Toronto Press.
Swartz, David
1997 *Culture and Power: The Sociology of Pierre Bourdieu.* Chicago: University of Chicago Press.
Swedberg, Richard
1996 "Analyzing the Economy: On the Contribution of James S. Coleman." In Jon Clark (ed.), *James S. Coleman.* London: Falmer Press: 313–328.
Symbolic Interaction
1981 Fall. Entire issue devoted to George Herbert Mead.

1983   Review symposium on J. David Lewis and Richard L. Smith, *American Sociology and Pragmatism* 6:127–174.
1988   Special issue on Herbert Blumer's legacy. 11:1–160.
Szacki, Jerzy
1979   *History of Sociological Thought.* Westport, Conn.: Greenwood Press.
Szmatka, Jacek, and Mazur, Joanna
1996   "Theoretical Research Programs in Social Exchange Theory." *Polish Sociological Review* 3:265–288.
Sztompka, Piotr
1974   *System and Function: Toward a Theory of Society.* New York: Academic Press.
1991   *Society in Action: The Theory of Social Becoming.* Chicago: University of Chicago Press.
forthcoming "Robert Merton." In George Ritzer (ed.), *The Blackwell Companion to Major Social Theorists.* Oxford, England, and Cambridge, Mass.: Blackwell.
Sztompka, Piotr (ed.)
1994   *Agency and Structure: Reorienting Social Theory.* Amsterdam: Gordon and Breach.
Takla, Tendzin, and Pope, Whitney
1985   "The Force Imagery in Durkheim: The Integration of Theory, Metatheory and Method." *Sociological Theory* 3:74–88.
Tannen, Deborah
1990   *You Just Don't Understand: Women and Men in Conversation.* New York: William Morrow.
1994   *Gender and Discourse.* New York: Oxford.
Tannen, Deborah (ed.)
1993   *Gender and Conversational Interaction.* New York: Oxford.
Tar, Zoltan
1977   *The Frankfurt School: The Critical Theories of Max Horkheimer and Theodor W. Adorno.* London: Routledge and Kegan Paul.
Taylor, Verta
1989   "Social Movement Continuity: The Women's Movement in Abeyance." *American Sociological Review* 54:761–775.
Taylor, Verta, and Rupp, Leila
1993   "Women's Culture and Lesbian Feminist Activism: A Reconsideration of Cultural Feminism." *Signs* 19:1–61.
Tax, Meredith
1970   "Woman and Her Mind: The Story of an Everyday Life." In S. Firestone and A. Koedt (eds.), *Notes from the Second Year: Radical Feminism.* New York: Radical Feminism.
Telos
1989–1990   "Does Critical Theory Have a Future? The Elizabethtown *Telos* Conference (February 23–25, 1990)." *Telos* 82:111–130.
Ten Have, Paul
1995   "Medical Ethnomethodology: An Overview." *Human Studies* 18:245–261.
Theory, Culture and Society
1997   "Gilles Deleuze: A Symposium." 14:1–88.
Thibaut, John W., and Kelley, Harold H.
1959   *The Social Psychology of Groups.* New York: Wiley.

Thomas, William I., and Thomas, Dorothy S.
1928   *The Child in America: Behavior Problems and Programs.* New York: Knopf.
Thompson, Becky W.
1994   *A Hunger So Wide and So Deep: American Women Speak Out on Eating Problems.* Minneapolis: University of Minnesota Press.
Thompson, E. P.
1978   *The Poverty of Theory.* London: Merlin Press.
Thompson, John B.
1989   "The Theory of Structuration." In D. Held and J. B. Thompson (eds.), *Social Theory of Modern Societies: Anthony Giddens and His Critics.* Cambridge: Cambridge University Press: 56–76.
Thompson, Kenneth
1975   *Auguste Comte: The Foundation of Sociology.* New York: Halstead Press.
Thompson, Linda, and Walker, Alexis J.
1989   "Gender in Families: Women and Men in Marriage, Work and Parenthood." *Journal of Marriage and the Family* 51:845–871.
Thompson, William E., and Harred, Jackie L.
1992   "Topless Dancers: Managing Stigma in a Deviant Occupation." *Deviant Behavior* 13:291–311.
Thomson, Ernie
1994   "The Sparks that Dazzle Rather Than Illuminate: A New Look at Marx's 'Theses on Feuerbach.' " *Nature, Society and Thought* 7:299–323.
Thorne, Barrie
1993   *Gender Play: Girls and Boys in School.* New Brunswick, N.J.: Rutgers University Press.
Thorne-Finch, Ron
1992   *Ending the Silence: The Origins and Treatment of Male Violence against Women.* Toronto: University of Toronto Press.
Tilly, Charles
1997   "James S. Coleman as a Guide to Social Research." *American Sociologist* 28:82–87.
Tilman, Rick
1984   *C. Wright Mills: A Native Radical and His American Intellectual Roots.* University Park: Pennsylvania State University Press.
Tinker, Irene (ed.)
1983   *Women in Washington: Advocates for Public Policy.* Beverly Hills, Calif.: Sage.
Tiryakian, Edward A.
1979   "The Significance of Schools in the Development of Sociology." In W. Snizek, E. Fuhrman, and M. Miller (eds.), *Contemporary Issues in Theory and Research.* Westport, Conn.: Greenwood Press: 211–233.
1981   "The Sociological Import of Metaphor." *Sociological Inquiry* 51:27–33.
1986   "Hegemonic Schools and the Development of Sociology: Rethinking the History of the Discipline." In R. C. Monk (ed.), *Structures of Knowing.* Lanham, Md.: University Press of America: 417–441.
1992   "Pathways to Metatheory: Rethinking the Presuppositions of Macrosociology." In G. Ritzer (ed.), *Metatheorizing.* Beverly Hills, Calif.: Sage: 69–87.
Tiryakian, Edward A. (ed.)
1991   "Symposium: Robert K. Merton in Review." *Contemporary Sociology* 20:506–530.

Toby, Jackson
1977   "Parsons' Theory of Societal Evolution." In T. Parsons, *The Evolution of Societies*. Englewood Cliffs, N.J.: Prentice-Hall: 1–23.
Touraine, Alain
1977   *The Self-Production of Society*. Chicago: University of Chicago Press.
1995   *Critique of Modernity*. Oxford: Blackwell.
Travers, Andrew
1992   "The Conversion of Self in Everyday Life." *Human Studies* 15:169–238.
Trebilcot, Joyce
1973   "Sex Roles: The Argument from Nature." Paper presented at the meeting of the American Philosophical Association, Western Division, April.
Trebilcot, Joyce (ed.)
1984   *Mothering: Essays in Feminist Theory*. Totowa, N.J.: Rowman and Allanheld.
Trexler, Richard C.
1995   *Sex and Conquest: Gendered Violence, Political Order, and the European Conquest of the Americas*. Ithaca, N.Y.: Cornell University Press.
Trifonas, Peter
1996   "The Ends of Pedagogy: From the Dialectic of Memory to the Deconstruction of the Institution." *Educational Theory* 46:303–333.
Troyer, William
1946   "Mead's Social and Functional Theory of Mind." *American Sociological Review* 11:198–202.
Tseelon, Efrat
1992   "Is the Presented Self Sincere? Goffman, Impression Management and the Postmodern Self." *Theory, Culture and Society* 9:115–128.
Tucker, Robert C. (ed.)
1970   *The Marx-Engels Reader*. New York: Norton.
Tumin, Melvin
1953   "Some Principles of Stratification: A Critical Analysis." *American Sociological Review* 18:387–394.
Turbin, Carol E.
1992   *Working Women of Collar City: Gender, Class, and Community in Troy, New York 1864–1886*. Urbana: University of Illinois Press.
Turner, Bryan S.
1981   *For Weber: Essays in the Sociology of Fate*. Boston: Routledge and Kegan Paul.
1985   *The Body and Society: Explorations in Social Theory*. Oxford: Blackwell.
1995   "Karl Mannheim's *Ideology and Utopia*." *Political Studies* 43:718–727.
Turner, Jonathan
1973   "From Utopia to Where? A Strategy for Reformulating the Dahrendorf Conflict Model." *Social Forces* 52:236–244.
1974   "Parsons as a Symbolic Interactionist: A Comparison of Action and Interaction Theory." *Sociological Inquiry* 44:283–294.
1975   "A Strategy for Reformulating the Dialectical and Functional Theories of Conflict." *Social Forces* 53:433–444.
1982   *The Structure of Sociological Theory*. 3rd ed. Homewood, Ill.: Dorsey Press.
1985   "In Defense of Positivism." *Sociological Theory* 3:24–30.
1986   *The Structure of Sociological Theory*. 4th ed. Chicago: Dorsey Press.

1987 "Social Exchange Theory: Future Directions." In K. S. Cook (ed.), *Social Exchange Theory.* Beverly Hills, Calif.: Sage: 223–238.

1989a "Introduction: Can Sociology Be a Cumulative Science?" In J. Turner (ed.), *Theory Building in Sociology: Assessing Theoretical Cumulation.* Newbury Park, Calif.: Sage: 8–18.

1990 "The Past, Present, and Future of Theory in American Sociology." In G. Ritzer (ed.), *Frontiers of Social Theory: The New Syntheses.* New York: Columbia University Press: 371–391.

1991a "Developing Cumulative and Practical Knowledge through Metatheorizing." *Sociological Perspectives* 34:249–268.

1991b *The Structure of Sociological Theory.* 5th ed. Belmont, Calif.: Wadsworth.

1994 "The Failure of Sociology to Institutionalize Cumulative Theorizing." In J. Hage (ed.), *Formal Theory in Sociology: Opportunity or Pitfall?* Albany: State University Press of New York: 41–51.

1995 "Can Symbolic Interactionism Really Contribute to Macro Sociology?" *Current Perspectives in Social Theory* 15:181–197.

forthcoming "Herbert Spencer." In George Ritzer (ed.), *The Blackwell Companion to Major Social Theorists.* Oxford, England, and Cambridge, Mass.: Blackwell.

Turner, Jonathan (ed.)

1989b *Theory Building in Sociology: Assessing Theoretical Cumulation.* Newbury Park, Calif.: Sage.

Turner, Jonathan, and Maryanski, A. Z.

1979 *Functionalism.* Menlo Park, Calif.: Benjamin/Cummings.

1988a "Is 'Neofunctionalism' Really Functional?" *Sociological Theory* 6:110–121.

1988b "Sociology's Lost Human Relations Area Files." *Sociological Perspectives* 31:19–34.

Turner, Ralph

1968 "The Self-Conception in Social Interaction." In C. Gordon and K. J. Gergen (eds.), *The Self in Social Interaction.* New York: Wiley: 93–106.

Turner, Roy

1970 "Words, Utterances and Activities." In J. Douglas (ed.), *Understanding Everyday Life.* Chicago: Aldine: 161–187.

Turner, Stephen Park

1983 "Weber on Action." *American Sociological Review* 48:506–519.

1991 "Social Constructionism and Social Theory." *Sociological Theory* 9:22–33.

1993 "Introduction: Reconnecting the Sociologist to the Moralist." In S. P. Turner (ed.), *Emile Durkheim: Sociologist and Moralist.* London: Routledge: 1–22.

1998 "Who's Afraid of the History of Sociology?" *Schwezerische Zeistschrift fur Soziologie* 24:3–10.

Turner, Stephen Park, and Turner, Jonathan H.

1990 *The Impossible Science: An Institutional Analysis of American Sociology.* Newbury Park, Calif.: Sage.

Uehara, Edwina

1990 "Dual Exchange Theory, Social Networks, and Informal Social Support." *American Journal of Sociology* 96:521–557.

Ungar, Sheldon

1984 "Self-Mockery: An Alternative Form of Self-Presentation." *Symbolic Interaction* 7:121–133.

Urry, John

1995 *Consuming Places.* London: Routledge.

van den Berg, Axel
1980   "Critical Theory: Is There Still Hope?" *American Journal of Sociology*
            86:449–478.
Van den Berghe, Pierre
1963   "Dialectic and Functionalism: Toward Reconciliation." *American
            Sociological Review* 28:695–705.
van Krieken, Robert
1998   *Norbert Elias.* London: Routledge.
Varcoe, Ian
1998   "Identity and the Limits of Comparison: Bauman's Reception in Germany."
            Theory Culture and Society 15:57–72.
Veblen, Thorstein
1899/1994   *The Theory of the Leisure Class.* New York: Penguin Books.
Vetter, Betty M., Babco, Eleanor, and Jensen-Fisher, Susan
1982   *Professional Women and Minorities: A Manpower Resource Service.*
            Washington, D.C.: Scientific Manpower Commission.
Vidich, Arthur J., and Lyman, Stanford M.
1985   *American Sociology: Worldly Rejections of Religion and Their Directions.*
            New Haven, Conn.: Yale University Press.
Vogel, Lise
1984   *Marxism and the Oppression of Women: Towards a Unitary Theory.* New
            Brunswick, N.J.: Rutgers University Press.
1993   *Mothers on the Job: Maternity Policy in the United States Workplace.* New
            Brunswick, N.J.: Rutgers University Press.
1995   *Woman Questions: Essays for a Materialist Feminism.* New York:
            Routledge.
Wacquant, Loïc J. D.
1989   "Towards a Reflexive Sociology: A Workshop with Pierre Bourdieu."
            Sociological Theory 7:26–63.
1992   "Toward a Social Praxeology: The Structure and Logic of Bourdieu's
            Sociology." In P. Bourdieu and L. J. D. Wacquant (eds.), *An Invitation to
            Reflexive Sociology.* Chicago: University of Chicago Press: 2–59.
Wade-Gayles, Gloria
1993   *Pushed Back to Strength: A Black Woman's Journey Home.* Boston: Beacon.
Wagner, Gerhard
1998   "Differentiation as Absolute Concept? Toward the Revision of a Sociological
            Category." *International Journal of Politics, Culture and Society*
            11:451–474.
Wagner, Helmut
1964   "Displacement of Scope: A Problem of the Relationship between Small Scale
            and Large Scale Sociological Theories." *American Journal of Sociology*
            69:571–584.
Wagner, Peter
1994   *A Sociology of Modernity: Liberty and Discipline.* London: Routledge.
Walby, Sylvia
1990   *Theorizing Patriarchy.* Cambridge, Mass.: Basil Blackwell.
Walder, Andrew G.
1994   "Collective Behavior Revisited: Ideology and Politics in the Chinese
            Cultural Revolution." *Rationality and Society* 6:400–421.

Waldfogel, Jane
1997   "The Effect of Children on Women's Wages." *American Sociological Review*
            62:209–217.
Walker, Alice
1983   *In Search of Our Mothers' Gardens.* New York: Harcourt Brace Jovanovich.
1988   *Living by the Word.* New York: Harcourt Brace Jovanovich.
1989   *The Temple of My Familiar.* New York: Pocket Books.
Walker, Rebecca
1995   *To Be Real: Telling the Truth and Changing the Face of Feminism.* New
            York: Anchor.
Walkerdine, Valerie
1997   *Daddy's Girl: Young Girls and Popular Culture.* Cambridge, Mass.: Harvard
            University Press.
Wallace, Ruth A. (ed.)
1989   *Feminism and Sociological Theory.* Newbury Park, Calif.: Sage.
Wallace, Walter
1969   "Overview of Contemporary Sociological Theory." In W. Wallace (ed.),
            Sociological Theory. Chicago: University of Chicago Press: 1–59.
1988   "Toward a Disciplinary Matrix in Sociology." In N. Smelser (ed.), *Handbook
            of Sociology.* Newbury Park, Calif.: Sage: 23–76.
Wallerstein, Immanuel
1974   *The Modern World-System: Capitalist Agriculture and the Origins of the
            European World-Economy in the 16th Century.* New York:
            Academic Press.
1980   *The Modern World-System II: Mercantilism and the Consolidation of the
            European World-Economy, 1600–1750.* New York: Academic Press.
1986   "Marxisms as Utopias: Evolving Ideologies." *American Journal of Sociology*
            91:1295–1308.
1989   *The Modern World-System III: The Second Era of Great Expansion of the
            Capitalist World-Economy, 1730–1840.* New York: Academic Press.
1992   "America and the World: Today, Yesterday, and Tomorrow." *Theory and
            Society* 21:1–28.
1995   "The End of What Modernity?" *Theory and Society* 24:471–488.
Walum-Richardson, Laurel
1981   *The Dynamics of Sex and Gender.* Boston: Houghton Mifflin.
Ward, Kathryn B.
1984   *Women in the World System: Its Impact on Status and Fertility.* New York:
            Praeger.
1985a   "The Social Consequences of the World-Economic System: The Economic
            Status of Women and Fertility." *Review* 8:561–594.
1985b   "Women and Urbanization in the World System." In M. Timberlake (ed.),
            Urbanization in the World Economy. New York: Academic Press: 305–324.
1988   "Women in the Global Economy." In B. Glick et al. (eds.), *Women and Work.*
            Beverly Hills, Calif.: Sage 17–48.
1993   "Reconceptualizing World System Theory to Include Women." In P. England
            (ed.), *Theory on Gender/Feminism on Theory.* New York: Aldine de Gruyter:
            43–69.
1994   "Lifting as We Climb: How Scholarship about Women of Color Has Shaped
            My Life as a White Feminist." In G. Young and B. Dickerson (eds.), *Color,
            Class, and Country: Experiences of Gender.* Atlantic Highlands, N.J.:
            Zed Books.

Ward, Kathryn (ed.)
1990   *Women Workers and Global Restructuring.* Ithaca, N.Y.: Cornell
                University Press.
Ward, Kathryn B., and Pyle, Jean Larson
1995   "Gender, Industrialization, and Development." *Development* 1:67–71.
Wardell, Mark L., and Turner, Stephen P.
1986b   "Introduction: Dissolution of the Classical Project." In M. L. Wardell and
                S. P. Turner (eds.), *Sociological Theory in Transition.* Boston: Allen and
                Unwin: 11–18.
Wardell, Mark L., and Turner, Stephen P. (eds.)
1986a   *Sociological Theory in Transition.* Boston: Allen and Unwin.
Ware, Vron
1992   *Beyond the Pale: White Women, Racism and History.* New York: Routledge.
Warner, Michael (ed.)
1993   *Fear of a Queer Planet: Queer Politics and Social Theory.* Minneapolis:
                University of Minnesota Press.
Warsh, David
1990   "Modern Thinkers Merge Sociology, Economics to Explain Today's World."
                Washington Post Aug. 15:D3.
Warshay, Leon, and Warshay, Diana H.
1986   "The Individualizing and Subjectivizing of George Herbert Mead: A
                Sociology of Knowledge Interpretation." *Sociological Focus* 19:177–188.
Wartenberg, Thomas E.
1990   *The Forms of Power: From Domination to Transformation.* Philadelphia:
                Temple University Press.
Wasserman, Stanley, and Faust, Katherine
1994   *Social Network Analysis: Methods and Application.* Cambridge: Cambridge
                University Press.
Waston, Kath
1991   *Families We Choose: Lesbians, Gays, Kinship.* New York: Columbia
                University Press.
Weakliem, David, and Heath, Anthony
1994   "Rational Choice and Class Voting." *Rationality and Society* 6:243–270.
Weber, Marianne
1975   *Max Weber: A Biography.* Harry Zohn (ed. and trans.). New York: Wiley.
Weber, Max
1904–1905/   *The Protestant Ethic and the Spirit of Capitalism.* New York:
1958   Scribner's.
Weigert, Andrew
1981   *Sociology of Everyday Life.* New York: Longman.
Weingart, Peter
1969   "Beyond Parsons? A Critique of Ralf Dahrendorf's Conflict Theory." *Social
                Forces* 48:151–165.
Weinstein, Deena, and Weinstein, Michael A.
1992   "The Postmodern Discourse of Metatheory." In G. Ritzer (ed.),
                Metatheorizing. Newbury Park, Calif.: Sage: 135–150.
1993   *Postmodern(ized) Simmel.* London: Routledge.
1998   "Simmel-Eco vs. Simmel-Marx: Ironized Alienation." *Current Perspectives
                in Social Theory* 18:63–77.

Weinstein, Eugene A., and Tanur, Judith M.
1976   "Meanings, Purposes and Structural Resources in Social Interaction."
            Cornell Journal of Social Relations 11:105–110.
Weitzman, Lenore
1985   *The Divorce Revolution.* New York: Free Press.
Weldes, Jutta
1989   "Marxism and Methodological Individualism." *Theory and Society*
            18:353–386.
Wellman, Barry
1983   "Network Analysis: Some Basic Principles." In R. Collins (ed.), *Sociological
            Theory—1983.* San Francisco: Jossey-Bass: 155–200.
Wellman, Barry, and Berkowitz, S. D. (eds.)
1988/1997   *Social Structures: A Network Approach.* Greenwich, Conn.: JAI Press.
Wellman, Barry, and Wortley, Scot
1990   "Different Strokes for Different Folks: Community Ties and Social Support."
            American Journal of Sociology 96:558–588.
Wellman, David
1988   "The Politics of Herbert Blumer's Sociological Method." *Symbolic
            Interaction* 11:59–68.
West, Candace, and Fenstermaker, Sarah
1993   "Power, Inequality and the Accomplishment of Gender: An
            Ethnomethodological View." In Paula England (ed.) *Theory on
            Gender/Feminism on Theory.* NY: Aldine de Gruyter: 223–254.
1995   "Doing Difference." *Gender & Society* 9:8–20.
West, Candace, and Zimmerman, Don
1987   "Doing Gender." *Gender & Society* 2:125–151.
Wexler, Philip (ed.)
1991   *Critical Theory Now.* London: Falmer Press.
Whalen, Jack, Zimmerman, Don H., and Whalen, Marilyn R.
1988   "When Words Fail: A Single Case Analysis." *Social Problems* 35:335–361.
Whalen, Marilyn R., and Zimmerman, Don H.
1987   "Sequential and Institutional Contexts in Calls for Help." *Social Psychology
            Quarterly* 50:172–185.
Wharton, Amy S.
1991   "Structure and Agency in Socialist-Feminist Theory." *Gender & Society*
            5:373–389.
White, Harrison
1992   *Identity and Control: A Structural Theory of Social Action.* Princeton, N.J.:
            Princeton University Press.
White, Harrison C., Boorman, Scott A., and Breiger, Ronald L.
1976   "Social Structure from Multiple Networks: Parts 1 and 2." *American Journal
            of Sociology* 91:730–780, 1384–1446.
White, Hayden
1973   *The Historical Imagination in Nineteenth-Century Europe.* Baltimore: Johns
            Hopkins University Press.
Whitmeyer, Joseph M.
1994   "Why Actor Models Are Integral to Structural Analysis." *Sociological
            Theory* 12:153–165.

Whittier, Nancy
1995   *Feminist Generations: The Persistence of the Radical Women's Movement.*
            Philadelphia: Temple University Press.
Wiggershaus, Rolf
1994   *The Frankfurt School: Its History, Theories, and Political Significance.*
            Cambridge, Mass.: MIT Press.
Wiley, Norbert
1979   "The Rise and Fall of Dominating Theories in American Sociology." In W.
            Snizek, E. Fuhrman, and M. Miller (eds.), *Contemporary Issues in Theory
            and Research.* Westport, Conn.: Greenwood Press: 47–79.
1985   "The Current Interregnum in American Sociology." *Social Research*
            52:179–207.
1986   "Early American Sociology and *The Polish Peasant.*" *Sociological Theory*
            4:20–40.
1988   "The Micro-Macro Problem in Social Theory." *Sociological Theory*
            6:254–261.
1989   "Response to Ritzer." *Sociological Theory* 7:230–231.
Willer, David, Markovsky, Barry, and Patton, Travis
1989   "Power Structures: Derivations and Applications of Elementary Theory."
            In J. Berger, M. Zelditch, Jr., and B. Anderson (eds.), *Sociological
            Theories in Progress: New Formulations.* Newbury Park, Calif.: Sage:
            313–353.
Williams, Francis
1962   *The American Invasion.* New York: Crown.
Williams, Patricia
1991   *The Alchemy of Race and Rights: Diary of a Law Professor.* Cambridge,
            Mass.: Harvard University Press.
1995   *The Rooster's Egg: On the Persistence of Prejudice.* Cambridge, Mass.:
            Harvard University Press.
Williams, Robin
1980a   "Talcott Parsons: The Stereotypes and the Reality." *American Sociologist*
            15:64–66.
1980b   "Pitirim Sorokin: Master Sociologist and Prophet." In R. Merton and M. W.
            Riley (eds.), *Sociological Traditions from Generation to Generation.*
            Norwood, N.J.: Ablex: 93–107.
Williams, Simon Johnson
1986   "Appraising Goffman." *British Journal of Sociology* 37:348–369.
Willmott, Robert
1997   "Structure, Culture and Agency: Rejecting the Current Orthodoxy of
            Organisation Theory." *Journal for the Theory of Social Behaviour*
            27:93–123.
Wilner, Patricia
1985   "The Main Drift of Sociology between 1936 and 1982." *History of
            Sociology: An International Review* 5:1–20.
Wilson, John
1993   "The Subject Woman." In P. England (ed.), *Theory on Gender/Feminism on
            Theory.* New York: Aldine de Gruyter.
Wilson, John, and Musick, Mark
1997   "Who Cares? Toward an Integrated Theory of Volunteer Work." *American
            Sociological Review* 60:694–713.

Wilson, Thomas P.
1970   "Normative and Interpretive Paradigms in Sociology." In J. Douglas (ed.), *Understanding Everyday Life*. Chicago: Aldine: 1–19.

Wiltshire, David
1978   *The Social and Political Thought of Herbert Spencer.* London: Oxford University Press.

Winterer, Caroline
1994   "A Happy Medium: The Sociology of Charles Horton Cooley." *Journal of the History of the Behavioral Sciences* 30:19–27.

Wippler, Reinhard, and Lindenberg, Siegwart
1987   "Collective Phenomena and Rational Choice." In J. C. Alexander et al. (eds.), *The Micro-Macro Link*. Berkeley: University of California Press: 135–152.

Wolf, Frederick M.
1986   *Meta-Analysis: Quantitative Methods for Research Synthesis*. Beverly Hills, Calif.: Sage.

Wolf, Naomi
1991   *The Beauty Myth: How Images Are Used against Women*. New York: William Morrow.

Womack, James P., Jones, Daniel T., and Roos, Daniel
1990   *The Machine That Changed the World*. New York: Rawson.

Wood, Ellen Meiksins
1986   *The Retreat from Class: The New "True" Socialism*. London: Verso.
1989   "Rational Choice Marxism: Is the Game Worth the Candle?" *New Left Review* 177:41–88.
1995   *Democracy against Capitalism*. Cambridge: Cambridge University Press.
1997   "Modernity, Postmodernity or Capitalism?" *Review of International Political Economy* 4:539–560.

Wood, Ellen Meiksins, and Foster, John Bellamy (eds.)
1997   *In Defense of History: Marxism and the Postmodern Agenda*. New York: Monthly Review Press.

Wood, Michael, and Wardell, Mark L.
1983   "G. H. Mead's Social Behaviorism vs. the Astructural Bias of Symbolic Interactionism." *Symbolic Interaction* 6:85–96.

Woody, Bette
1992   *Black Women in the Workplace: Impacts of Structural Change in the Economy*. Westport, Conn.: Greenwood Press.

Wright, Erik Olin
1985   *Classes*. London: Verso.
1987   "Towards a Post-Marxist Radical Social Theory." *Contemporary Sociology* 16:748–753.

Wrigley, Julia
1995   *Other People's Children: An Intimate Account of the Dilemma Facing Middle-Class Parents and the Women They Hire to Raise Their Children*. New York: Basic Books.

Wrong, Dennis
1994   *The Problem of Order: What Unites and Divides Society*. New York: Free Press.

Wuthnow, Robert, Hunter, James Davidson, Bergesen, Albert, Kurzweil, Edith (eds.)
1984   *Cultural Analysis*. Boston: Routledge and Kegan Paul.

Yamagishi, Toshio
1995   "Social Dilemmas." In K. S. Cook, G. A. Fine, and J. S. House (eds.), *Sociological Perspectives on Social Psychology.* Boston: Allyn and Bacon: 311–335.

Yamagishi, Toshio, and Cook, Karen S.
1993   "Generalized Exchange and Social Dilemmas." *Social Psychology Quarterly* 56:235–248.

Yamagishi, Toshio, Gillmore, Mary R., and Cook, Karen S.
1988   "Network Connections and the Distribution of Power in Exchange Networks." *American Journal of Sociology* 93:833–851.

Yeatman, Anna
1987   "Women, Domestic Life and Sociology." In C. Pateman and E. Gross (eds.), *Feminist Challenges: Social and Political Challenges.* Boston: Northeastern University Press: 157–172.

Young, Robert L.
1997   "Account Sequences." *Symbolic Interaction* 20:291–305.

Zablocki, Benjamin
1996   "Methodological Individualism and Collective Behavior." In Jon Clark (ed.), *James S. Coleman.* London: Falmer Press: 147–160.

Zandy, Janet
1990   *Calling Home: Working Class Women's Writings.* New Brunswick, N.J.: Rutgers University Press.

Zaretsky, Eli
1976   *Capitalism, the Family and Personal Life.* New York: Harper Colophon.

Zaslavsky, Victor
1988   "Three Years of *Perestroika.*" *Telos* 74:31–41.

Zavella, Patricia
1987   *Women's Work and Chicano Families: Cannery Workers of the Santa Clara Valley.* Ithaca, N.Y.: Cornell University Press.

Zeitlin, Irving M.
1981   *Ideology and the Development of Sociological Theory.* 2nd ed. Englewood Cliffs, N.J.: Prentice-Hall.
1990   *Ideology and the Development of Sociological Theory.* 4th ed. Englewood Cliffs, N.J.: Prentice-Hall.
1994   *Ideology and the Development of Sociological Theory.* 5th ed. Englewood Cliffs, N.J.: Prentice-Hall.
1996   *Ideology and the Development of Sociological Theory.* 6th ed. Englewood Cliffs, N.J.: Prentice-Hall.

Zhang, Xianghuan
1993   "A Cross-Cultural Study of Gender Personality and Socialization: Voices from the People's Republic of China." Ph.D. dissertation, Washington, D.C.: George Washington University.

Zhao, Shanyang
1991   "Metatheory, Metamethod, Meta-Data-Analysis." *Sociological Perspectives* 34:377–390.
1993   "Realms, Subfields, and Perspectives: Differentiation and Fragmentation of Sociology." *American Sociologist,* Fall/Winter:5–14.
forthcoming "Metatheorizing in Sociology." In George Ritzer and Barry Smart (eds.), *Handbook of Social Theory.* London: Sage.

Zimmerman, Don
1978   "Ethnomethodology." *American Sociologist* 13:5–15.
1988   "The Conversation: The Conversation Analytic Perspective."
            Communication Yearbook 11:406–432.
Zimmerman, Don, and Pollner, Melvin
1970   "The Everyday World as a Phenomenon." In J. Douglas (ed.), *Understanding*
            Everyday Life. Chicago: Aldine: 80–103.
Zimmerman, Don, and Wieder, D. Lawrence
1970   "Ethnomethodology and the Problem of Order: Comment on Denzin." In J.
            Douglas (ed.), *Understanding Everyday Life.* Chicago: Aldine: 285–298.
Zinn, Maxine Baca, and Dill, Bonnie Thornton
1993   *Women of Color in United States Society.* Philadelphia: Temple
            University Press.
Zipes, Jack
1994   "Adorno May Still Be Right." *Telos* 101:157–167.
Zuboff, Shoshana
1988   *In the Age of the Smart Machine.* New York: Basic Books.
Zukin, Sharon
1991   *Landscapes of Power: From Detroit to Disney World.* Berkeley: University
            of California Press.

NAME INDEX

Aboulafia, Mitchell, 217
Abrahamson, Mark, 114–115
Abrams, Philip, 36–37
Addams, Jane, 57, 207, 318
Adorno, Theodor, 48, 64, 148, 446
Agger, Ben, 136
Alexander, Jeffrey C., 49, 80, 93, 108, 118–122, 133, 360, 365–369, 385, 415, 491–492
Alfino, Mark, 432
Alger, Janet M., 209
Alger, Steve F., 209
Althusser, Louis, 49, 396, 456
Amsterdamska, Olga, 52
Anderson, Margaret, 339
Anderson, Perry, 231
Anderson, R. J., 262
Appadurai, Arjun, 435
Archer, Margaret S., 81, 183, 387, 392–396, 414, 416–417
Aristotle, 94
Aron, Raymond, 398
Aronson, Ronald, 77, 176–179
Arthur, C. J., 491
Ashton, David, 392
Atkinson, J. Maxwell, 256
Atkinson, Paul, 249, 266–267

Bailey, Kenneth D., 181, 490–491
Baker, Patrick L., 490
Baldwin, Alfred, 105
Baldwin, John C., 209, 220, 237–238
Ball, Richard A., 182
Baran, Paul, 153–155, 179
Barber, Bernard, 103
Barthes, Roland, 455
Bartsky, Sandra L., 319
Baudrillard, Jean, 49, 80, 83, 87, 437, 447, 453, 469, 471–473, 477–482, 486
Bauer, Bruno, 491

Bauman, Zygmunt, 176, 440–444, 452
Beck, Ulrich, 82–83, 429, 432, 439–440, 452
Becker, Howard, 67
Bell, Daniel, 281
Bellah, Robert, 120
Benjamin, Jessica, 78, 339
Berger, Brigette, 319
Berger, Peter, 49, 73–74, 111, 319
Bernard, Jessie, 319, 323, 325
Bernard, L. L., 325
Bernard, Thomas, 93–94
Bernstein, Eduard, 136
Bernstein, Richard J., 389
Best, Raphaela, 319
Best, Steven, 469, 472, 477
Blau, Peter, 49, 71, 271, 282–287, 304–305, 360, 501
Blumer, Herbert, 48, 63–64, 71, 201, 203–205, 222–223, 225–226, 234–238, 244, 360, 373, 396
Boden, Deirdre, 267–270
Bogen, David, 253
Boorman, Scott A., 360
Bordo, Susan, 341
Bottomore, Tom, 147
Boudon, Raymond, 398
Bourdieu, Pierre, 81–82, 396–408, 413–414, 417, 489, 493–494
Bourricaud, Francois, 102
Braverman, Harry, 49, 155–158, 179
Breiger, Ronald L., 360
Breuer, Joseph, 37
Brinton, Crane, 49
Broadhead, Robert, 297
Buckley, Walter, 181–185, 199–200, 414
Bulmer, Martin, 52
Burawoy, Michael, 159, 178–179
Burgess, Ernest W., 53

Burns, Tom R., 388, 413–415
Burt, Ronald, 293–296
Button, Graham, 75, 262

Cabet, Etienne, 491
Calhoun, Craig, 407
Campbell, Colin, 110
Caputo, John S., 432
Carnegie, Andrew, 40
Castells, Manuel, 151, 449–452
Chafetz, Janet S., 312–313
Charcot, Jean M., 37
Chodorow, Nancy, 78, 319, 339
Cicourel, Aaron, 372–373
Cixous, Helene, 320, 324
Clayman, Steven E., 249, 257–258, 264, 268
Cohen, G. A., 170–171, 173
Cohen, Percy, 115–117
Coleman, James S., 49, 75, 81, 296–303, 305, 360, 369, 374, 385
Collins, Patricia H., 308, 337, 339–340
Collins, Randall, 70, 72, 93, 128–132, 134, 228, 371–374, 385, 416
Colomy, Paul, 93, 118–121
Comte, Auguste, 4–6, 8–9, 13–16, 18, 20, 25, 36, 38–39, 41–43, 46–47, 50, 94, 220
Cook, Karen S., 271, 274, 287, 289–292
Cooley, Charles H., 48–49, 53–56, 63, 201, 221, 225–226, 244
Cooper, Anna J., 77, 338
Coser, Lewis, 69, 75, 126–127, 132, 491
Cottrell, Leonard, 206
Craib, Ian, 392–393, 430
Crenshawe, Kimberle, 337
Cress, Daniel, 231
Crozier, Michel, 414
Curtis, Charles, 62

Dahrendorf, Ralf, 49, 69–70, 93–94, 123–128, 131, 133–134, 360
Daly, Mary, 319
Darwin, Charles, 39, 41
Davis, Kingsley, 59, 66, 94–96, 114, 133
Dawe, Alan, 387
Dean, Mitchell, 460, 468
de Beauvoir, Simone, 319–320
de Bonald, Louis, 5, 11–13
Deleuze, Gilles, 469
de Maistre, Joseph, 5, 11–13
Demerath, Nicholas, 94–95
Denzin, Norman, 240–242, 244, 253, 304
Derrida, Jacques, 457–459, 468, 471
de Saussure, Ferdinand, 396–397, 455
Descartes, Rene, 10
DeVille, Phillippe, 416
Dewey, John, 54, 202, 204, 207, 221, 242
Dietz, Thomas, 414–415
Dilthey, Wilhelm, 5
Dingwall, Robert, 264–265
Dreyfus, Alfred, 18–19
Duncan, Otis D., 286 360
Durkheim, Emile, 4–9, 12–13, 16–19, 25–26, 32, 36, 39, 42–43, 47, 48, 53, 57, 59, 74, 81, 83, 87, 94, 98, 105, 112, 119, 121, 128, 131, 162, 220, 233, 237, 247, 300–301, 360, 373, 384, 396, 399, 408, 414, 422–423, 445, 479, 491, 497, 500–501

Eco, Umberto, 482
Edel, Abraham, 362
Edwards, Richard, 158
Eisenstadt, S. N., 361
Elias, Norbert, 37, 80, 374–385, 415, 417
Elster, Jon, 169, 171–172
Emerson, Richard, 49, 71, 271, 274, 286–289, 292, 305

Engels, Friedrich, 22–23, 43, 136, 332–333, 446
England, Paula, 304
Eriksson, Bjorn, 13

Faris, R. E. L., 205, 207
Featherstone, Mike, 474
Ferguson, Adam, 13
Ferree, Myra M., 319
Ferry, Luc, 87
Feuerbach, Ludwig, 5, 23–24, 491, 500
Fine, Gary A., 64, 71, 225, 236, 241–242
Fitzhugh, George, 46
Flam, Helena, 413
Ford, Henry, 159
Foucault, Michel, 49, 79–80, 85, 343, 397, 424, 453, 459–468, 470, 485, 487
Fourier, Charles, 491
Frank, Andre G., 127
Fraser, Nancy, 469 471
Freud, Sigmund, 37, 48, 79, 105, 145, 314, 324, 326, 372
Friedberg, Erhard, 414
Friedman, Debra, 272–273
Friedman, George, 142
Friedrichs, Robert, 494
Frisby, David, 423
Fromm, Erich, 64
Fuhrman, Ellsworth, 46–47
Fuller, Margaret, 318, 387
Furfey, Paul, 492

Garcia, Angela, 262–263
Garfinkel, Harold, 49, 73–75, 121, 228, 246–249, 250–253, 266–267, 270, 361, 396
Gartman, David, 175
Gay, E. F., 112
Geertz, Clifford, 121
Geras, Norman, 179
Gerth, Hans, 67–68
Giddens, Anthony, 49, 75, 81–83, 248, 367, 388–395, 413–417, 423–430, 439–440, 452
Giddings, Franklin, 54
Gilligan, Carol, 319

Gillmore, Mary R., 289–290
Gilman, Charlotte P., 57, 318
Gindoff, Pamela, 492
Glenn, Phillip J., 256
Godelier, Maurice, 456–457
Goffman, Erving, 49, 71–72, 201, 225–233, 235, 244, 250, 315, 372–373
Gonos, George, 232
Goodman, Douglas, 185
Goodwin, Charles, 258–259, 260
Gouldner, Alvin, 67, 94, 109, 115–116
Gramsci, Antonio, 135, 137, 139–140, 174
Granovetter, Mark, 294
Greatbatch, David, 256, 264–265, 268
Green, Donald, 304
Gregory, Derek, 392
Greisman, Harvey C., 147
Griffin, Susan, 319
Gross, Llewellyn, 492
Guattari, Felix, 469
Gurvitch, Georges, 362, 501–502

Habenstein, Robert, 64
Habermas, Jurgen, 49, 64, 76, 81–83, 98, 135, 145, 147–151, 179, 198, 408–414, 417, 421, 444–449, 452, 491
Hankin, Thomas, 496
Harrington, James, 4
Hartsock, Nancy, 343
Harvey, David, 175–176
Hayim, Gila, 454
Hays, Sharon, 394
Heckathorn, Douglas D., 297, 303
Hechter, Michael, 272–273
Hegel, G. W. F., 5, 21–24, 26–27, 30, 320, 491–492, 500
Hegtvedt, Karen A., 291
Heidegger, Martin, 320
Heilbron, Johan, 14
Held, David, 389, 391
Helle, H. J., 361

Henderson, Lawrence J., 62, 112, 280
Heritage, John, 251, 256, 259, 268
Hilbert, Richard A., 74, 248, 253, 269
Hinkle, Gisela, 46–47
Hinkle, Roscoe, 52
Hobbes, Thomas, 10
Hofstadter, Richard, 47
Holton, Robert J., 98
Holub, Robert C., 448
Homans, George, 49, 62–63, 70–71, 82, 274–285, 287, 305, 360
Horkheimer, Max, 48, 64–65, 446–447
Horowitz, Irving, 67, 115–116
Huaco, George, 68
Hughes, Everett, 53, 63
Hughes, J. A., 262
Hunter, Allen, 178
Husserl, Edmund, 48, 73
Huxtable, Ada L., 482

Ibn-Khaldun, Abdel R., 6, 8
Irigaray, Luce, 320, 324

Jackman, Mary, 501
Jackman, Robert, 501
James, William, 202 221
Jameson, Fredric, 83–84, 453, 469–478, 484, 487
Jaworski, Gary D., 491
Jay, Martin, 43, 141, 145
Jefferson, Gail, 255
Jenkins, Richard, 397, 407
Joas, Hans, 202
Johnson, Miriam, 311–312, 319
Jones, Mark P., 388
Jonge, Matthias, 185
Jung, Carl, 37

Kalberg, Stephen, 30
Kant, Immanuel, 5, 26, 30
Kautsky, Karl, 5, 43, 48, 136
Kelley, Harold H., 273–274 305

Kellner, Douglas, 143, 151–152, 469, 472, 477, 479
Kemeny, Jim, 361
Kendall, Patricia, 113
Kilbourne, Barbara S., 304
Kleinman, Sherryl, 225
Kluckhohn, Clyde, 280
Knorr-Cetina, Karin, 371–372
Kolb, William, 235
Kollock, Peter, 290–291
Korsch, Karl, 137
Kuhn, Manford, 48, 64, 235
Kuhn, Thomas, 494–495
Kurzweil, Edith, 324, 456

Laclau, Ernesto, 139, 174, 178–179, 469
Lash, Scott, 454
Layder, Derek, 392
Lazarsfeld, Paul F., 67, 112, 300–301
Lefebvre, Henri, 76
Lemert, Charles, 457, 469
Lengermann, Patricia M., 307–355
Lever, Janet, 319
Levi-Strauss, Claude, 48, 79, 396–399, 453, 456–457, 487
Levidow, Les, 161
Levine, Donald, 82
Lewis, J. David, 56, 202–203
Lewis, Reba R., 82, 503
Lilla, Mark, 87, 485
Lipman-Blumen, Jean, 325
Lipovetsky, Gilles, 87, 485–486
Lipset, Seymour M., 300
Liska, Allen, 81, 369–371, 385
Locke, John, 10
Lockwood, David, 67, 116
Lorde, Audre, 338
Lowenthal, Leo, 120
Luckmann, Thomas, 49, 73–74
Luhmann, Niklas, 49, 83, 181, 183, 185–194, 196–200

Lukacs, Georg, 5, 29, 43, 48, 65, 135, 137–140, 144, 179, 445
Lyman, Stanford, 47
Lynch, Michael, 251, 253
Lyotard, Jean F., 83, 199, 447, 470–471, 473

Mackay, Robert W., 265
Maines, David R., 234 238
Malinowski, Bronislaw, 109
Mandel, Ernest, 473–474
Mandelbaum, Jenny, 259
Manent, Pierre, 87
Mann, Michael, 132
Mannheim, Karl, 48, 65–66, 376
Manning, Philip, 71, 230–231, 233, 260–261
Marcuse, Herbert, 64, 142–143, 145–146, 155, 179
Markovsky, Barry, 287
Marshall, Alfred, 491
Martineau, Harriet, 38
Marx, Karl, 4–5, 7–10, 13, 16, 19–30, 32–33, 36, 42–43, 47–48, 53, 59, 62, 65–66, 68, 76–77, 79, 83, 86, 94, 98, 119, 121, 123, 126, 128–129, 131, 135–137, 139–141, 143–144, 146, 148–150, 152–153, 155–159, 161–162, 168–171, 174, 177–179, 220, 237, 241, 309, 332–333, 340, 344, 388, 399, 413–414, 422–423, 436–437, 445–447, 454, 456–457, 470, 473–474, 477, 479, 491–492, 500–501, 505
Maryanski, Alexandra, 94–95, 360
Masterman, Margaret, 495
Matthews, Fred H., 57
Mayer, Tom, 171, 173
Mayhew, Bruce, 360
Maynard, Douglas W., 249, 253
Mayo, Elton, 280
McCarthy, Thomas, 150

McCreary, Edward A., 434
McLean, Paul D., 232
Mead, George H., 48, 51, 53–54, 56, 63, 82, 184, 201–226, 234–239, 243, 269, 350, 408–409, 414, 491
Mehan, Hugh, 253, 265
Meltzer, Bernard, 203, 221, 235
Merton, Robert, 49, 59, 61, 66, 82, 93, 99, 108–114, 133, 300–301, 499
Mestrovic, Stjepan G., 83
Michels, Alfred, 29
Michels, Robert, 29
Mill, James, 491
Miller, David, 203, 212
Mills, C. Wright, 49, 67–69, 76, 364, 472
Mizruchi, Mark, 295
Molm, Linda D., 271, 274, 289, 293
Montesquieu, Charles, 5, 9, 18
Moore, Wilbert, 59, 66, 94–96, 114, 133
Morrione, Thomas J., 238
Morris, Charles, 204
Mosca, Gaetano, 5
Mouffe, Chantal, 139, 174, 178–179, 469
Munch, P. A., 361
Murray, Gilbert, 112
Musolf, Gil R., 202

Nash, Bradley Jr., 499
Nedelmann, Birgitta, 82
Nicholson, Linda, 469, 471
Nicolaus, Martin, 492
Niebrugge-Brantley, Jill, 307–355
Nietzsche, Friedrich, 5, 30, 459–460, 470
Nisbet, Robert, 94

O'Brien, Jodi A., 290–291
O'Neill, John, 483
Owen, Robert, 491

Pareto, Vilfredo, 5, 32, 42–43, 59, 62, 491
Park, Robert, 33, 48–49, 53–54, 56–57, 63
Parker, Mike, 161
Parsons, Talcott, 16–17, 19, 32, 37, 42–43, 48–49, 58–63, 66–67, 69–70, 73–74, 82, 93–94, 97–110, 112, 114–116, 118–122, 133, 183, 185, 190–191, 237, 275, 281, 311, 360, 365, 367, 372, 377, 408–409, 414, 470, 472, 491
Patton, Travis, 287
Perinbanayagam, Robert, 239
Peterson, Richard, 94–95
Petras, James, 221 235
Plato, 94
Poggi, Gianfranco, 422
Pollner, Melvin, 247, 265–268
Poulantzas, Nicos, 456
Proudhon, Pierre, 491–492
Przeworski, Adam, 173

Quist, Theron M., 289

Radcliffe-Brown, A.R., 109
Ray, George, 260–261
Reader, George, 113
Renaut, Alain, 87
Reynolds, Larry, 221 235
Ricardo, David, 5, 24, 491–492
Rich, Adrienne, 78
Risman, Barbara, 319
Ritzer, George, 363, 385, 492, 496, 503–504
Robbins, Derek, 401
Robertson, Roland, 435
Rock, Paul, 221, 225, 233–234
Roemer, John, 168–173
Rose, Arnold, 63–64
Rosenau, Pauline M., 84, 469
Ross, E. A., 47, 49
Rossi, Alice, 319
Rousseau, Jean J., 5, 10
Ryan, William, 38

Sacks, Harvey, 228
Saint-Simon, Claude H., 5, 12–14, 20
Sarton, George, 112
Sartre, Jean P., 48, 320, 396, 398–399, 454
Saunders, Peter, 392
Sawicki, Jana, 343
Say, Jean B., 491
Schegloff, Emanuel A., 228 254–256
Schneider, Mark, 480
Schnore, L. F., 360
Schroyer, Trent, 142
Schutz, Alfred, 48, 73–74, 248, 350, 396, 408–409, 414
Schwendinger, Herman, 46
Schwendinger, Julia, 46
Seidman, Steven, 12, 20, 85, 444, 472
Shalin, Dmitri, 234
Shapiro, Ian, 304
Sharrock, Wes, 262
Sheridan, Alan, 460
Shils, Edward A., 104
Simmel, Georg, 5, 7–9, 20, 27, 29, 32–36, 47–48, 53, 55–57, 59, 63, 65, 83, 87, 94, 112, 122, 127, 132, 138, 204, 237, 360, 422–423, 434, 445, 471–472, 497
Simon, Herbert, 154
Skinner, B. F., 48, 63, 70, 276, 281, 498, 501
Slaughter, Jane, 161
Small, Albion, 33, 46, 48, 52
Smart, Barry, 432, 469
Smelser, Neil, 120, 304, 361
Smith, Adam, 5, 13, 25, 36, 436, 491–492
Smith, Dorothy, 319, 330–331, 336, 353
Smith, Richard L., 56, 202–203
Snizek, William, 498
Snow, David, 231
Sorokin, Pitirim, 48, 58–61, 99, 112, 325
Speier, Matthew, 265

Spencer, Herbert, 4–5, 13, 16, 38–43, 46–50, 445
Stone, Gregory, 46
Strauss, Anselm, 63
Stryker, Sheldon, 236, 239–240, 244
Sumner, William G., 46, 48–51
Sung, Johnny, 392
Swartz, David, 492, 494
Sweezy, Paul M., 49, 153–155, 179
Sztompka, Piotr, 82

Tanur, Judith, 235–236
Tar, Zoltan, 141
Taylor, F. W., 157
Tax, Meredith, 319
Terrell, Mary C., 338
Thibaut, John W., 273–274, 305
Thomas, Dorothy, 53, 224–225
Thomas, W. I., 52–53, 55–56, 63, 201, 221, 224–225, 232
Thompson, Elaine A., 291
Thompson, John B., 389, 391
Tilly, Charles, 303
Tiryakian, Edward A., 52
Toby, Jackson, 97
Touraine, Alain, 388, 398, 413–414
Trow, Martin A., 300
Turner, Bryan S., 98

Turner, Jonathan H., 16, 94–95, 115, 117–119, 236
Turner, Roy, 265

Uehara, Edwina, 287
Ungar, Sheldon, 227

Veblen, Thorstein, 48, 51–52, 87, 404
Vidich, Arthur, 47
Virilio, Jean P., 486

Wacquant, Loic J. D., 397, 401
Wagner, Helmut, 361
Wallace, Walter, 361, 492
Wallerstein, Immanuel, 43, 49, 162–167, 180
Ward, Kathryn B., 313–314
Ward, Lester, 48–51
Wardell, Mark L., 234, 499
Warner, W. Lloyd, 228
Washington, Booker T., 53, 55
Watson, D. R., 259
Watson, John B., 203–204, 242
Webb, Beatrice P., 7, 57
Weber, Marianne, 7, 57, 376
Weber, Max, 4–5, 7–9, 20, 27–33, 35–36, 42, 47–48, 53, 57, 59, 65, 74, 83–84, 87, 98, 121, 128–129, 131, 138, 142, 149–150, 162, 220, 237, 360, 369, 373, 376, 399,

408, 412, 414, 422–423, 432, 439–440, 445, 459, 480, 491, 497–498
Weil, Felix J., 64
Weinstein, Deena, 471–472
Weinstein, Eugene, 235–236
Weinstein, Michael A., 471–472
Weldes, Jutta, 178
Wellman, Barry, 293
Wells-Barnett, Ida, 7, 57
Whalen, Jack, 263
Whalen, Marilyn R., 262–263
White, Harrison C., 360
Whitmeyer, Joseph M., 290
Wieder, Lawrence, 266
Wiley, Norbert, 52, 57, 80, 367–369, 385
Willard, Frances, 318
Willer, David, 287
Wisely, Phillip A., 289
Wolf, Frederick, 490
Wood, Ellen, 174, 178
Wood, Houston, 253, 265
Wood, Michael, 234
Wright, Erik O., 172–173
Wundt, Wilhelm, 18
Wynyard, Robin, 432

Yamagishi, Toshio, 289–291

Zeitlin, Irving, 10–11, 42
Zimmerman, Don H., 249, 250, 262–263, 265–266, 314
Znaniecki, Florian, 52
Zuboff, Shoshana, 465

SUBJECT INDEX

Academic Women, 325
Accounts and accounting,
    248
Accumulation in capitalism,
    175
Acts, as units of study, 72,
    208–209
  four stages of, 208
    consummation, 208
    impulse, 208
    manipulation, 208
    perception, 208
  social, 234
Actes de la Recherche en
    Sciences Sociales, 398
Action(s), 119, 363, 368, 503
  communicative, 148–149,
    408–409, 412
  individual, 33, 43, 139, 184
  instrumental, 148
  and interaction, 33, 224
  joint, 234
  opportunity costs of, 272
  purposive-rational,
    148–149, 302
  rational, 366
    paradigm of, 297
  social, 498
  strategic, 148
  structural theory of, 296
  systems, 62, 97–106, 108
    behavioral organism,
      97, 100, 106
    cultural system, 97,
      100, 103–104, 119
    personality system, 97,
      100, 119
    social system, 97,
      100–101, 108, 119
  theory, 60, 110, 295, 408,
    491, 498
"Action and Its
    Environments," 121
Actor(s), 70–71, 202, 223,
    503
  collective, 294
  consciousness of, 213–214
  corporate, 302–303
  individual, 294

natural person, 302
rational, 287
social, 389
Adaptive upgrading, 106, 311
After Marxism, 77, 176–178
Ageism, 345
Agency-structure integration,
    49, 80–82, 242, 269,
    291, 352, 354, 359,
    375, 387–418, 454,
    496
  differences in, 413–415
  dualism vs. duality, 81, 394
  habitus and field
    (Bourdieu), 396–408
    applying, 403–408
    dialectical relationship,
      404
  and micro-macro linkage,
    298, 302, 415–417
  similarities with micro-
    macro linkage, 415
Aggregation, 273, 370
AGIL scheme (Parsons), 97,
    103, 185, 311
  adaptation, 97, 311
  goal attainment, 97, 311
  integration, 97, 311
  latency, 97, 311
Agnes, 253
Alienation of workers, 26,
    151, 475
Ameliorism, 36, 38
America, 479
American Journal of
    Sociology, 52, 57, 60,
    63
American Occupational
    Structure, The, 286
American Revolution, 321
American Sociological
    Association (ASA),
    52, 75–76, 98, 228,
    286, 297
American Sociological
    Review, 57, 63, 75, 325
American Sociological
    Society (ASS), 51–52,
    55, 57, 63

Americanism, 434
Americanization, 432,
    434–435
Anomie, 111–114, 422, 475,
    500–501
Anti-Semitism, 16, 18–19, 35
Applause, generating,
    256–257, 268
Artificial intelligence, 291
Assembly line:
  automobile, 84, 157,
    159–160
  fast-food industry, 161, 433
  predictability of, 442
Association, 125
  imperatively coordinated,
    124, 126, 360
  (see also *Interaction*)
Attribution theory, 291
Authority:
  corporate, 302
  roles, 124
    expectations, 105
    latent interests, 125
    manifest interests, 125
  types of, 31, 124–125
    charismatic, 31
    large-scale, 124
    rational-legal, 31
    traditional, 10, 31
Automobile industry:
  American, 185
  Japanese, 161
    management by stress,
      161
Autopoietic systems,
    185–188

Behavior, 71, 368
  civilized, 378
  collective, 299–300
  control, 274
  costs, 272–273
  covert, 224
  economic, 370
  fate-control, 274
  individual, 276
  overt, 224
  patterns of, 363

Behavior—*Cont.*
reinforcement, 71, 287
rewards, 272–273,
277–278, 280, 282
altruistic, 278
extrinsic, 282
intrinsic, 282
materialistic, 278
social, 497–499, 501, 505
at the table, 378–379
Behaviorism, 203–204, 269,
271–273, 279–280,
282, 287
operant conditioning, 272,
276, 287
radical, 203
reductionist, 275
Skinner's, 70, 360
social, 203, 283–284, 498
Watsonian, 204
Being and Nothingness, 454
Bellagio (Las Vegas), 481
Beyond Right and Left: The
Future of Radical
Politics, 426–427
Birth of the Clinic, The,
462–463
Black Feminist Thought, 339
Blade Runner, 470
Body and Society, 467
Body Heat, 475
Body posture, 260
Booing, 257–258, 264, 268
Bourgeoisie, 138, 139, 384
Breaching experiments,
251–252
Bricoleur, 471
British sociology, the
development of, 5,
36–42
Bureaucracy(ies), 17, 30–31,
74, 113, 159, 186, 414,
433, 441–442, 500,
504
German, 441, 443
rational, 441
structures, 503
Bureaucratization, 12, 30–31

Calculability, 438, 442
Calls to emergency centers,
262–263

Calvinism, 31
Capital, 313, 333, 402
cultural, 373, 402, 404
economic, 402, 404
and labor, 152–159
monopoly, 153–155
private ownership of, 424
social, 402
symbolic, 402
Capital, 23, 32, 137, 492
Capitalism, 3, 7, 25–26,
31–32, 46, 50, 74, 86,
136, 138, 140, 143,
159, 164, 169, 176,
316, 332–333, 347,
369–370, 412–413,
422, 424, 427, 436,
473
alienating effects of, 360,
422
class relations under, 334
coercive effects of, 360
and colonization, 163
competitive, 152–153,
158
domination within, 140
economic structure(s) of,
79, 146, 187, 505
economy in, 33, 422
exploitative nature of, 85,
176, 413, 422
and exploration, 163
global, 311, 313, 336, 341
historical stages of,
473–474
imperialist, 474
late, 474
market, 473–474
informational, 449
Marx's theory of, 30, 491
modern, 474
monopoly, 155, 474
multinational, 474
oppressiveness of, 26
rise of, 5–7
spirit of, 27
structures of, 24
technology in, 142–143
worldwide, 179
(See also *Division of labor;*
Money; Private
property)

Capitalist societies, 36,
141–142, 146
Carceral system, 464
Care of the Self, The, 466
Catholic Church, the, 11
Chains of interdependence,
382
Chaos theory, 490
Character and Social
Structure, 68
Chicago, The University of,
33, 50, 52
Chicago school, 8, 33, 52–57,
63, 71, 87
second, 64,
waning of, 57, 63–64
Choice(s):
collective, 302
individual, 302
Circus Circus (Las Vegas),
482
City(ies), 3, 54, 422–423,
486
sociology of, 20
Civilization, 376, 378–379,
381
process of, 378, 384–385
Civilizing Process, The, 375,
378, 381
Clan(s), 220
Class (See *Social class*)
Class and Class Conflict in
Industrial Society, 70
Class and Class
Consciousness, 43
Class Structure of Advanced
Societies, The, 430
Classes, 172
Cognitive:
anthropology, 291
maps, 476–477
processes, 293
science, 291
Collective conscience, 17
Collectivities, 12, 101, 285,
388, 413, 500
Colored Woman in a White
World, A, 338
Commodification, 152
Commodities, 137
fetishism of, 137
Marx's conception of, 436

Communication, 113,
150–151, 241, 349 447
high-speed, 486
systems of, 456
theory, 491
Communism, the death of,
176, 179
Communist Manifesto, 23
Comparable worth, 323
Computer(s), 476
as a modern Panopticon,
465
and technology, 158
*Conceptual Practices of
Power, The,* 331
*Condition of Postmodernity,
The,* 175
*Condition of the Working
Class in England,
The,* 22
Conflict:
theories of, 132
theory, 49, 69–70, 76, 87,
93–94, 122–134, 360,
498
analytic, 310–313
integrative, 128–132
Marxian, 131
synthetic nature of,
131–132
Conflict Sociology, 128, 373
Confucianism, 31
Consciousness, 21–24, 43,
54, 56, 71, 73, 120,
145, 170, 281, 335,
342, 350, 362, 368,
371, 389, 397
bifurcated, 351–352
class, 138–139, 477, 500
discursive, 390
false, 138–139, 144, 500
human, 391
individual, 145–146, 184
practical, 390
revolutionary, 145
self-, 184
Consensus theory, 93–94,
116
*Consequences of Modernity,
The,* 427
*Constitution of Society:
Outline of the Theory*

of Structuration, The,
388, 430
Constructivism, 397
structuralist, 397
Consumer Society, 87, 437
Consumerism, 341, 485
Consuming Places, 87
Consumption, 436–437
cathedrals of, 483
conspicuous, 51, 87, 154,
404
luxury, 436
new means of, 432,
435–439, 480–483,
497
casino-hotels, 436,
438, 497
chains, 437
cruise lines, 436, 483,
497
cybermalls, 436, 497
discounters, 436, 438,
483
fast-food industry, the,
436–437
home shopping
television, 497
Las Vegas, 481
megamalls, 497
shopping malls, 436,
438–439
superstores, 436,
497
theme parks, 436,
497
Parisian drugstore, the,
437
patterns of, 175
sociology of, 497
subsistence, 436
theories of, 49, 52, 87–88
*Contemporary Sociological
Theories,* 60
Contingency, 185
double, 190–191
*Contribution to the Critique
of Political Economy,
A,* 492
Control:
machinery as means of,
157
of management, 159

Conversation(s):
analysis, 248–250,
253–261, 266,
268–269
context-renewing, 250
context-shaped, 250
telephone, 254–255
*Cours de Philosophie
Positive,* 15
Creativity, 220
Credential Society, The, 373
Credit:
card(s), 364–365
debt, 364–365, 434
preapproved, 365
and students, 365
McDonaldization of,
433–434
Critical school, 48, 64, 76
Critical theory, 44, 65, 81,
137, 140–152, 308,
335, 408, 486
actor in, 171
authentications, 146
criticisms of, 147–148
critique of modern society,
141–143
and the liberation of
humankind, 146
of techno-capitalism,
151–152
of television, 143
of today, 151–152
*Critique of Dialectical
Reason,* 454
Critique of Domination, The,
142
*Critique of Political
Economy, The,* 492
Cross talk, 263
Crosscutting Social Circles,
286
Cultural conditioning, 395
Cultural determinism,
103–104, 360
Cultural elaboration, 395
Cultural explosion, 476
Cultural forms, 240
Cultural materialism, 336
Cultural products, 405
Cultural relationships, 403
Cultural reproduction, 410

Cultural sociology, 394
Cultural studies, 240
Cultural system(s), 103–104
Cultural theory, 122, 407
Culture, 17, 80, 103, 116,
    222, 304, 350, 363,
    414, 416, 478, 504
  and agency integration, 81,
    393–396
  critical approach to, 241
  critique of, 143–144
  death, 479
  high, 403
  industry, 143–144
  mass, 143
  modern, 143
  objective, 422
  popular, 78,
  and society, 33
  sociology of, 240
  structures in, 397
  subjective, 422
  and taste, 403–405
  tragedy of, 87, 422, 471

Debt:
  consumer, 364
  credit card, 364
Debunking, 111
Decision theory, 291
Decivilization, 378
Deconstruction, 242, 342,
    457–458
Dedifferentiation, 478
Democracy(ies), 143,
    485–486
  radical, 173–175
  theory of, 121
Deviance, 114
Deviant behavior, 113–114
Dialectic(s), 135–136,
    145–147
  diachronic view of, 146
  and Hegel, 21–24
  Hegelian, 500
  and Marx, 24, 169
  synchronic view of, 146
Dialectical materialism, 24
Differentiation, 106,
    192–197, 199,
    283–284, 311, 383,
    445

center-periphery, 193–194
code(s), 195–196
  functional, 193–195
    problems of, 196–197
  gender role, 313
  limits of, 192
  segmentary, 193, 195
  stratificatory, 193–194
  theory, 118
Disciplinary matrix, 492
Discipline and Punish,
    463–465, 485
Discourse, 150, 173, 179,
    342, 347, 460, 463
  hegemonic, 342
  medical, 462
Discrimination, 111, 322
  job, 323
  race, 337
  sex, 337
Dispute resolution in
    mediation hearings,
    263–264
Distinction, 403–405, 493
Distributive justice, 279
Division of labor, 17, 74, 87,
    156, 163, 313
  economic, 163
  gendered, 321–322
  household, 315
  pathologies of, 17
  social, 112
  worldwide, 164, 426
*Division of Labor in Society,
    The,* 17–18
"Doing shyness," 260–261
Domination, 142, 311, 326,
    328–329, 332, 334,
    347, 353, 478
  agents of, 353
  critique of, 144–145
  of culture, 34
  dominant, 324, 334, 337
  ideological, 347
  interactional, 349
  matrix of, 337
  resistance to, 353
  social, 347
  structures of, 331, 333, 353
  subordinate, 324, 334, 337
Dramaturgical analysis,
    71–72, 226–230

appearance, 227
back stage, 72, 229–230,
    372
front stage, 72, 227,
    229–230, 372
manner, 227
mystification, 229
personal front, 227
team, 229
Dromology, 486
Dyad, 34, 273, 290–291
Dysfunction(s), 111

Eastern Sociological Society,
    57
Economic(s):
  determinism, 5, 27, 43, 48,
    135–136, 152, 173,
    360, 366
  institutions, 392
  Keynesian, 175
  structures, 457
*Economic and Philosophic
    Manuscripts of, The,*
    22–23, 137, 491
Economic base, 143–144
Economist, The, 40
Economy(ies), 4, 27, 30, 103,
    186, 335, 414
  market, 311
  money, 34
  multinational, 476
  world-, 163
Economy and Society, 29
Efficiency, 30, 433, 438, 442
*Elementary Forms of
    Religious Life, The,*
    17–18, 233
Emergence, 234, 368, 370
*Empire of Fashion: Dressing
    Modern Democracy,
    The,* 485
*Enchanting a Disenchanted
    World: Revolutionizing
    the Means of
    Consumption,* 87, 497
Enlightenment, the, 5, 10,
    11, 12, 13, 16, 20, 25,
    321
  Conservative reaction to, 5,
    11–12
  Counter elements, 10

Enlightenment, the—*Cont.*
    philosophy, 42
Environmentalism, 341
Ethnomethodology, 49,
        73–76, 128–129, 131,
        228, 245–270,
        314–315, 360, 396,
        414, 498, 501
    accomplishing sex, 253
    criticism of traditional
        sociology, 265–266
    defining, 245–249
    diversification of, 249–250
    early examples of, 251–252
    indifference, 248
    stresses and strains in,
        266–267
    and symbolic
        interactionism,
        268–269
    synthesis and integration
        in, 267–269
Everyday life, 448
    organization of, 247
    sociologies of, 72–76, 228,
        266
*Everyday World as
    Problematic, The,* 331
Evolutionary theory, 5,
        39–41, 106–108, 114,
        150–151
    and Comte's law of the
        three stages, 14–16, 39
    metaphysical stage,
        the, 15
    positivistic stage, the,
        15
    theological stage, the,
        14
    and Hegel, 21
    and Parsons, 107
    selection, 191
    stabilization, 191–192
    variation, 191
Exchange, 184
    collectivity-individual, 285
    direct, 284
    dyadic, 288
    dynamics, 293
    economic, 477
    history of, 290
    indirect, 284

individual-individual, 285
interpersonal, 285
network, 287–288,
        290–291
structures, 293
symbolic, 477, 479–480
theory, 49, 63, 75, 82, 130,
        132, 271–293, 360,
        371, 498
    aggression-approval
        propositions, 279
    assumptions of,
        287–288
    birth of, 70–71
    of Blau, 282–286
    comparison level, 274
    comparison level for
        alternatives, 274
    cost, 279
    deprivation-satiation
        proposition, 278–279
    discrimination, 278
    of Emerson and his
        disciples, 286–293
    generalization, 278
    of Homans, 274–282
    integrative, 287,
        289–293
    outcome matrix, 274
    power and dependence
        in, 289
    profit, 279
    rationality proposition,
        279–282
    stimulus proposition, 277
    success proposition,
        277–278
    synthetic version of,
        291
    value proposition, 278,
        281
    (See also *Behaviorism*)
*Exchange and Power in
    Social Life,* 71, 286
Executive negotiations, 262
Existential sociology, 49
Existentialism, 396, 398–399,
        414, 457, 498
Exploitation, 130, 169,
        171–172, 179, 346
        449, 478
    economic, 142

of labor, 154, 158, 333
political, 163
of sex, 142
of workers, 437
*Expressing America: A
    Critique of the Global
    Credit Card Society,*
        364, 497
Externalization, 368

Factories, 7
*Fads and Foibles in Modern
    Sociology and Related
    Sciences,* 59
Family, 12, 16, 39, 217, 220,
        224, 303, 311–312,
        321, 332, 502–503
    conflict in, 131
    institution, 117
    monogamous, 11
    organization, 313
    Parsons' theory of, 311
    patriarchal, 312
Fashion, 87, 485–486
Father Knows Best, 470
Feedback, 368
Female World, The, 325
*Female World from a Global
    Perspective, The,* 325
Feminism, 5, 7–8, 79, 242,
        484
    basic theoretical questions
        of, 308–310
    black, 315, 338
    chicana, 338
    conservatism, 315
    cultural, 316, 318, 320
    expressionism, 315
    First Wave, 338
    global, 321
    instrumentalism, 315
    intersectionality theory,
        316, 337–340
        gender and age, 338
        gender and class, 338
        gender and global
            location, 338
        gender and race, 338
        gender and sexual
            preference, 338
        race, gender, and class,
            338

Feminism—*Cont.*
  lesbian, 315, 330
  liberal, 315–316, 321–324
  Marxian, 315–316, 332
  materialist, 336
  polarism, 315
  and popular culture, 78
  postmodern, 242, 316, 338,
    340–343, 469
  poststructural, 242
  psychoanalytic, 315–316,
    320, 324, 326–328
  radical, 315–316, 328–332
  and rape, 78
  Second Wave, 338, 342
  separatist, 315
  socialist, 315–316,
    332–337
    relations of ruling, 336,
      353
    sociology of knowledge,
      344–345
  synthesist, 315
  Third Wave, 78
    of monogamy, 329
    of motherhood, 78, 329
    of work, 78
Feminist Studies, 78
Feminist theory, 77–79, 82,
  88, 307–355
  integrative, 352–354
  varieties of, 315–343
Feudalism, 163
Fiduciary system, 103–104
Field, 81, 401–403
  strategies, 402
*Fighting Words: Black
  Women and The
  Search for Justice,* 339
Figurational sociology,
  374–385
  natural functions, 379
  psychogenetic vs.
    sociogenetic, 382
Fordism, 152, 159–161,
  175–176
  in fast-food restaurants,
    161
  (See also *McDonaldization
    of society*)
Formulations, 259–260

*Foundations of Social
  Theory,* 296–305
  collective behavior, 299
  norms, 299–302
Frame analysis, 232–233
*Frame Analysis: An Essay on
  the Organization of
  Experience,* 232–233
Frankfurt school, 64, 140,
  143–144, 146, 407,
  446
  Institute of Social
    Research, 64, 140
Freedom, 143
  individual, 454
French Revolution, 6, 11, 13,
  20, 25, 165, 321
French sociology, 5, 16
  conservative, 20
  development of, 5–6, 10,
    13–20, 36
Freudian theory, 65, 171
Function(s), 109
  latent, 110–111
  manifest, 110–111
*Functions of Social Conflict,
  The,* 127, 491
Functionalism, 311–312,
  414
  Parsonsian, 311–312
  societal, 95
  universal, 109
Future of Marriage, The,
  322, 325
Future of Motherhood, The,
  325

Game theory, 272
Gaze, the, 260, 463–464
Gender, 58, 78, 314,
  336–337, 340, 346,
  400, 484
  deconstructing, 342
  difference(s), 316–320
    biological explanations
      for, 316
    essentialism of, 318
    existential and
      phenomenological
      analyses of,
      318–320, 331

  "doing gender"
    explanations, 319
    explanatory theories
      of, 318–319
    institutional and
      socialization
      explanations for, 316,
      319
      policy implications of,
        317–318
    social-psychological
      explanations for, 316,
      339–340
  displays of, 315
  equality, 321
  equity, 313
  how it is done, 314
  identity, 314–315
    internalization of,
      314–315
  ideology, 347
  inequality, 309, 312,
    316–317, 320, 322,
    324, 332, 349
  macro-social theories of,
    310–311, 345–347
  micro-social theories of,
    314–315, 348–350
  oppression, 311, 316–317,
    324, 328–329,
    331–334, 337–339,
    347, 484
    vectors of, 316–317,
      337–340, 345
  social construction of, 322
  stratification, 311–312
Gender and Society, 78
Generalized media of
  interchange, 108
Generalized other, the,
  217–218, 350, 352
Generalized texts, 353–354
German historicism, 5
German Ideology, The, 22,
  491
German Sociological Society,
  29, 32
German sociology, the
  development of, 5,
  20–36
Gestures, 210–211

Gestures—*Cont.*
  conversation of, 210
  nonsignificant, 210–211
  physical, 211
  significant, 210
  unintended, 230
  vocal, 210
Globalization, 432, 435
  ethnoscape, 435
  finanscape, 435
  technoscape, 435
Grand narratives, 241, 341
  liberal, 485
  and postmodernism,
      470–471, 473, 480,
      484
Grand theory, 69, 74, 241
Group(s), 39, 233–235
  cohesion, 283, 294
  conflict type, 125–126
  formal, 287
  formation, 283
  interest type, 125–126
  primary, 55,
  quasi type, 125
  social, 400, 500
Grundrisse, 492

Habitus, 81, 399–401, 404,
      413
  dispositions, 413
  hysteresis, 400
Harvard University:
  Department of Social
      Relations, 61, 63, 281
  the rise of, 58–63
Hegelian philosophy,
      Subjectivism of, 137
Hegemony, 139–140, 166,
      173–175
*Hegemony and Socialist
      Strategy,* 173
Hermeneutic(s), 121, 414,
      460
  double, 248, 389
Heterosexism, 332, 345
Heterosexuality, enforced,
      78, 329
Hinduism, 31
Historical materialism:
  feminist, 332, 335

Marxian, 144, 334–335
*History and Class
      Consciousness,* 137
History of Manners, The,
      375–381
History of Sexuality, The,
      465–468
*Holy Family: Against Bruno
      Bauer and Co., The,*
      22, 491
Homo Academicus, 405–407,
      493
Homo sociologicus, 303
Homosexuality, 85–86
Hotel Bonaventure, 476
Human Group, The, 280–281
Human emancipation, 147
Human potential, 148, 155,
      470
  (See also *Consciousness*)
Human rights, 87, 485
Hyperreality, 478–480
Hyperspace, 476

Idea systems, 66
  ideology, 66
  utopia, 66
Ideal speech, 150
Ideal types, patriarchal, 330,
      336
Idealism:
  German, 500
  and Hegel, 21
  subjective, 22
Ideology, 65, 144, 150, 335,
      345, 349–350
  patriarchal, 313, 322
  and power, 337
Impression management,
      227, 230
Individual(s), external control
      over, 142
Individualism, 485
Individuality, 143, 220
  semantics of, 198
Individuation, 327
Industrial Revolution, 5–7, 8,
      11, 25, 87, 165, 275,
      436
Industrial society(ies), 36,
      39–40, 84, 431

Industrialization, 12, 46, 48,
      52
*Industrialization as an Agent
      of Social Change,* 238
Infomercials, 478
*Information Age: Economy,
      Society and Culture,
      The,* 449
Informationalism, 449–452
Inside Edition, 478
Institutional settings, 249
Integrated sociological
      paradigm, 368, 388,
      492, 498–505
Integration:
  social and system, 410
  of theory and practice, 176
Intelligence, 212–213
Interactants, types of, 33, 35
Interaction(s), 33, 71, 80,
      202, 222–224,
      314–315, 363, 503
  and distance, 229
  face-to-face:
    civil inattention and,
        231
    involvement and, 231
    and situational propriety,
        231
  "Felicity's Condition," 232
  forms of, 33, 35
    conflict, 33
    subordination, 124, 298
    superordination, 124
  models of, 348
  patterns of, 184
  ritual chains, 132, 371
  social, 72, 148, 349
  sociocultural, 395
  thinking and, 222–223
  types:
    miser, 33
    prostitute, 33
    spendthrift, 33
    stranger, 33
  (See also *Action; Dyad;
      Thought; Triad*)
Internalization, 105, 368
  harmonious, 131
  of norms, 102, 301
Intersubjectivity, 73

Introduction to Pareto, An, 62
Introduction to Mathematical Sociology, 300
Introduction to the History of Science, 112
Introduction to the Science of Sociology, An, 53
Irrationality, 142
Italian sociology, the development of, 5, 42–43

Job interviews, 261–262

"K Is Mentally Ill: The Anatomy of a Factual Account," 331
Karl Marx's Theory of History: A Defence, 170
Kinship systems, 456
Knowledge:
   archaeology of, 459–462
   hierarchization of, 461
   and human interests, 147
   industry, 143–144
   postmodern, 471
   power and, 459–460
   production of, 143, 461
   scientific, 461
   semantics of, 198
   sociology of, 65–66
      Luhmann's, 197–198
   systems of, 65, 309
      analytic science, 147
      critical knowledge, 147
      humanistic knowledge, 147

L'annee sociologique, 20
Labor, 36
   capital and, 152–159
   household, 313, 315
   manual, 156
   markets, 36, 175
   mental, 156
   movements, 47
   process, 155, 175
   propertyless wage, 424
   simple, 157
   unions, 159–160

Labor and Monopoly Capital: The Degradation of Work in the Twentieth Century, 155
Language, 211, 389, 504
   deconstructed, 457
   structure of, 397
Langue and parole, 455
Laughter:
   initiating, 255–256
   within-speech, 255
Law(s), 17, 28, 137, 321, 349, 363, 392, 500, 503–504
   institutionalized, 17
   semantics of, 198
   sociology of, 20
Leadership, charismatic, 31, 52
Legal system, 186–187, 425
Legitimations, 145, 150
Leisure:
   class, 51
   conspicuous, 51
   time, 436
Liberalism and conservatism in sociology, 46
Libido, 145
Life-world, 73, 351, 409, 411
   colonization of, 81–82, 152, 408–413, 444–445
   condensation of, 445
   culture, 410
   domination within, 411
   impoverished, 445–446
   personality, 410
   rational communication of, 409
   rationalization of, 84, 409, 411
   secularization of, 445
   self-deception within, 411
   society, 410
   they relations, 73
   we relations, 73
"Limit experiences," 466
Linguistic(s), 173, 456, 459, 477
   structures, 455
Listen, Yankee: The Revolution in Cuba, 68

Local actualities of lived experience, 353–354
Logocentrism, 458–459
Lost Dimension, 486
Luxor (Las Vegas), 481

Macro-social order, the, 345–347
Macrosociology, 53, 247, 270
Madness, 461–462, 467
Madness and Civilization, 461, 463
Making Sense of Marx, 171
Mall of America, 482
Manager(s), 153–154
   rationality of, 153
Managerial control, 156–158
Market(s), 404, 427
   free, 7
Marriage, 322–323
   egalitarian, 323
   institutional, 323, 364
Marriage and Family among Negroes, 325
Marxian sociology, 25
   rise and fall of, 76–77
Marxian theory, 25, 27, 29, 32, 43, 68–70, 76–77, 82, 87, 107–109, 122, 126–129, 136, 138–142, 145, 147, 152, 177, 334, 346, 399, 413, 454, 457, 473, 477, 497
   conservative reaction to, 12
   criticisms of, 140
   decentering of, 342, 458–459
   developments in, 64–65
   economic, 141, 155
   postmodern, 173–176
   productivist bias in, 87, 436
   radical reaction to, 12
   rejection of, 42
   synthesis of, 477
Marxism, 30, 120, 139, 147, 177, 308
   analytical, 145, 168–173, 178
   cultural-, 120
   deterministic, 43

Marxism—*Cont.*
economic, 49
empirically oriented, 169,
172
European, 43–44
feminism's impact on,
177
game-theoretic, 169–171
Hegelian, 5, 43, 48, 64–65,
136–140
historical, 49, 161–167
mechanistic, 140
New Left, 120
phenomenological-, 120
post-, 82, 168–180
criticisms of, 178
postmodern, 82, 145, 178
psychoanalytic-, 120
rational choice, 169–172
and social transformation,
308
structural, 49, 360,
396–397, 399, 454,
456–457
vulgar, 120
Weberian, 65, 142
Western, 43
Marxist Studies, 76
Marxists, The, 68
*Mathematics of Collective
Action, The,* 300
McDonaldism, 161
McDonaldization of society,
84, 432–434, 439–440,
497
and credit cards, 433–434,
497
and the Holocaust,
442–444
(See also *Fordism*)
*McDonaldization of Society,
The,* 432, 497
*McDonaldization Thesis,
The,* 497
McDonald's, 435, 437
Meadian theory, 235, 237
Meaning(s), 121, 189, 214,
222, 269
learning, 223–224
pure, 368
shared, 349
Mechanization, 155, 158

Media, 321–322, 478–479
control of, 480
delinguistified, 411
political economy of, 143
Mediated messages, 315
Mental processes, 203, 223
and the mind, 212–215
Meta-Analysis, 490
Meta-data-analysis, 490
Metadiscourse, 470
Metamethods, 489–490
Metanarratives, rejection of
in postmodernism,
470–471
Metasociology:
neodialectical, 492
positivistic, 492
Metatheorizing, 489–494
external-intellectual,
490–491, 493
external-social, 491, 493
internal-intellectual,
490–491, 493–494
internal-social, 490–491,
493–494
Metatheorizing, 497
Metatheorizing in Sociology,
497
Methodological holism, 492
Methodological
individualism, 171,
492
Methodological relationism,
403, 492
"Metropolis and Mental Life
The," 34
MGM Grand (Las Vegas),
482
Micro-macro extremism,
359–361
Micro-Macro Link, The, 361
Micro-macro theory, 49,
80–82, 239–240, 242,
287, 290, 354,
359–385, 413, 496
and agency-structure
linkage, 415–417
and ethnomethodology,
270
integration, 361–362
examples of, 362–374
model of, 369–371

Micro-social order, the,
348–350
Microsociology, 122, 248,
270, 348
micro foundations of,
371–374
radical, 371
Militant society(ies), 39
Mind, the, 56, 214–215, 222,
368
collective, 362
deep structures of, 79
*Mind, Self and Society: From
the Standpoint of a
Social Behaviorist,*
56, 204–207, 219,
236
and the priority of the
social, 205–207
Mirror of Production, The,
477
Modern society(ies), 8, 159,
485
Modern World System, The,
162
*Modern World System II,
The,* 165
Modernism, 176, 341–342
469
essentialism of, 341
foundationalism of, 341
god-eye view, the, 341
representation of, 342
universalism of, 341
Modernity, 176, 341, 481
classical stage of, 421–423
consequences of, 424–427
design faults, 426
operator failure, 426
reflexivity of social
knowledge, 426
unintended
consequences, 426
utopian realism, 426–427
defenders of, 83–84
disembedding in, 424–425
distanciation, 424–425
high, 423
and the Holocaust,
440–444
as a product of
modernity, 440–441

Modernity—*Cont.*
and the Holocaust—*Cont.*
role of the bureaucracy
in, 441–442
and identity, 427–428
industrialism and, 424
and intimacy, 428
juggernaut of, 423–429
late, 423
limitations of, 469
and the nation-state, 311,
424
radical, 423
reflexivity in, 424, 426,
428–429
and the sequestration of
experience, 428
shattering impact of, 392
surveillance capacities of,
424
and symbolic tokens, 425
theories of, 49, 83–85,
421–452
time and space separation
in, 391–392, 424–425
time-space compression in,
175–176
unfinished project of,
444–449
violence in, 424,
(See also *Organic
solidarity*)
Modernity and Self-Identity,
427, 430
"Modernity versus
Postmodernity,"
447–448
Modernization, 422, 432, 434
theory, 434
Monarchy(ies), 11
Money, 87, 108, 186–188,
425, 451
economy, 422–423, 425
Moral disorder, 19
Moral education, 112
Morality, 123
collective/common, 17,
422
semantics of, 198
Morphogenesis, 183
Morphostasis, 183

Multicultural social theory,
49, 85–86, 88
Afrocentric theory, 86
Native American theory, 86
theories of masculinity, 86,
317
Multidimensional sociology
(Alexander), 80,
365–367
action, 80, 365
levels of analysis:
collective-idealist, 80
collective-materialist, 80
individual-idealist, 80
individual-materialist, 80
order, 80, 365
collective (macro) level,
365
individual (micro) level,
365
"My Four Revolutions: An
Autobiographical
Account of the
American Sociological
Association," 325

National Organization for
Women (NOW), 321
National Women's Studies
Association (NWSA),
78
Nationalism, 341
Natural selection, 39, 50, 191
*Nature of Social Science,
The*, 281
Need-dispositions, 102,
104–105
Neoevolutionary sociological
theory, 41–42
Neofunctionalism, 49, 82, 88,
93–94, 117–122, 311
491
Neofunctionalism and After,
122
Neo-Marxian sociology, 147
economic, 152–161
Neo-Marxian theory, 76, 87,
123, 135–180, 308,
335, 360, 408, 412,
454
Net balance, 110

Network society, 449–452
Network theory, 49, 132, 271,
289–291, 293–296
integrative, 295–296
strength of weak ties, the,
294
New Professors, The, 292
New School for Social
Research, 73
New York, New York (Las
Vegas), 482
Nihilism, 485
Nonfunctions, 110
Norms, 93, 101, 103, 116,
123, 150, 190, 204,
265, 275, 284–286,
293, 299–302, 304,
362–363, 366, 368,
371, 434, 500,
503–504
institutionalization of, 323
445
internalization of, 350
mythical, 338

Objectification, 368
Objectivism, 396–397
"On the Microfoundations of
Macrosociology," 371
One-dimensional society,
143, 146
Oppression:
responses to, 353
structural, 316–317,
331–340
theory, 324, 332
Organic solidarity, 422
Organization(s), 128, 500
political, 414
of social interaction,
254–255
*Origins of the Family Private
Property and the State,
The,* 332

Panopticon, 465
surveillance possibilities
of, 465
Paradigm(s), 494–496
integrated sociological, 80,
362–365, 368
multiple, 494–495

Paradigm(s)—*Cont.*
  postmodern, 499
Parsonsian theory, 61, 70,
    97–108, 366
  change and dynamism in,
    106
"Pastiche," 475
Paternalism, 346
Patriarchy, 11, 312, 316, 324,
    326, 329, 332–333,
    344, 347
  capitalist, 334
  critique of, 332
Pay equity, 323
Personality formation, 410
Personality systems, 104
Phenomenology, 73–75,
    128–129, 371, 390,
    396–397, 414, 498,
    501
*Phenomenology of the Social
    World, The,* 73–74
Philosophy of Money, The,
    33–34, 422
*Polish Peasant in Europe and
    America, The,* 52–53
Political economy:
  English, 5, 22, 36–38
  Marx's theory of, 24–25,
    477
Political institutions, 392,
    414
Political revolution(s), 5–6
Political system, 186
Polity, 4, 103–104, 335, 414,
    502
Positive philosophy (see
    Positivism)
Positivism, 12–16, 393
  critiques of, 140–141
Positivistic sociology, 47
Post-Fordism, 152, 159–161,
    175, 176
Post-industrialism, 433
"Post-Marxism without
    Apologies," 179
Postmodern social theory, 49,
    80, 84, 86–87, 449,
    454, 469–471,
    483–486, 497
  affirmative, 470

applying, 480–483
broad generalizations of,
    484
extreme, 477–479
as ideology, 484
moderate, 472–477
post-, 49, 86–87
skeptical, 470
Postmodern Social Theory,
    483
Postmodern society, 87, 159,
    470, 474
Postmodernism, 85, 173,
    175–176, 240–241,
    388, 423, 454, 458,
    468–487
  criticisms of, 483–486
  Disneyland, 84
  fatal theory of, 479
  feminism and, 331,
    340–343
  Habermas' criticisms of,
    448–449
  insanity of, 483
  intensities in, 475
  loss of historicity in, 475
  loss of temporality in, 475
  new technology, 476
  post-, 87, 485
  re-enchantment, 480–483
    and the role of
      spectacle, 481
  simulations, 84, 478,
    480–482
    Celebration, Florida,
      482
    Kentlands, Maryland,
      482
    Las Vegas, 481–482
    Seaside, Florida, 482
  and sociological theory,
    479–480
  and the waning of emotion
    or affect, 475
"Postmodernism or The
    Cultural Logic of Late
    Capitalism," 473
Postmodernity, 84, 341, 469
  and implosion, 84, 478,
    482–483
  theories of, 84–85

Postmodern(ized) Simmel,
    471
Poststructural theory, 483
Poststructuralism, 49, 79–80,
    121, 173, 240–241,
    388, 397, 454,
    457–468, 484–486
Poverty, 33, 36
  feminization of, 322
Power, 29, 313, 320
  disciplinary, 464–465
    examination, 464
    hierarchical
      observation, 464
    normalizing
      judgments, 464
  genealogy of, 459–461,
    463, 465
  and knowledge, 459–460
  micro-politics of, 459
Power and Civility, 375–376,
    381–384
Power Elite, The, 68
Pragmatism, 202–204
  nominalist, 202–203
  philosophical realism,
    202–203
Praxeology, 399
Praxis, 24, 139, 399
Predictability, 433, 438, 442
*Presentation of Self in
    Everyday Life,* 72, 226,
    230, 233
Primitive society(ies), 8, 18,
    26
Prisoner's dilemma, 171
Private property, 129
Production, 51, 478
  commodity, 424
  control of, 341
  economic, 313, 345
  flexible, 450
  household, 313
  Marx's theory of, 437
  mass, 159–160
  material, 352
  means of, 129, 333, 436
  owners of, 333
  process of, 26
  social, 345–346, 352–353
Profane, 19

Profit, 478
Proletariat, 86, 136, 139, 174, 413, 437
 class-consciousness of, 27, 138
 lumpen, 126
Property, 333
 relations, 333
 rights, the destruction of, 333
 the unequal distribution of, 172
Protestant ethic, 369, 373
Protestant Ethic and the Spirit of Capitalism, The, 27, 29
Protestantism, 27, 47, 369–370
Pruitt-Igoe housing project, 469–470
Psychic systems, 188–189
Psychoanalysis, 37, 149
Psychological behaviorism, 56, 63, 70, 202, 498

Race, 58, 78, 337, 340–341, 346
 inequality, 344
 relations, 53,
Race, Class and Gender, 339
Racism, 316, 321, 332, 345
Ragtime, 475
Rational choice theory, 49, 81, 83, 88, 130, 168, 271, 272–273, 276, 280, 291, 296–305, 360, 416
 criticisms of, 303–305
 deductive determinacy, 304
"Rational Reconstruction of Society, The," 297
Rationality, 42, 65, 84–85, 144, 150, 273, 434, 444
 formal, 30, 84, 142, 422, 433, 440, 444
 calculability, 438
 efficiency of, 30, 433, 438
 in fast-food restaurants, 30, 84, 433–434, 439
 nonhuman vs. human technologies in, 433, 438, 443

 predictability of, 433, 438
 quantity vs. quality in, 433
 iron cage of, 84, 144, 360, 391, 422–423
 irrationalities of, 142, 439, 443
 dehumanization, 433, 443
 demystification, 433
 of life-world, 84
 norms of, 304
 substantive, 142, 409
 system, 84
 Weberian theory of, 432, 439, 459, 497
Rationality and Society, 296–297, 300
Rationalization, 30–33, 149–150, 155, 390, 422, 439, 480, 497
 bureaucratic, 422, 441, 497
 of communicative action, 150, 411
 disenchantment with, 480
 of fast-food restaurants, 30, 497
 drive-through window, the, 30, 433
 iron cage of, 459
 of medicine, 497
 progressive, 153
 of punishment, 463–465
 of purposive-rational action, 149–150
 thesis, 433
 (See also *City(ies); Law; Religion*)
Reason, 10, 142, 321, 461
 communicative, 470
Recognition, 327
Reductionism, 204–205, 287, 340
 psychological, 275, 303
Reflexivity, 390
 radical, 267
 (See also *Modernity, reflexivity in*)
REI (Seattle), 482

Reification, 137–138, 151
 of social structures, 74
Relativism, 344
Religion(s), 8, 17–20, 22, 29, 31, 47, 52, 112, 414, 503
 irrational examples, 31
 ritual, 12
 totemism, 20
 worship, 12
 (See also *Religiosity*)
Religious change, 5, 9
Reproductive:
 freedom, 322
 process, 326–327
 technologies, 476
Rethinking Marxism, 77
"Revolution against 'Capital,' The," 139
Revolutionary subject, 427
Rio (Las Vegas), 481
Risk:
 concept of, 197
 coping with, 431
 creating, 431
 ecological, 197
 profile, 426
 society, 84, 429–432, 439
Risk Society: Towards a New Modernity, 82, 429
Role(s), 308, 311
 difference, 309
 expectations, 190, 222
 expressive, 311
 institutionalization of, 323
 instrumental, 311
 making, 240
 models, 113
 set, 113
 sex, 324
 taking, 350–352
Role distance, 230–231
Routinization, 390
Rules of Sociological Method, The, 17–18, 497

Science, 16, 47
 growth of, 5, 9
 sociology of, 113
 study of, 249
Scientific determinism, 43

Scientific management,
157–158
Scientific reporting, 53
Scientific system, 186
Scottish Enlightenment, 36
Scottish Moralists, 36
"Scream, The," 470, 475
Second Sex, The, 319
Seduction, 479–481
Self, 80, 215–219, 222, 350,
427–428
childhood development of,
216–217
game stage, 216
play stage, 216–217
definite personality, 218
as dialectically related to
the mind, 215
"I" and "Me," 218–219,
226
looking-glass, 54–55, 225
social processes of,
219–221
and the work of Erving
Goffman, 225–233
Self-actualization, 320–321
Self-Fulfilling Prophecy, The,
113
Self-mockery, 227
Self-restraint, 381
Semiotics, 121, 414, 455,
477
Sentences and stories,
258–259
Setting-talk, 261
*Sex Game: Communication
between the Sexes,
The,* 325
Sex roles, 308
Sexism, 321–323
Sexual preference/
orientation, 337,
340–341
Sexual relations, 380
uncivilized, 380
Sexuality, 335, 381, 465–468
inequality based on, 344
postmodern study of, 85
repression of, 465, 467
*Shelf Life: Supermarkets and
the Changing Cultures
of Consumption,* 87

Signs, a system of, 455, 478
Signs, 78
Simmelian theory, 43
Simulacrum(a), 474–475,
478–479
Simulation(s), social, 301
Social action, 120, 269
Social amelioration, 52, 58
Social analysis:
levels of, 33, 97–98, 369,
417, 499–501
micro and macro,
361–362, 499–500,
502
a model of, 501–505
objective-subjective
continuum, 500–502
subjective, 367–368
Ritzer's theory, 501–505
macro objectivity, 80,
363, 367, 416, 502,
504
macro subjectivity, 80,
363, 367, 416, 504
micro objectivity, 80,
363, 367, 416, 502,
504–505
micro subjectivity, 80,
363, 367, 416,
504–505
*Social and Cultural
Dynamics,* 58
"Social Behavior as
Exchange," 70
*Social Behavior: Its
Elementary Forms,* 70,
281
Social behaviorism, 348–349,
503, 505
Social change, 13, 16, 46–52,
59, 68, 93–94,
106–107, 115, 276
cyclical theory of, 42, 58
directional theory of, 42
process of, 114–115
Social class(es), 58, 78, 129,
138, 169, 174, 337,
340, 344, 346, 388,
400, 404, 413, 485,
500
conflict, 335
dominant, 129

inequality, 335, 344
oppression, 179
relationships, 313, 403
structure, 400
struggle, 46, 136, 449
subordinate, 129
system, 424
Social coercion, 123–124
violent, 129
Social cohesion, 311
Social conflict, 125, 360
functions of, 69, 127
and Simmel, 122
Social constraint, 381
Social construction of reality,
250, 363, 368, 389,
396, 499, 503
*Social Construction of
Reality, The,* 73–74
Social control, 102, 219,
368
Social Darwinism, 39, 48–50
Social definitionism, 335,
348–349, 497–499,
501, 503, 505
Social dilemma theory, 291
Social disorder, 14–16, 115,
360
Social disorganization, 52
Social dynamics, 13
Social equilibrium, 68, 99,
102, 119
Social evolution, 38, 106
compound societies, 39
doubly-compound
societies, 39
trebly-compound societies,
39
Social facts, 17–20, 94, 124,
182, 233, 247, 275,
283, 285, 360, 396,
497, 499–500, 503
material, 17, 500
nonmaterial, 17–20, 500
objectivity, 247
paradigm, 284, 497–498
Social identity:
actual, 231
virtual, 231
Social inequality, 46, 58, 66,
130, 311, 331, 335
geosocial, 78

Social institutions, 8, 12, 17, 39, 53, 60, 94, 220, 273, 501
  studies of, 261–262, 267
Social integration, 107, 115, 410–411
Social mentalities, 58–59
  idealistic, 59
  ideational, 58–59
  sensate, 58–59
Social Mobility, 60
Social movements, 152, 413, 445, 449
Social network(s), 225
Social Networks, 294
Social order, 6, 93–94, 98–99, 119–120, 269, 373
Social organization, 331
Social physics, 12–16
Social Psychology of Groups, The, 273–274
Social reality, public knowledge of, 347
Social reform(s), 16, 39, 41, 52, 58
Social reformism, 13–17
Social reproduction, 344
Social revolution, 17, 20, 36, 139
Social Statics, 40
Social statics, 13
Social status, 231, 320, 373
Social structure(s), 12, 16, 43, 62, 70, 80, 345, 389, 457, 501
  and anomie, 111–114
  dynamic equilibrium of, 61
  functions of, 62
  large-scale, 17, 30, 34, 36, 60, 71, 94, 128, 236, 281
  micro and macro, 270, 294
  recursive structure of, 389
Social system(s), 74, 100–101, 297, 391, 408
  actors and, 101–103
  ego and alter ego, 100
  evolution of, 191–192
  status-role, 101

Social System, The, 61, 98, 197
Social theory, 52, 303
  modern, 470
Socialism, 19, 25, 27, 112, 136, 176, 427
  French, 22
  rise of, 5, 7
Socialist societies, 26, 32
Socialization, 74, 102, 222, 265, 319, 324, 368, 385
  adult, 222
  childhood, 222, 265, 426
  dialectic of, 102
  harmonious, 131
  process, 11, 105, 222, 303
Societal community, 103–104
Society, 103, 219–222, 368
  consumer, a Marxian critique of, 477
  as organism, 39
Socioanalysis, 493
Sociobiology, 83
Sociological Imagination, The, 67, 69
  personal troubles and public issues, 69, 364–365, 471
Sociological Inquiry, 78
Sociological methods:
  ahistorical methods, 114, 132
  comparative research, 16, 132
  empirical research, 8, 10, 72, 74, 77, 113, 128, 483, 493
  ethnographic studies, 57
  experimentation, 16
  field studies, 37
  historical, 161–162
  observation, 16, 53
  participant observation, 54, 64
  questionnaires, 64
  statistical techniques, 57
  sympathetic introspection, 55, 64
Sociological Society of London, 36

Sociological theory, 303
  classical, 17
  development of,
    intellectual forces in, 9–44
    social forces in, 6–9
  early years of, 3–44
  early American, 46–57
  feminist, 49, 85, 307–355
  from mid-century, 66–80
  later years of, 45–89
  queer, 85–86
  recent developments in, 80–83
  synthetic, 49
  (*See also* Feminist theory)
Sociologism, 204–205
Sociologists for Women in Society (SWS), 78
Sociology:
  actionalist, 413
  applied, 51,
  behavioral, 498
  of the body, 317, 467
  conservative, 17
  criticisms of, 141
  general theoretical logic for, 492
  of gender, 317
  institutionalization of, 52
  meta, 489, 493
  metatheorizing in, 489–494
  a multiple paradigm science, 496–498
  occupational, 489
  phenomenological, 49, 73–75, 409
  process, 374
  pure, 51
  radical, 49, 68–69, 76
  reflexive, 493–494
  scientific conception of, 42, 52
  scientism, 141
  a socially and morally engaged, 471
  sociology of, 493
Sociology, 430
Sociology: A Multiple Paradigm Science, 496

Sociology and Modern Systems Theory, 181
"Sociology for Women, A," 331
Sociology of Sociology, A, 494
Sociometry, 292
Space:
  of flows, 450
  of places, 450
Specialization, destructive effects of, 156–157
Species-being (see *Human potential*)
Standpoint epistemology, 344
Standpoint theories, 86, 340
State, the, 39, 129, 137, 220, 503
  nature of, 317
  role of, 31–32
"Statistics on Women and Mental Illness: How Not to Read Them The," 331
Status, 29
  -set, 113
Stigma, 231–232
  discreditable, 231
  discredited, 231
Stigma: Notes on the Management of Spoiled Identity, 231
Stimulus, 204–205, 213, 277, 281
  and response, 208
Studies in Ethnomethodology, 74–75, 249
Stratification, 29, 66, 114, 128–131, 346, 372
  conflict theory of, 129–131
  economic dimension of, 28–29, 313
  functional theory of, 95–96
  Marx's theory of, 129
  microsociology, 129
  multifaceted, 129
  scientific study of, 130–131
  sex, 312–313
  structural-functional theory of, 96

system, 501
Structural Contexts of Opportunities, 286
Structural determinism, 295, 366
Structural elaboration, 393–395
Structural equivalence, 294
Structural functionalism, 43, 49, 57–63, 69, 74, 76, 82, 93, 94–118, 185, 187, 205, 237, 275, 360–361, 366, 371, 389, 390, 393, 416, 454, 492, 498
  criticisms of, 114–122
    logical, 116
    methodological, 116
    substantive, 114–116
  functions and dysfunctions, 66, 109–110
  Merton's, 108–114
  Parsons, 97–108, 119
  peak and decline of, 66–68
Structuralism, 49, 79–80, 173, 228, 360, 396–397, 399, 414, 416, 454–457, 459–460, 462–463
  anthropological, 456
  constructivist, 397
  French, 79,
  and French humanism, 454
  genetic, 397
  linguistic, 414, 455
  macro, 360
Structuration theory (Giddens), 81, 267, 388–393, 423, 426
  criticisms of, 392–393
  elements of, 390–392
Structure of Social Action, The, 19, 43, 59, 98–99, 112, 120
Structure of Scientific Revolutions, The, 494–495
Subjectivism, 137, 396–397
Subjectivity, 57, 87, 144–145, 238, 320,

335, 350–352, 367, 453, 397, 484
  macro, 80, 350
  micro, 80, 350
Suicide, 112, 360
  causes of, 17
  rates, 17, 370, 501
  types of:
    altruistic, 501
    anomic, 501
    egoistic, 501
Suicide, 17–18, 301
Superstructure, cultural, 143–144, 146–147, 151, 474
Surplus, economic, 154, 163
Survival-of-the-fittest, 39, 41, 50
Symbol(s), 222
  learning, 223–224
  nonsignificant, 113
  shared, 269
  significant, 211–213
Symbolic Exchange and Death, 479
Symbolic interactionism, 33, 48, 53–54, 56–57, 63, 71, 82, 201–244, 291, 304, 314–315, 360–361, 389, 396–397, 498, 501, 505
  adoption, 242
  basic principles of, 221–235
  criticisms of, 235–236
  ethnomethodology and, 268–269
  expansion, 242
  fragmentation, 242
  future of, 242
  historical roots, 202–205
  incorporation, 242
  integrative, 236–242
  Iowa school of, 64
  making choices, 224–225
  and objects:
    abstract, 222
    physical, 222
    social, 222
  synthetic, 236–242

Symbolic Interactionism and Cultural Studies, 240–242
Symbolic media of exchange, 108
Symbolic order, 392
Symbolism, 119
Systeme de Politique Positive, 15
System(s) theory, 49, 83, 181–200, 393, 395, 408, 414, 498
    applications to the social world, 184–185
    entropy, 183
    gains from, 181
    General (GST), 182
    general principles of, 183–184
    Luhmann's general theory, 185–199
    mechanical, 183
    mediating systems, 183
    morphogenesis, 183, 393–396
    morphostasis, 183, 393–394
    negentropy, 183
    neo-Marxian, 310–311
    organic, 183
    similarities with dialectical approach, 185
    sociocultural, 183

Taoism, 31
Tautology(ies), 117, 126, 173
Taylorism, 160
Technocratic thinking, 142
Technology, 504
    industrial, 35
    informational, 449
    modern, 142–143
Teleology, 95, 117
    illegitimate, 117
Television, 84, 476
Telos, 76
Ten Commandments, 470
Texts, Facts and Femininity, 331
Theatre of cruelty, 458

Theoretical Logic in Sociology, 120–121, 492
Theoretical syntheses, 80, 82–83, 120–121, 267, 496
Theories of Surplus Value, 492
Theory and practice, 146, 396–397
Theory and Society, 76
Theory, Culture and Society, 377
Theory of the Leisure Class, The, 51
Therapeutic critique, 149
Thought:
    capacity for, 221–222
    individual, 43, 139
Totalitarianism, 142
Toward an Integrated Sociological Paradigm, 496
Transformation of Intimacy, The, 428, 430
Triad, 34
Truth:
    consensus theory of, 151–152
    copy theory of, 151
Twenty Lectures: Sociological Theory since World War II, 121
Twin Peaks, 470
Typology, 267

Unanticipated consequences, 111, 391
Union Democracy, 300
Urban ecology, 53
Urban ethnology, 54
Urbanization, 5, 7–8, 12, 46, 52
Use of Pleasure, The, 466
Utilitarianism, 272

Value, 137
    generalizaion, 311
Values, 93, 101–103, 116, 123, 265, 272,

284–286, 293, 362–363, 368, 434, 500, 503–504
    collective, 362
    consensus, 190, 284
    individual, 369–370
    integration, 123
    internalized, 105
    Marx's labor theory of, 25
    particularistic, 285
    patterns, 102
    surplus, 25, 313, 333, 436
    system, 107
Violence, 38
    control of the means of, 129, 424
    by men against women, 329, 331
    symbolic, 402, 494
Voice from the South by a Black Woman from the South, A, 338

Wage(s), 160
WalMart, 482
Warfare, 40
Webbed accounts, 344
Weberian theory, 27, 31, 43, 68, 76, 129, 497
"What It Might Mean to Do a Canadian Sociology: The Everyday World as Problematic," 331
"Where There Is Oppression, There Is Resistance," 331
White Collar, 68
Women, 344
    in early sociology, 57–58
    and the second shift, 322
    social location, 320
        global location, 337, 340
    spheres of social activity, 322
    standpoint of, 344
    subordination of, 331–333, 346
Women and the Public Interest: An Essay on Policy and Protest, 325

"Women, Class and Family,"
331
*Women, Wives, Mothers:
Values and Options,*
325
Women's Christian
Temperance
Movement, 110
Work, 87, 314, 321
coercion of, 159
organization, 313
patriarchal patterning of,
322
Workbench practices, 249
Worker(s), 16, 25, 35, 87,
313–314, 344, 360
automobile assembly line,
158–159

blue-collar, 155
detail, 156
manual, 155, 157
service, 155, 157
white-collar, 155, 157
Working class, 155, 177, 449,
478
exploitation of, 25, 155
World-system(s), 368, 500
modern, 162–167
modern capitalistic world
economy, 163, 165
core, 163, 165, 313
development of,
164–165
external zones, 165
and geographic
expansion, 163–164

periphery, 163, 165–166,
313
semiperiphery, 163, 165,
313
socialist world
government, 163
theory, 166–167, 313–314

Young Hegelians, 5, 21–22,
491